THE OXFORD H

RELIGION AND
VIOLENCE

THE OXFORD HANDBOOK OF

RELIGION AND VIOLENCE

Edited by

MARK JUERGENSMEYER,
MARGO KITTS,

and

MICHAEL JERRYSON

OXFORD
UNIVERSITY PRESS

OXFORD
UNIVERSITY PRESS

Oxford University Press is a department of the University of Oxford.
It furthers the University's objective of excellence in research, scholarship,
and education by publishing worldwide.

Oxford   New York
Auckland   Cape Town   Dar es Salaam   Hong Kong   Karachi
Kuala Lumpur   Madrid   Melbourne   Mexico City   Nairobi
New Delhi   Shanghai   Taipei   Toronto

With offices in
Argentina   Austria   Brazil   Chile   Czech Republic   France   Greece
Guatemala   Hungary   Italy   Japan   Poland   Portugal   Singapore
South Korea   Switzerland   Thailand   Turkey   Ukraine   Vietnam

Oxford is a registered trademark of Oxford University Press
in the UK and certain other countries.

Published in the United States of America by
Oxford University Press
198 Madison Avenue, New York, NY 10016

Library of Congress Cataloging-in-Publication Data
The Oxford handbook of religion and violence / edited by Mark Juergensmeyer, Margo Kitts, and
Michael Jerryson.
p. cm.
Includes index.
ISBN 978–0–19–975999–6 (hardcover : alk. paper); 978–0–19–027009–4 (paperback : alk. paper)
1. Violence—Religious aspects.
I. Juergensmeyer, Mark.   II. Kitts, Margo, 1952–   III. Jerryson, Michael K.
IV. Title: Handbook of religion and violence.
BL65.V55O94 2013
201'.76332—dc23
2012012032

Contents

PART III   ANALYTIC APPROACHES

PART IV   NEW DIRECTIONS

CONTRIBUTORS

James Aho is professor emeritus of sociology at Idaho State University, Pocatello. He is author of many books, his latest being *Sociological Trespasses: Interrogating Sin and Flesh*.

Candace S. Alcorta is a research scientist in the Department of Anthropology at the University of Connecticut. Dr. Alcorta has conducted research in Thailand and the United States on impacts of religion on adolescent resilience. Her published works include articles on the evolution of religion, religion and adolescent brain development, and other related topics.

Gideon Aran is a professor of sociology and anthropology at the Hebrew University, Jerusalem, specializing in religious and political extremism. His forthcoming publication is *The Cult of Dismembered Limbs: Suicide Terrorism, Radical Religion, Contemporary Judaism, Body, Death and the Middle East Conflict*.

Reza Aslan is associate professor of creative writing at University California at Riverside and author of *No God but God: The Origins, Evolution, and Future of Islam*.

Hector Avalos is professor of religious studies at Iowa State University. He is the author of *Fighting Words: The Origins of Religious Violence* (2005) and *Slavery, Abolitionism, and the Ethics of Biblical Scholarship* (2011).

Walter Burkert is professor emeritus of classics at the University of Zürich. He writes on religion and philosophy from an anthropological perspective (*Homo Necans*, 1972, English ed. 1983), and on Oriental-Greek interrelations (*Babylon Memphis Persepolis*, 2004).

David Carrasco is a historian of religions and the Neil L. Rudenstine Professor of Latin America and director of the Moses Mesoamerican Archive at Harvard University. He is author or editor of more than twenty books including *City of Sacrifice, Quetzalcoatl and the Irony of Empire, The History of the Conquest of New Spain, Waiting for the Dawn: Mircea Eliade in Perspective*, and *The Oxford Encyclopedia of Mesoamerican Cultures*.

David Cook is associate professor of religious studies at Rice University. He is author or editor of six books, including *Studies in Muslim Apocalyptic, Understanding Jihad*, and *Martyrdom in Islam*, and numerous articles on Islamic history, apocalyptic literature, and contemporary radical thought.

Veena Das is Krieger-Eisenhower Professor of Anthropology and professor of humanities at the Johns Hopkins University. She is the author, among other books, of *Structure and Cognition: Aspects of Hindu Caste and Ritual*, *Critical Events: An Anthropological Perspective on Contemporary India*, and *Life and Words: Violence and the Descent into the Ordinary*.

David Frankfurter is professor of religion and Aurelio Professor of Scripture at Boston University and has published widely on Christianization and popular religion in Roman antiquity, addressing such themes as magic, demonology, domestic religion, ritual, and violence. His book *Evil Incarnate: Rumors of Demonic Conspiracy and Satanic Abuse in History* (2006) won the 2007 American Academy of Religion award for analytic/descriptive studies in religion.

John R. Hall is a professor in the Department of Sociology and a member of the graduate group in religious studies at the University of California, Davis. He has published extensively on issues of culture, religion, utopia, social theory, and epistemology. His most recent book is *Apocalypse: From Antiquity to the Empire of Modernity* (2009).

Ron E. Hassner is an assistant professor of political science at the University of California, Berkeley and co-director of its Religion, Politics, and Globalization Program. He is the author of *War on Sacred Grounds* (2009) as well as multiple articles on religion and conflict.

Julie Ingersoll is associate professor of religious studies at the University of North Florida where she teaches and writes about evangelicalism, fundamentalism, and the religious right. She is the author of two books, *Evangelical Christian Women: War Stories in the Gender Battles* (2003) and *Baptists and Methodists in America* (2003) and currently has a book under contract with Oxford University Press on Christian reconstruction.

Michael Jerryson is assistant professor of religious studies at Youngstown State University, Ohio. He is the author of *Mongolian Buddhism: The Rise and Fall of the Sangha* (2008), *Buddhist Fury: Religion and Violence in Southern Thailand* (2011), and co-editor with Mark Juergensmeyer of *Buddhist Warfare* (2010).

James W. Jones is professor of religion and adjunct professor of clinical psychology at Rutgers University and a senior research fellow at the Center on Terrorism at the John Jay College of Criminal Justice in New York. He is the author of *Blood That Cries Out from the Earth: The Psychology of Religious Terrorism* and *Terror and Transformation: The Ambiguity of Religion* and co-author of *The Fundamentalist Mindset: Psychology, Religion and Violence*.

Mark Juergensmeyer is professor of sociology and global studies and founding director of the Orfalea Center for Global and International Studies at the University of California, Santa Barbara. He is author or editor of more than twenty books, including *Terror in the Mind of God: The Global Rise of Religious Violence* and *Global Rebellion: Religious Challenges to the Secular State*.

John Kelsay is Bristol Distinguished Professor of Religion and Ethics at Florida State University, where he also serves as associate dean in the College of Arts and Sciences. His most recent book is *Arguing the Just War in Islam* (2007).

Charles Kimball is presidential professor and director of the religious studies program at the University of Oklahoma, Norman. He is the author of five books, including *When Religion Becomes Evil: Five Warning Signs* and *When Religion Becomes Lethal: The Explosive Mix of Politics and Religion in Judaism, Christianity and Islam.*

Margo Kitts is professor and coordinator of religious studies and East-West classical studies at Hawai'i Pacific University in Honolulu. She is the author of *Sanctified Violence in Homeric Society* (2005, 2012) and numerous articles on Homer, ritual, and violence, as well as co-editor of *State, Power, and Violence* (vol. 3 of *Ritual Dynamics and the Science of Ritual*, 2010) and *Princeton Readings in Religion and Violence* (2011).

Karen L. King is the Hollis Professor of Divinity, Harvard University's oldest endowed professorship (1721) and is the first woman to hold the chair. She is the author of numerous books and articles on ancient Christianity, gender, and heresy, including *What Is Gnosticism?*, *The Secret Revelation of John*, and *The Gospel of Mary of Magdala: Jesus and the First Woman Apostle.*

Bruce B. Lawrence is Marcus Family Professor of the Humanities Emeritus, professor of Islamic studies, and inaugural director of the Duke Islamic Studies Center. He has authored or co-authored, edited or co-edited, translated or co-translated eighteen books, including *Messages to the World: The Statements of Osama bin Laden* (2005) and *The Qur'an: A Biography* (2007).

Cynthia Keppley Mahmood is Frank Moore Chair of Anthropology and Professor of Anthropology at Central College. She is the author of *Fighting for Faith and Nation: Dialogues with Sikh Militants* (1996), *The Guru's Gift: Exploring Gender Equality with Sikh Women in North America* (2000, with Stacy Brady), *One More Voice: Interventions on South Asia* (in press), and more than twenty-five academic articles on the anthropology of religion and conflict in South Asia.

Brian McQuinn is a research associate at the Geneva-based Centre on Conflict, Development and Peacebuilding and a doctorate candidate at the University of Oxford. He investigates the way organizational rituals shape the social structure and cohesion of non-state armed groups.

Wolfgang Palaver is professor of Catholic social thought and chair of the Institute for Systematic Theology at the University of Innsbruck in Austria. He has written articles and books on Thomas Hobbes, Carl Schmitt, René Girard, and the relationship between religion and violence.

Daniel Philpott is associate professor of political science and peace studies at the University of Notre Dame, where he is on the faculty of the Kroc Institute for

International Peace Studies. He is the author of *God's Century: Resurgent Religion and Global Politics*, along with Monica Duffy Toft and Timothy Samuel Shah of the forthcoming *Just and Unjust Peace: An Ethnic of Political Reconciliation*.

Saskia Sassen is the Robert S. Lynd Professor of Sociology, Columbia University. Her recent books are *Territory, Authority, Rights: From Medieval to Global Assemblages* (2008) and *A Sociology of Globalization* (2007).

Michael A. Sells is John Henry Barrows Professor of the History and Literature of Islam and professor of comparative literature at the University of Chicago. He writes and teaches in the areas of religion and violence, Arabic poetry, the Qur'an, and mystical literature.

Meir Shahar is associate professor of Chinese studies at Tel Aviv University. He is the author of—among other books—*The Shaolin Monastery: History, Religion, and the Chinese Martial Arts* and *Crazy Ji: Chinese Religion and Popular Literature*.

Mona Kanwal Sheikh is a research scholar at the Danish Institute for International Studies, Copenhagen. Her doctorate in international relations at the University of Copenhagen focused on the Pakistani Taliban and its justifications for violence.

Susumu Shimazono is professor in the Department of Religious Studies of the University of Tokyo. He has published eight books in Japanese, one in Korean, and one in English entitled *From Salvation to Spirituality: Popular Religious Movements in Modern Japan* (Melbourne: Trans Pacific Press, 2004). Recently, he started working in the area of religion and medicine, including bioethics, and in the new interdisciplinary field of life and death studies.

Richard Sosis is professor of anthropology and director of the Evolution, Cognition, and Culture Program at the University of Connecticut. He is co-founder and co-editor of *Religion, Brain & Behavior*, an interdisciplinary journal on the biological study of religion.

Lloyd Steffen is professor of religious studies, university chaplain and director of the Center for Dialogue, Ethics and Spirituality at Lehigh University. An ethics scholar whose books include *Executing Justice: The Moral Meaning of the Death Penalty* and *Holy War, Just War: Exploring the Moral Meaning of Religious Violence*, Steffen has been a representative to the United Nations for the Religious Coalition for Reproductive Choice.

Andrew Strathern and Pamela J. Stewart (Strathern) are a husband-and-wife research team currently based at the University of Pittsburgh, Department of Anthropology, as Andrew W. Mellon Professor and senior research associate, respectively. They are the co-authors/co-editors of more than forty-five books and more than 200 articles, including their co-authored books *Violence* (2002), *Witchcraft, Sorcery, Rumors and Gossip* (2004), and *Peace-making and the Imagination* (2011).

Christopher C. Taylor is an anthropologist and independent scholar who has written extensively about Rwanda. His most recent book, *Sacrifice as Terror*, is about the historical and cultural dimensions of the 1994 genocide in that country.

Monica Duffy Toft is professor of government and public policy at the University of Oxford's Blavatnik School of Government. She is the author of three books, including *The Geography of Ethnic Violence: Identity, Interests and the Indivisibility of Territory*; *Securing the Peace: The Durable Settlement of Civil Wars*; and (with Daniel Philpott and Timothy Shah) *God's Century: Resurgent Religion and Global Politics*.

Jamel Velji is assistant professor of religious studies at Claremont McKenna College. Among his research interests are the history of Islamic thought, Islam and the history of religions; and apocalyptic and the rise and renewal of religious traditions.

Hent De Vries holds the Russ Family Chair in the Humanities and is professor of philosophy at Johns Hopkins University, where he is also director of the Humanities Center. He is also Directeur de Programme at the Collège International de Philosophie in Paris. His principal publications include *Philosophy and the Turn to Religion* (2000), *Religion and Violence: Philosophical Reflections from Kant to Derrida* (2002), and *Minimal Theologies: Critiques of Secular Reason in Theodor W. Adorno and Emmanuel Levinas* (2005). He is the editor of *Religion Beyond a Concept* (2008). Among the volumes he has co-edited are, with Lawrence E. Sullivan, *Political Theologies: Public Religions in a Post-Secular World* (2006) and, with Samuel Weber, *Religion and Media* (2001).

Harvey Whitehouse is chairman of social anthropology, professorial fellow of Magdalen College, and director of the Centre for Anthropology and Mind at the University of Oxford, England. He is author or editor of more than ten books including *Inside the Cult* (1995) and *Arguments and Icons* (2000).

Liz Wilson is professor of comparative religion and an affiliate in the women, gender, and sexuality and the Asian American programs at Miami University in Ohio. She is the author of *Charming Cadavers: Horrific Figurations of the Feminine in Indian Buddhist Hagiographic Literature* (1996), and she is editor of *The Living and the Dead: Social Dimensions of Death in South Asian Religion* (2003).

Nathalie Wlodarczyk is currently forecasting director at Exclusive Analysis, a specialist intelligence company in London. She received her PhD in war studies from King's College London and is the author of *Magic and Warfare: Appearance and Reality in Contemporary African Conflict and Beyond*.

RELIGION AND VIOLENCE

INTRODUCTION

THE ENDURING RELATIONSHIP OF RELIGION AND VIOLENCE

MARK JUERGENSMEYER, MARGO KITTS, AND MICHAEL JERRYSON

THE dark attraction between religion and violence is endemic to religious traditions. It pervades their images and practices, from sacred swords to mythic conquests, from acts of sacrifice to holy wars. Though much has been written about particular forms of religious violence, such as sacrificial rites and militant martyrdom, there have been few efforts to survey the field as a whole, to explore the studies of religious violence historically and in the present, to view the subject from personal as well as social dimensions, and to cover both literary themes and political conflicts.

The Oxford Handbook of Religion and Violence provides a comprehensive examination of the field and introduces new ways of understanding it. The forty original chapters in this volume are written by authoritative scholars who address four major dimensions of the topic: 1) overviews of major religious traditions, each of which is examined with an attempt to understand how violence is justified within the literary and theological foundation of the tradition, how it is used symbolically and in ritual practice, and how social acts of vengeance and warfare have been justified by religious ideas; 2) patterns and themes relating to religious violence, such as sacrifice and martyrdom, which are explored in cross-disciplinary or regional analyses; 3) major analytic approaches, from literary analyses to social scientific studies, which are surveyed with an eye to showing the diversity of analytic perspectives; and 4) new directions in theory and analysis related to religion and violence, which are presented by some of the most innovative contemporary scholars and provide novel insights into the understanding of this important field of studies. In its entirety, this volume forges new paths in the analysis of religion and violence, anticipating the way that this field of studies will continue to evolve. The book should be useful for students and teachers for generations to come.

Our hope is that the handbook will help to unravel some of the perplexing aspects of the relation of religion to violence and will show how acts of destruction in the name of God (or gods) or justified by faith have been rooted in historical and literary contexts from early times to the present. Contemporary acts of religious violence, of course, are profuse. Since the end of the cold war, violence in the name of religion has erupted on nearly every major continent, and many of its perpetrators have been revered by those who find religious significance for such actions. Although no longer novel, religious violence and the adulation of its prophets continue to confound scholars, journalists, policy makers, and members of the general public. Some of them have argued that religious violence is not really religious—it is symptomatic of something else and thus is an anomaly, a perversion of foundational religious teachings. Yet it is precisely foundational religious teachings that are claimed to sanctify violence by many of its perpetrators. Others cite bloody legends of martyrs and heroes and argue that religions, or some of them, are violent at the core, their leaders masterminds of criminal behavior. Yet the chapters in this volume show that there is a much more nuanced interpretation of the presence of violence in so many different traditions.

The relationship of religion to violence is vexing. The chapters in this handbook reveal a variety of ways in which religious violence can be understood. Some social scientists point to a resurgence of anticolonialism, poverty, and economic injustice; the failures of secular nationalism; cultural uprootedness and the loss of a homeland; and the pervasive features of globalization in its economic, political, social, and cultural forms. Alternatively, literary theorists and historians examine how scriptural traditions and founding cults are steeped in violent myths, metaphors, and apocalyptic expectations that support acts of violence in the contemporary world. Different still are analyses based in evolution, anthropology, and psychology. The various approaches represent the range of lenses from which one might view religion and violence within the total realm of historically situated human experience.

Is violence, then, the rare exception in religious traditions, or is it one of the rules? Adherents of most religious traditions almost universally regard their own faith as pacificistic, one that abhors violence and proclaims reconciliation among foes. Perhaps they are right, since the overwhelming message of scriptural writings and prophetic voices is that of love, peace, and harmony. Yet both historians and keen observers also see another side. They point to the legends of war, sacrifice, and martyrdom that cling to the histories of all the great religious traditions. The disconnect between these two points of view raises some profound questions: Is violence peripheral to the religious imagination or at its core? Is it religion that promotes violence or some other social or natural factor? Is religion even distinguishable from those factors? Some argue that the great global religious traditions, because of their long histories of intertwining clerical authority with political powers, are more inclined to violence than are local ones. Yet sources for local religions, collected often at the crossroad between tradition and modernity, also report many forms of ritualized violence, such as assault sorceries, martial initiations, and pre-battle sacrifices. Thus, for scholars of the global and the local, the question looms: What is the link between religion and violence and how profound is it?

As the scholars included here explore the answers to this question, they have to deal with semantic complications. *Religion* and *violence* are each ambiguous terms. The search for a suitable definition of religion has exercised the scholarly imagination for centuries, luring psychologists, sociologists, anthropologists, theologians, philosophers, ethologists, and others into debates over its meaning. Must a religion be centered on supernatural beings? Does the term refer to social or private behavior? Is dogma or praxis the key to its essence? Is it a philosophical system or a poetic structure, a matter of art? Violence, too, is not an easy thing to identify. Immediate bodily harm, verbal assault, social manipulations, cultural destruction, injurious magic, political oppression—the range of ways of thinking about violence is enormous. From whose perspective and at what point is an act to be deemed violent? What act cannot be construed as violent in some way? For instance, are we talking only about war and genocide, or psychological coercion, social restrictions, and binding categorizations? The contributors to this volume have wrestled with these issues and many more. Their collective work reflects the complex and contested meanings of both religion and violence. While the contributors do not operate with a collective definition for either term, they use these words in a manner that illuminates relationships and deepens the understanding of particular phenomena.

The chapters that make up the volume are rich in their interpretive and descriptive quality. The four sections—overviews of traditions, patterns and themes, analytic approaches, and new directions—provide a roadmap to the academic field of studies in religion and violence. The chapters in each section show both the range and diversity of areas of inquiry within this emerging field.

PART I: OVERVIEW OF RELIGIOUS TRADITIONS

Part I provides overviews of Hindu, Buddhist, Chinese, Sikh, Jewish, Christian, Islamic, African, and Pacific Island religious traditions as they have engaged with violence. While the ideas and adherents of most of these traditions have spread throughout the globe, they are anchored in distinctive histories and cultures that set them apart from one another. For instance, Jewish, Hindu, Chinese, and Buddhist traditions draw from their respective sets of sources that are thousands of years old. The Sikh tradition, however, emerged in the 1600s and is one of the youngest global religions. Some traditions, such as Christianity, Buddhism, and Islam, are united by core beliefs and ideological frameworks; others, such as Hindu, Jewish, Chinese, African, and Pacific Island traditions, tend to be rooted in particular places and are linked with specific communities and social systems. The traditional religious communities differ also by size; Islamic, Hindu, Christian, and Buddhist traditions have more than one billion adherents each, while the numbers of Jewish, Sikh, and Pacific Islander followers are only in the millions. Together, however, these traditions influence more than six and a half billion people around the world. The histories of their relationships to violence are a part of the fabric of global history.

Each of the chapters in this section introduces readers to the diversity within the religious traditions. Within Christianity, for instance, the Protestant history of religious violence is distinctively different from that of the Catholic. In the Hindu traditions, the theology and history of devotees of Vishnu (Vaishnavites) are dissimilar to that of devotees of Shiva (Shaivites), and both differ from the communities related to the earlier Brahmanical and Vedic traditions in India. Differences also emerge between theological pronouncements in scripture and the actual instances of religious violence in society. In some cases, sacred texts do not just pronounce but describe forms of religious violence, such as sacrifice and warfare; these accounts are found in the Jewish Torah, the Qur'anic surahs, the Buddhist sutras, the Christian gospels, and the Hindu epics. Violence is also embedded in religious symbols. The sword of the Buddhist bodhisattva Manjushri, for instance, symbolizes the cutting away of illusion; the cross that represents Jesus's persecution and death signifies the atonement of Christians from sin; the two edges of the blade in the Sikh symbol, the khanda, represent the spiritual and temporal power of the faith; the warlike tattoos of the martial Chinese gods are believed by adherents to invigorate warriors. The chapters review these theological and symbolic connections to violence and also the historical and social manifestations, including warfare, torture, ritual, or suicide. Through a historical lens, contributors intimate with the religious traditions provide intricate perspectives on the various ways in which each religious tradition is linked with violence. In addition to these nine chapters, other traditions are touched on in later sections of the volume. (See, for instance, the discussion of Mesoamerican religion in Chapter 11, "Sacrifice/Human Sacrifice in Religious Traditions" by Davíd Carrasco.)

The essay on Hindu traditions, by Veena Das, sets out the complex dynamic of religious attitude and violent practice as represented in the history of Indian ideology and poetics, focusing on ambivalent nuances in reports of animal (and human) sacrifice and in gendered violence. The essay on Bhuddist traditions, by Michael Jerryson, explores the paradox of irenic abstractions about Buddhist nonviolence versus culturally embedded customs prescribing acts of coercion and self-immolation, represented within Buddhist texts and social realities. By looking at the exception to the rule, Jerryson isolates key doctrinal passages that allow for violence and connects them to physical manifestations. The Sikh tradition is placed by Cynthia Keppley Mahmood within the context of the shifting sands of India's religious history; she describes the reverence for certain Sikh gurus as being associated with martyrdom and violence and relates this history of religious violence to the militant drive for a Sikh homeland—Khalistan—in recent decades. In exploring the theme of religious violence in the Jewish tradition, Ron E. Hassner and Gideon Aran begin with divergences among ethnic Jews with regards to identity and scriptural adherence and then explore the way that violence is portrayed in biblical prescriptions and stories, as well as in postbiblical history and interpretation; they also cover the extracanonical books and Talmud and the legacy of violence in Jewish mysticism and messianism. In covering the diversity within the Christian tradition, Lloyd Steffen probes the multilayered Christian imagination with regards to violence, from the tradition's inception in political executions and apocalyptic dreams, through the intertwining of Christianity with political empires, wars, and crusades to its internal struggles over heresy, slavery, missionary zeal, just war, and social justice. In examining the role of violence in Islam, Bruce Lawrence contrasts Islam in 611 with the Islam associated with terrorism on 9/11. He summarizes a complex trajectory of defiant moralism as well as ethical compromise, from Islam's revolutionary roots in human rights through its early rules for how to and when to wage war, through the eventual (post-Mohammed) establishment of jihad as an instrument of state, the crystallization of its rules in response to the Crusades, the founding of "gunpowder empires" such as the Ottoman, and finally Muslim responses to European colonization.

A wide range of African customs and legends are examined by Nathalie Wlodarczyk who shows, among other things, that African traditional religion provides notions of a thriving spirit world that offers "sacred warriors" ritualized protections and martial enhancements when defense of community is urgent. Among the variety of Pacific Island religious cultures described by Andrew Strathern and Pamela J. Stewart, notions of violence vary hugely—from physical harm to slights of honor to mystical assault—but, generally speaking, more hierarchical societies have tended to be supported by ritual and cosmological structures that may be harnessed for revenge and war. Discussing religion in China, Meir Shahar points out that the category of religion eludes traditional Chinese thinking; nonetheless, he summarizes the periods of harmony between official Buddhism, Daoism, and Confucianism, pointing out also the historical reverence for martial gods and practices of religiously sanctioned human sacrifice and self-mortification.

PART II: PATTERNS AND THEMES

In the second section of the book, leading scholars in their fields write on fourteen topics related to religion and violence that frequently occur within religious traditions or that cut across religious diversity. Some of these are patterns—activities that reveal the religious dimensions of political violence, cosmic war, genocide, terrorism, torture, and abortion-related conflicts—that are found in the social histories of many religious traditions. Others are themes—concepts and practices more centrally related to religious ideas and conduct, such as the concepts of evil, just war, martyrdom, and sacrifice. Still other chapters may be regarded as discussing both patterns and themes; these include topics such as contested sites, self-mutilation, death rituals, and violent death.

Through careful historical examination and innovative analysis, each of these chapters provides thick descriptions for critical terms such as self-mutilation or torture and how they connect to the discussion of religion and violence. For instance, the label of martyr was glorified in early Christianity, then highly restricted and contextualized at the inception of Islam; but at the end of the twentieth and in the first decades of the twenty-first century, the idea of martyrdom has gained a certain political notoriety. The theme of sacrifice is regarded in most contemporary religious communities as a concept or a symbol, yet it has a history in actual practice, including cases of human sacrifice in religious ritual. Its appearance among early Greeks and Romans, northwestern African Dahomey, Chinese, Mesoamericans, and others demands a fuller examination. The comparisons made in these chapters are not intended to generalize or blur the lines between different religious traditions but rather to burrow beyond limited religious frameworks of a concept in order to excavate its deeper meaning. In some cases the chapters are comparative, such as those on evil and on the concept of violent death across religious traditions. Other chapters, such as those on martyrdom and genocide, focus on one particular culture to explore the various aspects of concepts and practices.

The chapters that make up this section move roughly from themes in the religious imagination to social acts and practices and, finally, to conceptions of death. The opening essay is James Aho's treatment of the anthropodicies of evil, which he identifies as "horrifying and beguiling, terrifying and wonderful," paradoxically tied to the sacred. Aho surveys evil's causes, motives, and purposes as perceived in a range of traditions. Animal and human sacrifice—diverse theories about it, its geographical and historical range, and its various forms—are studied by Davíd Carrasco, who delves especially into the Aztec cosmovision behind large-scale human sacrifices and the sacrificial symbolism extending from the heavens to earth.

The theme of martyrdom is explored within Islamic history by David Cook, who identifies respect for martyrs in the earliest battles, wherein the *shahid* who died fighting selflessly to defend the faith was understood to ascend to heaven and to intervene there on behalf of the living. The label later was extended to victims of plague, defenders of markets, and warriors fighting invaders, and, with the development of explosive devices, perpetrators of the controversial "martyrdom operations" associated with suicidal activists. Of course suicide and killing innocents are proscribed by traditional Islamic jurispudence. Violence to one's self, as in self-mutilation and starvation, is explored by Liz Wilson, who illustrates how these behaviors have been used as strategies for change across traditions.

Several of the chapters are about warfare and the contest between good and evil. This confrontation is often portrayed in images of the apocalypse, as described by Jamel Velji. Great battles between absolute good and absolute evil, temporal urgency, compelling authority in the form of prophets or texts, and, of course, millennial expectations are some of the features of apocalyptic visions of the end of history.

The notion of divinely sanctioned warfare is explored with relation to the concept of cosmic war, described by Reza Aslan, who outlines ten of its common features and traces its origins to ancient Near Eastern spectacles of warrior gods who exercise cosmic commands on earthly battlefields and secure sacred spoils for humans.

An imagined confrontation of cosmic forces can justify not only warfare but the extermination of whole populations of people and their cultures. The violent imaginaries that informed reports and deeds of the 1994 Rwandan genocide are the focus of the essay on genocide written by Christopher C. Taylor. To the violent demise of President Habyarimana and his supporters, Taylor traces the perseverance of precolonial notions of a sacred king whose "wild sovereignty" and inability to promote the flow of *imaana*—a diffuse, fecundating fluid understood to nourish the social and natural world—earns him fateful sacrifice. Images of a cosmic war between good and evil can justify also acts of terrorism. In his chapter on this topic, Mark Juergensmeyer describes religious terrorism as "performance violence"—acts that are performed for the purpose of creating a public event. These acts present a dramatic scene into which observers are unwittingly drawn; they are compelled to enter into the perception of cosmic warfare imagined by those who perpetrate the acts. Based on his conversations with accused terrorists, Juergensmeyer shows that performance violence is designed not only to achieve tangible goals but also to theatrically enact and communicate an imagined reality. Religious justifications for and against torture are addressed by Karen L. King, who points to the torturous narratives at Christianity's foundations, the notion of redemptive martyrdom, and the various ways in which Christian ideology has challenged as well as supported the torturous suffering of fellows and foes.

Other chapters deal with public conversations about violence and the religious arguments that allow or disallow it. The ethical justification for war is famously promoted by the concept of just war. John Kelsay outlines Western just war thinking, from Roman Cicero's exhortations for honorable treatment of conquered populations to the United Nations' trial of Slobodan Milosevic for crimes against humanity. Particularly within Christianity, Kelsay identifies traditional motivations for forcibly resisting anarchy and transgressions against public order, as well as for moral constraints on fighting and aggressive force. Abortion is a contentious public issue in the United States. After a glance at religious positions on abortion around the world, Julie Ingersoll surveys the thinking of the extreme end of the prolife movement in the United States, exploring its link with Christian reconstructionism, its use of violent and nonviolent strategies of resistance, and its identification of abortion with genocide and sin.

Public space and the impact of globalization are emergent themes in the conversation about religion and violence. Ron E. Hassner explores the conflicts over contested religious sites by communities invested in their integrity and for whom partition is abhorrent. States mistakenly overlook the complex forces at play in these contests, such as cultural memory and iconic identity, the felt presence of spiritual powers, and the expectation of sanctuary for fugitives. Monica Toft analyzes the resurgence of both religion and religious violence over the last decades, locating that resurgence at the intersection of local politics and three trends: modernization, democratization, and globalization.

The section's final chapters are about death. Susumu Shimazono and Margo Kitts outline the rituals related to death and burial, such as corpse treatments, conceptions of death, and the etiquette of remembrance from ancient times to the present, highlighting the nexus of cultural themes that emerge at the site of burial. Finally, Margo Kitts explores the peculiar obsession of world religions with violent death, under three rubrics: when death is perceived as primordially wrong, when violent death is seen as cosmically right, and when violent death, particularly in the form of suicide, is enshrined as martyrdom.

PART III: ANALYTIC APPROACHES

The third section provides insights into analytic approaches from specific disciplinary fields. The authors of the chapters represent six different academic disciplines in which scholars have wrestled with explanations of and treatments for religiously motivated violence: sociology, anthropology, psychology, literature, theology, and political science.

The chapters in this section have two objectives. On the one hand, they are attempts to provide an overview of the way that the aspect of religion and violence has been conceived as a field of studies within each discipline and how it has evolved. The sociological tradition of studies in religion and violence, for instance, reaches back to such important nineteenth-century theorists as Émile Durkheim and Karl Marx. Anthropological studies of this subject go back to the nineteenth-century theorist William Robertson Smith and the early twentieth-century scholar Bronislav Malinowski. Theological and literary analyses date back even earlier.

On the other hand, the chapters provide an opportunity for the authors to develop analytic approaches that they think are particularly appropriate to the disciplinary perspective from which they approach the topic. For this reason, the discussions are critical analyses of the studies of religion and violence in the various disciplinary areas.

In some cases, the authors reach across disciplinary boundaries to incorporate ideas from scholars from other fields, such as the anthropologist Clifford Geertz or the literary theorist René Girard. Although guided by their fields of study, theorists of religion and violence connect well beyond their methodological homes. It is fair to say that, except within the interdisciplinary field of religious studies, typically scholars in particular disciplines are not brought into conversation with one another. They are here. Through short, concise summations of key theorists and their advances, this section provides a theoretical blueprint of interdisciplinary academic discourses on religion and violence.

The chapter from a sociological perspective, by John R. Hall, is qualitative in its analysis and draws on the tradition of reflective social thought. Hall combines insights from sociological case studies, comparative structural studies, and the humanities. After caveats about the interwoven categories of religion, violence, nation, and ethnic community, Hall explores the formations and circumstances that shape violent expressions of religion, particularly among apocalyptic groups, and suggests that understanding multitiered social processes is intrinsic to understanding the complex interplay of religion and violence. Anthropologists Pamela J. Stewart and Andrew Strathern succinctly outline a variety of anthropological approaches to religion from the work of Émile Durkheim through the contemporary cognitive theory of mind, exploring the culturally vast interplay of imagination with, for instance, divinatory processes that legitimate war, witch hunting, and revenge and with cosmic postulates that sanctify the imposition of suffering on others and on oneself.

In the chapter from a psychological perspective, James W. Jones disavows a singular perspective on the psychology of religion and violence, surveying studies that focus on individual psychology, social influences, psychodynamics, and trauma (as well as the lack of it) as expository models for understanding why some individuals are drawn to religious terrorism and others not. From the perspective of political science, Daniel Philpott surveys a variety of potential relationships between state and religion and degrees of accepted theological autonomy to account for two forms of religious violence: communal conflict and terrorism. He concludes that religious violence is least likely to originate—though it will sometimes operate—in settings of consensual, institutional independence, as found most commonly in religion-friendly liberal democracies.

A range of literary approaches are offered by Margo Kitts, who surveys theories that attempt to explain how and why violence pervades foundational religious texts, as well as the imaginative dynamics that emerge from those texts and shape acts of violence. Christian theological approaches are summarized by Charles Kimball, who traces the early Christian cult from its pacific origins through its nationalization and militarization with Constantine, Charlemagne, and the Crusades. He also addresses internal movements that complexly administered and mitigated violence, such as the Inquisition, internal church discipline, religious wars, just war thinking, monasticism, and what has been called the just peacemaking paradigm. Christian theological perspectives on violence resonate with other theological perspectives such as Jewish and Islamic, which are covered in the handbook's first section.

PART IV: NEW DIRECTIONS

This fourth section is a platform for describing new models for the study of religion and violence and for addressing new directions in the established approaches. A group of innovative scholars considers new directions in which the field is moving and offers novel analytic approaches. Some have taken as their task a consideration of the relationship of religion to violence in general. Others focus on particular components of religion and violence—such as religious conflicts within cities. Still others search for causation, attempting to produce an explanation for the phenomena of religious violence. Together the chapters in this section point to productive new possibilities in the study of religion and violence that will illuminate not only this specific topic but the range of ways in which religious culture interacts with other social phenomena.

The first chapter in this section takes an enduring theme in the study of religion and violence, sacrifice, and focuses on religious practices in the ancient Near East and Mediterranean. Walter Burkert shows that religion is perpetrated in the arena of death, that is, in the killings we call sacrifice. Such sacrificial killings—highly circumscribed by taboos, ritual prescriptions, and ceremonial significance—initiated all major collective institutions and decisions in ancient societies, accompanied often by a feast on the victim's flesh. Why should killing animals for food become a religious act? To explore this question, Burkert ponders studies of empathy across species. He deduces, among other insights, that religious sacrifice harbors the truth of the "struggle for existence," while creating an optimistic superworld that displaces it.

The next chapter shifts the focus from the ritual act of sacrifice as a concentrated locus of violence to the grand scenarios of violence as envisaged by war. Saskia Sassen sees some cities as ascendant theaters for asymmetric war—war between a conventional army and armed insurgents—and examines the instructive elements, both variable and contradictory, within the contemporary conflicts in Mumbai and Gaza. She describes the shift from an epoch dominated by secularizing forces to one in which organized religions are structurally part of cities in their global modernity. Warfare is also a part of one of the most important aspects of religious thinking—apocalypse—explored by Michael A. Sells, who compares contemporary militant apocalypticism in its American Christian (Dispensationalist) and Middle Eastern Islamic versions. Sunni Salafi illustrations are drawn from Saudi Arabia's Safar al-Hawali and American Ali al-Timimi, whereas Shi'a illustrations stem broadly from Twelver traditions and American speculation about them. Each of these apocalyptic dreams anticipates messianic triumph, although the Salafi and Christian versions are more emphatic in portraying the religious other as evil, human peace efforts as demonic, and war as total, global, and culminating in the annihilation of everyone other than the faithful.

Philosopher Hent de Vries reflects on the deconstruction of religion and religious violence from the perspective of Jacques Derrida's thought. Based on Derrida's "*Violence et métaphysique*" (1961–1962) and his reflection on wars of religion waged by finger and thumb (that is, mediatized, so less localized and predictable than ever before), de Vries observes that war and violence cannot be expunged from global politics and global religions, which are capable of astonishing evil masked by enlightened and universalistic intentions. On a similar theme, David Frankfurter contemplates the myriad religious suspicions of an evil that warrants preemptive purging—from witch burnings to ethnic cleansing. He sees prurient

fascination and righteous revulsion with sinister conspiracies and stories of preda-
torial monstrosities as emboldening crowds as well as the charismatic authorities
who instigate violent remedies to quell that evil.

Wolfgang Palaver focuses on the mimetic theory of René Girard in analyzing
foundational myths of violence. Palaver sees Girard's notion of the scapegoating
mechanism, whereby a substitute victim absorbs the mimetic animosities of the
entire group and thereby promotes peace, as applicable to the disturbing tendency
to direct violence toward exogenous groups. Hector Avalos also sees violence as
being endemic to the religious imagination, though he argues that this is due to
scarcity, not competition. Avalos claims that all religions tend to create artificial
shortages of supernatural blessings or beings and thereby promote violence.

The next chapters in this section also focus on the nature of religion in order to
understand the phenomenon of religious violence. Candace S. Alcorta and Richard
Sosis explain why, from an evolutionary perspective, the same religions that can at
times inspire joy, love, and awe can also involve terror, pain, self-mutilation, deprivation, violence, and feelings of revulsion. Examining ritual communication and
costly signaling theory, they show how emotionally powerful and highly memorable experiences—such as rites of passages—can trigger autonomic and neuroendo-
crinal changes in individuals and bonding experiences in groups. The chapter by
Harvey Whitehouse and Brian McQuinn also looks at religious ritual in relationship to social conflict, as based on Whitehouse's theory of divergent modes of religiosity and ritual. In the chapter in this volume, they contrast the social dynamics
of contemporary rebel groups engaging in high-frequency, low-arousal rituals (the
doctrinal mode) with groups bonded tightly by traumatic ritual ordeals (the imagistic mode), such as high-arousal and emotionally costly initiation rites. The latter
tend to intensify cohesion and tolerance within groups while heightening hostility
and intolerance toward outgroups.

The final chapter in this section looks at a recent shift in the social sciences and
humanities that enables scholars to better understand the religious dimensions of
social pheonoma such as acts of terrorism and violence. Mark Juergensmeyer and
Mona Kanwal Sheikh observe that there is a "sociotheological turn" in contemporary scholarship that encourages social scientists to take stock of the religious justifications for social action and for theologians and scholars of religious studies to
be more aware of the social significance of spiritual ideas and practices. Focusing
on "epistemic worldviews" as the appropriate subject for sociotheological analysis,
the authors outline useful guidelines for research, such as undertaking interviews
and case studies with an empathetic awareness that allows for the emergence of
relational knowledge.

*****

The images and acts of destruction described in all four sections of this book can
be collectively described as religious violence, though it is clear that there are many
ways of interpreting that phrase. In some cases the ideas related to violence are

rooted in the basic beliefs of the tradition; in other cases, they and the practices associated with them are not narrowly theological. Aside from ritual sacrifice, real acts of violence are seldom intrinsic to any specific religious experience—wars are often justified in the name of religion, for instance, when the primary purpose is to extend political power. Yet, because violence in both real and symbolic forms is found in all religious traditions, it can be regarded as a feature of the religious imagination. Almost every major tradition, for example, has some notion of sacrifice and some notion of cosmic war, a grand moral struggle that underlies all reality and can be used to justify acts of real warfare.

Thus the study of religious violence and the religious dimensions of violent situations do much to shed light on the intrinsic nature of religion. The chapters that make up this volume are intended to provide a guide to the emerging field of studies in religion and violence, but they will also be useful in understanding religion in all of its complexity, its myriad social, psychological, and theological forms.

PART I

OVERVIEW OF RELIGIOUS TRADITIONS

CHAPTER 1

....

VIOLENCE AND NONVIOLENCE AT THE HEART OF HINDU ETHICS

....

VEENA DAS

A starting premise on any reflection on violence is the acknowledgment that violence is not a self-evident transparent category.[1] While the application of physical force on an unwilling person in order to injure might seem to be the most obvious and manifest sign of violence, even this minimal definition confronts such issues as who counts as a person, what counts as consent, and is intentionality to injure necessary for an act to count as violence? In this overview, I take an engagement with these questions at the very heart of my project, which is to examine how we might render a certain anxiety around violence as integral to the imagination of an ethical life in Hindu texts and practices. But how is one to define what would count as a Hindu (versus, say, Vedic) text? As many scholars have argued, the term *Hindu* cannot be projected back into time for it is a product of a long history in which it becomes a word at hand for a dispersal of names, places, objects, gestures, and schemes for living a good life (Llewellyn 2005).

It is important to state that problems of definition are not unique to Hinduism. The philosopher of religion Hent de Vries offers us the following provocation: "Nothing allows us to determine in advance, let alone on the basis of some philosophically or transcendentally construed a priori, what, precisely religion in its very 'concept'—may still (or yet again) make possible or necessary, visible and readable, audible and palpable" (de Vries 2010: 1). The texts coming from the Hindu tradition (however retrospectively defined) face the additional problem that there have been powerful forms of repudiation of these texts' claims to philosophical or theoretical intervention made by philosophers of great repute (e.g., Hegel 1995; and for a critical discussion of such views, see McGetchin, Park and SarDesai 2004). Despite attempts to reclaim Hindu texts for a philosophically informed ethics (Billimoria, Prabhu and Sharma 2007; Paranjpe 1998) the difficulties of treating them as more than exotic traditions have been formidable.[2] Then how should one read these archives so that we neither romanticize them as bearers of some superior mystical traditions nor assume that they already belong to a past that has little to contribute to our lives now?

Given the enormity and range of the sources (from textual sources to ethnographies) that can come under the rubric of the term *Hindu*, it is not possible to give a chronological account of debates on violence and nonviolence within the confines of a chapter. I have, therefore, chosen to present two domains of discussion on which I track the reflections on violence and nonviolence and ask, especially, What is the imagination of how human societies can find a way out of cycles of violence? These two domains are defined by (a) the relation to animals as sacrificial offerings and as food in the language of ritual and (b) gendered violence in the imagination of sovereignty in the mythic register. I follow this discussion with some contemporary examples of violence and nonviolence and ask how new forms of collective life such as the imaginary of the nation shape the expression and experience of violence. However, I also claim that in the figure of Mahatma Gandhi we have some important experiments with these questions, and I signal these moments at various points in the text. My attempt here is not to give a history of these concepts but to construct an archive in which different temporalities are embedded. As Cavell puts the argument for inheritance so well: "It is not for the text to answer the questions you put to it, but for you to respond to the questions you discover it asks (of itself, of you)" (2003: 248). Toward the end of the chapter, I reflect on the question of whether the forms that contemporary Hinduism has taken are able to respond at all to the questions the texts ask of us—or if the place where the archive lives is in ordinary actions that turn away from the nationalist imaginings of Hinduism today? Is the task of scholarship, then, to patiently establish if texts and practices of Hinduism can offer a view of the moral life that can bring to the fore a different conceptual furniture than that which privileges the relation of philosophy, antiphilosophy, and political theology to essentially Greek, Judaic, and Christian traditions?[3]

The Claims of the Animal

In a text written in the thirteenth century of the Common Era, titled *Dharmaranya Purana* to depict the "history" of the Modh Brahmins and Baniyas of Gujarat,[4] we get an interesting glimpse of an argument between the Brahmins, who are depicted as those who perform sacrifice, and the Jains, who are shown as upholders of *ahimsa* (nonviolence). The debate is staged in the court of a Jain king. Jain monks accuse the Brahmins of indulging in violence and urge the king to withdraw patronage from the Brahmins. The Brahmins retort that it is hypocritical to assume that anyone can live without violence for, in order to live, it is necessary to eat, and that act means that we are bound to inflict violence, whether on animals or plants. They argue further that violence is much more expansive than physical harm and who, they ask, is free of harboring anger and jealousy, which are also forms of violence (see Das 1977). This debate, despite its local character, resonates with an important cultural theme enacted at various levels of Hindu texts and practices—that is, can the killing of animals in sacrifice be regarded as a dramatization of everyday acts of violence that we commit simply in order to live? Instead of thinking of sacrifice as primarily an act of communication between humans and gods with the animal offering as the object that mediates the two, as dominant theories of sacrifice in anthropology are inclined to do (Hubert and Mauss 1964),⁵ I point to a different cultural logic in which the eating and killing of animals in sacrifice are integrally linked with the violent preconditions of our life. From this perspective, sacrifice provides a dramatic expression of the ambivalence that surrounds the topic of violence and nonviolence—one might regard ritual violence as enacting puzzles about the costs we pay in order to live. Let us first consider the logic of sacrifice in the Vedic texts and in the Brahmanas (texts that provide explanations of Vedic injunctions of sacrifice), composed roughly from 1500 to 500 BCE. The Vedic texts distinguish between domestic animals (*pashu*) and wild animals (*mriga*)—killing of animals could take the form of either sacrifice, in which the offerings are domestic animals (including humans), or hunting that was oriented to wild animals. Here I choose to amplify three different strands that speak to the problem of converting the facts of violence into nonviolence—or at least into violence that we can live with. These three strands are (a) the ritual words and acts that convert the animal from a victim to a willing participant and, hence, the euphemistic expressions that redefine violence as a kind of pacification, (b) ritual substitution that keeps the symbolic presence of violence very much in the picture without actually committing the acts of killing, and (c) shifting the weight of ritual action from the act of killing to that of regeneration.

KILLING AS PACIFICATION: EUPHEMISTIC CHARACTER OF RITUAL VOCABULARY

In his classic work on the religion of the Vedas, Oldenburg (1988) describes the moment of the killing of the animal by strangulation as follows:

> The sacrificial animal was killed with the expressions, common also to other people, of efforts to free oneself from the sin of a bloody deed and from impending

revenge. It was told 'You are not dying, you are not harmed, you are going to the gods along beautiful paths'…the killing was called euphemistically 'to get the consent of the animal.' (Oldenburg 1988: 292)

The exact ritual term for this process was *sangyapan* (Sen 1978), which literally meant "taking the consent." As Émile Benveniste has shown in a short essay on euphemisms, this region of linguistic expressions hinges on the paradox that one wishes to bring to mind an idea while avoiding naming it specifically (1971: 266). Euphemisms are distinct from taboos on speaking certain words. In the latter case the issue is that of avoidance—in the former case, different words are substituted for those words that must not be uttered, thus concealing the nature of the act and yet bringing it to mind. Benveniste concludes his essay with this stunning observation: "Just as in the Vedic ritual of sacrifice, the victim is 'appeased' (*samayati*) or 'made to consent' when in actual fact it is 'strangled,' so the fire that is extinguished is 'appeased'" (1971: 270). Thus, language transforms the killing the animal into the creation of a beatific path for it to reach the gods. The sacrificer's (yajaman's) desire for heaven is made to merge with the animal's desire to reach heaven through this ritual. By becoming the sacrificial victim voluntarily the animal is seen to reach heaven directly without going through endless cysles of rebirth.

Now what is the nature of the idea that is brought to mind while avoiding its naming in the ritual characterization of strangulation as "consent"? I suggest that what is at stake in the euphemistic sacred vocabulary is the question of death—not the death of the animal that is being ritually strangled but the sacrificer's death that is being warded off. Thus the violence being done to the animal in the public (*srauta*) ritual is an anticipation or prefiguration of the violence that will be done to the sacrificer in a final sacrifice that he will perform—the sacrifice of the self as an offering to the gods in the final death rituals.

Mariasusai Dhavamony (1973) noted that it is through sacrifice that man ransoms his being from the gods in Vedic sacrifice, and scholars such as Anand Coomaraswamy (2000) explicitly drew attention to the offering of squeezed soma plant in sacrifice, saying that when soma and *agni* ("fire") are united in sacrifice they jointly overcome the force of death and redeem man since man is born in debt to death (see also Dalmiya 2001). Anthropologists have shown that the structure of the cremation rituals is best understood through the vocabulary as well as the spatial and temporal organization of sacrificial rituals (see Das 1977; Parry 1994). In his brilliant analysis of the cremation rituals, Charles Malamoud (1996) uses a culinary vocabulary to think of the transformation of the corpse through the cremation fire that "cooks" it to make it into an oblation fit to be offered to the gods, similar to other fires such as the cooking hearth and the digestive fire in the body.

The implications of the euphemisms used in the sacred vocabulary pertaining to killing as well as the strict analogy between cremation and sacrifice, or rather cremation as sacrifice, has an important bearing on our argument on the close braiding of violence and nonviolence. The ritual words and acts do not so much expel violence as make it the general condition of our lives in which we share with animals the common condition of being ransomed to death. It is understandable that the Jains (and Buddhists) with whom the Brahmins debate about whether violence committed in sacrifice is violence at all accused the Brahmins of ritual trickery. It is also a fact that for the Brahmin sacrificer as well the interpreters from the hermeneutic school of Mimamsa, there is no respite from the reality that all violence mimes the ultimate violence of death. As Wendy Doniger summarizes this melancholy sense, the texts are saying that "human beings are, like all other animals, fit to be sacrificed to the gods, they are, as it were, the livestock of the gods" (Doniger 2009: 152).

Ritual Substitution

The logic of substitution is widely acknowledged to be at the heart of sacrifice by social theorists (Beistegui 1997; Das 1977, 1983; Doniger 2009; Evans-Pritchard 1954; Girard 1997; Lévi-Strauss 1963, 1969). However, how to interpret the fact of substitution is the subject of considerable debate. Among these theorists, Lévi-Strauss is famous for his distrust of sacrificial logic. In his words:

> (Totemism) is a quantified system while (sacrifice) permits a continuous passage between its terms; a cucumber is worth an egg as a sacrificial victim, an egg a fish, a fish a hen, a hen a goat, a goat an ox. And this gradation is oriented; a cucumber is sacrificed if there is no ox but the sacrifice of an ox for want of a cucumber would be an absurdity. (Lévi-Strauss 1969: 224)

Lévi-Strauss founded his theoretical observations on the ethnography of sacrifice among the Nuer. Matters are much more complicated when it comes to understanding Vedic sacrifice, for, as noted in the last section, there is a different temporal horizon to these matters. Animals fit for sacrifice (pashu) are defined in a series of five, and man is included in the series as among those who can be sacrificed. One of the Brahamanic texts notes that the gods first used man as a sacrificial beast—as the sacrificial quality went out of him it entered the next in the series— thus the bull, then the stallion, then the billy goat, and so on. It is interesting that, after the enumerated animals are exhausted, the sacrificial quality then goes to rice and barley, which become complete sacrificial oblations. One text draws attention to the silent screaming of the rice and barley as they are offered in sacrifice (see Doniger 2009). The series is an oriented one, as Lévi-Strauss saw, but this is not a matter of mere contingency (for want of an ox, an egg, etc.); rather, even if each substitution leads to a lesser degree of violence and even if we cannot hear the silent screams of rice and barley, we cannot escape violence altogether, for, in the final sense not only human, but all existence entails violence. In the later devotional cults, vegetarian offerings are substituted for the sacrificial victim for many of the gods and goddesses who required sacrifice, but the memory of the original sacrifice is retained by such acts as the forceful smashing of the coconut and the red color put on the coconut; an origin myth in which a goddess explicitly states that she will accept the offering of a coconut in lieu of a head is often evoked to explain this change (Doniger 2009: 561). Unlike the idea of a scapegoat that is from outside the community and can carry away the sins of the community (see Girard 1977), the substitution here only points to temporal dislocations—either a past is evoked in the form of a myth in which the coconut represents the original violent event of sacrifice, or the animal sacrifice points to the future in which the sacrificer will be the victim. In either case, the horizon of thought is that of death and its intimacy with violence.

SACRIFICE AS REGENERATION

The third strand that I mentioned is that of converting the violence of sacrifice into regeneration. Consider the *purusha sūkta*, hymn 10.90 of the Rigveda, which describes the original sacrifice of *purusha* or the primeval man. It is from his dismembered body that both the natural and the social order are created, as different parts of the sacrificed body become the furniture of the universe. The *varna* (caste) hierarchy, as is well known, is created at this sacrificial moment with the mouth becoming the Brahmin, the arms the Kshatriya, the stomach the Vaishya, and the feet the Shudra. In a repetition of the original sacrifice, death rituals re-create death as an act of sacrificial offering and regeneration (Das 1977, Parry 1994). However, not everyone buys into the story of sacrifice as beatific regeneration and, as persistent critiques from not only the Buddhists and the Jains but also from the later devotional cults show, a shift of perspective from man to that of animal and from the future to that of the present moment has the potential of stripping the story of its comforting moment to make visible the utter devastation that sacrifice might bring to the world.

One such thought is present in the epic Mahabharata that will be analyzed in the next section when King Janmajeya performs the infamous snake sacrifice in which, instead of the prescribed horse, the king vows to burn every snake in the sacrificial pyre to avenge the death of his father by snakebite. In an act reminiscent of this terrible sacrifice, the Mahabharata details the *abhichara* (magical, clandestine) sacrifice performed by Drupad who wanted to generate a son who would be so powerful as to wipe out his enemies, the Kshatriyas or warrior kings, from the earth. Thus the texts recognize that not all sacrifice can achieve the aim of regeneration and that sacrifice contains in itself the dark energies fueled by such passions as anger and vengeance that can lead to massive destruction. As Doniger (2009) observes, "The Mahabharata sees a vice behind every virtue, a snake behind a horse, and a doomsday behind every victory" (Doniger 2009: 276).[6]

On the positive side, the Vedic sacrificial ritual contains many other acts than killing. In the interpretations of the Mimamsa scholars, the theme of gift, renunciation, and transfer of properties plays an important role in interpretation as does the question of how a reorganization of desire (from objects to heaven, not as a place but as an empty signifier), might take place (see Das 1983).

The Eating of Animals

The debates on violence and nonviolence that we tracked in the case of sacrifice find an interesting resonance in the dilemmas on the eating of animals. I focus on three specific issues and then consider how we might connect these with the question of what Cora Diamond (2008) called the difficulty of reality and the difficulty of philosophy. Here are the questions I want to discuss.

First, how are rules of interpretation in sacrifice applied to other domains of life and especially to the question of the consumption of meat? Second, in what manner does the notion of ahimsa (nonviolence) join the eating of animals conceptually to other forms of cruelty? Davis (2010) has convincingly argued that the scholastic tradition of the Dharmashastras relied on Mimamsa principles of interpretation, but it also translated its core elements into the mundane world of human society. The focus of theological reflection then became the everyday world of *varna* and *ashrama* (caste and life stages). For our purposes, it is interesting to reflect on the application of the principles of Mimamsa on the eating of meat. Davis gives the example from the fifth chapter in *The Laws of Manu,* in which there seem to be contradictory injunctions on this issue. Thus, one of the rules states that one can never obtain meat without causing injury, and therefore one should abstain from eating meat (5.48); while another rule says that there is no fault in eating meat, drinking liquor, or having sex for these are the natural activities of creatures, though abstaining from such activities carries great rewards (5.56). Davis shows how, applying the notion of what is rule in the Mimamsa, the tenth-century commentator Medhatithi argues that not all rules carry the same force since explanations and exhortations are not at the same level as the rules with injunctive force (Jha 1999). More interestingly, the text makes a distinction between what is primary and what is secondary in any act—concluding that killing the animal is secondary and eating the meat is primary (Davis 2010: 58). This is an interesting commentary precisely because it brings intentionality into the question of what constitutes violence. Was the pleasure of the act centered on the killing or on the eating? Further, I suggest that this reflection on the everydayness of ethical acts brings into view the more profound issue of whether our motives are transparent to us—a point that has relevance to how we might understand what is a violent act.

Let us suppose for a moment that our theoretical stakes are not centered on *what* we can learn about the Hindu notions of violence and nonviolence but *how* such notions might provide an archive for reflecting on contemporary dilemmas. Then, one of the most interesting figures we might turn to is Mohandas Gandhi. Gandhi is widely recognized as having brought the principles of nonviolence or

ahimsa to the political arena in the struggle against colonial rule. However, scholars have wrestled with the question of influences behind the depth and range of
Gandhi's ideas on ahimsa. We should note that ahimsa for Gandhi is not limited
to the eating or killing of animals—his ideas of both violence and nonviolence
are more expansive. Thus, for instance, he stated that not hurting a living thing
is a part of ahimsa, but it is its least expression—it was hatred of any kind that
Gandhi defined as violence (Gandhi, M. K. 1938). We might refer back to the debate
between the Brahmins and the Jains in which Brahmins offered this expanded
notion of violence. However, for Gandhi, the matter does not stop there for he also
shows in his life and his politics that resisting injustice is also part of his definition
of ahimsa. This is why his expanded idea of nonviolence includes for him *satyagraha* (truth force or tenacity in the pursuit of truth) and *brahmacharya* or celibacy (Gandhi, R 1982). Among his recent interpreters, Akeel Bilgrami (2002), Leela
Gandhi (2006), and Bhrigupati Singh (2010a) offer some fascinating insights into
this range of Gandhi's thought. For Leela Gandhi (2006), Gandhi's early interactions with the various late Victorian animal welfare societies in London and their
hospitality to him decisively influenced the affectivity and anti-constitutionalism
behind his ideas of ahimsa. What was at stake in human-animal relations for both
the proponents of vegetarianism in London and for the later Gandhi was a vision
of how nongovernmental sociality might be imagined. Thus, Leela Gandhi draws
attention to Gandhi's essay on enlightened anarchy, written in 1939, in which he
argued that true ahimsa could only be achieved in independent India if it agreed
to an experiment with statelessness. The structure of governance, he argued,
whether British or Indian, becomes contaminated by violence or *himsa*. The claim
that Gandhian politics owed some of its inheritance to the radicals who lived and
worked on the margins of late Victorian culture is unexceptionable—the difficulty
is that the other parts of Gandhi's inheritance are left unexamined. For instance,
while it is true that Gandhi rejected the governmentality of the biopolitical state,
surely he did not reject the government of the self. It is in this rift that the inheritance of an expanded notion of himsa and ahimsa in varied Hindu traditions found
expression in Gandhi's politics.

Akeel Bilgrami (2002) disregards the practice of dietetics and concentrates
instead on asking: How did Gandhi reconcile the idea of satyagraha as moral resistance with the exhortation that his satyagrahis must abstain from any moral judgment against the British rulers, which he saw as a sign of violence? The result is a
highly original reading in which Gandhi's differences from, for example, Mill's
idea of tolerance or from the Western philosophical traditions in which moral
action and moral judgment are integrally linked are brought out with great finesse.
The question that Bilgrami does not ask, however, is this: In what regard might
we consider Gandhi's thought as anchored on the expanded notions of violence
and nonviolence that were the subjects of much debate between Indic traditions—
Brahmanism versus Buddhism and Jainism and later debates among Hindus sects
elaborated in discursive forms as well as ritual practices? Alternately, to what
extent, might we see Gandhi as a critic of the apologetics offered by Hindu scholars

and practitioners? Singh (2010a) takes an important step toward the direction of linking dietetics with control over sexuality through the contrast between eroticism and asceticism in the government of the self (both at national and individual level), but his essay veers toward comparisons with Thoreau and Nietzsche rather than in the direction of engaging the archive from Hinduism. It seems to me that after some early leads in Ramachandra Gandhi (1982), the attempts to grapple with these difficult issues have remained sporadic.

Why Animals?

In his famous formulation on animal symbolism in totemism, Lévi-Strauss (1963) formulated his famous proposition that "animals are good to think with." In privileging the question of the animal as a concrete other to the human for articulating how we might think of the braiding of violence and nonviolence in texts and practices of Hindus, I am trying to tap into a different region of thought. In considering what death is to an animal, we might find that we are not able to inhabit its body in our imagination. I have suggested that in thinking of what it is to kill an animal in sacrifice and for food, the Vedic texts on sacrifice are struggling to find a language for depicting the cost of living that we pay—the violence of sacrifice is the way in which they imagine that one could ransom oneself from death. Ironically, we find that when the figure of the cow appears in the nationalist mobilization during the late nineteenth and early twentieth centuries, it now appears as an animal that condenses a Hindu cosmology and that also signifies the inability to imagine what it is for the other (as in the figure of the Muslim) to die as witnessed in brutal riots in which Muslims could be freely killed as revenge for the killing of the cow (see Freitag 1989; Pinney 2004; Yang 1980). Simultaneously it signals to a profound issue—the incapacity to imagine one's own death—to have a genuinely embodied sense of being extinguished. Cora Diamond (2010) in her profound reflections on J. M. Coetzee's (1999) Tanner Lectures on the lives of animals, articulated through the literary figure of Mrs Costello, in the novel *Elizabeth Costello*, says the following:

> I want to describe Coetzee's lectures, then, as presenting a kind of woundedness or hauntedness, a terrible rawness of nerves. What wounds this woman, what haunts her mind, is what we do to animals. This, in all its horror, is there in our world. How is it possible to live in the face of it? And, in the face of the fact, that for nearly everyone, it is as nothing, as the mere accepted background of life? (Diamond 2008: 47)

I suggest that the figure of the animal is important in understanding violence, precisely because in the contemplation of the killing of animals in sacrifice, it brings to the fore that accepted background of life that Diamond finds to be so wounding. If there is a glimmer of a hope here, it is that we learn to live with the awareness of the way our lives are entangled with other lives and forms of suffering entailed in our living, to which we might not normally give another thought.

I am not suggesting that the texts resolve these issues—just that they make us think of the violence we routinely commit. My deep disappointment with the way that these issues are made to disappear in the new guises in which Hinduism seems to tackle the issue of violence and nonviolence in the period we might name as that of the modern, and especially the deflection of the problem of what it is to imagine doing violence to another can hardly be overstated. So I will let a different voice, that of Gandhi on the issue of the cow protection movement that had led to riots in 1893 and subsequent episodes of violence between Hindus and Muslims, have the last word on this.

> But just as I respect the cow, so do I respect my fellowmen.... Am I, then, to fight with or kill a Mahomedan in order to save a cow? In doing so, I would become an enemy of the Mahomedan as well as of the cow. Therefore, the only method I know of protecting the cow is that I should approach my Mohemadan brother and urge him for the sake of the country to join me in protecting her. If he would not listen to me I should let the cow go for the simple reason that the matter is beyond my ability. If I were overfull of pity for the cow, I should sacrifice my life to save her but not take my brother's. This, I hold, is the law of our religion (Gandhi in Hind Swaraj, 1938).

Women, Warfare, and Sovereignty

With this section we shift the scene of violence from that of sacrifice to that of warfare especially as it pertains to the way in which kingship is imagined within what I have elsewhere called an alternate founding story of sovereignty (Das 2010a). While the connection between sovereignty and the subjugation of violence is the dominant theme of any story of sovereignty, we can treat the epic war of Mahabharata as educating us in a different kind of story in which one mode through which men seek their way out of cycles of violence is to join their own destiny to that of creatures lower than the human. The scene of sovereign violence then turns out to be one of vulnerability in which to be in the grip of violence is also to be in danger of losing the self. The voice of the woman appears as the voice of interrogation so that one might read the epics Ramayana and Mahabharata as an argument with the gods (Das 1998).

Sheldon Pollock (2007), among other scholars, has noted the complementary relationship between the two great epics, Ramayana and Mahabharata. Most important to the texts is the agon—the Ramayana, as Pollock says, is a tale of othering, the enemy is nonhuman, even demonic and the war takes place far away; the Mahabharata is a tale of "brothering," the enemy are kinsmen and the war takes place at home. It is also well known that both epics have spawned many versions in Sanskrit as well as in the vernacular languages and that stories from the epics provide a staple diet for oral epics as well as traditions of recitation, performance, and image making.

For reasons of space, I limit myself to the Mahabharata and refer to only one episode from Rama's story. The question remains similar to the earlier question asked—how is society to imagine a way out of cycles of violence? Out of the scenes of intense sexual violence depicted in the Mahabharata, we come to a different way of thinking about sovereignty and sexuality, not through concepts of contract and obligation as in European theories of sovereignty but through the intense debates on violence and nonviolence, cruelty and noncruelty. I suggest that it is not in the kinship with gods but in kinship with animals that the epic sees a way out of the cycles of violence in which the agonistic kingly lineages get implicated. And nature is not the scene of unmitigated violence for which social contract provides a way out, as in a Hobbesian view of the world[7]—rather it is the earth that is tired of the endless violence that men perpetrate on one another, and it is from within the scene of intimacy that a way out of violence is found.

Striving for Noncruelty

The epic tells us on many occasions that *anrishansya* or noncruelty is the highest *dharma*. Why noncruelty and not nonviolence? Doniger (2009) suggests that the text offers a "compromise." In her words, "The issue of non-cruelty to animals is a minor variant on the heavier theme of non-violence (ahimsa)...in an age when violence toward both humans and animals in inevitable" (Doniger 2009: 270). But the issue is not that of a particular age or a society mired in violence but rather that the accepted background of our lives as humans is put into question. The epic mode dramatizes the question of violence and asks: What does it mean to relate to the other if the self is lost—an inevitable risk of violence as the epic sees it. Instead of thinking of non cruelty as a compromise, what is being suggested is a new modality of relationships even when, and especially when, the self of the male subject is lost as it comes into the grip of the violence of warfare (see Lath 2009; Hiltebeitel 2001; Dalmiya 2001).

I begin with two observations fundamental to this story. First, a strong theme of the Mahabharata is to show how even the tragedy of great events and decisions is contained in the every day. Second, the epic dramatizes the moral as the point when we are put in the grip of an uncertainty—in the text this uncertainty hangs over the every day as the female voice emerges in the interrogation of various male characters and even of Krishna, the god who is present in every scene of violence.

The Scene of Violence and the Loss of Self

The argument in this section will be developed neither through plot and narration nor in terms of characters since the text uses multiple frames, embedding stories within stories and using techniques of side-shadowing to suggest other lives that the characters might lead (Hiltebeitel 2001). Further, we can regard the epic as a living tradition and will, indeed, make reference to literary creations that contribute to the story (see Sharma 2009). Doniger (2009: 263) summarizes the bare bones of the central story in the following terms:

> The five sons of King Pandu, called the Pandavas, were fathered by gods...all five of them married Draupadi. When Yudhishthira lost the kingdom to his cousins in a game of dice, the Pandavas and Draupadi went into exile for twelve years, at the end of which, with the help of their cousin the incarnate god Krishna, who befriended the Pandavas and whose counsel to Arjuna in the battlefield of Kurukshetra is the Bhagvad Gita, they regained their kingdom through a cataclysmic battle in which almost everyone on both sides was killed.

The bare bones of the story of course tell us nothing, (as Doniger's ironic condensation shows) about the texture of the text or its place in moral argumentation in the making of Indian sensibilities. I will therefore turn to two kinds of scenes[8]—the first I call the scene of the loss of self as one comes within the force field of violence, and the second I call the scene of instruction, in which the virtue of noncruelty is offered as a way out of violence enunciated sometimes through animal stories. It is of the utmost importance that the value of noncruelty is advocated precisely at some juncture in which violence or some form of violent death has taken place. It is as if noncruelty, defined simply as a desire not to injure others, is seen as a realistic starting point for imagining how humans make their way out of cycles of violence. Otherwise said, one might define anrishansya or noncruelty as a mode of being that re-creates the theme of nonviolence but on a minor key humanizing the impersonal force of both violence and blind adherence to dharma.

The Dice Game

Let us place ourselves in the public assembly of the Kaurava King. Here the dice game is in progress. Having lost everything else, Yudhishthira has waged Draupadi, the wife he shares with his brothers, and has lost the wager. An usher is sent to bring her to the public assembly. But she presents him with a cascade of questions of which the most important is "Go to the game. Having gone, ask Yudhishthira in the *sabha* (assembly), what did you lose first, yourself or me?" As Hiltebeitel interprets this question, the term *atmanam* in the question could be translated as "yourself" but also as "the self." Behind the legal question then, as to whether one who has already lost himself can wager another or whether the wife is the property of the husband, lurks the philosophical question, were you in possession of your self when you entered the contract? In the sabha the question will snowball reducing the most learned to utter silence.

Draupadi, having been dragged to the assembly stands now in a completely dishevelled condition in public before all the assembled kings, which include her elders. Here she is insulted, called a whore for having five husbands; invited to sit on the bare thigh of Dushasana, a younger brother of Duryodhana; and yet, the elders assembled do nothing. When Draupadi again asks if Yudhishthira had lost himself before he put the wager on her, she gets no response. Challenged by the questions of Draupadi, Bhishma, the eldest patriarch, can only say that the course of dharma is subtle and that only Yudhishthira, the most learned in the ways of dharma, would be able to answer her question. As readers, we are astonished that the same Yudhishthira who is able to answer the subtlest of questions on dharma is now reduced to silence. The crisis is temporarily resolved by the intervention of the blind king Dhritrashtra but not before terrible oaths of revenge have been uttered and the destruction of the entire Kuru race is predicted on the inexorable logic of insult and vengeance.

The most important lesson we learn from this episode is that dharma, on which the stability of the earth rests, becomes mute in the face of a question asked by a woman. Draupadi's question hovers on the text and, though she is saved from the ignominy of standing naked in the full court of men by the miraculous intervention of Krishna, a cycle of violence has been let loose. A public debating forum on the righteousness or otherwise of moral conduct fails in the presence of violence that is simultaneously public and intimate. Even if the war will be won, the self and all forms of relatedness will become frayed, if not lost.

The Hesitation of Arjuna

The second scene I consider is the famous battle scene in which Arjuna is standing in the battlefield and refusing to go into a battle that will result in the death of his kin. Krishna advises him that the violence is not only necessary but that, in the broader scheme of things, it is no violence. I cannot go into the literature on the philosophy of action to which notions of violence and war in the Bhagvad Gita have contributed, but I note that the text shows in full light how nonviolence, which Krishna propagates as the highest dharma, is enmeshed in violence.[9] There is also a difference between how Arjuna is to be consoled for he is facing future actions as he is about to wage violence and how Yudhishthira is to be consoled as he faces the old king Dhritarashtra and his wife, Gandhari, who have lost all their sons *after* the battle. In the latter event, even though the scene is that of reconciliation, dark residues of anger remain, for even as Yudhishthira touches Gandhari's feet, his nails go black from the anger that is transmitted from Gandhari's body to his. Further, it is not Krishna, the god, who can speak of noncruelty to either Arjuna or Yudhishthira, since he stands accused of encouraging the war. Even contemporary Indian literature retains this sense of the unjustness that was committed by not only the Kauravas but also the Pandavas. If Draupadi's voice showed dharma to have been silenced in the scene of sexual violence witnessed earlier, it is Gandhari, the mother of the Kauravas, who has lived her married life in voluntary blindness, whose grief leads to her cursing of Krishna. In Alok Bhalla's lovely translation of the Hindi play *Andha Yug* (Bharati 2010), we can hear her rage against Krishna:

What have you done Krishna! What have you done!
If you wanted...You could have stopped the war...
You may be a god...You may be omnipotent
Whoever you are...
I curse you and I curse all your kinsmen.

Krishna accepts the curse, which then leads to the complete extinction of his lineage, while he is killed like a wild animal in his old age. What is haunting, though, is Bharati's depiction of what Krishna has taken on himself in this terrible war. He says:

In this terrible war of eighteen days,
I am the only one who died a million times.
Every time a soldier was struck down,
Every time a soldier fell on the ground.
It was I who was struck down,
It was I who was wounded,
It was I who fell to the ground.

It seems that in order to get out of the cycle of violence, it is not the divine voice but the human voice, or one on a scale even lower than the human that will have to be recovered. The text of the Mahabharata goes in that direction, but Bharati of the Andha Yuga tried to capture the terrible violence done to women during the Partition riots of 1947 through the analogical rendering of the epic, and this had no such consolation. The question of how to break this cycle of violence was simply set aside in nationalist imageries as the question of violence between Hindus and Muslims, especially through the enactment of violence against women, became a recurring feature of independent India. But let us return to the epic.

Noncruelty or the Humanization of Dharma

Explaining the concept of noncruelty Mukund Lath asks us to look for its meaning in the actions of various characters of the Mahabharata, since the word does not seem to carry much importance outside the epic. In Lath's words,

Literally the word *anrhamsya* means the state, the attitude, of not being *nrhamsa*. The word *nrhamsa* is common enough in Sanskrit literature; it literally means one who injures man.... But the word (*anrshmsya*) has more than a negative connotation; it signifies good-will, a fellow feeling, a deep sense of the other. A word that occurs often with *anrhsamsya*, therefore, is *anukrosha*, to cry with another, to feel another's pain. All these meanings are brought out in the stories. (2009: 84)

I do not have the space to visit all the stories that would be relevant here. Let me briefly allude to the moment when in answer to a question posed by a divine being (Yaksha, who turns out to be the Dharma himself), Yudhishthira answers that noncruelty is the highest dharma. As we saw, it was the same Yudhishthira whose actions in the dice game had led to the unleashing of a cycle of violence, but more importantly his actions have shown that any learned public discourse on right and wrong becomes impossible for the one whose self is lost. So, is the modality of noncruelty as a way of being in the world what Yudhishthira *arrives* at, learning this virtue only after his silence in the assembly? Would it be possible to say that noncruelty lowers the sights from Dharma with a capital *D* to dharma in the lower key, as a way by which he might recover his lost self?

Humanizing Dharma

The different stories through which a human scale or at any rate a scale lower than that of the gods might be found to speak about noncruelty do not parse out the concept into different parts. Rather they allow us to circle around the concept so that a swarm of ideas is generated around it. The first such idea is that of breaking the rigid lawlike regularity of the relation between karma or action and its fruits, its consequences for humanizing the force of dharma. The second is the exploration of the meaning of togetherness, and the third is that of the obligation of a writer toward his (by extension her) character—thus not simply how one *is* in the world but also how one *imagines* others might live in the world. A common thread uniting these ideas is that noncruelty is generated from within the scene of intimacy and is hence perhaps to be distinguished from compassion as an impersonal virtue that is to be extended to all beings.

Since I do not have the space to tell the corresponding stories in any detail, I will simply summarize how each dimension of noncruelty is summarized in a particular story. The point about the humanization of dharma is related through the story of the sage Mandava and Vidura, the youngest uncle of the Kauravas born through a Shudra woman. Mandava curses Yama, the god of Dharma to be born as a human through a Shudra woman as punishment for the fact that he (Mandava) was cruelly punished for a childhood prank on the logic that every action has its consequences. Mandava decries that henceforth no one will be held responsible for childhood pranks, thus loosening the severe and impersonal logic of action and consequences through the modality of noncruelty. The second point, that noncruelty is to be learnt from mutual intimacy, comes out in various animal stories of which the most famous story is that of the parrot and the tree. A tree withered and died because a fowler mistakenly pierced it with a poisoned arrow. All the birds left the tree, but a parrot stayed on and slowly began to wither away for lack of nourishment. When asked to explain why he did not leave the withered tree for another with foliage and fruits, the parrot replied that since he was born there, had grown up, and received protection from the tree, out of noncruelty and sympathy, he would not leave the withered tree.

Contrasting the qualities of nonviolence and noncruelty, Hiltebeitel (2001: 213) interprets this story to say, "While ahimsa tightens the great chain of beings, anrishamsya softens it with a cry for a *human* creature-feeling across the great divides." Dalmiya, interpreting the same story sees it as a parable of the relational (Dalmiya 2001: 297). In both Hiltebeitel and Dalmiya, the force of a concept such as noncruelty comes from the fact that a disposition is generated through the experience of togetherness—if the parrot had gone to a different tree no one would have termed it as betrayal. The second animal story is the iconic one of Yudhishthira refusing to abandon a dog that had attached itself to him even though Lord Indra, who ruled the heavens, threatens that this act will mean a loss of the promised heaven to the king. Yudhishthira, too, explains that, out of a feeling of noncruelty, he could not abandon the dog even though it was pure contingency that the dog had attached itself to him.

Two features stand out in these animal stories. First, the quality of noncruelty is demonstrated across species and at moments when it is not through language or through appeals to such distant moral concepts as obligation or rule-following but through a sense of togetherness that has developed by the sheer contingency of having been brought together—the fated circumstances of togetherness. Second, it is from within a scene of intimacy that dispositions toward noncruelty develop.

At this point, we might recall the two women, Draupadi and Gandhari, who became the causes for the destruction of the Kshatriyas and of Krishna's dynasty, respectively, thus ending the cruelty of the warrior clans. From the ashes of the heroic project of warrior castes emerges the possibility that there is another kind of intimacy between men and women, humans and animals that can offer a noncruel way of inhabiting the earth. The Mahabharata names it noncruelty. We could name the epic as an argument with gods rather than a resolution about the connection of sovereignty, violence, and sexuality. In showing that the most powerful are also the most vulnerable, especially to the ever-present threat of the loss of self, the Mahabharata enacts this argument through a proliferation of figures, both minor and major. It reminds us that the stirring message about the necessity of war given by Krishna on the battlefield must one day come full circle when war ends, in the grieving prince, Yudhishthira, who seeks not incentives to wage war but consolation—for when all have been destroyed, what is left for the prince to take pleasure in?

***

In selecting how problems of violence and nonviolence are voiced in relation to sacrifice and warfare, I hope to have shown that the traditions harbor a deep ambivalence about even the most revered myths and rituals. There is no doubt that the same religious archive that can justify killing in sacrifice and remain silent in the face of the sexual humiliation of a woman can, and has been used to legitimate violence against lower castes or against women in other contexts. However, scholars have often been content to take explicitly formulated rules (as in Manu or, in particular, episodes of violence against lower castes or forest tribes in epics) to be sufficient for understanding Hinduism without paying attention to how divided these traditions could be in confronting profound questions about violence and nonviolence. Even Rama, a king regarded as the most righteous of all, has been faulted for following his kingly dharma in killing a Shudra ascetic whose pursuit of Vedic knowledge was said to have violated the correct order of caste. However, in the hands of a poet such as Bhavabhuti (eighth century), when Rama performs the hateful task of killing the Shudra, he experiences a repetition of the violence he had inflicted on his beloved Sita in exiling her to the forest, also in fulfilment of his kingly duty. In verse 2.70 of the *Uttararamacharita* (Rama's Last Act), translated by Pollock (2007), Rama says:

> O my right hand,
> bring down this sword
> upon the Shudra monk
> And bring the dead son of the Brahman
> back to life. You are a limb of Rama's—
> who had it in him to drive
> his Sita into exile,
> weary and heavy with child.
> Why start with pity now?
> (*somehow striking a blow*) There, you have done
> a deed worthy of Rama. Let the
> Brahman's son live again.

One might say that such laments and the utter contempt with which Rama utters his own name do not console the Shudra who has been killed, but they do show that there is room for critique here. It is in the conflict of voices, both in the social order and within the self, that the possibility of reclaiming a religious archive becomes attractive, not in opposition to other traditions but in company with them. One final question one might ask is whether modernity completely alters the nature of the questions that Hinduism can ask of itself? I have indicated in various places in the essay that the braiding of violence and nonviolence and the profound ambivalence toward violence finds expression in contemporary India in the figure of Gandhi, but one might ask if the question identified as central to the archive on sacrifice and on sovereignty in Hindu texts and practices, namely, how can human societies find a way out of cycles of violence, find any resonance in contemporary India?

Hinduism's Modernity or Modernity's Hinduism?

The transformation of Hinduism in contemporary India is a vast subject in its own right. My aim here is a limited one. I ask, has the religious archive become irrelevant under conditions of modernity and postmodernity? For some scholars there is an inherent discordance between Hinduism and modernity. Thus, for instance, David Smith writes, "Hinduism is threatened by modernity, and modernity is threatened by Hinduism.... Hinduism is the best or at least the largest single instance of a traditional culture. As such it can stand as the type, the very image of tradition, as modernity's opposite" (Smith 2003: 6). For several other scholars, modernity and its institutions, such as the nation form, have distorted the nature of Hinduism to the extent that its contemporary forms have become unrecognizable as forms of faith (Nandy 1983) and become new forms of identity politics. Striking a somewhat different note, Dilip Gaonkar suggests the idea of creative adaptation as the site where "people 'make' themselves modern as opposed to being 'made' modern by alien and impersonal forces, and where they give themselves an identity and distinction" (Gaonkar 1999: 2).

In this spirit, I take three regions of thought to consider how questions of violence and nonviolence fold into practices of self-making in relation to contemporary challenges. First, I ask, how does the notion of satyagraha (soul force) as developed in Gandhian thought and practice draw on the languages of sacrifice we discussed earlier? Second, I take the emergence of Dalit writings as recasting the relation between sovereignty and violence, from the perspective of the Shudras—the lowest caste in the varna hierarchy. Finally, I examine the frequent claim that alignment between nationalism and Hinduism has led to the casting of the Muslim in India as the figure of the absolute other (Ludden 2005). For reasons of space, I will not be able to offer a comprehensive analysis of these issues but will confine myself to a few examples of the complex ways in which the ideas embedded in the religious archive appear to find life but not in places where one would expect them to be.

In her comparative study of sacrifice, Kathryn McClymond asks what the study of traditional sacrifice has to do with life today? Her answer is that "[t]raditional forms of sacrifice are continually being transformed into metaphoric sacrifice through new configurations of the various sacrificial procedures... [and that]... sacrificial imagery and rhetoric carry tremendous weight beyond religious arenas" (McClymond 2008: 160). She also asserts that national imageries of sacrifice carry as much weight as traditional sacrifice. The idea of sacrifice in the commentarial literature on Vedic sacrifice is not that of simply killing but of making visible and dramatizing one's own inevitable death. In Gandhi's hands, this idea gets transformed into several notions—satyagraha that goes straight to offering oneself as the object of violence and thus overcoming the fear of death, fasting as the ability to heal the body politic through the purification of one's own body (Alter 2000), and cultivation of the ascetic self as tapas (penance) to relate to the others who are affirmed in their difference by an identification with their suffering (Skaria 2009, 2010). Ajay Skaria has made sustained attempts to show how Gandhi's ideas of tolerance and political friendship challenge secular and liberal notions of what it is to inhabit the world with the other. A specific concept that he draws on in Gandhi's writings is that of tapasya (practices of asceticism). During the Khalifat movement, Skaria says, Gandhi insisted that the only way to create friendship between Hindus and Muslims was to create bonds through unconditional suffering on behalf of the Muslims by the Hindus. Consider his statement, "The test of friendship is a spirit of love and sacrifice independent of expectation of any return" (Gandhi as cited in Skaria 2009: 224). As Skaria rightly concludes the tapasya or suffering one undergoes on behalf of another is to create a bond between two people who consider themselves apart, not joined by shared history or syncretism as in liberal ideas of what would be the conditions of possibility for building tolerance. While Gandhian techniques of the body—fasting, nonviolent protests, sitting in silence—have become part of the repertoire of political action in India, there is further scope for thinking the form and content of political theology that can stand as an alternative (for better or for worse) to the strongly Christianized political theologies on offer now (Singh 2011).

It is precisely this issue that is taken up by Debjani Ganguly (2002, 2005) in a compelling and original understanding of Dalit discursive forms, especially the works of B. R. Ambedkar. Ganguly argues that life-forms within which caste is embedded are not available to the "rational, systemic, disembodied public self of the modern social scientist" or even to the Dalit activists because they are all implicated in the social scientific representations of caste that are invested in a normative modernity that can only render caste in a retrogressive light. Ganguly gestures to a heterotemporality and argues that appreciating the multifarious ways in which caste comes to be written on the body politic needs a nonpedagogical sensibility that could decipher how the various kinds of pasts among which the history of caste oppression is but one such past are layered on each other. She shows how the mythic register operates in Ambedkar's writings to make parallel claims over a past from a Shudra perspective. Ganguly calls such appropriations principled forgetting—others might call these wilful forgetting. The point, however, is that various Indian archives (Hindu and Buddhist) speak in Ambedkar's writings as they do in other oral mythologies of Dalit castes. When Ambedkar pronounced that he was in some genealogical continuity with Vyasa, the author of Mahabharata, and Valmiki, the author of Ramayana, who were both outcasts, since he, too, though an outcast, was called on to write the Constitution of Independent India, we come to appreciate the complex ways in which he saw himself in relation to Indian (including Buddhist) archives. It is surely not accidental that the texts he evokes are the authoritative texts on sovereignty.

As my last example of the transformation of Hinduism in the contemporary era, I consider the question of the presence of the Muslim as an other within Indian polity. Several authors have argued that the most decisive transformation of Hinduism was its conversion into a political identity, announced in V. D. Savarkar's (1942) notion of "Hindutva" to distinguish it from matters of faith, belief, or ritual (van der Veer 1994). For Sarvarkar, a Hindu is any person who considers the land from Indus to Sindhu as his fatherland (*pitribhu*) and regards it as *punyabhu*—sacred or pure land. By this definition, Muslims, who simultaneously define themselves as Indian as well as members of a transnational *umma* or religious community, are disqualified from being Indians. The political aspirations for Sarvarkar is to make India a Hindu nation. Many scholars who have argued that for a militant Hindu Right the Muslim is wholly other see the roots of Hindu rage against Muslims in a variety of conditions, but a loss of "masculinity" as a result of colonization is identified as a major concern (Hansen 1996; Nandy 1983, 1990). The position of the

Hindu Right has been vigorously opposed by proponents of secularism, who nevertheless avoid the issue of how communities within a national polity could learn to inherit a divided and contentious past (but see Amin 2002).

As an illustration of this issue, let us discuss the possibilities of multiple and conflicting pasts with regard to the destruction of the Babri mosque in a prolonged dispute over sacred spaces that many see as emblematic of the politics of religious nationalism. Van der Veer (1994), in his analysis of Hindu nationalism, has argued that it is not Sarvarkar's ideas per se but their deployment for bringing together Hindus across sectarian, regional, or caste divides that makes them politically relevant. The discourse on Hinduism as a political entity seems to rely primarily on the idea of historical hurts and traumas caused the Hindus through Muslim invasions and the destruction of Hindu temples (Cohen 2010). Yet Muslims and Hindus have a long history of both intimacy and conflict—I have elsewhere called this agonistic belonging—the conflicts assuming a shared symbolic space (Das 2010b and 2010c). Second, there are many levels at which such conflicts are mediated, and the technologies of mediation are sufficiently different for us to give far more careful thought to what is at stake for understanding the nature of these conflicts. First, it is important that law courts have been involved in addressing disputes such as those over sacred spaces (as well as many others), showing that parties to the dispute find vocabularies to convert what would be purely theological or historical questions into questions for the law that allow for a deferral if not a resolution. Second, we have evidence from both historical and ethnographic writing that, while involved in different kinds of conflicts, Hindus and Muslims living in proximity engage in the commerce of life in which they are able to evoke different kinds of pasts making the identities Hindu and Muslim unstable (Ahmad and Reifeld 2004; Das 2010b; Gilmartin and Lawrence 2000).

In the case of the Ram Janambhumi and Babri Masjid dispute, which has been lingering in courts since 1885, Deepak Mehta (2011) shows that over a period of time legal questions altered as new parties were added to the dispute. Thus the courts have had to deal with such issues as the nature of religious property; whether a deity is a juristic personality; and also whether parties to the dispute are consolidated groups of Hindus and Muslims or if there are different legal personalities involved—for example, Sunni Waqf Board versus Shia Waqf Board as well as different Hindu sects; and finally, what did right to worship mean in legal terms? Mehta shows that the category of "status quo" is used by judges to get over the impasse these questions create, because no resolution of the questions seems possible without endangering what the courts call "public order." There is the fascinating question here as to whether any principles of interpretation derived from the hermeneutic traditions of Hindus or Muslims can be deployed by judges who must speak in secular languages, but answering that question would require an investigation into the thousands of pages generated by the case in the forms of legal briefs, judgements, and so on with an analytical eye rather than one that transports current political concerns into reading this archive. Perhaps a new way of addressing the question of conflicted pasts is being crafted, though we do not yet have the vocabulary to render this explicit.

A long route has been traversed in this chapter. To address the question how do human societies find a way out of cycles of violence, I first took the case of sacrifice and argued that the defence of killing is not so much an indifference to the suffering of animals as an occasion to dramatize and make visible the fact of one's own inevitable death. Yet, as we saw, the animal might not consent, and the earth might get tired of the wanton destruction of the beings that reside on it. In the case of the fraternal wars described in the epic Mahabharata, stories of sexual humiliation, wrongful killing, vengeance, and deceit blow up the cover of honorable exchange of violence among equals. We saw that the voice of the woman becomes the voice that interrogates the conceits of Dharma. In each case, the texts are not satisfied with offering prescriptive rules but rather, they zone in on a problem that cannot be resolved and is thus carried on, taking new forms into the future.

In the case of contemporary Hinduism, I do not find much engagement by the prominent political actors (such as Vishwa Hindu Parishad or RSS) with an archive, at least in the public domain. However, I do find that hints of ways of inheriting multiple pasts are present in the register of everyday life, such as when a Hindu healer in a low-income neighborhood begins to dream of ayats in the Quran as a way of healing those afflicted with malignant spirits or a Hindu mother makes room for her Muslim daughter-in-law to be able to say her prayers (Das 2010c). Or for that matter, when a Jain finds that he can make an alliance with an animal rights activists and find a language for saying how much the suffering of animals wounds him, thus bridging the divide between religious and secular languages (Laidlaw 2010). These moments are easily suppressed in official discourses of both Hindus and Muslims now. So I will conclude with two moments of resonance with the thoughts on violence and nonviolence traced from the texts. The first resonant moment is in Gandhi's words when he says that, if he cannot persuade a Muslim to relinquish the killing of a cow as a gesture of friendship with the Hindus and for the good of the country, then he will let the cow go on the grounds that the matter is "beyond my capability." In other words, if I am a beaver, I should not carry the guilt of not being able to build a dam. When does one simply accept and endure the fact that the world has a say in the projects through which we carve our moral selves? However disappointed in each other we might be, we are not allowed to carry that fact to the point where we end up cursing the world and unleashing our own violence on it.

The second resonant moment for me is of women who had witnessed their husbands and sons burnt to death in the violence against Sikhs in Delhi in 1984 sitting in the streets in a stonelike posture—dirty, disheveled, refusing to bathe, until the government publicly acknowledged the violence done to their community (Das 2007). The moment is etched forever in my memory as if it were the story of Draupadi who lived in the gestures through which dirt and pollution were made to speak. Out of such gestures—as those of Gandhi turning away from the violence against Muslims or the slum-dwelling women in Delhi refusing to consent to keeping silent about violence—I know that the archive has a life. Can contemporary social science recover such gestures from everyday life, recognize the waxing and waning of religious conflicts rather than letting them imprison her in a fascination with the horror of our present condition, and still recognize itself as "social science"?

NOTES

1. I am grateful to the editors and, especially, to Michael Jerryson for their insightful comments on earlier versions of the paper that helped me to knit the main arguments together.
2. I am not suggesting that such repudiations go uncontested but rather that it is not easy to move from the position in which the task of students of Indian texts is to simply render their content, to the position where they would be taken as texts to be developed, repudiated, accepted within the normal give and take of theoretical discussions.
3. The centrality of these traditions is taken for granted in the long history of theorizing on the political-theological where terms such as *philosophy* and even *antiphilosophy* are assumed to be about the tensions between the Greek, Judiac, and Christian inheritance of scholarly traditions (see Badiou 2011; Deutch and Nicgroski 1993; Dickinson 2011) Yet the difficulties of overcoming such restriction of vision cannot be laid simply on the doors of European hegemony which becomes nothing more than a lament.
4. This text is to be distinguished from the Dharmaranya Purana in the Pauranic canon (see Das 1977).
5. For a detailed critique of this model for a general theory of sacrifice see Das (1983) where I argue that the sacrificer is not defined in Vedic sacrifice as a bearer of sin but rather as a desiring being. Sacrifice then is about reordering of desire and not about expiation of sin.
6. I have not specifically taken up the issue of horse sacrifice that referred to the display of kingly power, but it is worth noting that the substitution of the horse by the snake also shows the dark side of kingship.
7. Such a view of nature in which sheer force is the operative principle of life is not unknown to the Hindu imaginary—*matsya nyaya*—or the law of the fishes in which the bigger fish eat the smaller fish is used to describe the direction of violence in nature. However, in the Mahabharata, there is layering of another thought in which it is the violence perpetrated by men that makes the earth as a living entity, tired of the burden she has to bear.
8. This is a very small selection of the scenes—a fuller description would take a monograph but see, especially, Hiltebeitel (2001).
9. See, for instance, Bilwakesh (2009) on this point. The concepts of the Bhagvad Gita might have gone important transformations, as it was translated into Persian on Dara Shikoh's behest as *Sirr ol Asrar,* then into Latin by Anquetil-Dupperon, followed by A. W. Schlegel's annotated translation into Latin. Although recent scholarship notes the importance of the German debate on the Bhagvad Gita in the critical engagement with the text and especially its theory of inaction in action, the issue of translation of concepts across philosophical traditions has not received much attention. See, however, Mehta (1989) and McGetchin et al. (2004). I am grateful to Andrew Brandell for tracking the various translations of the Bhagavad Gita.

Bibiliography

Ahmad, Imtiaz and Helmut Reifeld ed. *Lived Islam in South Asia: Adaptation, Accommodation and Conflict.* Delhi: Social Science Press, 2004.

Alter, Joseph S. *Gandhi's Body: Sex, Diet and the Politics of Nationalism.* Philadelphia: Pennsylvania University Press, 2000.

Amin, Shaid. "On Retelling the Muslim Conquest of North India." In *History and the Present.* Eds. Partha Chatterjee and Anjan Ghosh, 19–33. Delhi: Permanent Black, 2002.

Badiou, Alain. *Wittgenstein's Antiphilosophy.* Trans. with an introduction by Bruno Bosteels. London: Verso, 2011.

Beistegui, Miguel de. "Sacrifice Revisited." In *The Sense of Philosophy: On Jean-Luc Nancy.* Eds. Darren Shepards, Simon Sparks, and Colin Thomas, 152–169. London: Routledge, 1997.

Benveniste, Émile. "Euphemisms Ancient and Modern." In *Problems in General Linguistics.* Trans. Mary E. Meek, 265–271. Coral Gables, FL: University of Miami Press, 1971.

Bharati, Dharamvir. *Andha Yug: The Age of Darkness.* Trans. Alok Bhalla. Manoa: Hawaii University Press, 2010.

Bilgrami, Akeel. "Gandhi's Integrity: The Philosophy behind the Politics." *Postcolonial Studies* 5.1 (2002): 79–93.

Billimoria, Purhottam, Joseph Prabhu, and Renuka M. Sharma eds. *Indian Ethics: Classical Traditions and Contemporary Challenges.* Burlington: Ashgate Publications, 2007.

Bilwakesh, Nikhilesh. "Emerson, John Brown and Arjuna: Translating the Bhagvad Gita in a Time of War." *ESQ: A Journal of the American Renaissance* 55.1 (2009): 27–58.

Cavell, Stanley. *Emerson's Transcendental Etudes.* Palo Alto, CA: Stanford University Press, 2003.

Coetzee, J. M. *The Lives of Animals.* Ed. and introduced by Amy Gutmann. Princeton, NJ: Princeton University Press, 1999.

Cohen, Lawrence. "Ethical Publicity: On Transplant Victims, Wounded Communities and the Moral Demands of Dreaming." In *Ethical Life in South Asia.* Eds. Anand Pandian and Daud Ali, 253–275. Bloomington: Indiana University Press, 2010.

Coomaraswamy, Anand. *Perception of the Vedas.* Ed. Vidyanivas Misra. Delhi: Indira Gandhi National Center for the Arts, 2000.

Dalmiya, Vrinda. "Dogged Loyalties: A Classic Indian Intervention in Care Ethics." In *Ethics in the World Religions.* Eds. Jospeh Runzo and Nancy M Martin, 293–308. Oxford, UK: One World, 2001.

Das, Veena. *Structure and Cognition: Aspects of Hindu Caste and Ritual.* Delhi: Oxford University Press, 1977.

Das, Veena. "The Language of Sacrifice." *Man,* new series 18.3 (1983): 445–462.

Das, Veena. "Narrativizing the Male and the Ffemale in Tulasidas's Ramacharitamanasa." In *Social Structure and Change: Religion and Kinship.* Eds. A. M. Shah, B. S. Baviskar, and E. A. Ramaswamy, 65–92. Delhi: Sage Publications, 1998.

Das, Veena. *Life and Words: Violence and the Descent into the Ordinary.* Berkeley: University of California Press, 2007.

Das, Veena. "Sexuality, Vulnerability and the Oddness of the Human: Lessons from the Mahabharata." *Borderlands* 9.3 (2010). www.borderlands.net.au/vol9no3/html.

Das, Veena. "Moral and Spiritual Striving in the Everyday: To be a Muslim in
    Contemporary India." In *Ethical Life in South Asia*. Eds. Anand Pandian and
    Daud Ali, 232–253. Bloomington: Indiana University Press, 2010.

Das, Veena. "Engaging the Life of the Other: Love and Everyday Life." In *Ordinary
    Ethics: Anthropology, Language and Action*. Ed. Michael Lambek, 376–400. New
    York: Fordham University Press, 2010.

Davis, Donald R. *The Spirit of Hindu Law*. Cambridge, UK: Cambridge University
    Press, 2010.

de Vreis, Hent. "Introduction: Why Still Religion?" In *Religion Beyond a Concept*. Ed.
    Hent de Vries, 1–100. New York: Fordham University Press, 2008.

Deutch, Kenneth L., and Walter Nicgroski eds. *Leo Strauss: Political Philosopher and
    Jewish Thinker: The Return to Maimonides in the Jewish Thought of Leo Strauss*.
    Albany, NY: SUNY Press, 1993.

Dhavamony, Mariasusai. *Phenomenology of Religion*. Rome: Universitá Gregoriana
    Editrice, 1973.

Diamond, Cora. "The Difficulty of Reality and the Difficulty of Philosophy." In
    Philosophy and Animal Life. Eds. Stanley Cavell, Cora Diamond, John McDowell
    et al., 43–91. New York: Columbia University Press, 2008.

Dickinson, Colby. *Agamben and Theology*. London: T & T Clark International, 2011.

Doniger, Wendy. *The Hindus: An Alternate History*. New York: Penguin Press, 2009.

Evans-Pritchard, Edward E. "The Meaning of Sacrifice among the Nuer." *Journal of
    the Anthropological Institute of Great Britain and Ireland* 18.1/2 (1954): 21–33.

Flood, Gavin. *An Introduction to Hinduism*. Cambridge, UK: Cambridge University
    Press, 1996.

Freitag, Sandra B. *Collective Action and Community: Public Arenas and the
    Emergence of Communalism in North India*. Berkeley: University of California
    Press, 1989.

Gandhi, Leela. *Affective Communities: Anticolonial Thought, Fin De Siecle Radicalism
    and the Politics of Friendship*. Durham, NC: Duke University Press, 2006.

Gandhi, Mohandas K. *Indian Home Rule or Hind Swaraj*. Ahmadabad: Navjivan
    Publications, 1938.

Gandhi, Mohandas K. *The Collected Works of Mahatma Gandhi*. New Delhi:
    Ministry of Information and Broadcasting, 1958–1990.

Gandhi, Ramchandra. "Brahmacharya." In *Way of Life: King, Householder,
    Renouncer*. Ed. T. N. Madan, 205–223. Delhi: Vikas Publications, 1982.

Ganguly, Debjani. "History's Implosion: A Benjaminian Reading of Ambedkar."
    Journal of Narrative Theory 37.3 (2002): 326–347.

Ganguly, Debjani. *Caste, Colonialism, and Counter-Modernity: Notes on a
    Postcolonial Hermeneutics of Caste*. London: Routledge, 2005.

Gaonkar Dilip. "On Alternative Modernities." *Public Culture* 1.1 (1999): 1–18.

Gilmartin, David, and Bruce A. Lawrence, eds. *Beyond Turk and Hindu: Rethinking
    Religious Identities in Islamicate South Asia*. Gainesville: University of Florida
    Press, 2000.

Girard, René. *Violence and the Sacred*. Trans. Patrick Gregory. Baltimore: Johns
    Hopkins University Press, 1977.

Hansen, Thomas Blom. "Recuperating Masculinity: Hindu Nationalism, Violence and
    the Exorcism of the Muslim Other." *Critique of Anthropology* 16.2 (1996): 137–172.

Hegel, W.G.F. 1827. *On the Episode of the Mahabharata Known by the Name
    Bhagvad-Gita*. Trans. Herbert Herring. Delhi: Manohar Publications, 1995.

Hiltebeitel, Alf. *Rethinking the Mahabharata: A Reader's Guide to the Education of the Dharma King.* Chicago: University of Chicago Press, 2001.

Hubert, Henri and Marcel Mauss. *Sacrifice: Its Nature and Functions.* Trans. W. D. Halls. Chicago: University of Chicago Press, 1964.

Jha, Ganganath. *Manusmrti: With Manubhashya of Medhatithi*, 10 vols., 2nd ed. Delhi: Motilal Banarisidas, 1999.

Laidlaw, James. "Ethical Traditions in Question: Diaspora Jainism and the Environmental and Animal Liberation Movements." In *Ethical Life in South Asia.* Eds. Anand Pandian and Daud Ali, 61–83. Bloomington: Indiana University Press, 2010.

Lath Mukund. "The Concept of Anrshamsya in the Mahabharata." In *Reflections and Variations on the Mahabharata.* Ed. T.R.S. Sharma, 82–89. Delhi: Sahitya Academy, 2009.

Lévi-Strauss, Claude. *Totemism.* New York: Beacon Press, 1963.

Lévi-Strauss, Claude. *The Savage Mind.* Chicago: University of Chicago Press, 1969.

Llewellyn, J. E. ed. *Defining Hinduism: A Reader.* London: Routledge, 2005.

Ludden, David E. ed. *Making India Hindu: Religion, Community and the Politics of Democracy in India.* New York: Oxford University Press, 2005.

Malamoud, Charles. *Cooking the World: Ritual and Thought in Ancient India.* New York: Oxford University Press, 1996.

McClymond, Kathryn. *Beyond Sacred Violence: A Comparative Study of Sacrifice.* Baltimore: Johns Hopkins University Press, 2008.

McGetchin, Douglas, Peter K. J. Park, and D. R. SarDesai. *Sanskrit and "Orientalism": Indology and Comparative Linguistics, 1750–1958.* Delhi: Manohar, 2004.

Mehta, Deepak. "The Ayodhya Dispute: Law's Imagination and the Function of the 'Status Quo.'" Paper presented at the Sociological Research Colloquium, University of Delhi, 2011.

Mehta, J. L. "Problems of Understanding." *Philosophy East and West* 39.1 (1989): 3–12.

Nandy, Ashis. *The Intimate Self: Loss and Recovery of Self under Colonialism.* Delhi: Oxford University Press, 1983.

Nandy, Ashis. "The Politics of Secularism and the Recovery of Religious Tolerance." In *Mirrors of Violence: Communities, Riots and Survivors in South Asia.* Ed. Veena Das, 69–93. Delhi: Oxford University Press, 1990.

Oldenburg, Hermann. 1894. *Religion of the Vedas.* Delhi: Motilal Banarisidas, 1988.

Paranjpe, Anand C. *Self and Identity in Modern Psychology and Indian Thought.* New York: Plenum Press, 1998.

Parry, Jonathan P. *Death in Banaras.* London: Cambridge University Press, 1994.

Pinney, Christopher. *Photos of the Gods: The Printed Image and Political Struggle in India.* London: Reaktion Books, 2004.

Pollock, Sheldon trans. *Rama's Last Act by Bhava-bhuti.* New York: New York University Press, 2007.

Savarkar, Vinayak Damodar. 1922. *Hindutva.* Poona: S. R. Date, 1942.

Sen, Chitrabhanu. *A Dictionary of the Vedic Rituals: Based on the Sratua and the Grihya.* Delhi: Concept Publishing, 1978.

Sharma, T.R.S. "Introduction: Many Makers Many Texts/Contexts." In *Reflections and Variations on the Mahabharata.* Ed. T.R.S. Sharma, 1–37. Delhi: Sahitya Academy, 2009.

Singh, Bhrigupati. "Asceticism and Eroticism in Gandhi, Thoreau, and Nietzsche." *Borderlands* 9.3 (2010a). www.borderlands.net.au/issues/vol9no3.html.

Singh, Bhrigupati. *Gods and Grains: On the Political Theologies of Popular Hinduism.* PhD dissertation. Baltimore: Johns Hopkins University, 2010b.

Singh, Bhrigupati. 2011. "Agonistic Intimacy and Moral Aspirations in Popular Hinduism. A Study in the Political Theology of the Neighbor." *American Ethnologist* 38.3 (2011): 430–450.

Skaria, Ajay. "Gandhi's Politics: Liberalism and the Question of the Ashram." In *Enchantments of Modernity: Empire, Nation, Globalization.* Ed. Saurabh Dube, 119–234. New Delhi: Routledge 2009.

Skaria, Ajay. "Living by Dying: Gandhi, Satyagraha and the Warrior." In *Ethical Life in South Asia.* Eds. Anand Pandian and Daud Ali, 211–232. Indiana University Press, 2010.

Smith, David. *Hinduism and Modernity.* Oxford, UK: Blackwell Publishing, 2003.

Veer, Peter Van der. *Religious Nationalism: Hindus and Muslims in India.* Berkeley: University of California Press, 1994.

Yang, Anand A. 1980 "Sacred Symbol and Sacred Space in Rural India: Community Mobilization in the 'Anti-Cow Killing' Riots of 1893." *Comparative Studies in Society and History,* Vol. 22.4 (1980): 576–596.

CHAPTER 2

BUDDHIST TRADITIONS AND VIOLENCE

MICHAEL JERRYSON

IN recent studies, psychologists have found that the color orange releases more serotonin into our brain, which calms and relaxes us. It simply might be a coincidence that this hue is most frequently used for Buddhist monks' robes in Asia; however, the sensation of calm is also associated with Buddhism itself. The saffron robes have become a trademark of Buddhism around the world. Their colors usually range from bright orange to dark brown to black (Japanese *unsui*), depending on the ordination lineage of the school (*nikaya*). Corresponding to the neurological associations is the general conception that Buddhist traditions are irenic, encapsulated in the practice of meditation and complete withdrawal from worldly affairs (*lokiya*).

It is thus unusual to encounter such militant nomenclatures as Saffron Army or Saffron Revolution in the discussions of contemporary Buddhist monastic movements. Although some saffron armies, such as those of the Sri Lankan Janatha Vimukthi Peramuna (People's Liberation Front) are armed, others are not (Abeysekara 2002: 222–229). In September 2007, Burmese Buddhist monks employed Gandhi's nonviolent methods of protest against their government and were met with violence (Skidmore & Wilson 2010; Schober 2010). Whether violent or peaceful, these militant characterizations illustrate the Buddhist ambivalence toward violence.

Violence is a social phenomenon that pervades every religious tradition. In regard to physical acts of violence, there is a robust history of Buddhists who commit suicide and engage in conflicts and wars. Buddhist monasteries have served as military outposts, monks have led revolts, and Buddhist principles have served as war rhetoric for heads of state. Some of these acts of violence draw on Buddhist scriptures; others invoke Buddhist symbols. In addition to Buddhism's history of violence, Buddhist traditions globally influence religious acts of violence. Contemporary attacks of suicide martyrdom can be traced back to Japanese kamikazes during World War II, which influenced the communist-leaning Japanese Red Army. On May 30, 1972, Red Army gunmen Tsuyoshi Okudaira, Yasuyuki Yasuda, and Kozo Okamoto committed the first contemporary suicide attack in the Middle East during the Lod Airport Massacre in Israel (Reuter 2004: 136–137).

Perhaps the core element that draws Buddhist traditions into the social realm of violence is their identification: "I am a Buddhist," which often is coterminous with a number of ethnic and national markers, (e.g., Tibetan Buddhist, Thai Buddhist, etc.). The construction of an identity requires the distinction between those within and outside the imagined community. This politicized element has been the genesis for many structural forms of violence over the centuries. In early South Asian societies, Buddhist traditions were aniconic and without strict identity markers, but as early as the first century CE, this changed. The crystallization of a Buddhist identity introduced adherents of the *Buddhadharma* (Buddhist teaching) to a new arena of politics and forms of alterity.

Since the third century BCE, Buddhists have clashed with opponents of different faiths, Buddhists from different countries, and even Buddhists of different ordination lineages within the same country. On most occasions, the mixture of Buddhist authority and political power has provided the recipe for violence. Early scriptures were ambiguous as to the relationship between Buddhist principles and sovereignty, due in part to the crucial patronage of the Buddha by the north Indian monarchs of Magadha and Kosala in the fifth century BCE. As states developed, Buddhist authority served to legitimize kings and rulers by granting them religiopolitical titles such as *chakravartin* (universal rule; literally, "one who turns the wheel"), *dhammaraja* ("ruler of the Buddhist doctrine"), or *dalai lama* ("ocean of wisdom"). Buddhist states have used violence externally as well as internally. Early South Asian religious literature charged rulers with protecting their subjects from external forces (which involves warfare) and with upholding the law by inflicting physical punishments.

In the era of nation-states and nation building, Buddhists such as Tibetan, Thai, Cambodian, and Burmese consider their nationality intimately connected with Buddhism. Due to this collusion of identities, an attack on the nation becomes an attack on Buddhism (and vice versa). The issue of multiple interrelated identities raises a larger and more problematic question: What is Buddhism?

Similar to other religions, the Buddhist system is a theoretical construct that becomes tradition through the imputation of culture. Officially there are more than 350 million Buddhists in the world; however, if we include unofficial estimates from China and other countries, there are over 1.3 billion adherents. There are Buddhist communities in more than 135 countries, and each community possesses unique characteristics endemic to its school and location. In such a way, Buddhism is a global religious system that encompasses a canopy of people, rituals, scriptures, and beliefs. But what is the theoretical construct that binds these communities together?

The Buddhist theoretical construct is predicated on the teachings of the Buddha. Buddhists worldwide take refuge in the Buddha, whether he is conceived as historical or cosmological (Jerryson 2010: 5). Although the teachings vary among Buddhist communities, all acknowledge the Four Noble Truths (Sanskrit: *catvari aryasatyani;* Pali: *cattari ariyasaccani*): Life is suffering, there is a cause to this suffering, there is a cessation to this suffering, and there is a path to cessation. There is no uniform initiation into Buddhism as in the case of a Christian baptism or the Islamic declaration of faith (*shahadah*), although some Buddhist traditions have initiation rites. Perhaps the closest to a lay profession of faith in Buddhist traditions is to seek refuge in the three jewels (Sanskrit: *triratna;* Pali: *tiratana*): the Buddha, the Dhamma (the doctrine), and the Sangha (community that upholds the teachings). That said, Tantric practitioners take refuge in a fourth jewel: their guru.

In drawing the parameters for Buddhist traditions, it is clear that there is a high variance of cultural practices and beliefs. This chapter will cover the history of Buddhist traditions and violence with special attention to the scriptural justifications, symbols, and actual manifestations of violence.

Ethical and Scriptural Justifications for Violence

Every global religion contains scriptural interdictions on violence; Buddhist traditions are no exception. There are numerous passages within Buddhist scriptures that uphold the notion of *ahimsa* (nonviolence) and equanimity. Nonetheless, like every other global religion, Buddhist traditions have adherents that commit violence and justify their acts with scriptures. These Buddhist scriptures either condone the use of violence or are hermeneutically ambiguous.

Most canonical sources lack a specified author because an indication of an author would impose a sense of temporality and reduce a scripture's sacrality. Thankfully, the nature of these scriptures is not germane to this overview, rather what the scriptures say and the influence they carry are. Buddhist scriptures are organized into three baskets of texts (Sanskrit: *Tripitaka;* Pali: *Tipitaka*): the scriptures on monastics (*Vinaya*), the scriptures of discourses (Sanskrit: *Sutras;* Pali: *Suttas*), and the scriptures of higher knowledge (Sanskrit: *Abhidharma;* Pali: *Abhidhamma*). The orthodox language in Theravada is Pali; the orthodox language in Mahayana and Vajrayana is Sanskrit. In addition, many important Buddhist scriptures are in the local or regional vernacular.

Because Buddhist traditions began in South Asia in the fifth century BCE, early Buddhist thought was largely influenced by South Asian worldviews that include

Brahmanism and Jainism. Each religious tradition that emerged from the subcontinent before the Christian era (or even the Buddhist era), was heavily influenced by the laws of action (Sanskrit: *karma*; Pali: *kamma*). Buddhism was no exception to this. According to Buddhist scriptures, a person accrues demerit through violent actions or even intentions to commit violence. The most severe of these actions is murder.

The esteemed Buddhist scholar Paul Demiéville argues that no other precept is so strictly followed by all Buddhists and goes so far as to say that not killing is a characteristic "so anchored in Buddhism that it is practically considered a custom" (Demiéville 2010: 18). This custom is perhaps best understood as one of five moral precepts (Sanskrit: *panchashila*; Pali: *panchasilani*), which are to abstain from killing sentient beings, stealing, lying, partaking of intoxicants that cloud the mind, and sexual misconduct. This practice is analogous to the five restraints (*yama*) in Hindu traditions, and underscores the social ethics of South Asian traditions. In addition to lay practices, there are canonical and commentarial sources throughout the different Buddhist schools that contain severe interdictions on violence. They also contain the exception to the rule. Analogous to Carl Schmitt's notions of *Ausnahmezustand* (state of exception), Buddhist exceptions empower or legitimate kings and rulers.

These exceptions are not generated in a vacuum and did not remain simply "exceptions." The scriptures that condone or justify violence are connected to physical acts of violence. Either Buddhist authors try to rationalize the previous violence of Buddhist rulers—such as the early Magadha king Ajatashatru who killed his father, Bimbisara—or condone the current acts of a Buddhist state (often in defense of the religion), such as the Japanese imperial violence from the start of the Meiji period (1868) and onward.

In most cases, the state of exception depends on three variables: the intention of the person who commits the violence (e.g, is it accidental or deliberate, and if deliberate, is the mind clear of hatred and avarice?), the nature of the victim (e.g., human, animal, or supernatural), and the stature of the one who commits the violence (e.g., is the person a king, soldier, or a butcher?). Buddhists have applied these variables to condone or, at times, even to advocate murder. Although there are some texts (Sanskrit: *sutra*; Pali: *sutta*) that traverse doctrinal boundaries, in order to preserve the distinctions between schools I will treat these exceptions within their doctrinal categories of Theravada (Path of the Elders), Mahayana (Great Vehicle) and Vajrayana (Diamond Vehicle) and, when necessary, indicate, regional specificities.

Theravada Scriptures

The teachings of Theravada are predominantly practiced in Sri Lankan, Thai, Burmese, Cambodian, Lao and early Indian traditions. Within the Theravada doctrine (*dhamma*), violence is categorically condemned as an unwholesome act (*akusala*); however, there are degrees of condemnation, especially in regard to the state.

Theravada doctrine on violence derives from the three baskets, which is commonly referred to as the Pali Canon and its commentaries. Since ordained men and women model behavior as bearers of the dhamma, one of the ethical corner-stones in the Pali Canon is the *Vinaya,* the monastic codes. Interestingly, within the monastic tradition murder is ranked third out of four defeats (*parajika*) and results in permanent expulsion from the Sangha (the four defeats are sex, stealing, murder, and false claims of enlightenment). Although ranked third out of the four, murder is among the greatest sins (*adhamma*) a person can commit.

The *Vinaya* is replete with examples of violent scenarios. In most occasions, the prominent factors in the monk's penalty are whether the act was successful or not, and (2) her/his intentionality. The nature of one's kamma (literally, one's action) is predicated on the outcome of the action; failed attempts to commit violence are penalized because of the intention but do not carry the full penalty of a successful action. Correspondingly, accidents are generally critiqued in Buddhist scriptures as a result of a lack of mindfulness, and the penalties are not as severe as deliberate acts of violence. The Buddhist emphasis on intention distinguishes the tradition from other regionally prominent religious traditions, such as Jainism.

Intention

The first book of the *Vinaya* is the "Suttavibhanga," or "The Analysis of the Rules." It distinguishes the acts of manslaughter and attempted murder from the act of murder in numerous accounts. In one particular instance, an accidental death caused by pushing one's father yields no offense; the failed attempt to kill one's father by pushing him results in a grave offense. However, a death caused by the deliberate intention to kill results in expulsion (Horner 1938: 139). The same rationale is applied to issues of euthanasia and abortion. If a monk or nun advocated a quick death or techniques to abort a pregnancy and the advice led to a death, the person was expelled from the Sangha. Advice that was not heeded carries lesser penalties. Insanity also plays a role in assessing the act of murder. In a previous life as the Brahman Lomakassapa, the Buddha killed hundreds of creatures but was not in the correct state of mind. Lomakassapa was "unhinged" with desire, and the text explains that a madman's crimes are pardonable (Horner 1963–1964: 14–17).

Nature of the Victim

Regardless of intention, a monk's murder of a nonhuman does not result in expulsion. Monks who kill fearsome dryads (*yakkha*) and other nonhuman beings commit grave offenses (*thullaccaya*), which requires confessions (Horner 1938: 146–147). The monk Udayin's killing of crows (or of any other animal) also only merits a confession (Horner 1942: 1).

The commentaries offer similar interpretations of offenses related to murder. The famous Indian scholar monk Buddhaghosa (fifth c. CE) analyzed the monastic laws on murder in his *Sumagala-vilasini* and claimed:

> In the case of living creatures without [moral] virtues, such as animals, [the act of killing] is less blameworthy when the creature has a small body, and more blameworthy when the being has a large body. Why? Because the greater effort

[required] in killing a being with a large body; and even when the effort is the same, [the act of killing a large-bodied creature is still more blameworthy] because of its greater physical substance. In the case of beings that possess [moral] virtues, such as human beings, the act of killing is less blameworthy when the being is of little virtue and more blameworthy when the being is of great virtue. But when the body and virtue [of creatures] are equal, [the act of killing] is less blameworthy when the defilements and force of the effort are mild, more blameworthy when they are powerful. (Gethin 2004: 171–172)

The *Vinaya* rules and Buddhaghosa's accounts explain, among other things, Theravada dietary habits. Thai, Lao, Burmese, and Sri Lankan lay Buddhists will generally eat chicken and pork and avoid beef, because the cow is a much larger animal. They also provide an area of ambiguity in regard to humanity and virtue. This distinction between human/nonhuman and virtuous/nonvirtuous humans has been raised in other Buddhist sources.

One of the more popular accounts comes from the Sinhalese mythohistorical chronicle, the *Mahavamsa*. The Buddhist king Dutthagamani wages a just war against the Damil invaders led by King Elara. After a bloody and victorious battle, Dutthagamani laments for causing the slaughter of millions. Eight enlightened monks (*arahant*) comfort him with the explanation"

From this deed arises no hindrance in thy way to heaven. Only one and a half human beings have been slain here by thee, O lord of men. The one had come unto the (three) refuges, the other had taken on himself the five precepts. Unbelievers and men of evil life were the rest, not more to be esteemed than beasts. But as for thee, thou wilt bring glory to the doctrine of the Buddha in manifold ways; therefore cast away from thy heart, O ruler of men! (Geiger 1993 [1912]: 178)

The monks' explanation includes the prerequisites discussed earlier for being a Buddhist, in this context the taking of the three refuges, and following the five moral precepts. By distinguishing Buddhists from non-Buddhists, the murders in this narrative are dismissed, since the non-Buddhists possess such little virtue they are on par with animals. Furthermore, the king has pure intentions with the desire to support and defend the Buddhist doctrine. The *Mahavamsa*'s rationale and context was not overlooked by Sri Lankan Buddhists centuries later in their twenty-six year civil war against the Liberation Tamil Tigers of Eelam (LTTE, 1983–2009) and has permeated Southeast Asia as a form of rhetoric, such as during the Cambodia anticommunist campaign in the 1970s.

A similar rationale was used by the prominent Thai Buddhist monk Kittiwuttho in the 1970s during the Thai campaign against communism. For Kittiwuttho, a communist was a bestial type of a person and not a complete person at that. More importantly, her or his death served to support the Buddhist doctrine (Keyes 1978: 153). Kittiwuttho drew on the *Anguttara Nikaya*, "To Kesi, the Horse Trainer," to justify his stance on killing communists. Not widely used for this purpose, "To Kesi the Horse Trainer" is about the Buddha's conversation with a horse trainer on the similarities between training people and horses. At one point, the Buddha explains that if a tamable person does not submit to any training, the untamable person is killed. However, shortly after this statement the Buddha explains that death is meant as the Buddha's abandonment of that person's needs, thus meaning the death of the person's ultimate potentiality (Thanissaro 2010). While Kittiwuttho's use of this text is problematic, it is demonstrative of how Buddhist exceptions have been applied to justify violence.

Stature of Those Who Kill

Monastic ethics serve as exemplary rules for others to model, but the 227 rules for Theravada monks are not required for the laity. Different roles merit different ethics; the ethics for a monk is not the same as it is for a butcher or a soldier (although butchers were noted for having to spend many anguishing lifetimes to redress their negative karma). As for soldiers, Buddhist scriptures remain ambiguous in certain places as to the ramifications of their occupations. Some impose restrictions on monastic interactions with soldiers or declare that soldiers may not ordain while serving the state, but most do not directly condemn a soldier for following her or his duty. Instead, what is repeatedly emphasized in the ethics of this position is the soldier's state of mind.

One example of this comes from the fourth book and eighth chapter of the *Samyutta Nikaya*, "Gamanisamyutta" or the "Connected Discourses to Headmen." The Buddha counsels a headman Yodhajiva, who is a mercenary under the assumption that mercenaries who strive and exert themselves in battles will be reborn in the heavens. The Buddha explains that, when a mercenary dies with the debased thoughts of slaughtering and killing other people, he is reborn in either the hell or animal realms (Bhikkhu Bodhi 2000: 1334–1335). In this scenario, Yodhajiva is cautioned to avoid debased thoughts at the time of death but not to avoid the act of killing. This warning against ill thoughts is relevant whether a person commits an act of aggression or even an act of self-defense. However, the ambiguity about the act itself is present and is found in contemporary contexts as well. In the recent civil war with the LTTE, Sri Lankan Buddhist monks preached to soldiers in order to suffuse their minds with mercy and compassion. Buddhist soldiers with "cool heads" are less apt to make mistakes on the battlefield and harm civilians (Kent 2010: 172).

A unique set of ethical parameters is for kings and just rule, which in the contemporary context apply to nation-states. According to the commentaries (*atthakatha*), Theravada's earliest model of a just ruler was the Mauryan emperor Ashoka. After a successful and bloody campaign against the Kalinga in which more than 100,000 died and 150,000 were enslaved, Ashoka repented and turned to the Buddhist doctrine. Typically, Ashoka's reign is praised after his turn to the Buddhist doctrine (and thus, after his conquests). However, Ashoka never disbanded his army after his Buddhist epiphany. He maintained the state policy of capital punishment and, according to literary records, killed more than 18,000 Jains and committed other atrocities well after his turn to righteous Buddhist kingship (Jenkins 2010: 63).

Early Buddhist scriptures tacitly support states, which may be due partly to the fact that the Buddha received most of his principle support in his early years from

the kingdoms of Magadha and Kosala. The Buddha's relationship to the two kingdoms was stressed at times by their internecine conflict. As a moral and ethical
liaison for both kingdoms, the Buddha responded on these occasions by condon-
ing wars of defense over wars of aggression. This endorsement of defensive violence employs one of two modes on the ethics of state violence. According to Steven
Collins, Theravada scriptures present on occasion a categorical imperative to avoid
violence. On other occasions, the doctrine offers an ethics of just war through reciprocity; the Buddha counsels kings to administer judgments and punishments, but
with a clear and calm mind (Collins 1998: 420).

This latter mode is best evident in the 239th rebirth story of the Buddha, the
"Harita-Mata-Jataka," or the "Blue-Green Frog Birth Story," in which the Buddha
addresses a recent attack by the kingdom of Kosala on the kingdom of Magadha.
As in other rebirth stories, the narrative serves as a didactic for the particular context as well as general readership. The story tells of a water snake that falls into a
trap and is attacked by a throng of fish. Appealing to a blue-green frog for help,
the frog, which is the Buddha-to-be, replies to the entrapped snake, "[i]f you eat
fish that get into your demesne, the fish eat you when you get into theirs. In his
own place, and district, and feeding ground, no one is weak." Following the frog's
explanation, the fish seize and kill the snake (Cowell 1895: 165).

Ethics of state violence are mentioned several times in the *The Questions of
King Milinda*. Throughout the text, the Indo-Greek king Menander I questions the
Buddhist monk Nagasena about Buddhist principles. In the fourth book, called
"The Solving of Dilemmas," the king lists eight classes of men who kill living
beings: lustful men, cruel men, dull men, proud men, avaricious men, needy men,
foolish men, and kings in the way of punishment (Davids 1894: 17). As in the case
of the other seven types of men, a king by his nature adjudicates punishments and
kills living beings.

This aspect of rule is further described in a later conversation, when the king
explains that, if a man has committed a crime, the people would request that the
criminal be deprived of goods, bound, tortured, put to death, or beheaded (Davids
1894: 239). In neither conversation does Nagasena dispute the king's views on murder, and the presence of these duties in a book on Buddhist ethics is unmistakably
notable. This approach to just rule is found in other canonical sources such as the
twenty-sixth and twenty-seventh books of the *Digha Nikaya*, "The Sermon on the
Knowledge of Beginnings," and "The Lion's Roar at the Turning of the Wheel." In
both books, the king is entrusted with the moral responsibility to uphold the law
and mete out punishments. Balkrishna Gokhale argues that early Buddhist thinkers had a Weberian conception of the state: "For them the state is an organization
of force or violence the possession of which is largely restricted to the king and his
instruments" (251).

While this concept of the state was taken for granted by early Buddhist thinkers, it became emboldened by modern Buddhist advocates and rulers, such as the
Sri Lankan government in its indiscriminate use of force against the LTTE and the

Thai state and its use of *lèse majesté* to impose corporal punishment on those who disrespect the Buddhist monarchy.

Mahayana Scriptures

The Mahayana doctrine can be found primarily among Indian, Chinese, Korean, Japanese, and Vietnamese traditions, and its scriptures cover a vast array of sub-schools and corresponding soteriologies. Mahayana's doctrinal stances on violence are similar to those found in Theravada in many respects. Its scriptures condemn violence and hold murder as an unwholesome act (*akushala*). In some Mahayana traditions, this abhorrence of violence requires that practitioners maintain a strict vegan diet. Yet ethical exceptions also exist in Mahayana doctrine. Most of the exceptions in regard to these variables derive from two principal ideas within Mahayana: skill in means (*upaya*) and emptiness (*shunyata*).

Mahayana ethics on violence are found primarily within the second of the three baskets (*Tripitaka*), the *Sutras*, and the commentaries. Some traditions refer to multiple sources in their ethical discussions, while other traditions base their ethics solely on one text, such as the *Perfection of Wisdom* texts (*Prajnaparamita*) or the *Lotus Sutra*. Although there are some commentators, such as Asanga and Vasubandhu, who address violence within their treatment of ethics, most of the scriptures on violence are in a narrative style.

Intention

Even though Mahayana notions of skill in means and emptiness provide justifications for violence, or in these instances murder, the actors must not have ill thoughts or intentions when they perform the violence. Rather, their intentions should be compassionate and imbued with skill in means. In this vein, most exceptions require that the actor be a bodhisattva—an enlightened being. However, this is not always the case; in some cases the absence of any ill intent is sufficient to pardon an act of violence. In Chan Buddhism, the *Treatise of Absolute Contemplation* explains that murderous acts are analogous to brush fires. "The man who renders his mind similar [to the forces of nature] is entitled to do equally as much" (Demiéville 2010: 56). Likewise, Japanese Zen interpretations of killing stress the vacuity of the act. Killing puts an end to the passions of a person's mind and fosters the Buddha-nature within (ibid., 44). Intentionality is a critical component in Mahayana ethics of violence. It is not simply whether a person engages in an accidental or deliberate action, but there are also exceptions that allow for intentional violence.

At times, violence by lay practitioners is permitted; of particular note is the act of suicide in the Chinese traditions. Within the Chinese traditions, the *Lotus Sutra* provides a literary blueprint for self-immolation practices. The chapter

"The Original Acts of the Medicine King," tells of a bodhisattva who covers himself with oil and fragrance, wraps his body in oil-soaked clothes, and burns himself (the self-immolation lasts for 1,200 years). The Buddha explains to the reader that the bodhisattva's act is one that anyone meritorious may do:

> Gifts of his own body, such as this one, number in the incalculable hundreds of thousands of myriads of millions of *nayutas*. O Beflowered by the King of Constellations! If there is one who, opening up his thought, wishes to attain *anuttarasamyaksaṃbodhi* [consummation of incomparable wisdom], if he can burn a finger or even a toe as an offering to a *Buddhastūpa* [Buddhist relic shrine], he shall exceed one who uses realm or walled, wife or children, or even all the lands, mountains, forests, rivers, ponds, and sundry precious objects in the whole thousand-millionfold world as offerings. (Benn 2007: 61)

Here, the exception to intended violence is the conscious sacrifice of one's body. Suicide is also noted in other sources such as the "Hungry Tigress Jataka," in which the Buddha-to-be offers his body to a starving tigress so that she may feed her cubs.

Skill in means is a method employed by awakened beings to help others awaken. Perhaps the most famous example of this comes from a section in chapter 3 of the *Lotus Sutra*, "The Burning House." The *Lotus Sutra* is one of the core scriptures in the Chinese Tiantai and the Japanese Tendai and Nichiren schools and is considered sacred. In the text, the Buddha tells a parable to his disciple Sariputra about an old man and his children. The man attempts to rescue his children from a burning building, but they are enthralled by their games and do not heed his warnings. In order to get them to leave, he promises them three gifts; when they escape the building, they receive the greatest of these gifts. Sariputra praises the Buddha and correctly interprets that the man should not be condemned for lying, even if he had not given the children any gifts. His action was just because he was trying to liberate the children from a very painful experience.

The *Lotus Sutra* provides not only the strategy of skill in means but also ambiguous excerpts on violence. In 1279 CE, Nichiren writes to his devoted samurai follower, Shijo Kingo, and explains that Shijo's faith in the *Lotus Sutra* helped saved him from a recent ambush. He enjoins Shijo to employ the strategy of the *Lotus Sutra* in his future work and quotes a section from chapter 23 of the *Lotus Sutra*:

> "'All others who bear you enmity or malice will likewise be wiped out.' These golden words will never prove false. The heart of strategy and swordsmanship derives from the Mystic Law. Have profound faith. A coward cannot have any of his prayers answered." (Nichiren 2009: 1001)

The sentence quoted from the *Lotus Sutra* is generally regarded as metaphorical, but in this context Nichiren applies it literally in his address to a samurai about past and future acts of violence.

Another seemingly metaphorical use of violence is found in the Chinese text *The Sutra of the Forty-two Sections*. In one of the aphorisms by the Buddha, the text compares fighting in battle with attaining the Way:

> A man practicing the Way is like a lone man in combat against ten thousand. Bearing armor and brandishing weapons, he charges through the gate eager to

do battle, but if he is weakhearted and cowardly he will withdraw and flee....
If a man is able to keep a firm grip on his wits and advance resolutely, without
becoming deluded by worldly or deranged talk, then desire will disappear and
evil will vanish, and he is certain to attain the Way. (Sharf 1996: 370)

The use of war as a metaphor was also used by the Indian Buddhist monk
Shantideva in his commentary, *Engaging in Bodhisattva Behavior*. However, in neither the *Lotus Sutra* nor the *Sutra of the Forty-Two Sections* (or even in *Engaging in
Bodhisattva Behavior*) do we find direct advocacy of violence; instead we encounter ambiguous passages for such an interpretation.

Perhaps the most extreme measure of skill in means to justify violence is found
in the chapter "Murder with Skill in Means: The Story of the Compassionate Ship's
Captain" from the *Upayakaushalya Sutra*, or the *Skill-in-Means Sutra*. In one of
his many previous births, the Buddha is the captain of a ship at sea and is told by
water deities that a robber onboard the ship intends to kill the five hundred pas-
sengers and the captain. Within a dream, the deities implore the captain to use
skill in means to prevent this, since all five hundred men are future bodhisattvas
and the murder of them would invoke on the robber immeasurable lifetimes in
the darkest hells. The captain, who in this text is named Great Compassionate
(Mahakarunika), wakes and contemplates the predicament for seven days.
He eventually rationalizes:

> "There is no means to prevent this man from slaying the merchants and going
> to the great hells but to kill him." And he thought, "If I were to report this to the
> merchants, they would kill and slay him with angry thoughts and all go to great
> hells themselves." And he thought, "If I were to kill this person, I would likewise
> burn in the great hells for one hundred-thousand eons because of it. Yet I can
> bear to experience the pains of the great hells, that this person not slay these
> five hundred merchants and develop so much evil *karma*. I will kill this person
> myself." (Tatz 1994: 74)

The captain subsequently murders the robber, and the Buddha explains, "For me,
sam☐sāra was curtailed for one hundred-thousand eons because of that skill in
means and great compassion. And the robber died to be reborn in world of paradise" (ibid.). Here, the skill in means is motivated by compassion, which ameliorated the karmic results of murder.

Nature of the Victim

The School of Emptiness (*shunyavada*) derives its teachings in part from the
pan-Buddhist positions of no-self (Sanskrit: *anatman;* Pali: *anatta*) and of the two
truths model: conventional truth and ultimate truth. Buddhists recognize that
there is no eternal self (or, no-soul) and that everything we perceive in this world
is impermanent and thus constitutes conventional truth. The philosopher
Nagarjuna is the most prominent and respected advocate of this principle and
extends the idea of no-self to reality in its entirety, claiming that all phenomena are
empty of essence. While emptiness serves to explain reality ontologically and epis-
temologically, it also provides a lens for valuing human life. This line of reasoning

raises the query: If human life is empty of any true nature, what is destroyed in a murder?

One element that is commonly presented when justifying murder is the dehumanization of the intended victim(s). This dehumanization is present in Theravada when monks consider communists or the followers of the Tamil king Elara less than human and thus meritoriously expendable. Within Mahayana doctrine, some humans are designated as *icchantikas,* those who are those barred from enlightenment.

Mahayana doctrine typically advocates proselytizing, with people undertaking the bodhisattva vows to work toward liberating all sentient beings (*bodhicitta*). This all-encompassing ethos has an exception with the *icchantika*. Considered the most vile and debased creatures, they have either committed the worst of deeds or repudiated the basic tenets of the doctrine; they are classified at a lower level than animals. Some texts, such as the Chinese version of the Mahayana *Mahaparinirvana Sutra,* consider it more harmful to kill an ant than an icchantika. Within this text, the Buddha explains that no negative karma accrues from killing them:

> "Just as no sinful *karma* [will be engendered] when one digs the ground, mows grass, fells trees, cuts corpses into pieces and scolds and whips them, the same is true when one kills an *icchantika,* for which deed [also] no sinful karma [will arise]." (Ming-Wood 1984: 68)

Perhaps the most extreme religious rhetoric of dehumanization occurs within Mahayana doctrine: If a person is empty of substance, what is being murdered? One scripture that offers an answer is the Chinese text called the *Susthitamati-Paripriccha,* which is often referred to as *How to Kill with the Sword of Wisdom.*

Within the text, the fully enlightened being Manjushri explains to the Buddha that, if one were to conceive of sentient beings as only names and thoughts, she or he should kill those names and thoughts. However, as long as a person clears the mind of holding a knife or killing, to kill the "thoughts of a self and a sentient being is to kill sentient beings truly. [If you can do that,] I will give you permission to cultivate pure conduct [with me]." (Chang 1983: 65). Later in the text, Manjushri attempts to assuage bodhisattvas of their guilt from committing violence and advances to kill the Buddha with his sword. The Buddha explains that there is neither killing nor killer. Hence, Manjushri does not suffer any negative repercussions for attempting to kill the Buddha, since ultimately "there is no sword and no karma and no retribution, who performs that karma and who will undergo the karmic retribution?" (Chang 1983: 69). The acts in this reality are empty of true existence; therefore violence is empty of any true repercussion. Another Chinese text, *The Catharsis of Ajatashatru's Remorse,* justifies an act of matricide in a similar fashion. Manjushri defends the criminal and explains that since the actor's thoughts were empty at the time of the deed, he should be exonerated (Demiéville 2010: 42).

Stature of Those Who Kill

In some texts, killing or war is justified so long as it is done to defend the religion. In the Tibetan version of the Mahayana *Mahaparinirvana Sutra,* Buddhists, especially kings, are expected to take up weapons and fight to defend their religion (Schmithausen 1999: 57–58). Similar to Theravada doctrine, Mahayana doctrine contains different ethics for rulers than for lay practitioners. The Mongolian text *White History of the Tenfold Virtuous Dharma* instructs rulers to destroy those against the Buddhist teachings and to implement harsh measures when necessary (Wallace 2010: 93). The South Asian *Arya-Bodhisattva-gocara-upayavishay a-vikurvana-nirdesha Sutra (Satyakaparivarta)*, which is loosely translated at *The Noble Teachings through Manifestations on the Subject of Skill-in-Means within the Bodhisattva's Field of Activity,* also provides instructions for rulers, which includes ways to administer Buddhist-sanctioned torture, capital punishment, and other forms of violence. In the text, the king is warned to avoid the exercise of *excessive* compassion and to imprison, terrorize, beat, bind, or harm "uncivilized people" (Jenkins 2010: 64).

Mahayana doctrine provides a similar structure of exceptions for violence as Theravada. However, the principles of emptiness and skill in means create a distinctive set of ethical considerations. These principles are shared in Vajrayana doctrine, which is often said to have evolved out of Mahayana doctrine.

Vajrayana Scriptures

Vajrayana is a contested term, and scholars are not in agreement as to the traditions that fall under its canopy. Some scholars argue that it is principally an offshoot of Mahayana doctrine that is specifically Tibetan and Mongolian, while others identify the term with similar appellations such as Tantrayana or Mantrayana and consider the term to include Indian, Nepali, Tibetan, Mongolian, and Japanese traditions. Whether one considers Vajrayana a Tibetan nomenclature or a descriptor of various traditions, it inevitably involves tantras. Tantra is another term that is highly contested, and a replete discussion of it would stretch beyond the parameters of this chapter.

Tantra texts often prescribe transgressive actions. For the *tantrika,* if one is bound by conventional taboos, then s/he is not truly free of the world and its fetters. Often acts of transgression are sexual or violent in nature. In addition to its transgressive inclinations, Tantra texts are intended to be esoteric. Most traditions require special ordinations for their initiates and gurus to explain the doctrine. This complexity adds several lays to the texts and often leads to the Buddhist hermeneutics of provisional meanings (*neyartha*) and definitive meanings (*nitartha*). With the help of one's guru, provisional meaning can be discarded for the highest truth of the scripture. Some texts, such as the Indian and Tibetan *Kalachakra Tantra (Wheel of Time Tantra)*, may prescribe violence, but this is argued to be a provisional interpretation. When the text encourages readers to kill, lie, steal, and commit adultery, commentators explain the metaphorical nature of it (Broido 1988: 100). In this vein, a venture into an ethics of violence is fraught with distinct hermeneutical challenges.

Vajrayana doctrine is suffused with texts and commentaries that reject the use of violence. Many of the Tantra texts criticize Hindu texts and their position on animal sacrifices, or their contextual advocacy of justified violence in the *Bhagavad Gita* and other sources. However, Vajrayana texts offer arguments that are quite similar in nature to those that they critique. For instance, the Tibetologist Jacob Dalton locates in the *Kalika Purana* detailed instructions for human sacrifices to Kali or to the *heruka* Buddha and his mandala assembly. In such cases, the position in which the severed head comes to rest reveals signs of a kingdom's success (Dalton 2011: 90).

The seemingly contradictory status of Vajrayana texts serves as a poignant reminder that texts are not ahistorical and bereft of contexts; rather, they were born at different times, from people with various schools of thought. The texts display various accounts for justified violence. Of particular distinctive prominence among the texts are those pertaining to intentionality, such as defensive violence and liberation killing, and the stature of those who kills, which is primarily found in the bodhisattva.

Intention

Many of Vajrayana's ethical foundations for justified violence are coterminous with those in Mahayana doctrine. A motif that justifies violence in Vajrayana scriptures is defense; one of the most ubiquitous of reasons to commit violence. The questions arise though: What are the determinations of the aggression that necessitates the defense, and what does that defense entail? Within Vajrayana scriptures, defense is mounted through rituals of sacrifice and cosmic battles.

Tantra texts range from ritual to practical and yogic purposes. Most germane to our discussion is the tantric ritual goals, which involve the pacification of diseases, enemies, and emotions; augmentation of money, power, and merit; control of opponents, gods, and passions; and the killing of enemies, gods, sense of self, and so on (Davidson 2005: 35). Among the defensive rituals is the rite of fire sacrifice (*abhichara-homa*), which in the Indian *Mahavairochana-abhisambodhi Tantra* subdues hated foes. There are disparate but concerted commentaries on the fire sacrifice that expand on its transgressive and violent nature. The Indian Buddhist scholar-monk Bhavyakirti writes on the *Chakrasamvara Tantra*:

> Then the destruction of all, arising from the vajra, is held [to be accomplished] with the great meat. It is the dreadful destroyer of all the cruel ones. Should one thus perform without hesitation the rites of eating, fire sacrifice (*homa*), and sacrificial offerings (*bali*) with the meats of dogs and pigs, and also [the meat of] those [chickens] that have copper [colored] crests, everything without exception will be achieved, and all kingdoms will be subdued. (Gray 2007: 252)

Whereas Bhavyakirti's commentary invokes the violent sacrifice of animals for defensive purposes, other texts have more inclusive and aggressive positions. Vajrayana doctrine differs considerably from Theravada doctrine on the killing of animals, especially for dietary purposes. In Mongolian and Tibetan traditions, adherents are encouraged to eat larger animals instead of smaller ones. The death of one large animal such as a cow could feed many, whereas the death of one shrimp would not satisfy a person.

Defense does not pertain to simply threats of the state but also include preemptive attacks due to an imminent cosmic war. The most notable of these is found in the Indian and Tibetan *Kalachakra Tantra*, referred to as the *Wheel of Time Tantra*. As mentioned by the Buddhologist Lambert Schmithausen, the text describes an eschatological war in which the army of the bodhisattva king of Shambhala finally conquers and annihilates the Muslim forces in order to destroy their barbarian religion and to reestablish Buddhism. We should not overlook the historical context of this text; it is estimated by scholars that it was composed during the Muslim invasions of northern Indian in the eleventh century.

In some texts, the Mahayana principle of skill in means is applied to show violence as a redemptive act, which is often referred to as liberation killing. Such is the case of the bodhisattva Vajrapani, who kills the Hindu god Mahesvara and revives him as an enlightened follower of the Buddha. Tibetan Buddhists from the Nyingma school have killing rituals that are meant to liberate their enemies (Mayer 1996: 108). The *Sarvadurgatiparishodhana Tantra*, translated as *The Purification of All Misfortunes*, advocates the killing of those "who hate the Three Jewels, those who have a wrong attitude with regards to the Buddha's teachings or disparage the [Vajrayana] masters" (Schmithausen 1999: 58). This position is partly justified through the notion of compassion, where killing an evil person prevents that person from committing further negative actions (karma).

One of the most famous of these examples comes from the Tibetan *Chos 'byung me tog snying po*, which details the Buddhist assassination of the Tibetan ruler Lang Darma in 841. At the time, the Tibetan king Lang Darma oversaw policies that reduced the power and control of monasteries and was viewed as anti-Buddhist. The author Nyang Nyi ma 'od relates that the Buddhist monk received a vision from a protective Buddhist deity, who directed him to kill the ruler. This killing both liberated the country from an anti-Buddhist ruler and also liberated the ruler—through his murder. The narrative of this liberation killing is part of the Tibetan collective memory, and the murder is recalled in ritual yearly in Tibetan monasteries in their dance—the *cham* (Meinert 2006: 100–101). This violent practice of liberation did not end in the ninth century, nor was it restricted to ignoble kings. The presence of Tibetan Buddhist Tantric ritual killings and blood sacrifice was widespread enough for King Yeshe O (942–1024 CE) to publicly oppose them and to argue hermeneutically for a distinction between the tantric practices of liberation rites and sacrifice (Dalton 2011: 106–108).

Stature of Those Who Kill

Among the Vajrayana foundational principles is the Mahayana conception of the bodhisattva, a being who is either enlightened or on the path to enlightenment. In some texts, these individuals, who are endowed with perfected compassion and wisdom, gain the benefits from an ethical double standard. As seen in the scriptures about the bodhisattva Manjushri, ordinary people are bound by the provisional ethics; however, bodhisattvas may do anything, even commit murder. Fully enlightened beings are not hindered by the attachments of ill thoughts, so their actions are different from others. In addition, they use skill in means to liberate people and protect the religion. Within the Mergen Gegen tradition, Tibetan lamas identify the Mongol emperor Chinggis (Ghengis Khan) as an incarnation of the bodhisattva Vajrapani. As Vajrapani, his function is to protect Buddhism and destroy heretics. This rationale applies to Tantric masters: Buddhist yogis. In the Tibetan *Song of the Queen Spring*, the Fifth Dalai Lama explains that advanced Buddhist yogis can commit just acts of violence because of their command over mental states and emotions (Maher 2010: 85). It is in this context that the Fifth Dalai Lama justifies violence committed by his school's protector, the Mongol ruler Gushri Khan. In addition to the fact that Gushri Khan was defending the dharma, the Fifth Dalai Lama explains that the ruler was a bodhisattva (ibid., 88).

SYMBOLIC REPRESENTATIONS OF VIOLENCE

The Four Noble Truths focus on suffering (Sanskrit: *dukkha*; Pali: *duhkha*), a painful theme that serves as the bedrock for Buddhist worldviews. Although the Four Noble Truths discuss the suffering of the world (and the need to liberate oneself from it), there is violent rhetoric, imagery, and legends in Buddhist traditions as well. Some of these are global, whereas others are culturally specific to their locality. Whether global or locally relevant, symbolic representations of violence are generally found in eschatological accounts, legends about nemeses, or tantric imagery.

Military metaphors and similes abound in Buddhist scriptures. We find examples these in places such as the *Dhammapada,* where the "conqueror of the battlefield" is compared to the "conqueror of the self," or in the *Lotus Sutra* with references to bodhisattvas who conquer the evil one, Mara. One of the most the more popular parables, the "Chulamalunkya Sutta" in the *Majjhima Nikaya,* uses the example of a soldier to illustrate the distinction between beneficial and unbeneficial questions. The Buddha discusses the problems of a soldier wounded by a poisoned arrow. The soldier is more intent on learning who shot the arrow and why than on addressing the imminent issue of the poison and dying. Often times, military metaphors and similes are related to kingship in Theravada scriptures (Bartholomeusz 2002: 41).

The Buddhist system presents time as cyclical in nature but linear in its progression. In this manner there is no ultimate end time, rather a beginning and an end to every cycle. Throughout Buddhist and Hindu societies there is the general consensus that we are living in the fourth era: the age of destruction (*kali yuga*).

According to Buddhist scriptures, the end of a cycle is signaled by the disappearance of the teachings and the marking of a new cycle. At times, Buddhist relics symbolically mark the new cycle, such as the reconstitution of the Buddha's bones (*sarira*), the coming of the next Buddha (Sanskrit: *Maitreya*; Pali: *Metteya)*, or the reappearance of his begging bowl and robes (in some cases, the destruction of the Buddha's begging bowl signals the end). Millenarian movements are not necessarily violent, but the ones that are violent use these and other signs to justify their actions.

Often, violent millenarian movements invoke the imagery and rhetoric of Mara, the maker of death and desire. In the narrative of the Buddha's enlightenment, Mara is his principal adversary, who tries to prevent the Buddha from reaching enlightenment. Violent millenarian movements view Mara as their adversary, such as the one led by the Chinese Buddhist monk Faqing in 515. Faqing announced the coming of the new Buddha, Maitreya, and commanded 50,000 men to battle against the forces of Mara. The more people a soldier killed, the more he advanced in the prescribed bodhisattva paradigm (Demiéville 2010: 25).

Mara is one of the elite among Buddhist literary adversaries. Another nemesis in Buddhist lore is the Buddha's cousin Devadatta, who vied for control of the Sangha and has become a literary scapegoat. In many scriptures, he tries to repudiate the Buddha's authority and to kill him. In one famous encounter present in children's books, Devadatta sends a crazed and furious elephant named Nalagiri at the Buddha. The elephant comes close to crushing a baby in its path, but the Buddha intervenes and calms the wild elephant. Of all his actions, the worst Devadatta purportedly committed were causing a schism in the Sangha, killing a nun, and wounding the Buddha. This last act resulted in the earth swallowing up Devadatta and condemning him to Avichi, the darkest of hells. Often, religious persecutors call on the memory of Devadatta to denounce Buddhist practitioners and their practices as heretical.

The violent and persecuted caricature of Devadatta is almost the reversal of another person who tried to kill the Buddha. Angulimala was a robber who had committed himself to completing his vow of killing 1,000 people. Angulimala had a necklace of fingers, one finger for every death, and as it turned out, his last intended victim was the Buddha. On meeting the Buddha, Angulimala renounced his bloody path and joined the Sangha. During his time in the Sangha, he endures attacks from lay communities but attains enlightenment under the guidance of the Buddha. Images of Angulimala represent the far-reaching redemptive power of the Buddhist path for the most violent of initiates.

In the Sri Lankan *Mahavamsa's* legendary war between the Buddhist king Dutthagamani and the forces of King Elara, Dutthagamani wields a royal spear endowed with a Buddhist relic. During scriptural accounts of battles, rulers are purportedly given amulets or relics that sacralize their weapons. Most of the time, these weapons or artifacts bestow on a person protection. In Thailand, soldiers believe that by consuming the wild animal one may absorb their spiritual and physical prowess. They wear various amulets, often images of Buddhist saints that prepare them for battle; some shield them from bullets while others repel bombs. These amulets became transnational commodities during the US war in Vietnam, when Thai Buddhist soldiers shared their amulets with US soldiers (Richard 2011: 134 and 189).

Buddhist images are suffused with brilliant colors and complex lines. Like the doctrine, tantric imagery is remarkably complex and contains several interpretative layers. Sand mandalas represent the microcosm of the body and the macrocosm of the universe, all the while reminding us of their impermanence. The Buddhist pantheon contains violent depictions of deities, bodhisattvas, and spirits—many wield bloody weapons with ferocious countenances such as the skull-crowned Mahakala. The bovine-headed Yama, the lord of death, is killed by the bovine-headed Yamantaka (which means "terminator of Yama"). There is even Kojin, the fiery, fanged bow-and-arrow-wielding Japanese god of the hearth. These violent depictions most often are meant not for practitioners but for the evil spirits that would prey on the practitioner, or they serve the metaphoric purposes of attacking the negative qualities within ourselves.

There are also myths about demons that are ritually murdered but are reborn as protectors of Buddhism. This transformation from foe into protector illustrates the power of compassionate violence. This notion of violence as a means of burning away the vices of an entity transcends Buddhist traditions (it is quite common with the use of Agni, god of fire, in Vedic and Hindu traditions). However, it has become a central theme for some Buddhist traditions. One prominent example comes from a Tibetan Buddhist foundational myth found in the Nyingma *Compendium of Intentions Sutra* in which tantric buddhas battle with the demon Rudra. In his analysis, Jacob Dalton considers the murder of Rudra "essential for anyone seeking to understand the place of violence in Tibetan Buddhism" (2011: 3). After numerous rebirths and confrontations, the conflict ends when a *heruka* buddha plunges a trident into Rudra's chest and swallows him whole. Within the heruka's stomach, Rudra is purified (ibid., 19–21). From Rudra's subjugation, death, and then rebirth emerges a protector deity of Tibetan Buddhism. This motif of demon into protector is found in other myths and legends, such as cannibalistic evil spirits who protect the *Lotus Sutra*, the sword-wielding Dorje Shugden that protects Tibet and its people, and damned Cittipatti, skeletons who after living lives of sin and misdeeds must work off their negative karma and guard the entrances to Tibetan and Mongolian Buddhist sites.

In addition to the Tantric images that contain violent figures, there are other images of notoriously nonviolent deities and bodhisattvas that are placed in violent contexts. When the Manchus conquered the Mongols in the late seventeenth century, they considered their rule an emanation of the bodhisattva of wisdom, Manjushri, even in their use of the death penalty (Wallace 2010: 96–97). The benevolent image of Manjushri is seen in other contexts, such as in tenth-century Japan, when Tendai abbot called on monks to embody Manjushri by carrying bows and arrows into battle. A thousand years later, the Japanese gave the bodhisattava of compassion, Avalokiteshvara, the rank of a shogun or generalissimo in World War II (Victoria 2006: 142).

Although tantric rituals of defense invoke symbolic (and actual) violence on animal sacrifices, the bulwark of symbolic violence comes from narratives and images. Buddhist traditions have their share of violent symbols, relics, and images, but a cursory review of these also reveals the dominant presence of context. Even the most peaceful of images, such as Avalokiteshvara, the bodhisattva of compassion, may become associated with violence given the specific circumstances.

MANIFESTATIONS OF VIOLENCE

People commit various atrocities upon themselves and others, but what is distinctive about their violence that makes the actions Buddhist? To return to the parameters drawn earlier, Buddhists are people who follow the Four Noble Truths and hold the Buddha as the penultimate figure/deity. However, being Buddhist does not necessarily mean that one's acts are "Buddhist"; rather, Buddhist worldviews and codes of conduct influence one's behavior. Various Buddhist elements are embedded in acts of violence. Tanks have patrolled with Buddhist amulets on them, monasteries have served as military compounds for soldiers, and monastic Buddhist reliquaries (stupas) and pagodas have been used for military defenses. However, to narrow our focus, the most notably "Buddhist" acts are human actions that reflect the core values of the religion: The Three Jewels of Buddha, Dhamma and Sangha (or in Tantric Buddhism, the Four Jewels). Self-proclaimed bodhisattvas, *arahants* and buddhas (Buddha) have engaged in violence, violent acts are done in the name of Buddhist teaching (Dhamma), and monks have committed violence (sangha). This section will review these elements in regard to war, punishment, and social control.

War

Buddhists have engaged in wars since the time of Ashoka in the third century BCE. These wars contain a myriad of causes and factors but become sanctified to the participants through enlightened leaders, Buddhist rhetoric (dhamma/dharma), and Buddhist monks. Most Buddhist-inspired wars are either the result of a closely aligned monasticism and state or a movement that contains millenarian elements.

It was in the first century CE that Buddhist monks brought their traditions to China. Three hundred years later, there were Chinese Buddhist millenarian revolts and insurrections, often led by monks. Buddhist-inspired revolts also occurred under the Tabgatch Empire against the villainous Mara (402–517 CE), and messianic monks rebelled during the Sui and Tang dynasties (613–626 CE). It was in the Tang Dynasty that Faqing led his soldier-monks on a revolt in which ten deaths would enable them to complete their bodhisattva path (815 CE). The White Lotus Society incorporated messianic elements into its Pure Land practices. By the thirteenth and fourteenth centuries, they had staged armed uprisings to establish their own states and to overthrow the Mongol Dynasty.

Mahayana Buddhist traditions were transported from China to Korea in the fourth century CE. Korea embraced Buddhist practices during the bloody Chinese interregnum (220–589 CE.). The nascent Silla kingdom credited Buddhist protectors for causing the Chinese to make peace with them in 671 CE. Then Koreans brought Buddhist practices and beliefs to Japan in the sixth century CE. In Japan, powerful Buddhist monasteries gradually emerged, and armies were solicited to protect their landholdings. The close political ties between monasteries and state in the Heian period (794–1185 CE) drew monks into conflicts. During the twelfth century, Chinese and Korean monks fought in wars against the Jurchens, the Mongols, and the Japanese. In the next century, Japanese Shin adherents fought apocalyptic battles over Amita paradise.

Within the Theravada traditions, Thai chronicles in the sixteenth century reveal monks as spies and conspirators. From 1699 until the mid 1950s, Lao and Thai holy men (*phumibun*) staged dozens of messianic revolts against Thailand. The leaders claimed to possess extraordinary powers and drew on the lore of Phra Si Ariya, the Thai version of Maitreya, the Buddha-to-be (Nartsupha 1984: 112). This claim of supernatural powers was not solely a phenomenon of revolts. The Thai king Taksin liberated his people from Burmese occupation in 1767 and declared himself a stream enterer—the first of four stages to sainthood in Theravada Buddhism.

Monks became warriors in Chinese, Japanese, Korean, Thai, and Sri Lankan traditions. Perhaps the most widely known of these are the Shaolin monks of the Chinese Chan tradition, who developed martial arts for meditation and fighting. Japanese peasants, inspired by Pure Land teachings, fought a battle of cosmic relevance to promote a Buddhist paradise during the Warring States period of the 1500s, and Japanese Zen monks fought as soldiers in the Russo-Japanese War of 1904 and 1905 (Victoria 2006). Within the Tibetan traditions there is a fraternity of fighter monks (*ldab ldob*). Although these monks are not soldiers, they equip themselves with at least one weapon. They are notable fighters and have served in special all-Tibetan frontier forces in the Indian Army of the Republic. In recent years, Thai soldiers serve in covert operations as military monks (*tahan phra*). Unbeknownst to their abbots, these men fully ordain and retain their military status, guns, and monthly stipends (Jerryson 2011: 116–127).

In the colonial and postcolonial periods, Buddhists rebelled against the predominantly Christian colonialists and reasserted their identities. Burmese monks such as U Ottama led anticolonial movements against the British in the 1930s. During the early 1940s, Korean monks equated the United States' growing military influence with "Christian power" and sought to cleanse the world from demons and the evil of Mara (Tikhonov 2009: 8). Their sentiments were mirrored by Chinese

Buddhists during the Korean War (1951–1953). Influential Chinese monks like Ven. Juzan challenged Chinese Buddhists to fulfill their patriotic duty and assist North Korea by resisting the encroachment of US influence, which he saw as the same as subduing evils (Xue Yu 2010: 142). However, Korean Buddhist movements against external forces turned internal in the 1950s. Korean Buddhist Chogye monks engaged in bloody conflicts with married monks over the issue of celibacy, claiming that monastic marriage practices were a by-product of Japanese colonialism.

In the twentieth century, monks became part of the intelligentsia that supported socialist revolutions. In the early 1900s, Mongolian monks were principal members of the socialist revolutionary party (Mongolian People's Revolutionary Party). After the revolution, the government embraced a more militant socialism and targeted and killed tens of thousands of monks (Jerryson 2007: 93). In a similar fashion, Cambodian monks were also early supporters of Pol Pot's efforts, only to find themselves victims after the regime was installed. Communist movements such as these concerned Thai Buddhists. One of the most notable political activists was Kittiwuttho, who in the 1970s called on Thais to eradicate the communist rebels.

During the US war in Vietnam (1963–1975), Buddhist monks demonstrated their opposition to the suppression of Buddhism and US involvement by self-immolation. The most prominent of these was Thich Quang Duc's immolation in Saigon on June 11, 1963. Although Buddhist self-immolations were largely a Chinese or Vietnamese phenomenon, Tibetan lamas have adopted this practice of self-immolated for political protest. The earliest reported self-immolation was Thubten Ngodup who lit himself on fire during an Indian police crackdown on the Tibetan Youth Congress in 1998. The Tibetan self-immolation gained international attention in 2009 when it was used to protest the Chinese human rights violations and suppression of Tibetan Buddhism. Since then, more than thirty-six have died by self-immolation, the most recent a 20-year-old Tibetan monk from Kirti monastery in Aba county, China, on March 28, 2012 (see McGranahan and Litzinger 2012).

In South Asia, Sri Lankan monks became politically active and advocated strong forms of Buddhist nationalism. The socialist-leading Janatha Vimukthi Peramuna enlisted monks in an armed uprising during the 1980s. Lao monks have supported resistance movements against the Lao communist government since the 1980s.

After the fall of the Berlin Wall, the Buddhist world changed. Among the more costly sites of Buddhist conflict in contemporary times was the Sri Lankan civil war against the LTTE (1983–2008), the current Tibetan uprisings in Chinese-controlled Tibet, Burmese Buddhist rebellion efforts in Myanmar, and Buddhist and Muslim conflicts in Ladakh, India, and southern Thailand.

Punishment

Throughout the many iterations of the state over the centuries, Buddhists have supported their government's right to adjudicate punishments in order to maintain the Buddhist ethos. In addition to the state's function of preserving the dhamma, some interpret corporal punishments as executions of the law of kamma. For others, the system of punishment is itself an application of negative actions. As indicated earlier under doctrinal justifications, the majority of Buddhists condone corporal punishments, which includes torture as well as capital punishment.

The Buddhist position on punishments has changed over the centuries. In the sixteenth century, the Mongolian Khutukhtu Setsen Khung Taiji edited the *White History of the Tenfold Virtuous Dharma*, which advised measures such as blinding someone for stealing or cutting out a tongue for a lie (Wallace 2010: 93). Various punishments were carried out in Mongolia until the social revolution in 1921. Thailand does not maintain laws like those found in the *White History*, but it has been cited by nongovernmental organizations such as Amnesty International and Human Rights Watch for their torture techniques of suspects. Some torture techniques retain Buddhist connotations, such as the Sri Lankan *dhammacakke ghahana* (hitting the wheel of the dhamma). For this torture, people were forced to contort their bodies into the shape of a wheel; their bodies were then spun and beaten until the person passed out or bled to death (Abeysekara 2002: 230–231). Tortures are not always inflicted by force. Buddhists have applied forms of self-mortification in order to gain merit, display filial piety, or express devotion. These practices are most frequently seen in Chinese traditions, wherein Buddhist monks wrote in blood, sliced off parts of their body, and engaged in extreme ritual exposures to the sun (Jimmy Yu 2012).

Some nation-states are not supportive of the death penalty. Sri Lanka has had a long history of opposition to the death penalty. In 1815, the British implemented the death penalty, but in 1978 it was revoked. Subsequently there have been periodic attempts to reinstate this policy.

Social Control

Social control is maintained through hegemonic systems, as well as through the execution of particular laws. Because of the visible state advocacy of Buddhist principles, Buddhist traditions have been used in authoritarian regimes such as Myanmar and its *karaoke fascism*, a term Monique Skidmore uses to describe the form of oppression and the Burmese response to a life of domination (Skidmore 2004: 7).

Religious texts are suffused with gender and racial stereotypes. In the heterosexually dominated narrative, women are subservient to men—either in recollections of the Buddha and his past lives or in the pantheon of deities and bodhisattvas. Buddhist traditions were among the earliest to grant women ordination (along with Jains), but this was not without contest. The Buddha's favorite disciple Ananda had to ask three times for their admittance, and after the Order of Nuns was created, the Buddha explained the life of the dhamma was cut short because women were included. There were early female Buddhist saints such as those found in the collection of female hagiographies (*Therigatha*), but South Asian Buddhist women have learned to identify themselves from the perspective of male heroes (Wilson 1996: 5). Through the centuries most countries did not sustain their Order of Nuns; some, such as Thailand, never initiated it. In the alternative practices of Tantra, the division of sexual bodies and sacrality are not much different. Charlene Makley points out that paradigmatically male bodies of Tibetan incarnate lamas (*trulkus*) act as crucial indexes of the local divine cosmos (2007: 25). There is much to say about a religion that focuses on overcoming attachment and depicts women as seductresses in texts and images (such as Mara's daughters). Viewed from this perspective, it is not a coincidence that sex ranks higher than murder among the highest offenses (*parajika*).

Buddhist practices have been used to sustain racial impositions. The earliest of these dates back to the South Asian Brahmanical caste system, which was officially rebuked by the Buddha. However, the monastic guidelines contain a wealth of physical restrictions for those who wish to ordain, and the vast majority of his followers were of the higher castes (particularly of the merchant and priest castes). Within the early South Asian social system, racial divisions were physically mapped by skin tones; those people with darker skin pigmentations were designated as the lower castes. The preference for lighter skin pigmentation is largely the result of labor conditions. Those of the lower castes worked outside in the sun, whereas the wealthy could afford to stay indoors. This early method of racializing bodies is present within cotemporary Buddhist societies of South and Southeast Asia and has been reinforced by global media and entertainment.

Sri Lankan society still maintains a caste system, and Thai society retains a preference for lighter skin tones as well. Within these nation-states, it is generally the White tourists who visit the beaches to tan; whitening creams are commonly advertised. The preference for lighter skin pigmentation is mapped onto Buddhist images, with light skin tones for the Buddha and darker skin tones for his adversaries. In some accounts, Mara and his minions are depicted with darker skin tones, such as in Thai Buddhist murals. These features suggest a structural level of violence that integrates Buddhist lore and racialized subjects (Jerryson 2011: 143–177).

In regard to slavery, Buddhist traditions do not have canonical prohibitions. We find examples of Buddhist intolerance toward slavery, such as in "Assalayana" in the *Majjhima Nikaya*, in which the Buddha rejects the view that people are born into servitude and are lesser beings than others. He espouses that all people, no matter the color of their skin, are equal to one another. However, Buddhist states (and monasteries) employed slaves until the late nineteenth century. In China, slavery continued under Buddhist influenced states, (the earliest records of slavery predate the introduction of Buddhism in the fourth century BCE), and there is record of the Sri Lanka Sangha receiving slaves as gifts as early as the first century BCE.

Laws on euthanasia and abortion differ with each nation-state and doctrinal grouping. The majority of Buddhist nation-states do not support the use of euthanasia or abortion. Humans must endure the fruits of their negative actions; in this light, the dying persons expiate their past kamma through their suffering. And because Buddhist notions of the self pinpoint life at conception, the abortion of a fetus is the ending of a self. This stance has created problems in some countries such as Thailand, where abortion is prohibited but abortions are performed. Thai Buddhists believe that the fetuses' spirits must be appeased, and so aborted fetuses are brought to monasteries for cremation. Japanese Buddhists perform a fetus memorial service (*mizuko kuyo*) for stillborn, aborted, or miscarried fetuses. During these ceremonies, offerings are made to the bodhisattva Jizo (Ksitigarbha), the guardian of children.

CONCLUSION

There is great strength in the Buddhist calls for compassion and acceptance. Among the various examples in the scriptures lies one from its founder Siddhattha Gotama, who abandoned his own familial allegiance for the sake of reconciliation. In the *Sutta Nipata Atthakatha,* the Sakya and Koliya kingdoms were close to declaring war over the use of the river Rohini, which flowed along the borders of both kingdoms. Each kingdom needed water for irrigating their crops, and a recent drought had deepened the severity of that need. However, instead of choosing his own kingdom of Sakya, Siddhattha counseled both sides to share the water since blood was more important than water.

We find more recent examples of Buddhist-inspired reconciliation in the Nobel Peace laureate, the Fourteenth Dalai Lama, whose recent advocacy of diplomacy with the Chinese government limits the violence within the Tibetan region to small disparate acts. In the last several decades, movements such as the Sarvodaya Movement in Sri Lanka and the recent Burmese monks' use of civil disobedience in their Saffron Revolution exemplify the power of Buddhist peace activism. Like all religious systems, Buddhist traditions contain a great capacity for reconciliation. In order to make use of these strengths, we should not turn a blind eye to its shortcomings.

BIBLIOGRAPHY

Abeysekara, Ananda. *The Colors of the Robe: Religion, Identity, and Difference.* Columbia: University of South Carolina Press, 2002.

Bartholomeusz, Tessa J. *In Defense of Dharma: Just-War Ideology in Buddhist Sri Lanka.* New York: Routledge Curzon, 2002.

Benn, James A. *Burning for the Buddha: Self-Immolation in Chinese Buddhism.* Honolulu: University of Hawai'i Press, 2007.

Bhikkhu Bodhi, trans. *The Connected Discourses of the Buddha: A Translation of the Saṃyutta Nikāya.* Boston: Wisdom Publications, 2000.

Broido, Michael M. "Killing, Lying, Stealing and Adultery: A Problem of Interpretation in the Tantras." *Buddhist Hermeneutics.* Ed. Donald S. Lopez Jr., 71–118. Honolulu: University of Hawai'i Press, 1988.

Chang, Garma Chen-chi, ed. "How to Kill with the Sword of Wisdom." *A Treasury of Mahayana Sūtras: Selections from the Mahāratnakūṭa Sūtra,* 41–72. University Park and London: Pennsylvania State University Press, 1983.

Chatthip Nartsupha. "The Ideology of Holy Men Revolts in North East Thailand." *Senri Ethnological Studies* 13 (1984): 111–134.

Collins, Steven. *Nirvana and Other Buddhist Felicities: Utopias of the Pali Imaginaire.* Cambridge, UK: Cambridge University Press, 1998.

Cowell, E. B., ed. *The Jataka or Stories of the Buddha's Former Births.* 1895. Delhi: Motilal Banarsidass Publishers, 1990.

Daishonin, Nichiren. "139: Strategy of the Lotus Sutra." Trans. Soka Gakkai International. *Writings of Nichiren Daishonin.* 1000–1001. Soka Gakkai International, n.d. 17 January 2009. www.sgilibrary.org/view.php?page=1000.

Dalton, Jacob P. *Taming the Demons: Violence and Liberation in Tibetan Buddhism.* Princeton, NJ: Yale University Press, 2011.

Davids, Thomas Williams Rhys. *Questions of King Milinda, Part II.* Oxford, U.K.: Clarendon Press, 1894.

Davidson, Ronald M. *Tibetan Renaissance: Tantric Buddhism in the Rebirth of Tibetan Culture.* New York: Columbia University Press, 2005.

Demiéville, Paul. "Buddhist and War." Trans. Michelle Kendall. *Buddhist Warfare.* Eds. Michael Jerryson and Mark Juergensmeyer, 17–58. New York: Oxford University Press, 2010.

Geiger, Wilhelm, trans. *The Mahāvaṃsa or the Great Chronicle of Ceylon.* New Delhi and Madras: Asian Educational Services, 1993 [1912].

Gethin, Rupert. "Can Killing a Living Being Ever Be an Act of Compassion? The Analysis of the Act of Killing in the Abhidhamma and Pali Commentaries." *Journal of Buddhist Ethics* 11 (2004): 167–202.

Gokhale, Balkrishna. "Dhamma As a Political Concept" *Journal of Indian History* 44 (August 1968): 249–261.

Gray, David B. "Compassionate Violence?: On the Ethical Implications of Tantric Buddhist Ritual." *Journal of Buddhist Ethics* 14 (2007): 238–271.

Horner, Isaline Blew, trans. *The Book of the Discipline (Vinaya-Pitaka): Vol. I (Suttavibhanga).* Oxford, UK: Pali Text Society, 1992 [1938].

Horner, Isaline Blew, trans. *The Book of the Discipline (Vinaya-Pitaka): Vol. III (Suttavibhanga).* Oxford, UK: Pali Text Society, 1983 [1942].

Horner, Isaline Blew, trans. *Milinda's Questions.* London: Luzac & Company, 1963–1964.

Jenkins, Stephen. "Making Merit through Warfare and Torture according to the Ār ya-Bodhisattva-gocara-upāyaviṣaya-vikurvaṇa-nirdeśa Sūtra." *Buddhist Warfare.* Eds. Michael Jerryson and Mark Juergensmeyer, 59–76. New York: Oxford University Press, 2010.

Jerryson, Michael. *Mongolian Buddhism: The Rise and Fall of the Sangha.* Chiang Mai, Thailand: Silkworm Books, 2007.

Jerryson, Michael. "Introduction." *Buddhist Warfare.* Eds. Michael Jerryson and Mark Juergensmeyer, 1–16. New York: Oxford University Press, 2010.

Jerryson, Michael. *Buddhist Fury: Religion and Violence in Southern Thailand.* New York: Oxford University Press, 2011.

Kent, Daniel. "Onward Buddhist Soldiers." *Buddhist Warfare.* Eds. Michael Jerryson and Mark Juergensmeyer, 157–177. New York: Oxford University Press, 2010.

Keyes, Charles. "Political Crisis and Militant Buddhism." *Religion and Legitimation of Power in Thailand, Laos, and Burma.* Ed. Bardwell L. Smith, 147–164. Chambersburg, Penn.: ANIMA Books, 1978.

McGranahan, Carole and Ralph Litzinger, eds. "Self-Immolation as Protest in Tibet." *Cultural Anthropology* (special edition, April 9, 2012). Last modified on April 9, 2012. www.culanth.org/?q=node/526.

Maher, Derek F. "Sacralized Warfare: The Fifth Dalai Lama and the Discourse of Religious Violence." *Buddhist Warfare*. Eds. Michael Jerryson and Mark Juergensmeyer, 77–90. New York: Oxford University Press, 2010.

Makley, Charlene E. *The Violence of Liberation: Gender and Tibetan Buddhist Revival in Post-Mao China*. Berkeley: University of California Press, 2007.

Mayer, Richard. *A Scripture of the Ancient Tantra Collection, The Phur-pa bcu-gnyis*. Oxford, UK: Kiscadale Publications, 1996.

Meinert, Carmen. "Between the Profane and the Sacred? On the Context of the Rite of 'Liberation' (*sgrol ba*)." *Buddhism and Violence*. Ed. Michael Zimmermann, 99–130. Lumbini, Nepal: Lumbini International Research Institute, 2006.

Ming-Wood, Liu. "The Problem of the Icchantika in the Mahayana *Mahaparinirvana Sutra*." *Journal of International Buddhist Studies* 7.1 (1984): 57–81.

Reuter, Christoph. *My Life Is a Weapon: A Modern History of Suicide Bombing*. Princeton, NJ: Princeton University Press, 2004.

Ruth, Richard A. *In Buddha's Company: Thai Soldiers in the Vietnam War*. Honolulu: University of Hawai'i Press, 2011.

Schmithausen, Lambert. "Buddhist Attitudes toward War." *Violence Denied: Violence, Non-Violence and the Rationalization of Violence in South Asian Cultural History*. Eds. Jan E. M. Houben and Karel R. Van Kooij, 39–67. Leiden, Netherlands, and Boston: Brill, 1999.

Schober, Juliane. *Modern Buddhist Conjunctures in Myanmar: Cultural Narratives, Colonial Legacies, and Civil Society*. Honolulu: University of Hawai'i Press, 2010.

Sharf, Robert H. "The Scripture in Forty-Two Sections." *Religions of China in Practice*. Ed. Donald S. Lopez, Jr., 360–371. Princeton, NJ: Princeton University Press, 1996.

Skidmore, Monique. *Karaoke Fascism: Burma and the Politics of Fear*. Philadelphia: University of Pennsylvania Press, 2004.

Skidmore, Monique, and Trevor Wilson. *Dictatorship, Disorder and Decline in Myanmar*. Canberra: The Australian National University Press, 2010.

Tatz, Mark, trans. "Murder with Skill in Means: The Story of the Ship's Captain." *The Skill in Means (Upāyakauśalya) Sutra*, 73–74. New Delhi: Motilal Banarsidass, 1994.

Thanissaro Bhikkhu trans. "Kesi Sutta: To Kesi the Horsetrainer." *Anguttara Nikaya*. Access to Insight, 25 July 2010. www.accesstoinsight.org/tipitaka/an/an04/an04.111.than.html.

Tikhonov, Vladimir. "Violent Buddhism—Korean Buddhists and the Pacific War, 1937–1945." *Sai* 7 (2009): 169–204.

Victoria, Brian Daizen. *Zen at War*. Lanham, MD: Rowman and Littlefield Publishers, 2006.

Wallace, Vesna. "Legalized Violence: Punitive Measures of Buddhist Khans in Mongolia." *Buddhist Warfare*. Eds. Michael Jerryson and Mark Juergensmeyer, 91–104. New York: Oxford University Press, 2010.

Wilson, Liz. *Charming Cadavers: Horrific Figurations of the Feminine in Indian Buddhist Hagiographic Literature*. Chicago: University of Chicago Press, 1996.

Yu, Jimmy. *Sanctity and Self-Inflicted Violence in Chinese Religions, 1500–1700*. New York: Oxford University Press, 2012.

Yu, Xue. "Buddhists in China during the Korean War (1951–1953)." *Buddhist Warfare*. Eds. Michael Jerryson and Mark Juergensmeyer, 131–156. New York: Oxford University Press, 2010.

CHAPTER 3

SIKH TRADITIONS AND VIOLENCE

CYNTHIA KEPPLEY MAHMOOD

THERE has been a martial aspect to the Sikh tradition since the early stages of Sikh history. This is due, in part, to the social context of the emergent community. Were historical maps of resistance on the geographical peripheries of the Indian subcontinent constructed, they might show conflicts piled on one another like colored transparencies glowing through time, though expressed in differing idioms, sometimes religious, sometimes political. The Sikh tradition arose in one of these contested cultural regions and geographical peripheries and expressed itself in its own religious and political terms.

THE SIKHS

Sikhism is among the youngest of the global religions. The seminal figure who is regarded as the founder, Guru Nanak, was born in 1469 in what is now Pakistani Punjab. While orthodox Sikhs believe that Nanak's message was totally new and divinely inspired, some Western scholars point to Hindu and Islamic elements in his teachings (e.g., McLeod 1989). It is clear that Nanak rejected much of what he observed in both religious communities and critiqued particularly the empty ritualism of Brahmanical Hinduism that he saw as an impediment to true spiritual understanding. He founded a community that would eventually comprise 2 percent of the Indian population, and count some 20 million members worldwide.

Nanak traveled through the subcontinent and beyond and gathered disciples or *Sikhs* (the term *sikh* comes from the verb *to learn* and implies those who learn from a spiritual teacher, a "guru"). He emphasized the importance of meditation on a unitary divine spirit and on rightful living in this world. In direct contrast to the position of Orthodox Hindus, the Sikh community strove to ignore caste distinctions by interdining in a communal kitchen (*langar*). Also open to all were the Sikh temples or *gurudwaras* (a term that literally means "the doorway to the guru"). After Nanak died, the status of guru was passed to a loyal disciple, and the authority of guruship was subsequently passed from one to another through a series of ten gurus.

Three gurus are of particular interest here. Guru Arjun, the fifth guru (1563–1606), was not only the compiler of the *Adi Granth* ("the Ancient Scripture"), writings that would become in their final form the Guru Granth Sahib ("the scriptural lord guru"), the holy book of the Sikhs, but he was also the first of the Sikh Gurus to be martyred. Through the hideous tortures by the Mughal emperor Jahangir, Guru Arjun is described as remaining "unruffled" and "calm as the sea." Portraits of this first martyr adorn the walls of the homes of many Sikhs, including those who have attained political asylum abroad after suffering torture in contemporary Punjab.

The sixth guru, Hargobind (1595–1644), is a key to understanding another important strand of the Sikh martial tradition. He was the first to take up arms in defense of the faith. The double swords of Guru Hargobind represent the complementarity of temporal and spiritual power (*miri* and *piri*). Important to the Sikh understanding of "the just war" (*dharm yudh*) is the recognition that, while Hargobind was a valiant fighter, his battles were entirely defensive in nature. Hargobind also supplemented the symbol of the sword to defend the weak, with that of the kettle to feed the hungry. "Kettle-Sword-Victory" (*Deg Teg Fateh*) is a Sikh motto that remains popular in the militant community. Its symbolism is integrated into the *khanda*, an icon sewn onto flags, pinned into turbans, and representing the miri-piri philosophy. Today it is second only to the image of the words *Ek Oankar*, one god, in its prominence in Sikh life.

The tenth and last guru, Gobind Singh (1666–1708), took the most important step toward full militarization of the Sikh tradition: He established the army of the Khalsa, a group of respected Sikhs who vowed commitment to the faith. This took place in 1699, when Guru Gobind Singh called for a gathering of the entire *panth* (Sikh community). According to an account of this occasion that is remembered in the Sikh community, he drew his sword and demanded volunteers who would be willing to give their heads for their faith. Five volunteered, willing to make the ultimate sacrifice for their guru. They were called *panj piaray* or "five beloved ones" and were initiated by Guru Gobind Singh into a new order called the Khalsa, "the pure." They were to be "saint-soldiers" (*sant-sipahi*) and were regarded as having the wisdom of saints and the courage of soldiers.

Rather than pass the guruship to another individual as his predecessors had done, Guru Gobind Singh chose to pass his spiritual authority to the holy scripture; it was after this occasion that the *Adi Granth* became known as the *Guru Granth Sahib* ("the Scriptural Lord Guru"). Sikhs today venerate the sacred book as a living Guru and do not accept intermediaries such as priests (although there are clergy who are scripture readers and caretakers of the *gurudwaras*). Insults to the *Guru Granth Sahib* are taken as direct affronts to the guru, a factor that plays a role in the development of the sense of outrage militant Sikhs feel toward those considered to have committed blasphemy against the holy book and, by extension, against their faith. Guru Gobind Singh passed his worldly authority to the community, or panth. Thus the book, and the community, were the two manifestations of Divinity in the ongoing Sikh tradition.

By the time of India's independence in 1947, Sikh activists had mobilized their community, reformed the gurudwara system, and won recognition as an important political force. Many Sikhs believe that it was at this moment of the political partition of the Indian subcontinent in 1948 that the Sikh nation of Sikhistan or Khalistan might have been established. Instead, Sikh leaders at the time chose to stay with the secular pluralist India led by Pandit Jawaharlal Nehru. They lost much of their territorial base to Pakistan, but the Sikh population in India's east Punjab formed a significant minority. In 1966, after the redrawing of Punjab's boundary lines to match the boundaries of the Punjabi language, Sikhs became a slight majority in the newly defined Punjab state of India. However, economic inequalities and rising unemployment in the 1970s resulted in a disenfranchised, unemployed rural youth, who formed the backbone of the Sikh militancy in the 1980s (see Fox 1985; Kapur 1986).

In the early 1980s, Sikh separatists began fighting for an independent state of Khalistan to be located in place of the Indian state of Punjab. This struggle connected the past with the present, with a central theme of martyrdom within the separatist discourse drawn from the valorization of death in battle expressed in Sikh religious history. The struggle for Khalistan was a resistance movement against the perceived injustices of the Indian state and a political movement aimed at sovereign rule, but it also provided an existential means of being a Sikh, independently of instrumental political goals (Mahmood 1996, 1–16). This combination is a particular point of interest to those concerned with religion and violence.

SIKHS AND MILITANCY

Following the rise of the militant Khalistan movement in the 1980s, there has been a popular misconception in India and around the world that Sikhism is a violent religion and that Sikhs involved in the movement for Khalistan were terrorists. Some Sikhs attempted to defend their tradition by arguing that Sikhism is a peaceful religion and that members of the Khalistan movement were nation builders like Washington and Jefferson; but this position also ignored the complexity that

actually characterized the state of *Sikhi* ("the Sikh way of life") during the insur-
rectionary period of the 1980s and 1990s. It is only now, in a period of reflection,
that Sikhs and those in dialogue with them are finding ways to talk about militancy in more nuanced terms.

The discussion about Sikhism and militant protest begins with the debates
about the nature of the first guru, Nanak. Though often portrayed as a reclusive
meditative figure like the Buddha, with his eyes half shut in spiritual rapture, he
was also recorded as having challenged the prevailing socioreligious order. The
pacifist image of Guru Nanak was promoted by scholars who regarded him as a
reconciler, taking the best of Islam and Hinduism and merging them into a new
religion. Some British colonial observers such as Ernest Trumpp (1828–1885) went
so far as to define Sikhism as a synthesis of Hindu and Muslim traditions. Sikhs
almost uniformly reject the idea that Sikhism is a blend of Hinduism and Islam.
Most Sikhs see Guru Nanak as a critic of both religions, since he quite firmly criticized what he saw as flaws in the Muslim and Brahmanical Hindu traditions, saying clearly that a Sikh was neither a Muslim nor a Hindu. It is true, however, that
the Guru Granth Sahib contains ideas from Hindu, Muslim, and other predominant idioms of the times. The fact remains that the teachings of Guru Nanak were
spiritually rebellious as much as they were politically benign.

As the community of Sikhs grew and the mantle of the guru's spiritual authority was passed from one to another, questions about definitions arose. Islamic
dynasties were in power during the evolution of the Sikh community, and it was
clear by the increasing persecution they faced that Sikhs were not regarded as
Muslims. Were these Sikhs some sect of Hindus, then, who also bore the burden of
Muslim political oppression? Sikh and Hindu communities at the time had perme-
able boundaries in the region; they intermarried; they worshipped at each other's
temples; they enjoyed each other's festivities. In particular, the Sikhs of Punjab,
who ended up fighting the long line of invaders coming into the subcontinent from
the west, became colloquially known as "the sword arm of Hinduism." Many of the
eldest sons in Hindu families were reared as Sikhs, just as a family might send one
son off to military duty.

In the flurry of academic cogitations around the question "Who is a Sikh"
(McLeod 1989), one thing that scholars cannot fail to note is the increasing stri-
dency of the tone of the stories about the nine gurus who succeeded Guru Nanak.
It is common to place the kind, fatherly, gentle visage of Guru Nanak, the first
guru, next to the proud, martial and regal Guru Gobind Singh, the tenth and
last, in Sikh homes and in classrooms teaching the development of Sikhi. Clearly,
something has been transformed during the course of the teachings of the lineage
of ten gurus from approximately 1500 to 1700 CE. The Sikhs were persecuted by
either Hindu or Muslim rulers during nearly the entirety of this period. The revo-
lutionarily egalitarian message of the gurus can be seen as a threat to any ruler of
India, especially one who is dependent on a hierarchical social structure. Thus it is
understandable that the Sikh tradition would be characterized with conflict, even
violence, throughout its history.

In the mid twentieth century, the Sikhs were among the communities that were affected by the independence of India and the partition of the subcontinent that created the countries of India and Pakistan. Some of the Sikhs at the time considered the possibility of a homeland defined by religion. Just as there would be a Pakistan for the Muslims, some representatives argued that there should be a Sikhistan for the Sikhs. For various reasons that historical opportunity passed, and the Sikhs, for the most part, threw their lot in with India on promises of secularism by the Central Government and room for all religious communities in India "to breathe," as it was said. So the need to define just who was a Sikh was put off for a time, but the issue arose again during the Punjabi Suba movement of the 1960s, which led to redrawing the state boundaries of Punjab on the basis of speakers of the Punjabi language. The issue became even more salient during the Khalistan insurgency of the 1980s and 1990s.

Sikhs wielding AK-47s and using RDX explosives were responsible for large numbers of deaths in the Punjab of the 1980s and 1990s, but it was a tiny minority of all Sikhs who engaged in this action and probably a minority who supported them. Moreover, the government of India, in the form of Punjab Police and other military and paramilitary groups, was responsible for at least as many, and probably more, deaths. Sikhi (the Sikh way of life) was irrevocably linked to violence in the Indian mind, and Sikhs were then seen as unworthy victims when desperate cries for solidarity against human rights abuses went unheeded by a frightened population.

This picture is out of sync with the Sikh army officer that every Indian knew from childhood as a figure to be trusted and respected. That moment of slippage from military defense to bloody violence is critical to a historical narrative of India that recognizes the interaction of minorities with the Centre as the key to civilizational structure. For scholars of Sikhi, it is the key to understanding how militancy became defined as a posture that is now linked to violence. Citizens of India showed themselves willing to tolerate, even applaud, the abrogation of their civil rights in the name of national security as threats such as Sikh separatism reared their heads.

A conflation of militancy with violence in the Sikh tradition has led to a widespread misunderstanding of Sikhi in the modern world, has contributed to the unfortunate "Sikhs as terrorists" propaganda, and has distorted the theological message of the tradition. This conflation has indeed led to a *meconnaissance* of a people with its own historical identity, limiting to some extent the current discourse that appears possible and the range of futures that appear feasible even within the Sikh community. My twenty years of ethnographic research among *amritdhari* and other Sikhs leads me to propose that elucidating the razor-thin line between militancy and violence opens a way forward for studies of comparative religion and violence, for dialogue between Sikhs and non-Sikhs in the Indian postconflict context, and for a healing dialogue within the Sikh community that has been badly damaged by the Khalistan conflict as well.

Recall that the Sikh stance of militancy evolved through the leadership of the ten gurus who originated and led the community; violence emerged as a last resort when all other means of maintaining Sikhi had failed. It is a narrow line when viewed etically (from outside) and particularly from an accusational posture, but it is a key distinction when analyzing Sikh tradition from within (emically). We can find a useful and new angle into Sikh discourse through this little-noticed distinction. Sikhs may find a path to a more peaceful and more unified future if they come to terms with just who their gurus asked them to be, contemplating not only when the time arrives to remove the sword from its sheath but also when it may be time to put the sword once again to rest, seeking alternate means of fulfilling the duties of Sikhi.

THE SIKH IDENTITY TODAY

Although the first several gurus did not explicitly teach about violence or nonviolence, the martyrdom of the fifth guru, Arjun, was seminal. This led the sixth guru, Hargobind, to take up the classic icon of double swords, *miri* and *piri*, denoting worldly power and spiritual truth. By implication, one could only find spiritual truth when worldly sovereignty was assured. And the Sikhs did attempt to ensure the political space for their search for truth by becoming *sant-sipahis* or saint-soldiers, trained as well in the martial as in the spiritual arts.

It was Guru Gobind Singh, the tenth guru, "rider of the blue steed," who in 1699 established the Khalsa, which committed five sant-sipahis, known as the Beloved Ones, to live with their heads in their hands, or in complete service and egoless dedication. Long ago Guru Nanak had described such service as the best way to "play the game of love" that was human life. In 1699 the five were given five Articles of Faith to keep at all times: uncut hair bound into a turban, a wooden comb signifying purity, a steel or iron bangle on the right wrist, a martial loincloth used for horsemanship, and, perhaps most important, the *kirpan* or sword. All were called Singh, lion (the women were called Kaur or princess), and were to live as one family. This lifestyle since has become a goal for all Sikhs, whether or not they adopt the five articles or take on the vows of lifelong dedication.

Today, the initiation into the Khalsa through *amrit* is a visually stunning, deeply moving ceremony. The applicant, who is "of age" in terms of conscience and conscious choice, has usually prepared for months or years for the amrit. It is an irrevocable change in status that can therefore not be undertaken lightly. Men and women both often wear the five articles for some time in preparation, and study the holy book day and night. There being no intercessors in Sikhism, every individual knows the prayers, the readings, the ways to approach the Spirit. Walking the path of guru is seen as an ambition that will demand a life's work, so the amrit ceremony—overseen by the Five Beloved Ones—is held in a spirit of deep humility. The vow to give one's head, to live one's life, for one's community and one's faith is the moment of martyrdom for a believing Sikh; the battlefield death, the physical death, is but an incidental in a guru-permeated life. This is why *amritdhari* Sikhs (those who have undergone the ceremony of amrit) are said to be "fearless." It is not exactly courage in the Western sense that is praised here; it is more akin to the Buddhist notion of "living as if already dead," that is, in a state of detachment. That is the Sikh state of grace.

The actual use of the kirpan (and, derivatively, other weapons) is governed by specific rules. It is to remain on the body at all times but is to remain sheathed. One may remove it from its sheath only to protect the weak, to correct an injustice, and to defend the faith and only when all peaceful means have failed. It is not to be used offensively, not even for the sake of one's own family. The level of defense must be when the identity of Sikhi itself is in trouble; that is, when it is existentially under assault. That is why Jarnail Singh Bhindranwale, the charismatic preacher who roused the Sikhs to action in 1984, emphasized the danger that Sikhism could disappear in India unless Sikhs did something about it. He saw the decline of the faith all around him, but never issued a call for separatism. A separate state would be necessary, he said, only if the Golden Temple itself came under attack.

Bhindranwale's urging that Sikhs become sant-sipahis by way of the amrit ceremony was prompted by several grievances. A major one was article 25 of the Constitution, which for purposes of marriage law groups Sikhs and Buddhists within the Hindu category, thereby eliding Sikhs with Buddhists and, ultimately, Hindus. There were other serious grievances such as the diversion of river waters to other states, agricultural pricing detrimental to Punjab's Sikh farmers, and the lack of a separate capital city for Punjab. However, these other grievances received little air time at the Golden Temple, because Bhindranwale understood well that the "the faith in danger" was the trigger point at which amritdhari Sikhs would take action. He spent much of his time initiating thousands of young Sikhs into the Khalsa, an activity which some criticized as a waste of (political) time. But in theological terms, the strategy makes sense. When Indira Gandhi proclaimed a state of national emergency from 1975 to 1977, the base of newly initiated Sikhs was motivated to "save the faith." These were the core of the Khalistani activists. They set their revolt in terms of the precondition laid down by Guru Gobind Singh—"all peaceful means having failed." In their perception, the move from militancy (the protesters refusing to comply with Indira Gandhi's emergency and instead being jailed by the thousands) to violence (the guerilla warfare of the Khalistan movement) was fully justified.

The political implications of the *panth-granth* principle are often overlooked. When Guru Gobind Singh noted, as did the Buddha and the Prophet Mohammed before him, the tendency of human beings to idolize charismatic leaders and form a cult around them rather than continuing to devote themselves to Spirit, he took radical action in announcing that there would be no more human gurus after him. Guru had always been a vaguely defined concept, not exactly "both human and divine" but conceived more as a human being who holds within himself or herself the flame of divinity—which is passed on to the next guru, as a candle lights another candle. Guru Gobind Singh, reflecting the two-in-one approach of miri-piri, the world and the spirit together, said that the whole of the worldly power he held as guru would be passed into the Sikh *panth* or community. His spiritual power, on the other hand, would be passed into the sacred texts, the *granth*. Hereafter there would be no human leaders; there would be instead, Guru Granth Sahib, the holy book, and Guru Panth, the community of Sikhs. This doctrine became known as *granth-panth*, and is one of the clearest expressions of the "religion and politics combined" thesis in existence.

Few theologians, philosophers, or political theorists outside the tradition have commented on the radical quality of this development, the vesting of Godhead in a book open to anyone to interpret (from the beginning there had been no priesthood or intercessor class in Sikh tradition) and, correspondingly, the deeply democratic affirmation that the people, students on the path toward God, hold the ultimate authority over themselves. This reality is the Sikhi in which Sikhs understand themselves to be the primary actors. A Sikh saint-soldier is one who lives in the state of grace allowed to those who have "already died" through committing themselves heart and soul to God (becoming Khalsa by amrit initiation), and martyring himself with joy in defense of God (the book/the community). The Sikh does not look forward to a further life in heaven, far less at the right hand of God the Father. Nor does he imagine a heaven in which seventy-odd virgins await his arrival. The Sikh's martyrdom is existential: an afterthought to the well-lived life on the guru's path.

As founder of the Khalsa, Guru Gobind Singh also defined the use of force within the Sikh path. "When all peaceful means have failed," he said, "then it is justified to take to the hilt of the sword." It is on this point that the internal controversy over the twentieth-century Sikh separatist movement in Punjab centered. Were the members of the Babbar Khalsa, and the Sikhs gathered with Jarnail Singh Bhindranwale in the Golden Temple Complex in 1984, "terrorists" the Indian state had the right to rout out of there, or were they revolutionary Singhs who were standing up for Sikh rights after more than a decade of peaceful protest and sacrifice in the name of democracy? Certainly there was violence, but what kind of violence? For the years during Indira Gandhi's emergency rule, Sikhs led the civilian protests, courting arrest in the thousands. Did this fulfill Guru Gobind Singh's caveat that "all peaceful means" had to be tried first, before taking up "the hilt of the sword"? If so, the militant violence of the Khalistanis in the 1980s may be seen as religiously valid. The Anandpur Sahib Resolution of 1973 (there were later iterations), had called for a centrifugal dispersion of power from the Center to the states. This had been supported by many of India's minorities and peripheral states but was initiated by Sikhs working for the good of the community. The later "terrorist" label for Sikhs supplanted a considerable respect for the courage of the Sikhs in these early peaceful protests. (Likewise, historians agree that Sikhs contributed heavily to the Gandhian project earlier, at the front lines of peaceful protest against the British Empire; another fact easily forgotten once the accusation of terrorism took hold after 1984.) There are those, however, Sikh as well as non-Sikh, who believe that the avenues for peaceful protest had not been fully explored when, in the early 1980s, Sikh militancy became Sikh violence—pulling it thus beyond the validation offered by Guru Gobind Singh's maxim.

Guru Gobind Singh is said to have attached nuggets of silver to his arrows, so that the families of the enemies he had slain would have the money to sustain themselves. Bhindranwale, leader of the band of militants at Amritsar in 1984, also carried arrows around with him as a reminder of Guru Gobind Singh. But in discourses over the morality of killing, one notes a distinct failure of imagination to consider the victim, both historically and in the present time. One saw Khalistani fighters evaluated according to their courage, their brilliance, their clever strategies, and so on, with no room for the question of victims. The key humanitarian question was whether the victims were innocent bystanders or combatants? The way of thinking that valorizes the soldier but ignores his victims is a characteristic of warrior cultures but not of a professional soldiers in a modern war, who must uphold the humanitarian laws of war.Likewise, the granth/panth formulation of authority in Sikhism meant that it was virtually every person for him- or herself in terms of understanding what the sacred texts say about the morality of violence, and the "five beloveds" form of leadership meant that every small community on the local level had the power to take matters into its own hands (i.e., decide its own missions). Khalistani Sikhs expressed pride in these features of their religion and culture, saying they expressed basic democracy in action. In the battlefield setting, however, they meant, practically speaking, chaos. They also meant many innocent deaths.

The guerilla organizations organized themselves according to military ranks, but it would be hard to argue that these had much meaning except as honors for jobs well done. No one knew who was responsible for what, no one had the authority to establish rules over things such as the treatment of civilians and cross-border smuggling and, though they upheld the Sikh tradition of fighting and dying with stunning valor, the desire for martyrdom played at odds with the instrumental military goal of living to fight another day. Although the Sikhs had real grievances with the government of India and a generation of men and women gave themselves over to one more chapter in the rich narrative of Sikhs in revolution, in the end the movement faded away for two reasons. First, the population on which all guerilla movements depend simply grew weary of violence, death, fear, and the crime that had overwhelmed the military aspects of the moment. Second, the government of India had the power to crack down on Punjab with complete impunity, which it did not only during the Khalistan movement but even after it had bled away its existence. The core of true sant-sipahis simply had no resources left.

CONCLUSION

Sikhs in the past had been known for turning defeats into victories. But the fight for Khalistan was different, in large part because their side took all the blame for the violence that overtook Punjab while the Indian government, despite all manner of human rights reports and other attempts to publicize the atrocities Sikhs

suffered in repercussion against Khalistani insurgency, got off scot-free. The
Sikh-as-terrorist icon has spread across the whole world.

Interestingly, the theological formulation of *Guru Granth/Guru Panth* continues to be at issue today. In the first decade of the twenty-first century, there has
been an increasing tendency, often unmarked, to cite *Guru Granth* and simply not
mention the complementary *Guru Panth* at all. As the Khalistan movement wound
down in the 1990s, many Sikhs lamented that all their community needed was a
strong leader—a comment entirely contrary to the traditional Sikh notion of leadership by community. So powerful is the traditional notion of the panth that it is
depicted iconographically by the scene in which the first Five Beloved Ones, having received amrit from Guru Gobind Singh, turned around and initiated him.
On bended knee, head humbly bowed, sword on the ground by his side, the guru
sipped from the bowl of nectar proffered by one of the newly sworn Khalsa. This
early panth had the power even to initiate a guru; today, however, for some at least,
faith in the community has apparently been shattered.

In an intriguing attempt to analytically separate the elite leadership of the
Khalistan movement from the broad base of Sikhs who, in the late twentieth century, became alienated from the state of India and developed a collective forward
identity, Jasdev Rai distinguishes between the first as a modernist movement for a
territorial Sikh state, which failed, and the *lehar*, the body of ordinary Sikhs that
has resisted assimilation to any other collectivity before and after the moment in
time marking the Khalistan movement with its attendant violence. The Sikh lehar
could never fit into a secular state that demands separation of the sociopolitical
from the spiritual, because for Sikhs they are intertwined. Yet the response to the
secular territorial state of India need not be a contrarian Sikh territorial state (of
Khalistan). Rai's concept of lehar allows for a wider, postmodern range of futures
for a Sikh panth that need not defer to the territorial state model of sovereignty (see
Rai 2011).

In the twenty-first century, when it has been made clear that the path of arms
has not led Khalistani Sikhs to victory in their struggle for a sovereign Sikh state,
many Sikhs have turned to their holy book to try to figure out when the kirpan is
to be appropriately returned to its sheath, even if Guru Gobind Singh's standard
of when a turn to violence is justified had been met. Significantly, the guidance of
the book is that Sikhs are only to return to a peaceful path when victory has been
achieved. "All Victory to the Khalsa!" is a daily greeting of the initiated (amritdhari) Sikh. Unfortunately there is no advice as to when it may be appropriate to
resheathe the swords and again attempt a peaceful path to the assertion of rights
(or protection of the weak or the correction of an injustice—the other two grounds
for the use of arms). Sikhs had been always expected to win, so the "if…then…" is
not present in the text to offer guidance in the current situation. Facing a modern
nation-state with a vast military machinery, Sikh warriors of course could never
have won their war through the use of arms. Today groups of young Sikhs all over
the world are rethinking what to do next; other means of achieving justice and sustainable coexistence consistent with Sikhi. (Jasdev Rai's proposal is one of these.)

Some are reevaluating whether the bar had been met for the use of violence in 1984; perhaps there had been an overemotional rush to fight rather than a considered plan for the protection of the religion, the resolution of the economic issues, and the establishment of a capital city. Working to retain the militant, principled, and uncompromising stance that has kept Sikhi alive through the centuries and made Sikhs the embodiment of courage, integrity, and respect in all of India (prior to 1984), young men and women defining a new, global panth have high ambitions as they attempt to think through more thoroughly how Sikhi can avoid the chaos of unwarranted violence, while upholding its gloried principles

Bibliography

Asad, Talal. *Genealogies of Religion: Discipline and Reasons of Power in Christianity and Islam.* Baltimore: Johns Hopkins University Press, 1993.

Embree, Aislee T. *Utopias in Conflict: Religion and Nationalism in Modern India.* Berkeley and Los Angeles: University of California Press, 1990.

Fox, Richard G. *Lions of the Punjab: Culture in the Making.* Berkeley and Los Angeles: University of California Press, 1985.

Kapur, Rajiv. *Sikh Separatism: The Politics of Faith.* London: Allen and Unwin, 1986.

Mahmood, Cynthia Keppley. *Fighting for Faith and Nation: Dialogues with Sikh Militants.* Philadelphia: University of Pennsylvania Press, 1996.

Mahmood, Cynthia Keppley. "Why Sikhs Fight." In *Anthropological Contributions to Conflict Resolution*, edited by Alvin Wolfe and Honggang Yang, 11–30. Athens, GA: University of Georgia Press, 1994.

Mamdani, Mahmood. *When Victims Become Killers: Colonialism, Nativism, and the Genocide in Rwanda.* Princeton, NJ: Princeton University Press, 2002.

McLeod, W. H. *The Sikhs: History, Religion and Society.* New York: Oxford University Press, 1989.

Oberoi, Harjot. "Sikh Fundamentalism: Translating History into Theory." In *Fundamentalisms and the State*, edited by Martin E. Marty and R. Scott Appleby, 256–285. Chicago: University of Chicago Press, 1993.

Rai, Jasdev. "Khalistan is Dead! Long Live Khalistan! *Sikh Formations* 7.1 (May 4, 2011): 1–41.

Tully, Mark and Jacob Satish. *Amritsar: Mrs. Gandhi's Last Battle.* Calcutta: Rupa and Company, 1991.

CHAPTER 4

RELIGION AND VIOLENCE IN THE JEWISH TRADITIONS

RON E. HASSNER AND GIDEON ARAN

THIS essay presents the traditional violent themes in religious Judaism as they appear in sacred texts, rites, customs, and chronicles. It offers a survey of the components of Jewish religion relating to violence while analyzing and illustrating their development and influence throughout history.

Religious tradition is a reservoir of ideas and symbols, norms and values, information and moods handed down from generation to generation and stored in written and oral texts or objects, available for contemporary cultural, social, or political use. Tradition is not just a fixed rigid body inherited from the past, a fossil imposing itself on passive consumers of tradition. It is a vital and open-ended organism that lends itself to a wide variety of understandings and manipulations.

Jewish tradition preserved a harmony among countless interpretations, homilies, metaphors, sayings, ethical teachings, legends, and testimonies, which together constituted the material contained within the Aggadic (homiletic) and normative components of the Talmud, Midrash, Halakha, and Kabbalah. This included a fair number of categorical, embellished, and provocative statements that, in their wider contexts, were considered acceptable despite their problematic nature. All these sacred texts provided a wealth of ideas that proved crucial in the tradition's survival. They can be said to contain everything: arguments, on all their variants, including their opposites. This reservoir, limited but large, was harnessed by a wide range of ideological leanings and historical requirements. It also legitimated a vast array of interests and moral stances by providing them with a "traditional" authority. This included an abundance of materials that supported religious violence and an abundance of materials that opposed it.

Religious violence is, firstly, violence sponsored or performed by individuals or groups who self-define and are identified by those around them as religious. Secondly, these actors account for their violence in a religious language, invoking religious symbols and referencing religious norms and values.

The case of Jewish violence is especially complicated since Judaism is characterized by a close relationship and a substantial overlap between religious association and ethnonationalist ties, akin to the ethnic nationalism that characterizes Tibetan Buddhism, Tamil Hinduism, Shintoism, and Sikhism. In Christianity and Islam, religious affiliation does not necessarily involve attachment to any particular nation or ethnic group. In contrast, affiliation with the Jewish religion implies affiliation with the Jewish people and vice versa. For more than three millennia, until the late eighteenth or nineteenth century, it was difficult to differentiate between the religious and the "tribal" components of Jewish identity. In the modern era, however, this tight linkage was disentangled. With the disintegration of the traditional, basically medieval, Jewish community, new Jewish phenomena emerged, including Jewish secularism, on the one hand, and varieties of Jewish religion, on the other hand. Though one cannot be a religious Jew without belonging to the Jewish people, the vast majority of contemporary Jews are not religious, let alone Orthodox. Consequently if, before, the term *Jewish violence* was sufficient to describe our phenomenon and by definition referred to a complex of both religious and ethnonationalist violence, the recent two centuries require us to distinguish between two types of Jewish violence: secular Jewish violence, which is mainly associated with Jewish nationalism (i.e., Zionism), and religious Jewish violence, on which this chapter focuses.

Our intention in the following pages is not to depict Judaism as a violent tradition nor is it our intention to portray Judaism as a nonviolent tradition. The reality is far more complex, as it is in all religious traditions. Jewish tradition includes an abundance of material that has clearly violent implications but also a profusion of materials that support a nonviolent ethic. Jewish religious motifs are as apparent in the past and present struggle against Jewish violence as they are in justifying such violence. Most contemporary observant Jews have no violent tendencies and in today's Jewish world there are religious figures and movements dedicated to opposing violence. Many of these actors justify their peaceseeking positions by means of religious ethics and base their resistance to animosity and aggression on sacred texts.

We begin our survey by tracing the violence in Jewish tradition to its roots in biblical prescriptions and descriptions (the second and third parts, respectively). In the chapter's fourth part, we explore how postbiblical interpretation and mediation blunted the Bible's violent elements by discussing the motif of zealotry, exemplified in the Bible by the acts of Phinehas. Our survey then traces the development of the violent tradition from the four great revolts that occurred from 2 BCE to 2 CE, through the composing of the extracanonical books (the fifth part), to the compilation of the Talmud (the sixth part). In the seventh and eighth parts of this chapter, we discuss the violent implications of two religious elements that are distinct and central in the Jewish legacy: mysticism and messianism. We conclude with a critical assessment of the nonviolent tradition attributed to medieval and early modern Judaism (the ninth part).

Biblical Prescriptions for Violence

The most fundamental element in the Jewish cultural reservoir, its very axis, is the Hebrew Bible. The Bible provides a rich source of antiviolent themes, humanist ideals, and descriptions of idyllic peace and justice. At the same time, the Bible, like its counterparts in other ancient Near Eastern civilizations, is a remarkably militant text that includes an extraordinary range of aggressive themes and models, often confusing and contradictory. Violence is evident in the image of God, his treatment of humanity, the manner in which he demands to be worshiped, and the rules he sets forth for social control. Violence is also apparent in the chronicles of the Israelites, replete with war, genocide, and internecine conflict, as well as in prophecies that envision a turbulent end of times.

The violence inherent in the Hebrew image of God is particularly significant because the divine serves as a model for human emulation (*imitatio dei*). The Hebrew God is a "Lord of Hosts", vengeful and militant. He ruthlessly kills individuals, annihilates groups, and punishes humanity with plagues, brutal wars, and natural disasters. He also commands killing on a "chauvinist" basis: His chosen people are instructed to implement his fury against inferior peoples that are accursed from the moment of their inception, like the Ishmaelites, Moabites, Ammonites, and Edomites.

The implications of God's wrath are both direct and indirect: God is wrathful, and he commands others to do violence on his behalf. Since he is a model of emulation, his exemplar permits or even requires mimetic violence, as exemplified by Phinehas. At the same time, violence committed in the name of God and in emulation of God can absolve the perpetrator of agency and responsibility.

Violent divine discrimination is twofold: God is intolerant toward lesser peoples but reserves his most extreme expressions of fury for the people he holds to the highest standard. His entire relationship with Israel, even in its ideal form, is based on the ritualization of violence: It begins with Abraham's "Covenant between the Parts" (*brit bein habetarim*), which involves a dismembering of animals, continues with the covenant of circumcision (*brit milah*), and ends with the cultic butchering, eating, and burning of animals in the Jerusalem Temple (*korban*). God requires constant sacrifice. Sacrificial offerings, ranging from sheep, bulls, and doves to wine, grains, and incense, were offered at regular festivals, as thanksgiving, after birth or disease, as atonement for sin, in fulfillment of vows, or as a voluntary deed.

The ritual slaughter industry in Jerusalem was vast, requiring colossal administrative, architectural, and economic machinery. But it also undergirded a prohibition on human sacrifice, the likes of which had occurred in the valleys around Jerusalem. Prebiblical memories of child sacrifice to Moloch survive in the ominous tales of the sacrifice of Isaac and the story of Jephthah's daughter.

In prohibiting human sacrifice, homicide, and even the consumption of blood, the Bible places limits on violence. At the same time, the divinely ordained procedures designed to prevent crime, including violent crime, involve violence as a form of social control. The Bible commands capital punishment as a reprisal for violent acts such as murder, negligent homicide, brutality against parents, rape, and kidnapping. But it also requires capital punishment for sexual crimes (ranging from incest and bestiality to adultery) and for a long list of religious offenses (worshiping false gods, desecration of the Temple, blasphemy, desecration of the Sabbath, and witchcraft). The response to minor violent crimes is violent as well, in accordance with the *lex talionis* principle of "an eye for an eye."

BIBLICAL DESCRIPTIONS OF VIOLENCE

Beyond prescriptions for violence, the Bible abounds in descriptions of violence. Key historical moments in the chronicles of the Israel stand out in their carnage. The Exodus begins with Egyptian genocide against the Israelites, features the retaliatory killing of a violent Egyptian by Moses as its turning point, culminates in the ten plagues (including genocide against the Egyptians), and ends in the drowning of Pharaoh's army in the Red Sea to the rejoicing of the Children of Israel. There follows the conquest of Canaan by Joshua, including the destruction of Jericho and Ai, the enslavement of the Gibeonites, the defeat of the Amorites, and the destruction of Hazor, all aided by divine intervention. Once settled in the land, the Israelites follow judges and kings in a sustained campaign against neighboring ethnic groups, including the Aramites, Moabites, Midianites, Amalekites, Ammonites, and, their most threatening rivals, the Philistines. These conquests are accompanied by a sustained struggle against idolatry, exemplified in the Prophet Elijah's massacre of four hundred priests of Ba'al. The period of peace and flourishing under King Solomon is brief: Civil wars, conquest by regional empires, and exile follow. Even in exile, the Jews suffer but also sanction violence, as described in the book of Esther.

The brutal wars that assume a central role in the Bible are regulated by laws of war that prohibit particular tactics but also compel ruthless killing. Deuteronomy 20, for example, prohibits surprise attacks and requires sparing women and children in wars outside Canaan. But it suspends these constraints in wars against the six peoples of Canaan (the Hittites, Amorites, Canaanites, Perizzites, Hivites, and Jebusites), in which none may be spared. Wars against these groups were regulated by the laws of the ban (*herem*), in which all the spoils of war were dedicated to God. Refusal to abide by these strictures, as in the case of Achan, prompt swift retaliation. Famously, King Saul loses his crown and his sanity for his refusal to execute the Amalekite king, a task that the Prophet Samuel promptly completes on his behalf.

The war against the six peoples of Canaan bore distinctly religious characteristics. The confederacy of tribes made a sacred commitment to participate in it. Combatants, their weapons, and their camp were consecrated. This purity was prompted by virtue of God's presence in the midst of the camp and by a perception of the enemy as unclean and contaminating. In battle, the Israelites were accompanied by the arc of the covenant, priests equipped with trumpets, and temple vessels. The victims and loot were "consecrated to destruction," gifts to God akin to sacrifices in gratitude for victory. While composed in the context of an existential struggle and confined to a particular time and space, the virulent hostility towards neighboring groups depicted in the scriptures beckoned the reader to relive and reimplement ruthless enmity in every passing generation, as epitomized in the commandment to "remember what Amalek did to you."

Even the rare moments of peace in the Bible's historical account are interwoven with brutality. The origins of man, depicted in the early chapters of Genesis, involve betrayal, expulsion, pain, multiple homicides, and the annihilation of all living things by means of flood. The Hebrew patriarchs engage in theft, deceit, abduction, and physical combat; conduct war; commit incest; and attempt fratricide and infanticide. The latter is of particular significance, because Abraham's willingness to sacrifice his son by divine edict, the *akedah*, supplies a model for Jewish martyrdom in later ages.

In the Bible, civil conflict also pits Israelites against one another as rival kings, clans, tribes, cities, and the two kingdoms, Judea and Israel, struggle for supremacy. For example, in Judges 19–21, a Levite avenges the rape and murder of his concubine by his Benjaminite hosts by hacking the concubine's corpse into twelve pieces and sending the sections throughout the territory of Israel. This macabre call to arms prompts a civil war in which the other tribes nearly exterminate the tribe of Benjamin.

The Bible, thus, offers an infinite yet paradoxical repertoire from which true believers can draw precedents, inspiration, and virtual blueprints for violent activity. The herem offers a script for violence but tempers the laws of war. The active role played by God in war suggests the feebleness and even innocence of the combatant, but the Bible's historical account emphasizes his pervasiveness and brutality. At times, the Bible glorifies war as a chivalrous game in which warriors prove their cunning and courage. At other times, it prophecies an end to war. These prophetic scenarios for the end of times can be equally shocking. Isaiah, Micah, Zechariah, and Jeremiah may envision a distant future devoid of arms, poverty, and aggression. But, on closer reading, these prophecies of global peace result from the death, devastation, or enslavement of the enemy. Apocalyptic visions are suffused with bloodshed, torture, and the annihilation of entire populations. Only the winners enjoy relief from fighting.

Even innocuous passages from the prophecies have received interpretations that are charged with intolerant implications. For example, Ezekiel 34:31 states: "And ye my flock, the flock of my pasture, are men [*adam*]." The Talmud interprets this quote to signify that "You [Israel] are called Man and gentiles are not called Man" (Talmud, Baba Me'zia 114b). A statement in the Mishnah that expresses unconditional love toward all humans received similar treatment. "Beloved is man, for he was created in God's image" (Avot 3:17) was interpreted by several leading rabbis as referring to Jews only. In his commentary on this passage of the Mishnah, the sixteenth-century rabbi Judah Loew of Prague argued: "Though it says 'Beloved is man' this does not include all of mankind, because the sages said 'You are called man and gentiles are not called man.'"

COPING WITH THE VIOLENT IMPLICATIONS OF THE BIBLE

Judaism has distanced itself from the Bible by placing interpretation (the Oral Torah) as an intermediate between itself and the Bible (the Written Torah). With the passage of time, this interpretation assumed primacy. The Talmud, intended as an exegesis of the Bible, became its substitute. The essence of Judaism became the interpretation and application of the Bible to historical realities. This involved a neutralization of the Bible and a defusing of any embarrassing and complicating segments that encumbered this adaptation to changing circumstances. Thus, Judaism is at one and the same time a religion in which the Bible is crucial and a different religion that developed after the Bible was sealed, canonized, yet rendered less relevant with the destruction of the Temple in Jerusalem and the Jewish exile from the holy land. In the absence of a kingdom, a territory, or priesthood, the wars of the Bible, its sacrifices, and other violent elements lost their validity as a model for emulation.

Interpretation and mediation have blunted the Bible's violent elements. Biblical violence experienced the same process of castration as biblical eroticism did: Both underwent symbolization, spiritualization, and ritualization. The foundation of postbiblical religion, which forms the core of Jewish tradition, is a product of the systematic effort to "deviolence" the ancient Israelite inheritance. The rabbinical treatment of zealotry in the Bible is instructive of this process.

Numbers 25 narrates the paradigmatic case of zealotry. While the Israelites were camping in the desert of Moab before crossing the Jordan River on the way to Canaan, they whored with Midianite women, and worshiped a pagan deity. This double sin angered God who ordered Moses to hang the wayward Israelites, but Moses did not dare to confront the people. At that point, a prominent Israeli aristocrat challenged the divine power, transgressing both the sacred law and the authoritative leadership by committing an outrageously wicked act of blasphemy:

He had sex with a local princess while worshiping the local gods. The act took place in public, near the Tabernacle. In reaction, God punished his people with a plague that caused the death of thousands. However, Moses and the judges did nothing to stop the scandalous situation. In contrast to the impotence of established authority, a man named Phinehas took the initiative and slew the mixed couple. His impulsive brutal action, committed out of true belief, appeased God, thus stopping the plague.

Phinehas's zealotry was rewarded highly. He was granted God's covenant of peace and the high priesthood was guaranteed for him and for his descendants. According to this biblical precedent, zealotry is defined as religious violence aimed against those who are perceived as opposing the divine will, particularly by violating the boundaries of the collectivity and thus threatening its identity. From this formative religious moment on, zealotry in general, and Phinehas's zealotry, in particular, were sanctified. For more than two thousand years, Phinehas and his zealous act have been a quintessential ideal of monotheistic religious virtuosity. His epic deed became a morally, if not legally, binding precedent among Jewish and Christian devotees.

Yet the text can be read in many different ways, as the Judeo-Christian record has shown. It can be read literally as an incontrovertible precedent calling for brutal action. It can also be interpreted critically, a move that necessitates a great deal of creative sophisticated religious rationalization. Between these exegetical alternatives lies a vast array of resourceful maneuvering.

Phinehas had embarked on his deadly mission without any official license, ignoring all legal procedures. Yet he was not sentenced even after the fact. Zealotry amounted to undermining authority, law and order, thus threatening anarchy. It threatened to harm the very religiopolitical culture whose banner it bore. The traditional Jewish handling of the Phinehasic issue, developed through hundreds of years of exilic rabbinic life, is a qualified and reluctant attempt to diffuse the sting of zealotry.

Over the course of generations, the Jewish zealotry tradition has become mostly subterranean or marginal, while the antizealot tradition became the dominant traditional culture. The religiopolitical leadership sought to avoid presenting zealotry as a guiding ideal lest it endanger the status of traditional authority, threaten the internal integration of the collectivity, and endanger its ability to cope with its external environment.

These mixed feelings are reflected in the Palestinian Talmud, which argues that Phinehas and his zealot act are contrary to the rabbinic spirit (Jerusalem Talmud, Sanhedrin 27:2). The Mishnah rules that a person who "copulates with a Syrian (Gentile) woman…zealots are permitted to hit [i.e., kill] him" (Babylonian Talmud, Sanhedrin, 81b). At the same time, the traditional convention is to effectively annul this rabbinical decision by introducing this passage into the peculiar category of "this is religious law but the rabbis do not so instruct" (halakha ve'ein morin ken). The ruling regarding zealotry is one of those rare cases referred to in the Oral Torah in which there is a general consensus about the legitimacy of a certain behavior in principle, but it is modified by the fear that license for such behavior would be expanded beyond acceptable bounds.

The sages demanded that zealotry should be enacted in a public place, witnessed by many. A zealous act witnessed by less than ten people was regarded a punishable crime. The sages also placed time constraints on the act. Zealotry is a matter of a clear-cut specific moment. The sages declared religious violence that is initiated a few seconds too early or terminated a few seconds too late to be illegitimate. Thus the distance between the most elevated zealous act and sheer murderous criminality is miniscule but, nevertheless, critical. The Talmud contends that a zealot who approaches religious authorities to ask for their advice and sanction should not be granted such a license: "The one who comes to consult, they do not approve" (ha'ba lehimalech, eyn morin lo). Zealotry has to be an individualist and spontaneous act. A person who commits religious violence can be defined as a zealot only in retrospect, never beforehand. The Talmud also sets a terminal time limit on the act: Had Phinehas killed the couple after their bodies had parted, the act of killing would have been considered illegal and liable for punishment. Furthermore, had the would-be victim reacted quickly enough to kill Phinehas, he would have been found innocent. Seconds suffice to turn an exemplary deed into a despicable act.

Between the Torah and the Halakha, on the one hand, and the implementation of the precepts derived from them, on the other hand, thick strata of rabbinical interpretation qualify and refine the law based on changing historical circumstances. The interpretation, rationalization, adaptation, and application of Phinehas's zealotry are representative of the rabbis' sustained effort to disarm violent motifs in the Bible. This marks the transformation of the ancient Israelite cult to what became known as rabbinical Judaism, represented in modern times mainly by Jewish orthodoxy. This old-new religion, basically an exegetical enterprise, became the crux of Judaism's distinct religious tradition.

It is contained in a corpus that can be divided into four parts. The first, and least important, is the extracanonical books. The second consists of the writings of the sages, starting with the Mishna and continuing with the Halachik and Aggadic elements in the Talmud, composed between the second and the sixth centuries CE. The third consists of the medieval heritage that includes explanatory reading of the Torah (e.g., Rashi), Halachik rulings (such as responsa and treaties, including those by Saadia Gaon, Maimonides, and Joseph Karo), theology and philosophy (e.g., Nachmanides, Yehuda Halevi, and Judah Loew of Prague), and mystical writings (particularly the Zoharic and Lurianic Kabbalah). The fourth component consists of rabbinical writings in recent centuries and in modern times, mostly Halakha (notably Chafetz Haim, Chazon Ish, and Ovadia Yosef) and Machshava. The latter combines simplified versions of theology and politics, moral-didactic teaching (musar), and mysticism (prominently, work by Abraham Isaac Kook and his son Zvi Yehuda Kook).

A Legacy of Rebellion and Destruction

In the period between second century BCE to the second century CE, the Jewish community in the Land of Israel experienced four great revolts: the Hasmonean Revolt against the Seleucid Empire (167–160 BCE), the Great Revolt (66 CE–73 CE), the Revolt of the Diasporas (also known as the Kitos War, 115–117 CE), and the Bar Kokhva Revolt (132–136 CE) against the Roman Empire.

These four revolts shared three characteristics. First, all exhibited a clear nationalist component in addition to their religious facet. All occurred against the background of a Jewish striving for overthrowing foreign occupation and establishing political sovereignty and religious autonomy. Second, each revolt was suffused with a messianic spirit. Third, in all revolts, violence was directed not only against a foreign occupier, as part of a liberation struggle, but was also inwardly directed, aimed at political and religious deviants or collaborators who were not sufficiently radical. During the Hasmonean Revolt, much of the bloodshed was directed at Hellenisers, seen as undermining both the ritual and the ethnic purity of Judaism. During the Great Revolt, the Sicarii assassinated many who rejected their suicidal stance of combat without restraint against all odds.

Due to the excessive violence of these rebellions, particularly the inwardly directed violence, and because they ended in military, political, and religious catastrophes (primarily the destruction of the Temple and exile), they are remembered as traumatic events in Jewish historiography. After all, the violence resulting from repression of these revolts exceeded by far the violence initiated by Jews. Of the Bar Kokhva rebellion, for example, the Jerusalem Talmud notes that the Romans "went on killing until their horses were submerged in blood to their nostrils" (Ta'anit 4:5). As a result, traditional Judaism has a deeply ambivalent attitude toward each of these episodes, which tend to be condemned or repressed and forgotten. The Masada episode, at the culmination of the Great Revolt, was absent from Jewish chronicles until it was rediscovered by Zionists. Bar Kokhva was initially perceived not only as a national savior but as a veritable messiah (hence his name, son of the star). But after the failure of his revolt, the sages described him as "Bar Koziba" (meaning both "son of a lie" and "son of disappointment," i.e., a false messiah), until his image was rehabilitated by Zionists.

The period of the revolts was a period in which Jewish violence was conspicuous and consequential. At the same time, this period was distinguished not merely by its disastrous violence but by virtue of being the only such episode in Jewish history. No less significant than its occurrence was the systematic effort by the guardians of Jewish traditions to relegate this interlude to oblivion or to regard it with loathing, from the period of the sages until the modern era.

This period, in which the last books of the Bible were written, the centuries before the Common Era, was a tumultuous period of changing governments, wars, civil wars, rebellions, the destruction of the Temple, and exile. All were momentous events in ancient Israel, upheavals of geopolitical, national, and religious dimensions. It seems that different varieties of Judaism existed side by side in this period in the Land of Israel and its surroundings. One of these Judaisms was the Pharisee movement that ultimately prevailed to imprint itself on Jewish tradition, which in retrospect was considered the most authentic and legitimate and which found its expression in the writings of the sages. Another movement was to eventually become Christianity. In the range between the two, a variety of movements provided textual innovations in response to the decline of the Jerusalem-centered priestly cult.

Several of these more-or-less Jewish books were excluded from the scriptures due to theological resistance or because they were completed after the sacred writings were sealed. Some of these texts have been lost, some survived only in Greek translation, and some were only recently discovered. For these reasons, this literature has had a negligible influence on later Jewish worldviews and on Jewish behavior, but the apocrypha and other documents from this period can testify to the moods prevailing in this revolutionary period. The status of these documents, in particular their representativeness and influence, continues to be hotly debated. The Dead Sea Scrolls, discovered in the 1940s and 1950s, offer a dramatic example. The texts are replete with violence, concentrated particularly in the scroll about the "War of the Sons of Light against the Sons of Darkness." This scroll offers a detailed Manichean account of a brutal confrontation in the future between Israel and a coalition of nations that will result in redemption.

The expressions of violence in texts from the Second Commonwealth period take one of two literary forms: apocalyptic visions and mythohistorical accounts. The prophecies, such as the books of Enoch, Ezra, and Baruch, are reminiscent of the catastrophic visions of the biblical prophets, such as the book of Daniel and the New Testament prophets, such as the book of Revelation. Among the mythohistorical accounts, Jewish tradition respects but has not canonized the books of Maccabees, which describe the Jewish rebellion against Seleucid rule in Judea. These two books are our most important source about this period. First Maccabees, a Hebrew text addressed to local Judeans, is sympathetic to the rebellion's leaders, the Hasmonean priestly family, who strain for ritual purity and national militancy, emphasizing heroic zealotry. Second Maccabees, written in Greek and addressed to Jews in the Diaspora, tends to be more critical of the revolt. It argues that it was not an inevitable clash between two cultures but unnecessary bloodshed caused by corrupt and alien parties.

These texts have also offered behavioral models for later Jews, in particular Zionists. This includes the most gruesome incident of Jewish martyrdom: the legendary tale of the woman and her seven children who are willing to undergo horrific torment and, ultimately, painful death rather than agree to consume pork. The narrator comments: "Most admirable and worthy of everlasting remembrance was the mother, who saw her seven sons perish in a single day, yet bore it courageously because of her hope in the Lord" (2 Maccabees 7:24). Sure enough, generations of schoolchildren in Israel have been taught to revere this woman as a symbol of Jewish courage and dignity.

THE ORAL TORAH AND RABBINIC RULING

Present day orthodoxy is a Judaism that is centered on the Halakha. It inherited, fostered, and developed the normative ritual code from traditional Judaism, which now regulates its way of life. The Halakha dictates how a Jew is to behave in any situation. Orthodox doctrine considers the source of these laws to be divine and regards the laws as having been transmitted to the Jewish people in a revelatory act at Mount Sinai. The laws were initially recorded in the Written Torah (i.e., the Hebrew Bible, particularly the Pentateuch). The Oral Torah is a sequel and interpretation of the Written Torah. Officially, the Oral Torah is slightly inferior to the Written Torah in holiness and authoritativeness but in practice it replaces and supersedes the Written Torah.

The writings of the sages and the Halakha combine elements from different sources with different agendas, expressing various schools, periods, and places. Nonetheless, future generations, including contemporary Orthodox Jews, conceived of these as made of one cloth. Moreover, they are organically bound with the great pillars of the medieval and early modern Halakhic literature.

The number of rabbinical rulings has grown exponentially over time. Generations of rulings, rendered generally as answers (*responsa*) to questions from community members analyzed the commandments and adapted them to the changing situations with which Jews had to contend. In this manner, the rabbis compiled a rich corpus covering almost every conceivable topic. Thousands of compendiums have since collected, reworked, and updated these rulings.

The oral law, in general, and the Halakha, in particular, are not merely an exegesis of past writings but also a foundation for future writings, an infrastructure for a new Judaism that would have to survive unknown circumstances. The Bible, composed in ancient times, had to be adapted for a people without a temple, a homeland, territorial concentration, a shared language, independence, or politics. The oral law can be seen as Judaism's adjustment project to thousands of years of life in exile. To so adjust, the Oral Law and the Halakha had to suppress nationalism and repress messianism. This also involved a sublimation of the Bible in an effort to supervise and qualify the violence of Judaism, until it could no longer be expressed. This denationalizing and demessianism required the severing of the Gordian knot between religion and territory and religion and politics. Thus, the sages emphasized the sanctity of the Land of Israel and its ritual significance over its historical significance and its function as a sovereign base. In the first four or five centuries of the Common Era, the counterviolent trend may well have been one current among others, perhaps not even the primary current. Only later on, given the exilic reality, did this current prove to be the most adaptive. It alone prevailed and became identified with Jewish tradition.

The sages used several strategies in order to curb the violent elements of Judaism, particularly those hidden in the religion's national and messianic aspect. First, Jewish tradition underwent a fundamental theological transformation: It transferred the focus of responsibility to the heavens and placed sovereignty exclusively in the hands of God. The Jewish collective and the individual were absolved of the need to take an active role in history. Second, Jewish fate was reinterpreted: The failure of rebellions and exile were presented as a divine punishment for transgressing religious law, "because of our sins" (*mipney chata'enu*) as evident in the *musaf* prayer that Jews continue to recite on holy days. This allowed the believer to come to terms with his circumstances and to turn his efforts to contemplation and ritual and away from politics. Since persecution was divinely ordained, failure to submit to God's instruments (the Assyrians, Babylonians, Greeks, or Romans) merely invited further suffering and delayed redemption. The focus of conflict shifted away from military clashes between Jews and their enemies and to the tension between Israel and God. Here, Israel's power lay in the opposite of self-determination: in negating power, subjecting itself to God, and repenting.

Changes in religious conceptions were accompanied by changes in Jewish identity that had implications for violence. A clear example was the revolution in the masculine image in Judaism. The biblical hero, who worked the land, administered the state, and participated in combat was gradually replaced with the man of books and the man of faith. The great virile conquerors underwent near effeminization: Joshua became a Torah scholar, and David became the head of a yeshiva. From now on, their distinction was wisdom and piety. An exemplary expression of this revolution can be found in the tale of an emperor who asked a rabbi: "Who is a hero?" According to the Mishnah, the rabbi replied: "He who conquers his lust" (Avot 4:1).

A parallel twist occurred in stories about the Bible and the Second Commonwealth. The emphasis shifted from physical to spiritual force and from the political to the miraculous. The Passover *Hagadah* retold the Exodus as deliverance by divine hand in which Jews were passive participants and Moses, the Bible's charismatic leader, was completely absent. Similarly, the Chanukah epic ceased to be about a war in which the weak cunningly and courageously overcame Seleucid troops equipped with elephants, as reported in First and Second Maccabees. The Talmud transformed this military account into a story about the miracle of the small pot of oil. Here, as in the rabbinical treatment of Bar Kokhva, the rabbis strove to ensure that violent legacies would not lead to risky imitation.

This new Jewish stance also led to significant Halakhic innovations, including a moderation and restraining of the laws of war. The Halakha suggested that the launching of war involved prudence and caution. It distinguished between mandatory war (*milkhemet mitzvah*), which was essentially defensive, and discretionary war (*milkhemet reshut*) that could be launched only with permission from the Sanhedrin (the parliament of seventy-one sages) and with the support of the high priest. Since both the Sanhedrin and the priesthood had been dissolved, some argued, these conditions precluded war altogether.

Other Halakhic changes related to the regulation and humanization of war. It was said that even Amalek must be offered peace conditions before attacking. Maimonides, for example, ruled that one cannot surround a city from all sides but only from three sides so that the enemy can escape. Nachmanides prohibited pillaging the enemy's livestock and property. Judah Loew of Prague ruled that one could not harm civilian bystanders.

At the same time, the sages placed limits on violent criminal penalties. Though the list of capital offenses in the Bible was long, in practice the death penalty was enacted only under the most extreme circumstances and only after particularly complex legal procedures, so much so that Rebbi Elazar ben Azaryah regarded a court that executed one criminal in seventy years as a "murderous court." Maimonides stated that that it is better to set a thousand criminals free than to punish a single innocent man.

KABBALAH AND MYTHOLOGY

Analyses of the traditional sources of Jewish violence tend to focus on the Bible and the Halakha while ascribing a significantly lesser role to the mystical or moralistic literature. Yet even these disregarded texts have shaped the ethos of Jewish believers, particularly in the modern era. Like any religious mysticism, the Kabbalah deals with the secret of the divine and the wonders of creation and of man. Mysticism seeks to create an unmediated link between the believer and his God and to arrive at a knowledge of a reality that is both sublime and internally hidden. This reality is authentic, while apparent reality is only its symbolic reflection.

The roots of Jewish mysticism lie in the Second Commonwealth era. It flourished in the Middle Ages, both in the Land of Israel and in the Diaspora, in parallel to Jewish philosophy, its rival and complement. Because of its esoteric and individualist tendency and its preoccupation with higher realms, mysticism is usually associated with the tendency to withdraw from worldly matters, with an indifference and alienation toward the surrounding environment or a striving toward harmony with the environment. Consequently, the Kabbalah has a naturally quietist and conciliatory dimension. At the same time, the Kabbalah has a facet that can lead to worldly activism and even to Jewish violence.

Jewish mysticism can be divided into two currents. The ecstatic Kabbalah focuses on meditative procedures to create a direct contact with God. This type of Kabbalah has a prophetic and an occult aspect, which can gravitate to practical Kabbalah. The second type of Kabbalah is theosophical. It develops an elaborate theological system to intimately and profoundly know God, his environment, deeds, and plans. For hundreds of years, the ecstatic Kabbalah has been linked to violent rituals that have a clear magical element. This violence is neither central nor prominent in the Kabbalah, but it is a noteworthy offshoot of this tradition. These rituals include complex cultic procedures aimed at affecting the well-being of individuals and groups, such as rituals that can cause material and physical harm, even death. The best known of these is the secret spell Lashes of Fire (*pulsa dinura*), rumored to be in use even today by Israeli political activists who wish to neutralize opponents.

More surprisingly yet are the subtle and effective implications of theosophical Kabbalah for Jewish violence. First, the Kabbalah gives rabbinical Judaism vitality by introducing a mythical component to what is otherwise an intellectual and legalistic tradition. The Kabbalah overflows with mythology, in the strict sense of the word: the epic exploits of the divine. Second, the Kabbalah offers tools for theurgy, the ability to influence God and manipulate the heavens. The Kabbalah does so by supplementing the halakhic practice with *kavana*, a concentrated awareness of the mystical implications of one's normative actions. With kavana, the believer can redeem the divine and thus redeem the world. The Kabbalah makes possible an activism pregnant with religious energies. It presents historical reality as a mirror and integral component of a larger cosmic drama in which the Jew and the people of Israel can play a vital role.

The two most influential Kabbalistic texts are the Zohar, composed in thirteenth-century Spain, and the Lurianic Kabbalah, composed in Galilee in the sixteenth-century. The Zohar allows the reader to become thoroughly acquainted with the nature of God and to fathom the secrets of the universe by means of the ten *sefirot*, emanations of the divine that create and sustain the world. Of the many interesting ideas in the Zohar, the most relevant to Jewish violence is the distinction between the exalted Jew and inferior non-Jew. The Zoharic tradition treats the Jew as unconditionally and undeniably holy whereas the gentile is of low moral standing, regardless of his behavior. The Jew draws from the divine light whereas the gentile is impure, beastly, corrupt, and sinister. This dehumanization of non-Jews makes them potential targets of Jewish violence.

The Lurianic Kabbalah can be read as confirming this discriminatory attitude toward gentiles and can be exploited to back calls for violence against non-Jews. For example, according to the Lurianic myth of *berur* ("selection"), evil achieves its reign over human existence and can struggle against the divinity and harm humans by capturing sparks (*nitzotzot*) in shells (*klipot*). Whereas divinity is the sole supplier of life energy, evil, the essence of matter, has no independent source of power. It draws its vitality from its hold on holiness, which is the substance of the sparks. The devil can only exist by joining the divine source, taking it hostage by stealth or force and drawing it out. Rescuing the sparks from the grasp of matter is the key to destroying the powers of evil. There is no repair (*tikkun*) for heaven and earth without a clear selection between the emissaries of good and evil. This esoteric account has been read as identifying the sparks with Jews and the shells with gentiles, whose force derives entirely from their hold on Jews. Destroying the gentile will release the Jew from captivity, will eliminate chaos (*tohu vabohu*), and will restore order to the world.

The Lurianic Kabbalah has an even greater impact on violence by virtue of linking mysticism with messianism. This mystical messianism is suffused with national ideas and symbols that encourage the believer to become an agent for change. For these and other reasons, this Kabbalah is particularly popular and has impacted multiple facets of Judaism, including normative Halakha, the seventeenth-century Sabbatian messianic surge (discussed ahead), and eighteenth-century Hassidism. It has many followers among religious Jews in Israel, particularly those of Middle Eastern origins.

According to Luria, at the root of all evil and chaos was a primal event, the breaking of the vessels (*shvirat kelim*), a cataclysmic cosmic rupture. Overcoming this catastrophe requires repair (*tikkun*), which means redeeming the divine and the world, in particular Israel. This process is not merely cosmic in which good and evil struggle over the future of the universe but delegates a seminal role for the individual Jew. Redemption does not occur of its own accord but requires human awakening from below (*itaruta diletata*) through the improvement of religious behavior. This unites the mystical and the messianic goals: perfecting the world (*tikkun olam*). It creates an overlap between the redemption of God and the cosmos from a state of fragmentation, the redemption of the nation from its exile, and the redemption of the individual Jew's soul. This is an activist and protonationalist approach that places responsibility on each and every Jew and on the Jewish people as a whole. The Jews' task is to usher in the Messiah by separating from the gentiles and discarding them. They do so by fulfilling the commandments of the Torah in a focused matter that leads to awareness of their deeper significance, a penetration of the heavens and their manipulation. A particular mystical-messianic power is ascribed to the commandment to conquer the land and settle in it. Thus the force-ful treatment of Palestinians has cosmic significance.

The atmosphere of mystery and awe that surrounded the Kabbalah, in addition to the explicit rabbinical ban on the study of the Kabbalah, limited its circulation. Only in certain periods did the preoccupation with the Kabbalah become relatively widespread. In these periods, it underwent concretization and simplification. This occurred in the seventeenth century, when the trauma of the expulsion from Spain created fertile ground for redemptive ideas.

Messianic Ideas and Messianic Movements

Messianism is one of Judaism's most important contributions to the Western heri-tage. This motif is not to be found in a distinct corpus of sacred books or in a particular genre of Jewish thought. Rather, it is manifested in a broad variety of sources that have infused Jewish tradition throughout the ages. Judaism conceived of messianism, developed it, and spread it. Judaism has also done its best to restrain messianism and neutralize it of its revolutionary and aggressive elements. Even the sages of the first centuries of the Common Era espoused messianism while pro-claiming it to be detrimental "to awe" (of God) "and love" (of man).

As in other religions, Judaism displays an affinity between messianism and violence. The books of Isaiah and Daniel, the apocrypha, the legends of the Talmud, the Kabbalah, and even current prophecies envision the end of days in apocalyptic terms. It is difficult to think of historical incidents of acute messianism that did not degenerate into violence. In Jewish history, the variable intervening between messianism and violence is nationalism. The rebellions of the Second Commonwealth are prime examples of outbursts of Jewish national messianism that involved violence.

As a rule, with the exception of several brief episodes, Jewish tradition has treated messianism with ambivalence. It praised the messianisms of the past and future but deplored present-tense messianism. Excessive messianism would endanger the existing order, make tradition superfluous, undermine the authority of the Halakha and the rabbis, and undercut political power. An example for this attitude is the famous Talmudic assertion that "There will be no difference between the current age and the Messianic era except for [our emancipation from] subjugation to the [gentile] kingdoms" (Berachos, 34b). Maimonides interpreted this as a bold claim to defuse the explosive revolutionary and miraculous element of messianism and turn redemption into a normal political process. At the same time, Judaism took care to maintain messianism on the back burner because it recognized that a measured and contained drive was necessary for sustaining religious vitality.

Exilic quietism was interrupted by messianic incidents that are mere historical curiosities, as in the case of Shlomo Molcho (a sixteenth-century Portuguese Marano and mystic who is recorded in Jewish historiography as a "pseudo-Messiah"). The famous exception that problematizes the linkage between messianism and violence is the seventeenth-century Sabbatean movement. This was a particularly intensive messianic outburst that lasted two years and swept much of Judaism, from the Middle East to Europe. Yet the movement provoked no violence at all. The Turkish sultan was threatened by Sabbatai Sevi's "kingdom" and arrested the messiah, but the enthusiasm that seized hundreds of thousands of Jews from all sectors of society was contained within the bounds of religion and did not cross the line into social and political unrest. It most certainly did not manifest as rebelliousness and violence. Sabbatai alone was assigned the burden of realizing redemption while his followers were expected only to focus on his personality and deeds by means of faith and rite. It is tempting to hypothesize that the presence of a figure that personifies the messianic urge releases the followers from the burden of activism.

The Sabbatean movement was echoed in several movements in the century after its decline, such as the Frankists. Their messianism became more esoteric and antinomian over time, until it lost all political and activist potential. A final element of Sabbateanism appeared in yet another great historical Jewish movement, the eastern European Hassidism of the eighteenth century. This movement was also messianic, but its messianism was curbed by displacing mundane religious energies into the soul.

The paradox of messianic quietism in the Middle Ages is even more surprising in light of several characteristics of Jewish messianism. First, both the redeeming agent and the redeemed unit are not the individual but the collective, namely the Jewish people. Second, redemption occurs not merely on the spiritual level but first and foremost on the historical level. Both characteristics distinguish Jewish messianism from its Christian counterpart and grant it a national-political quality. Even at its most fanciful, when it conjectured the redemption of God and the cosmos, Jewish messianism maintained a nucleus of Jewish territorialism and sovereignty. The fulfillment of the messianic vision, in all its variants, posited the ingathering of the exiled in the Land of Israel and the establishment of an independent state that will guarantee security, affluence, and dignity for Jews. It can be said that the Jewish conception of redemption always contained a proto-Zionist element.

In regard to the human role in God's redemptive plan, Jewish scholars tended to adopt an intermediate stance. Although redemption is up to heavenly forces, man has a role to play, be it minor. Human behavior is not a sufficient but a necessary condition. Human involvement is limited to ethical and ritual behavior at some times and necessitates historical action at other times. Religious behavior that contributes to redemption can be limited to the fulfilling of commandments and the strengthening of faith, or it can necessitate an involvement in the social and political order. The latter involvement risks being interpreted as a signal of distrust in divine providence. Consequently, activism is trivialized and minimized as an effort to "merely" hasten the pace of redemption, as a trial of determination to signal to the divine that one is deserving of redemption, or as a mechanism of selection that sets apart those willing to take action into their own hands. Yet, even though it fulfills a minor role, human participation in the dynamics of redemption is often violent.

Human intervention in the messianic process can take on a paradoxical character. When belief in messianic determinism is particularly strong and the redemption is particularly imminent, when redemption is practically behind the door, logic dictates passive waiting with full trust in the divine. Ironically, it is precisely then that the believer loses his patience and violently bursts through the door in a manner that tends to be cruel and deadly. When the messianist is active in history, his action tends to be assertive precisely because he is playing a role in a divine process, feels omnipotent, is released from ethical restraint, and can overcome all political hurdles. After all, the responsibility for his actions is not truly his. These conditions create the perfect storm for messianic violence.

In Jewish history this has occurred two times, separated by two millennia: once in the period immediately before and after the destruction of the Temple and once in the last four decades. The most resourceful and dominant Jewish revival movements in recent times are the overtly messianic movements Gush Emunim, the Lubavitch Hassidism (Chabad), and, to a lesser extent, the Breslav Hassidism. All three contributed substantially to the remessianization of religious Judaism and all involve right-wing militant ethnonationalism. Members of the first have been implicated in violent acts whereas members of the latter two movements seem to sympathize with and even admire perpetrators of Jewish violence.

Several idioms related to the messianic tradition involve catastrophic eschatology that is unavoidably violent. The pangs of the Messiah (*chevley mashiach*,
often also *ikvata demeshicha*) refer to the period that precedes the realization of
the full redemption, typically characterized by a radical deterioration in religious
and political conditions. This concept suggests that the messianic process is not
necessarily linear but involves digressions, regressions, and most importantly, a
dramatic crisis just prior to the consummation of the process. This catastrophe has
a moral-spiritual and a physical-historical aspect. The pangs of the Messiah can
take the form of heavy wars involving Israel. There are those who seek such a war
to ensure redemption in their time.

The messiah from the Davidic branch is the idyllic messiah whose appearance
signals the End of Days. He is the embodiment of harmony and peace. Some Jewish
traditions claim that his reign is preconditioned by a different messiah, "Messiah,
son of Joseph" (*mashiach ben yoseph*), a man of war, who fiercely fights for the fulfillment of redemption. According to the Talmud (Sukkah 52a–b), as interpreted in
the rabbinical apocalyptic literature, only his death in battle opens the opportunity
for the arrival of the Davidic messiah.

Redemption is a matter of timing. Its date is clouded in mystery and dread.
This tormenting uncertainty can be overcome by anxiously searching for hints
(*simanim*) in regard to the definite time and by calculating the end of days (*chi-
shuvey kitzin*). On occasion, this search can escalate into taking impatient action to
provoke the appearance of these indices. For example, those who read Jeremiah's
prophecy that "evil begins from the North" (1:14) as a precondition of messianic
timing find a degree of comfort in Israel's armed confrontations with Syria and
Lebanon.

The War of Gog and Magog (the equivalent of the Christian Armageddon) is
the ultimate military clash between Jews and the nations that hate Israel and seek
to conquer Jerusalem. After great suffering and sacrifice, the Jews will be victorious and will usher in the full redemption. Any identification of a contemporary
military confrontation with the War of Gog and Magog might encourage certain
Jews to support the war enthusiastically and take great risk in the certain knowledge that the end will involve victory and redemption. The Jewish messianic tradition describes this war as a day of judgment (*yom ha'din*) on which all accounts
will be settled. This will be a day of darkness, suffering, blood, and death but also
a day in which justice will prevail.

When messianic Jews lose their patience, they seek at all costs to change reality
in order to force it to match their vision. A different strategy to fulfill the vision is
to turn it from a future aspiration to a present reality by declaring that the current
order, as it stands, is a redeemed world. Both approaches are potentially dangerous
from the religious establishment's point of view. It is no coincidence that orthodox
authorities are deeply concerned about the realization of the dream held high by
their followers. Rabbinical authorities, from ancient times to this day, have fought
every messianic phenomenon by declaring it to be a false messianism as soon as

it manifests itself. In addition to endangering traditional religion and conventional morals, which are rendered obsolete by the messiah, there is also a danger of violence. Believers experience a dissonance between their internal reality, which acknowledges redemption, and external reality, which they experience empirically, that is abundant with the characteristics of an unredeemed world. The frustrating gap between these levels of consciousness has to be bridged without reservations, even violently if necessary.

1,800 Years of Nonviolence?

Between the suppression of the Bar Kokhva Revolt and the modern era, most Jews settled in the European and Middle Eastern diasporas as a minority that survived by virtue of Christian and Muslim tolerance. This relative peace was interrupted occasionally by violence against Jews. The survival of Jewish communities, let alone their well-being and prosperity, depended on curtailing violent initiatives. Gradually, this nonviolence transformed from an existential expediency into a religious principle.

In the Middle Ages, the effort to curb violence was accompanied by a parallel effort to neutralize messianism, gradually distance Judaism from the written Bible (the Torah) in favor of the Oral Torah (the Talmud), condemn violent episodes, and reduce the nationalist elements associated with Jewish violence, such as territory and sovereignty, to a symbolic level. For example, rituals and memories of the holy land, such as prayer eastward, came to replace immigration and settlement. Techniques for neutralizing the threat of activist messianism include spiritualization, ritualization, and co-optation.

A well-known example is that of the "three oaths." At the origin of this principle is a verse in the Song of Songs: "I adjure you, O maidens of Jerusalem, by gazelles or by hinds of the field: Do not wake or rouse love until it please!" (2:7). The Babylonian Talmud invokes this verse and relates that God made the Israelites swear to "not ascend the wall," traditionally understood as a prohibition against mass immigration to the Land of Israel. The second oath is "not rebel against the nations of the world," interpreted as a command to refrain from politics and violent activism. Many quote a version of these oaths that imposes an additional prohibition: "Do not press the end," abstain from coercing God to bring the redemption before its preordained time.

In this protracted exilic period, which provided the roots of religious Judaism as we know it today, violence was rare and a tradition of victimhood developed. But in this same period, new cannons, customs, and rituals developed that undoubtedly had a grain of violence in them. The two most prominent examples are the Passover *Haggadah* that was compiled over the course of the Middle Ages and Purim celebrations that drew on the book of Esther. The reader will be familiar with the ceremonial Seder meal in which religious Jews repeat the line from the *Haggadah* "Pour out your wrath on the nations that refuse to acknowledge you—on the peoples that do not call upon your name. For they have devoured your people Israel." Participants sing hymns of victory accomplished through cruel acts of violence against Egyptians (which are often identified with contemporary villains). They also recount with triumphalism each of the ten plagues with which the Egyptians were afflicted, including the killing of their firstborns.

The violence in Purim celebrations takes two forms. The first, not unlike Passover, revolves around a ritual reading of a biblical text, the book of Esther, which expresses superiority over gentiles, hatred, and a great deal of verbal violence. Readers rejoice at the hanging of Haman, the villain of the tale, with his ten sons at gallows intended for the hanging of Jews. The second element is a carnival atmosphere that may have led on occasion to modest physical violence against gentiles.

The prototypical medieval carnival involved not only the overturning of fortunes, which is a central principle of this holiday, but the upending of all social hierarchies and categories. This reversal found expression in the donning of costumes and in the commandment to consume alcohol until one cannot distinguish friend from foe. But this carnival atmosphere also confined aggression in time and space (such as the synagogue, on one particular day of the year). The same emancipating subversiveness that enabled measured expressions of Jewish violence during Purim also contributed to restraint during the rest of the year and thus bolstered the existing social order in which Jews were passive and subordinate.

There is a clear gap between the Halakhic, theological, and ceremonial preoccupation with violence and the ability to actualize that violence. It is precisely the certain knowledge that violence cannot be exercised that gave free reign to violent fantasies. One can speculate that the textual and ritual acting out of violence betrays impotence as an overcompensation for the inability to take violent action.

Three final comments conclude this discussion of Jewish quietism and bring to a close our survey of violence in Jewish tradition. First, there is some evidence of violence directed by Jews against other Jews in the context of social control. This violence relates primarily to rabbinical rulings designed to penalize deviants in the community by means of humiliation or excommunication. A conspicuous example is the struggle against informers, particularly in periods of Jewish persecution in Europe. The community's fear that its autonomous social and economic arrangements would be exposed to the authorities and the Christian environment led it to view informers as one of its greatest menaces. Ashkenazi communities often circumvented Jewish legal institutions when dealing with informers (categorized as *moser* in Halakhic law). On rare occasions, Sepharadic communities condemned informers to death, with the assent of Christian rulers. The most common and effective control mechanism was the herem that, in distinction from its biblical namesake, was akin to an excommunication. This banishment was proclaimed in a terrifying ceremony and was experienced as a particularly violent measure, given the precarious nature of Jewish life outside the community.

Second, the ancient Jewish tradition of "sanctifying the name of God" (*kiddush ha'shem*) reached its apex during the Middle Ages. This martyrdom tradition developed in response to extreme acts of violence directed against Jewish communities, such as the slaughters of the Crusades. As part of this tradition, Jews murdered their families or committed suicide to avoid conversion. These defiant acts contained a measure of aggressiveness toward the Christian perpetrator, perhaps even an internalizing of the perpetrators' aggressiveness. Medieval Jewish and Christian martyrdom traditions influenced each other in mutual and cunning ways. Several elements of the medieval Jewish martyrdom tradition diffused from Christian models of martyrdom and assimilated them until they appeared to be authentically Jewish. Such martyrdom was violent not merely by virtue of the aggression directed toward oneself and one's family. The martyr also snatched the prerogative of killing from his opponent, thus appropriating mastery over his own death. Finally, by undergoing a noble death that sanctified the name of God, the martyr provoked the divine to avenge his death, unleashing God's violence against his opponent.

Third, the medieval period saw the emergence of a Jewish tradition of victimhood. For long and formative periods in history, Jews were targets of violence by non-Jews, as exemplified by forced conversions and expulsions in fifteenth-century Spain, nineteenth-century pogroms in Russia, and so forth. This violence tended to be lethal and was driven by ideological-religious (mostly Christian) justifications in addition to an economic and political logic. Moreover, it was directed against Jews as a collective, affiliated with a particular ethnic and religious group. In the two millennia in which Jews were victims of anti-Semitism and its violent derivatives, an elaborate tradition of Jewish victimhood emerged.

The issue of victimhood is particularly conspicuous in the post-Holocaust era. Contemporary Jewish life takes place under the shadow of the most extreme case of anti-Jewish violence, the Shoa. Jewish collective memory and collective identity as victims of violence has two implications. On the one hand, it has led Jews to be acutely aware of issues concerning violence, leading to toleration and moderation. On the other hand, a distinct minority of Jews use their own victimhood as a license to inflict violence on others by way of compensation or revenge.

Thus, to the two parallel and complementary Jewish traditions, violence and antiviolence, one should add another Jewish tradition, that of victimhood. These three traditions can be viewed as an integral triangle, each corner of which has a dialectical relationship with the other two.

BIBLIOGRAPHY

Ben-Sasson, Haim Hillel, A. Malamat, et al., eds. *History of the Jewish People.* Cambridge, MA: Harvard University Press, 1976.

Berger, Michael S. "Taming the Beast: Rabbinic Pacification of Second-Century Jewish Nationalism." In James K. Wellman, ed. *Belief and Bloodshed: Religion and*

Violence across Time and Tradition, 47–62. Lanham, MD.: Rowman and Littlefield Publishers, 2007.

Eisen, Robert. *The Peace and Violence of Judaism: From the Bible to Modern Zionism.* Oxford, UK: Oxford University Press, 2011.

Horowitz, Elliott. *Reckless Rites: Purim and the Legacy of Jewish Violence.* Princeton, NJ: Princeton University Press, 2006.

Idel, Moshe. *Kabbalah: New Perspectives.* New Haven, CT: Yale University Press, 1988.

Inbar, Efraim. "War in Jewish Tradition." *The Jerusalem Journal of International Relations* 9 (1987): 83–99.

Niditch, Susan. *War in the Hebrew Bible: A Study in the Ethics of Violence.* Oxford, UK: Oxford University Press, 1995.

von Rad, Gerhard. *Holy War in Ancient Israel.* Grand Rapids, MI: Wm. B. Eerdmans Publishing, 1991.

Scholem, Gershom. *Major Trends in Jewish Mysticism.* New York: Schocken, 1995.

Scholem, Gershom. *The Messianic Idea in Judaism: And Other Essays on Jewish Spirituality.* New York: Schocken, 1995.

Schwartz, Regina M. *The Curse of Cain: The Violent Legacy of Monotheism.* Chicago: University of Chicago Press, 1997.

Steinsaltz, Adin. *The Essential Talmud.* New York: Basic Books, 1984.

Urbach, Efraim Elimelech. *The Sages: Their Concepts and Beliefs.* Cambridge, MA: Harvard University Press, 1979.

Yuval, Israel. *Two Nations in Your Womb: Perceptions of Jews and Christians in Late Antiquity and the Middle Ages.* Berkeley: University of California Press, 2008.

CHAPTER 5

RELIGION AND VIOLENCE IN CHRISTIAN TRADITIONS

LLOYD STEFFEN

OVER the centuries Christian people have engaged in acts of violence believing that they were, on religious grounds, justified in doing so. This is a matter of historical record, as is the fact that Christian people have also opposed violence on the same grounds. Any discussion of violence in this faith tradition must acknowledge at the outset that Christianity, with more than 2 billion adherents the world's largest religion, does not advance a single consistent perspective on the issue of violence despite the assertion of many Christians that it does—the religion is simply too large and too complex for any such claim to uniformity in belief or practice on this or any number of other issues.

Christianity continues to be today what it has been historically: not one religion but three distinct overarching faith traditions—Catholicism, Orthodoxy, and Protestantism. Each of these Christianities houses a multiplicity of discrete, sometimes ethnically distinct, smaller groupings of Christian communions, to the point that it is estimated today that what we perhaps too confidently refer to as "Christianity" breaks down into more than 34,000 denominations, rites, or distinct "sects" worldwide, many of them independent churches or church collectives not wanting to affiliate with larger ecclesiastical bodies or denominations (ReligiousTolerance.Org).

Each of the major Christianities has a history of involvement with violence. Theological differences have naturally arisen among the wild diversity of Christians who have believed their particular interpretation of the faith possesses an exclu-sive—and excluding—access to the truth of God's way with humanity. These dif-ferences have occasioned conflicts that Christian people have sometimes sought to resolve by resorting to force.

The conflicts have been many, but they have occurred in basically three arenas.

1. Christians have come into conflict with other Christians, not only one Christianity against another but sometimes within the same tradition, denomination, or even within the same local church body.
2. Christians have resorted to violence against people of other faiths. Christian anti-Jewishness is perhaps the most notable example of a nefarious and sometimes murderous bigotry directed against another religion, but a more broadly conceived anti-Semitism has historically been directed as well against Muslims and the religion of Islam.
3. The close relationship of Christian authority to political power, especially in Europe, has led to numerous situations over the centuries in which the state has called on Christian spiritual authority to sanction and legitimate uses of force against perceived enemies. This development affected Christian theological reflection on the state as well as on the state's use of coercive force as it pertains to war, punishment, and social control.

Added to these general reasons for involvement with violence is the status of Christianity as a conversion religion. People engaged in the work of spreading the Christian faith have often resorted to coercion in the effort to "Christianize" the world or, in a more inward turn, to purge the faith of perceived theological impurities. So Christianity has had a major role to play in colonialist missionary efforts that have been coercive and oppressive to indigenous peoples, and the three Christian traditions, in their own claim to exercise coercive power, have had occa-sion to direct violence against those who self-identified as Christian but who were deemed subversive to church authority. Historically, Christians have claimed the power to use force as an instrument of institutional self-governance.

The story of the Christian religion traces back to an execution, an act of polit-ical violence directed at a first-century itinerant teacher, a Palestinian Jew, and leads, according to the final book in the Christian scriptures, Revelation, to an apocalyptic vision of the end of history. Violence and destructiveness are insepa-rably linked to the Christian self-understanding, from beginning to end, and are clearly integral to the unfolding story of Christianity in the Western historical record. The involvement with violence is not a surprising development given that the religion early in its history became the official religion of the Roman Empire and thus became a player embedded in the world of power politics. That Christian people have resorted to violence to settle conflicts believing that using force is con-sistent with Christian values contrasts, however, with other, more irenic teachings in the tradition that offer a compelling, even beautiful vision of forgiveness, reconciliation, and peacemaking. The twentieth-century ecumenical movement and interfaith dialogue efforts designed to turn from religious conflicts based on differences among Christians and between Christianity and other faiths serve as an implicit acknowledgement that Christian people have in the name of their religion too often acted in ways at odds with the noblest values of the faith. Such efforts have constituted an attempt to repudiate the violence and destructiveness that have been so much a part of Christian history.

The story of the Christian involvement with violence is long and complex, but some summarizing, highlighting of major developments, and an inescapable simplifying can be useful in the effort to clarify how Christianity relates to questions about violence, coercion, and uses of force in particular issues such as war, punishment, and social control. In the overview that follows, three issues will be discussed. The major focus will be to examine the theological justifications for violence within the sources of the traditions. A brief look at the symbolic representations of violence in the history of the tradition will be followed by a consideration of some specific issues that have provoked Christian people to condone or even resort to violence while believing themselves faithful to Christian teachings and values. We turn first to theological justifications.

THEOLOGICAL JUSTIFICATIONS

Paul

Christianity began as a Jewish reform movement intended to reorient Jews to a belief that the long-expected promise of a "messiah," an "anointed one" or in Greek, *Christos*, had in fact been realized in the life and work of Jesus of Nazareth. Oppression of the Jewish people by Rome in first century Palestine lent regional fervor to the hope for a messiah, who, for many Jews, was to be a new King David sent by God to unite the people of Israel and usher in an age of justice and peace. Aggressive missionary work by early church leaders took Christian ideas beyond the originally targeted Jewish audience, and Christianity owes its status as a world religion to the vision and work of Saint Paul, who can rightly be said to be the true founder of the religion of Christianity, for it was he who took the message of Christianity to the gentile world, connecting Jewish and Greek thought in a way that offered a universal message that attracted a diverse following of people. Jewish and gentile converts formed the communities of faith that became institutionalized as "church" (Gk: *ecclesia*), and Saint Paul articulated ideas that would become the theological basis for Christian doctrine. Saint Paul endorsed a notion of basic human equality before God, freedom from Jewish legal constraints, an eschatological hope for Christ's return and a preaching pronouncement that, because of the person and work of Jesus Christ, sinful humanity had been restored to a right relationship with God.

The successful organizing activity of the early church in the Mediterranean basin did not escape the watchful eye of the Roman authorities. Tacitus and Suetonius, two first-century Roman historians, both reported that Rome viewed Christianity suspiciously, considering it an atheistic superstition out of line with the older religious traditions that helped order the state. The early Christian church did experience persecutions, especially under the emperors Nero and Domitian. According to Tacitus, Nero held Christians responsible for the great fire of Rome in 64 CE and in retaliation had Christians rounded up and summarily executed, which included hoisting them on pikes and setting them afire in his garden to illumine the walkways (Tacitus 15.4).

Although the violence directed against Christians by Rome was probably not as widespread as is sometimes portrayed, the dangers some Christians faced were real. Saint Paul was arrested and executed, and there is no doubt that despite efforts to evade persecution—Paul, a Roman citizen, appealed to Rome to defend his preaching activity—the early Christian community became a victim of state-sponsored violence due to repression by the Roman authorities, and suffering persecution at the hands of governmental authority is a major theme in the Christian scriptures. Saint Paul had been an active opponent of Christians prior to his conversion, even participating in the killing of the first church martyr, Stephen (Acts 7:58–8:1a), after which "a severe persecution began against the church in Jerusalem" (Acts 8:1b). Jesus noted the potential for violence and persecution against his followers when he offered the beatitude in the Sermon on the Mount: "Blessed are those who are persecuted for righteousness sake" (Matthew 5:10). Christians came to honor as "saints" those victims of lethal violence "martyred" at the hands of the enemies of the faith; and Christians came to understand "persecution" as important to their history and integral to their identity.

Paul's writings, the earliest we have in the Christian Scriptures, advance an ethical view in which the faithful are charged to love one another, to extend hospitality to the stranger, to bless one's persecutors, to live in harmony, and to refuse to repay evil for evil but overcome evil with good. He does not advocate any uses of coercive force in response to harms and persecution but takes the psychological view that by returning kindness to one's enemies "you will heap burning coals on their head"(Romans 12:20). Romans 13:1–7a, however, offers these comments from Saint Paul about the state and what it is owed:

> Let every person be subject to the governing authorities; for there is no authority except from God, and those authorities that exit have been instituted by God. Therefore whoever resists authority resists what God has appointed, and those who resist will incur judgment. For rulers are not a terror to good conduct but to bad...if you do wrong you should be afraid, for the authority does not bear the sword in vain! It is the servant of God to execute wrath on the wrongdoer. Therefore one must be subject, not only because of wrath but because of conscience. For the same reason you are also to pay taxes, for the authorities are God's servants.

In this passage, it appears that Paul is recognizing the right of government to use coercive force to maintain the social and political order, for he acknowledges the power of the sword, an image of lethal power, although he also is saying that Christians should recognize and accede to this power not out of fear of wrath or terror, but out of conscience—because all authority comes from God. Christians will, then, pay their taxes and meet other obligations to the state because the state wields power on authority from God who sanctions the state's activities, including the coercive power to tax and even the power of the sword itself, which would appear to fall justifiably on one who offends the state through bad conduct.

Mennonite theologian John Howard Yoder has argued against a theological view that justifies state violence on the grounds that there exists "a very strong strand of Gospel teaching which sees secular government as the province of the sovereignty of Satan" (Yoder 1972:195). Government may have a legitimate ordering function to perform, but the power of the state is restricted and akin to that of the librarian who puts the books on the shelves in an orderly way so that they might be readily found and used effectively. Government has such an ordering function, but Yoder will argue that it does not receive any blessing from God for the use of violence or coercive force. Violence and coercion are anti-Christ—activities appropriate to the province of Satan.

Romans 13, because it invokes and acknowledges the "power of the sword," undoubtedly provides Scriptural support for the perspective that the coercive powers of the state are divinely sanctioned, but what those powers are specifically is not spelled out. The reference to the power of the sword apparently endorses the view that such power is an extension of God's own. Important as this passage is in providing a justification for state-sponsored uses of coercive power, Paul's invocation of "the power of the sword" challenges and even befuddles Christian interpreters, who cannot agree on its exact meaning. Nevertheless, this passage does provide a Christian scriptural warrant to justify the use of force—thus violence—by governing institutions, which includes not only the state but also the church when it has acted as a governing authority.

Jesus

Saint Paul had almost nothing to say about the actual life of the person who became the focus of the Christian faith, Jesus of Nazareth. For one thing, he believed, as his own earliest writings make clear, that Jesus as the victorious Christ would return in Paul's own lifetime—Christianity was an eschatological faith awaiting an imminent "end time" (Gk: *eschaton*). Paul's interest, therefore, was not in past history but in the person and work of Jesus as the Christ, and his letters to the various Christian churches in the Mediterranean area established the backbone of theological interpretation concerning Christ that are still affirmed in the main by Christians the world over. In his theology of the cross, Paul presented Jesus's execution and subsequent resurrection as the salvific events and atoning means whereby

God and humanity were ultimately reconciled and even the power of death was overcome. Stories about Jesus's life and his teachings, however, are not to be found in Paul but in later writings—the Gospels. These writings were produced in and for Christian communities acting to preserve memories of Jesus as they awaited his eagerly anticipated return—that eschatological "second coming."

Jesus is well known to Christians but obscure to history. The Gospels must necessarily contain historical truth about Jesus, but the extent of it cannot be determined with confidence. Jesus was no doubt a healer, a teacher, and a person who attracted a significant and deeply loyal following. The Gospels present the church's understanding of Jesus's teaching on a variety of subjects, including the appropriate response to enemies and even to the government. With reconciliation, forgiveness, and equitable sharing among his followers hallmarks of his ethic, Jesus offered, as Paul had earlier averred, a message that emphasized love of one's enemies, returning good for evil and doing good even to one's persecutors. The Gospels portray Jesus preaching about a kingdom of God that would exclude those not willing or ready to accept it but that demanded of the faithful a life lived in and toward love of God and neighbor and opposed to violence, vengeance, retaliation, and hatred—all that is opposed to love of God and neighbor. According to the Gospels, Jesus, upon being asked his views on the question of taxes, acknowledged a role for government and the obligation to "render to Caesar what was Caesar's" (Matthew 12:17), but he offered no specific justification for uses of force or a defense of the "power of the sword" except to say that "all who take the sword will perish by the sword" (Matthew 26:52). Furthermore, he did not condemn people who served the state but was known—and criticized—for associating with tax collectors, one of whom, according to Matthew 10:3, became a disciple (Matthew), and with members of the military, once doing the kindness of healing the paralyzed servant of a Roman centurion whose faith Jesus praised (Matthew 8:13).

The Gospel's picture of a nonviolent even pacifist Jesus, however, does have some cracks in it, and it cannot be said with certainty that what breaks through is historical truth. One crack is to be found in the cryptic comment, "I did not come to bring peace but a sword" (Matthew 10:34). He offers this comment in an "instruction" that finds Jesus saying in acknowledgment of the many conflicts his followers will experience: "I have come to set a man against his father, and a daughter against her mother" (Matthew 10: 35a). Although many Christians interpret this entire passage as a metaphor for ideological conflict, Jesus is not making an impartial observation about the inevitable consequences of following him; he is claiming as his intention that setting such conflict in motion is his mission. A more significant crack appears in the story of the cleansing of the temple, where, according to the Gospels, Jesus in a fit of rage overturned the tables of merchants selling goods and animals for sacrifice and chased them out of the Jerusalem temple. The Gospel of John adds the detail that he did this having fashioned a "whip of cords" to drive out the animals and apparently the money changers as well (John 2:15). So Jesus not only showed anger but engaged in what from a moral point of view must be considered acts of violence even if Christians would interpret this event as completely justifiable righteous indignation. Jesus did not peacefully negotiate or reason with the temple merchants but resorted to a use of coercive force in this instance—the Gospels are all agreed on this point.

A central issue related to the Christian understanding of violence involves the Crucifixion. For all that Christians would do to pin the death of Jesus on the Jews, there is no doubt at all that his death was a rather ordinary dispensing of Roman justice. Although the Gospels tell a story of Jewish leaders scheming for that death because of Jesus's apparent blasphemy, Jesus does not suffer the punishment for blasphemy set down in Mosaic law—stoning. Moreover, scholars are skeptical of such details in the Gospel passion narratives as the midnight trial before the Jewish elders at the Sanhedrin, which never met at night. The historical fact evident in the passion narratives is that Jesus was accused and tried under Roman law and sentenced to a specifically Roman means of death—crucifixion—for a specific crime—sedition.

Despite the overwhelmingly pacifistic portrayal of Jesus in the Gospels, it is possible that Jesus actually posed some kind of threat to the established order of his day and that he was guilty of sedition. One challenge to the Jesus-as-pacifist portrayal surmises—it is all surmising—that because the first-century church was suffering persecution from Nero, one way to blunt any possible justification for Roman action against the Christian community was to reassure Rome that Christianity posed no threat to its authority. As part of that effort at reassurance, the church presented Jesus as an otherworldly preacher of love and forgiveness, a peacemaker. To support the point, the passion narratives in a sense exonerate the Romans from their obvious part in Jesus death, for as Jesus will say to the Roman procurator, "My Kingdom is not from this world," for if it were "my followers would be fighting to keep me from being handed over to the Jews" (John 18:36). No one fights for Jesus, evidence that his is an otherworldy kingdom and, thus, of no threat to Rome, but he here imagines a justifiable use of force. Even in the moment he faces Roman legal judgment Jesus displays no hostility to Rome—he is portrayed as one who understands that it is the Jews who are making the trouble, with Rome caught unwittingly in a political drama and forced to accede to Jewish demands for Jesus's death.

The Gospels misrepresent and excoriate Jews, especially the Pharisees, who were liberal interpreters of the Torah, and present Jewish leaders as not only plotting Jesus's death but taking responsibility for it and even welcoming any consequences. When Pontius Pilate, the Roman governor hearing Jesus's case, addresses the Jewish crowd assembled by "the chief priests and elders," they shout back at him, according to the Gospel of Matthew: "His blood be upon us and our children!" (27:25). The Gospel of Matthew was written sometime between the years 70 and 100 CE, more than thirty years after Jesus's death, so that this story, despite its inclusion in a Gospel addressed primarily to a Jewish audience, reflects the deep anti-Jewish sentiment rampant in the early Church. The Gospels are infected with anti-Jewish attitudes, and the story of a Jewish crowd calling for Jesus' blood would undoubtedly provide comfort to later Christians seeking justification for acts of violence against Jews.

The Gospels shift blame for Jesus's death from a cruel Roman justice to Jewish conspiracy, and in the first century CE the refusal of many Jews to convert to a belief in Jesus as messiah would have further fueled Christian animosity toward Jews. Attributing Jesus's death to Jewish intrigue added an additional support and justification for anti-Jewish attitudes and actions that might not have led to profound consequences except for an unforeseeable accident of history, which Christians of the time did not see as fortuitous but as God willed. Emperor Constantine converted to the faith in 312 CE and following his victory over the Eastern emperor, Licinius, he consolidated power and became sole Emperor in 324 CE, a date that traditionally marks the beginning of the "Christian Empire." What this meant for Christians was this:

> The Kingdom of God had come down to earth. Christians now accepted the sacred nature of the emperor, whom they naturally enough looked to as the head of the Christian people: a new Moses, a new David.... The clergy obtained legal privileges; the Episcopal tribunals had a civil jurisdiction, and the bishops were considered to be on an equal footing with governors. (Comby 1992: 68, 75)

In 380 CE, Emperor Theodosius proclaimed Christianity the official religion of the state.

As Christianity and the developing religion of rabbinic Judaism broke into separate religions over the first four centuries of the Common Era, conflicts between the two intensified, with each tradition undergoing transformation and taking on a new historical role. James Carroll writes:

> Christianity went from being a private, apolitical movement to being a shaper of world politics. The status of Judaism was similarly reversed, from a licit self-rule, a respected exception within a sea of paganism, to a state of highly vulnerable disenfranchisement. What might be called history's first pogrom, an organized assault on a community of Jews, because they were Jews, took place in Alexandria in 414, wiping out that city's Jewish community for a time. Even in Palestine, Jews became a besieged minority. (Carroll 2001: 176)

Theologically, the Christian community came to understand itself as having replaced the Jews as God's chosen people—the conflict is referred to in Christian theology as supersessionism. What made this self-understanding dangerous was that Christian people involved with the wielding of imperial power could take political, legal, and even military action consonant with supersessionist beliefs. Jews were a target of deep animosity and viewed, as reflected in anti-Jewish Gospel stories, as dangerous enemies of Christian faith. Accordingly, Emperor Constantine, a powerful Christian scornful of Jews, issued an edict in 315 that made it a crime for Jews to proselytize. This offense would be upgraded a century later to a capital crime. This latter action symbolizes what can happen to a religion, even one that remembers its founder as nonviolent and as the victim of unjust state violence, when it becomes enmeshed in governmental power. Jews came to be viewed as fair game for political exclusion and legal retaliation. Justification for acts of violence against these perceived enemies of the faith was found in the fact that Christians had actually come to hold the levers of imperial power, that is, Christians came to believe that they were justified in their hostility toward Jews by history itself, for unfolding in history was God's own divine plan for Christian supremacy.

Justification for Christian involvement in violence is not found so much in explicit Scriptural sources, with Saint Paul's "power of the sword" notion a possible exception, but in an interpretation of history. Christianity, like Judaism and Islam, is a historical religion, meaning that the faithful believe history is the arena of divine activity where God acts to reveal the divine will. On this belief, Christians came to understand that their rise to power was an expression of God's will, the successful advance of Christianity evidence that God was authorizing Christians to seize the power of the sword in order to use it to God's greater glory. On this understanding Christians were authorized to use coercive power to maintain the supremacy of Christian faith against all adversaries, be they from within the faith or external to it.

Christian theological justifications for violence continued to develop over the course of European history. The development of a tradition of just war thinking, the Crusades, the internal purging of dissidents, and missionary activity represent arenas in which such justifications were advanced.

Just War

The Christian approach to the problem of violence includes an important tradition of pacifism, but Christian thinkers have also addressed in a "realist" mode the possibility that force or violence might be used justifiably even to go to war. Since the fourth century, Christian moral theology has advanced a tradition of thinking about justified uses of force associated with the idea of just war.

Just war thinking harkens back to Cicero and to older natural law philosophy, so this is not explicitly a Christian doctrine. Just war thinking, however, was developed within the Roman Catholic Church by significant natural law theologians so that that it can be said that it emerged as a teaching of the church. Just war realism is today advocated by many Christians, including Roman Catholics but other Christians as well. It enjoys wide acceptance in various secular arenas and is used by governments and militaries, and it frames international law on the question of war. Just war theory, as it is understood today, advances several criteria that structure the morally relevant issues that must be examined in light of empirical particulars. These broad, nonspecific guidelines or *jus ad bellum* criteria include legitimate authority, just cause, right intention, last resort, an outcome in which the good achieved outweighs the pain and destruction of war, preservation of values that could not otherwise be preserved, reasonable hope of success, with two other criteria governing the conduct once hostilities have commenced (*jus in bello*): noncombatant immunity and a proportionality of means, also called the prohibition on inherently evil means of waging war. These criteria taken together, if satisfied, outline a justification for violence and uses of force in a "just war."

Just war thinking as a Christian-friendly philosophical tool in specifically Roman Catholic moral theology has its origins in Saint Augustine (354–430). Augustine's view was that war was a great evil because it expressed human self-ishness and the disorder that arose from "love of violence, revengeful cruelty, fierce and implacable enmity, wild resistance and the lust of power and such like" (Augustine 21). For Augustine, a justified war was not a war of self-defense but a punitive action: "It is generally to punish these things [these disorders just mentioned], when force is required to inflict the punishment, that, in obedience to God or some lawful authority, good men undertake wars" (Augustine 22). Augustine famously said that wars are waged for peace and order, that they are the result of necessity and not choice, and he advanced three ideas that are still vital to the contemporary formulation of just war criteria: legitimate authority, just cause, and right intention.

Saint Thomas Aquinas (1225–1274) moved away from the punitive notion of just war and developed what is considered the classic form of just war thinking. Aquinas adds to Augustine's "criteria" a different content to the "just cause" criterion, arguing that wars could be justly waged if they were for the purpose of righting wrongs, which would include restoring what has been unjustly taken away or punishing a nation that has failed to punish crimes committed by its own people. As Thomas wrote ("Of War"):

> In order for a war to be just, three things are necessary. First, the authority of the sovereign by whose command the war is to be waged. For it is not the business of a private individual to declare war.... Secondly, a just cause is required, namely, that those who are attacked should be attacked because they deserve it on account of some fault. [Quoting Augustine] "A just war is wont to be described as one that avenges wrongs, when a nation or state has to be punished, or to restore what it has seized unjustly." [and] Thirdly, it is necessary that the belligerents have a rightful intention, so that they intend the advancement of good, or the avoidance of evil. (Aquinas 578)

Aquinas made another significant contribution to just war thinking. In discussing the permissibility of natural self-defense in the *Summa Theologica* (II-II, qu. 64, art.7)—"Whether it is permissible to kill a man in self-defense?" was his actual question—he introduced the principle of double effect. "Nothing hinders one act from having two effects, only one of which is intended, while the other is beside the intention.... Accordingly, the act of self-defense may have two effects: one, the saving of one's life; the other, the slaying of the aggressor."(190–191) The "double effect" came into play to emphasize that individual Christians subjected to unjust aggression could justifiably repel attackers with a use of force that could prove lethal but only as long as any killing occurred as an unintended and secondary consequence (double effect) of the legitimate just war aim of repelling the unjust attack.

The intention and just cause criteria of just war have long centered on self-defense and resistance to unjust aggression, and these notions are current today in article 51 of the United Nations Charter, which acknowledges an "inherent right" of both individual and collective self-defense. Thomas held that it was natural for individuals to act to preserve their "being," but the repelling of an unjust attack must be proportional and not excessive and "it is not lawful for a man to intend killing a man in self-defense" (191). Thomas emphasized that using force with the specific objective in mind of killing an enemy is not a legitimate aspect of just war, and a criterion of proportionality developed over the centuries to indicate that a use of force must always be proportional to the end of restoring peace.

After Aquinas, the Spanish Scholastics Vitoria (d. 1546) and Suarez (d. 1617) and the Protestant Dutch theologian Hugo Grotius (d. 1645) offered further developments in the idea of just war. Often regarded as the founder of international law, Grotius, for instance, held to the view that "war is not in conflict with the law of nature," so that the rules of war were naturally binding. His treatment of war in the context of "the laws of nations" included the premise that "[b]y nature all men have a right of resistance against injury" and that this natural right could not be changed, not even by God (Grotius, 385–437). As the idea of a Christian commonwealth disintegrated during the Reformation, with the nation-state emerging along with increasingly secularized political and cultural shifts, just war thinking began to attend to the problem of limiting the destructiveness of war, a development caused by the devastation of the religious wars of the sixteenth century.

In both the Reformation and post-Reformation era, just war thinking shifted to address conduct of war or *jus in bello* concerns for means. New attention was paid to the issue of proportionality, and double effect was invoked beyond killing of combatants to include justification for the killing of noncombatants. Under just war thinking, such deaths, regrettable as they would be, could be deemed morally permissible as long as they were not intended and every effort was made to avoid them. Just war theory came to have more and more of an influence in international law and in secular thinking in general, and appeals to just war ideas play an important role in international law today, appearing often in United Nations deliberations and resolutions (Vaux 1992: 120–145).

Just war has evolved and modified over the centuries, but one constant in the background of just war thinking is the view that war is a terrible state of affairs, much to be avoided, and even if uses of force are considered legitimate, they must be restrained. Roman Catholic theologian Richard McBrien has written, "The purpose of just-war theory ... was not to rationalize violence but to limit its scope and methods" (McBrien 1981: 1036).

Today, both the secular and the religious worlds invoke just war ideas, but the action-guides do not of themselves settle any particular issue in any particular conflict. The criteria provide, rather, the structure within which uses of force can be deliberated. The criteria serve to guide the moral reflections of policymakers, the military strategists and critically minded citizens who worry about violence and its use by the state.

A widely noted and inescapable criticism of just war thinking concerns the ease with which just war ideas can be used self-servingly, even cynically, to "rationalize violence" and to justify political and military incursions that require the patina of moral justification to garner public support. Despite those dangers, however, the great value of the just war structure lies in its ability to call reasonable people of good will together to employ a common language within a rational structure designed to assist in the public deliberation over the appropriateness of considering the use of force.

Just war thinking is Christianity's clearest institutionalized, church-related justification for using coercive force. Just war ideas have been criticized for rationalizing violence and serving national self-interest while failing to serve justice and peace. Many Christians join other reasonable people in holding that just war is an oxymoron given that wars, however justified they may seem at the start, spin out of control into injustice, with the just war idea of imposing rational constraint on violence lacking the realism about war that its proponents criticize pacifists for ignoring.

Although now thoroughly secularized, just war thinking still represents the major Christian perspective on justifying uses of force to resist evil and restore peace, and in as much as it provides a structure for determining when and under what circumstances violence might be applied to resist injustice, it continues to expresses the central justification for violence in Christian moral theology.

The Crusades

The Crusades offer another justification for violence that has arisen within the Christian experience—holy war. Holy war means, in its simplest generic sense, a war undertaken because it is divinely authorized, and all the monotheistic religions of the West have had their experiences with generic holy war. *Crusade* was the name for holy war given by the church, and eight Crusades to Palestine were undertaken from the eleventh to the thirteenth centuries (1095–1291)—this age of Christendom when Christianity was both the temporal and spiritual backbone of European society.

The origins of the Crusades can be traced to two causes: Christian pilgrimage and Turkish threats to the Eastern Byzantine Empire. European Christians had often made pilgrimage to Palestine, Jerusalem especially, to experience the early life and sufferings of Jesus and as an act of penitence for sins. Muslims and the eastern empire centered in Constantinople, Byzantium, had been in constant conflict for centuries, but in 1071 Muslim Turks defeated the Byzantine forces at Manzikert, took over Asia Minor and threatened the Byzantine Empire. This created serious problems for continued pilgrimage to Muslim-controlled Jerusalem, and the threat to the eastern empire affected all of Christendom. The Byzantine emperor Alexis asked Pope Urban II for assistance, and in 1095 the Pope convened the Council of Claremont from which he issued the first call to crusade. Pope Urban saw the Crusade as a way to heal the rift between eastern and western Christendom, which had divided in the Great Schism of 1054, and it is estimated that by spring and autumn 1096, ten armies of more than 160,000 soldiers accompanied by numerous pilgrims and church officials joined in the first Crusade (Armstrong 2001: 3).

Pilgrims to the holy land had previously been forbidden to take weapons, but now they were authorized to do so. The Crusades became armed pilgrimages.

The official justification for the Crusade was religious. The Pope, Christ's vicar on Earth, was sending forth an army with a holy commission to return Jerusalem and Christ's tomb to Christian hands. One twelfth-century report of the Council of Clermont—no contemporary account of Urban's speech exists—observed that "the pope, a prudent man, summoned to war against the enemy of God all those who were capable of bearing arms and, by virtue of the authority which he holds from God, absolved from all their sins all the penitents from the moment they took up the cross of Christ," that is, resolved to go on the Crusade (Vitalis 1992: 156). In his call to crusade, Urban II described the Muslim Turks as "an accursed race, a race utterly alienated from God, a generation, forsooth, which has neither directed its heart nor entrusted its spirit to God," so that Christians were duty bound "to exterminate this vile race from out lands" (Armstrong 2001: 3). Urban endorsed taking up arms to liberate Jerusalem from the Muslims, to which his crowd of listeners responded, "*Deus hoc vult* [God wills this]" (Armstrong 2001: 67).

Pope Urban had hoped by his call to crusade to expand the territorial reach of the papal church into Byzantium and improve relations between the eastern and western empires. The Pope cast the Crusade as a spiritual journey, reminding his listeners at Clermont that Jesus had said that those who followed him should be prepared for death. Urban even quoted the words of Jesus traditionally offered to monks entering the cloister: "Everyone who has left houses, brothers, sisters, father, mother or land for the sake of my name will be repaid a hundred times over" (Matthew 19:29; Armstrong 2001: 67). There is no doubt that, for all the political purposes served by the Crusades, the justification for the call to crusade was religious. The Crusades were a call to arms authorized by God, a holy war against the enemies of Christianity—Muslims. Karen Armstrong observes that with this move "Urban had made violence central to the religious experience of the Christian layman and Western Christianity had acquired an aggression that it never entirely lost" (Armstrong 2001: 67).

Anti-Islamic sentiment would prove to be a central factor in uniting Christendom for war on Muslims. Justification for holy war goes directly to divine authority, and the Pope acted explicitly as God's representative and directly on God's behalf. The Crusades may have created for knightly European societies "a perfect way to unite their love of God with their love of war," in Karen Armstrong's words (Armstrong 2001: 150), speaking about the Franks; and there is no doubt that Christians faced a military threat. But any appeal to a defensive "just war" was overshadowed by the holy war justification, which is always difficult to counter, for if God, the ultimate arbiter of truth and justice, commands an action, it is the duty of the faithful to respond with the question of right and wrong being beyond question and settled because God has willed the action. In response to the Pope's call, significant numbers of people would for the next two centuries be involved in bloodletting, demonstrating how sacred places can give rise to destructive behaviors, a phenomenon still seen today.

Although they fostered interaction between East and West and helped to consolidate papal power and even a sense of Christian unity and solidarity, the Crusades failed to accomplish the original end of expelling Muslims from the Holy Land. They also created what would turn out to be even greater divisions between eastern and western Christians. The attempt to create unity among Christians was accomplished by identifying a common enemy—Muslims—who were vilified and demonized as a "vile race" outside God's protection. The Crusades may have failed to defeat Islam, but they did succeed in exposing a Christian supremacist attitude toward yet another Semitic group of non-Christian monotheists, who, along with the Jews, were to be viewed as enemies of God whom God wanted resisted and defeated through violence. The Crusades left a legacy of bloodshed and massacre and reinforced the view of many Christians that God willed the use of violence to settle conflicts against enemies of the faith.

Heresy and Inquisition

If the Crusades were an example of Christians using violence to respond to external threats to the faith, the church also resorted to violence to deal with internal threats. Saint Augustine had expressly forbidden execution for heretics, a view maintained until the eleventh century. Heresy was a religious offense, a denial of the articles of faith, but because society in the Middle Ages was theocratic, heresy was also a form of treason—it challenged the claim of rulers that their authority came from God and tore at bonds of societal unity. The Second Lateran Council (1139) had stipulated imprisonment and confiscation for heretics; and in 1231 Emperor Frederick II, following legal precedents, issued this legislation:

> Anyone who has been manifestly convicted of heresy by the bishop of his diocese shall at the bishops's request be seized immediately by the secular authorities of the place and delivered to the stake. If the judges think his life should be preserved, particularly to convict other heretics, they shall cut out the tongue of the one who has not hesitated to blaspheme against the Catholic faith and the name of God. (Comby 1992: 167)

In February 1231, Pope Gregory IX issued *Excommunicamus*, which set up courts to try heresy cases, pronounce judgment and dole out punishment, although the convicted were handed over to civil authority to carry out sentences (O'Brien 9). Thus Pope Gregory set in motion what would become by 1233 the Inquisition tribunals, which relied on Dominican inquisitors who received under papal power the authority to bring suit against any person even rumored to be a heretic. The purpose of the Inquisition was to suppress heresy, to return heretics to the Catholic Church and to punish those who would not recant their errors (McBrien 1998: 9). The most common punishment was burning at the stake.

Following the medieval Inquisition, other inquisitions would follow, including the Spanish Inquisition (1478–1834), which was independent of the Pope and royally administered; it addressed political issues as well as heresy and was directed at Muslims, Jews, and, later, Protestants. Various groups, including the Bogomils, Waldensians, Cathars, and Lollards (Edwards 1997: 43, 266–268) suffered persecution and execution for heresy; and these groups, along with many others, were the target of Frederick II's legislation, for heretics were believed to threaten the stability of the government. Although inquisitions are associated with Roman Catholicism, Protestants rooted out heresy by means of ecclesiastical tribunals as well. In John Calvin's theocratic Geneva, for instance, the governing council condemned Michael Servetus to the stake as a heretic in 1553. Calvin defended the action on the grounds that it is the duty of the state to establish true religion. The state, he wrote, "exists so that idolatry, sacrilege of the name of God, blasphemies against his truth and other public offenses against religion may not emerge and may not be disseminated" (Calvin 123). The severe reaction to a humanist and non-Trinitarian such as Servetus arose from fear of the consequences of letting heresy proceed unchecked. For false doctrine destroyed souls; heretics tore the church apart; and the great fear was that heretics would bring down on the faithful a divine wrath, which could take the form of war, famine, or plague.

Inquisition and heresy trials employed violence on the grounds that if a heretic was not reclaimed, others would be endangered. Thomas Aquinas had said as much when he defended execution "if the church gives up hope of his conversion and takes thought for the safety of others, by separating him from the church by sentence of excommunication, and further, leaves him to the secular court, to be exterminated from the world by death" (*Summa Theologica*, IIa, IIae, 11, art. 3). The Inquisition used torture to extract confessions, sometimes resorted to mass executions, and in the Inquisition period, between the fourteenth and seventeenth centuries, a war on witchcraft was undertaken with Protestants and Catholics in apparent competition to put witches to the stake. Luther said, "I would burn them all" (McBrien 1997:122), and a chronicler of the day noted that the Holy Office had burned 30,000 witches who, "if left unpunished, would easily have brought the whole world to destruction" (O'Brien 123). It is estimated that the number of witches killed as enemies of Christian faith numbered anywhere from hundreds of thousands to millions (McBrien 1997: 127). Although women were not the exclusive target of the witch mania, most were women—the move by the male-dominated churches to exterminate witches expressed a murderous repression of women, an assault on women that one historian has described as "a vast holocaust" (McBrien 1997: 126).

Missionary Movements

Being a religion that actively seeks converts, Christianity has had a missionary history since the time of Saint Paul. Christianity spread through the Mediterranean basin and had become the official religion of the Roman Empire by the time of the empire's fall in 476. Missionaries took Roman Catholicism to the kingdom of the Franks and into Germany as early as the fourth century; Saint Patrick helped establish monasteries in Ireland; and by the seventh century monasteries were to be found in England and Scotland with missionaries spreading out over the European continent.

As Europe extended itself into the world, Christian mission work was deemed an extension of colonial power. Christian missionaries undertook evangelizing activity in the Americas, in Asia (India, China, and Japan), Africa—all over the world. Missionaries from Spain, France, and Portugal were sometimes persecuted in various settings due to resistance from indigenous people. Japan, for instance, outlawed Christianity in 1614 with a subsequent massacre of 35,000 Christians in 1636, after which missionaries were prohibited in the country. But in their service to Empire and imperial ambitions, missionaries contributed to the colonial efforts that brought warfare deaths and such European-based diseases as measles and smallpox to indigenous people, at times decimating the populations subjected against their will to colonial rule. When the Spanish and Portuguese invaded Latin America in the sixteenthth century, estimates are that native populations decreased from 70 million to about 3.5 million due to massacre, European-based diseases, overwork in mines, and enslavement (Edwards 1997: 512–513). Spaniards enslaved Indians, and replacing Indians killed by war and disease opened up a slave trade in the Christian West. The demand for labor after the discovery of the Americas gave rise to trade in Africans, with an estimated 20 million blacks being transported from Africa to the Americas, one of the justifications for it being that it allowed the African blacks to come into contact with the Christian faith. Some missionaries actually had slaves and participated in the slave trade (Comby and McCullough 1992: 69).

Serious students of missionary activity may argue, as Lamin Sanneh has, that assessing this evangelizing and conversion work is difficult, because "missions in the modern era has been far more, and far less, than the argument about motives customarily portrays" (Sanneh 1989: 331), but there can be no doubt that Christian missionary activity colluded with colonialism and participated in some heinous activities, including enslavement, warfare, murder, rape, and economic exploitation. Christian missionaries have performed positive, life-affirming, and self-sacrificing chores on behalf of the Christian faith and the church, including founding schools and building hospitals, providing health care, and working to support the development of indigenous peoples in many ways. But in assessing the relationship of Christianity to violence, missionary work must be included as having played a role in subjecting non-Christian people to violence and at times atrocity, and even today accusations are made that Christian missionary activity continues to pursue its goals through violence ("Conversion Tactics").

Concluding Statement

In discussing the problem of Christianity's relationship to violence, it is worth noting that Christian people have, in the name of their faith, also acted in ways opposed to violence. The Reformation spawned what are known today as the historic peace churches. The Protestant churches that hold pacifistic positions include the Quakers, the Mennonites, and the Church of the Brethren. Christian involvement in the ecumenical movements and inter-religious dialogue efforts begun in the twentieth century and that continue today constitute implicit recognition of the violence Christians have engaged in over the centuries with those both inside and outside the faith. These efforts at dialogue and understanding across the barriers of tradition and belief represent a repudiation of the legacy of violence that has characterized Christian history. The easy association of Christianity with a willingness to resort to violence has of course been offensive to many Christians over the centuries who have stood opposed to violence, war, and social injustice. Martin Luther King, Jr. repudiated violence as a means for achieving social and racial justice, locating his source of justification for active but nonviolent resistance to evil in the teachings of Jesus (and Gandhi). The Christian Peace movement of the 1970s and 1980s, a time when Protestants and Catholics were engaged in mutual terrorist actions against each other in Northern Ireland, put forward a Christian opposition to war and the means of war, nuclear weapons especially. The important work undertaken by Christians as citizens informed by their faith or working through their faith communities in support of environmental integrity, economic justice, women's rights, and inclusion of gays and lesbians and transgendered people in the life of the church express contemporary efforts to oppose violence—the violence of environmental degradation, structural injustice, and attitudes of discrimination. Christians have justified violence over the centuries by appealing to scripture and by developing theological interpretations that sanction violence in the belief that it is in accord with God's will, but many are today working with a new consciousness of this history and a new resolve to create dialogue in religious affairs and to connect faith to action in ways that repudiate reliance on uses of force.

SYMBOLIC REPRESENTATIONS OF VIOLENCE IN THE CHRISTIAN TRADITION

Symbols, rites, and rituals permeate all aspects of Christian belief and practice, and violence is disclosed in various symbolic representations. Christian symbols, being multifaceted, can suggest meanings in the context of religious faith at odds with obvious historical or empirical connections to violence, suppressing moral meaning while effecting a transformation to transcendent meaning. Consider Christianity's most important symbol, the cross.

Every Christian knows that the cross was a brutal mode of Roman execution and that Jesus of Nazareth suffered a tortuous death on the cross, having been scourged and then crowned with thorns by Roman soldiers. For Rome, the cross symbolized imperial power and effective criminal justice. Crucifixion was a mode of execution designed to maximize pain and suffering so that its terror and brutality would serve the utilitarian purpose of deterring any who might want to foment resistance or rebellion against the state.

For Christians, the cross could certainly symbolize state power in service to injustice, for Christians believe in the main that Jesus was an innocent man who had done nothing to deserve such a death. It might be expected that Christians would hold the cross in contempt as a symbol of the worst injustice human beings can deliver to one another—using the enormous power of the state to crush and cruelly kill an innocent. Some Christians undoubtedly hold firm to this meaning of the symbol, but this represents a moral interpretation of the cross.

The cross came to represent something other than injustice. It came to represent sacrifice and redemption. Theological interpretation, offered by Saint Paul and transmitted through the tradition, has long held that the cross provided the means of human salvation. The logic of this line of theological interpretation is that God's justice demanded human accountability for sin but that the atoning and sacrificial death of Jesus as the Christ was sufficient to appease the divine wrath and thus that death provided the means of salvation for all of humanity. The cross, then, rather than being simply a symbol of violence, became a symbol for preventing a more important metaphysical violence than the Romans could imagine—the damnation and loss of souls due to God's just but wrathful judgment. The cross was transformed in the Christian community into a symbol of human salvation—and it is Christ's sacrifice that is honored by Christians and actually reenacted at every Mass in the Roman Catholic Church.

The cross, then, as horrible as it was for Jesus to experience, was more importantly a metaphysical or theological necessity, for without it, there would have been no resurrection and thus no salvation. The cross, a symbol of earthly injustice, was transformed to symbolize a most fortunate boon for fallen humanity, now redeemed and saved. The cross endures as a violence-bearing symbol that identifies Christians as Christians—and it has been worn on the breastplates of crusaders going off to war and by contemporary Christians going off to the office. The cross came to symbolize membership in the Christian community and to demonstrate confidence that the wearer is among those whom the cross has saved. Christians have transformed the cross from a symbol of violence into one of salvation and eternal life, and on such a reading the cross is actually a good thing indeed.

This transvaluation of symbolic meaning can be found in other symbols important to Christians. Blood, for instance, transforms bloodshed in the violence of crucifixion into a sign of Christ's enduring presence. Blood is of course a symbol of life, but rather than the horror of the blood loss Jesus experienced through crucifixion leading to death, which it did, that loss of blood is transformed in and by the faith community to symbolize the "new life" to be enjoyed "in Christ." Christ shares his blood, and imbibing this blood in the memorial ritual of Eucharist or communion, for all the many different meanings this sacrament can have, takes the life that Christ has to offer into oneself, so that the violence that results in bloodshed is suppressed and transformed through a sacramental ritual to express thanksgiving and symbolic union with Christ, the transcendent source of the blood that symbolizes life eternal. Blood comes to represent the presence of the Christ and the new life the Christian can have with Christ and "in Christ."

Another important symbol for Christianity is fire, which can be a destructive as well as a creative power. In the story of the founding of the Christian church in the book of Acts, fire comes to serve as a symbol of God's presence and spirit—the Holy Spirit; yet in the book of Revelation, the apocalyptic punishment of the enemies of God is accomplished by consigning them to eternal torment in a lake of fire that does not consume them, fire now a symbol of violent purification and judgment.

Christianity has other symbols associated with violence, some of which have been obscured by history. For instance, in one nonlethal punishment imposed by the medieval Inquisition, some repentant individuals found guilty of offense were compelled to wear a yellow cloth star on the outside of their clothing, a punishment particularly detested by those who received it, because it was humiliating and elicited jeering (McBrien 1981: 18). Christian images or religious statements, including those that were musical and incorporated into hymnody, such as "Onward, Christian Soldiers," found their way into Christian practices, even worship, as well as into the broader life of Christendom. So, since the time of Constantine, Christian images or religious statements consistent with a Christian majority's status have appeared on imperial or national currencies, thus demonstrating the close relationship of the state with Christian values and wishes. The use of clergy, mainly chaplains, to provide religious connection to government continues to exist to this day in various governmental settings, including the US Congress, which holds power to declare war and authorize violence in support of national defense and policies; and military chaplains have been employed to provide not only counsel and comfort to soldiers but to pray for God's protection and support of military causes. One of the important rites of the Christian church that was practically involved in violence during the Middle Ages was excommunication, because this ecclesiastical rite of cutting individuals off from the church was usually preliminary to delivering offenders to the state for execution. Christian clergy and prison chaplains have traditionally been fixtures at state-sponsored executions.

Christianity preserves connection to its history of involvement of violence—both as recipient as well as dispenser—in a variety of symbols, rites, and rituals. Christians have of course been on the receiving end of violence as is made clear in Christian art, with Jesus's crucifixion a major theme, but also with portrayals of martyred saints and their icons of violent death hallmarks of the tradition. Such symbols preserve a Christian memory of persecution and honor martyrs who died for the faith. But Christians have also been dispensers of violence in such matters as war, execution, serving governments, and providing religious sanction for acts of state violence. What is most remarkable about the valence of meaning attached to these the various symbols, rites, and rituals associated with violence in Christianity is the way in which they come to be used by the faithful as disclosures of transcendent meaning. By attending to a transcendent meaning, Christian symbols come to emphasize transcendence while relativizing and even suppressing the "earthly" violence that naturally associates with them, the result being that religious sensibilities are not directed to the rational moral meaning of those justice issues to which the symbol point but beyond morality and justice to theological matters such as salvation and redemption.

Manifestations of Violence: Warfare, Punishment, Social Control

Although it would be a philosophical mistake to attach agency to religion and argue that religion is a direct cause of violence, there is no doubt that religions sponsor viewpoints and attitudes that affect the decisions people make about what to do and how to act, and this is certainly true on the issue of violence. Christian people have turned to their faith tradition to seek justification for what they do even when their actions are morally suspect. Religion and morality are not equivalent notions, and what may be questionable, unjustifiable, or even wrong from a moral point of view may yet find religious justification because religion involves ultimate matters and transcendent resources that can effectively trump the ordinary moral thinking of reasonable people of good will. Christian people have appealed to such transcendent resources—a "higher" authority—over the centuries to justify actions involving violence that are not only morally questionable but which are at odds with values and ideals also endorsed in the tradition. A brief examination of several issues where the issue of violence is at stake will expose how Christian thinking about violence is manifest in the world of practical affairs.

War

Christians have a long history of involvement in warfare, not only against other religions, as in the Crusades, but among other Christians. In the post-medieval period of Protestant Reformation and Roman Catholic Counter-Reformation, wars between these two Christianities were pervasive in Europe. The sixteenth-century French wars of religion pitted the royal Catholic League against the Protestant Huguenots (1652–1698); and the Great Peasant War in Germany (1524–1525) protested, with religious overtones, the injustices of medieval serfdom. When Luther's attempt at reconciling the parties failed, he encouraged landlords to "stab, strike, strangle these mad dogs" thus ensuring that Catholics would continue to dominate southern Germany (Edwards 303). The seventeenth century saw civil wars in Sweden and Poland, and the Thirty Years War in Germany (1618–1648) began to separate the longstanding partnership of pope and emperor. These national and civil wars led to political upheavals, including the Protestant challenge to Catholic monarchy, which culminated in the overthrow and execution of England's Charles I in 1649. The bloodshed and political instability in Europe from religious wars led to a begrudging realization that religious tolerance was necessary if there was to be peace and stability in political life. As far away as such conflicts seem, it is also the case that Protestant and Catholics fought against each other in Northern Ireland for most of the twentieth century.

Christians have in their history advocated, defended, and justified war, viewing it essentially as a way of combating evil and defending values, such as one's nation or the faith itself, by means that may be undesirable and contrary to Christian ideals but that practical realities necessitate as a lesser evil. Christians who stand willing to support the use of force to resolve conflicts, presumably on the basis of just war thinking, have been designated Christian "realists" in contrast to Christian pacifists. Realists have included such influential theological minds as the twentieth century's Reinhold Niebuhr (1892–1971), realism's major advocate and arguably not a defender of classic just war thinking. Niebuhr recognized the love and nonviolence ethic of Jesus as the Christian ideal but advocated a pragmatic ethic of responsibility that would allow decisions for the use of force to be made as lesser or necessary evils. For Niebuhr, a theologian influenced by Augustine's view of human fallenness and sin, resisting with force of arms the evil and destructive power of the Nazi regime was a necessary and lesser evil that constituted responsible action. Niebuhr was a champion of anticommunism during the cold war and supported the development of nuclear weapons as a way of balancing power. This attitude of realism and a willingness to use violent force in the realm of practical politics expresses an attitude toward the use of force widely held by many Christians who would justify force similarly today in the face of threats like terrorism.

Just war thinking is still a useful tool for many Christians, and its employment has taken some interesting turns. In the 1980s, the American Catholic Bishops declared themselves nuclear pacifists on the grounds that nuclear weapons were a disproportionate means for conducting warfare since the effect of such weapons would prove damaging to innocent human life long after use in a tactical situation. This position did not receive Vatican approval but indicated, nonetheless, that just war's demand for restraint on violence could provoke a critical response to modern warfare, which was also extended to biological and chemical weapons on the same grounds. Many Christians opposed the United States' preemptive invasion of Iraq in 2003 as unjustified under various just war criteria last resort, just cause, just intention, and reasonable hope of success. Appeals to just war, as said earlier, go well beyond the Christian community, but this approach to the question of war and violence, which has maintained life due to the active transmission of just war in and through the church continues to have effect. Many Catholics and Protestants invoke just war, and Orthodox Christianity has supported just war thinking and armed defense against oppression and violence in certain circumstances but considers any killing that takes place in war a sin for which repentance is required. Holy war is not in favor in Christian circles, although it may appear in the unwavering support many evangelical Protestant Christians extend today to Israel and its often violent actions toward Palestinians on the grounds that doing so is prophetic of the end time and presages Christ's Second Coming.

Christianity's long history of involvement with power politics, contributing theological and ethical resources in support of using force of arms to resist evil and oppression, will prevent it from ever unifying around the pacifism so much associated with Jesus's ethic of forgiveness and love of enemies. A challenge facing Christians who continue to support the use of force concerns consistent application of this ethic of resistance to evil, for if Christians apply the ethic selectively and do not call for the active defense of those suffering persecution and genocide, as happened in Cambodia under Pol Pot or in Rwanda or Darfur, it might appear as if this ethic of justified uses of force is in reality a tool of nationalistic self-interest rather than a true moral perspective grounded in faith. The argument could be made that a Christian moral perspective that endorses just war ought not to consider geographical location when innocent people—all being equal in the eyes of God—are in need of active protection from evils such as genocide. The options of realism and just war, on the one hand, and pacifism and nonviolent resistance, on the other, identify a constant tension in Christian ethics, and the challenge of consistent application is a difficult moral issue for realists who want to maintain a Christian identity when addressing the question of war.

Punishment

Christian people have supported both the state and the church in dispensing retributive justice that has as its purpose the inflicting of pain and suffering on offenders and miscreants. They have supported everything from public humiliation, shunning, corporeal punishments, and imprisonment to executions. Christians have also opposed the death penalty and worked for prison reform, with Quakers in Philadelphia creating the first penitentiary 1829 designed to provide work and solitary confinement as penance in place of corporeal punishment—little did the reformers realize the cruelty of solitary confinement. Christian clergy have provided spiritual support for prisoners as visitors and prison chaplains.

Christians have supported harsh retributive justice on the model of "an eye for an eye," a notion that harkens back to the Code of Hammurabi and was picked up and transmitted through Hebrew scriptures and culture (Leviticus 24:20). Jesus explicitly repudiated the retribution teaching and did so in a story in which a woman accused of blasphemy was about to be stoned. Jesus stopped it (John 8:3–11). That story would seem to lend serious scriptural support to a Christian antideath penalty stance, but as on other issues, Christians are divided. Many Protestants oppose the death penalty but many also support retention of the death penalty on the grounds that the practice is biblical, and the Hebrew Bible, to which appeal is made, reports thirty-six different capital crimes (Steffen 1998: 147). Official Catholic teaching supports the right of the state to execute but Pope John Paul II moved closer to an abolitionist stance on the grounds that society can be protected by means other than killing an offender. Various Orthodox Christian statements have condemned the death penalty because it eliminates the possibility of an offender's repentance.

That so many Christians support capital punishment may seem odd given that at the heart of the Christian story is an execution considered by Christians to be unjust and the victim innocent. The symbol the cross is multivalent and is so framed metaphysically that its meaning as an instrument of moral terror is dissipated; so for many Christians, the cross is not charged with negativity. In addition, many Christians appeal to the "power of the sword," believing Saint Paul gave executions legitimacy by that image, overlooking the fact that Paul made this reference in a prison letter when he was facing execution—why would he provide the temporal powers a justification to kill him when he had appealed his case to avoid such a fate?

The death penalty is a direct and intentional killing of a human being, a practice of extraordinary violence by whatever method, and many Christians continue to support the retributive practice even as many Christian bodies, including many Protestant denominations, Orthodox councils, and patriarch and papal statements, oppose it.

Social Control

Christians have been concerned to both preserve and extend their faith by various means of social control. Missionary efforts, the founding of Christian schools and institutions of higher learning, and support for hospitals, nursing homes, and orphanages point to the kinds of institutional developments that have been concerned to structure societies in conformity with Christians values and beliefs. Christians have sometimes entered the political arena with the express purpose of advancing Christian values or specific church teachings.

Christian people have expressed discriminatory and even demeaning attitudes toward people outside the community structures of faith. The exclusion of certain people from full societal participation as well as from various church communions expresses the primary means by which this is accomplished. In society, attitudes of discrimination and exclusion have been directed for centuries toward Jews and Muslims and peoples of non-Christian faith traditions; in the church it has expressed support of racial supremacy as well as in patriarchal structures to the exclusion of women—women still cannot become priests in Roman Catholicism, Orthodox Christianity, and in many Protestant denominations. Hatred of gay, lesbian, and transgendered people has led to their censure and exclusion in many Christian communities, highlighted in the contemporary United States by the nondenominational, independent Westboro Baptist Church of Topeka, Kansas, whose members actually advocate making sodomy a capital crime in accordance with Leviticus 20:13. Of course there are Christians who are working for full inclusion of women and gay persons into church life and leadership, but attitudes of hatred and discrimination express violence in that they inflict injury on people by disrespecting them and denying them their full humanity.

Many Christians in the twenty-first-century United States consider same-sex marriage a moral abomination or at least a violation of the Christian understanding of marriage; thus many same-sex couples are denied certain civil liberties in virtue of being denied the legal protection of marriage. The abortion issue is very much related to social control and violence. The Roman Catholic Church hierarchy, the undisputed leader of the opposition to abortion rights in the United States, has associated abortion with murder and denied that a fetus could ever be a material aggressor. This stance however puts women at risk of losing their own lives since some abortions are therapeutic for life-threatening situations, but no abortion as an intentional killing, even to save mother's life, is permitted under Catholic teaching. Several American abortion providers have been murdered by individuals claiming religious sanction for their action. Religious advocates of abortion rights, such groups as Catholics for Choice and the Religious Coalition for Reproductive Choice, provide a counterpoint faith perspective and oppose the violence to women they hold is at issue in denying women reproductive freedom.

Christian people will reflect—as well as instigate—many of the conflicts that arise in contemporary society. At one time churches in the United States in regions where slavery was legal defended slavery on biblical grounds, the Pauline book of Philemon in the New Testament carrying an instruction that slaves should return voluntarily to their masters. Christian people have endorsed and supported the institution of slavery, and even when slavery has been abolished, attitudes of racial superiority have led to social structures of extreme discrimination and oppression, as was certainly the case in South Africa and the United States. Racial discrimination and attitudes of racial superiority have been a part of Christian culture in many settings and persist to this day. Christian churches are racially segregated today in the United States, as are American public schools, although the churches are so voluntarily.

In all manner of social justice issues, Christians have played important roles on both sides of the violence question as advocates and opponents. Christianity contributed to the identity of the Ku Klux Klan, a murderous vigilante lynching group that terrorized blacks beginning in the post Civil War era. On the other hand, the black Southern Baptist Church was the institutional foundation for the American civil rights movement and Jesus's Gospel teachings an inspiration for Martin Luther King's nonviolent resistance.

On social issues, on questions of war and punishment, Christianity fails as a religion to present a fixed consistent message. Some Christian people have expressed through their faith enormous respect for God's creation and for human life, while others have appealed to their faith to justify acts of horrendous violence. The violence in Christian history is unmistakable and not to be denied or diminished. But the story is complex, and the brightest hope for the faith being an instrument of peace comes from Christian people making moral decisions about how they will express their faith. Violence is a moral issue even when religion plays a role in motivating it, for people can appeal to religion to justify even horrendous or despicable acts: religion is infinitely interpretable and can serve many masters. In the end, Christian people are moral agents who have to make decisions not only about how to act but how to act religiously; they have to make decisions about what kind of Christian they shall choose to be. This is a moral rather than a religious question, but it is relevant to every religious person and will determine, finally, if the religion they practice expresses values that are life affirming or destructive (Steffen 2007).

BIBLIOGRAPHY

Aquinas, Saint Thomas. "On War." *Summa Theologica, II, II Q. 40.* Trans. Fathers of the English Dominican Province. Chicago: Encyclopedia Britannica, 1952.

Aquinas, Saint Thomas. "Whether It Is Permissible to Kill a Man in Self-Defense?" *Summa Theologica,* II-II, Q. 64, article 7. Reprinted in *The Ethics of War: Classic and Contemporary Readings.* Eds. Gregory Reichberg, Henrik Syse, and Endre Begby, 169–198. Malden, MA: Blackwell 2006.

Armstrong, Karen. *Holy War: The Crusades and Their Impact on Today's World.* New York: Anchor Books, 1988, 2001.

Augustine. St. *Contra Faustum Manichaeum.* In John Langan, "The Elements of St. Augustine's Just War Theory," *Journal of Religious Ethics,* 12.1 (Spring 1984): 19–38.

Bible. New Revised Standard Version. Oxford, UK: Oxford University Press, 1989.

Calvin, John. *Defensio orthodoxae fidei.* In T.H.L. Parker, *John Calvin: A Biography.* Philadelphia: Westminster Press, 1975.

Carroll, James. *The Sword of Constantine: The Church and the Jews.* Boston: Houghton Mifflin, 2001.

Comby, Jean. *How to Read Church History, Volume 1: From the Beginning to the Fifteenth Century.* New York Crossroads, 1992.

Comby, Jean and Diarmaid MacCulloch. *How to Read Church History, Volume 2: From the Reformation to the Present Day.* New York: Crossroads, 1992.

"Conversion Tactics." 20 December 2010. www.christianaggression.org/tactics_violence.php.

Edwards, David L. *Christianity: The First Two Thousand Years.* Maryknoll, NY: Orbis Books, 1997.

Grotius, "The Theory of Just War Systematized (On the Law of War and Peace)." Reprinted in *The Ethics of War: Classic and Contemporary Readings.* Eds. Gregory Reichberg, Henrik Syse, and Endre Begby, 385–436. Malden, MA: Blackwell, 2006.

McBrien, Richard P. *Catholicism: Study Edition.* Minneapolis: Winston Press, 1981.

ReligiousTolerance.Org. "Number of Adherents." 4 December 2010. www.religioustolerance.org/worldrel.htm.

Sanneh, Lamin. "Christian Missions and the Western Guilt Complex." *The Christian Century* (8 April 1987). 2 December 2010. www.religion-online.org/showarticle.asp?title=143.

Steffen, Lloyd. *Executing Justice: The Moral Meaning of the Death Penalty.* Cleveland: Pilgrim Press, 1998.

Steffen, Lloyd. *Holy War, Just War: Exploring the Moral Meaning of Religious Violence.* Lanham, MD: Rowman & Littlefield, 2007.

Tactius. *The Annals*, 15.44. 28 December 2010. http://mcadams.posc.mu.edu/txt/ah/tacitus/TacitusAnnals15.html.

Vaux, Kenneth L. *Ethics and the Gulf War: Religion, Rhetoric, and Righteousness.* Boulder, CO: Westview Press, 1992.

Vitalis, Ordericus. *History of the Church* (1135). Cited in Jean Comby. *How to Read Church History, Volume 1: From the Beginning s to the Fifteenth Century.* New York: Crossroads, 1992.

Yoder, John Howard. *The Politics of Jesus*, Grand Rapids, MI: Eerdmans, 1972.

CHAPTER 6

....

MUSLIM ENGAGEMENT WITH INJUSTICE AND VIOLENCE

....

BRUCE B. LAWRENCE

In thinking about Islam and violence, when do we begin to track the connection of the two? Do we begin with 9/11 or 611? 9/11 is all too familiar: It conjures the stealth attack of Arab/Muslim suicide bombers, co-opting two planes, on the twin towers of the World Trade Center, a third plane attack on the US Pentagon, and a fourth crashed plane in Pennsylvania. After 9/11 and as a result of the traumatic death of more than 3,000 people, the US government declared war on two majority Muslim nations, global airport security forever changed, and American Muslims, as well as Muslims coming to the United States, became potential terrorist suspects.

But if 9/11 redefines Islam and violence, does it not also distort the long histori-cal view of Muslims and their multiple responses to violence? If one begins not with 9/11 but almost 1,400 years earlier with 611, the story of Islam and violence changes dramatically. There was no Islam in 611, just an Arab merchant who felt called to be a prophet. The previous year, 610, when Muhammad ibn Abdullah experienced rev-elation for the first time, only his wife and a few others accepted his claim. His claim to prophecy depended on intermittent revelations, delivered in the face of hostility from local tribesmen, merchants, and idolaters in his hometown of Mecca. When Muhammad began preaching publicly, as he did in 612, the public reaction was not only negative but violent. From 612 till 622, there was continual, punitive violence directed against Muhammad and his tiny band. It was expressed at many levels: dis-regard of his lineage, since he had been orphaned, then raised by an uncle; disdain for his relative poverty, since he was not among the wealthy elite of Mecca; and outright rejection of his claim to represent a superior divine channel, a single all-encompassing God called Allah, rather than a pantheon of competing deities with several names.

VIOLENCE IN THE EARLIEST PHASE
OF ISLAMIC HISTORY

The Time of the Prophet: Societal versus Military Violence

If we begin in 611 rather than 9/11, the first expression of violence and Islam is not violence directed by or sanctified through Islam but rather violence against Muslims. Often that violence was a response to efforts by early Muslims to curtail pre-Islamic forms of violence. Throughout human history, societal violence has been as prevalent as military violence, and in early seventh-century Arabia one finds numerous forms of societal violence. These included, for instance, female infanticide, along with the abuse of orphans, the poor, and marginal. Against such forms of societal violence, the revelations mediated through Muhammad were clear, incontrovertible challenges to the social order of tribal Mecca. For instance, they prohibit the pre-Islamic Arabian practice of female infanticide as well as other bodily and social abuses through directives set down, transmitted, and encoded in the Qur'an. Consider the following:

> And when the infant girl who was buried is asked
> For what offense she was killed
> [the person who killed her will have to answer
> for his sin on Judgment Day].
> (Surah al-Takvir, Qur'an [Q] 81: 8–9)[1]

> Do not kill your children out of fear of poverty;
> We will provide for them, and for you.
> Indeed, killing them is a great sin. (Surat al-Isra, Q 17:31)

What these two passages reflect is that in pre-Islamic Arabia killing of female infants was very common; often the moment a female was born she was buried alive. Islam not only prohibits female infanticide, but it forbids all types of infanticide, irrespective of whether the infant is a male or female. Consider the following:

> You should not kill not your children on account of poverty—
> We provide for you and for them.
> And do not approach the property of the orphan,
> except with what is better till he comes of age.
> Take not life which God has made sacred. (Surat al-Anam, Q 6:151–152)

In 2011 it is difficult to imagine how precarious life was in 611 and not just for children and women but also, and especially, for orphans. Consider the following directive, set forth in the chapter dedicated to women:Give orphans their property,

> Without exchanging bad for good;
> —And if you fear you cannot
> Do justice by the orphans,
> Then marry women who please you,
> Two, three, or four;
> But if you fear you won't be equitable,
> Then one, or a legitimate bondmaid of yours,
> That way it is easier for you not to go wrong. (Surat an-Nisa, Q 4:2–3)

The irony of the preceding passage is its misapplication during subsequent Muslim history. In the course of centuries, Islamic law overlooked both the context for this revelation—to care equitably for the orphan—and its qualification—if you cannot be equitable to two, three, or four women (who have been previously married and have children now orphaned without a father), then marry but one woman or cohabit with a legitimate bondmaid, as Abraham did with Hagar producing Ishmael. Caring for orphans is the crucial rationale for plural marriage during the earliest period of Islamic history. It could even be argued that it is the sole rationale for plural marriage, and so the first signpost of violence in Islam is not the violence inherent in Qur'anic dicta but rather the greater violence of the preceding, non-Islamic period known as *jahliyya*, or period of ignorance. And the revelation of the Qur'an, along with the formation of a Muslim community (*ummah*), was intended to curtail rather than to expand or export violence.

The Qur'an as Guidepost for Early Muslims

It was difficult, however, to sustain the purity of thought and the dedication of purpose indicated in those early surahs. They were revealed to the Prophet intermittently over twelve years, from 610 to 622, and during that time Muslims were the nonviolent members of Arabian society, in general, urban Mecca, in particular. At one moment, it seemed that Muhammad's nonviolent responses to the provocations of his hostile countrymen would jeopardize the entire Muslim experiment. In 617 the Prophet sent some of his closest followers and relatives next door, across the Red Sea, to Abyssinia (Ethiopia). Their enemies followed them and demanded that the traitorous Muslims be handed over to them and returned to face justice, that is, certain death, in Mecca. When the Christian king asked the fearful Muslims to explain their faith, one of their band recited to him a revelation that had just come to the Prophet. It included the first forty verses of Surat Maryam, and so closely did it parallel Christian scripture, belief, and hope that the king granted them asylum. That first *hijrah*, or exodus, was yet another instance when violence was prevented, rather than abetted, by the earliest Muslims, and the medium of their pursuit for justice, peace, and equality were those revelations that later became the Noble Book, the Holy Qur'an.

Later the bar of restraint moved higher and higher for Muhammad and his followers. By 622, life had become intolerable for the hardy cohort of Muslims.

Consider the power of their enemies. All of them were connected to Mecca, either to Muhammad's close relatives or to tribesmen who had resolved to defeat him and, if possible, to kill him. The early followers faced curses and death threats from prominent Meccans, some of whom were relatives of the prophet. Public spectacles were made of converted slaves, for instance, who were targeted for verbal shame and physical harassment. In instance after instance, violence was directed at Muslims, not perpetrated by Muslims.

The First Instances of Muslim-Initiated War

Once Muhammad established a community of followers in Medina, he had no choice but to fight his Meccan enemies who continued to pursue him. As the Qur'an represents it, God had declared:

> Permission to fight is given
> to those on whom war is made. (Surat al-Hajj, Q 22:39)

But war was always and everywhere to be defensive. The war Muhammad waged against Mecca was not a struggle for prestige or wealth; it was, in his view, a war for survival, of both the community and the faith. His helpers from Medina joined the migrants from Mecca. They provided the migrants with food and with shelter from their own resources, but they were all stretched to the limit. They had to raid caravans. They raided only small caravans at first and never attacked during those times when fighting, especially blood feuds, was prohibited by Meccan custom. As someone who had guided many a successful caravan to its destiny, Muhammad knew the routes. He knew the seasons. He also knew the wells where Meccan traders would pass with their camels and their goods.

In December 623, more than a year after the beleaguered Muslims had fled to Medina, Muhammad ordered a small detachment to spy on a caravan to the south. It was proceeding along the route to Yemen, at the oasis of Nakhlah that links Mecca to Taif. Since it was a holy month, he had ordered his followers not to attack but they disobeyed. Killing some, they took others captive and brought the caravan back to Medina. Muhammad was appalled. Not only had his followers disobeyed him; they had disobeyed the divine command to fight only in defense of one's own life and property. Their actions mirrored his leadership. He was responsible. The prophet who had pledged to be a divine mediator had betrayed his own prophecy. Riven with distress, he prayed to God. He needed guidance from above. And when it came, it was at once clear and compelling:

> They ask you about war in the holy month.
>   Tell them:
>   "To fight in that month is a great sin.
> But a greater sin in the eyes of God is
> to hinder people from the way of God,
> and not to believe in Him,
> and to bar access to the Holy Mosque
> and to turn people out of its precincts.

And oppression is worse than killing."
They will always seek war against you till
They turn you away from your faith, if they can.
But those of you who turn back on their faith
and die disbelieving will have wasted their deeds
in this world and the next.
They are inmates of Hell,
and abide there forever. (Surat al-Baqarah, Q 2:217)

This revelation had replaced a rule of principle with one of practical moral value. Yes, killing is forbidden in the sacred month (Q 2:191), but worse than killing is oppression, hindering people from the way of God. Empowered by this divine dictum, Muhammad accepted and divided the spoils of war from his followers at Nakhlah.

More war would follow. Muhammad and his followers entered into an unending conflict with their Meccan kinsmen and opponents. From 623 to 632, Muhammad planned thirty-eight battles that were fought by his fellow believers. He led twenty-seven military campaigns. The nonviolent protestor had become a general, waging war again and again. The first full-scale military campaign came at the wells of Badr, in 624, less than four months after the skirmish at Nakhlah. Muslims chose to attack a caravan coming south from Palestine to Mecca. The Meccans learned of their attack, opposing them with a force that far outnumbered the Muslim band. Muhammad and his followers should have lost; they would have lost, except for the intervention of angels (Q 3:122–127).

While the Battle of Badr projected the small Muslim community onto a stage marked as cosmic, with divine intervention as the basis for military victory, its outcome provoked fear in the Meccans. It also made them resolve even more firmly to defeat the upstart Muslims. By 625 the mighty Meccan general Abu Sufyan had assembled a huge army of both foot soldiers and cavalry. He marched toward Medina. The Muslims countered by moving out of the city proper. They engaged their rivals on the slopes of a nearby mountain, Uhud. Despite the superior numbers of the Meccans, it went well for the Muslims till some of Muhammad's followers broke ranks too early, in anticipation of another victory such as Badr. The Meccans then counterattacked, and Khalid ibn al-Walid, one of the brilliant Meccan nobles, led his squadron to the unprotected rear of the Muslim formation and, catching them unawares, began a great slaughter. The Muslims were soundly defeated, Muhammad wounded in the mayhem that day.

Yet the Prophet resolved to learn the deeper lesson behind this bitter defeat. He regarded the defeat of Uhud to be as important for Islam as the victory of Badr, for in defeat as in victory the Muslims had to acknowledge that their fate was not theirs but God's to decide.

> He knows what lies before them and what lies after them (i.e., what is in their future and in their past), and they understand nothing of His Knowledge expect what He wills (to disclose to them). (Surat al-Baqara, 2:255)

The aftermath of the Battle of Uhud also reinforced Muhammad's resolve to secure the loyalty of all his followers—both those who were Muslims and those who were non-Muslims yet bound to him by treaty. There followed some difficult, often bloody purges of tribes near Medina, and then the major Battle of the Trench in 627. A mighty Meccan army was led again by Abu Sufyan, the architect of Uhud. Abu Sufyan had tried to invade Medina, to defeat and destroy Muslims once and for all. Yet as understood by Muslims, God—and God alone—granted Muslims victory there. In the aftermath of this victory, fierce foes such as Abu Sufyan and the fiery Khalid ibn al-Walid ceased to oppose the Muslims and instead joined their ranks.

Beyond the battlefield, Muhammad never ceased trying to convert his Meccan opponents to the religion of Islam. Though he had forsaken nonviolence, he had not embraced violence as a way of life, only as an expedient to a higher end. He contacted the Meccans to propose a peaceful pilgrimage. He assured their leaders of his intention, but they doubted him. It took until 629, seven years after he had left Mecca, before he and his followers were allowed to reenter their native city. At last all Muslims—those Meccans who initially had emigrated to Medina, those Medinans who had joined them, and other tribes who had become their allies—then also submitted to God, and all were able to return to Mecca in a peaceful pilgrimage.

When they returned in January 630, Muhammad made a singular decision. Instead of vengeance, Muhammad forgave all but his bitterest enemies. Yet another military encounter quickly followed on the heels of the peaceful pilgrimage. It happened one month later, in February 630. It was a bigger battle than any Muslims had seen since Uhud, and it came not from Mecca but from beyond. Many Bedouin tribes who were opposed to Islam saw the reentry to Mecca as provocation for their own ferocious, full-scale assault on the Muslims. Hunain was a fierce battle. Many of Muhammad's followers panicked. Once again, from the Muslim point of view, it was the Almighty and the angelic host—not Muslim numbers or their military prowess—that brought them victory. The Qur'an once again marked the event:

> Indeed God has helped you on many occasions,
> Even during the battle of Hunain,
> When you were elated with joy at your numbers
> Which did not prove of the least avail,
> So that the earth and its expanse became too narrow for you,
> And you turned back and retreated.
> Then God sent down a sense of tranquility
> On His Apostle and the faithful;
> And sent down troops invisible
> To punish the infidels.
> This is the recompense of those who do not believe. (Surat al-Tawbah, Q 9:24b)

Muslims had scarcely moved beyond the victory of Hunain when other challenges beyond their borders arose. They had to engage the Byzantines, they had to levy taxes among recalcitrant Bedouin tribes, and above all, they had to purify their central rite, the pilgrimage or hajj, removing every vestige of pagan practice.

Muslim Wars after Muhammad: The Special Case of Ridda and the Problem of Retaliation

After the death of Muhammad in 632, his experiment, based so squarely on his personal authority, almost came unhinged. It was a delicate moment when a new leader, one of his trusted followers, Abu Bakr, was elected his successor, or *khalifa*. When several tribes tried to withdraw from the treaty that bound them to Muhammad, Abu Bakr fought them in what became known as the Ridda wars, the wars of apostasy or repudiation of Islam. For many scholars, this period initiates the practice of open warfare in the name of Islam. It is said to be the time when jihad, or war in defense of the faith, came to be associated with Islamic expansion. Yet according to Fred Donner, the Ridda wars, while testing the new Muslim state's capacity to integrate and organize Arabia's tribesmen, did not meet the standard of jihad, and neither the Ridda wars nor the expansionary wars that continued through the next period of nascent Islamic history should be defined as jihad.

According to Donner, three interlocking concepts defined the nascent Muslim experiment. They were: a single, indivisible community united by faith, that is, "the universal community of believers, reflecting its character as the body of worshipers of the one and universal God"; an absolute authority mediated through a binding, divine law; and the notion of a central human authority transferable from Muhammad to his successors (Donner: 54–61). The second concept—absolute authority mediated through divine law—was crucial since it curtailed without quite eliminating the pro-tocol of retaliation, requital, or *lex talionis*. Qur'anic passages support this shift:

> Believers, requital is prescribed
> For you in cases of murder;
> The free for the free, the slave for the slave,
> And the female for the female.
> But if anyone is forgiven
> Anything by his brother,
> Let fairness be observed,
> And goodly compensation. (Surat al-Baqarah, Q 2:178)

> And do not take a life
> That God has made sacred,
> Except for just cause
> And if anyone is killed unjustly,
> We have given his next of kin
> A certain authority;
> But he should not be excessive in killing;
> For he has been given divine support
> (to be restrained). (Surat al-Isra, Q 17:33)

Especially crucial is the protocol for requital among believers, announced in Surat an-Nisa. It is long but pivotal and consequential for Muslim attitudes toward inter-personal violence:

> It is never right
> For a believer to kill a believer,

Except by mistake;
And one who kills a believer by mistake
Is to free a believing slave,
And compensation is to be handed over
To the family of the deceased,
Unless they forego it to charity.
If the deceased was from a people
Warring against yours,
Yet was a believer,
Then free a believing slave.
But if the deceased was from a people
With whom you have a treaty,
Then compensation is to be paid
To the family of the deceased,
And a believing slave is to be freed.
And if one has not the means,
Then one is to fast
For two consecutive months,
As an act of contrition granted
As a concession from God.
And God is all-knowing, most judicious. (Surat an-Nisa, Q 4:92)

All of these conditions—God as authority, the community as resource, the successor as leader—are crucial for defining both the Islamic state and its impetus for expansion through war. Jihad, when it does occur, appears only as an ancillary, incidental concept. Of course, early Muslim warriors were motivated by the prospect of either booty (if they survived) or paradise (if they were slain), but jihad entered as "a product of the rise of Islam, not a cause of it—a product, to be exact, of the impact of the new concept of the *umma* on the old (tribal) idea that one fought, even to the death, for one's own community (Donner: 295–296)." While there is a lot of fighting depicted in Islamic histories, such military encounters are known mostly as *maghazi* ("raids") or *futuh* ("conquests"). Whenever jihad is invoked, it is a sidebar, not a central feature of the narrative of early Muslim warfare.

Jihad Invoked, Redefined, and Reawakened

Over time what had been an incidental, qualified part of the Qur'anic message, and the earliest Islamic worldview became an independent force on its own, so much so that some have declared jihad to be a sixth pillar (beyond the standard five) that defines Islamic belief and practice. The seminal text cited by all proponents of jihad as a collective duty incumbent on all Muslims is Surat at-Tawbah (Q 9). Here, Muslims are told that idolaters must be fought, polytheists leveled, and that the reward for those who struggle will be paradise:

(But) the messenger
And those who believe with him
Struggle with their possessions and their persons.
So the good things are for them,

And they are the successful ones.
God has prepared gardens
Under which rivers flow,
Where they will abide.
That is the great attainment. (Surat at-Tawbah, Q 9:88–89)

Yet neither this verse nor other Qur'anic verses motivated Muslims to engage in perpetual warfare against Byzantines, Sassanians, and other "people of the Book" after the death of Muhammad. In an analysis marked by consummate concern with detail and context, Carole Hillenbrand has shown how by the early eighth century, Muslim navies had given up their century-long quest to conquer Constantinople. "It became the practice for both empires to engage in annual campaigns, described in the Islamic sources as jihad but these gradually became a ritual, important for the image of the caliph and the emperor, rather than being motivated by a vigorous desire to conquer new territories for their respective faiths" (Hillenbrand: 93).

It was not until the eleventh century, with Saladin and the crusader conquest of Jerusalem, that jihad was revitalized. The crucial events were the fall of Jerusalem to the Crusaders in 1099; the recapture of Edessa from the crusaders by Saladin's father, Zengi, in 1144; and then, in 1187, Saladin's recapture of Jerusalem. It was during the fateful twelfth century that the doctrine of jihad was revived and heralded as a paramount duty to preserve Muslim territorial, political, and symbolic integrity. "The process of the reawakening of jihad," notes Hillenbrand, "must have been slow and gradual, and in some part at least it must have come as a direct response to Crusader fanaticism, witnessed first-hand (Hillenbrand: 108)."

One scholar has even gone so far as to argue that "the Crusades triggered the jihad mentality as we know it now." It was in response to the Crusades that Zengi and Saladin produced, for the first time in Islamic history, "a broad scale propaganda effort to praise jihad and jihad-warriors. Jerusalem became the center of jihad propaganda, and Saladin extended its sanctity to Syria, reminding everyone that Syria (too) is the Holy Land and that Muslims are responsible for defending and protecting it (against foreign assaults) (Mourad)."[2]

Later, the doctrine of jihad was amplified and applied anew in the thirteenth and fourteenth centuries after the Mongols plundered Baghdad, ravaged the Muslim world, and then themselves became Muslims. It was Ibn Taymiyya (d. 1328), one of the most influential jurists in Islamic history, who inveighed against the Mongols, and his favorite tool for anathematizing them was jihad. "With Ibn Taymiyya," observes Hillenbrand, "jihad to (save) Jerusalem is replaced by an internal movement within the Dar al-Islam itself, both spiritual and physical.... Ibn Taymiyya sees the Muslim world assailed by external enemies of all kinds, and in his strong desire to purify Islam and Islamic territory from all intrusion and corruption, he advocates as "the only solution to fight [is] jihad so that 'the whole of religion may belong to God.'" (Hillenbrand: 243).

VIOLENCE IN THE GUNPOWDER EMPIRES

The Ottoman Case

Is violence waged by an Islamic empire or nation always an expression of jihad, or religious violence? One could argue that it is less jihad than other features of structural violence that came to characterize the major Muslim empires of the premodern era. Beginning in the fifteenth century and, in part, due to the violence unleashed by the Mongols, a simpler political map of the Nile-to-Indus region, or the core Islamic world, emerged. It was characterized by three regionally based empires: the Ottoman, Safavid, and Mughal. They represented the core population of the Muslim world by 1800, perhaps 70 percent of all Muslims, and much of what today is regarded as Muslim expressions of violence can be traced to the structural elements that characterized each of these empires.[3] For clarity of insight into violence—its causes, expressions, and outcomes—the focus will be on the Ottoman Empire. The Sunni Ottomans, based in Anatolia and southeastern Europe, absorbed nearly all of the Arabic-speaking lands with the exception of Morocco and parts of the Arabian Peninsula. Theirs became the dominant regional power, although Shia Iran emerged as a formidable foe and bloody conflicts between the two countries erupted periodically. Mughal India, officially a foe of neither the Ottomans nor the Safavids, benefited from their mutual antagonism. Especially the persecution and expulsion of non-Shia Muslims from Safavid Iran provided some of the human resources—artistic, intellectual, and religious—that made possible the splendor of the Great Mughals. Islam remained a central focus of identity as well as the ideological underpinning for a variety of social and political movements. The period saw the establishment of Shiism as the state religion of Iran, with the forced conversion of its largely Sunni population under Safavid pressure. New Sufi orders emerged throughout the region, one of them actually serving as the precursor to the state sponsored Shiism of Safavid Iran. Often Sufi orders became vehicles of protest against the establishment, nowhere more evidently than the Naqshbandi-Mujaddidi movement of north India. Toward the end of this period in Arabia, the Muslim puritanical movement of the Wahhabis rose to challenge Sufi practices and Ottoman authority.

Violence must also be traced through its implication in the political order, not least in the way that it was managed for the preservation of the empire so that the rulers of various Muslim empires, like their non-Muslim counterparts elsewhere, became the sole legitimate purveyors of violence. There was never a question of eliminating violence but rather justifying its use for higher ends.

One must instead ask again the question Is warfare, when declared by a Muslim ruler, always and everywhere a reflex of Islamic norms and values? That was the question that occupied Ibn Taymiyya, but its practical consequence was nil, as much of the violence that characterized premodern Islamic polities was intra-Islamic, that is, Muslims were fighting Muslims for imperial gain, better taxation, and public prestige. Consider the case of the Ottomans.

In its origins, the Ottoman Empire goes back to the thirteenth century and the Seljukids. The first of the newly converted Turkish nomads to expand beyond their central Asian homeland, the Seljuks had overrun Buyid Iran in the eleventh century and conquered Baghdad by 1055. The Seljuks created a new empire in the name of Islam, but they also drew on Sasanian traditions still in place with their conquered subjects. They had a graduated taxation system that depended for its efficiency on *iqtas* or land grants. Warriors were supported through iqtas in return for their service on behalf of the Seljukid rulers.

The Seljuks were also assisted and tested by Turcomans, nomadic frontiersmen with less interest in settled or city life than the Seljuks. The Turcomans helped the Seljuks by operating as *ghazis*, or warriors for the faith, on the frontiers with the Byzantine Empire. They readily invoked jihad in their cause. After the Battle of Manzikert, where the Seljuks defeated the Byzantines in 1071, the Turcomans helped to Islamize and Turkify the region of Anatolia, still culturally linked to Byzantium.

The Seljuks might have become the masters of Anatolia and survived much longer had they not become victims of the Mongols. The same Mongol invasion that led to the sack of Baghdad in 1258 had earlier led to a Seljuk defeat in 1243. The Seljuks survived as a reduced polity in Asia Minor but as a vassal Mongol state; their last Sultan died in 1306. In the meantime, between 1260 and 1320, the Turcomans, mobilized by their *ghazi* tribal chiefs, and in tandem with the Seljuks, waged jihad against Byzantine forces that still held parts of Anatolia. Their leader was Osman Ghazi, who held the frontier land in western Asia Minor that was farthest north and closest to the Byzantines. He gained immense prestige when he defeated an imperial Byzantine army in 1301 at the Battle of Baphaeon. Many other nomadic Turkish soldiers came to Konya, Osman's capitol. They became known as *beys*, commanders of complements of fighters who were loyal to them, just as they, in turn, were loyal to Osman. At Osman's death, his son, Orhan expanded the empire still further, capturing major strategic and commercial cities in Anatolia. Bursa became the new Osmanli capital after 1326 and remained so until 1402.

At the same time as they were expanding in the east, the Ottomans were also making inroads into the Balkans, and a measure of their success is that one of Orhan's successors, Murad, made Adrianople (also referred to as Edirne) his capital in order to consolidate Ottoman conquests in Rumeli.

The success of the Ottomans invoked Islam and the doctrine of jihad, but it was banked on the logic and limits of conquest. They formed a pyramidal military state, with roots that went deep into local society, and allowed the Ottoman Sultan at the apex to control the beys, who also represented geographical and economic interests crucial to the burgeoning state.

As ideal as the system sounds, it had limits inherent to the very strengths that made the system possible. Ottomans were heirs to the Byzantine as well as the Sasanian empires. Like their Umayyad predecessors, it was the Byzantine model, especially as reflected in Istanbul, which both fueled and restricted their imagination. They expanded by conquest, making the army responsible for two fronts, one in Asia and one in Europe. Yet the army could only fight when the Sultan was on the battlefield to lead his troops in person. The competitive pull of two war zones produced a major donnybrook for the fledgling Ottoman state in 1387. Murad I had to confront an Anatolian resistance movement, the Karmanids, at the same time as the Serbs, joined by dissatisfied Bosnians and Bulgarians, were posing a challenge in the Balkans. Though the Ottomans won the Battle of Kosovo in 1389, Murad was killed in the fray, and in its aftermath his son and successor, Bayazid, executed the Serbian king, Lazar.

More threatening to the state than Anatolian or Balkan rivals, however, was the emergence in the East, in Rum, of a threat from central Asia. It came from the Chagatai Turkish successor to the Mongols: Timur Leng, or Tamerlane. When Ottoman and Timurid forces clashed in Ankara in 1402, the Timurids were victorious. Bayazid, humiliated as well as defeated, died at his own hand a year later in 1403. The Ottoman experiment, like many of its *ghazi* emirate neighbors, might have vanished with Bayazid, but it survived for several reasons. First, it had attained legitimacy as a Muslim polity when Bayazid, anticipating the threat of Timur, had invested himself with recognition as an official Muslim ruler: The Mamluk ruler of Cairo had become the caliph or nominal leader of all Muslims after the Mongol sack of Baghdad in 1256, and in 1394 he made Bayazid the sultan of Rum. Second, he had introduced a system of recruitment and administration that conjoined the *timar* system with the expansion of territory. Like his Seljukid predecessors, he recruited non-Muslim youth, then, after converting them to Islam, had them trained as slaves, or *ghulams*, for military and palace duty. In effect, Murad began what became known as the janissary system, a backbone of later Ottoman state policy.

The religious establishment was important as a third element of regime enhancement. Bayazid fostered it as he did the janissary or slave system, extending patronage to its recipients but at a price: preferential deferral or even outright acquiescence in the authority of the state. Muslim scholars and teachers, Sufi masters, and juridical experts came from neighboring Islamic polities to Anatolia and to the Ottoman court. They came because of patronage from the emperor, and they were expected to assist him in his effort to be not just a conquering ghazi but also a Muslim Sultan. In other words, Islam became an explicit ideology, and building block of public prestige, for the newest Turkish Muslim empire.

The defining moment for the new Ottoman polity came in 1453 when Muhammad II, also known as Mehmed the Conqueror, achieved an ambition that had eluded all his Muslim predecessors: the conquest of Constantinople (Istanbul). It was a singular moment that saw not just the collapse of the truncated Byzantine Empire but also the rededication of Constantinople as a Muslim capital city.

Following the conquest of Istanbul, Syria, Egypt, and the Hijaz region of Arabia were conquered in the early sixteenth century. The conquest of Egypt conferred further Islamic legitimacy, as the caliphate devolved from the defeated Mamluks to the victorious Ottomans. With the possession of Jerusalem, Mecca, and Medina, they controlled the three holiest cities in Islam. Rumeli remained no less important to the imperial ambitions of the Sultans: By the sixteenth century, Belgrade and Hungary, Moldavia, and Wallachia and Transylvania had all become tributary principalities under nominal Christian rulers. But the Ottomans were limited by the need to maintain supply lines to their sources. On the European front, they could not go beyond Vienna, where the time frame for sieges was limited and so never succeeded. On the southern rim of the Mediterranean, they continued to expand beyond Egypt, annexing Algiers, Tripoli, and Tunis and establishing beys and *deys* as rulers or surrogates on behalf of the Ottoman sultan, who was now also the commander of the caithful. Thus, at its apogee under Suleiman I in the mid-sixteenth century, the Osmanli realm was the most powerful empire in the world. Overshadowing his nearest European rival, Suleiman I enjoyed revenue twice that of Charles V.

But the state had limits both theoretical and empirical. In theory, it sustained an Islamic empire, with the sultan the uncontested source of religious as well as secular authority. He combined in himself the apogee of *shari'a* (religious) and *qanun* (civil) law. Suleiman was known as Suleiman *qanuni*. The notion of the state as a harmonious structure permeated the state military and civilian bureaucracies. It derived from the classic Perso-Turkish source, Nasir ad-din Tusi (d. 1273). No theory or account of Islam and violence can be complete without reference to Tusi's circle of justice. The circle of justice became the basis for Ottoman consciousness. Since the Sasanian social ethic emphasized order, stability, legality, and harmony among the theoretical four estates of priests, soldiers, officials, and workers, Tusi recycled Sasanian principles within an Islamic program. Tusi projected a dual function: hierarchical duties mirroring a consensual reciprocity between different groups, each aware of its specific role in the hierarchy. While the loyalty structure is a pyramid, its function is projected as a circle, the circle of justice. There can be no royal authority without the military (*askeri*):

> There can be no military without wealth
> The reaya or agriculturalists produce the wealth
> The sultan keeps the loyalty of the *reaya* by ensuring justice
> Justice requires harmony in the world
> The world is a garden, its walls are the state
> The state's axis is the religious law
> There is no support for religious law without royal authority.[4]

The elegance of this formulation belies its inner tension. The accent is on justice rather than right religion as the basis for effective rule, not eliminating conflict or violence but redirecting its force to the benefit of the state. While the ruler and the ruled depend on each other, theirs remains an asymmetric relationship, for the circle begins and ends with the state and its supreme subject, the ruler. Only the middle line suggests that harmony and justice are coterminous one with the other, yet justice is not justice between equals but rather justice as "just" rewards or allotted payments for participation in the system. It never approaches parity much less equality. The religious classes, custodians of religious law, require state support, just as the state, in turn, requires the askeri or military classes who are its foundation. One could either label this system as controlled violence or the harmonious balance of competing self-interests, but it projects a consistent stress on justice.

Enlightenment notions of nonreligious loyalty to a state marked by both equality and justice for all are confounded in the Sasanian, then Ottoman notion of justice as a circle with the ruler at its center and also its apex. The pyramidal nature of authority becomes clear when one traces the circle via the four classes or differentiated orders, also derived from Tusi. The men of the sword dominate, with the men of the pen as their closest allies, while all other groups, whether Muslim or non-Muslim, urban or rural, have a lesser stake in the system but cannot escape its influence.

A review of its empirical limits demonstrates the faultlines within the Ottoman Empire. The system could only work as long as the conquests continued. Suleiman's reign may have been the apogee of power, but it also cast a shadow on the subsequent period of Ottoman history. The last significant conquest in the Mediterranean theater was Cyprus in 1570 (soon after his reign), and no other conquest came till Crete in 1664 almost a century later. The battles to the east of Rum, specifically with the Iranian Safavids, did not produce any major territorial gains. Without conquests, the Ottoman state could not claim to be the major Muslim empire of its day. Lack of conquest undermined its own logic, signaling its reduction in status and eventual demise. The empire's ideology was two pronged. It was dominated by and oriented toward the bureaucracy and governing institutions, yet at the same time it was reinforced by the religious schools and courts. The focal point of the ideology was the emperor. The success of the system depended on his personal stature. The emperor was at the same time the supreme religious leader, the owner of all land, and the commander in chief of the armed forces.

So there were indices of autocratic violence—structural, societal, and political—that characterized not only the Ottoman Empire and also its rivals, the Safavids and Mughals, but also its regional subsets, later to become independent polities, from Morocco on the edge of the Atlantic to Egypt at the base of the Mediterranean.

Overshadowing these rivalries, however, was engagement with Europe, above all, a response, sometimes cooperative but more often oppositional to European initiatives to control parts of Africa and Asia. Commercial trade became the Achilles heel for Ottomans as for other Muslim polities. Closely controlled by the state, trade was primarily in luxury items (Ottoman silk and Asian spices). It did not propel the economy out of its sense of self-sufficiency nor did it enable the state to control the number of competing centripetal forces within the empire that put Ottoman officialdom at risk in dealing with external polities, whether European or Muslim. Diplomatic relations with France revealed the strength as well as the weakness of the Ottoman system. A French-Ottoman alliance, forged in order to combat Charles V and the Holy Roman Empire, effectively delayed the Ottoman need to enter into permanent relations with other European powers until 1793, with the result that the Ottomans actually knew little about their future rivals, including the Russians. There were efforts to recuperate lost opportunities in the nineteenth century, but the great chase deprived not just the Ottomans but other Muslim polities from any sense of parity vis-à-vis their European rivals, then rulers.

Comparative Perspectives on Regional Empires

Comparable political economic processes informed the Ottomans along with their neighbors and rivals, the Safavids and Mughals. The rise of each empire involved the imposition of a strong state with tribal origins on a predominantly agrarian economy and society. In all three cases, after a prosperous period of stable reproduction of social relations and expansion of wealth in the sixteenth century, a retreat or decline seems to have been registered in the seventeenth century in the form of agrarian crises with political economic causes and political outcomes.

Several major developments altered the political scene in the seventeenth and eighteenth centuries: the Ottoman Empire became decentralized as Istanbul's hold on the provinces weakened and autonomous authorities sprang up almost everywhere; the Safavid regime collapsed, giving way to several decades of internal fragmentation and turmoil; and Mughal India reached its apogee, only to be sacked by Nadir Shah, an Afghani adventurer, in the early eighteenth century.

Alongside the shifts in the internal power relations came changes in the region's position in regard to Europe. While Safavids, Ottomans, and Mughals remained virtually untouched by European culture, they now fought and traded with Europeans on a more extensive basis than before and on increasingly unfavorable terms. Military conflict with European countries raged along a wide front extending from the Black Sea area and the Balkans to the western Mediterranean and the Indian Ocean. The region's armies were able to hold their own until the second half of the eighteenth century, when disastrous defeats by Russia and the easy fall of Egypt to Napoleon brought home to the Ottoman leaders the recognition that global power had shifted definitely in favor of Europe.

European Colonial Presence and Violent Muslim Responses

There is no generic category of religious protest that applies to the modern period of world history, from 1600 to the present.[5] Instead, there are three distinct phases of Islamicly valorized protest. In each phase, certain Muslim groups revolted against the ascendant, which has become the dominant, world order linked to western Europe. Only the first phase is properly speaking revivalist. It is succeeded by a second that can and should be termed reformist, and it is only after the revivalist and reformist phases and, in large part, due to their failures that there what is now termed Islamic fundamentalism or Islamism emerged.[6]

All three—revivalism, reformism, and fundamentalism—are historically specific socioreligious movements propelling marginalized male leaders into public view as they attempt to reclaim the space challenged and reduced, impoverished and redefined, by the expanding sea powers of western Europe. From the eighteenth century to the present, all the major Muslim polities experienced financial crises, demographic disruption, and agricultural stagnation. If there is a case to be made for structural violence as the backdrop and often the catalyst for physical violence, then the European interlude must be considered when addressing the topic of Islam and violence. Some of the malaise in early modern Muslim polities resulted from indigenous challenges. Provincial Arabs chafed under Ottoman Turkish rule, Afghans protested Qajar control within Iran, and Marattas rebelled against Mughal hegemony in South Asia. In each instance, however, the situation of ruling elites was complicated and worsened by: the external diversion of commodity trade from the Mediterranean and Indian Ocean routes to the Atlantic Ocean following the discovery and exploitation of the New World and the internal infiltration of European trade through a nexus of foreign merchants and local middlemen or *compradores* cooperating to establish new products, new markets, and new communication networks also as new sources of profit and reinvestment. Islam, in effect, became an idiom of protest against the gradual contraction of internal and external trade, brought about by the mercantile activities of European maritime nations, specifically, the Portuguese, Spanish, Dutch, British, and the French. What was contested in the name of Islam by Islamic revivalists was control over vital commodities—slaves, textiles, coffee, tea, and spices—as well as gold, all trafficked along the major trade routes from the Atlantic coast of West Africa to the Indonesian archipelago.

The major Muslim revivalist movements were without exception preindustrial. Their leaders mobilized followers in response to the European redirection of global trade, even when they did not acknowledge the extent to which European advances were reshaping their lives.

One of the earliest instances of European influence concerns the upstart Wahhabis. In western Arabia, the Wahhabis aligned with a Najdi chief named Ibn Sa'ud. That combination in time produced what is now regarded as a legitimate government, though it remains the only Muslim polity named after a tribal group: the present-day Kingdom of Saudi Arabia. Both Ibn Sa'ud and his appointed ideologue, Ibn 'Abd al-Wahhab, benefited from the loss of revenues suffered by their chief rival, the sharif of Mecca, who in the eighteenth century reigned as the legitimate ruler of the Hijaz. Dependent as he was on the lucrative Indian trade, primarily in textiles, indigo, and spices, the sharif could not sustain its diversion away from the Arabian Peninsula by the British. Weakened economically, he also became vulnerable militarily. His Najdi rivals rallied to their side other groups who had been deprived by the British ascendancy in trade, and toward the end of the eighteenth century they were able to dislodge and replace the sharif of Mecca. Although the Wahhabis had other battles to wage, with the Turks and also with

Muslim loyalists from rival tribes who did not accept their leadership, their initial success was a by-product of incipient European colonialism.

Unfortunately, the influence of Muhammad ibn 'Abd al-Wahhab on both Muslim and non-Muslim scholarship of Islamic revivalism has led his movement to be overvalued beyond its actual historical achievement. It is often presumed that a literal, text-restricted reading of the Qur'an prevailed from the origins of Islam. It did not, nor has it ever been the practice for most observant Muslims. Ibn 'Abd al-Wahhab had a narrow reform agenda not shared with other eighteenth-century and later Muslim reforms. Even his notion of the boundaries of faith were limited to exploring and explaining the concepts of *tawhid* and *takfir, iman* and *kufr,* that is to say, how you make God exclusively one and declaim all other Muslims who fail to express the same level of creedal commitment. Ibn 'Abd al-Wahhab never claimed to be a reinterpreter of the scholarly legacy of the past. He never concerned himself with the wider Muslim community and its integrity. He never addressed issues of tyranny and social justice.

Yet the Wahhabi paradigm created numerous analogues elsewhere on the seams of commercial activity that became increasingly under British rule. In northwestern India, the Brelvis tried to wage war against indigenous groups the Sikhs and Hindus, but the latter were better positioned than the Brelvis in regard to British commercial interests. The Brelvis were strategically isolated before being defeated on the battlefield by Sikhs. Elsewhere, in northeastern India, the Faraidis perceived the shift to a moneyed, international economy as advantageous to Hindu landlords while impoverishing Muslim peasant laborers. They mobilized resistance, at first in local protests, later in region-wide acts of defiance; neither succeeded in reversing the tides of change.

It was the same story, with different actors but a similar outcome in Africa. The best documented of the revivalist movements, the Fulani-Qadiris in Nigeria, pitted Muslim herdsmen and traders against British markets and middlemen who were often being recruited from rival Muslim tribes. Though the revivalists enjoyed superb Islamic credentials, they were eventually defeated on the battlefield. There were temporary successes: the Sanusis prevailed in the Cyrenaica region near the Ottoman province of Libya, strengthening Islamic identity for more than fifty years until the Italian invasion of 1911. A Somali chieftain, too, was able to mobilize interior tribes against British, Italian, and French forces in the coastal areas near Mogadishu. He won several battles and continued to rule for more than twenty years, only to have the British bomb and machine gun their way to victory in 1920. Finally, on the other side of the Muslim world in Southeast Asia, a puritanical movement known as the Padris galvanized Sumatran Muslims dispossessed by the shift from gold and pepper trade to a new cash crop, coffee. During the course of the nineteenth century, the Padris were harassed and coerced, enduring defeat after defeat in bloody encounters before finally succumbing to the Dutch authorities.

All these revivalist movements were violent, but they followed a pattern of responsive violence. It is not accidental that they all occurred at crucial seams in the expanding imperium of maritime Europe. All were Sunni Muslim movements.

The single parallel within Shia Islam were the Bahais, a group still despised by Twelver Shia clergy. The vilification masks a deeper fear: The first Bahais embodied and projected the latent messianic impulse of Twelver Shiism. Yet the Bahais became harbingers of ecumenical pluralism and so represent a graphic example of how Islam and violence cannot be neatly matched.

Apart from the Bahais, Islamic revivalist groups were succeeded by Islamic reformers. Interposed between Islamic revivalism and Islamic fundamentalism, Islamic reformers are closely linked to nationalist movements, and in retrospect it can be seen that, despite their universalist rhetoric, almost all the Islamic reformers were shaped by the influences of the colonial period. Especially keen is the emphasis on science and technology in education, constitution and parliamentary democracy in politics, and the revised role of women in social life. If Muslim nationalism became mimetic, it is due to the fact that movements that claimed a loyalty to Islam were also mimetic, picking up elements of the West that they hoped could be transformed into an Islamic system. Far from reacting with violence to European presence and control, they attempted to accommodate to an emergent, if asymmetric, world system. There is no independent Muslim movement after the colonial period; all are reacting to some force or series of forces that emanate from the Western world, which is to say northern Europe and the United States.

Muslim reformers recognized the power of the institutions that were propelling European maritime nations to a unique position of global prestige. The reformers came from those countries whose Muslim elites were most engaged by the specter of European commercial and military penetration—Egypt and India, Iran and Turkey before World War I, but then, following the war, also Tunisia, Algeria, and Morocco. The North African reformers coalesced into a movement known as Salafiya, or Islamic traditionalism. Criticized for their unwitting promotion of historical retardation, its leaders seemed to hark back to a golden age that never existed or at least could never be reconstructed, and so their passionate pleas merely drained energies away from the task at hand, to accommodate to the new reality of a European world order. Yet most of the reformers acted in good faith, as committed Muslims conflicted by the gap between Europe's pragmatic success and what seemed to be its spiritual vapidity. It was as though they were witnesses to a novel and "unholy" revelation. For them, "the arbiter of truth and knowledge suddenly ceased to be enclosed in the revealed word of God. Another text, with no specific author or format, had made a permanent intrusion. It was the West in its political systems, military presence and economic domination which now appeared in the background as an authoritative code of practice."[7]

But the authoritative code was not uniform. The intervening European powers quarreled with one another. Some Muslim polities, such as the Sharifian kingdom of Morocco, benefited from these quarrels, able to resist direct rule because no Mediterranean power wanted its rivals to control the seat of the Arab/Muslim West. But all polities were affected by the great wars, sometimes known as the Christian wars, which were waged by these self-same powers twice in the twentieth century. It was only due to the enormous expenditures and consequent destruction of these wars that protest movements among Muslims and others were able to mobilize into national liberation movements. Gradually, as the smoke cleared from the second of these horrific Christian wars, most Muslim ruling elites were able to grasp the laurel of independence. Even so, not all were marked by the same political order.

Even countries that were not colonized directly, such as Saudi Arabia and Iran, still experienced the effects of colonial economic penetration into the eastern Mediterranean and Indian Ocean, and the structures that arose after independence reflect this influence, above all in the sphere of politics and law. It was because the nature of self-rule was shaped as much by European as by indigenous models that one must speak of "mimetic nationalism." Though Arab, as also non-Arab, Muslim leaders embraced nationalism to chart the path to independence, the models of governance were derived from the departing colonials. Whether one looks to constitutional charters or to the adoption of separate executive and legislative bodies, the impress of European precedents is evident. At the same time, the boundaries of new nations reflected a patchwork of compromise that was worked out by the European powers not by their Muslim subjects. Saddam Hussein's outburst in fall 1990 over the manipulation of Iraq's borders with Kuwait was at once justified and spurious. It was justified because the borders of all African and Asian countries were set in the colonial period or its immediate aftermath. It was spurious because many countries benefited as well as lost from such manipulation: Without the addition of parts of Kurdistan, especially the oil-rich region around Mosul, Iraq, for instance, would not have had the geopolitical resources that make it potentially the economic giant among all Arab states.

The truth about the process by which postcolonial borders were decided may be simpler, though no prettier, than conspiracy theories allow: Disparate communities of Asia and Africa had been welded together as parts of the British, French, or Dutch empires. They could not be dissolved and reconstituted in their precolonial form with independence. Often the conditions of self-rule had to be set by colonial authorities and imperial administration, because consent could not have been secured on any other basis. Yet the end result was to make the entire process of Arab/Muslim nationalism seem imitative or mimetic. It appealed only to a limited stratum of elites. The mechanisms to curb military control and to spur the emergence of a middle class were never set in place. Structural violence took on a new face, but it was still violent and its tensions, contradictions, and excesses continue to the present day.

While most Europeans and Americans have lived within "secure" national borders for several generations and see themselves as beneficiaries from the tradition of nation-state loyalty, many third world citizens, and Afro-Asian Muslims, in particular, do not share either their experience or their trust. For most Muslims, it is hard to applaud the random, top-down process by which almost all their polities came to assume their present form.

Not only the external boundaries of territory but also the internal boundaries of identity are open to challenge and reformulation. In thinking about Islamic protest, it is especially important to note how the clash at the core of all other clashes between nationalists and fundamentalists is the totalizing impulse guiding each. In the Muslim world, the state functions as an obedience context, and the rulers of the Muslim state demand total compliance with the state's vision of Islam. Tacitly it recognizes that the norms it imposes are not universally shared by all Muslims, yet publicly it arrogates to itself and to its custodians the right to decide which elements of Islamic belief and practice are to be supported. The memory of other Islams is too strong, however, to be erased. In each instance, Muslims have to decide how to preserve their symbolic identity within a public order that is antireligious at worst, as in the Union of Soviet Socialist Republics, China, Indonesia, and Turkey or pseudoreligious at best, as in most Arab states, Iran, Pakistan, and Bangladesh.

Twentieth- and now twenty-first-century nationalism produced for the entire Muslim world a cleavage of enormous magnitude. The most evident rift was between Muslims and the dominant culture of western Europe. But an equally great divide devloped among Muslim themselves, between those who were attracted to European achievements, seeking to appropriate their benefits, and those others who sought to oppose them.

While the legacy of colonialism reshaped the Muslim world into truncated territories and contested borders, capitalism left it with economies that could only function on the margins, benefiting the major powers of the high-tech era. These powers were the technologically advanced, professionally differentiated, and economically privileged societies of western Europe, North America, and, now, East Asia. Even before the rubric of first, second, and third worlds was invented in the 1950s, a third world existed. It embraced all Muslim societies, even those benefiting from the petrodollar infusion that began in the 1950s and 1960s but did not accelerate until the 1970s and 1980s.

JIHAD IN MODERN TIMES

Among the ongoing effects of the postcolonial legacy in Muslim polities has been the overwhelming attention to Islam and violence. From medieval to modern to contemporary history, the trope of Islam as violence has focused on jihad, and so it is important to note how those who came to be labeled fundamentalists invoked the early experience of the Prophet Muhammad and the Medinan state on behalf of their own authority to proclaim jihad. None did so more stridently or effectively than Sayyid Qutb, the Muslim brother who opposed Nasser, the Egyptian president from 1954 to 1970. Executed on charges of sedition in 1966, Sayyid Qutb produced a series of writings, some from prison, that exposed modern-day nationalism as itself a form of *jahliyya*. In effect, it was equated with the kind of tribal order that Muhammad had opposed and that he, together with his early followers, had to overcome in order to establish the ummah, or single supratribal Muslim community. In one of his most memorable string of homologies, Qutb reappropriated nationalism for "true" Islam: "[N]ationalism is belief, homeland is Dar al-Islam, the ruler is God, and the constitution is the Qur'an" (quoted in Lawrence 1998: 68).

Qutb's message and his resort to jihad as the just cause for Muslims under threat resonated through Egypt and the Arab world and with the Taliban and the attackers of 9/11. It is impossible to make this temporal transition from the seventh to the twenty-first century without noting how eschatological religion is instrumentalized through modern means, not least martyr operations. The connection has been nimbly charted by Hans Kippenburg:

> When they attacked the United States in September 2001, jihadists were interpreting the Middle East conflict in Islamic concepts, but they did so in a radically different manner from the mainstream of the Muslim Brethren (following the lead of Sayyid Qutb rather than his predecessors). The power of the United States and Israel has made Islam so rotten and corrupt that no external institution is now able to represent it credibly; it is only the pure intentions of the last surviving upright believers that can form the core of a new community of the elect. And this is what they demonstrate by means of martyr operations (carried out by Al-Qaeda and in the name of Osama bin Laden). (Kippenberg: 201)

The Legacy of Osama Bin Laden: The Cosmic Warrior Mediated

We now come full circle from 611, the beginning of a nonviolent protest movement led by an Arab merchant turned prophet, to 9/11, the day of infamy for twenty-first century Americans. The source of that violence that brackets Islam with the worst forms of violence was Osama bin Laden; but it was Bin Laden, the Islamic apocalypticist as mediated through modern visual and satellite technologies. Now that Osama bin Laden has been killed by a US Navy seal team in Abbotabad, Pakistan, in early May 2011, it is possible to reflect on his impact on Islamic notions of war and violence.[8]

There is probably no aspect of Bin Laden's profile that is more critical nor less understood than his use of the media, especially al- Quds al-'Arabi and al-Jazeera. One episode from late 2003 illustrates how intertwined the interests of the Saudi dissident and the major Arabic language media were. On December 10, 2003, the London-based Arabic daily *Al-Quds Al-Arabi* reported that Al-Qa'ida, headed by Osama bin Laden, "is gearing up for a big operation to coincide with Eid Al-Adha [February 2, 2004] … a new videotape of bin Laden will be circulated shortly before the holiday … it will surface in conjunction with 'a great event that will shake the region,' and it will be broadcast by Al-Jazeera television." The source explained that Al-Qa'ida had an agreement with Al-Jazeera by which it was committed to broadcast any videotape that the Sahab Institute provides about Al-Qa'ida.

He pointed out that the institute would sever its relations with the station if it refused to broadcast a videotape, and reiterated that the station is obligated to broadcast any videotape we send to it.[9]

In the several messages included in my collection of Bin Laden's writings, his relationship to Al-Jazeera proves to be almost as important as his decision to wage jihad. Prior to December 1998, when the United States and Britain launched an attack on Iraq, called Operation Desert Fox, Al-Jazeera had been a local satellite news service. Founded in February 1996 by the emir of Qatar, its goal was to promote freedom of information among Arabic-speaking citizens of the Gulf and its neighbors. In 1998, the Baghdad office got the big break when they filmed the missiles launched against Iraq from British and American airplanes. Bin Laden gave an interview that was broadcast on Al-Jazeera in December,[10] and he became an instant international attraction. So significant was the impact of this interview that, nine days after September 11, 2001, it was rerun by Al-Jazeera. Accompanying the ninety-minute video were pictures of Bin Laden firing a gun. The message, in images as well as in words, was that the war is religious, the war is between aggressive crusaders and defensive believers, and Muslims have a stark choice, either to side with the infidel oppressors or to support the beleaguered but pure and resolute Muslim defenders.

The same message was articulated in all of Bin Laden's subsequent epistles that were broadcast via Al-Jazeera. Each was tailored to the audience he addressed. Jason Burke observed that "bin Laden seemed to show an incredible instinctive grasp of modern marketing techniques" (Burke: 175). Flagg Miller goes further, explaining why the genre of epistles may be one of the best marketing techniques for his message:

> Epistles became a defining medium of eloquence in the 9th-century Abbasid court of Baghdad. In epistles colorful pleasantries, competitive verbal jousts, and political wrangling are all of a piece. Bin Laden deploys the genre with his own rhetorical flourishes. As pious public lecturer, militant *jihadist*, and now enfranchised literate scribe, Bin Laden excoriates ruling Saudi leaders for corruption, fiscal mismanagement, human rights abuses, and especially for their alliance with 'American Crusader forces' since the Gulf War of 1990. Such accusations gain religious significance for Bin Laden as apostasy (*shirk*) insofar as Saudi leaders are represented as recurring to man-made state law instead of to true Islamic law (*shari`a*), the latter of which remains confidently underspecified. Overall, the pious tenor of Bin Laden's epistle is consistently maintained as an act of remembrance (*dhikr*), so central to Islam's message that mankind is essentially forgetful, and is thus in need of constant reminding. (Miller)[11]

The epistles functioned as sermons, delivered from on high and projected globally in ways that enhanced Bin Laden's charismatic stature.

His epistles to the Iraqis were elaborated with scriptural and historical citations and also with poetic verses, some from his own pen. His epistle to the Afghans flowed with cascades of Qur'anic citations as he reminded them of his struggle on their behalf against the Soviets. His letter to the Americans and Europeans,

by contrast, contained an unadorned accusation: They were blindly following leaders who were dooming them to an endless war of attrition. In every instance, he
was an antiimperial polemicist on behalf of global jihad, shaping the message to
reach the audience.

In the sermon he delivered in 2003 on the holiest day in the Islamic calendar,
Id al-Adha, he combines elements from all his letters and declarations to address
Muslims around the world. He talks to individuals directly, commending each
one's worthiness to participate in global jihad and accusing their leaders of criminal corruption. Like the first encounters that the seventh-century Arabs had with
unbelieving Persians, the current jihad pits absolute good against absolute evil.
Psychologically speaking, it is as though Bin Laden is charged with a paranoid certainty about the end time, the apocalyptic moment in which all are living but only
he and the guided warriors from Al-Qa'ida understood fully. Numerous Qur'anic
citations and prophetic traditions are woven into his fervent appeal to believers
to take up arms against the United States, Britain, Israel, and their collaborators
in the Arab world. Like the Prophet Muhammad's followers, Bin Laden's Muslim
armies will prevail. They have a recent history of victories over the superpowers.
Who was it that defeated the Soviet Union in Afghanistan and the Russians in
Chechnya if not the Afghan-Arab mujahidin? Was it not they who conquered the
Americans in Lebanon, Somalia, Aden, Riyadh, Khobar, East Africa, at home, and,
most recently, in Afghanistan? The myth of American democracy and freedom
has been shattered, thanks be to God! And then, remarkably, he concludes with his
own poem in which he vows to fight until he becomes:

> a martyr,
> dwelling in a high mountain pass
> among a band of knights who,
> united in devotion to God,
> descend to face armies.

Unfortunately, due to the dizzying shifts of technology in the Information Age,
one loses all sense of just how dramatic Bin Laden's moves as a risk taker were.
As one analyst explains:

> Bin Laden's bald comparisons between hallowed personages of early Islamic
> history and contemporary actors and events subject him to decided risks. Not
> only does he hazard alienating Muslim listeners by compromising the unique
> role that the Prophet played in Islam; he also risks becoming a poor historian,
> one whose antiquarian zeal fails to re-connect narrated events with present
> concerns. It is precisely here that Bin Laden adopts an entirely new tactic, one that
> moves him from his role as pious public lecturer to the roles of tribesman, poet,
> and ultimately cosmic warrior. In the midst of this set of transformations, the
> temporal distinctions of 'then' and 'now' become entirely blurred, and listeners
> are invited, through the most sonorous and impassioned portions of the cassette,
> to mobilize as eternal holy combatants." (Miller)

The oracle who speaks has recast himself as a cosmic warrior, auguring both the
end time and its "certain" outcome.

While Bin Laden not only mastered modern media and was also its primary beneficiary, no one should assume that Bin Laden benefited from his use of the media, in general, and Al-Jazeera, in particular, without some cost to his project. The channel of influence and of risk taking runs two ways. Bin Laden advocated the maximal response to imperialism. He constantly called on sacrifice, especially of youths through martyrdom for a greater cause, yet he gave no hint of a future frame beyond the shibboleth "Islamic state" or "rule of God on earth." The emptiness of his political vision was made clear in the Taysir Alluni interview in October 2001 (MW # 11), when he declared that jihad will continue until "we meet God and get His blessing!" Yet earlier, in the Ladenese epistle of August 1996 (MW # 3), he had seemed to call for a deferral of apocalyptic rewards, insisting on the value of oil revenues for a near term Islamic state: "I would like here to alert my brothers, the Mujahidin, the sons of the nation, to protect this (oil) wealth and not to include it in the battle as it is a great Islamic wealth and a large economical power essential for the soon to be established Islamic state, by the grace and permission of God."

Still later, in his second letter to the Iraqi people (February 11, 2003; MW #18), he called again for establishing the rule of God on Earth but only through incessant warfare against multiple enemies, with no agenda for structure or network that succeeds the current world system.

While there are many ways to connect Bin Laden to the early generation of Islam, perhaps the crucial move is to see how he contrasted the perfection of early Islam with the desecration of the twenty-first century. In the same way that former President George W. Bush saw freedom and democracy as standards of global virtue, projecting both holistic soundness and indivisible oneness for "the axis of good," so Bin Laden saw sacrifice and war as the dual emblems of early Islam that persist until today as the axis of hope for all committed Muslims who recognize the seriousness of the moment. Yet his was a hope that could never be realized under the current world order because all its denizens were living in an end time of total crisis. There was no rush to restore the caliphate nor to remake the Ottoman Empire in the pre–World War I image of a pan-Islamic Muslim polity. Instead, the ultimate criterion was "meeting God and getting his blessing." That was a deferred hope, one that could not be achieved in this world during the lifetime of Muslim martyrs but was deferred for all humankind to experience in the terrible reckoning that God Almighty has prepared.[12]

The Muslim Legacy Post-Osama Bin Laden

The great unaccounted for in the scenario of Osama Bin Laden are those Muslims who still consider themselves custodians of the faith and followers of the Prophet yet do not see perpetual warfare in the name of jihad as the only measure of Islamic loyalty. Instead of opposing perfections, they try to see the will of God in this age through different instruments, affirming the current world order, at once trying to maximize its benefits while curbing its excesses. They need more than scriptural dictates, poetic balm, or binary shibboleths to chart their everyday life, whether as individuals or as collective members of local communities, nation-states, and the world at large. For them, Bin Laden's legacy, especially in the aftermath of his death and with seeds of hope sprouting from the Arab Spring (January–June 2011), is one of deviance and damage rather than persistence and profit in the cause of Islam. The world is not coming to an end, and other means have to be found to advance Islamic principles and the well-being of the Muslim community (ummah).

For pragmatists, Muslim as well as non-Muslim, the real work is to prepare for an eventuality beyond the diatribes of apocalyptic doomsayers. It is not easy but it is the only way forward, and if God wills, it may yet augur the next chapter in Islam beyond violence, mirroring the first phase of the life of the Prophet Muhammad as also the consistent intent of the full panoply of divine directives mandated in the Holy Qur'an and pursued through the major epochs of Muslim history.

NOTES

1. Unless otherwise noted, all the Qur'anic verses quoted here and subsequently derive from or are adapted from Thomas Cleary, *The Qur'an—A New Translation* (Starlatch, 2004).
2. Suleiman Mourad in an e-mail dated September 23, 2003. Elsewhere in an April 15, 2011, interview (http://www.smith.edu/insight/stories/jihad.php, Professor Mourad, who is co-authoring a book titled *The Radicalization of Sunni Jihad Ideology in the Crusader Period* (to be published by Ashgate Press), observed that: "Jihad is not what the Prophet initiated but what a scholar in 12th-century Damascus (Ibn Asakir)was paid by his political patron to promote and disseminate."
3. In the analysis that follows, I have benefited from the seminal work of Marshall G. S. Hodgson, *The Venture of Islam: Conscience and History in a World Civilization* (Chicago: University of Chicago Press, 1974), volume 3: The Gunpowder Empires and Modern Times, as also the more recent, by Stephen F. Dale, *The Muslim Empires of the Ottomans, Safavids, and Mughals* (Cambridge, UK: Cambridge University Press, 2010), but neither Dale nor Hodgson is responsible for my inferences about the interconnection between Islam and violence during the long span of these premodern Muslim empires.
4. For the elaboration of this concept among Ottoman ruling elites, see Cornell Fleischer, "Royal Authority, Dynastic Cyclism, and 'Ibn Khaldunism'" in Bruce B. Lawrence, ed. *Ibn Khaldun and Islamic Ideology* (Leiden, Netherlands: E. J. Brill, 1984): 48–51
5. The issue of Muslim responses to European colonial presence in Afro-Eurasia has been explored in Bruce B. Lawrence, *Shattering the Myth: Islam beyond Violence* (Princeton, NJ: Princeton University Press, 1998), and in what follows, I have relied on the analysis provided in chapter 2 "Islamic Revivalism: Anti-Colonial Revolt," especially pp. 41–52.
6. On the debate between Islamic fundamentalism and Islamism as analytical categories, see Richard C. Martin and Abbas Barzegar, eds., *Islamism: Contested Perspectives on Political Islam* (Palo Alto CA: Stanford University Press, 2010). My essay, "Islam at Risk: The Discourse on Islam and Violence" (93–98), challenges assumptions behind the more recent terms, *post-Islamism* and *neofundamentalism*, especially as deployed by Olivier Roy (98).

7. Youssef M. Choueiri, *Islamic Fundamentalism* (Boston: Twayne, 1990): 35. I am indebted to Choueiri for his clear exposition of Islamic fundamentalism, but I demur from his use of "radicalism" to refer to the last or most recent phase of Islamic protest. The term *radical,* unlike *revivalism* and *reformism,* has no positive referent. It presupposes some other norm, and in my view, that norm is a strict religious code or sense of inalterable, all-encompassing fundamentals, thus my use of *fundamentalism* in preference to *radicalism* to denote the last and most significant phase of Islamic protest.

8. Much of the material that follows comes from the final section of my article "Osama bin Laden—The Man and the Myth," in Charles B. Strozier, ed. *The Leader: Psychohistorical Essays,* 2nd edition (New York: Springer, 2011): 119-134.

9. See the (too) brief reference to Al-Sahab in Hugh Miles, *Al-Jazeera: How Arab TV News Challenged the World* (London: Abacus, 2005): 180. Other sources are equally dismissive or neglectful of this crucial conduit to the Osama bin Laden media strategy.

10. Osama Bin Laden, "A Muslim Bomb" in Bruce Lawrence ed. *Messages to the World—The Statements of Osama bin Laden* (London and New York: Verso 2005): 65-94.

11. W. Flagg Miller, "On 'The Summit of the Hindu Kush': Osama Bin Laden's 1996 Declaration of War Reconsidered," unpublished talk delivered at the University of Michigan in March 2005, cited here by permission of the author.

12. The notion that apocalypse as end of the world appeals to other contemporary Muslim audiences is also reflected and documented in Jean-Pierre Filiu, *Apocalypse in Islam* (Berkeley: University of California Press, 2011). His monograph also provides apt and striking parallels to Christian apocalyptic thoughts, movements and leaders.

BIBLIOGRAPHY

Burke, Jason. *Al-Qaeda: The True Story of Radical Islam.* London: Penguin, 2004.

Choueiri, Youssef M. *Islamic Fundamentalism.* Boston: Twayne, 1990.

Cleary, Thomas. *The Qur'an—A New Translation.* Burlington, VT: Starlatch, 2004.

Dale, Stephen F. *The Muslim Empires of the Ottomans, Safavids, and Mughals.* Cambridge, UK: Cambridge University Press, 2010.

Donner, Fred McGraw. *The Early Islamic Conquests.* Princeton, NJ: Princeton University Press, 1981.

Filiu, Jean-Pierre. *Apocalypse in Islam.* Berkeley: University of California Press, 2011.

Fleischer, Cornell. "Royal Authority, Dynastic Cyclism, and 'Ibn Khaldunism.'" In *Ibn Khaldun and Islamic Ideology.* Edited by Bruce Lawrence, 198–220. Leiden, Netherlands: E. J. Brill, 1984.

Hillenbrand, Carole. *The Crusades—Islamic Perspectives.* Edinburgh: Edinburgh University Press, 1999.

Hodgson, Marshall G. S. *The Venture of Islam: Conscience and History in a World Civilization.* Chicago: University of Chicago Press, 1974.

Kippenberg, Hans G. *Violence as Worship: Religious Wars in the Age of Globalisation.* Palo Alto, CA: Stanford University Press, 2011.

Lawrence, Bruce. *Shattering the Myth: Islam beyond Violence.* Princeton, NJ: Princeton University Press, 1998.

Lawrence, Bruce. *Messages to the World—The Statements of Osama bin Laden.* London and New York: Verso, 2005.

Lawrence, Bruce. *The Qur'an—A Biography.* New York: Atlantic Books, 2007.

Lawrence, Bruce. "Osama bin Laden—The Man and the Myth." In *The Leader: Psychohistorical Essays.* Edited by Charles B. Strozier, 2nd edition, 119–134. New York: Springer, 2011.

Martin, Richard C. and Abbas Barzegar, eds. *Islamism: Contested Perspectives on Political Islam*. Palo Alto, CA: Stanford University Press, 2010.

Miles, Hugh. *Al-Jazeera: How Arab TV News Challenged the World*. London: Abacus, 2005.

Mourad, Suleiman, with James E. Lindsay. *The Radicalization of Sunni Jihad Ideology in the Crusader Period*. Aldershot, UK: Ashgate, 2011.

CHAPTER 7

AFRICAN TRADITIONAL RELIGION AND VIOLENCE

NATHALIE WLODARCZYK

IN Africa, the religious beliefs and practices that predated the arrival of Christianity or Islam existed as oral traditions. When, as a result of the slave trade, some of these beliefs were exported to the Americas, they were equated with the savage traditions of the African slaves—more carnal and bloodied than the sanitized religious beliefs of the slave traders and owners. On the plantations in the Americas, the beliefs became associated with the wild, uncontrollable, and angry African population. On the African continent, Christian and Muslim missionaries also sought to counter the indigenous beliefs of the tribes and communities they came across to bring them what they saw as both salvation and civilization. This view of African traditional religions as something savage and brutal has retained currency and is regularly reflected in writings on Africa. In particular, attempts to explain and understand the brutality of civil wars since the end of colonialism have been peppered with references to traditional practices as an illustration of an apparent return to a savage past.

In reality, African Traditional Religion is no more or less of an ancient or modern tradition than other religions. The cosmologies predate colonialism by centuries, but over the years they have come to incorporate aspects of the various cultures and other religions on the continent. The ability to adapt to changing realities without being subsumed has been the strength of African Traditional Religion, a strength in large part derived from the same lack of central doctrine and hierarchy that has given it an appearance of insignificance. The peoples who subscribe to the traditional religious beliefs find in it not only answers to most practical and esoteric questions but also a means of drawing directly on the spirit world to affect events in the material world. Perhaps unsurprisingly these means have been drawn on repeatedly and regularly, both to promote peace and healing and to provide strength and power to ensure victory in conflict.

WHAT IS AFRICAN TRADITIONAL RELIGION?

The vast majority of people who subscribe to traditional African religious beliefs reside on the African continent. In areas of the world with large African diasporas such as Britain, France, and the United States, some of these beliefs have accompanied the migrant communities. When Africans first began to leave the continent in large numbers, under duress during the slave trade, some of these beliefs were also brought to the Caribbean and South America where they blended with local religions to form the Vodun, Santería, and Obeah of today. Nonetheless, African Traditional Religion remains primarily an African phenomenon, and as a result, it is tightly connected to the cultures and realities of the continent. To talk of African religion is, therefore, to a large extent to talk of religion in Africa.

Common Themes

African Traditional Religion is the set of beliefs that originated on the African continent before the introduction of Christianity, Islam, or other religions from further afield. It is a repository of oral traditions without a single founder or central sacred text but, nonetheless, with a striking number of coherent themes across this vast continent. As opposed to variants of Christianity and Islam, the common themes of African religion are not so much enshrined in doctrine or even narrative but rather in non-text-based, yet shared approaches to the nature of power and to man's and the world's relationship to it. While the many peoples of Africa have their own deities and spirits as well as their own rituals and celebrations, their traditional belief systems share some core features. This means that individual societies and even communities will have their own names for spirits and deities and their own myths recalling the characters and adventures of these beings. It is rare that they translate exactly from one place to another. However, while the Yoruba in Nigeria refer to their spirits as *Orisha* and individual spirits such as Eshu, Yemaya, and Ologun have their own distinct personalities and abilities, they nonetheless share traits with the djinns of East Africa, the spirits of northern Uganda (referred to as *Jok*) and the spirits of Sierra Leone (commonly called "devils").

Some have referred to African traditional religion as simultaneously monotheistic and polytheistic (Lugira 2009). There is almost always a supreme being, usually the creator of the universe and all life, unrivaled by a multitude of nonetheless powerful lesser gods and spirits. However, while the supreme being holds the greatest power, it is also the furthest removed from daily human life. Although creation stories differ across the continent, a large number share the idea that the supreme being retreated from the earth as a result of human action. In some cases it is said that humanity became too demanding of the supreme being and retreat was the only way to find peace and quiet from the incessant demands of humans. In others, the aggressive and disobedient behavior of man is said to have led the supreme being to turn away and deny them his presence (Parinder, 1969). In contrast, the lesser gods and, even lower down the ranks, spirits tend to be both approachable and actively engaged in human affairs. Ancestors also play a significant role in most African religious traditions, usually as mediators who both guide their descendants from their new spiritual state—achieved through death—and intercede with nonhuman spirits and gods on their descendants' behalf.

The spirit world permeates the material world, and culture has become closely entwined with religion. Local cultures in Africa are often defined to a significant degree by the history of its people and heroes, many of whom have assumed places in the spirit world since their passing and whose history while walking the earth was shaped by the intervention of spirits. All events in the material world are assumed to be the cause of dealings in the spirit world, although these dealings could well have been instigated by people rather than the spirits themselves. As a result, everyday life becomes a spiritual affair, in which appeasing or beseeching ancestors, spirits, or deities is the key means of ensuring life progresses as planned. This appeal to the spirits is made more challenging by the fact that spirits and even the gods are assumed to be largely morally neutral. Their power can be used for positive or negative—constructive or destructive—purposes. This places significant onus on adherents to engage proactively with the spirit world to ensure they get the desired result.

The spirit world can be reached through spiritual practitioners, of which there are a number. Each culture has its own names for its spiritual practitioners and their functions vary somewhat, but most of them include versions of priests, spirit mediums, diviners, healers and witch doctors, and witches. Priests, or the acknowledged local authority on religious practice, usually officiate significant rituals and offer guidance on spiritual matters and practice to community members. Priests often double as mediums, healers, or diviners. Spirit mediums can effect possession by one or several spirits and allow people to communicate with "their" spirits in this manner. They also often offer consultations with individuals' spirits when they speak directly to the spirits without possession. Diviners use craft to consult with spirits or to find answers to specific questions, about the past, present, or future. Healers or witch doctors offer a mixture of medical craft and spirit access to heal illness and often also to counter the activities of witches or the destructive practices of spirits or other spiritual practitioners. The witch doctors along with witches also tend to be the ones able to compel spirits to do their bidding through their craft. Often the main distinction made by people between witches and witch doctors is simply the nature of the end to which they are using their craft—constructive use that is deemed good for the community is condoned, whereas destructive use that lets an individual benefit at the expense of another is not. But witches are a more elusive group and one that is defined mostly by their enemies rather than an identity they have claimed for themselves. In most societies, bad things are blamed on the activity of witches who are assumed to be consciously looking to upset the peace in their communities. They are generally thought to be born with their spiritual power, which can put them under the control of spirits with a bent for destruction. For this same reason, they often become the scapegoats for unwanted developments and events, and rarely do the accused witches own up to the activities of which they are accused.

The proactive nature of African traditional religion has allowed it to blend relatively easily with imported religions. Whereas Christianity or Islam are seen as concerned primarily with the afterlife—ensuring one's place in heaven—traditional religion offers a means of affecting life on a daily basis through the local spirits. Even though both Christian and Muslim authorities oppose this syncretism, it nonetheless remains a reality across Africa. In West Africa, the *mori* men and marabouts blend Islamic mysticism with local traditions to offer spiritual services to the local communities. The arrival of marabouts and Islam to an area with predominantly traditional beliefs has not tended to discourage beliefs in the power of charms; rather, the traditional forms of divining were replaced by new ones based on the Quran (Bledsoe and Robey 1986: 209). Similarly, as Christianity spread with missionaries across central and southern Africa, particularly in the nineteenth and twentieth centuries, traditional practice was incorporated in church worship using the same types of songs and dance to offer prayer as had been used to communicate with indigenous gods and ancestors.[1] Spirit possession traditions have since found new expression in Christian movements that emphasize communion with the Holy Spirit and, in the other direction, some traditional cults now use the Bible for divination.

African Traditional Religion is in many ways highly practical. The endgame is more often the immediate impact on daily life than eternal salvation. The relationship between humanity and the supernatural is in some ways more equal than in religions such as Christianity or Islam, in the sense that practitioners do not have to settle for requesting assistance from spirits and gods—if they are good at their craft they have a chance of compelling them to intervene. However in most traditional religion on the continent, this ability to force the spirits' hands also opens up for potential trickery by spirits that resent being used for human purposes. As a result, most rituals are a bargaining process. While practitioners are attempting to convince a spirit to do their will, they offer incentives to do so, usually through sacrifice but also through the maintenance of taboos or prohibited behavior.

POWER

The notion of power lies at the heart of the cosmology. In many ways, life is conceived of as a constant struggle for and balancing of power—between good and bad spirits, individuals in a family, community and state. Power is seen as something that is generally ambivalent and ambiguous. The power source and the use to which it is put can therefore be alternately positive or negative depending on the intent of the practitioner. The same power that can be used to inflict harm on an opponent can also be used to heal an ailment. This ambiguity extends further to turn what appears to be straightforward dichotomies of outcomes on their head. For example, the use of spirit power (*ashe*) to help an ambitious person enhance his or her position can be seen by the wider community as constructive if the person is thought to benefit the community, while the same power can also be used to curb people who are thought to be overly ambitious and disruptive to community good (Geschiere 1997). In a similar manner, the healing provided by spirits in northern Uganda included an act of retaliation against the aggressor that had caused the suffering in the first place, which could lead to his or her death (Behrend 1999). This ambiguity makes the use of spirit power a malleable tool for addressing personal and communal concerns, although it also creates ample room for challenges by people with a different view of what constitutes a destructive or constructive agenda.

Power is both spiritual and material and often explicitly so. Spiritual power is assumed to lead to material power—political influence and wealth. In some cultures, this link is made even more explicit in that the spiritually powerful are assumed to have a physical substance in their body that houses the spiritual power.[2] This has led to idioms of "power being eaten" across the continent. It is also reflected in the many rituals that involve the ingestion of herbs and potions or carrying them in pouches and amulets. In wartime, this same imagery has been taken to an extreme in human sacrifice and cannibalism. Overall, spirit power is assumed to permeate the material world, which makes this world both something to be wary of and something that can be used in interactions with the spirits.

The intimate connection between material and spiritual power has meant that those in positions of power are assumed to have gained these positions at least in part through spiritual prowess—whether traditional, Christian, or Muslim. Poor leadership and good leadership alike are explained with reference to the way the leaders have used their spiritual power. This does not mean that natural explanations—whether scientific or social—are discarded altogether, but they are placed in the context of the invisible world of spiritual power. Spirit power is assumed to give the impetus for worldly activity. For example, many would recognize that HIV/AIDS is caused by a virus but would point to the spirit world to explain why a certain person was infected at a certain time (Stadler, 2003). This understanding of causation also opens up for redress—if the underlying cause can be identified it can be addressed to revert the outcome.

Most societies in African use rituals to mark significant transitions in life as well as to effect change. For the former, rituals tend to accompany the transition from childhood to adulthood, marriage, births, and death. For the latter, rituals offer a means of inciting change of a particular kind, for example, to heal ailment or to ensure prosperity or wealth. Almost all rituals are physically tangible and involve the administering of potions, herbal remedies, or amulets alongside incantations, dancing, and prayers in various combinations. Some of these involve a sacrifice to thank, reward, or entreat the invisible world of spirits to intervene in the desired manner.

African Traditional Religion as a Driver of Violence

When looking at the role of religion in violence there are two main dimensions—the role of religion in inciting violence and its role in carrying out the violence.

Witchcraft and Witchcraft Accusations

Witchcraft is at the heart of most violence that can be said to be incited by African Traditional Religion. Accusations of witchcraft have become more common in conflict or postconflict countries in Africa where the strain of poverty and rebuilding lives and livelihoods shattered by war is most pronounced. Children, elderly people, and widows and widowers with no family left to protect them are often the most vulnerable to accusations of witchcraft. To the communities that accuse them, they offer an answer to why life is not improving despite the end of war. Although the accusations in recent years have tended to be led by revivalist Christian churches, for example, in the Democratic Republic of Congo and Angola, the belief and concept of a witch that they use is firmly traditional. Accusations leveled at children have attracted particular attention because of the often violent implications. The children are accused of knowingly and maliciously bringing harm to the community. But while the accusation is no dramatic departure from other settings, the means of redress through the new churches has tended to be much more violent than in most traditional religious contexts. In the new churches, exorcisms of the child witches often involve severe beatings and starvation and sometimes lead to the death of the child. Although adults are often more able to defend themselves, the administering of mob justice often involved in witchcraft cases can leave them equally vulnerable. In some instances, witches are simply executed by their accusers. An older woman in Tema, Ghana, was set on fire by a group of people accusing her of witchcraft, one of which was a pastor (BBC 2010). Incidents like this are becoming increasingly commonplace across sub-Saharan Africa. In contrast, "exorcisms" by traditional witch doctors or priests are often focused on ritual cleansing with a view to reintegrate the witch into the community. Of course, in many cases accused witches face mob justice when neither traditional nor church approaches to dealing with witchcraft are necessarily adhered to, often with even graver implications for the accused.

Whereas witch accusations are ultimately aimed at undoing the destructive magic caused by the suspected witchcraft, the power of witch doctors that is intended to provide this service sometimes requires destruction as well. Some of the medications and potions witch doctors provide require human body parts—some of which leave the donor dead. In smaller villages and communities, this type of magic and medicine has generally been tightly controlled but in the growing urban sprawls of many African countries today the relative ease of abducting victims for this purpose has led to an upswing in both supply and demand for this powerful magic. Although it is far from condoned by most practitioners of African Traditional Religion, most would nonetheless acknowledge the power of such medicines. This power, as much as the required death, is the reason these medicines are taboo, as their use is assumed to upset power balances dramatically.

War

Unlike some of the other world religions, however, African Traditional Religion has rarely been the cause (real or proclaimed) of wars. Because of the lack of central doctrine and, therefore, hierarchy and institutions, it has never become the powerful tool for state conquest that Christianity or Islam have become. Although traditional religious explanations for misfortune have helped legitimize the cause of many insurgent groups and aided their recruitment, this has tended to be on a smaller scale than state-sponsored warfare. In part, this is because of the cultural disconnect between most African states at a central level and the local authority structures within them—both during and after colonialism. The powerful African empires that reigned in East and West Africa prior to the arrival of colonizers from outside of course faced a different reality. Interestingly, however, the greatest of these empires (in reach and power) built their successes partly on their adoption of Christianity or Islam. In Ethiopia, the Aksumite Empire, while polytheistic, shared more religious traits with its neighbors on the Arabian Peninsula than those farther west and south, and its early adoption of Christianity became a core component of the identity of the empire as it spread across the Horn. The Malian Empire spread Islam through the Sahel region from the thirteenth through sixteenth centuries as rulers and traders gained access to the privileges associated with sharing the quickly spreading religion. Later, the Songhai Empire continued this tradition, also firmly grounded in Islam. Their wars of conquest were a combination of holy war to spread the faith and the extension of geographical power to support trade and the generation of wealth.

However, among the smaller empires and kingdoms, war was not imperial in outlook and rulers rarely sought to spread their power and influence far across the continent. Most wars were to settle grudges and disputes with neighboring kingdoms, to secure wealth through loot, or to avert threats from neighbors with similar ambitions. In the postcolonial period, these kingdoms had lost their power almost all across the continent, and the power to wage war had been limited to central governments or insurgent opposition. The secular ideologies that accompanied postcolonial governments made religious beliefs—whether traditional or otherwise—an awkward reference point, even for those that launched wars. However, in many cases, the reality beneath the secular surface was filled with traditional religious belief and practice. This can be seen most clearly in the civil wars that have afflicted the continent since colonialism but is also reflected in the approach taken for protection from crime in many African cities or even in domestic disputes.

Explaining misfortune is a key function served by African Traditional Religion. It is therefore only natural that political, economic, or social grievances will be related back to the spiritual world and that redress will be sought in part from it. In Zimbabwe, during the civil war in the 1970s, the rebel Zimbabwe African National Liberation Army (ZANLA) quickly learned that the way to gain the support of local populations was not to reference a secular socialist agenda but to present the group's cause with reference to local cosmology. When members entered Zimbabwe and sought to recruit from local communities, they were told to consult with the spirit mediums who would guide their strategy and whose blessing would give them access to prospective fighters (Lan 1985). The mediums accepted the insurgents, in part, because their struggle against the Rhodesian government resonated with local resentment of the collapse of traditional land rights and hierarchies but also because they fit within the local spiritual order: Some of the most prominent local ancestral spirits were warriors, and the newly arrived rebels could be given the authority of these spirits. This authority had previously been held by traditional chiefs, but as the chiefs became increasingly entangled with the Rhodesian state, the spirit mediums took over their authority in the eyes of many. As a result, when the war came, they were the ones able to bestow legitimacy on a cause. The mediums that represented the spirits of deceased chiefs (*mhondoro*) represented the authority and legitimacy of the respected chiefs of the past. This legitimacy they passed on to ZANLA guerrillas by naming them the successors of the mhondoro. With the aid of the mediums, the ZANLA fighters were therefore able to hold recruitment rallies at which they could explain their ideology and cause to local youth and bring them within their ranks.

By the time the insurgency of the Resistência Nacional Moçambicana (Renamo) was launched in Mozambique in the early 1990s, the traditional religions were the most potent in the country. Like ZANLA in Zimbabwe, Renamo therefore appealed to potential recruits on the basis of traditional religious beliefs. They denounced the government for suppressing traditional practitioners such as the *feiticeiros* (spirit mediums) and *curandeiros* (traditional healers) and blamed the drought of the early 1980s on the government's alienation of the ancestors. They explicitly said their struggle was "of the spirits" and "for the ancestors" (Weigert, 1995).

Similarly, in Uganda, the brief insurgency launched against the government of Yoweri Museveni in 1986 drew support from the Acholi population in northern Uganda by pointing to the need for a spiritual cleansing of the land to restore local peace and prosperity. The Holy Spirit Movement (HSM) and its armed wing the Holy Spirit Mobile Force (HSMF) blamed the social upheaval in the north on the sins committed by Acholi soldiers during the previous civil war (between the National Resistance Movement [NRA] and the Uganda National Liberation Army [UNLA] in 1981–1986), when they had been involved in killing civilians in the Luwero area farther south. When the soldiers returned home they failed to respect local traditions of cleansing following war, and as a result, the community was thought to be haunted by the vengeful spirits of the dead.[3] Alice Auma, a local Acholi spirit medium who channelled the spirit Lakwena (more commonly known as Alice Lakwena), organized the HSMF to wage war against the government and witches to redress the misfortunes brought on by this sin. Her rhetoric built on the spiritual tradition in northern Uganda that recognized spirits as responsible for misfortune and catastrophe but also as a power against disaster—a tradition echoed across the continent. It was a spiritual matter in need of spiritual remedy. For a population that had interpreted its misfortunes as a manifestation of witchcraft and mischievous spirits for some time, this rallying call engendered significant support (Behrend 1999).[4] However, while the HSMF came a long way on the power of their rhetoric alone (they marched almost all the way to the capital, Kampala, before being defeated), they had failed to combine their powerful cause with sufficient military capability—something subsequent rebel groups in northern Uganda tried hard to remedy. The most recent, the Lord's Resistance Army (LRA), that also claims spiritual legitimacy, has been the most long lived after more than twenty years of fighting. The LRA have shown that a spiritual agenda and rhetoric are not enough to win the support of a people. Their inability to win the support of key local leaders forced them to adopt a recruitment strategy reliant on abduction, which further alienated them from the community they claimed to be fighting for. As a result, they have come to be seen as using spiritual power for destructive rather than constructive purposes, just like the shunned but feared witches of most African societies.

AFRICAN TRADITIONAL RELIGION AS A COMPONENT OF VIOLENCE

The proactive nature of access to spirit power in African Traditional Religion makes it eminently suitable for people looking to enhance their ability to compel others forcefully, whether in outright warfare or other types of violence.

It offers a resource that can enhance power and strength with some immediacy. In contrast to religions that require long periods of prayer or even a lifetime of service to achieve rewards, African Traditional Religion generally offer the option of turning to a spiritual practitioner to gain access to spirit power, often as part of a simple financial transaction. This option has been exercised in almost all wars the continent has seen, and transactions to gain spiritual power regularly turn up also in smaller-scale violence, whether as part of criminal activity or political confrontations. The at times violent nature of rituals also means violence is visited on victims who fall prey to some spiritual practitioners. This has perhaps been most visibly illustrated by the high-profile cases of ritual killings of children in southern Africa but also beyond African shores in the United Kingdom.

As in any transaction, the more valuable the service or commodity is, the higher the price. Higher stakes, for example, amassing great wealth or winning political office, require more difficult and expensive rituals but often also costlier sacrifice. This has fueled trade in parts of rare animals as well as humans. While some animal and human body parts are widely acknowledged as being powerful ingredients for magic—notably hearts and livers but also bones and reproductive organs—others become sought after as a result of more short-lived trends. For example, in recent years, albinos in Tanzania and Kenya have been targeted for their body parts, especially their pale skin, believed to bring luck and offer potent ingredients for healers and witch doctors.

Yet while the powerful nature of human sacrifice is hardly ever in doubt in African Traditional Religion, it is equally widely acknowledged as a destructive form of spiritual practice and rarely condoned. Nonetheless, the market exists and especially in urban sprawls where the poor and vulnerable often go missing, the trade in human body parts is a reality. Some of these practices have been exported along with diaspora communities—initially with the slave trade to the Caribbean and more recently to Europe and North America. In Europe, the discovery of the torso of a young boy in London in 2001 shocked a community that believed ritual sacrifice had not been exported out of Africa.

The vast majority of sacrificial rituals, however, do not require human or even blood sacrifice. Nonetheless, the idea of the potency of blood rituals has fueled violent manifestations of traditional belief in conflict situations. Particularly during war when social control is loosened, the stakes are high and then the pursuit of power unchecked. But blood ritual also emerges in times of acute community distress or in the pursuit of great power and wealth.

In warfare, traditional religious practice offers a means of enhancing powers to fight, survive, and win. The practical nature of the belief system allows fighting parties to request specific types of power and protection from their priests and other spiritual practitioners, not unlike the requirements for designing offensive and defensive weapons.

Most commonly, fighters are offered protection from enemy fire and attack. This protection usually comes in the form of charms, amulets, and potions alongside behavioral rules and taboos that must be upheld. What has been given can therefore be taken away, which provides a strong incentive for fighters to uphold rules and maintain discipline.

Images of fighters covered in amulets and charms became prolific with the African civil wars of the 1980s and 1990s but are a reflection of a much longer tradition. It draws on a long tradition of warrior heroes and sacred warriors, which is part of the oral mythology of most African peoples and therefore a given point of reference for fighters. For example, the Malian warrior king Sundiata Keita (alternatively known as Sunjata) who founded the Malian Empire in the thirteenth century is also the central character of an epic that describes his rise to power through the assistance of spiritual power and objects, including a staff made from a sacred tree that allows the hunchbacked child Sundiata to stand up straight and walk (Janson 2001). Among the Dinka in southern Sudan, Aiwel Longar was the son of a water spirit and a human woman and through his power protected his warriors and founded the spear master tradition that still lives among the Dinka. In West Africa, the tradition of hunting societies in which the hunters drew on spiritual power to trap and kill animals in peacetime and enemies in times of war have become prototypes for more recent fighting groups. The Civil Defence Forces that emerged to counter the threat from rebels during the Sierra Leone civil war drew their imagery, identity, and practices from their traditional hunting societies. The traditional image of the hunter was of a man imbued with magic that allowed him to track and kill animals in the wild while surviving the tribulations of the forest. Because of their powers, these hunters were also the guardians of their communities who would return to protect their villages when external threats arose, cementing their identity as a hunter-warrior. When war broke out in 1991 and the government proved unable to counter the threat of the rebels, this tradition was reinvented to create a fighting force whose main purpose was to protect communities. Although these civil defence forces were a far cry from the hunter-warriors of local mythology they drew on the same spiritual traditions, albeit adapted to fit the challenges of the contemporary war (Wlodarczyk 2009). In a similar manner, LRA rebels in northern Uganda also drew on old traditions of ritualistic protection against death and injury to form part of their armor. The idea that warriors can be protected from death and injury through rituals and the application or ingestion of magical substances surfaces again throughout the continent, both in historical accounts of war and in contemporary conflicts.

The ways in which protective magic has been used in the wars of the last twenty years is not necessarily the same as they would have been a century ago. As political and traditional power structures have been renegotiated—some violently and some not—first in the colonial and then the postcolonial period, traditions have also changed. In wars in which the challenge of traditional authority lay at the heart of the conflict, this meant the rituals and spiritual means employed to fight the war also had to be reinvented to fit the agenda of the fighters. For example, in Sierra Leone, the Revolutionary United Front (RUF) rebels that took on the government in 1991 in what would be a decade long war explicitly opposed the power hierarchies of the existing elites as well as the traditional deference to elders. The youth that made up the bulk of the rebel force sought to overturn this order and therefore would have struggled to rely on the very beliefs and practices that represented that order. Nonetheless, whereas they may not have believed in the political system or even some of the rituals and practices of their communities, they believed in the power of the invisible spirit world. The result was a syncretic blend of new, secular rituals that echoed the old spiritual ones and an ambivalent attitude toward the potency of spirit power. In most Sierra Leonean communities outside the capital, initiation into traditional secret societies provides the transition from childhood to adulthood, usually through a time of seclusion in the forest along with other initiates and shared trials—physical and psychological—alongside teachings about the responsibilities and realities of being an adult. Initiation is steeped in ritual and presided over by those with spiritual power. The RUF, opposed to the hierarchies of the secret societies, nonetheless ended up closely mimicking the process of initiation for their own recruits to mark the transition from civilian to fighter. They secluded new recruits from the group and made them go through ritualistic trials and hardship as well as listen to preaching on the rebel cause (Richards 2006). Similarly, they derided the power of priests and witch doctors while at the same time claiming that their own leader possessed the ability to fly and to gather intelligence through the air across vast distances. This reflects the deeply engrained belief in an invisible and powerful spirit world, even among those who look to counter or reject parts of it.

In the same way, the Frelimo government forces in Mozambique ridiculed the Renamo reliance on witch doctors to enhance the power of their fighters but ended up employing the same tactics as the war dragged on and Renamo proved both persistent and powerful. In one instance, Frelimo managed to capture an important pro-Renamo medium and displayed him around a government-held town as a morale booster. They also described the capture of the medium as the result of spiritual might—a Frelimo soldier had supposedly gone into a Renamo camp protected by magic that allowed him to abduct the medium unseen (Wilson 1992; West 1997).

The attraction of incorporating spiritual practice in warfare is twofold. In a context in which belief in the existence of supernatural power is almost always a given, attempting to access that power in times of need is a logical choice. The fact that this belief is shared, usually across enemy lines, also makes it a powerful signal to the enemy, especially through the visible display of amulets and charms but also through the spreading of rumors. For example, Renamo would tell battle stories that interpreted the group's successes through a spiritual lens, which both raised the spirits of their own troops and intimidated Frelimo fighters.

Conclusion

African traditional religious practice is as much a reflection of the social dynamics in a given country or community as it is a frame of reference and source of power for the members of that community. The beliefs offer a means of engaging with the world that has the added edge of spirit power. But the ends to which it is directed is usually dictated by the concerns of the material world. This has made it at times a violent practice and at others a promoter of peace. Perhaps more so than other religions, African traditional beliefs put the onus of morality primarily on the practitioner. It provides the tools for shaping the world without clear moral guidelines for their appropriate use. Of course as in most communities, these guidelines have also emerged but not always as a direct result of religious authority.

A proliferation of news stories and images from across Africa of persecuted albino communities, victims of ritual sacrifice, or magically empowered rebels might give the impression that traditional religion and violence are more intertwined than ever. While the religion has not become more violent or changed in scope, social pressures and circumstances have pushed forward the more extreme features of the belief system. As the challenges become greater—whether as a result of political upheaval, poverty, or disease—the means for overcoming them also become more severe.

NOTES

1. This is still the case with many "Zionist" churches in southern Africa, for example, the Marange church in Zimbabwe or the Harris churches in Côte d'Ivoire.
2. This belief exists in communities across the continent and has been documented by Peter Geschiere in Cameroon, Evans-Pritchard among the Azande in Ghana, Joseph Tonda in Gabon and the Republic of Congo among many others. In each setting, this "witch substance" is referred to by a different name—*djambe* among the Maka in Cameroon, *mangu* among the Azande, and *ikundu* among the Mbochi in Congo—but is always understood as a physical substance that gives its host power.
3. Luwero is the area in the south where some of the worst atrocities were committed during the war between the UNLA that dislodged Idi Amin in 1979 and the NRA of Yoweri Museveni that took power in 1985, the perpetration of which was associated with the Acholi because of their prominent presence in the UNLA.
4. In this case, witchcraft was seen as the destructive practices inspired by bad spirits, and increasingly polarized by the Christian framework that was used by the HSM.

BIBLIOGRAPHY

Behrend, Heike. "Power to Heal, Power to Kill, Spirit Possession and War in Northern Uganda." In H. Behrend and U. Luig (eds.), *Spirit Possession: Modernity and Power in Africa*, 20–33. Oxford, UK: James Currey, 1999.

Bledsoe, C. H. and K. M. Robey. "Arabic Literacy and Secrecy among the Mende of Sierra Leone." *Man*, new series, 21.2 (June 1986): 202–226.

Geschiere, Peter. *The Modernity of Witchcraft: Politics and the Occult in Postcolonial Africa*. Charlottesville: University Press of Virginia, 1997.

Janson, Jan. "The Sunjata Epic—The Ultimate Version." *Research in African Literatures*, 32.1 (Spring 2001): 14–46.

Lan, David. *Guns and Rain: Guerillas and Spirit Mediums in Zimbabwe*. London: James Currey, 1985.

Lugira, Aloysius. *African Traditional Religion*. New York: Chelsea House, 2009.

Parinder, Geoffrey. *African Mythology*. London: Paul Hamlyn, 1969.

Richards, Paul. "The Emotions at War: Atrocity as Piacular Rite in Sierra Leone." In A. Treacher, et al. (eds.), *Public Emotions*, 62–84. London: Palgrave Macmillan, 2006.

"Shock in Ghana over Gruesome Death of 'Witch.'" *BBC News*, 26 November 2010 (http://www.bbc.co.uk/news/world-africa-11848536).

Stadler, Jonathan. "Rumor, Gossip and Blame: Implications for HIV/AIDS Prevention in the South African Lowveld." *AIDS Education and Prevention*, 15.4 (2003): 357–368.

Tonda, Joseph. *Le Souverain moderne. Le corps du pouvoir en Afrique Centrale (Congo, Gabon)*. Paris: Karthala, 2005.

Weigert, Stephen. *Traditional Religion and Guerrilla Warfare in Modern Africa*. London: Macmillan, 1995.

West, Harry G. "Creative Destruction and Sorcery of Construction: Power, Hope and Suspicion in Post-War Mozambique." *Cahiers d'études Africaines*, XXXVIII, 147.3 (1997): 675–698.

Wilson, K. B. "Cults of Violence and Counter-Violence in Mozambique." *Journal of Southern African Studies*, 18.3 (1992): 527–582.

Wlodarczyk, Nathalie. *Magic and Warfare: Appearance and Reality in Contemporary African Conflict and Beyond*. New York: Palgrave, 2009.

CHAPTER 8

....

RELIGION AND VIOLENCE IN PACIFIC ISLAND SOCIETIES

....

ANDREW STRATHERN AND
PAMELA J. STEWART

THE Pacific overall is a broad region, encompassing many historical and cultural variations, reflecting waves of prehistoric migrations and vicissitudes of colonial and postcolonial experience. Polynesia, Micronesia, and many parts of what has conventionally been called Melanesia (i.e., the southwest Pacific, see Strathern and Stewart 2002) were colonized by speakers of the vast Austronesian set of languages (see Blust 2009) and tend to be characterized by systems of rank and chiefship. Much greater cultural and linguistic diversity is found among older strata of populations, in which forms of nonchiefly leadership predominate. Where there is rank, there tend also to be gradations of ranked deity figures; where rank is absent or weakly developed, rituals center on ancestral spirits and spirits of the landscape with power over fertility. In all of these regions, deities and spirits are traditionally invoked in major concerns of social life, both integrative within the group and involving hostility toward others or in the mediation of intergroup relations. (For detailed accounts, see A. Strathern, Pamela J. Stewart, et al. 2002.)

The title of this chapter juxtaposes religion and violence, suggesting an exploration of relationships between these two categories. Our major purpose is to illustrate some of the complexities of these relationships in regard to materials from Pacific Islands ethnographies. Our perspective on these materials is holistic: If violence seems at times to be supported by religion, at other times religion is equally involved in supporting nonviolence or the production of peace. Ritual action is also frequently called into play in Pacific Island cultures to produce mock forms of violence, symbolic displays of strength that may lead to outright conflict but may equally lead to the avoidance of physical harm while expressing the ambivalence of social relations or a potential threat (epideictic displays as Rappaport 1967 put it). Sorcery, however, should be interpreted somewhat differently. If people suffer misfortunes, become ill, or die, this may be attributed to sorcery, which can be interpreted as a deflection of immediate physical violence into mediated forms of aggression utilizing symbolic projections of hostility and harm. The hermeneutics of sorcery and sorcery accusations, thus, are different from those surrounding immediate acts of physical harm. With sorcery, people's aims may be to trace back from the misfortune to its possible cause in hostile sorcery; with physically observed harm, this process is unnecessary, because the cause is generally known (other than in cases in which wounded bodies are discovered after their death and the killers are not known). Sorcery has to be considered as a part of the whole complex of ritual activities and their place in the control of social relations. For example, killings in physical conflict may provoke demands for compensation, may issue in revenge killings, or the protagonists may turn to secret forms of sorcery to pursue vengeance in a way that is less risky than open combat; and the "ghosts" of the dead may be brought into play in any of these contexts. Hostility can also be deflected into rhetorical speeches, in which issues are discussed in a coded way so as to avoid inciting further physical violence. Or, equally, language may be used as a venue for escalating conflict (Brenneis and Myers 1991, originally published 1984; see also, for subtle extensions of this perspective, Kitts 2010 and Noegel 2010). In general, in a processual analysis, violence and peacemaking may alternate over time, and religious and ritual practices can be called into play at specific moments of transformations in relationships between networks of groups.

We further recognize that violent acts can occur in many contexts, for example, in networks of kin or spousal relations. In these, religion as such may initially play no special part. However, in processes of reparation or in the "mystical" understandings of the disruption caused by such events, religious notions certainly may enter in. A central cultural concept for the Mount Hagen people of Papua New Guinea is the notion of *popokl* or "anger" (see Strathern and Stewart 2010) that can lead people to commit violent acts, either legitimately or otherwise, depending on the perspective adopted. It can also be a mark of a person's dissatisfaction with a current state of affairs and can make persons ill, so that their grievances must be attended to if they are to recover their health. Where popokl drives people to take revenge, it is said to be accompanied by the popokl of the ghost of the kinsperson who was killed by enemies. Within the domestic group, the illness that a person experiences may be interpreted by kin as a result of their popokl, which must then be revealed and steps taken to deal with its causes: In this case, also, the ghosts are thought traditionally to be involved, because it is they who may be implicated in causing sickness to afflict their living relatives. In a third scenario, the person may have done wrong, perhaps simply the wrong of not sacrificing to

the ancestral ghosts of the dead. In this instance, the ghosts/ancestors are traditionally said to withdraw their protection and to allow wild spirits of the bush
(*tipu römi*) to break through the fence of that protection and make the victim ill.
In all of these instances, it is evident that religion is centrally involved. (These scenarios have changed with the advent of Christianity from the 1930s onward, but the
basic ideas remain relevant.)

Because our aim is to illustrate and explore processes to show the intertwining of religion, violence, and other social practices, we do not aim at any kind of
encyclopedic coverage of Pacific societies. The cases we examine can, however, be
considered as more or less paradigmatic, using this term in the sense introduced by
Meyer Fortes in his work on the comparative study of kinship systems (Fortes 1969).
Our plan in the chapter, then, is to examine a few cases in some detail, while giving
an idea of parallels and variant complexities in other ethnographic contexts.

Another analytical point needs to be made at the outset. All Pacific societies
depended on some kind of social context in which peaceful relations were maintained. The elementary form of this context was expressed by Peter Lawrence with
his reference to the "security circle" among the Garia people of Madang Province in
Papua New Guinea (Lawrence 1971). Within the security circle, ritual practices are
likely to be supportive of the maintenance of co-operation and reciprocity between
people. Outside this circle, not only may hostile relations enter or prevail, but the
same religious forces that help to maintain peace inside the circle may be brought
into play in the production of violent action. When this is so, the violence involved
is no longer of contested legitimacy among the people but is regarded as legitimate.
War is the context in which violence is redefined in this way, by those involved, and
is then said to legitimize violence, perhaps even as a way subsequently to produce
peace through domination, incorporation, or grudging coexistence.

There is a considerable difference in this regard between societies without a
centralized chiefship and those in which chiefs and kings or queens emerged at the
centers of protostates, often with specialized warriors or armies. Somewhat paradoxically, it may be that the chiefless societies, conventionally portrayed as "without rulers" or even "anarchic," have historically equipped themselves better for
peacemaking, largely because they are not geared to the achievement of long-term
domination over one another. Centralization of power may bring peace at the center and strife at the peripheries (see Ferguson and Whitehead 1992): strife that over
time may reach back into the centers themselves. These considerations are pertinent to the cases we will examine, especially with regard to the Fijian polity of Bau.
Finally, here, within the security circle, however it is defined, in structural or situational ways, there is an ethic of settling disputes primarily by elaborate sessions of
talk rather than by hasty recourse to physical violence. This is the arena pinpointed
by the editors of and numerous contributors to the volume *Disentangling: Conflict
Discourse in Pacific Societies* (Watson-Gegeo and White eds. 1990). The term *disentangling* aptly points to the complex unravellings of causes of a dispute and possible ways to settle it. Ritual practices and religious notions may be involved, and
it is perhaps particularly here that Christianity has been able to slot into the roles

of previous indigenous customs. Thus Boggs and Chun, in their discussion of contemporary Hawaiian disentangling, note that the leader, in handling a dispute,
conducts opening prayers and lessons read from the Bible. Boggs and Chun suggest
that the leader's role is reminiscent of the *mana* or ritual power of persons to whom
suppliants could appeal as refugees (Boggs and Chun 1990: 128). At the same time,
Boggs and Chun make it clear that, at the level of practice, a great deal of careful
management and assessment has to be conducted by leaders, if disentangling is
to be successful. While mana is conceptualized as an external and spiritual force,
practical abilities feed into it.

Fiji: Hegemony and Its Limits

Marshall Sahlins (2004), basing his analyses partly on the extensive earlier work
of A. M. Hocart (e.g., 1927, 1952), has produced an interpretation of the rise and
fall of the influence of different rulers in the tiny island of Bau in Fiji. The Bau
chiefs extended their hegemony over a wide area through maritime activity, both
by trade (or tribute) and warfare culminating in struggles with Rewa during the
1840s (Sahlins 2004: 27). A complex cosmological history underlay the rise of Bau.
Common to all chiefly systems in Fiji, there is a division between war chiefs and
sacred rulers of the land (the Roko Tui). Usually, the Roko Tui was considered superior to the war chief, but in Bau this situation was reversed (Sahlins 2004: 27). The
rulers had also moved to Bau from the mainland of Viti Levu nearby, creating it
as an offshore fortress, after one sacred Roko Tui was assassinated. In Fiji, also,
the sacred rulers of the land are usually thought of as autochthons, but in Bau the
tradition was that it was the sea people (*kai wai* in Fijian) who first settled it and
remained its "owners" (Sahlins, 33). Many of these original sea people had also
been subsequently sent out to colonize other areas of eastern Fiji and they retained
their allegiance to Bau, bringing in tribute. One of the valued items brought in such
tribute was sperm whale teeth (*tabua*), which Sahlins characterized as "the most
valuable of all valuables" (34).

   Tabua were sacred. Sahlins goes on: "Presented as binding proposals of marriage and assassination, as offerings to gods and chiefs, or in return for providing
cannibal victims, the whale tooth" (34) was the equivalent of a human life. It was
thus used in the same way pearl shells and pigs were in the Papua New Guinea
highlands: They were also the equivalents of a human life. The implications of such
a cultural feature are twofold. These kinds of valuables, at the apex of a hierarchy of
values, could be used equally as instruments of destruction or as the means of making peace. In the case of Bau, its history took a turn to warfare (in the 1840s), partly
because of Bau's control over colonial trade and the introduction of guns (Sahlins, 35).
Tabua and other goods could be used to recruit allies. The Bau warriors were con-
tracted to aid their allies among the Cakaudrove people by attacking the people

of Natewa. They did so but took great tribute from the Cakaudrove people in the course of this process. Sahlins comments further that Bau's domination of the sea brought them into a politics of wealth and enabled them to bring down Rewa, a "traditional" polity based on the superiority of the land chiefs. The rulers in Bau were the Vunivalu, a name that translates as "the roots of war" (Sahlins, 60), and the war chiefs were seen as active in outside activities, while the sacred land chiefs or Roko Tui were portrayed as "sitting" and receiving wealth from outside. Both war chief and land chief had aspects of divinity. Of the Vunivalu, Sahlins notes that "as the procurer of human sacrifices by acts of transcendent violence, this 'God of War' was in some respects the more terrible of the two" (60). The land chief, on the other hand, was the one who was seen as "the ritual fount of its well-being" (61). It would be the land chief who made peace in internal conflicts, no doubt (compare Sahlins 1962: 289–362).

Over time and perhaps influenced by the British colonial policy of identifying a single chief rather than a complex diarchy such as existed in Bau, the position of the Roko Tui became further sacralized into that of a "sacred king," served by his subjects with his seat of power seen as the center of the kingdom, surrounded by a series of concentric circles marking greater or lesser proximity to the ritual center. This concentric empire was sustained not by the land people of the king but by the sea people of the Vunivalu, or war chief (Sahlins, 2004: 64), who were accepted as the "owners" of Bau Island, and were fierce warriors and procurers of victims (ibid.). Sahlins comments that Bauan power "depended not a little on a reputation for terror" (ibid.). Over time the Roko Tui of Bau was driven out by the Vunivalu, who installed one of their own as the new king (65) and ushered in the time of Cakobau, a noted military leader, whom Sahlins describes as "the master of the extensive Bauan imperial order" (Sahlins 2004: 269).

The longer-term history of Bau, which Sahlins delves into in great detail, involves fratricidal conflicts between older and younger brothers; the interstitial roles of the *vasu*, or sister's sons, within intermarrying dynasties; and a violent, protracted conflict between Bau and the kingdom of Rewa. This conflict ended with Cakobau's victory over his enemies, and his proclamation as Tui Viti, king of all Fiji, by the British in 1844, combined with his extraordinary conversion to Christianity that entailed the conversion of his followers as well, and the later cession of Fiji to British power in 1874 (Sahlins 2004: 289). It might seem that this conversion marked a new way of establishing peace under a Pax Britannica; but in some ways, it also ushered in a new arena of ritual conflict, because the defeated kingdom of Rewa espoused Catholicism, whereas Cakobau converted to Methodism (Sahlins 2004: 290).

It is clear, at any rate, from this brief account, that both war chiefs and land chiefs were considered legitimate because of the ritual and cosmological underpinnings that supported their power. The values of peace and war were ideally held in balance in the divisions of power, but this ideal balance could easily be subverted by specialisms of imperial-style trade and warmaking. Bau reached the apex of its imperialism in the persona of Cakobau, but the arenas of power were further transformed by Cakobau's conversion to Methodism and the entry of British sovereign power and the plantation economy the British brought with them. In theoretical terms, we see here that religion, violence, and peacemaking are all bound together. But, while tabua (whale's teeth) were supreme valuables like the pearl shells of the Papua New Guinea highlands, it is less clear that they were used for compensation payments to make peace as pearl shells and pigs were in Papua New Guinea: The cultural register may be the same, but social practices may differ.

BELLONA: THE DOMINANCE AND
DEMISE OF REVENGE

Another domain in which this observation applies is the ideology and practice of revenge (see, e.g., Stewart and Strathern 2002a: 108–136). An ideology or a requirement of revenge is built into the expectations of many peoples with autonomous kin groups that enter into violent conflict with one another. Unchecked, such an ideology can lead to unending chains of killings and counterkillings, and these are prototypically underpinned by the notion that it is the spirits of the dead kinsfolk who look to their living kin to avenge their deaths, on pain of their suffering the effects of ghostly displeasure. Obviously, such a process of ongoing violence is at least partly based in religious and ritual ideas. However, in practice, limitations are usually placed on killings, either by peaceful compensation payments or at least by a recognition that the scores are, for the time being, equal between the opposed groups. In the Papua New Guinea highlands, arrangements for compensation are highly elaborate and, historically, have led to extended sequences of exchanges that replace overt hostilities with ostensibly friendly competitive displays and disbursements of wealth. This microevolution from enchained killings to competitive exchange is most clearly exhibited among groups with strong clans, aspiring leaders known in the literature as "big-men," and intensive systems of agricultural production that enable the multiplication of pig populations that enter the arenas of exchange as prime forms of wealth along with shell valuables and, subsequently, state monetary forms (e.g., Strathern and Stewart 1999, 2000; Stewart and Strathern 2002b). Such an evolution is strongly marked in these highlands societies. A contrasting case from Bellona Island, an outlying Polynesian-settled area belonging politically to the Solomon Islands in the southwestern Pacific, provides a different picture (Kuschel 1988). Kuschel's analysis begins with the imputed first arrival of immigrants on this small island and ends in oral histories up to the year 1938, when Christian missionaries brought about the demise of much Bellonese indigenous culture and, with it, a considerable decrease in revenge homicides.

Bellonese genealogies of settlement apparently reached twenty-four generations (approx. five hundred years), in some cases, by 1938 (Kuschel 1988: 15, 40), although knowledge was lacking in detail about the first eight to ten generations (ibid.). Oral traditions suggest that the people arrived from Uvea in the Loyalty Islands and found an earlier people, the *hiti*, living on Bellona. Later, the immigrants exterminated the hiti in revenge for the killing of a relative (47). Slash-and-burn horticulture was practiced, with yams, taro, and bananas, and later sweet potato (54). Fishing was also important. The island was affected regularly by hurricanes. Land was held by a small number of patrilineal clans, reduced at the time of Kuschel's fieldwork (1968 onward) to only two clan groups (56). Separate subclans of an original clan could intermarry (60), and this fact seems to be connected with hostilities between groups that emerged in this way (ibid.).

One subclan was forced to become largely endogamous as a result of hostilities with others over revenge killings (61). Lineages were recognized subgroups within the subclan, controlling land and inheritance among males.

A review of kinship relations and social organization offers some clues as to why revenge killings were an endemic feature of life on Bellona. Affinal relations, especially between brothers-in-law, were polite but prickly. Marriages were entered into in a relatively simple way, and divorces were common, although mostly in earlier years of a marriage. Affines were expected to present each other with gifts and hold feasts in honor of each other. However, in one instance, a man killed his sister's husband over a slight: When he arrived at the husband's settlement, he had not been properly greeted. On the other hand, in a manner classic for many patrilineal systems, the exclusiveness of lineage ties was broken by the importance of warm and supportive ties between mother's brothers and sister's sons. Kinship ties were cross-cut by status differences, but social stratification was not elaborate. There was a distinction between persons of high status, ordinary status ("commoners" in Kuschels's usage), and low status. Kuschel seems to apply these terms largely but not exclusively to classify men. High-status men were called *hakahua*, and their position was gained by a combination of advantages of birth, such as descent from a line of original immigrants (i.e., rights of precedence), and personal achievements of character and generosity in giving feasts. The latter criterion aligns the hakahua as much with the New Guinea "big-man" type of leaders as with the ideal-typical Polynesian chief. Low-status men (76) were also like their counterparts in the Papua New Guinea highlands: They were dependants who could be ordered to do things, as others could not, and were thus the equivalent of those called *kintmant* ("workers/servants") in Mount Hagen (see numerous references in A. J. Strathern 1972 to "rubbish-men"). Status rivalry between brothers was frequent, leading to endless quarrels and, even if rarely, it could result in homicide.

All activities were considered to be dependent on the deities and ancestors. There were minor rituals to deal with the spirits of the original hiti inhabitants of Bellona (79). Bush spirits, 'apai, were blamed for otherwise unaccountable misfortunes. The sky gods and goddesses were the most powerful and were held "to assist the fighters, to localize, and kill their enemies" (82) and to protect them against harm. District gods, on the other hand, had more peaceful functions, helping people to gain children and to intercede with the sky gods (ibid.). The multiplication of district gods, Kuschel suggests, reflects the fragmentation of political identities over time as the population on Bellona increased after the arrival of the first immigrants (ibid.). However, district gods could not be mobilized for hostile purposes. Living men, on the other hand, sometimes predicted what they planned to do as ancestors, including taking vengeance for killings. High-status men and also women acted as mediums, interpreting putative statements from the district gods or ancestors. The rituals of great feasts brought together the deities, spirits, and living kin and affines (84). Ignoring kinsfolk at such a distribution was a cause of trouble and could lead to killings (84).

Physical acts of violence were not the only means by which vengeance killings could take place. *Kuba* sorcery rituals could be conducted against the *ma'ungi* or spirit of a victim (life force, comparable to the Duna tini in the Southern Highlands Province of Papua New Guinea; see Stewart and Strathern 2005: 35–47). This sorcery ritual requested a sky god to take the person's ma'ungi away and hide it in a sacred (*tapu*) place (84). An object or a small canoe replica with a figure inside could stand for the intended victim (86), and a formula was pronounced, addressing the deity whose assistance was solicited. The sorcerous act is really, therefore, a request to a powerful deity rather than a straightforward magical act; but it is not clear under what political circumstances redress via kuba, rather than a direct killing, might be chosen. In one case given, the intended victim had gone away elsewhere, to Rennell Island, and her offence was simply to have rejected the man making kuba against her for marriage. She might be hard to kill, then, and the grievance would not have been one that would justify vengeance between lineages. (See further below, on kuba.)

What this and other details make clear is the immense importance of senses of honor, shame, rivalry, and envy that are cited as motivations for action on Bellona. Such an ethos fits well with a stress on revenge killing. Kuschel begins his chapter 4, on disputes, with the statement that "Bellonese society has been in a constant state of strife and controversy" (102). Offenses are not forgotten and are made worse by verbal invective. Kuschel refers appositely to a Samoan proverb that makes the same point: "stones decay, but words last" (104). Cutting down valued coconut trees or destroying a canoe could end in retaliatory killings because these acts were symbolic equivalents of killing a man's sons. Atonement gifts could be made to halt escalation. Verbal abuse would heighten conflict and could be followed by threats of killing (104). Physical fighting could be accompanied by kuba rituals, Kuschel notes, so this negates the idea that kuba was only used as a safety device against physical violence. Disputes often occurred over the use of land. In marital disputes, a woman could insult or curse her husband, in some cases inducing suicide. A lineage could split over quarrels, making it vulnerable to enemies (109). People might try to move to a new settlement or go to nearby Rennell for a while, to let things cool down. Conflicts were inhibited generally by close kin ties; but Kuschel notes that every "conflict contained the germ of protracted disputes which could eventually mean the end of an individual, a family, a lineage or a clan" (110).

Revenge killings had to be open and carried out by raiding parties, mostly agnatic male kin, under leaders, for the occasion. They were accompanied by rituals (including kuba ritual) with appeals to the sky gods to weaken the ma'ungi of the intended victim. The raid was carried out in stealth but was followed by the overt performance of victory songs at the leader's settlement. Weapons used were dedicated to the sky gods. A man's district gods or ancestors might warn him of danger by means of omens (118). When the killing was carried out, the killer was supposed to tell the victim the reason for it, and these performative statements passed into oral traditions (120). Secret killings were despised. Killing, therefore, was a matter of honor. Sometimes a dead body was mutilated as a mark of dishonoring it; but skulls were not taken as trophies (121).

The victors in a raid retired to a hillock where they continued to sing their songs of the killing for a few days. Hillocks were considered sacrosanct. Presumably intended victims could take temporary safe refuge there too. The raiders later destroyed their victim's settlement and ritual possessions. Women kinsfolk of the victim then began mourning, and the body was given burial according to status: For example, a high-status man's corpse was rubbed with turmeric (132). Some mourners maintained prohibitions on eating any favorite food of the deceased for some months after the funeral. (The same practice held in Hagen: Such customs are the obverse of those emotions of hatred that informed killings.) Memories were held onto; vengeance might be delayed, but it would usually be attempted, sooner or later.

There were peacemaking rituals (144). These were stimulated by a kind of necessity. Both the raiders and the kin of the victims would live in isolation in bush areas until peacemaking was instituted. Women, or men related to both sides, could be the messengers for peace. Women were never killed in feuds, an important fact surely (144). If a peace proposal was accepted, the surviving kin of the victim went to the raiders' settlement, and later the visit was reciprocated. Preparations were then made for a feast. For the occasion, the victim's close male kin rubbed charcoal on their skin, and their leader put special gifts on his head (a special paddle, mat, and flying fox teeth), carrying these to the event. The leader made an opening speech and abased himself before the raid leader, who then wiped charcoal off the other's eyes and declared that he embraced the backside of his former enemies to finish their conflict (147). A speech maker then sprinkled coconut water sacred to the sky god and made a reconciliation speech, citing the coconut as a marker of peace. The raid leader responded, suggesting that in the past the groups had been friendly. A feast and dancing followed, and a few days later the sequence was repeated at the settlement of the victim's kin.

Peacemaking rituals, therefore, were practiced, and the same sky gods appealed to for assistance in killing presided over the rituals that brought about peace. Case histories show, nevertheless, that killings could start up again later between the same groups (Kuschel, chapter 7). Further, vengeance raids also took place between Bellona and Rennell Island (170). One of the factors that both perpetuated and to some extent contained these blood feuds was that strong rules governed who could legitimately be killed. For instance, retribution was limited to the members of the original raiding group and its lineage agnates. One's own close kin should not be killed, nor should any women (223, cf. 61). The range of killing and, therefore, the potential for feud to escalate into warfare was thus restricted. But it was difficult to preempt or circumvent a feuding process once it was set in hand, because there were no overarching authorities and no mediating roles between groups outside the periodic peace rituals. Marital alliances that linked high-status men together could eventuate in peacemaking between them; but high-status men were also involved in the protection of honor though killings. Only Christian mission teachings and the fear of government punishment eventually brought the feuding to a close in 1938. Reliance on government could come to replace self-reliance, the only principle on which agnatic groups had previously been able to operate. The injunction of the Christian God, "Thou shalt not kill," was able perhaps to supersede the earlier sky god's double favoring of both vengeance and peacemaking, because government and mission were seen as working together; and, Kuschel adds, punishment for killers involved exile in distant Honiara, the capital of the Solomons—something more terrifying, it seems, than living a life at home faced by the risk of being killed by those one knew quite well.

The conclusion from this Bellonese case is that the ideology of honor drove the pattern of vengeance killings; that this ideology primarily pertained to men and their agnatic kin; that it was supported by appeals to gods and ancestors, although some of these figures could equally be appealed to for protection from harm; that peace rituals were also presided over by the deities and eventually replaced after 1938 by the injunctions of the Christian God and the British district commissioner; and, finally, that peace rituals did not produce permanent effects nor did they involve any clear element of compensation payments such as are found in the New Guinea cases to be considered next. Instead, in keeping with the intensely emotional small-scale and intimate social relations involved, they involved the ritual reversal of the emotional markers of hatred and disrespect into marks of reconciliation and amity. Without this, nothing could have stopped the Bellonese men from simply annihilating one another to the point of extinction, as happened to some kin groups. Nothing could better demonstrate the importance of religion and its ritual enactments for preserving a see-saw balance between violence and peaceful co-existence. We see here also the "capstone" effect that British colonial control brought with it, just as we saw earlier for the case of Fiji, where the predatory and religiously sanctioned preeminence of Bau was brought both to its culmination and its end by the agency of Cakobau and his final conversion to Methodism.

Mount Hagen, Papua New Guinea: Cycles of Exchange

Materials on exchange and sacrifice in the Mount Hagen area of the Western Highlands Province in Papua New Guinea clearly fit our general argument in this essay, that religion is brought into play both in the cause of violent actions and in peacemaking activities, in each case because it provides an overarching and tak-en-for-granted legitimacy and motivation for actions. In the Fijian case, we have seen that there was an assumed balance between the powers of war and peace, a balance that was subverted in the case of Bau. We have seen also that valuables were used to pay allies in war but without, apparently, a complementary context of peacemaking. Finally, British centralized control and Cakobau's conversion to Methodism superseded the terms of the older political structures. In Bellona, feuds between small lineages were endemic, fueled by an ethos of honor, shame and revenge that impinged differently on men since women were not killed in feuds. Peace ceremonies were held in which there was a ritual rebalancing of relations, but wealth items, again, were not directly employed to make compensations for deaths. When we come to the context of the New Guinea highlands, however, we find that the life-giving and life-replacing power of valuables, given in compensation pay-ments, is clearly and forcefully brought into play. This power was embedded in sequential processes of exchanges that implicated generative acts of killings as well as regenerative acts of compensation and the re-creation of positive ties.

The argument can be presented here in a relatively brief form because we have written about these themes extensively in earlier publications. The ethnographic focus is on Mount Hagen, in the western highlands of Papua New Guinea.

Australian explorers first entered these highlands areas in the early 1930s, fol-lowed closely by Catholic and Lutheran missionaries. Administrative control and "pacification" proceeded through the 1950s, and national political independence was granted in 1975. Exchange practices of the kind we discuss here date back to precolonial times, with a complex history of expansion in the 1960s and turbulent experiences of change since the 1970s. Our account picks out important enduring features.

For the overall analysis, it is important to highlight the relationship between exchange and sacrifice (see Stewart and Strathern eds. 2008, especially our intro-duction and chapter 9). If we take a processual look at how acts of killing in Hagen could gradually be transformed into acts of positive alliance, we will see how sac-rifice enters at different moments of the process involved.

In precolonial times, a death of a man caused by physical violence in combat between groups would call for revenge, either through renewed collective fighting or by ambush. Similarly, a death attributed to hostile sorcery and traced to a partic-ular person or their group would call for retaliation, either by countersorcery or by holding a divination test and executing the one held responsible. In either case two interlinked concerns were at work: the maintenance of group strength and prestige, and duty to the ghost of the person originally killed or thought to have been killed. Whether in practice revenge would be sought might depend on the relative power and numbers of those involved by their status in implicitly agnatic groups of kin. A death set up a potentiality for vengeance, whether it was immediately carried out or not, and the potentiality would continue indefinitely until some resolution of it was reached. If vengeance was sought in war, a sacrifice of a pig or pigs would be made to the aggrieved ghost as well as to a collectivity of ancestral spirits.

The potentiality for vengeance did not have to result in an actual revenge killing. Actions taken were contingent on relationships between the parties of the victims and the killers, and on group alliances and enmities. Between major, traditional enemies there was little chance of a peaceful resolution, but starting a war was also hazardous. In that case, concealed countersorcery might be tried, utilizing marginal, interstitial persons with ambiguous loyalties, either male or female. In all other circumstances, matters were negotiable, and the likelihood of peacemaking by compensation was enhanced by the density of affinal ties between the groups of those principally responsible for taking action. Allies in warfare who lost men in battle would need to be compensated to avoid shifts of allegiance. These same allies might be, at times, minor enemies in restricted warfare, and again compensation could be arranged between them by their leaders, "big-men" who could influence others by their deployment of pigs and shell valuables and who encouraged the transformation of enmity into friendship by converting compensation payments into two-way competitive exchanges of wealth known as *moka* (see, e.g., Strathern and Stewart 2000, Strathern 1971[2007]), especially following "pacification" in the 1950s. So well-known did the Hagen moka and the use of pearl shells in it become in the highlands region that government patrol officers such as James Sinclair, working later to bring about peace settlements in a distant and remote area of the highlands (Lake Kopiago among the Duna people), applied the term, with the spelling *moga*, far beyond the Hagen area as a general expression for effective peacemaking (Sinclair 1966:207).

Since revenge was sanctioned by the putative and implied wishes of a victim's ghost and the ancestral dead kin, in general, and was sealed as an intention by the killing of pigs in sacrifice, the option to make and accept compensation instead had also to be made acceptable to the dead. Meat sacrifices, in which the pork was steamed or roasted in earth ovens, sent up a smell that was considered appealing to the dead kin, and this was therefore the way of getting the dead on the side of compensation.

Beyond this sacrificial act of soliciting support of the dead, an important and delicate process of diplomacy, negotiation, and making commitments was set in hand, ultimately involving more and more persons (both male and female) as potential exchange partners across the divide created by violent acts. In this process, leaders played a crucial role in raising wealth goods, marshaling support, sorting out conflicts, and making diplomatic and aesthetically powerful speeches to bring about peace. The more they succeeded with their efforts, the more they would be able to instigate the development of wide-ranging exchange relations that would become the vehicle for the expansion of their own careers as leaders. An initial motivation to pay for deaths and halt overt conflicts was thus transmuted over time into a powerful machine for the replication and multiplication of exchange ties founded on complicated "financing" ties masterminded by the big-men.

The religious and ritual background to this expansion remained, underpinning the economic activities. No moka ceremony, it was thought, could succeed without the assistance of the ancestors, whose displeasure might be shown by the decorations of the moka givers failing to appear bright and shining when they danced for the occasion or by a sudden unfavorable onset of rain that would curtail the dancing, singing, and drumming intended to establish the harmony, well-being, and prestige of the group under its ancestors' protection.

From the 1970s onward this expansion of peaceful exchanges was halted by a series of recessive outbreaks of violence between groups. These were caused by a number of influences: the advent of roads and vehicles, disputes over land for growing coffee, conflicts over national politics and electorates, the overall increase in the scale of social relations bringing into contention categories of people not related by language or "ethnicity," and the introduction of guns into warfare, increasing the numbers of deaths and making it harder to pay for them. These conditions continue today (up to the publication of this volume).

It is interesting that, *pari passu* with these changes, people began to turn more to various denominations of Christian churches, especially those with an urban base and new transactional connections with the outside world. It might be expected that because of the formal emphasis in these churches on peaceful relations, the rituals and rhetorics of the churches would be brought into play to transcend the dilemmas of scale brought about by economic and political change. Formidable obstacles stood in the way of this pathway, not least the complex segmented histories of conflict in local areas. There have been clear signs, however, that Christian ideology lends itself to the extension of peacemaking across group boundaries, with prayers and communal feasting and that none of this works without compensation payments.

CONCLUSION

The three case studies in this chapter have been intended to stand in partial counterpoint to one another. In all three cases, it is obvious that religion and violence were mutually implicated, but the terms of that implication were different.

In the Fijian case, with a chiefly society and centralization of power, we saw that war chief and land chief, both sacralized, were ideally balanced with each other, the one standing for external violence, the other for internal peace. In Bau, this balance was upset and inverted, because the seagoing war chiefs came to occupy a preeminent position by displacing the land chiefs. Bau's empire was established by conquest and by the use of wealth to pay allies in war.

Bellona is an example in which, on a small island occupied by Polynesian seafarers, a kind of hierarchy was established but without governmentality. Instead, relations between lineages were egalitarian and marked by competitive killings. Religion was implicated in these conflicts because the superior sky gods were thought of as supporting raids, while the less powerful district gods were seen as helping to protect people. As with Bau, the balance was tipped toward violence, here in the proliferation of vengeance killings. But there were also rituals for peace-making, with apologies and acts of reconciliation. Wealth goods were employed at feasts held for peace but not as a prime means as bringing the peace about. Sky gods presided over rituals for peace as for war, bringing ritual closure to vengeance killings.

In the New Guinea highlands societies, we find a higher development of an ideology of wealth used as a life-giving replacement for persons, whether for bride-wealth payments, payments to allies, or compensation to enemies. The big-men type of leadership, founded both on a ritual relationship with ancestors and on the deployment of wealth as an integrating medium of defining sociality, ensured that life was encompassed by wealth, and wealth could therefore be used to define both interpersonal and political relations. Sacralization of wealth ensured the possibility of peacemaking. At the same time, as with the other cases, violence could also by underpinned by values held to be sacred. Christianity impacted all three cases (Bau, Bellona, and Hagen) by providing a link with powers that cross-cut the previous structures of relations and made a rationale for creating peace on a different ritual basis, without necessarily removing the causes that could lead to conflicts.

Religion and violence in these societies are perhaps best seen as in a kind of see-saw dialectic. Where violence was practiced, religion might support it; but religion was also brought into play to halt violence and make peace. The broader background that explains how both of these processes could occur lies in the transformative framing powers of ritual and its underlying cosmological perceptions of order, producing self-justifying bases for the legitimization of actions. (See also Schirch 2005 and Strathern and Stewart 2011, ch. 7, on rituals and peacebuilding.)

Over all, religion and violence do not have to be seen as privileged or exclusive arenas of inquiry. One arena of discussion can be whether violent actions are sometimes required or incited by religious notions and ritual actions. Even if this is the case, violence may have other, independent causes and correlates, and religion may equally be founded on and foster other values. A holistic analysis is likely to show that, while religion and violence may intersect in various ways, peacemaking or the avoidance of conflict may equally involve religious ideas. In a processual analysis, cycles of political activity may alternate between violent conflict and quiet peacemaking, so the cycles need to be understood as a whole and not just in part. The definition of *violence* must give the analyst pause before deploying it as a counter in the investigation. For example, what the observer evaluates as violence may not be categorized in that way by the actors, if by the term *violence* we mean a transgressive or disruptive act that is antinormative—murder rather than an execution, for example. We have investigated questions of violence and its definitions, drawing on the work of David Riches and others (Riches 1986), in previous publications (e.g., Stewart and Strathern 2002a). We refer in that publication to the theme of contested legitimacy in relation to violent acts, because the evaluation (or even the classification) of an act as violent can vary between the performers, victims, and witnesses of the act (op. cit.: 25–51). In the English language, violence also tends to carry the sense of inflicting immediate physical harm on persons, but the term can also readily be extended in two further ways: one, to contexts in which people's emotional or social status is harmed or violated in ways they experience as hurtful and, the other, in terms of so-called mystical notions of attack or harm inflicted on others by means of sorcery, magic in general, cursing, and the like—all categories that bring us back into the domains of ritual and religion (see Stewart and Strathern 2004).

BIBLIOGRAPHY

Blust, Robert. *The Austronesian Languages.* Canberra: Australian National University, 2009.

Boggs, Stephen T. and Malcolm Naen Chun. "*Ho'oponopono*: A Hawaiian Method of Solving Interpersonal Problems." In Karen Ann Watson-Gegeo and Geoffrey M. White eds. *Disentangling: Conflict Discourse in Pacific Societies*, pp. 122–160. Palo Alto, CA: Stanford University Press, 1990.

Brenneis, Donald and Fred R. Myers eds. *Dangerous Words: Language and Politics in the Pacific.* Prospect Heights, IL: Waveland Press, 1991 [1984].

Ferguson, R. Brian and Neil L. Whitehead eds. *War in the Tribal Zone. Expanding States and Indigenous Warfare.* Santa Fe, NM: School of American Research Series, 1992.

Fortes, Meyer. *Kinship and the Social Order: The Legacy of Lewis Henry Morgan.* Chicago: Aldine, 1969.

Hocart, Arthur Maurice. *Kingship.* Oxford, UK: Oxford University Press, 1927.

Hocart, Arthur Maurice. "*The Life-Giving Myth, and Other Essays.*" London: Methuen and Co. Ltd, 1970 [1952].

Kitts, Margo. "*Poinē* as a Ritual Leitmotif in the Iliad." In M. Kitts ed. (Section I: Ritual and Violence), pp. 7–32, vol. III of *Ritual Dynamics and the Science of Ritual.* M. Kitts et al. eds. Wiesbaden, Germany: Harrassowitz Verlag, 2010.

Kuschel, Rolf. *Vengeance Is Their Reply. Blood Feuds and Homicides on Bellona Island.* Copenhagen: Dansk Psykologisk Forlag, 1988.

Lawrence, Peter. "The Garia of the Madang District." In Ronald M. Berndt and Peter Lawrence eds. *Politics in New Guinea, Traditional and in the Context of Change: Some Anthropological Perspectives*, pp. 74–93. Nedlands: University of Western Australia Press, 1971.

Noegel, Scott. "The Ritual Use of Linguistic and Textual Violence in the Hebrew Bible and Ancient Near East." In M. Kitts ed. (Section I: Ritual and Violence), pp. 33–46, vol. III of *Ritual Dynamics and the Science of Ritual.* M. Kitts et al. eds. Wiesbaden, Germany: Harrassowitz Verlag, 2010.

Rappaport, Roy A. *Pigs for the Ancestors: Ritual in the Ecology of a New Guinea People.* New Haven, CT: Yale University Press, 1967.

Riches, David. *The Anthropology of Violence.* Oxford, UK, and New York: Basil Blackwell, 1986.

Sahlins, Marshall D. *Moala: Culture and Nature on a Fijian Island.* Ann Arbor: University of Michigan Press, 1962.

Sahlins, Marshall D. *Culture in Practice: Selected Essays.* New York: Zone Books, 2000.

Sahlins, Marshall D. *Apologies to Thucydides: Understanding History as Culture and Vice-Versa.* Chicago: University of Chicago Press, 2004.

Schirch, Lisa. *Ritual and Symbol in Peacebuilding.* Bloomfield, CT: Kumarian Press, 2005.

Sinclair, James P. *Behind the Ranges: Patrolling in New Guinea.* Melbourne: Melbourne University Press, 1966.

Stewart, Pamela J. and Andrew Strathern. *Violence: Theory and Ethnography.* London and New York: Continuum Publishing, 2002a.

Stewart, Pamela J. and Andrew Strathern. "Transformations of Monetary Symbols in the Highlands of Papua New Guinea." For a special issue of the journal *L'Homme* on money (*Questions de Monnaie*) 162 (April/June 2002): 137–156, (2002b).

Stewart, Pamela J. and Andrew Strathern. *Witchcraft, Sorcery, Rumors, and Gossip.* New Departures in Anthropology series. Cambridge, UK: Cambridge University Press, 2004.

Stewart, Pamela J. and Andrew Strathern. "Cosmology, Resources, and Landscape: Agencies of the Dead and the Living in Duna, Papua New Guinea." *Ethnology* 44 (2005): 35–47.

Stewart, Pamela J. and Andrew Strathern eds. *Exchange and Sacrifice.* Durham, NC: Carolina Academic Press, 2008.

Strathern, Andrew. *The Rope of Moka.* Cambridge, UK: Cambridge University Press, 2000 [1971].

Strathern, Andrew. *One Father, One Blood.* Canberra: Australian National University Press, 1972.

Strathern, Andrew and Pamela J. Stewart. "Objects, Relationships, and Meanings: Historical Switches in Currencies in Mount Hagen, Papua New Guinea." In *Money and Modernity: State and Local Currencies in Melanesia,* 164–191. David Akin and Joel Robbins eds. ASAO (Association for Social Anthropology in Oceania) Monograph Series No. 17. Pittsburgh: University of Pittsburgh Press, 1999.

Strathern, Andrew and Pamela J. Stewart. *Arrow Talk: Transaction, Transition, and Contradiction in New Guinea Highlands History.* Kent, OH, and London: Kent State University Press, 2000.

Strathern, Andrew and Pamela J. Stewart. "The South-West Pacific." In *Oceania: An Introduction to the Cultures and Identities of Pacific Islanders,* pp. 10–98. Andrew Strathern, Pamela J. Stewart, Laurence M. Carucci, Lin Poyer, Richard Feinberg, and Cluny Macpherson. Durham, NC: Carolina Academic Press, 2002.

Strathern, Andrew, Pamela J. Stewart, Laurence M. Carucci, Lin Poyer, Richard Feinberg, and Cluny Macpherson. *Oceania: An Introduction to the Cultures and Identities of Pacific Islanders.* Durham, NC: Carolina Academic Press, 2002.

Strathern, Andrew and Pamela J. Stewart. *Curing and Healing: Medical Anthropology in Global Perspective.* Second edition, updated and revised. Durham NC: Carolina Academic Press, 2010.

Strathern, Andrew and Pamela J. Stewart. *Peace-making and the Imagination:Papua New Guinea Perspective.* St. Lucia, AU: University of Queensland Press, 2011.

Watson-Gegeo Karen Ann and Geoffrey M. White eds. *Disentangling: Conflict Discourse in Pacific Societies.* Palo Alto, CA: Stanford University Press, 1990.

....

CHAPTER 9

VIOLENCE IN CHINESE RELIGIOUS TRADITIONS

....

MEIR SHAHAR

ALTHOUGH the history of the Western monotheistic faiths is replete with inter-religious conflict, it is fair to ask whether China ever experienced inter-religious conflict. Did Chinese of one religious persuasion try to subdue or forcibly convert others, or was war waged in China for control of sacred places? The amorphous religious identity characteristic of China offers a convenient starting point for examining these questions.

INCLUSIVE RELIGIOSITY AND THE ABSENCE OF HOLY WARS

....

For the most part, Chinese people find it hard to define their religious identity. When asked about their faith, they might answer vaguely that one or another family member is a Buddhist or a Daoist, or they might reject the question, asserting that they succumb to no one label. Such answers should not be taken to mean that Chinese lives are devoid of a spiritual dimension or of cultic activities. The Chinese landscape is dotted with temples and monasteries, and the Chinese people worship a wide assortment of divinities, even as they consult with numerous clerics: Buddhist monks, Daoist priests, and the spirit mediums of the popular religion, to name just a few. Rather than the absence of religion, the difficulty to define it suggests an inherent difference between the Chinese faiths and the Western monotheistic ones. Before we probe it, a brief survey of the principal Chinese religions is in order.

Scholars usually distinguish between at least three Chinese religious traditions: Buddhism, which arrived to China from the Indian subcontinent in the first centuries CE; Daoism, which emerged as an organized religion with its own clergy and canonical scriptures during the same period; and the amorphous popular religion, which is also variously referred to as the village religion, the local religion, or as Chinese popular cults. To these three, some scholars add a fourth, Confucianism. The writings of Confucius (551–479 BCE) and his followers have served as the official ideology of the imperial Chinese regimes, providing the foundation for the Chinese educational system for more than two millenniums. Some Chinese literati have found in Confucian philosophy a spiritual dimension, in which sense it could be termed a religion. However, as theological questions occupy a minor place in it, many authors (including this one) prefer to describe Confucianism as an ethical and a political philosophy rather than as a religion. (Though largely in response to Buddhism, the neo-Confucian movement of the eleventh century onward is concerned with metaphysical questions).

Even as they significantly differ, the three (or four) Chinese religions share the important mark of inclusiveness. Neither one requires its followers to declare an exclusive adherence to it. Whereas the monotheistic faiths have forbidden their flocks following more than one—a Jew has not been able to become simultaneously Christian, for example—it is permissible for the Chinese laity to seek solace in diverse religions, alternately or concurrently. Rituals of conversion—which are of paramount significance in the monotheistic tradition—do not exist in China, where the laity freely shops in divergent religious establishments. Rather than committing herself or himself to a given faith by such rites as baptism or circumcision, a Chinese person may pray one day in a Buddhist temple and the next in a Daoist one, all the while seeking ethical guidance in the Confucian classics. Professing that they have no religion, the Chinese do not mean that they believe neither in gods nor in the efficacy of ritual. They assert, rather, that they do not adhere to the kind of exclusive religion that is familiar in the West. The word for religion, *zongjiao*, is a neologism that has been introduced to China—via Japan—following the encounter with the colonial powers. Exclusive as it is, the newly coined term is inapplicable to the native Chinese faiths.

The medical metaphor might illuminate the relative freedom that characterizes the Chinese religious market. Much as we might turn to several physicians—and diverse healing methods—until we find the proper one, a Chinese might seek spiritual help from various religious specialists, consulting one day with a Buddhist priest and hiring the services or a Daoist priest or a village spirit medium the following one. In cases of emergency, the Chinese might convene a consultation with several clerics simultaneously, just as an American hospital might summon a multidisciplinary medical conference. It has been customary in China to hire, concurrently, religious specialists of several faiths for important ritual passages, such as the one separating the living from the dead. If its financial resources permit, the family will commission for one and the same funeral an assortment of clerics: Confucian literati, Buddhist monks, and Daoist priests, no less than the geomancers and astrologers who are associated with the popular religion. Each one will employ his disciplinary tools—whether the reading of the Daoist scriptures or the intonation of the Buddhist sutras, for instance—for the salvation of the deceased, whose soul will be spiritually committed to neither.

Their religious identity unclear, the Chinese have been less prone than their Western counterparts to religious warfare. Where the population cannot be divided into identifiable communities of faith, conflict between them is unlikely. (The statistical attempts to differentiate between Chinese Buddhists, Daoists, or Confucians are artificial at best.) It probably would not be too much of an exaggeration to claim that traditional China never witnessed a holy war. To the best of my knowledge, prior to the encounter with the modern West, no Chinese religious community ever tried to gain military supremacy over—not to mention forcibly convert—another. There has never been an armed conflict between Chinese of diverse religious persuasions (such as Buddhists against Daoists). Significantly, the first Chinese war that has been colored by a proselytizing zeal occurred under Western influence. In 1850, the messianic leader Hong Xiuquan (1814–1864) led his followers into one of the deadliest crusades in history. Declaring himself the younger brother of Jesus Christ, Hong established the Taiping Heavenly Kingdom (1850–1864), in which a modified Christianity was to replace the native Chinese faiths. Hong's ideology combined ideas of social equality and women's liberation with a Christian vision in which he himself figured as a savior. Some twenty million people died before his messianic utopia was crushed by the reigning Qing Dynasty (Shih, 1972).

Whereas the Chinese laity has lacked a clear religious identity (and its concomitant hostility toward the religious other), its clergy has developed identifiable spiritual profiles. Unlike their lay followers, religious specialists have been required to undergo such initiation rites as the Buddhist tonsure and the Daoist ordination ceremony. Following their gradual immersion in a given scriptural tradition and its liturgies, Chinese clerics developed a quintessential ecclesial identity as Buddhist monks, Daoist priests, or ritual masters (*fashi*) of one or another ceremonial lineage. Whether or not Confucianism is considered a religion, its bearers—the male literati elite—likewise cherished a distinct identity. As they gradually climbed through the examination ladder that qualified them for government office, the literati acquired a sense of pride in the Confucian heritage that distinguished them from the ignorant masses. They were likely as conscious of their educational mission as Buddhist monks and Daoist priests were of their respective spiritual vocations. China's clerics have kept distinct identities, even as the religion of the laity has remained obscure.

Possessed of a quintessential religious identity, clerics (unlike their lay followers) vied with one another. The competition extended from the spiritual realm to the economic sphere. Buddhist monks, Daoist priests, ritual masters, and spirit mediums relied for their living on the same lay clientele. Lacking a following, however, their rivalry was rarely translated into physical violence. Religious specialists led no congregations that they could muster for a holy war. The only avenue possible for religious persecution extended through the imperial regime. Those clerics who wished to eliminate their rivals could try to convert the ruler for their cause. The Daoist Kou Qianzhi (365–448 CE) had been exceptionally successful in this regard. Under his spell, the Northern Wei emperor Taiwu (408–452 CE) proscribed the Buddhist faith, going as far as executing monks who were accused of sedition. Taiwu's successor, however, was quick to rescind his anti-Buddhist policies (Mather, 1979). Much like their subjects, most emperors were comfortable sponsoring diverse religious experts, rather than relying on some to the exclusion of others.

Chinese clerics—unlike the laity they minister to—have been conscious of their religious distinction to the extent of competing with others. The rivalry, however, has rarely been as acrimonious—not to mention as violent—as in Western monotheism. Well-known as early as the medieval period, the slogan of "the three teachings unite into one" (sanjiao heyi) gained special currency during the sixteenth and seventeenth centuries, when leading thinkers argued that Confucianism, Buddhism, and Daoism led to the same ultimate truth. The neo-Confucian philosopher Jiao Hong (1540–1620) advocated the study of Daoist and Buddhist scriptures, for they could elucidate the meaning of the Confucian classics, and Lin Zhaoen (1517–1598) advanced one step further, arguing that the three faiths were equivalent and hence interchangeable. Beginning in the late Ming period (1368–1644) and continuing to the present, numerous theologians have used interchangeably the Confucian vocabulary of sageness, the Buddhist terminology of enlightenment, and the Daoist parlance of immortality. Rather than quarreling over doctrinal differences, leading thinkers have conceived of their respective religions as diverse avenues to the same goal. Even as they reserve pride of place for their own, clerics have been mindful of the other faiths' spiritual merits (Berling 1980; Brook, 1993).

Sacred geography illustrates the relative tolerance that characterizes Chinese religions. Much like the Western monotheistic faiths, Chinese religions tend to adopt one another's holy places. But whereas in Jerusalem and in Constantinople (Istanbul) this has led to warfare, in China, divergent religious establishments often coexist harmoniously. Holy places are usually located atop sacred mountains, and it is not uncommon for Buddhist monasteries and Daoist temples to share them (Naquin and Yü, 1992). The renowned Buddhist Shaolin Monastery and Daoist Temple of the Central Holy Peak (Zhongyue miao), for instance, are situated on the same sacred Mount Song (in Henan Province). When several years ago I visited the former, a Buddhist monk drew on the Daoist experience to explain his choice of a retreat. "Mount Song is sacred," he told me. "That is why there is a Daoist Temple here." Rather than driving them out, the Shaolin monks cherish their Daoist neighbors for proving the sanctity of the Buddhist monastery's location.

Why have Chinese religions been relatively tolerant of one another? The question might be addressed from a theological angle no less than from an institutional perspective. We may want to consider the polytheistic worldview that has characterized the Chinese faiths, as well as their institutional weakness, which reflected the tremendous power of the Chinese state.

POLYTHEISM, TOLERANCE, AND STATE PERSECUTION

The Chinese religious tradition has, by and large, been polytheistic. Even though on the doctrinal level Buddhism does not recognize any god, in practice the religion arrived in China equipped with a substantial pantheon of heavenly beings. The Buddhist divinities have been ordered into an elaborate hierarchy of (in descending order) Buddhas, bodhisattvas, *arhats*, guardian deities, and other divine (or demonic) beings ranging from sexual harpies to cannibalistic ghouls. Daoism, likewise, celebrates a vast hierarchy of supernatural beings, ranging from carefree immortals to divine bureaucrats each appointed to a specific post in a heavenly government, which has been fashioned after the traditional Chinese state. As for the popular religion, the number of its gods has been greater still. Drawing on Buddhism and Daoism, it includes in addition to their divinities an endless array of historical figures who have been elevated to divine standing. Ranging from chaste maidens and lively clowns to fearless warriors and upright officials, some have been worshiped in a given locality only, whereas the cults of others have spread throughout the Chinese cultural sphere. Finally, to the degree that it sanctions ancestor worship even Confucianism might be described as polytheistic.

It might perhaps be argued that polytheism tends to be more receptive of other faiths than monotheism. The Hebrew Bible's dictum "you shall have no other gods before me" (Exodus 20:3) might have signaled the emergence of religious zealotry, as the "jealous lord" forbade the chosen people worshiping divinities other than him. Whereas the belief in one god implies one truth, polytheism tolerates many. Unlike monotheism, which by definition precludes other faiths, polytheistic religions have been inclined to adopt one another's gods. This has been the case in China, where divinities have been mutually borrowed by Buddhism, Daoism, and the popular religions. To give a minor example, a well-known figure in the Chinese popular religion is the child god Nezha whose cult was brought to China from India by Tantric (Esoteric) Buddhism during the Tang period (618–907). Originally a minor *yakṣa* spirit named Nalakūbara, the divine youth had been harnessed by Tantric ritual masters into their elaborate rituals. Summoned to China for the protection of the imperial court, his cult was quickly adopted by Daoist priests, no less than by village spirit mediums. The (originally Hindu)

Buddhist god became a major figure in Daoism and the popular religion. Rather than proscribing them, the Chinese religions have been inclined to absorb one another's mythologies.

If polytheism might have contributed to the mutual tolerance of the Chinese faiths, their institutional weakness has precluded violence. No Chinese religion has ever been strong enough to wage war on another. Neither Buddhism, nor Daoism, nor the popular religion, have been able to establish churches of lasting political, economic, or military influence. The institutional impotence of the Chinese faiths has been due to the tremendous power of the Chinese state. Their weakness has mirrored the enormous clout of the imperial—or, recently, communist—regimes. The ineffectiveness of the Chinese faiths alerts us to a prominent aspect of the Chinese experience of violence: Whereas China's diverse religions never fought among themselves, in varying degrees they have all been subject to state oppression. If China never experienced inter-religious warfare, it has witnessed a heavy dose of religious persecution by the state.

During the cold winter season of 1077, a barefoot European emperor was doing penance in the snow in front of the northern Italian castle of Canossa. Pope Gregory VII (1028–1085) was staying at the castle, and the Holy Roman emperor Henry IV (1050–1106) begged his clemency for the sin of intervention in the affairs of the church. The emperor was repenting, in particular, for the liberty he had taken in appointing bishops (in what came to be known as the Investiture Controversy). Such a scene could not have been imagined in China, where the "Son of Heaven" had always ruled supreme. By way of hyperbole, we might say that whereas God has been central to European history, in China he has always been overshadowed by the emperor. Chinese political thought has required that religion be subordinate to the state, and the bureaucracy has been careful to control all faiths. No Chinese religion has ever been permitted to create independent institutions, especially those that might coordinate activities across regional boundaries. In this respect, the Communist Party has inherited its predecessors' policies: Neither imperial China nor the People's Republic would tolerate a religious establishment threatening its absolute authority. Religions that challenged the state would be crushed.

The Tang period (618–907) persecution of Buddhism illustrates the Chinese state's abhorrence of religion. In the course of the first millennium, the Indian-born faith had become a powerful presence in Chinese society. Buddhist temples amassed great wealth in landed property (that for the most part was tax free), employing on their estates hundreds of thousands of peasants. The state eyed with envy the accumulated Buddhist wealth, irritated with the huge numbers of monks (and their serfs) who were exempt from corvée labor no less than from military service. In 845 Emperor Wuzong decided to put an end to the Buddhist church: Thousands of temples were destroyed and their lands confiscated. Hundreds of thousands of monks (and nuns) were forcibly laicized, sent back to their families and brought under the control of regional officials. Even though Buddhism was to have a lasting impact on Chinese religion and society, as an institution it never recovered. Buddhist monasteries of later periods could regain neither the wealth, prestige.

or freedom that they had enjoyed prior to the Tang purge (Weinstein 1987; Ch'en 1964).

During the Qing period (1644–1911), the government's wrath was directed less toward Buddhism and Daoism (both of which have been brought under firm government control) than independent religious movements that were labeled heterodox (*xiejiao*). The late imperial period witnessed the spread of millenarian sects, which mushroomed outside of the government-supervised Buddhist and Daoist temples. Commonly referred to as the White Lotus Religion (*Bailian jiao*), these sectarian movements were transmitted by lay masters and disciples. In their heightened sense of (often secretive) religious identity, no less than their strict cultic regimen, they somewhat resembled the exclusive and demanding religiosity familiar in Western monotheism (at least more so than Chinese Buddhism, Chinese Daoism, and the Chinese popular religion did). Furthermore, characterized by a strong millenarian zeal, at least some of these sects posed a threat to the existing political powers. Some White Lotus believers expected the imminent collapse of the imperial regime and its replacement by a messianic leadership establishing heaven on earth.

White Lotus religiosity focused on the cult of a female deity, whose sex made her suspect in the eyes of the bureaucratic elite. Whereas the state typically promoted the veneration of male scholars and generals, sectarian religion placed a goddess at the apex of the divine pantheon. Worship centered on the Eternal Mother (*Wusheng laomu*), from whose womb humankind had been banished and to which it would ultimately return. The cult of the supreme goddess was carried out by the recital of scriptures and magic spells (mantras), often coupled with a vegetarian diet (which had been borrowed from Buddhism), breathing exercises and calisthenics (drawing on the Daoist immortality techniques), and martial arts practice. Whereas the sects were commonly diffused, in times of heightened messianic expectations—or when pushed to it by state persecution—they could unite, mobilizing tens of thousands (Groot [1903–1904] 1970; Naquin 1976; Naquin 1981; Liu and Sheck 2004; ter Haar 1992).

Many White Lotus sects were likely peaceful, centering on personal salvation rather than political redemption. (Scholars have noted that the term *White Lotus* has been loosely used by state officials against all sects they wished to annihilate.) Such sects might have been driven to rebellion by their very oppression. Others, however, had been marked by a heightened messianic expectation, overtly expressed in rebellion. In 1813, White Lotus sectarians known as the Eight Trigrams coordinated an uprising in several cities, including the capital, Beijing. Approximately 80,000 people perished in the unsuccessful attempt to replace the existing sociopolitical system with a divine order, ushering eternal blessing. The messianic hopes of redemption—no less than their violent suppression by the state—have remained alive to this day. Active since the 1990s, the politically sensitive Falungong movement is a direct descendent of the White Lotus sects, combining their odd mixture of Buddhist eschatology with breathing exercises and calisthenics (that are referred to by sect members as *Qigong*). The panicked and brutal reaction on the part of the communist government likewise mirrors the violent suppression of sectarian religiosity by the Qing Dynasty. Dreams of salvation—and their ruthless repression—are as evident in today's China as they have been for centuries.

The state's control of religion has been achieved by the appointment of leading clerics, among other measures. As early as the medieval period, the state had established offices for the control of religious affairs, staffed by Buddhist monks and Daoist priests to its liking. The policy has remained in effect to this day, the ordination of leading abbots and head priests requiring the state's approval. Whereas government officials would not necessarily intervene in the selection of a head monk for a village hermitage, they would be careful to choose themselves the abbots of large temples (especially thoses that function as tourist and pilgrimage attractions and, thus, as sources of potential revenue). The policy has been a major source of friction between the People's Republic of China and the Catholic Church, whose bishops are universally appointed by the Vatican. Refusing to accept the Holy See's intervention in what it considers as its internal affairs, the Chinese government has established the Chinese Patriotic Catholic Association, for the purpose of nominating its bishops. The bitter argument over the clerical ordination—whether it should be decided by the Chinese government or by the Vatican—has been a principal reason for their ongoing breach of diplomatic relations.

MARTIAL GODS AND BLOODY SACRIFICES

Even though no war had been fought in traditional China on behalf of the gods (that is by the devotees of one, against the adherents of another), the gods regularly participated in warfare. Just as in Homer's *Iliad* the Greek divinities join the Trojan campaign, the Chinese gods have been regularly drafted to their believers' wars. Gods of Buddhist and Daoist descent no less than the martial divinities of the amorphous popular religion have assisted in armed conflicts that ranged from the defense of the Chinese state to the conquest of neighboring kingdoms, from struggles of dynastic succession to peasant rebellions. The earliest extant Chinese-language documents record divine participation in warfare. Dating from the second millennium BCE, the oracle bone inscriptions attest that the Shang kings consulted with their deified ancestors before heading for battle. Military campaigns would be undertaken only when sponsored by the gods.

Chinese emperors hired a wide assortment of ritual specialists, assuring their military victories. During the Tang period (618–907) these were often priests of the Tantric (also known as Esoteric) Buddhist tradition. Indian-born ritual masters such as Amoghavajra (705–774) conjured a panoply of Tantric martial divinities for the protection of the Chinese state. Many of these guardian divinities originated in Indian religion, before being drafted into the Buddhist pantheon. The Heavenly King of the North Vaiśravaṇa, (in Chinese, Pishamen), illustrates the long journey of the Hindu gods from the Sanskrit epics, through Tantric Buddhist mythology, into the martial pantheon of medieval China. Originally named Kubera, he had been celebrated as early as the second century BCE *Rāmāyaṇa* as the king of the semidivine semidemonic *yakṣa* troops. Later known primarily as Vaiśravaṇa, he was incorporated as the Heavenly King of the North into the Buddhist pantheon. Occupying a central place in the Esoteric rituals for state protection, he was brought to China, where he became the tutelary divinity of the Tang armies. Significantly, the Indian-born Vaiśravaṇa had protected not only the Chinese state as a whole but also its individual warriors. In order to be empowered by his superhuman strength, medieval wrestlers (and criminals) tattooed their bodies with the martial god's image (Demiéville 2010, 38–39; Strickmann 1996, 41; Chou Yi-Liang 1945, 305–306; Hansen 1993, 80–83; Zheng Acai 1997, 432).

The very names of some Chinese deities attest their military function. The "Perfect Warrior" (Zhenwu) also known as the Emperor of the Dark Heavens (Xuantian shangdi) has lent his martial prowess to rebels and emperors alike. In 1774 he was called on by the White Lotus leader Wang Lun to join his (ultimately failed) uprising, just as centuries earlier he had supported Emperor Chengzu's (r. 1403–1424) usurpation of the imperial throne. Posthumously known as the Yongle Emperor, Chengzu had attributed his military victories over his nephew, Emperor Huidi (r. 1399–1402), to the divine warrior's assistance. There is some evidence to suggest that he had participated himself in spirit medium seances in which, possessed by the martial god, he was taught his superhuman fighting skills. Once he became emperor, Chengzu (Yongle) embarked on a massive building campaign on his divine patron's behalf. Three hundred thousand corvée laborers built an enormous temple complex dedicated to the "Perfect Warrior" atop Mount Wudang (in Hubei Province). The martial god who had helped the reigning emperor was honored by seven large monastic complexes and numerous additional shrines, all staffed by government-sponsored Daoist priests (Naquin 1981, 39, 165; Seaman 1987, 23–27; Lagerwey 1992).

Martial gods have helped those who fought against the political order, no less than those who supported it. Throughout the late imperial period—and into modern times—rebels and revolutionaries headed to battle convinced of divine protection. The valiant gods they worshiped were, for the most part, the deified protagonists of such popular novels as the *Three Kingdoms* (*Sanguo yanyi*), the *Journey to the West* (*Xiyou ji*), and the *Water Margin* (*Shuihu zhuan*, also known in English as *The Outlaws of the Marsh*). The epic novels of either historical or mythological warfare have served as a source for oral literature and drama, reaching every segment of society, literate and illiterate. Familiar to every peasant, their heroic protagonists such as the *Three Kingdom*'s Guan'gong (Guandi) have been venerated as guardian divinities. The martial pantheon invoked in popular uprisings demonstrated, therefore, the inseparability of Chinese religion and popular culture. The divine warriors who empowered the rebels were those whose exploits were celebrated by itinerant storytellers and actors. Rebel armies such as the 1990s Boxers headed to battle possessed by the gods whose adventures were enacted on the village stage (Esherick 1987, 38–67).

The military gods protecting the peasant-rebel often share his mutinous ideology. Possessed of outstanding fighting skills, many are equally remarkable for their opposition to the existing order. Worshiped as tutelary divinities, the martial protagonists of late imperial fiction are often marginal figures who question accepted social norms, challenging the powers that be. The *Water Margin*'s heroes are Robin Hood–type bandits, distributing to the poor the spoils of the rich, and the *Journey to the West*'s Sun Wukong challenges divine, no less than earthly, authority. Rising in arms against the entire heavenly bureaucracy, the fearless Monkey aims to usurp its highest post. The Great Sage Equal to Heaven, as the defiant Monkey calls himself, struggles to occupy the Jade Emperor's throne. No wonder that he has been chosen as a rallying symbol by rebels ranging from the 1900 Boxers to the 1960s' Red Guards. Such unruly gods as Monkey illustrate the potential for resistance that is inherent in many Chinese martial divinities (Shahar and Weller 1996). Providing symbolic resources for insubordination, they have been cherished by all those who strayed from or challenged the existing order from late imperial insurgents and outlaws to contemporary gangsters. It might further be argued that military gods have contributed to the shaping of masculinity at large. Chinese men, especially but not only of the lower classes, often emulate the enticing combination of generosity and violence, loyalty and defiance that is characteristic of the deified warrior in popular culture (Boretz 2011).

Martial gods have conferred invulnerability on their warrior devotees. During the nineteenth and twentieth centuries, peasant armies headed to battle tragically convinced that divine protection would make them immune to swords, spears, and even firearms. The search for battle invulnerability has ancient origins. As early as the medieval period, Chinese masters of Tantric Buddhism conjured a magic shield around their bodies that protected them from the demons of disease no less than from enemy weapons. Called "Diamond Armor" (*Jin'gang jiazhou*), it reflected the centrality of the adamantine vocabulary in the Tantric movement, which had been known by the alternate name of the "Diamond Vehicle" or *Vajrayana* (Shahar 2012). By late imperial times, Chinese invulnerability techniques were commonly known by the generic names Golden Bell Armor (*Jinzhong zhao*) and Iron-Cloth Shirt (*Tiebu shan*). The impenetrable body was achieved by a combination of physiological and ritual practice. Adepts circulated their internal energy (*qi*) pounding the flesh with bricks and sandbags, even as they swallowed charms (burnt and mixed with water), making offerings to valiant deities. In some cases, magic immunity was obtained by rituals of possession, the martial divinities descending into the warrior's body as he headed to the battlefield. In others, the polluting, yet magically potent, power of women was put into use, as prostitutes were instructed to urinate from city walls so as to defend it against the enemy's artillery (Naquin 1976, 30–31; 37, 320 note 125; Naquin 1981, 100–101; Esherick 1987, 96–98, 104–109, 216–222; Perry 1980, 186–205; Shahar 2012).

Martial gods require meat-based offerings. In order for them to accomplish their heroic feats they have to be nourished by animal flesh. This leads us to another aspect of religion and violence—the aggression toward the sacrificial victim.

In ancient China, human sacrifices were not uncommon. During the second millennium BCE, the Shang kings ritually slaughtered war prisoners as offerings to deified ancestors (Shelach 1996; for further discussion of this, see David Carrasco's "Sacrifice/Human Sacrifice," chapter 11 in this volume). Slaves were similarly killed to accompany their deceased lord in his journey to the netherworld. By the middle of the first millennium BCE, such human sacrifices largely disappeared, being replaced by the offering of animals or, in the case of funerary ceremonies, by effigies (instead of real persons). To this day, animal sacrifices have remained widespread in the popular religion. Most gods are offered the flesh of slaughtered animals (most commonly pigs). Even though Buddhist monks and Daoist priests refrain from animal sacrifices (the former maintaining vegetarian offerings, the latter specializing in the oblation of written scriptures), their lay clientele have adhered to the offerings of the flesh. Daoist priests often participate in religious festivals that feature animal sacrifice, even though they do not take part in it. In the temple's inner shrine the priest performs the Daoist rites (that do not involve meat offerings), even as in the adjacent courtyard animals are slaughtered for the same religious occasion.

Even though human sacrifices no longer figure in China, human blood is still drawn in religious ceremonies. On major occasions such as a deity's birthday, spirit mediums and ritual specialists (*fashi*) mortify the flesh. The self-torture is a public spectacle in which the performer may stab his flesh with a spear, slash it with a sword, or hit it with a ball of nails. Mediums often go as far as piercing their cheeks with metal skewers, which are carried for hours, sometimes with weights attached. In one sense, the medium functions in the ritual as the community's sacrificial scapegoat, his streaming blood an offering to the gods (Dean 1993, 181–182; Elliott 1984 [1955]). From another angle, his sacrifice provides the village with magic protection. Ritual masters of the Lüshan lineage, for example, smear their blood on the flags of the Five Armies (*Wuying*) that are stationed in the Five Directions: north, south, east, west, and center. Made of divine troops, the Five Armies protect the village against demonic influences. In medieval times, the mortification of the flesh figured also in Buddhist circles, even though its purpose differed. Hoping for salvation or divine epiphany as depicted in the Lotus Sutra, monks and lay persons would burn body parts, experiencing liberation in a moment of excruciating physical pain (Benn 2007; Michael Jerryson's "Buddhist Traditions and Violence," chapter 2 in this volume).

Martial Arts and Spiritual Practice

The Chinese martial arts are a multifaceted system of physical and mental self-cultivation that combines military, therapeutic, and religious goals within the same training routine. Even though it sometimes makes use of weapons (including staffs, swords, and spears among others), practice is usually done barehanded, for which reason the Chinese fighting techniques are known by the generic term *quan* ("fist"). Gymnastic exercises that combined limb movements, breathing, and meditation had been practiced in China as early as the first centuries BCE. Intended for health and spiritual cultivation, they were integrated during the first centuries CE into the emerging Daoist religion, becoming an integral aspect of its immortality practice. During the late Ming and early Qing periods (the sixteenth and seventeenth centuries) the ancient Daoist gymnastic techniques (which originally were not intended for fighting) were integrated with the barehanded martial arts, creating the unique synthesis of martial, remedial, and spiritual aspects that, by the twenty-first century, has made the martial arts popular the world over (Shahar 2008; Wile 1996; Wile 1999).

The names of prominent martial styles attest their self-conscious spiritual goals: Taiji Quan ("Supreme-Ultimate Fist"), Xingyi Quan ("Form and Intent Fist"), Bagua Zhang ("Eight Trigrams Palm," so called after the *Classic of Changes'* eight primary configurations of the *yin* and the *yang*), and Shaolin Quan ("Shaolin Fist," named after the renowned Shaolin Buddhist Temple, which monks have been practicing fighting for more than a millennium). These diverse fighting techniques lead the practitioner into a mystical experience of liberation—or union with the divine—that is obtained in the body, by a combination of physiological practice and mental concentration. The sixteenth- and seventeenth-century creators of these martial arts drew on diverse sources: Daoist manuals of gymnastics, medical treatises of acupuncture, cosmological interpretations of the *Classic of Changes*, and Buddhist scriptures. The result was a unique amalgamation of physiological and spiritual vocabularies, as fighting manuals simultaneously employed diverse religious terminologies to articulate their spiritual goals. The imagination of Daoist immortality, the cosmology of the Supreme Ultimate, and the vocabulary of Buddhist enlightenment were equally harnessed to describe the practitioner's mystical experience.

We may want to conclude this chapter by quoting a brief passage from an influential martial arts manual. The early seventeenth-century *Sinews-Transformation Classic* or *Yijin jing* (which carries a forged preface attributing it to the semilegendary fifth-century Buddhist saint Bodhidharma) has played a major role in the emergence of the late imperial and contemporary martial arts. The treatise's combination of military, therapeutic, and religious goals is articulated by both Daoist and Buddhist vocabularies. Its postscript assures of not only the practitioner's physical health and mental well-being but also that he becomes an immortal and a Buddha:

> I have been studying the *Sinews-Transformation Classic* because I realize that in the two schools of Buddhism and Daoism those who seek the Way are as numerous as cattle's hair, but those who obtain it are as few as the unicorn's horn. This is due not to the Way being hard to achieve, but to the adepts not recognizing its gate. Due to the lack of a foundation, in Chan meditation there is the danger of insanity; in gymnastics there is the fear of exhaustion; in sexual practices there is the specter

of premature death; and in drug-taking there is the anxiety of being parched—all because people have not read the *Sinews-Transformation Classic*. If they obtain it and practice it—if they take it and expand upon it—then on a large scale they will render the state meritorious service, and on a small scale they will protect self and family. The farmer will by it diligently till the land, and through its practice the merchant will carry heavy loads on long journeys. The sick will regain his health, and the weak will be strengthened. The childless will abundantly reproduce, and the old will revert to his youth. The human will progress into a Buddha, and the mortal will be transformed into an immortal. Little practice will bring modest results; thorough practice will lead to great accomplishments. The *Sinews-Transformation Classic* is indeed the world's ultimate treasure. (Shahar 2008, 174)

BIBLIOGRAPHY

Benn, James A. *Burning for the Buddha: Self-Immolation in Chinese Buddhism.* Honolulu: University of Hawaii Press, 2007.

Berling, Judith A. *The Syncretic Religion of Li Chao-en.* New York: Columbia University Press, 1980.

Boretz, Avron. *Gods, Ghosts, and Gangsters: Ritual Violence, Martial Arts, and Masculinity on the Margins of Chinese Society.* Honolulu: University of Hawaii Press, 2011.

Brook, Timothy. "Rethinking Syncretism: The Unity of the Three Teachings and their Joint Worship in Late-Imperial China." *Journal of Chinese Religions* 21 (1993): 13–44.

Ch'en, Kenneth K. S. *Buddhism in China: A Historical Survey.* Princeton, NJ: Princeton University Press, 1964.

Chou Yi-Liang. "Tantrism in China." *Harvard Journal of Asiatic Studies* 8.3/4 (1945): 241–332.

Dean, Kenneth. *Taoist Ritual and Popular Cults of South-East China.* Princeton, NJ: Princeton University Press, 1993.

Demiéville, Paul. "Buddhism and War." Translated by Michelle Kendall. In *Buddhist Warfare.* Edited by Michael Jerryson and Mark Juergensmeyer, 17–58. Oxford, UK: Oxford University Press, 2010.

Elliott, Allan J. A. *Chinese Spirit Medium Cults in Singapore.* Taipei: Southern Materials Center, 1984 [1955].

Esherick, Joseph W. *The Origins of the Boxer Uprising.* Berkeley: University of California Press, 1987.

Groot, J. J. M. de. *Sectarianism and Religious Persecution in China.* Taipei: Ch'eng Wen, 1970 [1903–1904].

Hansen, Valerie. "Gods on Walls: A Case of Indian Influence on Chinese Lay Religion?" *Religion and Society in T'ang and Sung China.* Eds. Patricia Buckley Ebrey and Peter N. Gregory, 75–113. Honolulu: University of Hawaii Press, 1993.

Lagerwey, John. "The Pilgrimage to Wu-tang Shan." In *Pilgrims and Sacred Sites in China.* Edited by Susan Naquin and Chun-fang Yu. Berkeley: University of California Press, 1992.

Liu Kwang-Ching, and Richard Sheck, eds. *Heterodoxy in Late Imperial China.* Honolulu: University of Hawaii Press, 2004.

Mather, Richard B. "K'ou Ch'ien-chih and the Taoist Theocracy at the Northern Wei Court, 421–451." *Facets of Taoism.* Eds. Holmes Welch and Anna Seidel, 103–122. New Haven, CT: Yale University Press, 1979.

Naquin, Susan. *Millenarian Rebellion in China: The Eight Trigrams Uprising of 1813.* New Haven, CT: Yale University Press, 1976.

Naquin, Susan. *Shantung Rebellion: The Wang Lun Uprising of 1774.* New Haven, CT: Yale University Press, 1981.

Naquin, Susan, and Chün-fang Yü. *Pilgrims and Sacred Sites in China.* Berkeley: University of California Press, 1992.

Perry, Elizabeth J. *Rebels and Revolutionaries in North China, 1845–1945.* Palo Alto, CA: Stanford University Press, 1980.

Seaman, Gary. *Journey to the North: An Ethnohistorical Analysis and Annotated Translation of the Chinese Folk Novel Pei-yu-chi.* Berkeley: University of California Press, 1987.

Shahar Meir, and Robert Weller, eds. *Unruly Gods: Divinity and Society in China.* Honolulu: University of Hawaii Press, 1996.

Shahar Meir. *The Shaolin Monastery: History, Religion, and the Chinese Martial Arts.* Honolulu: University of Hawaii Press, 2008.

Shahar Meir. "Diamond Body: The Origins of Invulnerability in the Chinese Martial Arts." *Perfect Bodies: Sports, Medicine and Immortality.* Ed. Vivienne Lo. London: British Museum, 2012.

Shelach, G. "The Qiang and the Question of Human Sacrifice in the Late Shang Period," *Asian Perspectives.* 35.1 (1996): 1–26.

Shih, Vincent Y. C. (Shi Youzhong). *The Taiping Ideology: Its Sources, Interpretations, and Influences.* Seattle: University of Washington Press, 1972.

Strickmann, Michel. *Mantras et mandarins: le Buddhism Tantrique en Chine.* Paris: Gallimard, 1996.

ter Haar, Barend J. *The White Lotus Teachings in Chinese Religious History.* Leiden, Netherlands: Brill, 1992.

Weinstein, Stanley. *Buddhism under the T'ang.* Cambridge, UK: Cambridge University Press, 1987.

Wile, Douglas. *Lost T'ai-chi Classics from the Late Ch'ing Dynasty.* Albany: State University of New York Press, 1996.

Wile, Douglas. *T'ai-chi's Ancestors: The Making of an Internal Art.* New City, NY: Sweet Ch'i Press, 1999.

Zheng Acai. "Lun Dunhuang xieben 'Longxing si Pishamen Tianwang lingyan ji' yu Tang Wudai de Pishamen xinyang" ("On the Dunhuang Manuscript 'The Divine Efficacy of the Longxing Temple's Heavenly King Vaiśravaṇa' and the Vaiśravaṇa Cult of the Tang and Five Dynasties Period"). *Zhong'guo Tang dai wenhua xueshu yantaohui lunwen ji, di san jie.* Taipei: Zhong'guo Tang dai xuehui, 1997.

PART II

PATTERNS AND THEMES

CHAPTER 10

....

THE RELIGIOUS
PROBLEM OF EVIL

....

JAMES AHO

PRIOR to the modern era, evil was accounted for by what are technically known as theodicies, justifications of God's ways to man. Among these were the idea that evil is divine retribution for mankind's sins, that evil is an automatic consequence (according to the law of karma) that follows from disobeying one's obligations, that it is a test of one's faith (à la Job), or that in the next life those who suffer evil now shall inherit the earth and be blessed as peace makers.

From the beginning of the nineteenth century, however, for reasons we need not examine here, thoughtful minds began turning to the possibility of *anthropodicies* of evil, to accounts of suffering posed in human terms and that therefore allow for human remedies (Becker, *Structure* 15–19). The move toward anthropodicy eventually culminated in the modern sciences of mankind: psychology, political economics, and social anthropology.

All anthropodicies revolve around two questions: How does evil give itself to consciousness experienced; and, Why is there evil? This chapter reviews some of the answers to these queries.

HOW EVIL IS EXPERIENCED

....

Whether it is written as madness, disease, sin, pollution, noise, delinquency, or as the "militant ignorance" of those who kill and maim others under the pretense of love or patriotism (Peck), evil at bottom refers to what does not fit, to the unexpected, to disorder, or to what Mary Douglas calls "matter out of place.". The crucial insight afforded by this definition is that, at least from the standpoint of modern social science, no person, thing, or act is in itself evil. What makes it so, when it is, is that it does not comport to the normal and acceptable state of affairs. Evil irrupts into the everyday world unasked and unwelcome, shattering taken-for-granted routines.

To illustrate, Douglas cites the case of swine meat, an otherwise entirely edible substance (assuming it is properly cooked and preserved), but one that is experienced in both Judaism and Islam as toxic (*treif* [Heb.] or *haraam* [Arab.]). This is so much the case that one biblical anecdote has seven brothers brought before a Greek military commander in Palestine and given the choice between eating pig meat or being executed. Each man, refusing the proffered pork, is summarily detongued, scalped, and relieved of his extremities, in this way going to his death "undefiled and with perfect trust in the Lord" (2 Mac. 7).

Douglas's argument is that pork is vile, not because it harbors parasites but because the pig is a cloven-hoofed beast that does not chew a cud. Thus, unlike cattle, antelope, and deer, it does not "fit" into the category of licit animals. Instead, it is an "other thing" (*davar ahar*), an object so foul that even to mention it by name puts the speaker at risk of contamination.

An analogous argument can be made for what is considered human evil: people with misshapen bodies or a different skin color, those who adorn themselves in "impure" ways, individuals with "disgusting" sexual desires, speakers of *bar-bar* (Gk., "a foreign language"), or adherents of a heretical (literally, "other") belief; in short, folk who violate the template of comeliness, validity, and health, which, of course, is to say: us. Like bats (who fly through the air but have no feathers), snakes (who crawl on the earth yet have no feet), or crabs and shrimp (who reside in the sea but have neither fins nor scales), such beings are "icky," *cakka*, garbage. They are to be treated like refuse, which means they must be either denied entry into the community or, if they are already in our midst, cast out from it (for an extended conversation on this, see David Frankfurter's chapter in this volume).

Whether incarnate in human form or in beastly guise, evil presents itself to our consciousness as horrifying and beguiling, terrifying and wonderful (i.e., as occasioning jaw-dropping wonder), as something both awful and enchanting. In other words, like the sacred or holy (as analyzed by Rudolf Otto), evil evokes in witnesses a paradoxical combination of contrary feelings. Otto suggests that, at the most basic level, the sacred *is* evil. Or as he would say, "the devil is older than God." This possibility is suggested in both the Polynesian and Arabic equivalent to "sacred," taboo and *haraam*.

Haraam is cognate to the ancient Semitic term *herem,* the label used to designate the Canaanites who, in the biblical narrative, are displaced by the Israelites as the latter assume control of the land promised them by Yahweh. The First Testament describes *herem* as "most sacred to the Lord," meaning set apart for God's use alone. Thus, to intermarry with them, trade, or dine with them would be "the worst sacrilege of all" (Lev. 27:29). And what, precisely, is it that renders the Canaanites sacred? It is their evil, the fact that they worship alien gods? "Because of the abomination with which their impurities have infected [the Promised Land] from end to end" (Ezra 9:11), the *herem* must be "utterly destroyed" (Deut. 20:16,

13:13–19, 17:17). "You must not," Yahweh commands, "spare the life of any living thing" they have touched; except, that is, for the fruit tree.

It would be a serious mistake to think that the sacredness of evil is unfamiliar to contemporary experience. To take just one example, the scientists who detonated the first atomic bomb in 1945 immediately grasped that they were in the presence of something dreadful and wondrous. As a result, they felt compelled to use religious poetry to describe what they saw. "I am Death…Who shatters worlds," one uttered to himself, quoting the words of the skull-crushing, blood-lapping Hindu god Vishnu (Bhagavad Gita, 11:12, 26–30). Another was reminded of a famous painting by Matthias Grunewald. "He also pictured Christ in a ball [of fire] like this, even with the blue halo around. And I was almost scared by this contrast, between this instrument of death and the symbol of faith in Grunewald's picture." A third reported that the explosion "was like the grand finale of a mighty symphony…fascinating and terrifying, uplifting and crushing, ominous, devastating, full of great promise and great forebodings" (Aho, "I am Death," 50–54 184 n 25).

Evil has little inherent meaning apart from culturally contrived notions of orderliness, goodliness, or legality. This is to say, evil is relative. As it stands, however, this assertion is highly problematic, for it risks trivializing the lived experience of evil, what it is that gives evil its emotional resonance and enduring interest. Another and perhaps better way to approach the subject, then, is by considering what "matter out of place" points to and what it anticipates. This, simply enough, is death. However it is enframed, the little forms of chaos listed earlier—dirt, lunacy, disease, noise, crime, and so on—prefigure the Great Chaos: the eternal silence of the void. It is this that helps us access both the trembling that evil evokes and its paradoxical enchantment (Becker, *Denial*).

That evil stands for death explains its ghastliness. Think of the gaunt faces staring back at us from behind barbed wire in Auschwitz; the screaming Vietnamese child running naked down the road, frantically scraping at the napalm that is incinerating her flesh; the bloated, headless bodies of Tutsis floating down the Razizi River in Rwanda in 1994. The examples are countless. In all cases, the response is one of revulsion. Yet, like voyeurs, we seem powerless to avert our gaze. My argument is that this is because we glimpse in the victims something of ourselves—not directly, of course, or with full consciousness—but as "through a glass darkly." This something is our own personal death. To say it differently, what beguiles us most is ourselves. The evil we see in matter out of place "out there"—in madness, sickness, vice, and filth—reminds us of our own existential fragility and precarious "in here": our own mortality.

THE WHYS OF EVIL

Evil answers not just to one why but to three. The first is the why of its cause: What are the bio-psycho-social conditions independent of (an) evil, and prior to it, that remain statistically associated with (the) evil even when the effects of other possible causes (or "variables") are "controlled for" or eliminated? The second is the why of its motives: How do perpetrators of evil understand their behavior? What are the reasons they give for doing what they do? Third is the why of its purpose: What are social-psychological "functions," so to say, served by evil?

THE CAUSES OF EVIL

If evil is to be managed, if not eliminated, its causes must first be known. It was the search for evil's causes that inspired the original anthropodicies mentioned at the outset of this chapter. But as social scientists were soon to discover, there exists "a long procession of answers...each contingent in the parade...[having] its own body of argument and supporting evidence...each claiming possession of objective truth" (Burkhead 9). To get a taste of the daunting challenges faced by causal analysts of evil, let us focus on a single issue, crime (from Lat. *crimen*, "evil"). The reader should be able to make comparable itemizations in the cases of poverty, disease, pollution, war, and the like.

First of all, there are biologies of crime. Among other things, these would include the claim that crime's cause lies in the perpetrators' genes, perhaps lodged in a genetically transmitted retrovirus or in a head injury. Second are cultural anthropologies of crime. These argue that criminals are perfectly normal people biologically, who nonetheless have been nudged into wrongdoing by culture. That is, they have modeled themselves after what they have seen on television, in movies, and/or in violent video games or from what they have heard in misogynist, drug-extolling rock 'n' roll lyrics. Or they have become lawbreakers through being socialized into a "culture of poverty." As a result, their capacity to withhold immediate gratification is limited and/or they have no respect for private property. Third are political sciences of crime. Here we come across the theory of rising expectations, the hypothesis that crime originates from a lack of access to democratic means of redress for grievances and/or that crime is caused, for example, by the perpetrator's desire to compensate for his or her declining status. Fourth are the psychologies of crime, which theorize that criminals have low IQs and/or that they are psychopaths (i.e., they have no consciences). The former is because they lack access to modern education; the latter, because they have been physically and/or psychologically abused by their caretakers. In either case, their frustrations become manifest as criminal aggression. Fifth are sociologies of crime. Some sociologists hypothesize that criminality is a product of racism or that it grows from an absence of legitimate economic opportunities to achieve material success. Others say that crime emerges from the experience of alienation from the ordinary channels of community belonging, for example, marriage, religion, or work. Other sociologists maintain that peer pressure is the culprit; while still others assert that criminality is a rational adaptation to double-bind (maddeningly contradictory) messaging, or that society's laws are viewed by criminals as unworthy of being obeyed. Finally, a handful of sociologists claim that the main cause of crime is the victims themselves who inadvertently make themselves available to be preyed on.

Obviously, this is not the place to adjudicate the relative veracity of these various accounts. Instead, we will have to be satisfied with the following two comments.

First of all, from a causal perspective, wherein each act is assumed to be preconditioned by external and/or internal circumstances, by definition there is no free will. On the contrary, every supposed "choice" is always already determined, even if its causes have yet to be discerned. The concepts of free will and individual responsibility are from an entirely different "language game," one with its own limitations and possibilities. One implication of this is that, even as knowledge of evil's causes continues to accumulate, this will have no logical bearing on the notion of individual responsibility (although it may have a practical, political impact on determinations of guilt and on sentencing). As Jean-Paul Sartre once put it, human beings will always already be "condemned to freedom." Nothing can ever change that (Berger 121–150).

Looked at more closely, the question that causality asks of an evil act is this: What are the prior conditions of a rape, murder, theft, and so on without which it would likely not have occurred? The question asked in the language game of freedom and responsibility is: Who is responsible? Who is at fault? Inquiries into questions of causality are conducted through laboratory experimentation and/or by surveys of random samples drawn from large populations. Answers to questions of moral accountability, in contrast, are provided through finger pointing in public arenas and by the assignment of blame in courtrooms. Often the accusing eye of the fault finder settles on those whose "crime" is in having a different skin color, an "abnormal" sexual preference, or a "peculiar" belief.

Second, there is nothing in the language game of cause and effect that recommends it over the game of freedom and responsibility. More emotional satisfaction usually comes from inflicting retribution on a putative guilty one than it does from learning about the causes of (an) evil. In any case, the average person (including the causal analyst) typically skips from the cause game to the blame game and then back again with little awareness of doing so. Nevertheless, we would be well advised to temper the habit of conflating punishment with policies that actually hold some promise of making (an) evil less likely.

The Motives of Evil

Causal theories of evil approach evil from the outside, so to say, as an object separate from the investigator. Qualitative analysts, as they call themselves, seek instead to grasp it from the inside, from the standpoint of the perpetrators, seeing, thinking about, and recalling the evil in question as they do. This is done by investigators

imaginatively putting themselves into the perpetrator's shoes through a combination of nonstructured, goal-directed interviewing and participant observation.

Beginning in the late 1920s, the University of Chicago published a series of
qualitative studies of putative evils such as juvenile gangs; hobos; "taxi dance hall"
girls (prostitutes) and "unadjusted girls"; of professional pickpockets, pilferers,
shoplifters, cons, counterfeits, and extortionists; and of "jack-rollers" (those who
rob drunks). Eventually this approach was extended to encompass white-collar
corporate crime, international crime syndicates, war criminals, and politically and
religiously motivated terrorists (cf. Juergensmeyer).

Qualitative accounts of evil often lack analytic rigor. But this is more than
compensated for by their richness and depth. "Stanley," a one-time jack roller
whose life- story comprises the entire content of Clifford Shaw's classic oral history,
is typical in this respect (Shaw). It opens with Stanley describing his impoverished
youth, followed by the story of his being "lured" into making fast money illicitly,
as he "mingles" with a gaggle of similarly troubled boys. Stanley goes on to relate
how he supported himself "on the road" by means of petty theft until his travels
ended in arrest, conviction, and incarceration in what he calls a "house of corruption" (a reform school), from which he eventually "graduates" with a full panoply
of criminal skills and a well-honed vocabulary of criminal rationalizations, most
notably that he is a victim.

Causal and qualitative approaches to evil are more than just alternative methodologies. They can also have profoundly different outcomes. If done well, a causal
analysis will generate policies intended to control (an) evil. The end result of a
qualitative study, on the other hand, may be "reformation" of the investigators
themselves. Even if a qualitative researcher goes into the field intending to solve
an evil, he or she may well end up discovering his or her own complicity in it.
The reason for this is as follows: Georg Simmel writes that only after an investigator experiences the "aha" that he or she is not just "here" but also *there* in the
other person; only then can he or she be confident of having truly grasped that
other person's actions. (The German word for this is *Verstehen*, which means, literally, "standing there" in the other's place;Simmel). To say it differently, when I as a
researcher recognize myself in the hate-spouting neo-Nazi, in the Muslim suicide
bomber, the avaricious capitalist, or in the child predator who passes in public as
a defender of family values—only then do I see them in their full human subjectivity, as persons like me: fragile, fallible, and perhaps even worthy of forgiveness.
In Vajrayana Buddhism, this is known as *vajra,* the bolt of awareness that, like a
diamond, cuts through even the most obdurate illusion of my own purity and difference from them. Christianity calls the same shocking wound a "circumcision of
the heart" (Rom. 2:29).

There are three major reasons or rhetorics routinely invoked by evil doers
when called on to account for their acts. They are the arguments from affect, from
custom, and from rationality. By the argument from affect, we mean the voicing of
one or more of the familiar seven passions: pride, envy, rage, hunger, lust, greed, or
boredom. For example: "I kicked the homeless man to death because I wanted to

feel what it would be like to kill someone," "I murdered her because I felt jealous. If I can't have her, no one can!" or "I (a soldier) decapitated the little boy because I felt enraged for what his father (an enemy) had done to my best friend."

The rhetoric of custom finds its most elaborate expression in the philosophical doctrines of natural law and/or human nature. For example: "Slavery (warfare, male domination, greed, poverty, etc.) are given in the 'nature' of things." Hence, for all intents and purposes nothing can be done about it. By submitting with equanimity to the inevitability of nature and "loving fate" (*amor fati*), we can attain a measure of happiness.

In regard to the rhetoric from rationality, there are two variations. First are accounts of evil that insist that it is utilitarian, practical, or efficient. For example: "Dropping atomic bombs on the Japanese and fire-bombing defenseless German civilians was 'cost-effective.' The lives of millions of others were saved as a result." This is the kind of argumentation frequently heard in war rooms, as mathematical economists use differential equations to predict how to inflict maximum violence on putative enemies, while minimizing costs to one's own side.

The second rhetoric of rationality is ends oriented. Here the perpetrators claim that they have acted out of moral principle or duty alone, with no thought given to its costs or benefits, either to themselves or to others. This is the logic of the holy war or jihad. In a phrase, "God wills it!" or "Better dead than Red!" proclaims the anticommunist. "Better that life in its entirety be wiped from earth, than God's design be thwarted." Or again, as Adolf Hitler writes in justifying the Holocaust: "*By defending myself against the Jew I am fighting for the work of the Lord*" (Hitler 249, 65 his emphasis).

Even if it appears at first glance to be crazy, human evil is always "reasonable." It can always be rationalized, excused and/or justified. Excuses admit to an evil but deny responsibility for it; this, by claiming that it was "caused" by passions outside (*ex*) the evil doer's control. Justifications admit responsibility for the evil but either deny its harmfulness or relativize its damage by situating it in the context of a presumably higher good; or by insisting, as in the case of the Jews, that the victim deserved it: "They murdered our Christ!"

THE PURPOSES OF HUMAN EVIL

Emile Durkheim was one of the first sociologists to observe that human evil is "normal" and that "a society exempt from it is utterly impossible" (Durkheim 67, 71). This is because evil serves specific "functions." First of all, badness awakens people to prevailing standards of goodness, clarifying the limits of personal freedom and thereby helping to maintain social order. Secondly, evil doers teach others that, by comparison, they are exemplars of good. This enhances their pride and sense of well-being. "I may be down and out, but at least I'm not one of *them*!" This is to say nothing of the job opportunities that the problem of evil affords well-doers who are charged with rectifying it: psycho-social-rehab workers, genetic engineers, penologists, judges, lawyers, forensics experts, policemen, and the like, many of whom might be unemployable without it. To be sure, there may be more cost-effective, alternative ways to put people to work, instill in them how to behave, and convey a sense of self esteem. But ignoring this, there are two implications that follow from the basic proposition.

The first implication is that, in order to be pedagogically effective, encounters between well-doers and evil doers must always be made public. Or to say it another way, all viable societies will have some variation of public degradation ceremony, or what Durkheim calls a "piacular rite" (from Lat. *piaculum,* "sin offering"): criminal proceedings, insanity hearings, ecclesiastical inquisitions, courts of "love," senate investigations, and/or show trials at which deviants sobbingly confess their wrongdoing. In ancient times, piacular rites were conducted in plazas, agoras, or in theaters specially erected for this purpose. Today, they are frequently televised live or videotaped for evening viewing. In order to "work" in the ways previously specified, piacular rites must meet several preconditions (Garfinkel): One is that the accusers must be able to demonstrate orally and/or by written word that everything in the piaculum's life is an "index" of inherent perversity. This includes outward signs of abiding by the law, churchgoing piety, charity, and so on. These must all be reinterpreted as further proof of essential abnormality, duplicity, and greed. Another precondition is that the accusers must show that they are paragons of societal virtue. Third, the accusers must convince audiences that they are not testifying against the defendant out of a desire for personal vengeance or fear but solely out of concern for "tribal values."

The second implication is that, because evil doers are functionally necessary for society's viability, then it follows that if they did not already exist, they would have to be manufactured. So they are, following a time-honored recipe (Aho, *This Thing* 27–32, 36–47). The initial step involves "labeling": identifying certain rule breakers as troublemakers, heretics, delinquents, witches, and so on (Becker). This is followed by the devising of a corpus of demonic myths (that sometimes pass as scientific theories) that "explain" why those so labeled are as they are. In the final step, the evil one is submitted to a "treatment plan" (punishment): probation, imprisonment, reeducation, shock treatment, flesh cutting, hydrotherapy, exile, or in extreme cases, death. While treatments are ostensibly undertaken to rehabilitate, deter, or cure, what they accomplish in fact is the infliction of pain. The piaculum's reactions to the administration of pain—rage, screaming, withdrawal, vociferous denials of guilt, or groveling admissions of the same—have the effect of reconfirming in the audience the justice and rightness of the sentence imposed.

Those who undergo this three-step process are not rule breakers in general, but rule breakers who are isolated, poor, powerless, and members of racial, ethnic, and/or religious minorities. Rule breakers who are wealthy, well connected, and/or who can claim membership in the majority population are often able to deflect the pointed finger of blame. As for the former, however, in exchange for playing foil to society and helping instill the lessons mentioned, they will be housed, clothed, and fed with various degrees of security (and at taxpayer expense) in public facilities.

The modern piaculum bears an uncanny resemblance to the ancient biblical scapegoat (*kippurum*; Lev. 16), and to the *pharmakon* (*katharma*) of pre-Socratic Greece. These were the firstborn goat and the human grotesquery chosen in springtime to atone for the sins of their respective communities (Frazer 633–660). During Yom Kippur, high priests symbolically transferred the previous winter's sins, ills, and discontents onto the head of a goat that would be led to the gates of the city, released, and left to wander in the desert. This allowed Israel to "escape" its evils, at least temporarily. In the Greek feast of Thargelia, after a similar transfer of communal guilt, the so-called poison that heals would be executed. In both cases, elimination of the scapegoat would occasion collective catharsis, joy at community renewal.

These two rites are the probable sources of the Christian mythos of an unblemished "lamb of God" whose crucifixion is said to redeem the whole of mankind from evil, as opposed to that of the Jewish community alone (Girard). Furthermore and more to the point, in Yom Kippur and Thargelia we glimpse terrible/wondrous anticipations of the modern system of criminal justice. And not just this, but the perversity of modern war, the reputed goal of which is to save the world from "death" in the form of a so-called Axis of Evil, an Evil Empire, a Great Satan, or as *dar al-harb* (Arab., "the abode of the other"). In all of these cases, mankind becomes the occasion of evil not out of craven malignity, at least for the most part, but out of a yearning to triumph over evil.

CONCLUSION

It may be, as someone once said, that evil is in our DNA and that it is ultimately intractable. But it is equally true that "you'd need to be a madman or a coward or stone blind to give in tamely to [it]" (Camus 115). In these words, Albert Camus writes about the human response to "plague," a metaphor for the evils he had just witnessed during World War II.

Camus situates *The Plague* in the "glamourless, soulless…and restful" anytown of mundane imagination. There, for no apparent reason, flea-ridden wharf rats descend on its smug, whitewashed bungalows, bringing with them the plague bacillus. The question facing the citizenry is what to do. One local priest advocates humble submission, fervent prayer, and an attitude of thankfulness for the blessings of faith that plague confers. But a young activist angrily denounces this as appeasement, arguing that the only way to deal with evil is to confront it headlong and extirpate its carriers. Dr. Rieux, however, disagrees with both. To the priest, he replies with the words quoted in the previous paragraph. To the revolutionary, he says that one who longs for a rose should not plant a noxious weed, for the means we use to fight evil will determine what the end result will be. Instead, Rieux continues, given the choice between surrender and murder, we should struggle against evil but not allow our illusions (either about it or ourselves) to devolve into delusions. We must be neither victims nor executioners.

Camus fails to specify exactly what a disillusioned grappling with evil might entail. But I think he might agree that, at a minimum, it would involve clear thinking and speaking; that is, carefully parceling out evil's several *whys* and treating each separately, its cause(s), its motives (s), and its purpose(s); this, even as the immensity of evil's horror lures us into confusion.

Bibliography

Aho, James. "I Am Death…Who Shatters Worlds." *A Shuddering Dawn*. Eds. Ira Chernus and Edward Linenthal, 49–68. Albany: State University of New York Press, 1989.

Aho, James. *This Thing of Darkness*. Seattle: University of Washington Press, 1994.

Becker, Ernest. *The Structure of Evil*. New York: Free Press, 1968.

Becker, Ernest. *The Denial of Death*. New York: Free Press, 1973.

Becker, Ernest. *Escape from Evil*. New York: Free Press, 1975.

Becker, Howard. *The Outsiders*. Glencoe, IL: Free Press, 1963.

Berger, Peter. *Invitation to Sociology*. New York: Doubleday-Anchor, 1963.

Burkhead, Michael. *The Search for the Causes of Crime*. Jefferson, NC: McFarland, 2006.

Camus, Albert. *The Plague*. Trans. Stuart Gilbert. New York: Random House, 1947.

Douglas, Mary. *Purity and Danger*. London: Routledge and Kegan Paul, 1966.

Durkheim, Emile. *The Rules of Sociological Method*. New York: Free Press, 1938.

Frazer, James. 1922. *The Golden Bough*. New York: Macmillan, 1951.

Garfinkel, Harold. "Conditions of Successful Degradation Ceremonies," *American Journal of Sociology*, 61 (1956): 420–24.

Girard, René. *The Scapegoat*, trans. by Yvonne Freccero. Baltimore: Johns Hopkins University Press, 1986.

Hitler, Adolf. *Mein Kampf (My Struggle)*, trans. by Ralph Mannheim. Boston: Houghton Mifflin, 1943.

Jurgensmeyer, Mark. *Terror in the Mind of God*. Berkeley: University of California Press, 2000.

Otto, Rudolf. *The Idea of the Holy*, trans. by John Harvey. London: Oxford University Press, 1923.

Peck, M. Scott. *People of the Lie*. New York: Century/Hutchinson, 1983.

Shaw, Clifford. *The Jack Roller: A Delinquent Boy's Own Story*. Chicago: University of Chicago Press, 1966 (1930).

Simmel, Georg. *The Problems of the Philosophy of History*, trans. by Guy Oakes. New York: Free Press, 1977.

CHAPTER 11

SACRIFICE/HUMAN SACRIFICE IN RELIGIOUS TRADITIONS

DAVÍD CARRASCO

WHEN the archaeologist Saburo Sugiyama opened up a chamber in the center of the Pyramid of the Feathered Serpent at Teotihuacan, Mexico, he found a collection of eighteen male human bodies crowded together wearing greenstone nose pendants, earplugs, and beads. All had been sacrificed and appear to have been high status adults. Further excavating the pyramid, Sugiyama's team discovered human sacrificial burials along the four borders of the elaborately sculpted ceremonial precinct (Sugiyama 2005). Some wore necklaces of small shell beads while others had the unusual adornment of collars with human maxilla (upper human jaw) pendants. Back disks and abundant projectile points appeared in some burials as well as a number of females who had been sacrificed and wore shell earplugs and cylindrical shell beads. The surprising discovery began a reformation in our understanding of the ritual life and political worldview of the great capital that for decades had been viewed as the center of a "Pax Teotihuacana." Previously it was thought that this imperial city ruled large numbers of people and territories through a theocratic system of persuasion and intimidation with little need of practicing human sacrifice. Further studies of these ruins and the sites and inscriptions of the great Classic Maya civilization in southern Mesoamerica have transformed our understanding of how thoroughly ritual violence toward human beings and human sacrifice, in particular, created and maintained social order while also serving as instruments of communication about cosmology and moral life (López Luján and Olivier 2010). We now know that human sacrifice is embedded in the social, pictorial, and literary record of Mesoamerica, which presents a challenge to interpreters of not only this cultural area but of our understanding of religion and violence more broadly.

Spurred by these discoveries in Mesoamerica, scholars have asked about the uniqueness of the forms of Aztec and Maya human sacrifices in world religions (Lopez Austin and López Luján 2008). In a surprise to some, it turns out that many societies previously lauded for their sophisticated philosophies, magnificent building programs, and the "rise of civilization" carried out human sacrifices and massacres to their gods as part of their performative traditions, ethical justifications, and political philosophies. This widespread threading of human sacrifice within the urban societies of Mesoamerica and elsewhere justify following the lead of Walter Burkert who, even as he was focusing on animal sacrifices in Greece, wrote that "[m]ore can be said for the thesis that all orders and forms of authority in human society are founded upon institutionalized violence" (Burkert 1986).

This chapter begins with a survey of several contemporary, major definitions of sacrifice as forms of symbolic and performative violence. Following a modest discussion of patterns in the sacrifices of animals and their symbols in various traditions, the chapter turns to an interpretation of the more troubling topic of actual human sacrifices in various cultures with special attention to the best-documented traditions of Mesoamerica. Given the abundance of textual and archaeological evidence for a wide range of types and purposes of these ritual killings in public places, I choose to focus on two analogies and patterns of performative violence: human sacrifice as warfare, such as the human sacrifices that made the Aztec capital into the ideal battlefield, and human sacrifice as a moral imperative for the warrior. Even when a sacrifice of a woman is designed to produce agricultural renewal, its symbolism and the use of the body are redirected, in part, by the male warrior ideal. The ritual killing of human beings, in Mesoamerica at least, is often a public performance designed to communicate and persuade the populace that commitments to cosmic warfare, debt payments to the gods, and correct gender relations are being carried out to maintain the social and cosmic order. These human sacrifices are, in the words of Jon Levenson writing about child sacrifices in Judaism and Christianity, "extreme acts of devotion" (1995: 17) and also instruments in a cosmological conviction carried out by ritual specialists in order to make the city and society at large endure. Looking at the Mesoamerican cases will help us reflect on the broader claim made by one scholar, concerned about whether the origin of violence in human beings is to be located in biology or culture. He writes: "The one thing that cannot be denied is that violence is ubiquitous and tenacious and must be accounted for if we are to understand humanity" (Hamerton-Kelly 1987: vi).

SACRIFICE AND REBOUNDING VIOLENCE

Sacrifice comes from Latin sacrificium (sacer, "holy"; facere, "to make") denoting the act of killing an animal or person as an offering to a deity. Sacrifices are extraordinary processes involving dramatic communications leading to social and ontological changes (Henninger 2005). Its common usage today extends to such acts as giving up a valued object or status for a greater cause or good such as sacrificing a pawn in chess for tactical gain or a sacrifice bunt in baseball. But its more durable and powerful meaning of killing as a form of communication with a deity, gift giving, or expiation to a higher being points to its long association with performative violence.

According to scholars such as Henninger, a wide range of objects including animals, plants, stones, and human-made items are used in sacrifices in various traditions. Of special importance is that the performance of sacrifices, of whatever material, establishes or rejuvenates intimate relationships with supernatural beings considered crucial to a community's well-being. While there is disagreement over the definition of *violence* (see Das, chapter 1 in this volume) and the term *sacrifice* suffers from an instability of meaning, we can work with the following pattern of sacrificial rituals to explore similarities between distinct religious traditions. I call this pattern a performative scenario of sacrifice, which includes a) the forceful setting apart of a valued object (elevated or debased) b) in a liminal space where supernatural and social realms meet in a c) performance of cosmic significance d) focused by the symbolic and/or material injury or destruction of a creature representing a "life force" e) meant to sustain or rejuvenate what is valued as a greater life force or to bring about a social benefit to a community in need of supernatural power. In a performative scenario or public ceremonial sequence of events meant to develop intimate exchanges between humans and supernatural beings, relationships between cosmic levels are mediated through dramatic and symbolic gestures aimed at stimulating the human senses of sight, sound, smell, and often taste so as to make humans internalize the experience and meaning of sacrifice. In some religious traditions, there are myths that say the gods performed sacrifices *of themselves* in order to initiate life in the cosmos.

While it may be thought that bloodless offerings lack violence, Maurice Bloch's revealing work titled *Prey into Hunter* shows that "the irreducible core of ritual practice" organized two types of violence at work in New Guinea and elsewhere. Even when killings are only alluded to or remembered, this practice is marked by a violent separation of people, animals, and objects from domesticated spaces. This separation is followed by ritual acts that bring about a radical change in the vitality of the separated entities (actual and symbolic) within a sacred location. The final phase involves the return of these revitalized beings to the social order through a form of "rebounding violence." Humans create this two-way movement out of the awareness of a profound and deeply felt paradox. On the one hand, they are transient beings who live, die, and disappear. On the other hand they dwell "within a permanent framework which transcends the natural transformative process of birth, growth, reproduction, aging and death." The result is the invention of rituals that symbolically deny the transience of life and participate in a transcendent reality where spirits, gods, and ancestors live forever. The goal of these sacrifices and initiations is to acquire a long lasting "religious vitality" and bring it back into the community through specific kinds of actual and symbolic violence. These dramatic forms of violence strive in many traditions to acquire cosmomagical powers that Bloch refers to as "plundered vitality." In the case of the Orokovia children who are identified with vulnerable pigs (that are normally killed and eaten by humans), they are separated from their parents and village so they can be cosmomagically mixed with the "realm of spirits or gods" where they acquire a new kind of vitality, a spirit vitality. It is only after this supernatural change that the former prey, who is now a child-spirit combination, can descend back into the community as a potential hunter-warrior. This return requires a rebounding violence that brings back to the family and society the revered spirit powers of the spirit-dead that are immortal and transcendent. This sequence of two violences subsequently allows human children to legitimately express aggression toward humans and animals that they can now hunt and kill. Bloch believes this is the matrix that underlies many sacrifices and also gives power and wisdom to people.

A similar motive for sacrifice is found in a deep tradition of Indian thought and ritual, according to J. C. Heesterman in *The Broken World of Sacrifice* (1993). Human beings faced with the riddle of life and death, such as the awareness that each of these profound realities is intimately linked to its opposite, explored an answer to the riddle through sacrifices of various kinds. In the Indian case, pre-Vedic rituals were animated by conflict and contest and included three stages: killing, the ritual destruction of the sacrificed object, and its distribution in a ritual meal. Symbolic violence and physical violence were woven closely together in the search for a resolution to the puzzle. In Heesterman's view human sacrifice was, after a long period of application to the puzzle, deemed unsatisfactory for the Indian communities that eventually broke the world of sacrifice and created new ritual strategies filled with substitutes for human killing.

The crucial role of emotion and aggression in sacrifice appears in a number of Greek rituals and cultural expressions such as oracles, games, mysteries, dramas, and funeral and royal ceremonies. Apparently modeled on human-animal relations as expressed in the Paleolithic hunt and the shared sacrificial meal, the handling of animal bones signals feelings and thoughts of intimacy among humans and between humans and animals (Burkert 1986). The hunt was a supremely collective, dramatic experience that demanded not only knowledge of disciplined movement and behavior in the outdoor pursuit of game, but also the skillful handling of unwieldy human aggressions—often felt toward other humans—by refocusing them onto the animal prey that became the sacrificial victim. In Burkert's view, the dramatic scenes and emotions associated with the killing of animals after careful planning and intense physical and mental exertions resulted in new cultural processes of perception and reflection, including the telling of stories and the creation of mythologies about the events. In a formulation that assists our efforts to fathom the patterns of human sacrifice, Burton Mack summarizes well Walter Burkert's achievement in linking the hunt and sacrifice of animals to a profound understanding of religion when he summarizes:

> [T]he hunting ritual gave rise to the full range of articulations that we understand to be mythic or symbolic, articulations characteristic of religion. The naming of the "'Master of the Animals", the songs and "prayers" that address the prey, the gestures surrounding the kill, the care of the bones, the narration of the ritualized hunt as a sequence of events (myth), and the eventual articulation of social codes and honors, including honors due the Master of the Animals ("worship") all are

found to be generated by the complex experience of the act of killing. Thus a theory of the ritualization of the hunt becomes a theory of the origin of religion. (Burton Mack 1987: 26)

In this theory of religion and sacrifice, the effectiveness and emotionality of the kill as well as its intense planning and coordination are not only the dramatization of a new social ordering, it actually restructures society for the satisfaction of basic human needs. We are then led to ask if the same kind of social achievement and source of new religious sensibility can be assigned to the ritualization of human killing?

Much of the literature on human sacrifice in religions of the world speaks of either a transformation or evolution of human sacrifices into animal sacrifices or substitutions of animals or other objects for human kind. In the words of another scholar writing in this volume about violence and nonviolence in the Vedas, we see the pattern of "ritual substitution that keeps the symbolic presence of violence very much in the picture without actually committing the acts of killing" (Das 2012). Jon Levenson's excellent study of child sacrifices in Judaism and Christianity shows how even when the practice of human sacrifice was eradicated, the religious idea of child sacrifice remained "potent and productive." He celebrates this transformation "as highly positive, one that metamorphosized a barbaric ritual into a sublime paradigm of the religious life" (1995: x). What, then, do we say of the humanity and ritual practices of many human communities including those of some Native Americans who in many locations and eras continued to carry out the ritual destruction of human beings even while they were sacrificing animals and creating cities, great art, complex calendar and writing systems, and sophisticated philosophies and theological systems. More than one Spanish priest noted, even while they condemned the sacrifices of the Maya and Aztecs, that they had never been in societies in Europe where people cared as much for their children and families as the Mesoamericans. When we get to the many Mesoamerican examples of ritual violence toward human beings we find another kind of "substitution" at work. It is the gods who were "substituted" for humans, and the human sacrificial object was ritually emptied of human identity and filled with the living spirits of the divinity who was, in the theological twists and turns of various cultures, the entity that was now beheaded, followed by a heart extraction and sometimes immolation. The result in this theological system was a new birth for the god who had just been destroyed, reappearing in vital substances of plants, animals, stars, and even the kings. Before turning to the performative scenarios of these Mesoamerican human sacrifices, a short tour of human sacrifice elsewhere will set the backdrop.

HUMAN SACRIFICES ELSEWHERE

Human sacrifice in many parts of the world fit into a broader set of sacrificial practices that include the intentional disposal of animal parts, animals, and highly valued objects (including bronzes and jades in China, ceramics and paper in

Mesoamerica, and other materials), with roots that extend back into the Neolithic and Paleolithic periods. Among the human objects sought in sacrifice were human heads. Headhunting for religious purposes appears in many parts of history around the globe including among the Scythians as reported by Herodotus who tells that they hung the heads of enemies around the neck of their horses to display their accomplishments. The Celts in Ireland, the Iroquois in the United States and the Dayak of Borneo also killed humans for the purpose of gathering heads and gaining supernatural power. In sensational performative acts, Saiva ascetics ate from human skulls and meditated on cadavers. Headhunting has more recently received illuminating attention in a series of studies showing and debating the meanings of the practice of taking heads and the ceremonial remembering of headhunting in the Philippines and elsewhere (Rosaldo 1980; George 1996).

Human sacrifices were also carried out to restore authority and rejuvenate the well-being of towns and cities. According to Robert Turcan, the Athenians purified their polis with the sacrifice of two humans called *pharmakoi*—one representing the guilt of all Athenian men and the other carrying the guilt of all the women in the city. More to the point, human sacrifices often occurred in the ritual cult around kings and social elites whose potency in this world and destiny in the next required the killing of other humans. Examples include, in Africa, the former requirement that the Rukuba king's installation ceremony included him ingesting small pieces of two different human beings, his deceased predecessor and an infant killed for this propitious event and thereby insuring the longevity of his reign. The tie between human sacrifice and the palaces of royal families was expressed in the Abomey where the king's house was built over the entrails of a conquered enemy chief. Sacrifices became the very stuff of the buildings as when human blood from ritual killings was mixed with the earthen materials used to build the palace walls (Monroe 2007).

The link between sacrifice, elites, and warfare is abundantly shown in periods of Chinese history. The scale of sacrificial activity grows tremendously in the Early Bronze Age, to an extent that states in China are famously said to have been founded and maintained on a basis of "sacrifice and warfare" (according to the *Zuozhuan*, a chronicle of the Springs and Autumns period [770–481 BCE] that was compiled during the subsequent Warring States period [480–221 BCE]). Sacrifices of humans are related to traditions of ancestor worship that have Neolithic roots (Liu 2000) and, ultimately, to practices that legitimated the hegemony of the state. It was during the Shang period that we have the first extensive evidence of large-scale human sacrifices, and scholars have postulated three broad types of human sacrifices that have considerable overlap (Campbell 2007: 177; Fiskesjö 2003: 60–61). The first are foundation sacrifices, which were those used as dedicatory offerings in the context of construction events of special buildings. These typically comprise human remains (and other offerings) found in pits in or under foundations of important buildings. The second are sacrifices to spirits or ancestors, typically found in individual pits otherwise associated with rammed earth (i.e., elite) structures or elaborate burials. The third type of human sacrifice has been designated as death attendants, typically considered to be members of the households or entourage of elites who were interred in tombs. In some cases, a kind of spatial hierarchy is present as the attendants are found in special contexts within elite burials, such as shallow pits called waist pits beneath the main occupant's chamber. Humans buried with horses and chariots in separate sacrificial pits are included in this broad category of sacrificial victims. Among the most famous locations where these different sorts of human sacrifice can be distinguished is the royal cemetery at Xibeigang. Located northwest of Yinxu, the last capital of the Shang Dynasty, Xibeigang contained nine huge cruciform-shaped tombs attributed to the Shang kings and several other large tombs with one or two entry ramps (also considered royal tombs). These large tombs were surrounded by thousands of small graves and sacrificial pits, and human sacrifices have been found in the large tombs as well (Chang 1980: 110–123).

SELF-SACRIFICE

Human destruction is also turned toward the self in a number of traditions. It is a surprise to many to learn that the most common form of sacrifice among the Aztecs and Maya was self-sacrifice in many forms of bloodletting, a practice that started during infancy when parents drew blood from children during special calendar rituals (Klein 1987). More dramatic self-sacrifice appeared in the Hindu practice of sati with the self-immolation of widows (sometimes forced, sometimes voluntary) on their husband's funeral pyre (Geertz 1981). It is believed that the widow is only half alive and, at least during the Brahmanical period, she faced three choices: remarry the younger brother of her husband, a lifetime commitment to servitude in a widow's ashram, or *sati*. These "voluntary" sacrifices are justified by the cosmological belief that two human bodies are united in the fire to make one indivisible body (Weinberg-Thompson), thus enabling the couple to escape the cycle of birth-death and rebirth.

A form of self-sacrifice continues today in Japan where suicides in various forms are carried out under the influence of Confucian concepts of honor and in the shadow of the rubric of samurai who were compelled to commit seppuku for any number of reasons, including atonement for transgressions or to complete a code of honor. The classic case of self-sacrifice through ritual disembowelment is known as the Forty-Seven Ronin, in which a group of samurai was forced by the government to commit *seppuku* in punishment for murdering a high official. This event has become extremely popular in Japanese art and theater because it represents the ideal of how one should live a life of honor, loyalty, and commitment to authority. It is evident that kamikaze pilots toward the end of World War II followed this tradition with their suicide attacks on naval vessels thereby following the code of death instead of defeat or shame.

A huge, one-time example of group self-sacrifice or "revolutionary suicide" occurred in Jonestown, Guyana, in 1978 when nearly 909 people were persuaded to drink cyanide poison by their charismatic leader James Jones, who instead shot himself to death. It was the greatest single loss of life of American civilian life in a non-natural event until the attacks on 9/11.

THE CITIES OF SACRIFICE

A recent, comprehensive volume with twenty-four essays *El sacrificio humano en la tradición religiosa mesoamericana* (López Luján and Olivier 2010) opens new challenges for understanding not only the technique and performances of human sacrifice in Mesoamerica but also for scholars attempting new theories about religion and violence. It is something of a scandal in religious studies and anthropology, which the present publication attempts to address, that all significant theories of ritual sacrifice, from Robertson Smith through Henri Hubert and Mauss, Wilhelm Schmidt, Alfred Jensen, René Girard, Walter Burkert, J. Z. Smith, and Robert Hamerton-Kelley ignored, with minor exceptions, the most fulsome record of real, historical human sacrifices from Mesoamerica while instead favoring animal sacrifice or literary accounts of human sacrifices from Western classics to form their interpretations.

I can identify with the urge to turn our thinking heads away from this record because it challenges so much of what we say and hope to find in the history of human violence. I remember when my own academic deadpan, confident as a stone mask, cracked in the face of an offering cache at the Great Aztec Temple filled with the skeletal remains of forty-two children. I was the father of a young child and here before me was a ritual chamber filled with children's skulls and infant bones strewn and tangled in a chaotic and wild looking arrangement. I could see traces of green stone beads near several mouths, flakes of blue pigment sprinkled on the bodies, necklaces of greenstone and several disks with appliquéd turquoise mosaics and turtle shell touching the little bodies of these sacrificed children. When I stood up and gazed around at the site with its giant grinning serpent heads, stone warriors leaning against a stairway, and the monumental disk sculpture of a dismembered female warrior, it was evident that public violence against humans was viewed as a profound human necessity and benefit for the Aztecs in their capital city. I wondered, how could we come to understand these not so distant neighbors, in space and time, who played such a dramatic role in the foundations of the Americas when the Europeans arrived and unleashed an even greater violence on local bodies, settlements, and souls? Does it help, I mused, to know that these children were mainly males who were suffering from anemia, parasitism, and gastrointestinal diseases and that sacrifice was thought to alleviate their suffering and make creative, reproductive use of their lives? This event taught me that questions about human sacrifice were much bigger and more complex and grim than I and most theoreticians had wanted to admit.

The Aztec record does not show an evolution away from the sacrifice of the firstborn in a human family to a replacement animal. It does not record the "satanization" of the humans to be sacrificed (Juergensmeyer, "Performance Violence," chapter 17). The people sacrificed in Tenochtitlan were always turned into living gods, the most valued or feared gods, and then led along by male and female ritual specialists on the pathway to the sacrificial altar. The surviving record does not theologize these killings as gift exchanges. The Aztec name for sacrifice was *nextlaoalli* ("the paying of the debt") and the victims were called *netlahualtin* ("restitutions") showing that the sacrifices did not emphasize gifts but rather debts (Sahagún 2002: vol. 2). Human children were sacrificed in the first month of every ritual year. Women were sacrificed in a third of the yearly sacrificial ceremonies. The term repeated again and again in the most reliable accounts provided by elders who participated in and witnessed the spectacular ceremonies is *debt payment*. Debts are a long way from "gifts," though many gifts were exchanged during the paying of debts in the many ceremonial precincts where these performative scenarios were acted out (Carrasco 1999).

Given the abundance of textual and archaeological evidence for a wide range of types and purposes of these ritual killings in public places and the interpretive challenges they present, I now return to the aforementioned two performative scenarios: human sacrifice as warfare, such as human sacrifices that made the Aztec capital into the ideal battlefield and were instruments of empire, and human sacrifice and moral order, the teaching that the ideal death, the "true" death for the warrior and others, is by sacrifice. A primer on the worldview of human sacrifice will be useful.

THE COSMOVISION OF HUMAN SACRIFICE

The evidence for human sacrifice is both obvious and controversial. The archaeological and documentary accounts make it clear that human sacrifice was widely practiced in Mesoamerica for more than 1,500 years and increased in the festivals of the Aztecs and other polities during the Postclassic period between 1100 and 1521 CE. But the Spanish accounts are filled with huge exaggerations, in several cases up to 80,400 victims in a single ceremony, grossly inflated to justify the aggressions, massacres, rapes, and executions carried out by the conquistadores and their entourages.

Regardless of these exaggerations, we now have a grasp on the worldview and cosmovision of human sacrifice in the Aztec Empire. In short form, the Aztecs saw the world as having two distinguishable parts of the universe: the space-time of the gods and the space-time of the creatures of this world that the gods created.

Human beings, animals, plants, celestial objects, minerals, and rain occupied this visible space-time world that divine beings penetrated into through malinalli, or double-helix-shaped portals located in trees, creeks, caves, and elsewhere. In Aztec mythology, divine beings temporarily departed their space-time and infiltrated everything on Earth giving earthly beings their identities, energies, and powers to live and procreate. All creatures and forces on the earth and in the air were made up of subtle, eternal divine substances and b) hard, heavy, destructible, worldly substances that served as shells to the divine substance. All life-forms on Earth were hard shells covering the divine substance within.

The origin of human sacrifice comes into the story when during various stages of the creation of the world some gods violated divine laws and were expelled from their cosmic region and came to the surface of the Earth. Two cosmic events took place that led to human sacrifice being an imperative for human life. First, to create the cycles of life of the sun and plants on Earth these deities sacrificed themselves in Teotihuacan and descended into the underworld. Now within the Earth, these subtle substances or gods acquired the skins, shells, and other heavy, destructible coverings. Then they reappeared on and above the surface of the earth first as the sun in the sky and then as moon, stars, animals, waters, trees, and so on, and life on Earth was reborn. This journey to the below and back up to the surface of the Earth and the sky became the pattern for earthly creatures who, when they died (or were killed in sacrifice), lost the corporeal covering of their divine substance. Their divine substances went into the underworld waiting for an opportunity to arise again with skins and bodies into the world of humans in the form of new individuals of the same type (López Austin, López Luján 2008). Secondly, the deities eventually grew weary after their sacrifices, descents and reemergence, and required nourishment: "That is why they created the human beings, creatures who were forced to worship them and feed them with offerings and sacrifices. Man perceived himself to be a privileged being because of his close relationship with the gods, but at the same time he was indebted to them because they had created him" (López Austin and López Luján 2008: 145). Human labor and gifts were not sufficient to pay this cosmic debt, and blood offerings and human sacrifice became the solution to this cosmological conviction. The belief was that once a person was ritually transformed into a "god image" and died in sacrifice he or she (the god within the human body) repeated the primordial journey of the gods and traveled to the region of the underworld to recover their strength.

Human Sacrifice, Warfare, and the Ideal Battlefield

When the Spaniards along with thousands of allied Mesoamerican warriors assaulted the main temples of Tenochtitlan, they saw the huge circular stone altar, where some human sacrifices were carried out in the month of Tlacaxipeualiztli (the Flaying of Men). Spaniards and Mexica warriors fought hand-to-hand combat on and around the stone of sacrifice and when they gained the upper hand, the Spaniards mounted one of their cannons on it to strengthen their assault on the Great Temple. Years later, when the Franciscan chronicler Bernardino de Sahagún interviewed Aztec elders, they told him the following story, in stunning detail, about a colossal stone altar and a particular nextlaoali or ritual of "debt payment" that came to be known as "the gladiatorial sacrifice."

Captive warriors were transported from enemy territories to the capital of Tenochtitlan where they were paraded through the city before each was ritually transformed into a *teotl ixiptla*, a living image of the great god Xipe Totec. During the next forty days, these foreign warriors were, step by step, stripped of their culture, human identity, given new names after deities, and forced to dance with their captors but as living representatives of deities. These ixiptla are much more than symbols of deities. López Austin writes of deity impersonators as

> teteo imixiptlahuan...men possessed by the gods, who, as such, died in a rite of renewal. The idea of a calendric cycle, of a periodic returning, in which the power of a god was born, grew, decreased, and concluded made it necessary in a rite linking the time of man to mythical time that a god would die so his force might be reborn with new power. *It was not men who died, but gods—gods within a corporeal covering that made possible their ritual death on earth.* If the gods did not die, their force would diminish in a progressively aging process. Men destined for sacrifice were temporarily converted into receptacles of divine fire, they were treated as gods, and they were made to live as the deity lived in legend. Their existence in the role of ixiptlatin, or "images," could last from a few days up to four years. (López Austin 1988 [italics added])

Some of the *ixipylatin* were taken to the Great Temple and forced up the steps to the war god, Huitzilopochtli's temple. Some captives resisted or fainted, but some

> did not act like a woman; he became strong like a man, he bore himself like a man, he went speaking like a man...he went shouting...he went exalting his city.... Already here I go: You will speak of me there in my home land. (Sahagún, vol. 2: 48)

Six offering priests stretched him out on the sacrificial stone, extracted his heart, called "precious eagle-cactus fruit," and offered it to the sun (the text says it "nourished" the sun) before it was placed in the *cuauhxicallli* or "eagle vessel," a finely carved stone jar or a huge stone receptacle.

This body was cut to pieces and distributed, with one thigh going to the palace for Moctezuma and one piece of flesh eaten by the blood relatives of the captor in a bowl of dried maize stew. Then the victorious captor was decorated with bird down, covered with chalk, and given gifts as well as the names *sun, chalk,* and *feather* because he "had not died there in war, or else because he would yet go to die, would go to pay the debt [in war or by sacrifice]."

The second stage of this ritual month began with "the entire city" present at the public spectacle of other captives and their captors in procession to the gladiatorial stone. The procession was led by the elite eagle and ocelot warriors who—amid whistles, singing, and blasts of a conch trumpet—danced, pranced, and displayed shields and obsidian-bladed clubs raised in dedication to the sun. Surrounded by a huge crowd of commoners and royal families alike, a captive was made to drink *pulque* and forced up on the round stone where a priest dressed in bearskin, the "Old Bear," tied his leg with the "sustenance rope" to the center of the stone. Given a war club decked with feathers, the captive was attacked by a dancing jaguar warrior armed with a war club filled with obsidian blades. When the *teotl ixiptla* was wounded, weakened, and defeated, a figure called the Night Drinker, in the image of the warrior god Xipe Totec, sacrificed the captive, extracting his heart saying, "Thus he giveth the sun to drink." These gestures aimed at linking the city to the celestial realm were followed by the dispersion of the blood along an earthly path as the captor took the eagle bowl filled with the captive's blood to "every place...nowhere did he forget in the *calmecacs*" where on the lips of the stone images he placed the blood. The body was taken to the local temple school where it was flayed and then taken to the captor's home, where it was cut up for a ritual meal, and those who ate "would be considered gods" (ibid., 2: 67). Then the captor lent the skin to his assistants who begged for gifts for twenty days, after which the gifts were divided among them. This begging ritual, called *Neteotoquiliztli*, or "the impersonation of a god," involved friends of the captor, now wearing the divine skin of the sacrificed individual, dashing through the streets engaging other youths in little war games, boisterous skirmishes, and mock battles. Part of the game was to try and get a little piece of the skin under one's fingernail so as to acquire a bit of the charisma of the warrior god. Rough-and-tumble fights ensued, eventually calming down so the skin wearers and their entourages could visit family homes where ears of maize were given by the common people and nobles were offered clothes, feathers, and jewels. These war games spread throughout many neighborhoods alerting the populace to the completion of debt payment ceremonies and inviting their involvement in the giving of valued objects to the kids and teenagers.

I left out one crucial detail until now because it reveals the political purpose of this scenario and brutal destruction of human beings. The elders told the Spanish chroniclers that this ceremony, in particular, was attended by foreign rulers and nobles "from cities which were his enemies from beyond (the mountains)...those with which there was war, Moctezuma secretly summoned" to the ceremony and placed behind an arbor of flowers and branches so they would not be seen by the citizens of Tenochtitlan or their own warriors in this carnival of death. According to Diego Durán's account, the lords of foreign provinces and cities dispersed full of "*temor y espanto*," dread and fear.

I provide this ample description of just one of the eighteen ceremonies focused by human sacrifice carried out in the Aztec capital because it shows us both the sophistication of these performances and the cosmological conviction that performing sacrifices in this way creates an ideal battlefield inside the city where Aztecs were completely triumphant and revitalized city and cosmos. To do this, the Aztecs created a theater where a living warrior god was ritually dismembered so that his highly potent skin and blood could be seen, touched, and smelled throughout the neighborhoods where the next generation of warriors were excited into war games and visual experiences with sacrificial beings. The message was that, in our city, we win all battles, intimidate our enemy rulers in public sacrifices (debt payments to gods), and distribute supernatural power to the next generation of warriors who learn the Aztec way.

Historians have been able to show that as Mesoamerican states grew more complex, their rulers used larger scale human sacrifices as a method to expand their domains and gather in larger tributary payments. We now know that between 1250 and 1521 wars of conquest were used as a way for men to fulfill their holy mission to perpetuate the existence of the world through human sacrifice. Aztec armies and those of their allies carried out ambitious military campaigns from which they returned victorious with numerous prisoners for display and killing in large sacrificial festivals. The central symbol of this worldview was the Templo Mayor of Tenochtitlan and it is remarkable that as it grew in size (enlarged seven times during its 150 year existence), there were two other amplifications. The numbers of human sacrifices increased and the amount of territory controlled in Mesoamerica was progressively enlarged, ensuring a tremendous growth in tributary payments to the capital and its royal families.

THE MORAL IMPERATIVE OF HUMAN SACRIFICE/DEBT PAYMENT

In my study of the human sacrificial festivals, I was impressed with the extraordinary detail the Mexica elders recited to Sahagún. Songs, tones of voices, clothing from head to toe, dance movements, precise gestures with occasional references to emotional responses fill the reader with a sense of motion and color, complexity, and wonder. The actual moments of killing in the narratives are, while not avoided, given much less weight and focus than the preparations of the *teotl ixiptla* or the descriptions of the ritual treatment of the bodies, hearts, blood, and skin as they are worn, sipped, carried, tenderly prayed to, and sometimes immolated. One sensational sacrifice suggests that moral teachings were also at stake in some of the ceremonies.

In the month of Toxcatl (the dry season) a captured warrior with "no blemishes upon his body" was changed into a teotl ixiptla of the great deity Tezcatlipoca, (Lord of the Smoking Mirror). This handsomest of individuals lived for one year in "all luxuries" while being trained in music, singing, speaking, flower arranging, and walking among the populace as a deity. The first extraordinary dimension of the festival of Toxcatl was that the most physically attractive male from among a special group of captive warriors had to conform to this official description of the ideal male.

> He was like something smoothed, like a tomato, like a pebble, as if sculptured in wood; he was not curly-haired...he was not rough of forehead...he was not

> long-headed .... He was not of swollen eyelids, he was not of enlarged eyelids, he
> was not swollen-cheeked...he was not of downcast face; he was not flat-nosed;
> he did not have a nose with wide nostrils; he was not concave-nosed...he was
> not thick-lipped, he was not gross-lipped, he was not big-lipped, he was not a
> stutterer, he did not speak a barbarous language. He was not buck-toothed, he
> was not large-toothed...His teeth were like seashells...he was not cup-eyed, he
> was not round-eyed; he was not tomato-eyed; he was not of pierced eye....He was
> not long-handed; he was not one-handed; he was not handless; he was not fat-
> fingered...He was not emaciated; he was not fat; he was not big-bellied; he was
> not of protruding navel; he was not of hatchet shaped buttocks....For him who
> was thus, who had no flaw, who had no (bodily) defects, who had no blemish,
> who had no mark,...there was taken the greatest care that he be taught to blow
> the flute, that he be able to play his whistle; and that at the same time he hold all
> his flowers and his smoking tube. (ibid.: 71)

Tezcatlipoca was escorted throughout the city for nearly a year, greeted as a living god, enjoying luxuries even while in training in Aztec arts. He was eventually
given four female companions, themselves teotl ixiptla, for sexual coupling during
the last month of his existence. The elders, who had lived during these ceremonies,
said of this *hieros gamos*, "For only twenty days he lived lying with the women, that
he lived married to them." The symbolism of this ceremonial coupling is powerful
as each of these wives was also a *teotl ixiptla* representing the goddesses of love,
corn, salt, and water. The five of them, representing the five-part universe (four
quarters and the center), sang and danced in public and distributed food and gifts
to people at specific locations.

It was reported that at the place of his death on the outskirts of the city,
"he ascended by himself, he went up of his own free will, to where he was to die."
As he ascended the temple, he broke his flutes and whistles on the steps. Then the
scene speeded up as the offering priests seized him, "threw him upon his back on
the sacrificial stone: then cut open his breast, he took his heart from him, he also
raised it in dedication to the sun" (ibid.: 71). The *ixiptla's* body was carefully lowered from the temple and his head severed from his body, emptied of its contents,
and eventually hung on the public skull rack.

Then, according to Sahagún's informants, this journey from imprisonment to
lavish deification to sexual extravagance to death on the stone led to a pronouncement of human destiny, a kind of moral understanding that humans needed to realize and follow. The ceremony reaches its climax and then the code of meaning.

> And this betokened our life on earth. For he who rejoiced, who possessed
> riches, who sought, who esteemed our lord's sweetness, his fragrance—richness,
> prosperity—thus ended in great misery. Indeed it was said: "No one on earth went
> exhausting happiness, riches, wealth." (ibid.: 71)

Tezcatlipoca had another name which was the "Enemy on Both Sides," and his performative scenario warns everyone from top to bottom and along all pathways in
the city, who certainly watched him with the knowing eyes of what was in store for
him, namely that the correct death of the male warrior, even of those who live in the
highest potency and privilege, is the misery of the sacrificial death, the ideal death.

WOMEN IN SACRIFICE

As Inga Clendinnen has shown so well, this warrior ideal saturated the lives of women even as they created distinctive ways of living, caring, and dying (Clendinnen 1995). The most challenging accounts of Aztec human sacrifice to read are those involving women and children, which took place during a number of ritual months. Space requires that I simply make the following point. Even when female "debt payments" were focused on the crucial need for seasonal fertility of plants, the intrusion of the warrior imperative of death and dismemberment invades the performative scenario of regeneration. The itinerary of the festival of *Teteo innan* (Mother of the Gods) moves a female teenager, under the control of female priestesses, from a marketplace to Moctezuma's bedchamber to the sacrificial stone and, finally, to the frontier of a war zone. The girl is ritually distracted for four days amid mock public fights by groups of women-physicians, pleasure women, and elder women. The purpose was "to banish her sorrow," keep her merry and laughing for it was believed that many jaguar warriors would die in war and many women would die in childbirth if she wept in knowledge of her sacrifice. After spreading her corn seeds in an act of magical fertility, she is taken to the royal palace and told by her women handlers, "My dear daughter, at last the ruler Moctezuma will sleep with thee. Be happy... they did not tell her of her death."

Once the ruler has inserted his potency into her and drawn her deified power into his, she is taken by the women and soon dressed for the kill. Once sacrificed, her body is skinned and worn by a male priest who displays himself before the community. Finally, a piece of the skin is taken by members of a warrior society out to the edge of the empire where it is used to taunt enemies into conflict.

CONCLUSION

In this chapter, I have indulged the Aztec records of human sacrifice because of the pressing need for us to confront these practices to learn what they tell us about human cultures in the past and perhaps our own violent ritual actions today. The Mesoamerican religious traditions did not only seek substitutes for human "debt payments" or sublimate in rituals their aggressive drives toward humans in ways that eliminated human sacrifice, as many other peoples did. Yet when the European Christians, who self-righteously claimed to have substituted symbolic violence onto one man, i.e. Jesus, instead of killing the many, arrived in Mesoamerica, they raped, killed, and injured more natives in two years than the Aztecs had sacrificed in ten. One question this raises is, where does the violence toward humans actually go once human sacrifices are given up for the fire sacrifices of animals? While we may all proclaim that we are certainly opposed to human sacrifices, the variety of ways that humans in all corners of the globe invent new forms of torture, massacre, and human sacrifice leads us to question, so what if official rituals of human sacrifice were replaced in Christian, Hindu, and Chinese traditions? Did that change have any significant impact in the lessening of human violence toward other humans in ritual or other ways? Or is the real change simply in the hopeful stories and theologies we tell each other about ourselves, our cultures, and our hopes for humanity? Do these inspiring stories actually lead to less violent societies?

The contemporary reader of Bernardino de Sahagún's detailed descriptions, supplied by Aztecs who saw and participated in the many "debt payment" ceremonies, will be amazed by how much they tell us about Aztec humanity beyond the norms of Mexica warfare. Many levels of Aztec existence are revealed in exquisite detail—the monumental city in its color and sound, the dancing techniques, the complex rhetoric and philosophy of the nobles, the clowns, the gender relations of teenagers joking about sex and affection, the diversity of clothes among the women whose singing voices travel through the rituals. The intense crescendo leading to and then beyond the thrust of the ceremonial knives takes us back to those silent burials of men and women found by Sugiyama in the city named the "Place Where the Gods Were Born." Looking into these festivals and tombs from the sway of the terrorisms and performances of extreme acts of devotions of our own time, we are forced to wonder about our own rituals and to what they might give birth.

Bibliography

Bloch, Maurice. *Prey into Hunter: The Politics of Religious Experience.* Cambridge, UK: Cambridge University Press, 1992.

Burkert, Walter. *Homo Necans: The Anthropology of Ancient Greek Sacrificial Ritual and Myth.* Berkeley: University of California Press, 1983.

Campbell, R. B. *Blood, Flesh and Bones: Kinship and Violence in the Social Economy of the Late Shang.* Department of Anthropology, (unpublished PhD dissertation) Cambridge, MA, 2007.

Carrasco, David. *City of Sacrifice.* Boston: Beacon Press, 1999.

Chang, K.-C. *Shang Civilization.* New Haven, CT: Yale University Press, 1980.

Clendinnen, Inga. *Aztecs.* Cambridge, UK: Cambridge University Press, 1995.

Das, Veena. "Violence and Nonviolence at the Heart of Hindu Ethics." In *The Oxford Handbook of Religion and Violence*, edited by Mark Juergensmeyer, Margo Kitts, and Michael Jerryson. New York: Oxford University Press, 2012.

Fiskesjö, M. "Rising from Blood Stained Fields: Royal Hunting and State Formation in Shang China." *Bulletin of the Museum of Far Eastern Antiquities* 73 (2003): 49–191.

Geertz, Clifford. *Negara: The Theatre State in Nineteenth Century Bali.* Princeton, NJ: Princeton University Press, 1981.

George, Kenneth M. *Showing Signs of Violence: The Cultural Politics of a Twentieth-Century Headhunting Ritual.* Berkeley: University of California Press, 1996.

Hamerton-Kelly, Robert. *Violent Origins: Walter Burkert, Rene Girard, and Jonathan Z. Smith on Ritual Killing and Cultural Formation.* Palo Alto, CA: Stanford University Press, 1987.

Heesterman, J. C. *The Broken World of Sacrifice: An Essay in Ancient Indian Ritual.* Chicago: University of Chicago Press, 1993.

Henninger, J. "Sacrifice." *Encyclopedia of Religion*. Ed. L. Jones, vol. 12: 7997–8008. New York: Macmillan Reference, 2005.

Jay, Nancy. *Throughout Your Generations Forever: Sacrifice, Religion and Paternity*. Chicago: University of Chicago Press, 1992.

Jones, Lindsay (ed.). *Encyclopedia of Religion*. New York: Macmillan Distribution, 2005.

Klein, Cecelia. "The Ideology of Autosacrifice at the Templo Mayor." In *The Aztec Templo Mayor*. Ed. Elizabeth Boone, 293–395. Washington, DC: Dumbarton Oaks, 1987.

Levenson, Jon. *The Death and Resurrection of the Beloved Son: The Transformation of Child Sacrifice in Judaism and Christianity*. New Haven, CT: Yale University Press, 1995.

Liu, Li. "Ancestor Worship: An Archaeological Investigation of Ritual Activities in Neolithic North China." In *Journal of East Asian Archaeology* 2.1–2 (2000): 129–164.

López Austin, Alfredo. *Human Body and Ideology*. Salt Lake City: University of Utah Press, 1988.

López Austin, Alfredo, and Leonardo López Luján. "Aztec Human Sacrifice." In *The Aztec World*. Eds. Brumfiel, Elizabeth M., and Gary M. Feinmann, 137–152. Chicago: Field Museum of Natural History, 2008.

López Luján, Leonardo, and Guilhem Olivier. *El sacrificio humano en la tradición religiosa mesoamericana*. Mexico City: Instituto Nacional de Antropología e Historia, Coordinacíon Nacional de Arqueología, 2010.

Mack, Burton. "Introduction: Religion and Ritual." In *Violent Origins: Walter Burkert, Rene Girard, and Jonathan Z. Smith on Ritual Killing and Cultural Formation*, 1–70. Palo Alto, CA: Stanford University Press, 1987.

Monroe, J. C. "Continuity, Revolution or Evolution on the Slave Coast of West Africa? Royal Architecture and Political Order in Precolonial Dahomey." *Journal of African History* 48 (2007): 349–373.

Rosaldo, Renato. *Ilongot Headhunting, 1883–1974: A Study in Society and History*. Palo Alto, CA: Stanford University Press, 1980.

Sahagún, Bernardino de. *The Florentine Codex: General History of the Things of New Spain, 12 volumes*. Trans. Arthur J. O. Anderson and Charles E. Dibble. Salt Lake City: University of Utah Press, 2002 [1957–1982].

Sugiyama, Saburō. *Human Sacrifice, Militarism, and Rulership: Materialization of State Ideology at the Feathered Serpent Pyramid, Teotihuacan*. Cambridge, UK: Cambridge University Press, 2005.

Yuan Jing and R. K. Flad. "New Zooarchaeological Evidence for Changes in Shang Dynasty Animal Sacrifice." In *Journal of Anthropological Archaeology* 24.3 (2005): 252–270.

CHAPTER 12

MARTYRDOM IN ISLAM

DAVID COOK

MUSLIM martyrdom is almost as old as Islam itself and is closely related to similar martyrdom narratives in both Judaism and Christianity. The first Muslim martyrs appeared shortly after the preaching of Islam in Mecca during the early seventh century. These martyrs were those Muslims who were in weak positions, usually under the authority or influence of polytheists, and when presented with the choice of giving up their faith or submitting to torture and sometimes death, they chose the latter. This paradigm is strikingly similar to the martyrdoms that are the norm in Judaism from the Hellenistic period, especially from the Maccabean Revolt (ca. 167 BCE) and in Christianity from the Roman period (ca. 70–300 CE). However, this early phase of passive martyrdom did not persist in Islam, nor is it the norm. After the Prophet Muhammad's *hijra* (emigration) to the oasis of Medina in 622 and especially after the great Muslim conquests of the seventh and eighth centuries, Islam became closely associated with power, and for the most part, Muslims were not martyred solely for their faith.[1]

Starting with the first Muslim military victories during the time of the Prophet Muhammad's ministry in Medina (622–632), Muslim martyrdom became connected largely with death in battle. The term used in Arabic, *shahid* (pl. *shuhada'*), and in all other Muslim languages has almost the same semantic field as the Christian word *martyr,* meaning both a "witness" and "one who dies or suffers because of his beliefs" (and thus bears witness to the truth of those beliefs). But the Muslim shahid is usually not a passive martyr; he or she is encouraged to seek out circumstances under which martyrdom can be attained. The reasons for a Muslim's wanting to attain martyrdom are clear: The martyr is accorded a lofty and certain place in heaven together with other rewards such as intercession for family members. This reward is attested to by the Qur'an 3:169–170: "And do not think those who have been killed in the way of Allah as dead; they are rather living with their Lord, well-provided for. Rejoicing in what their Lord has given them of His bounty, and they rejoice for those who stayed behind and did not join them; knowing that they have nothing to fear and that they shall not grieve." In the hadith (tradition) and jihad literature many additional rewards are specified (e.g., al-Nahhas). Probably the best known of these rewards lists is contained in the authoritative collection of al-Tirmidhi (d. 892):

> In the sight of God the martyr has six [unique] qualities: He [God] forgives him at the first opportunity, and shows him his place in paradise, he is saved from the torment of the grave, he is safe from the great fright [of the Resurrection], a crown of honor is placed upon his head—one ruby of which is better than the world and all that is in it—he is married to 72 of the houris [women of paradise], and he gains the right to intercede for 70 of his relatives. (al-Tirmidhi: 106)

The popularity of the title shahid probably caused it to be extended well beyond the defined limits of those killed in battle and includes a range of other circumstances such as those killed unjustly by rulers, plagues, or in defense of their homes or merchandise and other categories. It is not necessary for a Muslim to die in battle in order to be considered a shahid; merely the intention to go and fight is sufficient as well (for all the categories see al-Suyuti).

Martyrdom is closely related to the topic of jihad, which is a major theme of Muslim history. Jihad is defined as religiously sanctioned and regulated warfare with the objective of augmenting the territory of Islam or defending it from an invader. In the Qur'an, jihad is presented as part of a contract between God and man:

> Allah has bought from the believers their lives and their wealth in return for Paradise; they fight in the way of Allah, kill and get killed. That is a true promise from Him in the Torah, the Gospel and the Qur'an; and who fulfils His promise better than Allah? Rejoice then at the bargain you have made with Him; for that is the great triumph. (Qur'an 9:111; translations by Fakhry)

However, jihad, despite the way it is commonly portrayed in the media (and in the colloquial usage) is not an unrestrained form of warfare. The basic goal of jihad is to raise the Word of God to the highest (Qur'an 9:41), and in order to accomplish this, jihad must be qualitatively different from other forms of warfare. Goals such as fame and wealth are enough to disqualify the Muslim from waging true jihad, and the fighter is encouraged to examine his own intentions in order to make certain that when he fights he is fighting with the purest of intentions. Muslim religious literature is full of descriptions of jihad and includes a number of boundaries that must be observed in order for the warfare to be jihad and for the martyr to be granted the title shahid (collections include Ibn al-Mubarak, al-Bukhari, and Ibn al-Nahhas). These boundaries include the process of declaring war, making certain that the enemy knows what the war is about, and under what terms it can be concluded. Other boundaries include fighting only combatants and making certain that particular implements of mass slaughter are avoided in battle and that the captives taken during the campaign are treated humanely.

While these restrictions were the ideal described in the jihad literature and in the law books, the Muslim practice of jihad, practically speaking, showed a certain loosening during the aftermath of the crusader period and the Mongol invasions (twelfth through fourteenth centuries). This was the time when Muslims had to face a series of invasions of the core lands of Islam (Syria-Palestine, central Asia, Iran, and Iraq), and endured a number of reverses (the loss of Spain). Under these circumstances, doctrines of defensive jihad became much more flexible and Muslim jurisprudents came to allow some methods of warfare that had previously been frowned on. For the purposes of this chapter, the primary method in question was the use of the mangonel, a rock or explosive lobbing device used in medieval times to bombard the walls of a city or to terrorize the inhabitants. By analogy, during the present time, the medieval acceptance of the mangonel is frequently adduced to support the use of suicide attacks (that terrorize and kill indiscriminately) as well as weapons of mass destruction (such as nuclear weapons) (see al-Fahd). However, after the crusader and Mongol threat had been repelled, this jihad literature was largely ignored until the present time.

Following the rise of radical Islam during the 1970s and 1980s, the discussions of jihad became more central to Muslim identity. Repeated defeats of Arab regimes at the hands of Israel; unresolved Muslim minority issues in Kashmir, the Philippines, Bosnia and Herzegovina and Chechnya; and the problem of the lack of shari`a (Islamic divine law) throughout the Muslim world have fueled a powerful reaction known as radical Islam. Although radical Islam is too diffuse for any single characterization, several common elements bind the tendency together: a desire to implement the shari`a in its totality, a willingness to declare that Muslims who do not share the vision of radical Islam are actually non-Muslims (takfir), a feeling that the entire world is party to a conspiracy to destroy Islam and a consequent need for Muslim unity, and a fixation on jihad as a salvific panacea for the problems of the Muslim world.

Radical Islam has many ideological currents, but this chapter focuses on those that generate martyrdom operations. They have a number of different sources. One is Shiite, as the radical Shiites of Lebanon were among the first contemporary Muslim groups to use martyrdom operations against the United States, France, and Israel during the mid-1980s (see Abu Diya). These martyrdom operations were successful in the long run, as the United States and France withdrew from Lebanon in 1984, and eventually Israel did the same in 2000 (although it is important to note that this withdrawal was not effected through martyrdom operations but through standard guerrilla warfare tactics). However, the more important focus of radical Islam during the past twenty years has been national resistance movements, especially those of the Palestinians, the Chechens, and the Kashmiris. They have been gradually radicalized and associated with radical Islam, but for the most part they each focus their violence on a single target state (Israel, Russia, or India). However, since the middle 1990s, the most flamboyant type of radical Islam has been globalist radical Islam (al-Qa`ida and its ideological affiliates), differing from the national resistance movements in that it seeks to globalize the conflict, which has taken martyrdom operations as its signature and popularized them throughout the Muslim world.

Contemporary Jihad Literature and
Martyrdom Operations

Jihad literature in support of martyrdom operations or in opposition to them takes either the form of a book or pamphlet discussing the subject in detail or a fatwa issued by a given scholar in response to a question. Starting from the mid 1990s, Muslim jihad literature in Arabic and Urdu began to discuss the legality of suicide attacks. The legal issues involved several separate categories of discussion. One was drawn from the classical legal category called "the single attacker who attacks a superior force." It is on the basis of this category—whether in support or in opposition—that most Muslim scholars have decided whether to permit suicide attacks. The classical literature is by no means unified in regard to this legal category, which, as its title suggests, deals with the question of whether a single soldier who charges a superior force is committing suicide. In general, the attitude of the scholars is that this soldier is not committing suicide as long as there is some positive benefit for the Muslim armies in his action. But even among these opinions, some cited Qur'an 61:4, "Allah loves those who fight in His cause arrayed in battle, as though they were a compact structure," to mean that fighting should be done as a group activity and there is no place in it for individual action (al-Nahhas: 535–536).[2]

However, contemporary jihad literature, especially that produced since the mid-1990s, has been far more tolerant of martyrdom operations. Starting with Muhammad Khayr Haykal's monumental three-volume study, *Jihad and Fighting According to the Shar'i Policy (al-Jihad wa-l-Qital fi al-siyasa al-shara'iyya)*, serious discussions of the legal issues involved are found. Although Haykal, writing in 1993, despite his comprehensiveness, does not discuss martyrdom operations, he brings out the two other issues that are foundational to allowing these operations: attacking human shields and using the mangonel. On the face of it, these do not appear to be relevant, but the legal issues of dealing with human shields are the focus for radical Muslims in deciding whether or not civilians can be attacked. The use of the mangonel, through analogy, also allows large-scale terror attacks that are likely to kill civilians indiscriminately. Haykal allows both of these tactics, saying that if the Muslims are likely to derive benefit from such tactics, then they should be used cautiously (Haykal: 1267–1268, 1343–1361).

The other most important treatise dealing with suicide attacks is Nawaf al-Takruri's *Martyrdom Operations in the Legal Balance (al-'Amaliyyat al-istishhadiyya fi al-mizan al-fiqhi)*, which in its four editions issued since 1997 has come to be the authoritative guide for the legal issues. Taken together with the Internet material, it is possible to speak of the general legal opinion of Sunni Muslim scholars as a whole, totally sixty-one fatwas that I have gathered. In general, theyspeak of the attacks against Islam and the need for Muslims to use any efforts to repel them. For Qur'anic support, they usually cite 2:205, "And some people sell themselves for the sake of Allah," a verse that is rarely found in classical jihad literature, with the interpretation that the passage allows for the possibility of dying for the sake of God. (One should note, however, that the use of this verse is ill-defined and does not support much more than martyrdom in battle.) The more detailed fatwas usually cite examples of fighters from the time of the Prophet Muhammad who were willing to attack an enemy in an extraordinarily brave or suicidal fashion. None of them seems to consider the differences between these stories and an actual suicide attack as is known during contemporary times. The legal category cited in support of suicide attacks is that of the single fighter charging a larger number of enemies.

Of the sixty-one fatwas, thirty-two mention the Israeli-Palestinian situation specifically, and a number of these would confine suicide attacks to this arena alone. The remaining fatwas either do not mention a specific geographic location for possible suicide attacks or mention other areas. The other areas are Chechnya (2), India (1), and the entire world (2), and an additional two of the fatwas mention both Palestine and the entire world. The fatwas, from a geographical point of view, are taken from Bosnia, Egypt (6), Iran (5), Iraq (5), Jordan (3), Kuwait (3), Lebanon (3), Pakistan (2), Palestine (3), Qatar (2), Saudi Arabia (10), Sudan (2), Syria (8), the United Arab Emirates (1), Yemen (1), in addition to those from non-Muslim countries (Australia, Great Britain, Russia, Chechnya, and South Africa) and one from al-Qaʿida. This material strongly indicates that martyrdom operations, despite their weak basis in Muslim law, have the support of a sizable percentage of the Sunni Muslim religious leadership, especially in the core areas of the Muslim world.

It is clear from reading fatwas issued by prominent mainstream Muslim leaders, such as the Shaykh of al-Azhar University, Muhammad Sayyid al-Tantawi, the Saudi Grand Mufti, ʿAbd al-ʿAziz Al al-Shaykh, and the famous Muslim Brethren leader and television personality Yusuf al-Qaradawi, that they wish to confine martyrdom operations to specific situations, usually the struggle of the Palestinians against Israel. All three of these leaders have regularly issued "clarifications" of their stance on martyrdom operations after the radical Muslim attacks of September 11, 2001, and have clarified themselves yet further after the appearance of martyrdom operations directed against Muslims in Saudi Arabia (2003), Morocco (2003), and Iraq (2004–2005 and following). However, it remains to be seen whether "clarifications" of this nature have the desired effect.

Not all jihad and fatwa literature, even that associated with radical Islam, discusses martyrdom operations favorably. Critiques of martyrdom operations fall into several categories:

1. Religiously based critiques. Examples of these critiques are those of Nasir al-Din al-Albani, the famous Syrian traditionalist, who maintained that martyrdom operations were suicide and that no amount of semantics would avoid that fact (al-Takruri: 105–107). Another critique appears in the radical Muslim jihad primer, *al-ʿUmda li-Jihad fi sabil Allah*. This treatise critiques suicide attacks on the basis of the fact that they are sought by those who desire fame and that the true *mujahid* would not seek out such flamboyant operations (al-Qadir: 353–358).
2. Critiques emphasizing tactics. Since martyrdom operations frequently kill civilian innocents (even by the loose standards of radical Muslims) and/

or Muslims and violate other laws of jihad, Muslim scholars have critiqued or questioned the tactics involved.[3] Usually these critiques do not actually prohibit suicide attacks per se, but they would place such limitations on the use of them (making certain that civilians or Muslims are not part of the target population) that effectively the advantages gained by their use would be nullified.

3. Critiques emphasizing strategy and propaganda. Martyrdom operations are occasionally critiqued by Muslims for bringing the reputation of Islam into disrepute, destroying the moral basis for an otherwise legitimate cause (such as that of the Palestinians, the Kashmiris, or the Chechens) or because they do not accomplish the military or propaganda goals claimed for them by their proponents.[4]

It is apparent from reading radical Muslim discussions of suicide attacks and their effects that the most potent critique leveled against them is that they kill civilians and/or Muslims. Ultimately this carelessness in regard to non-Muslim and Muslim civilians goes back to one of the foundational aspects of radical Islam, the use of takfir, which is making the claim that large numbers of apparent Muslims are apostates. Because this is true according to their analysis, Muslims who are located either permanently or temporarily in the vicinity of non-Muslims (who are legitimate targets according to the radical Muslim viewpoint) are likely to be apostate Muslims. To date, there are no known Muslim critiques of martyrdom operations that employ an objective moral criticism of the practice of terror.

Although there is a certain logic behind this takfir-based critique of contemporary Muslim society, it is unlikely that most Muslims will be swayed by it because of its totalizing and divisive character. This is a critical weak point in radical Islam and needs to be exploited in the effort to detach Muslim sympathy from causes. The same holds true for killing civilians in martyrdom or other terrorist operations. The killings at Beslan (2005) in southern Russia by the Chechen rebels had a profound (if brief) effect on the Muslim perception of the rightness of the Chechen cause. These types of situations demonstrate the line that radical Muslims must walk: Their operations must be flamboyant enough to gain attention, yet targeted against those objectives that will be seen (at least in the Muslim world) as legitimate from a religious and strategic point of view. This makes the planning of martyrdom operations a difficult problem.

MARTYRDOM OPERATIONS

Martyrdom operations or suicide attacks are often referred to as the weapons of the weak and poor against stronger opponents. The process is deceptively simple: choosing a vulnerable target; preparing a martyr, who has usually volunteered for the job; indoctrinating him or her; providing that person with the explosives needed and the means to arrive at the target; and then making certain that it is difficult for investigators to find the true perpetrators. This type of smart bomb, in which the detonator theoretically can make the last-minute changes possibly necessary to maximize the number of casualties, is effective in certain situations and in accomplishing several goals.

First, it is important to note, as Robert Pape has in his important study of suicide attacks during the past twenty years, that these types of operations are primarily useful against democracies and, most especially, against civilian targets. Pape lists the democracies targeted: Israel, the United States, Russia, Sri Lanka, India, to which we can add Indonesia, Kenya, Tanzania, Turkey, Bangladesh, and Iraq (to the extent to which Iraq can be spoken of as a democracy). However, since then he wrote that the use of suicide attacks has migrated to other less democratic states under the influence of al-Qaʿida and its affiliates: Saudi Arabia, Morocco, Uzbekistan, Pakistan, Algeria, and Somalia (Pape).

Second, the goals of martyrdom operations can be varied. One goal that is common to radical Muslims is that the martyr demonstrates a self-sacrificial type of Islam that stands in contradistinction to the governmentally supported religious elites they despise. As ʿAbdallah ʿAzzam, the mentor of Usama bin Ladin, stated:

> History does not write its lines except with blood. Glory does not build its lofty edifices except with skulls. Honor and respect cannot be established except on a foundation of cripples and corpses. Empires, distinguished peoples, states and societies cannot be established except with examples. Indeed those who think they can change reality or change societies without blood, sacrifice and invalids, without pure, innocent souls, do not understand the essence of this *din* [religion] and they do not know the method of the best of Messengers [Muhammad]. (Azzam: 25)

This process of leading by example is designed to be transformative of the Muslim societies that are the principal audience of radical Muslims. According to this analysis, the examples set by such martyrdom operations should lead inexorably to a future Islamic state.

But the propaganda aspect of martyrdom operations is also designed for the non-Muslim audience as well. Fundamental to this propaganda is the sense that there is no true defense against suicide attackers and that democratic societies must somehow confront the issues they represent because they will not go away or be defeated. Inherent in this statement is the fear and lack of understanding of true belief that is shared by most elites in secular democratic states. Because they cannot conceive of the type of belief that would lead someone to blow themselves up, usually in the midst of civilians, there is a certain sense of inevitability that goes along with the actual terror.

Of course, one cannot deny the reality of the terror caused by suicide attacks. As the writer of the "Islamic Ruling on the Permissibility of Martyrdom Operations" (probably Yusuf al-ʿAyyiri, the leader of al-Qaʿida in Saudi Arabia until his death in June 2003) stated:

> As for the effects of these operations on the enemy, we have found, through the course of our experience that there is no other technique which strikes as much terror into their hearts, and which shatters their spirit as much. On account

of this they refrain from mixing with the population, and from oppressing, harassing and looting them. They also become occupied with trying to expose such operations before they occur, which has distracted them from other things. (al-Ayyiri: 2–3)

What the author stated here is essentially correct: A population can be driven by martyrdom operations into a hysterical or catatonic state because any group of people in a given state or society anywhere can be a target. Martyrdom operations are truly democratic in that sense; they go where the people are. These different types of propaganda-communication are effective in achieving the goals of radical Islam, in addition to communicating the message of Islam from a missionary point of view. Although this final point is difficult to quantify, it is clear that people are actually attracted to Islam and convert to it as a result of martyrdom operations.

Martyrdom operations can be carried out by anyone—men and women—but there are certain categories of Muslims that are more likely to carry them out. Despite the fact that one can no longer exclusively confine martyrdom operations to single, unemployed males under the age of 30, this category is still a dominant one. Another group that is highly likely to carry out martyrdom operations is Muslims who have been compromised in some way. For men, that means perhaps collaborating with an enemy or criminal activities, while women are usually compromised by illicit sexual activity. Yet another group that is inordinately represented among martyrs is converts, who are under extraordinary pressure to find acceptance in their new community. Overarching all of these groups is the ideal of sincere piety and pure intentionality; that is,, that the intention of the martyr is to die solely for the sake of Islam (e.g., al-Amili: 2–3). However, in many cases one strongly suspects—especially among the Palestinians—that this ideal is not lived up to (after one looks at the situations or stories of the martyrs) and that a number of martyrs have been manipulated or psychologically abused. Given the categories previously listed, all exhibit some type of vulnerability to pressure, either because of their actions or their marginality in their societies. This fact is incompatible with the legal definitions of martyrdom operations.

THE ISRAELI-PALESTINIAN CONFLICT

Of all the conflicts between Muslims and non-Muslims, that of the Palestinians against Israel is both the most straightforward and the most varied (in terms of who participates). The use of martyrdom operations by radical Palestinian groups is usually held to have begun in 1994, as a reaction against the massacre perpetrated in the Tomb of the Patriarchs in Hebron, and was used selectively throughout the middle 1990s. As Robert Pape has demonstrated, Palestinian radical groups (Hamas and Jihad al-Islami) that used martyrdom operations effectively achieved their goals—Israeli withdrawals and other concessions—during this preliminary period. However, the radical Palestinian Muslim use of martyrdom operations was also a challenge to the Palestinian National Authority (PNA) from 1994 to 2000, as the latter was attempting to conduct negotiations with Israel at the same time. Between 1996 and 2000, the PNA suppressed a number of martyrdom operations and periodically punished the groups initiating them.

However, after the outbreak of the Second Intifada (2000–2007), the PNA has not made a serious attempt to suppress martyrdom operations, and they have become a hallmark characteristic of this Intifada (as opposed to the First Intifada, 1987–1993, which was largely mass protests and civil disobedience). These martyrdom operations demonstrate several patterns: an initial phase of exploratory martyrdom operations from October 2000 to September 2001, followed by an extreme period of escalation during January to June 2002 (forty-four attacks). This escalation resulted in the Israeli reoccupation of much of the West Bank during March and April 2002. Then there is a break until the resumption of attacks from late September 2002 until June 2003 (a further twenty-five attacks). Martyrdom operations have tapered off sharply from 2003 to 2007, although when they do happen they tend to be deadly (Shay: 225–242).

The Israeli-Palestinian conflict has thrown together a wide range of disparate groups, and one cannot speak of a substantive difference between the nominally secular-nationalist groups such as the al-Aqsa Martyrs Brigades, socialist-communist groups such as the Popular Front for the Liberation of Palestine, Islamic-national resistance groups such as Hamas, and globalist Islamic groups such as the Jihad al-Islami. Each has used more or less the same tactics, and each, with the exception of the PFLP, uses the same Islamic rhetoric in order to describe the martyr and their mission. There is no commonality between the martyrs, as rich, poor, and middle class; young and old; men, women, and children; educated and noneducated have all participated in martyrdom operations (for women's accounts see Victor, Brunner; for education of martyrs see Atran, McCauley). If there were any commonality, it would only be that when one group became too prominent (and therefore more easily identified by the Israeli security forces), then another less prominent group (such as women or children) would come to the fore as prospective martyrs. Of the Palestinian society, only Christian Arabs thus far have not taken part in martyrdom operations. Nor is there a commonality to the targets chosen or the geographic region. Buses and shopping areas have been hit hard but equally nightclubs, restaurants, hotels, and gambling operations. The martyrs, when choosing their targets, do not seem to discriminate between Israeli Jews and Israeli Arabs. Because of the physical similarity of Jews and Arabs, it would be difficult to make such discrimination possible.

Analysts have asked what the Palestinian strategy behind the martyrdom operations could possibly be. This is a difficult question because there are so many exceptions that a coherent strategy seems impossible to discern, and it may be with so many disparate groups pushing for martyrdom operations that there is no one strategy. However, on a local, personal level, many of the martyrs seem motivated by personal vengeance (Margalit). Some mention specific grievances, others speak of the situation as a whole and perhaps shaming others—usually Arab or Muslim governments and elites—into action. A minority of the martyrs use purely Islamic-salvific rhetoric and, within the context of the Palestinian society, even given the prominence of these slogans and the radicalization of the people, these ideas do not seem to be the primary motivation behind suicide attacks. However, it is also apparent that the collective sense of martyrdom that is fostered by so many disparate groups in Palestinian society makes up for the fact that the Second Intifada is not as popular as the first was. This collective ideal is promoted by the martyrologies published by the Palestinians and their supporters in the Arab world (see *Intifadat al-Aqsa*).

On a larger plane, it is apparent that the groups initiating martyrdom operations have a strategy. Although, in some cases, this strategy is nothing more than demonstrating to Israel that it is not immune from vengeance by Palestinians, it seems clear that during the period of January to June 2002, the Palestinians sought to bring Israel to its knees using martyrdom operations. However, this offensive brought an Israeli military response (reoccupation of the West Bank), and significantly detracted from the worldwide support that the Palestinians need in order to offset the military advantages that Israel has over them. This fact highlights the problems inherent to the use of martyrdom operations. Because of their indiscriminant slaughter of Israeli civilians (given the fact that few of the suicide attacks were actually directed at the Israeli military), Palestinians were not and have not been able to gain the world sympathy they needed to defeat Israel.

In hindsight, it seems clear that the Palestinian use of martyrdom operations fed off the easy access that the Palestinians had to Israel and the difficulties of dividing the populations of this thickly settled and intermixed land. Following the suicide campaign of 2002 and 2003, Israel decided to build a barrier to keep Palestinian suicide attackers out of its territory, and it appears that this barrier has been effective. The suicide attacks carried out since the erection of the barrier have only been directed against those areas in which the barrier has not been completed; other, previously hard-hit, areas of Israel have been comparatively peaceable. This suggests that the Palestinian martyrdom attacks relied overmuch on quick penetration of Israel and did not build up sleeper suicide cells for a long-term strategy of attack.

Chechnya

The appearance of suicide attacks associated with the Chechen national resistance to Russia was one of the signs that this struggle has become more of a global, Islamic one and less of a nationalistic one. After the reoccupation of Chechnya in 1999 by the Russian Army, the Chechen resistance resorted to guerilla warfare and, in June 2000, saw the first suicide attack. This suicide attack was the occasion of the writing of the "Islamic Ruling on the Permissibility of Martyrdom Operations," which according to the text was written to answer the question of whether Hawa Barayev (the woman who, with a companion, carried out the attack) had committed suicide. Nowhere in the text does the author—according to radical Muslim sources on the iInternet, probably Yusuf al-ʿAyyiri—address the question of whether women can carry out martyrdom operations.

As actual military operations by the Chechen rebels have diminished, martyrdom operations have become much more important. They usually strike in the Russian heartland and either take the form of suicide bomb blasts, according to the Palestinian model, or hostage taking by suicide squads who appear willing to commit suicide with their hostages if their demands are not met. This method of hostagetaking appears to be uniquely Chechen. The Chechen tactics are devised specifically for Russia, and like the Palestinians, they are careful not to widen the war by attacking other countries (although foreign nationals inside Chechnya are occasionally targeted). And unusual to radical Islam, many of the suicide attackers have been women (of forty-one major attacks until the beginning of 2011, fourteen were perpetrated by women or included women among the attackers).[5]

Starting with then president Aslan Maskhadov's proclamation of shariʿa law in 1999, the Chechen conflict has taken on an ever-increasing association with radical Islam, to the point at which there were links between al-Qaʿida and the Chechens, a number of the latter trained in Afghanistan. The other ideological link is with Saudi Arabia. Most of the fatwas that support suicide attacks in Chechnya have been written by Saudi religious figures, and the leader of the foreign radical Muslim faction in that country, Khattab (d. 2002), was from Saudi Arabia as well. No religious leaders from other countries (other than Chechnya) dealing with martyrdom operations are known to have written in support of them. It is probably due to this link that the Chechens came to be involved with al-Qaʿida.

AFGHANISTAN, PAKISTAN, CENTRAL ASIA, AND INDONESIA

In contradistinction to the two previous cases, the martyrdom operations associated with Afghanistan and central Asia do not have the character of a national resistance movement. They are purely formulated by the necessities of jihad against governments, deemed to be apostate Muslim (Afghanistan, Pakistan, and Uzbekistan) and with the larger goals of globalist radical Islam.

Martyrdom operations in Afghanistan since the fall of the Taliban in December 2001 have garnered little outside attention and do not seem to be differentiated from the overall Islamic resistance to the Hamid Karzai regime (which they see as infidel). Comparatively few martyrdom operations took place from October to December 2001 while actual fighting was taking place. Large-scale suicide attacks began as a Taliban war tactic as a result of the (perceived) success of radical Muslims in Iraq after 2005, with the major upswing in 2006 and 2007. In general, each year since then has seen between seventy and 120 suicide attacks. During the initial suicide campaign, most of the targets were military and caused few casualties other than that of the bomber and any unfortunate civilians close by. Mass civilian casualty attacks have been increasingly the norm since 2007, especially in Kabul and other major cities (Williams).

In Pakistan, the rise of suicide attacks has been equally dramatic, with the pattern being that from 2000 and 2007 attacks were directed by radical Sunnis against Shiites, together with major assassination attempts, such as the two on President Parviz Musharraf (December 14 and 25, 2003). The sectarian suicide attacks do not appear to be the work of globalist radical Muslims but are localized and are part of the sectarian violence that has plagued Pakistan since the early 1990s. It appears, when the goals of the attackers can be ascertained, that they desire revenge for specific issues—and thus deliberately attack places holy to their opponents—or desire to foment civil war. Since 2007 (the Pakistani Army attack against the Red Mosque in Islamabad), the warfare has taken on the characteristics of takfiri violence and has been directed against Pakistani government and especially military and intelligence organizations, together with other standard attacks against Sufi shrines (Lahore, July 2, 2010). During this phase of the suicide attack campaign, all nonMuslim targets have been avoided.[6]

Of all the martyrdom operations in this region, the most unusual were those carried out (apparently) by the Islamic Movement of Uzbekistan at the Charsu Bazaar in central Tashkent in March 2004. (One should note, however, that no one has ever taken responsibility for these attacks and that the IMU may have been blamed unjustly.) These were followed up by suicide attacks at the US and Israeli embassies in Tashkent on July 30, 2004. Like the Chechens, a number of the suicide attackers were women, but their goals, other than the foundation of a Muslim state, are not clear, so it is difficult to know whether the perpetrators of these operations considered them to have been a success or a failure.[7]

Starting with the Bali attacks on October 12, 2002, and then the repeated attacks in Jakarta (August 5, 2003, and September 9, 2004), Indonesia, on Western targets (the Marriott Hotel, the Australian Embassy), the radical Islamic group Jama'a Islamiyya located in Southeast Asia has begun using suicide attacks. These attacks stand out because they do not appear to be part of a pattern of response to grievances or governmental repression, nor do they seem obviously tied to the formation of an Islamic state. Instead, they serve the globalist radical Muslim necessity to drive non-Muslims out of Muslim countries. In all of these cases, while the terror created by the suicide attacks has temporarily driven foreigners away, there has been no groundswell of support among the Indonesian Muslim population for the goals of the radical Muslims (Sukma: 341–356).

IRAQ

Probably the most spectacular of all contemporary suicide attack campaigns is the one launched by Iraqi and foreign radical Muslims in the wake of the US invasion of Iraq in 2003. Although many groups have participated in this campaign, those associated with al-Qa'ida led by Abu Musa'b al-Zarqawi (d. 2006) undoubtedly contributed more to the approximately 1,200 suicide attacks carried out since 2004. Zarqawi, in his well-known assessment of the situation in Iraq, states that the use of suicide attacks is the basis for his strategy and that these attacks were designed, first of all, to create a sense of insecurity within the country so that the Iraqis would reject any government other than that of radical Islam and then to provoke a civil war between Sunnis and Shiites.[8] Although this latter goal may seem incomprehensible as Sunnis comprise only a small minority of the total Iraqi population, it is obvious from reading Zarqawi's work that he saw the conflict in Iraq as part of the larger one throughout the Arabic-speaking Muslim world, one that would only be resolved in the favor of radical Sunnis by involving the Sunni-majority populations of the countries surrounding Iraq.

As in so many other conflicts, however, Zarqawi and his successors overreached their goals and, by unleashing a civil war in Iraq through the use of suicide attacks, caused large numbers of both Iraqis and other Arabs (and those in the Muslim communities beyond them) to recoil from the indiscriminant violence and slaughter. As can be seen from Pakistan and Afghanistan Zarqawi's greatest legacy was to popularize the mythology of martyrdom through Internet videos (Hafez). These came to be highly stylized, containing initial footage of the martyr explaining his motivations and giving a rousing denunciation of the inaction of Muslims (couched in honor/shame terms already popularized by the Palestinians), and then follow-up footage of the actual martyrdom operation from up close, accompanied by *anashid* (war ditties) and citations from the Qur'an.[9]

The suicide campaign in Iraq can be easily divided into several periods: an early initial period in which the radicals had not organized themselves (spring 2003–spring 2004), but carried out terror attacks together with the remains of the Ba'thist regime, a second period of outright revolt together with Shiite radicals (spring 2004–November 2004), a third period of fomenting civil war between the Sunnis and the Shiites (end of 2004–mid-2007), a fourth period of belatedly focusing on military targets (2007–2008), mainly Iraqi or American, and a fifth period characterized by the foundation of the Islamic State of Iraq (2008 to the present), in which the focus of the suicide attacks has been sectarian once again, focused up Shiites, Christians, and the minority Yezidis. In all of these attacks, tens of thousands have been killed.

Most striking is the fact that, although Sunni radicals have killed thousands of Shiites, and despite the fact that the Shiites (in the form of Hizbullah in Lebanon) were early pioneers of the use of suicide attacks, there has yet to be a single documented case of Shiites in either Iraq or Pakistan responding to Sunni radicals by the use of a suicide attack. (Of course Shiites have responded by other violent means, such as targeted assassinations, and death squads.) This fact bespeaks the relative discipline of the Shia in regard to martyrdom operations as opposed to the chaotic and somewhat salvific character that martyrdom operations have acquired among Sunni radicals. Although until the middle 1990s suicide attacks were unknown among Sunnis, today they are actually emblematic of the militant side of the movement as a whole.

Contemporary Islamic martyrdom focuses almost exclusively on those Muslims killed in battle and ignores the heritage of spiritual martyrdom exemplified by the "greater jihad" of waging a struggle against one's lower soul. However, as a result of the comparative failure of Salafi-jihadis during the recent past, there has been a renewed interest in the spiritual jihad, and the martyrdom that was associated with the Sufis during premodern times.[10] There is a close link between the methodologies of the radicals in their contemporary martyrologies and those of Sufis in that both are viewed by the broader Muslim population as holy figures and both revered for their miraculous powers.[11] (It should be stressed, however, that radicals strongly oppose Sufis on theological grounds). Similarly, there is a mixture of martyrologies on a state level, as Muslims and sometimes even non-Muslims killed for nationalistic causes are given the title shahid by the population. Muslim martyrology is a reflection of popular sentiments and mixes together a wide range of Islamic, nationalistic, Sufi mystic, and sometimes even magical traditions.

Notes

1. At least not by non-Muslims; martyrdom of Muslims by Muslims continued and was quite prevalent.
2. Ibn al-Nahhas, *Mashari` al-ashwaq*, i, pp. 535–536; note that Nasir al-Din al-Albani, in Muhammad Tu`mat al-Qudat, *al-Mughamara bi-l-nafs* (`Amman: Dar al-Furqan, 1999), p. 37, took the same position.
3. For example, after the Riyad bombings of May 2003, see memri.org Special Dispatch series #505 "Saudi Press: Initial Reactions to the Riyadh Bombings" (May 15, 2003); and "A Statement from the Committee of Senior Scholars…Concerning the Riyadh Explosions" at islamica.com.
4. For example, both the Palestinian and Chechen suicide attacks have been critiqued in this manner: memri.org, Special Dispatch series #393 "A Palestinian Communiqué against Martyrdom Attacks" (June 25, 2002); #474 "Egyptian Opposition Daily Condemns Suicide Martyrdom Operations" (February 25, 2003); #780 "Arab and Muslim Reactions to the Terrorist Attack in Beslan, Russia" (September 8, 2004). For military and propaganda examples, Mari`i b. `Abdallah b. Mar`i, *Ahkam al-mujahid bi-l-nafs* (Medina: Maktabat al-`Ulum wa-l-Hikam, 2003), II, pp. 397–399; and the Saudi scholar Ibn `Uthaymin, cited in Tu`mat al-Qudat, *Mughamara*, pp. 38–39.
5. See bbc.com "Inside a Chechen Bomber's Mind" (September 4, 2003); "Russia's Suicide Bomb Nightmare" (February 6, 2004).
6. Interview with Amir Rana of the Pakistani Institute for Peace Studies (December 18, 2010); for Pakistani fatwas against suicide attacks, see *Daily Nation* (May 18, 2009),

http://www.nation.com.pk/pakistan-news-newspaper-daily-english-online/
Politics/18-May-2009/Ulema-issue-fatwa-against-suicide-attacks.

7. See "Violent Unrest Rocks Uzbekistan" bbc.com (March 30, 2004); and "Uzbekistan's Affluent Suicide Bombers," iwpr.net (April 20, 2004).

8. Al-Zarqawi, *Kalimat mudi'ya: al-Kitab al-jami` li-khutab wa-kalimat al-Shaykh Abi Musa`b al-Zarqawi* (2006), at http://www.e-prism.org/ (citation from p. 60), a partial translation in Giles Kepel and Jean-Pierre Milelli, eds., *al-Qaeda in its own Words* (trans. Paschale Ghazaleh, Cambridge, Mass.: Belknap Press, 2008), esp. 260–267.

9. Probably the best known is "Fatima's Fiancé," http://www.liveleak.com/view?i=f34_1219484173 (dating from 2004).

10. For example, the collection of *Jihad al-nafs* (Beirut: Jami`at al-Ma`arif al-Islamiyya al-Thaqafiyya, 2005) by senior religious figures in Lebanon.

11. Note the veneration of Taliban and al-Qa`ida martyrs in Kandahar, "Kandahar's Cemetery of 'Miracles'" http://news.bbc.co.uk/2/hi/south_asia/7193579.stm; http://www.counterpunch.org/fisk0813.html.

BIBLIOGRAPHY

Abu Diya, Sa'd. *Dirasa tahliliyya fi al-`amaliyyat al-istishhadiyya fi janub Lubnan.* Beirut: Jami`at al-`Ummal al-Matabi` al-Ta`awuniyya, 1986.

Al-'Amili, Abu Sa'id. "Wa-Yattakhidh minkum Shuhada." At aloswa.com. Accessed on 17 May 2002.

Al-Bukhari, Muhammad b. Isma`il. *Sahih.* Beirut: Dar al-Fikr, 1991.

Al-Fahd, Nasir. *Hukm istikhdam aslihat al-damar al-shamil.* At www.e-prism.org/articlesbyotherscholars.html. 2005.

Al-Suyuti, Jalal al-Din. *Abwab al-sa`ada fi asbab al-shahada.* Cairo: Maktabat al-Qiyyama, 1987.

Al-Takruri, Nawwaf. *`Amaliyyat al-istishhadiyya fi al-mizan al-fiqhi,* 4th ed. Damascus: al-Takruri, 2004.

Al-Tirmidhi, `Isa b. Salih. *al-Jami` al-sahih.* Beirut: Dar al-Fikr, n.d.

Al-Zarqawi, Musa`b. *Kalimat mudi'ya: al-Kitab al-jami` li-khutab wa-kalimat al-Shaykh Abi Musa`b al-Zarqawi,* 2006. www.e-prism.org/.

Atran, Scot. "Genesis of Suicide Terrorism." *Science* 299 (2003): 1536–1537.

'Azzam, Abdallah, *Fadl al-shahada.* Peshawar: Markaz al-Shahid `Abdallah `Azzam, n.d.

Brunner, Claudia. *Mannerwaffe Frauenkorper? Zum Geschlecht der Sebstmordattentate im israelisch-palastinensischen Konflikt.* Vienna: Wilhelm Braumuller Universitats Verlagsbuchhandlung, 2005.

Fakhry, Majid. *The Qur'an: A Modern English Version.* London: Garnet Press, 1997.

Hafez, Muhammad. *Suicide Bombers in Iraq.* Washington, D.C.: United States Institute of Peace, 2007.

Haykal, Muhammad Khayr. *al-Jihad wa-l-Qital fi al-siyasa al-shara`iyya.* Beirut: Dar al-Barayiq, 1993.

Ibn `Abd al-`Aziz,' Abd al-Qadir. *Risalat al-`umda li-jihad fi sabil Allah.* At tawhed.com, 1988.

Ibn al-Mar'i, Mari'i b. `Abdallah. *Ahkam al-mujahid bi-l-nafs.* Medina: Maktabat al-`Ulum wa-l-Hikam, 2003.

Ibn al-Mubarak, 'Abdallah. *Kitab al-jihad*. Ed. Nazih Hammad, Beirut: Muhammad 'Afif al-Zu'bi, 1971.

Ibn al-Nahhas. *Mashari' al-ashwaq*. Beirut: Dar al-Basha'ir al-Islamiyya, 2003.

Intifadat al-Aqsa. 'Amman: Dar al-Jalil, 2001–2003.

Jihad al-nafs. Beirut: Jami'at al-Ma'arif al-Islamiyya al-Thaqafiyya, 2005.

Kepel, Giles, Jean-Pierre Milelli eds. *al-Qaeda in its Own Words*. Trans. Paschale Ghazaleh. Cambridge, MA: Belknap Press, 2008.

Margalit, Avishai. "The Suicide Bombers." *New York Review of Books*. January 16, 2003.

McCauley, Clark. "Psychological Issues in Understanding Terrorism and the Response to Terrorism." In *The Psychology of Terrorism*. Ed. Christopher Stout, 1–29. Westwood, CT: Praeger, 2002.

Pape, Robert. 2006. *Dying to Win: The Strategic Logic of Suicide Terrorism*. New York: Random House.

Shay, Shaul. *The Shahids: Islam and Suicide Attacks*. Trans. Rachel Lieberman. New Brunswick, NJ: Transaction Publishers, 2004.

Sukma, Rizal. "Indonesia and the Challenge of Radical Islam after Oct. 12." In Kumar Ramakrishna and See Seng Tan, eds. *After Bali: The Threat of Terrorism in Southeast Asia*, 341–356. Singapore: Institute of Defense and Strategic Studies, 2003.

Tu'mat al-Qudat, Muhammad. *al-Mughamara bi-l-nafs*. 'Amman: Dar al-Furqan, 1999.

Victor, Barbara. *Army of Roses: Inside the World of Palestinian Women Suicide Bombers*. London: Robinson Publishers, 2003.

Williams, Brian Glyn. "Mullah Omar's Missiles: A Field Report on Suicide Attackers in Afghanistan." *Middle East Policy* 15 (2008). www.mepc.org/journal/middle-east-policy-archives/mullah-omars-missiles-field-repor t-suicide-bombers-afghanistan.

CHAPTER 13

STARVATION AND SELF-MUTILATION IN RELIGIOUS TRADITIONS

LIZ WILSON

THIS chapter explores the place of destructive acts against oneself—such as starvation and self-mutilation—in the spectrum of violent actions performed in the name of religion.[1] While many of the central cases taken up in this volume involve actions that harm others rather than harm the agent of the action, nevertheless there are forms of self-harm that share features with those actions that would clearly be considered as examples of religiously motivated violence against others. In this way, self-starvation and self-mutilation can be seen to share some of the ideological and performative features of violence in the name of religion.

Cases of fasting unto death and other forms of extreme self-denial or active self-harm most closely resemble violent actions in the name of religion when the person fasting or harming herself or himself does so in a public way that aligns the actor with a public cause or political objective. In this way, the actor's body becomes a site of protest or exhortation, an agent of expression. While fasting to death and self-mutilation can be private acts with no discernable public dimensions, it is those instances in which the act of fasting or self-mutilation is a public act in service of a larger cause that these actions are most clearly seen to be akin to acts of violence for religious causes. As public acts, starvation and self-mutilation often serve effectively as methods of assertions of the legitimacy of some cause. In this regard, a monk who self-immolates in protest against government persecution has something in common with a suicide bomber who blows herself up as a means of protest. Each action shows that the cause espoused is important enough to warrant great sacrifice. In this way, public starvation and self-mutilation transmit a message and work as assertions of the legitimacy of some cause shared by a larger group. In that they are intended to advance a collective goal and involve the assertion of the righteousness of that cause, public starvation and self-mutilation share some of the performative grammar that is demonstrated in cases of violence in the name of religion. Impulses toward violence that might be directed toward those who oppose one's goals are instead focused on one's own body, turning the body into a billboard for one's cause.

Probably the most influential modern example of a public case of self-harm done as a religious act of protest is that of Quang Duc, the Vietnamese Buddhist monk whose 1963 self-immolation in protest against the Vietnamese government's persecution of Buddhism caused an international media uproar. His death by burning was planned with precision and carried out with the media in attendance, cameras rolling. He doused his body with gasoline, ignited the flames, and sat peacefully with no distress showing in his face as he burned. Medical attention was prevented by assistance from others in his group who laid their bodies in front of the ambulances that were on the scene.

Quang Duc's death contained all the elements that make for an effective transmission of one's message: It was highly orchestrated, deftly executed, captured by journalists, and widely aired on multiple media formats. His death was not only performed in public but was essentially a public statement. One can clearly see the ideological, public dimension of Quang Duc's action. He requested permission to soak himself with gasoline and burn himself to death "as a donation to the struggle" (according to Thich Giac Duc, an activist in Saigon; see Thich Giac Duc 1986: 141).

Buddhist Self-Mutilation and Self-Immolation

Quang Duc's self-sacrifice drew on a time-tested Buddhist form of bodily practice known in Buddhist studies in the West as self-immolation. Self-mutilation through burning and other means of self-harm (practices collectively known as "abandoning the body") have played a significant historical role in Asian Buddhism, especially in China (Gernet 1960; Yün-hua 1964; Wilson 2003; Benn 2007). The *locus classicus* for the practice of self-immolation is an act of devotion narrated in the *Saddharmapundarika* or *Lotus Sutra*. In a previous life, the bodhisattva Bhaisajyaraja ingested copious amounts of flammable substances and then set fire to his body as an offering to the Buddhas. The burning of the entire body as a sign of one's willingness to abandon one's body can be symbolized by burning a part of the body (such as an arm or a finger). In Chinese Buddhist monastic ordinations, for example, the ordinand's willingness to make such an offering is signaled by the burning of several places on the head with moxa (mugwort herb that has been aged, ground up, and prepared for burning). Although the best known Buddhist cases of abandoning the body involve burning or self-conflagration, the practice of self-immolation historically includes a wide range of ways to take one's own life. Abandoning the body in East Asian Buddhist contexts could include drowning, death by starvation, feeding the body to insects, self-mummification, and other forms of voluntary death. Originally based on Mahayana scriptural precedents such as the *Lotus Sutra*, self-immolation eventually developed an aesthetic all its own in China, including such distinctive features as the death verse (a poem written near the end of one's life) and the mummified body. Such forms of self-harm appealed to all kinds of Buddhists of various sectarian orientations as a means of expressing devotion to religious figures and teachings. The idea of abandoning the body appealed not only to monks but to laypeople as well.

Early cases of self-immolation in China occurred in the context of religious persecution and are related to efforts at political legitimation on the part of Buddhists. The dying person displays the truth of the Buddha's teachings with the blazing fire that surrounds and consumes the body. Later instances of self-immolation in China tended to be performed by actors less concerned with establishing Buddhist legitimacy and more concerned with Buddhist goals such as the production of relics. In all of these cases, it is clear that for the actor who abandoned the body, the body thus abandoned functions as an offering, a witness to a cause or a means to promote a cause. Likewise, one can see a concern on the part of the actor about to die with the quality of life for those left behind. Those who undertake to die are not simply departing from the phenomenal world but are in many cases expressing their involvement in the world for the sake of specific goals such as defending Buddhism from persecution, enhancing fertility, preventing natural disasters, ending wars, and the like (Benn 2007: 202).

In modern times, a number of Americans followed the example of Quang Duc as a means of protesting US foreign policy in sustaining the war in Vietnam. Many of these were Quakers, members of a Christian sect committed to pacifism. For example, in 1965, 82-year-old Quaker Alice Hertz stood on a street corner in Detroit, covered herself with gasoline, and attempted to burn herself to death to protest (in her words) "a great country trying to wipe out a small country for no reason" (Ryan 1994: 21). Seven months later a Quaker man named Norman Morrison set himself on fire below the Pentagon office of Secretary of Defense Robert McNamara ("The Pacifists" 1965).

SELF-CONFLAGRATION AND POLITICAL RESISTANCE

Self-immolation has become a global phenomenon in the late twentieth and early twenty-first centuries. Michael Biggs speculates that this is the case because death by burning is a media-friendly form of protest. Self-conflagration makes for dramatic media footage—it is chilling but not so gruesome that it cannot be shown on television (Gallafent 2011). One example of the global reach of the phenomenon of setting oneself on fire as an act of protest is the spread of this form of action to places where it has not heretofore been a part of the repertoire of protest. Until recently, self-conflagration was uncommon in Muslim-majority nations, but this is changing in the twenty-first century. There is a growing trend of self-conflagration for political causes among women in Afghanistan (Rubin 2010), and self-conflagrations have contributed to public awareness of the democratic uprisings in North Africa and the Middle East known as Arab Spring. For example, the self-conflagration of a young Tunisian man by the name of Mohammed Bouazizi helped to inspire the protests that toppled Tunisia's authoritarian president Zine al-Abidine Ben Ali (Hendawi 2011). A number of self-immolations followed, not only in Tunisia but also in Egypt. Biggs estimates (2005: 174) that there have been between 800 and 3,000 individual acts of self-immolation (including nonfatal attempts) in the first four decades since Quang Duc's death in 1963. Although no change in policy resulted from the majority of these cases, Biggs notes (2005: 202–205) that some episodes of self-immolation have shifted the balance of power between protesters and their opponents in significant ways. It is clear that as a statement of commitment to a cause, self-immolation, especially self-immolation by fire, can be an extremely effective way to signal one's ideological commitments to the larger public and gain sympathizers for one's causes.

FLAGELLATION, LAMENTATION, AND PROTEST

We see from the Buddhist examples that self-directed violence can be both an act of devotion to a sacred being, sacred idea, or sacred symbol as well as an act of protest. The history of religions is full of examples of devotees whipping themselves as a means of identifying with the pain that revered martyrs and other sacred beings are said to have suffered. In Catholic Christianity, self-mortification offers the actor an intimate form of identification with deity (*imitatio Christi*) through imitation of the pain that Jesus withstood on the cross. Flagellation, for example, reproduces the scourging of Jesus during the crucifixion (Cooper 1868/1900; Weigel 1976). In Shi'a Islamic communities, collective ritual performances of flagellation and forms of lamentation that involve bodily self-harm have been both means of devotional expression and of protest against the perceived injustices that Shi'a Muslims have suffered at the hands of Sunni Muslims and others. During Muharram, one of the sacred months of the Muslim ritual year, Muslims practice various forms of abstention. Shi'a lamentation performances (including beating one's chest, flagellation, and other forms of self-harm) occur on the tenth day, commemorating a military battle in which Husayn, the grandson of the Prophet, perished from multiple wounds while his female relatives harmed themselves in lamentation and/or were abused by the victorious troops (Ayoub 1978). For Shi'i Muslims and also for those who join in ritual performances that commemorate Husayn's death, Husayn can serve as a symbol of legitimate political authority illegitimately routed by corrupt rulers. Muharram performances involve self-imposed suffering in ritualized re-enactments of bitter moments in history that can serve to mobilize public sentiment (Lincoln 1989: 35–36). For Shi'i Muslims and others who participate in lamentation rites, Muharram performances align the actor with fellow flagellants and with a public cause in the present. On occasion, Muharram performances have offered Shi'i Muslims politicotheological tools for expressing resistance to regimes seen as oppressive. In Iran during the 1978 and 1979 protests that led to the fall of the autocratic US-backed Shah, Muharram commemorations offered Ayatollah Khomeini the opportunity to galvanize support for the claims of the revolution; the Shah abdicated less than two months after the start of Muharram in 1978.

HUNGER STRIKES AND DEATH BY STARVATION

Hunger striking is another way to signal one's commitment to a cause by using one's own body as an advertisement for that cause. The hunger strike is closely related to self-immolation in the use of the body for instrumental purposes, but it is different in that it enmeshes the actor in a series of consequences over which she may or may not have control. Hunger strikes entail self-inflicted suffering through depriving the body of food, but the intent is not necessarily to fast until death. When someone undertaking a hunger strike threatens to starve to death, the striker's death can be avoided by conceding to the hunger striker's demands. By contrast, the self-immolator's death does not depend on the opponent's action or lack of action. In this sense, the hunger strike has a different structure and power dynamic than self-immolation. The hunger striker cedes control over her situation ("I will die if you don't agree to my concessions") and thereby, paradoxically, gains power that he did not have before he abstained from eating. It is by making her future contingent on the actions of others that the hunger striker accomplishes her goals.

As a tool that can be utilized in all sorts of situations, the hunger strike has a long and varied history. It has been employed in extremely effective ways in modern contexts, due largely to the use of mass media to draw widespread attention to hunger strikes in progress. The hunger strike has been used by many groups to further political causes that have few or no religious dimensions, such as women's suffrage. The man who utilized the hunger strike so effectively as to become, for many people, its iconic representation is Mohandas Gandhi. He earned the epithet Mahatma ("great soul") by putting his life on the line for others with great frequency. Through such tactics, Gandhi brought success to the movement to gain India's independence from Britain while drawing on religious resources that gave depth to the movement. In giving the hunger strike a place of prominence in the repertoire of tools employed in his movement, Gandhi may well have followed the example of British activists for women's suffrage. Marion Wallace-Dunlop was the first suffragette to hunger strike; she was arrested for militancy in July 1909 and refused to eat in prison unless her status as a political prisoner was recognized. After ninety-one hours without food, Wallace-Dunlop was released from jail. She is considered to be the first modern hunger striker, and her example was very much the topic of conversation at a meeting that Gandhi attended in London:

> Just three weeks after Wallace-Dunlop's release, he was in London and came to a WSPU [Women's Social and Political Union] meeting honouring the hunger strikers and crediting Wallace-Dunlop as "the founder." He noted the next day in a letter: "I attended a great suffragette meeting last night.... We have a great deal to learn from these ladies and their movement." In a subsequent article, Gandhi began to draw pointed lessons from women's protests: "If we want freedom, we shall not gain it by killing or injuring others (i.e., by the use of brute force) but by dying or submitting ourselves to suffering (i.e., by the use of soul force)." (Lennon 2009: 14)

The suffrage movement used hunger strikes quite frequently and effectively. In the five-year period from Wallace-Dunlop's hunger strike in 1909 until 1914, when the movement suspended the militant aspects of the campaign due to the outbreak of the war, suffragettes conducted more than 240 hunger strikes (Lennon 2007: 22). Scholars have suggested that the hunger strikes of the suffragettes influenced activists in Ireland and India (Grant 2006), but influence may have also flowed the other way, with examples from Ireland and India exerting influence on suffragettes like Wallace-Dunlop. Lennon speculates that Wallace-Dunlop may have known about Indian practice of "sitting *dherna*" at the door of someone to whom one has loaned money; in sitting dherna, one fasts so as to compel the debtor to pay debts owed (Lennon 2007: 25–27). Wallace-Dunlop's father was an Anglo-Indian magistrate who served in India during the Sepoy Revolt of 1857 and 1858. Two of Wallace-Dunlop's sisters had traveled in India and wrote a best-selling account of time spent there.

Recently, hunger strikers in India (including high-profile activists and religious leaders) have used this weapon effectively to galvanize politicians to strengthen anticorruption laws. In April 2011, a 73-year-old activist Anna Hazare won concessions from the Indian government on the issue after a four-day fast ("Anna Hazare on Indefinite Fast over Stronger Lokpal Bill" 2011; "India: Striker Claims Victory" 2011). Two months later, a populist yogi with a prominent media presence set up a protest in New Delhi. The telegenic yogi's gathering brought unwelcome attention to the ruling coalition that governs India when the government opted to break up the gathering by force even though a permit had been issued to allow the yogi to hold the event ("The Swami's Curse" 2011). But the hairy-armed yogi was photographed attempting to flee the scene disguised as a woman, undermining his own credibility as someone willing to put his life on the line for the anticorruption cause.

The hunger strike, like self-conflagration, can be an important tool to communicate a message. Both self-immolation and the hunger strike use the body as a means of resistance. Impulses toward violence that might be directed toward those who oppose one's goals can instead be fruitfully focused on the resistant body, turning the body into an agent of struggle. Both practices have been used to great effect in the twentieth and twenty-first centuries when the exposure provided by mass media makes these actions a spectacle performed on a public stage. Like self-conflagration, the hunger strike has become a global phenomenon utilized on every continent of the world.

NOTE

1. I would like to thank Randi Fredricks, who offered helpful bibliographic assistance on fasting and hunger strikes.

BIBLIOGRAPHY

"Anna Hazare on Indefinite Fast over Stronger Lokpal Bill." *Hindustan Times.* 5 April, 2011.

Ayoub, Mahmoud. *Redemptive Suffering in Islām: A Study of the Devotional Aspects of 'āshūrā' in Twelver Shī'ism.* The Hague: Mouton, 1978.

Benn, James A. *Burning for the Buddha.* Studies in East Asian Buddhism 19. Honolulu: University of Hawaii Press, 2007.

Biggs, Michael. "Dying without Killing: Self-Immolations 1962–2002." In *Making Sense of Suicide Missions.* Ed. Diego Gambetti, 173–208. New York: Oxford University Press, 2005.

Bynum, Caroline Walker. *Holy Feast, Holy Fast: The Religious Significance of Food to Medieval Women.* Berkeley: University of California Press, 1988.

Collins, Elizabeth Fuller. *Pierced by Murugan's Lance: Ritual, Power, and Moral Redemption among Malaysian Hindus.* DeKalb: Northern Illinois University Press, 1987.

Cooper, William M. [James Glass Bertram]. 1868. *Flagellation and the Flagellants: A History of the Rod in All Continents from the Earliest Period to the Present Time.* London, rev. ed. Paris: C. Carrington, 1868; 1900.

Gallafent, Alex. "Self-Immolation as Protest." *The World: Global Perspectives for an American Audience* (Public Radio International). January 18, 2011.

Gernet, Jacques. "Les Suicides par le feu chez les Bouddhistes Chinois du V' an X siècle," *Mélanges Publiés par l'Institute des Hautes Études Chinoises* 2 (1960): 527–558.

Grant, Kevin. "The Transcolonial World of Hunger Strikes and Political Fasts, c. 1909–1935." In *Decentring Empire: Britain, India and the Transcolonial World.* Edited by Durba Ghosh and Dane Kennedy, 243–269. New Delhi: Orient Longman, 2006.

Hendawi, Hamza. "Egyptian, Algerian, Mauritanian Set Selves Alight." *Associated Press.* Monday, 17 January, 2011.

"India: Striker Claims Victory." *Associated Press*. Appeared in *New York Times*, 9 April, 2011.

Korom, Frank J. *Hosay Trinidad: Muharram Performances in an Indo-Caribbean Diaspora*. Philadelphia: University of Pennsylvania Press, 2003.

Lennon, Joseph. "Fasting for the Public: Irish and Indian Sources of Marion Wallace Dunlop's 1909 Hunger Strike." In *Enemies of Empire: New Perspectives on Imperialism, Literature, and Historiography*. Ed. Eóin Flannery and Angus Mitchell, 19–39. Dublin: Four Courts Press, 2007.

Lennon, Joseph. "The Hunger Artist: Marion Wallace-Dunlop, Painter, Suffragette, and the First Modern Woman to Starve Herself for Politics." *Times Literary Supplement*, 13–14. 24 July, 2009.

Lincoln, B. *Discourse and the Construction of Society: Comparative Studies of Myth, Ritual, and Classification*. New York: Oxford University Press, 1989.

Michael, Maggie. "Self-Immolation Protests in Egypt Continue." *Associated Press*. 18 January, 2011.

"The Pacifists." *Time*. 12 November, 1965.

Rubin, Alissa J. "For Afghan Wives, a Desperate, Fiery Way Out." *New York Times*. 7 September, 2010.

Ryan, Cheyney. "The One Who Burns Herself for Peace." *Hypatia* 9. 2 (1994): 21–39.

Settar, S. *Inviting Death: Indian Attitudes toward Ritual Death*. Leiden, New York: E. J. Brill, 1989.

"The Swami's Curse." *Economist*, vol. 399, issue 8737. 11 June, 2011.

Thich Giac Duc. "Buddhists and Catholics." In *Portrait of the Enemy*. Eds. David Chanoff and Doan Van Toai, 39–42, 134–146. New York: Random House, 1986.

Weigle, Marta. *Brothers of Light, Brothers of Blood: The Penitentes of the Southwest*. Albuquerque: University of New Mexico Press, 1976.

Wilson, Liz. "Human Torches of Enlightenment: Autocremation and Spontaneous Combustion as Marks of Sanctity in South Asian Buddhism." In *The Living and the Dead*. Ed. Liz Wilson, 29–50. Albany: State University of New York Press, 2003.

Yün-hua, Jan. "Buddhist Self-Immolation in Medieval China." *History of Religions* 4 (1964): 243–268.

CHAPTER 14

....

APOCALYPTIC RELIGION AND VIOLENCE

....

JAMEL VELJI

EMBEDDED in the genetic fabric of virtually every religious tradition lie symbolic structures that can be manipulated to signal the imminent end of all things. Christian theological traditions have dubbed the study of these factors associated with the end of the world eschatology, the study of death, resurrection, heaven, and hell. While the terms apocalypse and eschatology are often used interchangeably, important differences exist between the two terms. This chapter begins by providing a working definition of apocalyptic. It discusses some of the term's most important constituent components and then focuses on relationships between these components and violence, shedding light on how structures of apocalyptic can be deployed to serve violent ends.

APOCALYPTIC TEXTUALITY

....

Apocalypse derives from the Greek *apokalypsis*, literally meaning an "uncovering" or a "revelation" (O'Leary 1994: 5–6). The term originally derived from the book of Revelation, or the Apocalypse of John, the last book of the New Testament (Aune). According to scholars such as John Collins, there are certain characteristics shared by apocalyptic texts that allow their classification as a distinct genre of literature.

An important part of Collins's definition is a revelation by an otherworldly being to a human recipient; this disclosure involves eschatological salvation and the disclosure of "another, supernatural world" (Collins 1984: 3–4). David Aune states that authors of apocalyptic narratives frequently employ pen names of "famous ancient biblical figures such as Adam, Abraham, or Enoch" in their writings (Aune 1993). These texts envision a strident division between this age—which is inherently evil—and an age of bliss that is to come, after intervention by a messianic agent or the divine itself. Apocalyptic texts, such as portions of Daniel and Isaiah, also envision a great conflict between the forces of good (which tend to be in the minority) and the forces of evil.

Apocalypses, though, are not only found in a relatively small selection of Jewish and Christian texts. Complicating our study is the fact that the term *apocalypse* is often tied to the Christian theological tradition. To talk about an apocalypse in Islam, or an apocalypse in Buddhism, requires rethinking the constituent components of the term. Furthermore, we must think about relationships between apocalyptic elements in texts and apocalyptically charged religious movements. How are the symbols we find in apocalyptic texts (re)deployed to construct movements that believe themselves to be upholders of truth at the edges of time? And how might these symbolic structures be used to serve violent ends?

Numerous scholars have proposed definitions of the constituent components of the term *apocalyptic*. Here I wish to highlight some of these elements and how they may help to bridge the distance between text and movement, as well as to help elucidate similarities between apocalyptic structures across distinct religious traditions.

Structures of Duality

Apocalyptic texts and movements illustrate a propensity to divide the world and its contents into absolute good and absolute evil. This dualistic battle—being locked in a struggle for truth against a majority under the influence of satanic forces—often characterizes one's existence at the end of time. Since time on earth is short, possession of true belief now becomes of utmost importance and guarantees salvation permanently in the life to come. All others will be destroyed, or condemned to hell or, at best, to nonexistence.

There are at least two implications of this polarization. First, mechanisms for salvation in apocalyptic texts or movements are often correlated with—or even motivated by—visions of utopia. It is not infrequent for these utopian visions to describe, in final divine judgment or the final battle between good and evil, the destruction of the wicked. Definitions of utopia, then, are predicated on the destruction of those who are evil as well as the strident upholding of boundaries that separate the elect from the cursed.

Dualistic thinking—the strict separation between forces of good and forces of evil—has frequently been observed by many scholars as a quintessential element of religious violence. Juergensmeyer, for instance, calls this phenomenon as it pertains to religious violence "cosmic war." He writes:

> I call such images "cosmic" because they are larger than life. They evoke great battles of the legendary past, and they relate to metaphysical conflicts between good and evil. Notions of cosmic war are intimately personal but can also be translated to the social plane. Ultimately, though, they transcend human experience. What makes religious violence particularly savage and relentless is that its perpetrators have placed such religious images of divine struggle—cosmic war—in the service of worldly political battles. For this reason, acts of religious terror serve not only as tactics in a political strategy but also as evocations of a much larger political struggle. (Juergensmeyer 2003: 149–150)

In evoking the "great battles of the legendary past" and eliding the characters in these battles with those on the plane of mundane history, perpetrators of religious violence are placing themselves, their followers, and their enemies in a construct governed by myth. This is why apocalyptically charged movements—violent or not—recur throughout history. Myth is "an expression of the sacred in words: it reports realities and events from the origin of the world that remains valid as the basis and purpose of all there is. Consequently, a myth functions as a model for human activity, society, wisdom and knowledge" (Bolle 2005: 6359). Interpretations of the myth of the apocalypse—regardless of religious tradition—provide ready-made templates from which characters and those who fight in these "great battles" can be (re)generated throughout history. And it is apocalyptic symbolism that has provided the mythical wellspring for the genesis and flourishing of apocalyptic movements throughout history—including the major religious traditions of Christianity and Islam.

If the apocalyptic is implicated so frequently in the rise and renewal of religious traditions, it is no surprise that some apocalyptically charged movements may turn violent. What are the factors that contribute to this violence? This is a particularly interesting question for those who study the structures and functions of apocalyptic symbolism, as symbols of cosmic destruction (which may include the destruction of a perceived enemy) so often give rise to and help maintain the contours of largely peaceful apocalyptically charged movements. To give one example: The "War Rule" of the Dead Sea Scrolls envisions in great detail the battle that will take place between the people of light and the people of darkness at the end of time. The text reads like a great work of eschatological choreography, complete with the texts to be written on the different trumpets that call different portions of the community to battle ("On the trumpets summoning the foot-soldiers to advance towards the enemy formations when the gates of war are opened they shall write, *Reminder of Vengeance in God's appointed Time*," Vermes 1987: 107); the exact text to be written on the congregation's standards (109); details of battle formation ("The formation shall consist of one thousand men ranked seven lines deep, each man standing behind the other. They shall all hold shields of bronze burnished like mirrors," 110); and visions of the enemy's destruction ("All these [formations] shall pursue the enemy to destroy him in an everlasting destruction in the battle for God.... Truly the battle is

Thine! Their bodies are crushed by the might of Thy hand and there is no man to bury them," 114, 116). While we are not certain concerning the actual uses of this text—was it used in ritual, liturgy, to motivate the community, or did it have other uses? (Weitzman 2009)—the community that produced it seems largely peaceful (Jassen). So how is it that some communities can move from domesticating a violent transcript to actually (re)enacting violence?

While there are many factors that contribute to violence, I wish to explore here three interrelated processes connected to duality that aid in the transformation of apocalyptic thinking into violence against others. First is the process of what Juergensmeyer calls "satanization"—the dehumanization of the individual, forming him into a collective "enemy;" this enemy becomes elided with a symbolic structure of pure evil (see Juergensmeyer 2003: 174–181; Sells 1998: 1–92; see also the discussion of enemy construction in James Aho, *This Thing of Darkness*). Secondly, there is the process of ritual purification. As part of the process of dehumanization, false attribution of guilt becomes imputed onto the "enemy." The purgation or sacrifice of the enemy becomes necessary to maintain the "purity" of the elect community (Jones 2008: 150–152; Berger and Luckmann). Such preoccupation with purity coupled with dehumanization and satanization were motive forces in the Crusaders' bloody cleansing of Jerusalem (Cohn 1970: 61–88) and the systematic destruction of the Jews in the Holocaust (Redles 2005: 160–189). Both the Crusades and Hitler's "Final Solution" were apocalyptically charged movements whose success—whose utopian vision—was contingent on the physical destruction of the enemy. Finally, there are the group's views on divine agency versus human agency. Jones, citing Juergensmeyer, posits that an apocalyptic group's propensity for violent action increases when there is "a shift in thinking from divine to human agency" (111); when humans, rather than the divine itself, harness control over events at the end of time.

Apocalyptic Temporality

The genesis and maintenance of strict boundaries between good and evil are aided through the "discursive manipulation" (O'Leary 1994: 44) of time. The manipulation of time is the second major feature of the apocalyptic mentality we find reflected in text and movement across religious traditions. Time acquires a sense of urgency in the apocalypse because it is rushing to its end. We find in the book of Revelation, the writings of Paul, or the Qur'an that the world is coming to a close; those who do not adhere to the truth will be destroyed in the imminent future and will simply not be saved—or will be vividly punished—in the hereafter. There are at least two ways in which apocalyptic temporality operates in the processes of community building and maintenance.

First, there is the issue of urgency. Temporal urgency forces an individual to make a decision, rapidly, to join the group that perceives itself as saved. This decision becomes infused with ultimate import, as one's salvation may be predicated on it. Group members, too, may experience a fervor of belief correlating with the expectation that the end of the world is at hand. For the individual or the group, then, apocalyptic urgency only serves to heighten boundaries between those who perceive themselves as saved and everyone else.

Secondly, apocalyptic temporality places the community in an exalted place in history. Time is interpreted to lead up to this unique moment—the edges of history—which has been predicted for millennia in some religious traditions. The process of apocalyptic fulfillment occurs through a variety of mechanisms—for Christopher Columbus, who believed that he was destined to discover the New Jerusalem, the "decoding" of scriptural texts such as Isaiah and Revelation to legitimate his claims to prophecy (Sweet 1986: 379–380). Columbus was also influenced by Joachim de Fiore (d. 1202), the "most important apocalyptic author of the Middle Ages" (McGinn 1979: 126) whose highly complex methods of scriptural interpretation organized history according to certain symbolic patterns. Joachim's conception of history, especially his belief that the third and final purely spiritual stage of history was just around the corner, sparked a renewed possibility of apocalyptic fulfillment among monastic orders and the laity (Reeves 1993).

Islamic history is punctuated by those who claimed to be the *mahdi*, literally "he who is rightly guided"—that figure who would come at the end of history to conquer injustice once and for all (see the overviews in Bashir 2003; Cook 2002; Filiu 2011; García-Arenal 2006; and Sachedina 1981). We cannot forget about Shabbatai Tsevi (d. 1676), the mystical messiah whose interpretations of Lurianic kabbalah (Scholem 1975) served as a uniting force among European Jews of the seventeenth century. Early Christianity was also grounded in messianic fulfillment: the book of Matthew, for instance, presents Jesus as the fulfillment of Jewish messianic expectation, the genealogical ancestor of David (1:1), the fulfillment of Hebrew Scripture (1:22 ff and 12:16ff, for instance) at the end of history (3:1–4). Those who articulated that we are at the end of time found "signs" all around them to legitimate their claims. In addition to numerical calculations and the decoding of symbols in scriptural texts, celestial or environmental phenomena could illustrate how they were in a time like no other; moral degeneration, too, was often cited as "proof" of the imminent end (Funkenstein 1993: 74–87).

The urgency and uniqueness associated with apocalyptic temporality, including processes of messianic fulfillment, provide a sense of increased meaning for apocalyptically charged religious movements. Apocalyptic duality is heightened through a sense of temporality that envisions all of time having led up to this unique moment in history in which only the elect exclusively possess the truth. Temporal urgency and uniqueness help to recruit members and to reify communal boundaries, but in many acts of religious violence, especially those of religious terrorism, the urgency and uniqueness associated with the end of time becomes suffused with a calendar of violence. Dates on which violence occurs become highly symbolic (Juergensmeyer 2003: 136–137) and potentially infused with sacredness, "commemorating" perceived divine progress against the constructed enemy.

Apocalyptic Authority

The last major component of apocalyptic I wish to discuss here is the concept of authority. O'Leary has argued that authority is, along with time and evil, a fundamental topos of apocalyptic discourse (20). There are myriad ways in which authority operates in the apocalypse. Apocalyptic symbolism, for instance, may foment the authority of a religious figure who claims to have access to the world of the unseen. Paul's authority as an apostle emanated largely from his spiritual vision (*apokalypsis*) of Jesus as Christ, as Paul never met Jesus in the flesh (Segal 1990: 70). This authority was heightened by his fervent belief that the end of the world was at hand (e.g., 1 Thess. 4:13–18; 1 Cor. 15).

Throughout history there has been no shortage of those who claim special knowledge of the end of days. Many of those who claim to be specific symbolic characters in the cosmic drama between good and evil—apocalyptic prophets, gurus, messiahs, or *mahdis*—have been particularly successful in engineering social transformations. One reason is because these figures may represent or even embody the collective utopian visions of a group. These figures, who by definition have access to the unseen, are able to impute new meaning onto symbols, reshape the trajectory of rituals (particularly ones that are seen as ineffective), and redraw religious boundaries. These divine disclosures may redefine fundamental aspects of religious practice, even refining the contents of and requirements for admission into heaven or hell (Velji forthcoming). The apocalyptic as a mode of thought and action, then, remains one of the most potent mechanisms religions have for accomplishing social transformation.

Those who harness apocalyptic authority to forward violent agendas have also come in many iterations. David Koresh, for instance, believed that he was "the christ or messiah who would die in Armageddon, be resurrected, and then conquer evil to establish God's kingdom" (Wessinger 2000: 84); Koresh (as well as the Branch Davidians) believed that he alone could unlock the secrets of the King James Bible (ibid.: 85). Koresh, using biblical texts, had developed a detailed scenario of the end of days, as well as his role in it (91). Wessinger argues that action by federal agents against the Davidians helped trigger violence since these actions validated prophecy, actualizing the community's role in Armageddon. The leader of Aum Shinrikyo, Shoko Asahara, "From 1987 on…styled himself as a Buddha who possessed psychic powers. Asahara claimed to have the power to levitate and to soul-travel out of body, and to have an infallible power of prophecy" (ibid.: 128). Further, he "identified himself as the Buddha of the current age and claimed to be teaching Mahayana Buddhism, and later, Vajrayana Buddhism. In 1992, Asahara published a book entitled *Declaring Myself the Christ* in English translation. He claimed to be the Lamb of God, who absorbed the bad karma of his disciples, even though it made him ill" (ibid.: 129). Asahara, symbolically eliding himself with Christ and Buddha, believed in impending Armegeddon and that he was the one who could save the elect. Simultaneously, he was orchestrating the development of weapons of mass destruction and a doctrine legitimizing the assassination of those who disagreed with the guru's teachings (Jones 2008: 74; Wessinger 2000: 143). Redles argues that Hitler saw himself as a prophet or messiah who had "revelatory experiences" (2005: 114–116) and whose goal was to usher in the "New Age of the millennial Reich" (145); this plan was inexorably bound to the genocide of the Jews.

Is there, then, a way to distinguish potentially violent prophets, gurus, or messiahs from nonviolent ones? In a discussion of the appeal of millenarian movements, Barkun writes: "The movement enfolds its members in a belief system that provides meaning and explanation for virtually all problems and in a round of activities that allays feelings of personal insecurity and builds a new and strong sense of identity" (Barkun 1986: 19). While membership in such groups is conducive to a symbolic restructuring of the universe and its contents to provide identity and meaning, there are numerous factors that Wessinger cites as causes for concern that do not necessarily correlate with a propensity toward violence (Wessinger 2000: 275–280). But if we look more closely at each of the three examples, we will find that each one of these claims arose in contexts of not just insecurity but humiliation. If alienation and humiliation help give rise to religious terrorism (Stern 2003: 9–62), and if "[r]esearch suggests that shame and humiliation may be crucial elements in most religiously sponsored violence" (Jones 2008: 121), then claims to apocalyptic authority—in addition to the uniqueness ascribed to apocalyptic temporality and "cosmic war"—might provide violent outlets as perceived antidotes to these conditions (ibid., citing Girard). There is, of course, a constellation of other factors that may predict propensity for violence.

LANDSCAPES OF THE JIHAD AND THE LANGUAGE OF TRANSFORMATION

Though perhaps the world's best known terrorist mastermind, Osama bin Laden framed his rhetoric in what has been classified as apocalyptic terms, the "landscapes of the jihad" are not apocalyptic. The jihad's rhetoric of of "metaphysical" categories such as "Islam" verses the "West," and the portrayal of Muslims as against Jews and Christians "should be seen for what it is—an effort to define the terms of global social relations outside the language of state and citizenship" (Devji 2005: 76). This is a movement, Devji argues, whose violent actions are motivated by disparate causes and help to reify these metaphysical categories through the media's portrayal of these actions, in turn forcing transnational action through the global act of witnessing. Another surprising aspect of the jihad is its lack of messianism. "There seem to be no *mahdis* or messiahs either predicted or expected" in the jihad (47). Since mahdism is closely linked with the concept of millenarianism in Islam (Filiu 2011: xi)—analogous or even equivalent to the utopian feature of apocalyptic—there is also no real utopia in the jihad, except perhaps for the hope that the entire Muslim community will respond to the jihad's calls for holy war (ibid.:48).

Because of its potential for societal transformation, it is not unusual for elements of apocalyptic rhetoric to infuse the language of foreign policy, as well as political or even revolutionary speech. The United States, for instance, has a history of perceiving itself as a chosen nation, a beacon of light to the world; the spreading of democracy and freedom is seen as an ideal value to be exported (Judis). Duality and utopia coalesce as motive forces for foreign intervention to "free" those who are "oppressed." In regard to political speech, the 2008 election was most telling—the candidate Barack Obama said "we are the ones we have been waiting for," an identification of this time as a time like no other, a time that unlocks our full political capital (including the potential for electing a candidate who was seen by many supporters as a messiah-like figure and by his detractors as the harbinger of the Antichrist, or the Antichrist himself). Messianic symbolism even became the subject of a television ad released by the McCain campaign called "the One." Revolution—whether secular or religious—also often reflects apocalyptic undercurrents—an identification of the enemy, a utopian vision, and an urgency driving change.

Scholars have made great progress in analyzing how each of the constituent components of apocalyptic can relate to violence. But more work must be done to assess how elements of apocalyptic—including the hermeneutics of uncovering; constructions of utopias, dualities, and enemies; the manipulation of time; and the process of elision of those on the plane of history with symbolic figures—may work together to fuel violent fires.

BIBLIOGRAPHY

Aune, David E. "Revelation: Introduction" in *The HarperCollins Study Bible, New Revised Standard Version*. Wayne Meeks, general editor, 2307–2309. New York: HarperCollins 1993.

Barkun, Michael. *Disaster and the Millennium*. Syracuse, NY: Syracuse University Press, 1986.

Bashir, Shahzad. *Messianic Hopes and Mystical Visions*. Columbia: University of South Carolina Press, 2003.

Bolle, Kees. "Myth: An Overview," in *Encyclopedia of Religion*, vol. 9, 2nd ed. Lindsay Jones, ed, 6359–6371. Detroit: Macmillan Reference, 2005.

Cohn, Norman. *The Pursuit of the Millennium: Revolutionary Millenarians and Mystical Anarchists of the Middle Ages*. Revised and expanded ed. New York: Oxford, 1970.

Collins, John, ed. *Apocalypse: The Morphology of a Genre*. Semeia 14. Missoula, MT: Scholars Press, 1979.

Collins, John. *The Apocalyptic Imagination: An Introduction to the Jewish Matrix of Christianity*. New York: Crossroad, 1984.

Cook, David. *Studies in Muslim Apocalyptic*. Princeton, NJ: The Darwin Press, 2002.

Devji, Faisal. *Landscapes of the Jihad: Militancy, Morality, Modernity*. Ithaca, NY : Cornell University Press, 2005.

Encyclopedia of Apocalypticism, 3 vols. New York: Continuum, 2000.

Filiu, Jean-Pierre. *Apocalypse in Islam*. Berkeley and Los Angeles: University of California Press, 2011.

Funkenstein, Amos. *Perceptions of Jewish History*. Berkeley and Los Angeles: University of California Press, 1993.

Garcia-Arenal, Mercedes. *Messianism and Puritanical Reform: Mahdis of the Muslim West*. Leiden: Brill, 2006.

Jassen, Alex P. "The Dead Sea Scrolls and Violence: Sectarian Formation and Eschatological Imagination." *Biblical Interpretation* 17 (2009) 12–44.

Jones, James. *Blood that Cries out from the Earth: the Psychology of Religious Terrorism*. New York: Oxford University Press, 2008.

Judis, John. "The Chosen Nation: The Influence of Religion on U.S. Foreign Policy." Carnegie Endowment for International Peace Policy Brief No. 37, March 2005. www.carnegieendowment.org/files/PB37.judis.FINAL.pdf.

Juergensmeyer, Mark. *Terror in the Mind of God: The Global Rise of Religious Violence*, 3rd ed. Berkeley and Los Angeles: University of California Press, 2003.

Lawson, Todd. "Duality, Opposition and Typology in the Qur'an: The Apocalyptic Substrate." *Journal of Qur'anic Studies* 10 (2008) 23–49.

McGinn, Bernard. *Apocalyptic Spirituality: Treatises and Letters of Lactantius, Adso of Montier-En-Der, Joachim of Fiore, the Spiritual Franciscans, Savonarola*. New York: Paulist Press, 1979.

McGinn, Bernard. *The Calabrian Abbot: Joachim of Fiore in the History of Western Thought*. New York: Macmillan, 1985.

McGinn, Bernard. *Antichrist: Two Thousand Years of the Human Fascination with Evil*. San Francisco: HarperSanFrancisco, 1994.

McGinn, Bernard. *Visions of the End: Apocalyptic Traditions in the Middle Ages*. New York: Columbia University Press, 1998.

O'Leary, Stephen. *Arguing the Apocalypse: A Theory of Millennial Rhetoric*. New York: Oxford, 1994.

Redles, David. *Hitler's Millennial Reich: Apocalyptic Belief and the Search for Salvation*. New York: New York University Press, 2005.

Reeves, Marjorie. The *Influence of Prophecy in the Later Middle Ages: A Study in Joachimism*. Notre Dame, IN: Notre Dame Press, 1993.

Reeves, Marjorie. *The Prophetic Sense of History in Medieval and Renaissance Europe*. Brookfield, VT: Ashgate Publishing, 1999.

Rusconi, Roberto, ed. *The Book of Prophecies Edited by Christopher Columbus*. Berkeley and Los Angeles: University of California Press 1997.

Russell, D. S. *Divine Disclosure: An Introduction to Jewish Apocalyptic*. Minneapolis: Fortress Press, 1992.

Sachedina, Abdulaziz. *Islamic Messianism: The Idea of the Mahdi in Twelver Shiism*. Albany: State University of New York Press, 1981.

Scholem, Gershom. *Sabbatai Sevi*. Princeton, NJ: Princeton University Press, 1975.

Sells, Michael A. *The Bridge Betrayed: Religion and Genocide in Bosnia*. Berkeley and Los Angeles: University of California Press, 1998.

Segal, Alan. *Paul the Convert*. New Haven, CT: Yale University Press, 1990.

Stern, Jessica. *Terror in the Name of God: Why Religious Militants Kill*. New York: HarperCollins, 2003.

Sweet, Leonard I. "Christopher Columbus and the Millennial Vision of the New
    World." *The Catholic Historical Review* 72 (1986) 369–382.
Velji, Jamel. "Apocalyptic Rhetoric and the Construction of Authority in Medieval
    Ismailism" in *Roads to Paradise: Eschatology and Concepts of the Hereafter in
    Islam*. Leiden: Brill, forthcoming.
Vermes, Geza. *The Dead Sea Scrolls in English*, 3rd ed. New York: Penguin, 1987.
Weitzman, Stephen. "Warring against Terror: The War Scroll and the Mobilization
    of Emotion." *Journal for the Study of Judaism* 40 (2009) 213–241.
Wessinger, Catherine. *How the Millennium Comes Violently: from Jonestown to
    Heaven's Gate*. New York: Seven Bridges Press, 2000.

CHAPTER 15

COSMIC WAR IN RELIGIOUS TRADITIONS

REZA ASLAN

A cosmic war reflects both a real, physical struggle in this world and an imagined, moral encounter in the world beyond. It is like a ritual drama in which participants act out on earth a battle they believe is taking place in the heavens. As such, cosmic war evokes a conflict, not between soldiers or armies but between the metaphysical forces of good and evil, belief and disbelief, order and chaos, and truth and false-hood (Juergensmeyer 2000, 2008; Aslan 2009).

The term *cosmic war* can encompass and transcend the terms *holy war* and *divine war,* each of which connotes an earthly battle between rival religious groups spurred by political, territorial, economic, and missionary impulses, insofar as that means the eradication of the worship of one god and its replacement with another. In biblical studies the terms *holy war* and *divine war* are delineated in such a way as to distinguish between the actual, historical battles fought by the Israelites (divine war) and the "theologically elaborate schema" (holy war) implanted on those bat-tles by biblical redactors (Von Rad, 1993; Snaith, 1964). In these instances, cosmic war can include the belief in the direct intervention of a deity on the battlefield on behalf of the deity's tribe, nation, or people.

The material and spiritual benefits of a cosmic war are many. By endowing warfare with what Mark Juergensmeyer calls a sense of "transcendent moralism" and "ritual intensity," cosmic war both sacralizes and legitimizes acts of violence (Juergensmeyer 2003: 149). Juergensmeyer outlines a number of characteristics that, when present in human conflicts, increases the likelihood of an earthly struggle being defined as a cosmic war:

1. When the struggle is perceived as being fought not over territory or political concerns but rather over identity and human dignity;
2. When the goals of the conflict become reified to the point that what is at stake is the survival of one's faith, culture, or way of life;
3. When the struggle cannot be won in real or material terms, either because the enemy is too strong or the goals are impossible to achieve in this world;
4. When the notion of losing the conflict becomes synonymous with loss of faith or identity, leading to the impossibility of compromise, negotiation, settlement, or surrender;
5. When victory is perceived as being achieved not through artifice or strategy but rather through the power of faith;
6. When the conflict is believed to be a participatory drama controlled by God, leaving no room for human conceptions of morality;
7. When acts of violence become ritualized, allowing fighters to be transformed into soldiers sanctioned by God and victims—particularly noncombatants—to be viewed in sacrificial terms;
8. When the symbols and metaphors that provide meaning and purpose to the conflict are derived from and linked to the mythological conflicts found in a community's sacred scriptures;
9. When opponents become dehumanized or demonized, so that the battle is waged not against opposing nations or their soldiers or even their citizens but against Satan and his evil minions;
10. When the ultimate goal of the confrontation is not to defeat an earthly force but to vanquish evil itself, ensuring that a cosmic war remains an absolute, eternal, unending, and ultimately unwinnable conflict (Juergensmeyer 2003: 164–166).

The occurrence of any of these characteristics in aggregate will, more often than not, gradually transform earthly conflicts between peoples, cultures, nations, or tribes into cosmic contests between metaphysical forces of good and evil.

The concept of a cosmic war is deeply rooted in the religious traditions of the ancient Near East, where God is not conceived of as a passive force in war but a supremely active soldier. A brief survey of literary and graphic sources from the Mesopotamian, Egyptian, Syro-Palestinian, Akkadian, Ugaritic, and Anatolian contexts highlights a few common themes in regard to the idea of cosmic war that can be found in most Near East cultures, particularly among the ancient Israelites, whose theological ruminations on divine warfare greatly influenced contemporary Jewish, Christian, and Islamic notions of cosmic war (Kang, 1989; Tadmor and Weinfeld, 1987; Hasel, 2005). For this reason, special emphasis will be placed on the development and evolution of cosmic war in the Hebrew Bible.

Perhaps the most common theme of cosmic war shared by the peoples and cultures of the ancient Near East is the depiction of god as warrior. In many narratives, god is the sole warrior on the battlefield. Marduk, Ashur, Amun-Re, and Baal were each martial deities who not only fought alongside (and sometimes in front of) their earthly representatives, but, more importantly, they were often presented as fighting each other for dominance over land and peoples.

This is certainly the case in regard to the Israelite god Yahweh, whom the Bible explicitly refers to as "a warrior" (Ex. 15: 3), a god who "goes forth like a soldier" and "shows himself mighty against his foes" (Is. 42:13; Lind, 1980; Miller, 1973). Yahweh's martial nature may be based in his likely origins as an Egyptian deity named after a seminomadic, militant tribe that resided somewhere near the Sinai. Some of the oldest hymns in the Bible, such as the Song of Deborah (Judges 5), celebrate Yahweh's triumphs in battle. Premonarchical Israelite poetry examined by Frank Moore Cross unambiguously depicts Yahweh as a warrior embroiled in a cosmic battle against other gods on behalf of Israel (*Canaanite Myth and Hebrew Epic*, 1973).

Perhaps because, unlike other traditions in the ancient Near East, the Hebrew tradition tends to have no firm concept of hero worship, the concept of Yahweh as warrior often results in the complete removal of human agents from the act of war, as when Moses at the Sea of Reeds instructs his followers that "the Lord will fight for you, and you have only to keep still" (Ex. 14:14). As John Wood puts it, Yahweh fights *for* Israel rather than *through* Israel, which is "active in faith but passive in battle" (*Perspectives of War in the Bible*, 1998). Throughout the Hebrew Bible it is Yahweh alone who singlehandedly delivers the enemies into Israel's hands (Josh. 2:24, 6:2, 6:16, 8:1, 10:8; Jud. 3:28, 4:7, 6:3, 7:9, 18:10, 20:28; 1 Sam. 13:3, 14:12, 17:46, 23:4, 24:4, 26:8; 1 Kings 20:28), making the size and strength of Israel's armies irrelevant. After all, "nothing can hinder the Lord from saving by many or by few" (1 Sam. 14:6).

At the heart of cosmic war traditions in the ancient Near East is the belief that it is not human beings who are fighting on behalf of god, but god who is fighting on behalf of human beings. Of course, divine intervention can take many forms, from direct action, as when Yahweh hurls "huge stones from heaven" on the fleeing army of Jericho (Josh. 10:11; here the text specifically emphasizes that "there were more who died because of the hailstones than the Israelites killed with the sword"), to the type of indirect action that Moshe Weinfeld refers to as "the excitation of nature" (e.g., the spreading of famine or disease among the enemy, the creation of hail, wind, or sandstorms, etc.: 124).

Regardless of the form or manner of the divine intervention, what must be recognized is the physical presence of the god in battle. Thus Yahweh "travels along with your camp, to save you and to hand over your enemies to you" (Deut. 23:14). While this presence can also be reflected either through emblems or standards (such as the Ark of the Covenant) or through the consecration of weapons, which essentially transforms them into instruments of the divine, what must not be lost is the fact that Yahweh remains the sole agent of war, striking terror into the hearts of the enemy (Deut. 7:23; Josh 10:10, 24:7; Jud. 4:15, 7:22; 1 Sam. 5:11, 7:10, 14:15). This is particularly true in regard to the conquest of Canaan, which, as Yahweh repeatedly reminds Israel, was done "not by your [Israel's] bow or your sword" (Deut. 6:11) but by Yahweh and Yahweh alone (Ex. 23:29–30, 34:11).

The second major theme found in most cosmic war traditions follows from the first. Because this is god's battle, not man's, divine consultation must first be attained through omens or oracles before a battle can be launched. The prior approval of the god was a requirement of cosmic war in nearly every context of the ancient Near East with the possible exception of Egypt, where war was not considered a "divine command" but rather part of the natural, divine plan of creation. Certainly in ancient Israel the first act of cosmic war always involved the consultation of Yahweh:

> David inquired of the Lord, "Shall I go up against the Philistines? Will you give them into my hand?" The Lord said to David, "Go up; for I will certainly give the Philistines into your hand." So David came to Baal-perazim, and David defeated them there. He said, "The Lord has burst forth against my enemies before me, like a bursting flood." Therefore that place is called Baal-perazim. The Philistines abandoned their idols there, and David and his men carried them away. (2 Sam. 5:19–22).

In the same way that the lack of human agency in Israel's wars is deliberately exaggerated in order to emphasize Yahweh's identity as warrior, so the narratives of the Hebrew Bible present Yahweh not only as a divine oracle but as a general commanding an army on the ground, making strategic, real-time decisions as the war rages around him. Thus, the passage quoted above continues: "Once again the Philistines came up, and were spread out in the valley of Rephaim. When David inquired of the Lord, he said, 'You shall not go up; go round to their rear, and come upon them opposite the balsam trees'" (2 Sam. 5:23).

The third major theme of cosmic war concepts in the ancient Near East involves the sanctification of spoils. Because victory in all divine wars is attributed solely to the divine, whatever spoils are won in battle must be set apart for the god. These spoils have become sacred and as such are inaccessible to the warriors who actually fought in the battle. Thus, they must be destroyed. This not only includes vanquished lands, livestock, and property but also captured enemy soldiers, their wives, and their children, all of whom are considered sacred and out of reach of mere mortals. "[K]eep away from the things devoted to destruction, so as not to covet and take any of the devoted things and make the camp of Israel an object for destruction, bringing trouble upon it. But all silver and gold, and vessels of bronze and iron, are sacred to the Lord; they shall go into the treasury of the Lord" (Josh. 6:18–19).

While sanctification of spoils is a common theme in divine war traditions throughout the ancient Near East, only in the Anatolian and Syro-Palestinian contexts does it lead to what is often the concluding act of the divine war: the utter annihilation (*herem* in Hebrew) of the enemy, combatant and noncombatant alike, as a holocaust to god. "Now go and attack Amalek, and utterly destroy all that they have; do not spare them, but kill both man and woman, child and infant, ox and sheep, camel and donkey" (1 Sam. 15:3).[1]

The themes of cosmic war, so prevalent in the Hebrew Bible, easily lent themselves to Christian appropriation both symbolically—as was the case in the first few centuries after Christ—and materially, after the adoption of Christianity as the imperial religion of Rome. The early followers of Jesus focused their ideas of cosmic war firmly on the apocalyptic plane—Christ would one day return as "a warrior on a white horse," his eyes "like a flame of fire," his vestments "dripping with blood," his tongue "a sharp-edged sword" with which he would "strike down the nations" with vengeance (Rev. 19:11–15). Because they were living in a state of constant persecution and political weakness, in which the enemy was too strong to be defeated in real or material terms, the early Christians transformed their struggle against Rome into a participatory drama controlled by God, wherein they were cast as actors in a divine script written before time.

With the merging of Rome and Christianity in the early fourth century, however, a long and steady process of Christian militarization began that would ultimately reach its zenith with the Crusades: the quintessential expression of a divine conflict thought to be taking place simultaneously on earth and in the heavens. The Crusades were consciously conceived of as a new means of earning salvation from the church, as spelled out by Pope Urban II in 1095 during the Council of Clermont, the ecclesiastical gathering that initiated the First Crusade. By placing the conquest of land and territory on the cosmic plane and transforming the Muslim enemy into a demonic force, the soldiers of God who embarked on the mission to "liberate" Jerusalem were given spiritual license to unleash unrestrained violence on the city's inhabitants, including on the women and children, who were viewed as sacrificial victims in the cosmic battle between the forces of good of evil.

A similar view of the conflict arose among the Muslim warriors fighting against Christendom. As with Christianity, the Islamic view of cosmic war is derived from the Hebrew Bible's characterization of God as warrior, as well as from the concept of cosmic duality that was so prevalent in the cultures and traditions of the ancient Near East, in particular, Zoroastrianism and Manichaeism. The term in Islam for this cosmic duality is *al-wala' wal-bara'*, which can mean "loyalty and enmity," "allegiance and disavowal," or even "love and hate" and which suggests that the whole of creation can be partitioned into believers and unbelievers, a category that in the minds of many contemporary Muslims includes non-Muslims, heterodox Muslims (e.g., Shi'ah or Sufis), Muslims living in Europe or the United States, the rulers and governments of the Arab and Muslim world, the clerical leaders of Islam's traditional religious institutions and schools of law, and anyone who accepts such political or religious authority. The concept of al-wala' wal-bara' allows for the cosmic partitioning of the world into black and white, good and evil, us and them. In such conflicts there is no middle ground. Soldier and civilian, combatant and noncombatant, aggressor and bystander—all the traditional divisions that serve as markers in real wars break down. Everyone must choose a side.

Such cosmic duality forms the theological basis for a great many of the contemporary militant religious groups in the world—from Christian militias in the United States to the Catholic Irish Republican Army in the United Kingdom; from

Islamist groups such as Hamas in Palestine and Hizbullah in Lebanon to transnational (or jihadist) organizations such as al-Qaeda; from the radical ideological settlers and Religious Zionists in modern-day Israel to the conservative American evangelical groups who support them; from the militant Sikh separatist movements in India to the Buddhist militants in Japan and Sri Lanka.

Perhaps no contemporary conflict has more clearly taken on the patina of cosmic war than the Arab-Israeli conflict. For a great many Jews, Israel's war with the Arab armies are viewed through the lens of the historical-cum-mythological battles fought by the Israelites against God's enemies; they are understood not in the earthly context of governments and political affairs but in the cosmic context of good fighting evil. God's command in the Hebrew Bible to cleanse the Holy Land of all "foreign" elements still lingers in the imaginations of a broad coalition of Religious Zionists, ultra-Orthodox *haredim*, ideological settler groups, and yeshiva students, who together have formed what the French scholar of religions Gilles Kepel terms a "re-Judaization movement" in Israel (*The Revenge of God*, 1994). These Jews insist on a state governed wholly by religious law, one in which the land is cleansed of its "foreign" inhabitants so as to hasten the return of the Messiah. As such, they are actively engaged in supplanting the secular Zionism that has defined Israel's political identity since its inception with a messianic Zionism whose ultimate goal is the dismantling of the secular state altogether.

The cosmic worldview of these radical Jewish groups is shared by militant Palestinian groups such as Hamas and Islamic Jihad, each of which relies on the concept of cosmic war not only to sanctify and legitimize acts of violence against Israeli citizens but also (and perhaps more importantly) to offer its followers hope for victory over a far mightier foe. Framing their struggle for resistance against Israeli occupation in cosmic terms—as a conflict not over land or territory but over identity and dignity—allows these Islamic militants to use the widely recognized symbols and terminology of Islam to frame their political platforms in religious terms as a metaphysical conflict between good and evil, rather than as a material conflict between opposing political ideologies.

The notion of transcending material concerns for metaphysical ones lies at the core of the ideology that propels transnational Islamic militant organizations such as al-Qaeda. In struggling toward global transformation, these so-called jihadist groups are fighting a war of the imagination, one that cannot be won in any real or measurable terms. The zealous devotion to the glories of martyrdom that so indelibly marks these groups is an implicit recognition that its objectives, unformed and indeterminate as they may be, are impossible to achieve in this life. That is why jihadist ideologues so rarely speak of achieving any kind of "victory," at least not in the sense of enacting some specific social or political agenda. Rather, they rely on the cosmic duality of al-wala' wal-bara' to propagate the notion that their struggle, as outlined by the Egyptian jihadist ideologue Ayman al-Zawahiri, is not between rival political ideologies but between belief and unbelief—or, in Zawahiri's words, "between Islam and the infidels."

The same cosmic duality can be found among Christian groups, whether the Christian revolutionaries in Latin America, who perceived their struggle for freedom from oppression as a cosmic contest in which God was actively engaged on behalf of the poor and dispossessed against the wealthy and powerful, or among the Christian militias in the United States that cast their struggle against the government in terms of a battle between good and evil (Juergensmeyer 2008: 182). Among American evangelicals, this cosmic contest has elevated the United States to sacred status, turning the nation's enemies into God's enemies. Surveys have repeatedly shown that large numbers of American evangelicals believe that God actively favors the United States in international conflicts. Perhaps this fact, more than anything else, explains why evangelicals in the United States appear more willing than other Americans to support state-sanctioned war. In the cosmic imagination of some American evangelicals, such wars are not merely conflicts between armies and nations; they are, rather, cosmic battles between the forces of good, represented by the United States, and the forces of evil, represented by the nation's enemies. This was particularly the case with the so-called War on Terror, which evangelical leaders such as Mike Evans labeled "a dress rehearsal for Armageddon." Indeed, the wars in Afghanistan and Iraq quickly took on the tenor of a cosmic conflict against demonic forces.

Ultimately, any religion whose adherents believe in the existence of good or evil in the universe can, by virtue of the belief that these metaphysical forces battle each other on earth through the words, actions, and thoughts of human beings, lend itself to a belief in cosmic war. Such a Manichaean worldview naturally leads to the belief that present earthly conflicts are merely reflections of the eternal, cosmic conflicts that are chronicled in sacred scriptures. Thus the Hindu nationalists of the Bharatiya Janata Party evoke the sacred wars of the *Mahabharata* and *Ramayana* in their political conflicts with India's Muslim minority, while militant Jews in Israel tend to view the conflict with Palestinians through the lens of the epic battles fought by the Israelites against their biblical foes. As Juergensmeyer notes, just as religion has the power to reaffirm the primacy of order, so, too, does it require that disorder be conquered, often through violence (Juergensmeyer 2003: 162). The notion that it takes violence to defeat violence is the hallmark of many religions' cosmology. Still, behind the cosmic impulse there often lurks real and earthly grievances that must be addressed if the drive toward cosmic war, which remains such a destructive factor in contemporary religious disputes, is to be stemmed.

NOTE

1. There is evidence for the practice of "utter annihilation" in Mari, Nabataean, Ugaritic, and even early Roman sources. However, the tradition of wiping out the vanquished enemy as an act of devotion to god seems to have been explicitly developed as a theological concept only among the Israelites and Moabites. It has often been noted that Moabite theology of warfare is strikingly similar to early Israelite doctrine. This is most dramatically depicted in the so-called Mesha stele, which seems to parallel the divine war concepts found in the Bible in almost every way except that it substitutes

Israel's national god, Yahweh, with the Moab national god, Chemosh. "And Chemosh said to me, 'Go, take Nebo from Israel. So I went by night and fought against it from the break of dawn until noon, taking it and slaying all, seven thousand men, boys, women, girls, and maid-servants, for I had devoted them to destruction for Ashtar Chemosh.'" From *Studies in the Mesha Inscriptions and Moab*, ed. Andrew Dearman (Atlanta: Scholars Press, 1989). Additionally, Assyrian propaganda explicitly connects decimating enemies with pleasing the heart of the god Ashur. The etiology is usually a violated oath, sanctioned by gods and avenged by the Assyrians. The same motif appears in the *Iliad* and in the curses that follow oaths in the ancient Near East.

BIBLIOGRAPHY

Aslan, Reza. *How to Win a Cosmic War*. New York: Random House, 2009.

Cross, Frank Moore. *Canaanite Myth and Hebrew Epic*. Cambridge, Mass.: Harvard University Press, 1973.

Dearman, Andrew. Ed. *Studies in the Mesha Inscriptions and Moab*. Atlanta: Scholars Press, 1989.

Hasel, Michael G. *Military Practice and Polemic*. Berrien Springs, Mich.: Andrews University Press, 2005.

Juergensmeyer, Mark. *Terror in the Mind of God: The Global Rise of Religious Violence*. Berkeley: University of California Press, 2003.

Juergensmeyer, Mark. *Global Rebellion: Religious Challenges to the Secular State*. Berkeley: University of California Press, 2008.

Kang, Sa-Moon. *Divine War in the Old Testament and in the Ancient Near East*. Berlin: Walter de Gruyter, 1989.

Kepel, Gilles. *The Revenge of God: The Resurgence of Islam, Christianity and Judaism in the Modern World*. University Park: Pennsylvania State University Press, 1994.

Lind, M. C. *YAHWEH Is a Warrior: The Theology of Warfare in Ancient Israel*. Scottsdale, Ariz.: Herald Press, 1980.

Miller, Patrick. *The Divine Warrior in Ancient Israel*. Cambridge: Harvard University Press, 1973.

Snaith, Norman Henry. *The Distinctive Ideas of the Old Testament*. New York: Schocken Books, 1964.

Tadmor, H. and Moshe Weinfeld. Eds. *History, Historiography, and Interpretation: Studies in Biblical and Cuneiform Literatures*. Leiden, Neth.: Brill, 1987.

Von Rad. Gerhard. *Holy War in Ancient Israel*. Trans. Marva J. Dawn. Grand Rapids, Mich.: Eerdmans, 1993.

Wood, John A. *Perspectives of War in the Bible*. Macon, Ga.: Mercer Press, 1998.

CHAPTER 16

GENOCIDE AND THE RELIGIOUS IMAGINARY IN RWANDA

CHRISTOPHER C. TAYLOR

IT is to Raphael Lemkin that we owe the legal concept of genocide. He first coined the term in *Axis Rule in Occupied Europe* (1944) to identify incidents of mass violence against Jews in World War II. As a Polish Jew, Lemkin lost many close relatives to the Nazi Holocaust. After the war, Lemkin's concept was used as one of the bases for the Nuremberg trials and was eventually adopted by the United Nations. But Lemkin's further efforts to stop "crimes against humanity" tended to encounter indifference. Perceived as something of a crackpot, sometimes humored, more often ignored, he died exhausted and impoverished at the age of 59. Since his death in 1959, similar incidents of mass murder have occurred in Indonesia, Nigeria, Cambodia, Guatemala, Burundi, Yugoslavia, Rwanda, Iraq, Sudan, Democratic Republic of Congo, and Sri Lanka. Despite a lot of hand wringing, the international community has done little or nothing in each instance, with the possible exception of Yugoslavia, where NATO's "no fly zone" prevented further genocidal acts against Bosnia's Muslims. Genocide, a "problem from hell," as Samantha Power has put it, is easier to criminalize than to prevent or stop.

Religion has been a component in a number of these genocides. The archetype is the Nazi Holocaust, but a religious component was unmistakable also in the earlier Armenian genocide, where most of the victims were Christian and most of the perpetrators Muslim. In Bosnia, on the other hand, most of the victims were Muslim and the perpetrators Christian. Religious differences, along with other factors, were also discernible in actions of mass violence that took place in Indonesia, Nigeria (Biafra), Cambodia, Iraq, Sudan, and Sri Lanka. It seems that no matter what a group's religious affiliation, that in itself does not prevent the group from committing mass murder, nor does it shield it from persecution. All too often yesterday's victims are tomorrow's killers.

Rwanda

A reputed exception to this pattern is the 1994 Rwandan genocide, usually attributed to ethnic rather than religious strife, since both the Tutsi victims and Hutu perpetrators tended to be Christian. Yet it is not correct to presume the irrelevance of religion. In this chapter, I contend that much of the violence in Rwanda cannot be fully understood without considering what I call the "religious imaginary." In this case, the religious imaginary involved cosmological and ontological notions specific to Rwandan culture and particularly apparent in earlier ritual practices having to do with sacred kingship. These penetrated ideas of leadership and moral personhood and can be discerned in images, such as cartoons, that were published in Rwanda's popular media in the time leading up to the 1994 genocide.

During violent conflicts information sources such as magazines and newspapers often fan the sentiments of hate against targeted groups (Dower 1986). Rwanda in 1994 was no exception, despite widespread illiteracy. Hutu propagandists used the media to arouse the passions of potential killers through radio broadcasts, cartoons, and writings. In other occurrences of mass violence, the targeted groups are convenient scapegoats because of their marginality. But in the case of Rwanda, the targeted group—the Tutsi—had once dominated the country. Much of the ferocity of Rwanda's genocide can be traced to the fact that even though the Hutu majority had wrested control of the country in the early 1960s, many Hutu did not feel confident that their rule was secure. This feeling was exacerbated when the Tutsi Rwandan Patriotic Front invaded the country in October 1990.

There were reasons, however ill founded, for Hutu suspicions. Some Tutsi had managed to do well despite decades of discrimination in practically every arena of public life. Moreover, many highly placed Hutu notables had taken Tutsi wives or mistresses. Such ethnic mixings were a thorn in the side of Hutu extremists and indicative of their contradictory sentiments of fear, desire, and envy—sentiments one expects more from an oppressed than from a dominant group. Unsure of their privileged position in the Rwandan state, Hutu extremists did everything they could to portray themselves as morally justified in inciting violent passions against the Tutsi minority. This resulted in state-sponsored violence against the Tutsis.

When any state implements a campaign of violence, it tries to legitimize its actions according to local moral perceptions and prevailing cultural codes, exploiting ideologies that make destructive acts appear justified for the maintenance of collective well-being. Frequently, public media serve as the means by which these ideologies are communicated to the mass of the state's citizens. However, these media also convey deeper, less immediately apprehensible desires and fears, especially when they rely on nonverbal means of communication. Certain images are less accessible to conscious apperception, are more archetypal in nature, and are less likely to be construed by social actors as having obvious and clear-cut ideological content. Prediscursive in nature, these images elude narrative form and are not, in themselves, political. In 1994 such images and the sentiments they evoked were undergirded by older Rwandan notions of power and sovereignty that were constitutive of the religious imaginary

Religious Imaginary, Wild Sovereignty, and Bare Life

Giorgio Agamben (1998) and Luc de Heusch (1982), discussing Roman and African notions of sovereignty, respectively, have noted a recurring pattern in which the sovereign is perceived as an outsider and, as such, possessed of wild potencies. Once inducted into the social fold, the sovereign then uses his preternatural force to impose order; yet, as an outsider, he is free to act independently of the laws and constraints that he imposes on others. However, many of the others against whom he asserts his control are also outsiders in the sense that they do not willingly submit to the sovereign order and are estranged, even enraged, by the sovereign's peculiar freedom to act with impunity. As an outsider, the sovereign can be reduced to "bare life." As Bruce Kapferer puts it, the sovereign is "that externality which asserts itself unconstrainedly against another externality…. This externality, like the sovereign, is defined as an a-social, a-moral being—in Agamben's analysis, 'bare life' and beyond the protection of the sovereign order, open to being killed with legal and moral impunity" (Kapferer 2005:7). Like the Roman sovereign, the African sacred kings discussed by de Heusch never completely shed their association with the wild and never permanently divested themselves of the risk of being reduced to "bare life" and summarily killed. In the case of the central African Luba, the group whose kingship symbolism preoccupies de Heusch the most and that bears close affinity to the Rwandan example, virtually every sacred king dies a violent death.

But it is not only sacred kings whose "wild sovereignty" predisposes them to being reduced to "bare life"; it is also those against whom these kings are simultaneously opposed and equivalent, those defined as external although dwelling within the state's borders—in the Rwandan case this would be the Tutsi. In Agamben's analysis, modernity does not radically change the pattern. He sees evidence of the continued wildness of sovereignty and its subjects in many times and places. This point is also taken up by Kapferer who says, "the examples are legion: the situation of Jews up to and including the Holocaust, of Romanies even today, of Palestinians in the West Bank and Gaza, of Tutsi and various other African populations, the prisoners of Guantanamo Bay, and those in refugee camps in Australia, Europe, and elsewhere" (ibid.). Oppression in all of these cases is associated with the perception of the parties as "bare life," as external to authentic social order.

De Heusch's analysis of the myths that surround sacred kingship in the Congolese savanna demonstrates that the Roman *Homo sacer* was not unique in the premodern world. De Heusch explores two opposed symbolic orders underlying central African sovereignty, *bufumu* and *bulopwe* (1982: 32). Bufumu, associated with the unbridled forces of nature, incest, and human sacrifice, may be compared to Agamben's "wild sovereignty." Bulopwe, associated with refinement, fecundity, and exogamy, constitutes the "rule of law" or the domesticated aspect of sovereignty. Rwandan sacred kingship, despite minor differences from the Congolese varieties, incorporates similar opposing principles in the persons of its mythical ancestors: One of them, Kigwa, was said to have fallen from the sky and to have practiced incest with his sister; a later mythical king, Gihanga, was well behaved and exogamous and "introduces a refined and truly royal cultural order" (ibid. 74). Also double-natured were the ritual and political functions of Rwandan kings in any single dynastic cycle of four kings. The first and fourth kings were supposed to follow the pattern established by Gihanga and thus be peaceful and forbidden to engage in wars of conquest. They were confined within the two sacred halves of the Rwandan kingdom. The second and third kings were supposed to be warlike, to traverse the sacred boundaries, and to conquer new territory (d'Hertefelt & Coupez 1964). Two of the four kings within each dynastic cycle thus had the responsibility of conquest, while the other two had the responsibility of consolidation and renewal. This opposition corresponds to bufumu and bulopwe, the mutually constitutive aspects of sovereignty in its wild and domesticated forms.

SPECIFICALLY RWANDAN SYMBOLIC FORMS

In order to understand the precolonial Rwandan state, it is necessary to know something about the religious concepts in which notions of the state were embedded. Let us begin with the Rwandan concept of *imaana*. Before Christian evangelization (early twentieth century), the term *imaana* referred to a supreme being and in a more generalized way to a "diffuse, fecundating fluid" of celestial origin whose activity upon livestock, land, and people brought fertility and abundance (d'Hertefelt & Coupez 1964). Elaborate state rituals called *inzira* or "paths" were performed to channel the fertility effects of *imaana* to the entirety of the Rwandan kingdom. The Rwandan king (*umwami*) and his coterie of ritual specialists (*abiiru*) were charged with the responsibility of enacting these rituals, and their credibility and tenure were dependent on tangible success. All Rwanda's kings as well as most of their closest retainers belonged to the pastoralist Tutsi group, who were a minority of the population.

In an earlier work I discussed the ritual functions of the Rwandan sacred king, the centrality of fluid symbols (rain, milk, blood, breast milk, and semen), and the symbolic opposition between disorderly states of fluid flows and orderly ones (Taylor 1988, 1992). In essence this opposition corresponds to the bufumu-bulopwe opposition discussed by de Heusch. For example, disorderly states of flow in early Rwanda included drought, inundation, incest, and two perceived infirmities concerning women's bodies: *impa,* or lack of menses in women of childbearing age, and *impenebere,* or lack of breast development in women of childbearing age. Orderly states of flow included rainfall in the proper measure, lactating cattle, honey-producing bees, fertile land, fertile people, and prosperity.

The king's legitimacy in precolonial Rwanda arose from his capacity to control the flows of such substances along hierarchically defined trajectories. But he could only control these by selectively interdicting them—the enactment of "wild sovereignty"—even though this carried the risk of total obstruction: drought, infertility, and death. The exercise of sovereignty, in other words, required a measure of "wild sovereignty," which had the potential of gaining the upper hand. Ideally, the king, as an embodiment of *imaana,* exerted just the right amount of pressure on the celestial udder. This is why in some instances he was referred to by the term *umukama,* which means "the milker." The king could enrich his subjects with his gifts of cattle and fertility or he could impoverish them, either by withholding these gifts or by being an unworthy repository of *imaana.* In this latter instance, with the qualities of wild sovereignty eclipsing those of domesticated sovereignty, the king would become reduced to "bare life" and killed.

Thus the king, as *imaana*'s earthly representative, channeled fertility to the rest of humanity. The king's body could be compared to a conduit through which celestial beneficence passed, but this passage was neither immediate nor direct. The royal body retarded the descent of *imaana,* the flow of fertility. By temporarily serving as the obstructing agent, the king catalyzed the proper pace of the channeling process and his role became tangible and visible. In one legend that I heard in 1987, for example, fertility power passed through the king's alimentary canal, according to this delayed rhythm:

> Ruganzu Ndori was living in exile in the kingdom of Ndorwa, a neighboring kingdom to the north of Rwanda. There he had taken refuge with his FZ (*nyirasenge*) who was married to a man from the region. In the meantime, because the Rwandan throne was occupied by an illegitimate usurper, Rwanda was experiencing numerous calamities. The crops were dying, the cows were not giving milk, and the women were becoming sterile. Ruganzu's paternal aunt encouraged him to return to Rwanda to retake the throne and save his people from catastrophe. Ruganzu agreed. But before setting forth on his voyage to Rwanda, she gave him the seeds (*imbuto*) of several cultivated plants (sorghum, gourd, and others) to restart Rwandan cultures. While en route to Rwanda,

Ruganzu Ndori came under attack. Fearing that the *imbuto* would be captured, he swallowed the seeds with a long drink of milk. Once he regained the Rwandan throne, he defecated the milk and seed mixture upon the ground and the land became productive once again. Since that time all Rwandan kings are said to be born clutching the seeds of the original *imbuto* in their hand.

The king's body was part of the polity, but it was also the part that resembled the whole. Since he was the conduit between sky and earth, his body had to be kept open and this was associated with his physiological processes (Taylor 1988). In essence, by attuning the king's body to the collective symbolic order and then metaphorically extending this to the cosmos as a whole, the Rwandan religious imaginary envisioned that the inherent randomness of weather, pestilence, and human social life might be kept in abeyance, if not stymied once and for all. However, keeping calamity at bay came at a price, which demanded sacrificial victims, in some instances the king himself. In instances of natural disaster (e.g., drought, epidemic, epizootic, flooding, or crop failure) or humanly caused disasters (e.g., military defeat, invasion by a neighboring kingdom), the king might be seen as an inadequate conduit of *imaana* and thus the ultimate human obstructor. Later his death might be idealized in dynastic legends as an *umutabazi* sacrifice, as if the king had heroically given his life for the survival of Rwanda (d'Hertefelt and Coupez 1964).

The umutabazi (pl., *abatabazi*) sacrifice was initiated by a mythical king named Ruganzu Bwimba who chose to sacrifice himself in order to save Rwanda from conquest by the neighboring kingdom of Gisaka (Coupez and Kamanzi 1962: 87–104). While Vansina (1960) has interpreted accounts in Rwandan court history of king sacrifice as attempts to conceal Rwandan military defeats, de Heusch (1982) maintains, following Frazer, that the sacrificial function was more than mere artifice to conceal a national humiliation. It was a quality implicit in kingship itself. There were moments of danger so extreme to Rwanda as a whole, that ordinary sacrificial victims could not be trusted to restore the flow of beneficence from sky to earth. In these instances, diviners would determine who, among those of royal blood, should sacrifice himself for the good of Rwanda. Often but not always, the lot fell on the king, for obviously his was the most potent royal blood. When this blood was spilled on enemy territory, it was thought to poison the area for its inhabitants, rendering it easy prey to Rwandan conquest (1982: 46).

The effect of royal blood spilled in sacrifice resembled that of two accursed beings: *impenebere* (women of childbearing age who had not developed breasts, i.e., deficient in milk) and *impa* (women of childbearing age who had never menstruated, i.e., deficient in blood). Such women, as embodiments of *ishyano* (impurity), were thought to be sources of aridity and infertility to the entire kingdom. Often Rwandan armies sacrificed them on enemy land. In certain instances, therefore, the king was equivalent to them and could be considered the final repository of impurity, the ultimate "blocked being," or in Agamben's terms, a *Homo sacer*, the overt embodiment of "wild sovereignty."

The person of Ruganzu Bwimba, the first king said to have died as an umutabazi, reveals something about the flow of royal blood while demonstrating principles about the symbolism of the body. In order for the body to be considered adequate in sociomoral terms, it had to be a good conduit for *imaana*. Let us consider the question of blood and consanguinity first. According to legend, the early predecessors of Rwandan royalty, beginning with Kigwa, practiced brother-sister incest. This hyperendogamy kept the blood of royalty flowing in a "closed circuit" and precluded all possibility of outsiders sharing in the privileges of royalty ("wild sovereignty" at its extreme). Later, the legendary king Gihanga instituted the practice of hyperexogamy by marrying women who were neither of royal blood, nor even from the Rwandan kingdom. Descendants of Gihanga continued a tempered version of exogamy by taking wives from Rwanda's three autochthonous clans (*abasangwabutaka*—lit., "those who were found upon the earth"): Zigaaba, Singa, and Gesera. Because of these exogamous kings, the blood of royal consanguinity began to flow in a more open manner. Kings with wild, incestuous ancestors married terrestrial women and engendered children who were mixed, yielding a form of sovereignty domesticated by establishing a connection to the earth.

Ruganzu Bwimba ended this practice when his mother's brother, Nkorokombe, a Singa, induced illness in himself in order to avoid having to sacrifice himself for Rwanda. Under threat from the neighboring kingdom of Gisaka, Rwanda's court diviners determined that a human sacrifice was necessary to save Rwanda from defeat and that the umutabazi was to be Nkorokombe. Instead of accepting this responsibility graciously, Nkorokombe took the flowers of an irritating plant and inserted them in his anus, then showed Ruganzu Bwimba that he was suffering from rectal prolapsus (Coupez & Kamanzi 1962: 97). Because a sacrificial victim must be healthy and whole, he had disqualified himself.

In effect, by stopping up his anus, Nkororkombe had turned himself into a "blocked being," someone capable of ingesting but not egesting. Metaphorically speaking, Nkorokombe had transformed himself into a closed conduit—someone capable of receiving but not passing on or giving up what he has received. No longer could a cycle of flow and exchange be constituted in which such a being was a participant, and by implication, no longer were "autochthones" like him suitable alliance partners with "celestials." To save Rwanda, Ruganzu Bwimba offered himself in Nkorokombe's place. Shortly before his sacrificial death, however, Ruganzu Bwimba decreed that never again should potential Rwandan kings take wives from groups that were not of celestial origin, from clans other than those termed *Ibibanda*. This excluded women from the abasangwabutaka, the three autochthonous clans.

PRESIDENT HABYARIMANA AS SACRED KING

At first glance, early kingship ritual and mythology would seem to have little to do with President Habyarimana whose assassination on April 6, 1994, triggered the Rwandan genocide. However, one of the ways in which this identification was clear was in the domain of fertility, as viewed from the perspective of the traditional Rwandan religious imaginary. In the 1980s Rwanda was relatively prosperous; by the 1990s, however, the economy had sustained several reverses, including currency devaluation and the collapse of world coffee prices. Although the perception of Habyarimana would change radically in the 1990s, during the 1980s many people made comments about the aptness of Habyarimana's name which comes from *imaana* (God or the "diffuse fecundating fluid") and *kubyara*—to engender. In other words his name, decoded, was "It is God who gives life." This concords well with the idea of the sovereign as the catalyst of fluid processes, the "diffuse fecundating fluid" of early Rwanda.

Popular news magazines of the 1990s occasionally compared the president to a Rwandan sacred king. At times, this was quite explicit and intended to be flattering, at other times, it was explicitly critical. These references to the former kingship institution were politically and ideologically motivated, which accounts for the differences seen among the various Rwandan political factions in their depiction of Habyarimana. However, in many instances the comparisons were implicit, an unwitting reflection of the religious imaginary. Here I will concentrate on the implicit symbolism in regard to the sovereign's body and to processes of flow.

This symbolism appeals to a deeper, more ontological level of imagination. Although the various Rwandan factions were contesting who would control the power of the state, the contest was being waged through the mediation of a common body of symbols, which were not in themselves being contested. For example, imagery of the body as a conduit is where ideological motivation gives way to a realm of thought having to do with a specifically Rwandan way of imagining the body as a being in time and space, one that acts as the focal point of physiological and social processes that are, nonetheless, redolent with cosmological import—a being through which *imaana* should pass in its descent from sky to earth.

Figure 16.1 manifests the symbolic pattern of "body as conduit," while also negating it. Political opponents of Habyarimana portray his body as a "flowing" conduit, but one that turns all flows back on itself. The headline reads: "In the MRND they continue to excrete on the plate from which they eat and into the water from which they drink." At the left an MRND (National Republican Movement for Democracy and Development) youth holds up a severed leg and says: "Let's kill them, let's get rid of them, let's eat them." Habyarimana replies: "Yes, let's descend on them all right." To his right, two Hutu extremists exclaim sarcastically: "In the Rwanda of peace, there sure is a lot of delicious food." Beneath the cartoon are the words: "The politics of the cattle thieves causes problems."

Much is condensed in this illustration. At an ideological level, Habyarimana and his Hutu extremist followers are being compared to cattle thieves. It is also quite obvious that the president, according to his detractors, is a man who eats excrement. But there are other elements that are not directly ideological or even logical in an ordinary sense. What serves as Habyarimana's toilet in the picture is Rwanda and its hapless population. The spoon that we see him moving from

Politiki y'abashimusi b'inka idukozeho.

Figure 16.1

beneath his anus and about to place in his mouth is labelled "taxes." The Rwandan people's taxes are swallowed by Habyarimana, defecated by Habyarimana, only to be swallowed by him again. Only if you are a follower of his are you likely to get anything to eat, as with these Hutu extremist party members who manage to grab the occasional severed limb or morsel of excrement. Habyarimana reverses the flow of beneficence. Instead of it descending downward from the sky, passing through his body, and then to the earth and people, it moves from down to up, from people to ruler. Once there, most of it is continually recycled in a sterile "closed circuit flow" within his body. What little passes through him gets gobbled up by his lackies.

At an ontological level, a more profound message is being communicated: Habyarimana is an inadequate conduit of *imaana* and thus not a worthy king. He is the antithesis of Ruganzu Ndori. A king like Ruganzu Ndori would never have allowed his bowels to selfishly retain the mystical powers of the original magical seeds (*imbuto*). Ruganzu Ndori's body was a moral "conduit," one through which *imaana* could pass from sky to earth, a body capable of performing "open circuit flow," a potentially good alliance partner, a giver and not simply a receiver of gifts, an adequate embodiment of *imaana* on earth. King Habyarimana is the opposite of Ruganzu Ndori; he is the embodiment of *ishyano* (ritual impurity). He has reassumed the mantle of "wild sovereignty" and, in doing so, reduced himself to "bare life." The cartoon evokes imagery of the inadequate king, the one who blocks the celestial flow. The implicit message is "Habyarimana must be killed."

CONCLUSION

So how does the ritualized death of the sacred king extend into genocidal acts against the Tutsi en masse?

The Rwandan genocide cannot be understood solely in political or even ethnic terms. Although recent contributions to the study of ethnonationalism in Rwanda are obviously of great importance in comprehending the 1994 tragedy, they accord little weight to what I have called the religious imaginary. My contention here has been that one of the best ways for gaining access to this level of genocide is to examine the symbolism implicit in both verbal and nonverbal means of communication—text certainly, but also cartoons and images that appeared in Rwanda's pregenocidal media. When we look beneath the surface of ideology and the avowed intentions of social actors in the genocide, we uncover a ritual and mythological component, one whose origins lie in the rituals of sacred kingship and one that reveals something about the deeper fears and desires of the *genocidaires*.

Despite the changes brought in the wake of colonialism, Christian evangelization, and incorporation into the world economy, there were lines of continuity in the cosmological conceptualization of the Rwandan state between the premodern period when the state was led by a sacred king and the modern period when the state was headed by a military dictator, President Juvenal Habyarimana. This continuity shows the importance of local mythological notions of wild sovereignty in the genocide of 1994 and can be discerned in representations of the President, which appeared in popular literature during the pregenocidal years between 1990 and 1994. Sovereignty in precolonial Rwanda depended on the balanced interplay of two metaphorical potencies that I have labeled "wild sovereignty" (following Agamben) and domesticated sovereignty. These correspond closely to the qualities of bufumu and bulopwe encountered in nearby Bantu-speaking areas of central Africa as discussed by Luc de Heusch. As long as these two potencies were perceived to act in tandem and for the benefit of the social group, the sovereign's externality, his origin in the realm of the wild, could be overlooked. It was only when the wild and domesticated aspects of sovereignty became detached from each other, rendering the king's externality visible, that the king exposed himself to the risk of being reduced to "bare life" and summarily executed. Wild and domesticated sovereignty in Rwanda were in turn dependent on another set of metaphors encapsulated in the cosmological notion of *imaana*, God or the "diffuse, fecundating fluid"—whose ordered descent to the earth was the central preoccupation of the rituals of Rwandan sacred kingship. The sacred king's responsibility was to catalyze and direct this process, but he could only do this by embodying aspects of "wild sovereignty." Yet the king forever risked being perceived as overly obstructing and thus overly wild and therefore responsible for the cessation of beneficial flows in times of crisis. This is when he could be judged an inadequate conduit for *imaana* and become reduced to "bare life." Collective remembering of such events in dynastic histories usually followed the model of umutabazi sacrifice, masking tragedy and making it appear as if the sovereign had died a selfless and heroic death.

We see a recurrence of this pattern in the person of President Habyarimana and in the intimation that he had become a "wild sovereign," an inversion of Ruganzu Ndori, for Habyarimana is portrayed as a sovereign who reverses flows, who retains beneficence within himself, and who blocks that which should pass through him. But the contagion of "bare life" did not stop with Habyarimana. With his externality made visible, it was then possible for Hutu extremists to insist on the externality of others, in this case, all Rwandan Tutsis, who were tarred with the accusation that they were "invaders from Ethiopia." Reduced to "bare life," Tutsis were a reminder that lingering externalities within the polity threatened its social and moral integrity. If a "sacred king" could not get rid of them, then the people must do it for themselves. Tutsis had become the "blocking beings," and they were everywhere—neighbors, colleagues, sometimes even wives and mistresses. No pity could be shown.

This assertion is not to insist on the persistence of the traditional within the modern, a dualism that persists in much anthropological thinking but rather to underline the important role of local mythological notions, the religious imaginary, in pushing people to commit mass murder when the integrity of the polity appears threatened. This is not confined to the Rwandan case. Although many elements within the religious imaginary may have premodern roots, virtually all heads of state in the modern world are embodiments of "wild sovereignty" in one way or another. Any one of them can be reduced to "bare life" under the right circumstances. Moreover, virtually all modern polities have people within them who could be perceived as external to the polity, and usually they are members of a minority. Mass collective murder is not only a political occurrence susceptible to rationalistic analysis, there are deeper levels of motivation, more covert and implicit, and it behooves us to try to understand them.

BIBLIOGRAPHY

Agamben, G. *Homo Sacer: Sovereign Power and Bare Life.* Translated by Daniel Heller-Roazen. Stanford, CA: Stanford University Press, 1998.

Coupez, A. and Kamanzi, T. *Les recits historiques du Rwanda.* Tervuren, Belgium: Musee Royal de l'Afrique Centrale, 1962.

Dower, J. W. *War without Mercy: Race and Power in the Pacific War.* New York: Pantheon Books, 1986.

Hertefelt, M. d'and Coupez, A. *Le royaum sacre de l'ancien Rwanda*. 1964.

Heusch, L. de. *The Drunken King or the Origin of the State*. Translated and annotated by Roy Willis. Bloomington, IN: Indiana University Press, 1982.

Kapferer, B. "New Formations of Power, the Oligarchic-Corporate State, and Anthropological Ideological Discourse." In *Anthropological Theory* 5.3 (2005): 285–299.

Lemkin, R. *Axis Rule in Occupied Europe*. Washington, D.C.: Carnegie Endowment for Internatonal Peace, Division of International Law, 1944.

Prunier, G. *The Rwanda Crisis*. New York: Columbia University Press, 1995.

Taylor, C., "Milk, Honey, and Money," Ph.D. dissertation, university microfilms, Ann Arbor, Michigan, 1988.

Taylor, C. *Milk, Honey, and Money: Changing Concepts in Rwandan Healing*. Washington, DC: Smithsonian Institution Press, 1992.

Taylor, C. *Sacrifice as Terror: The Rwandan Genocide of 1994*. Oxford, UK: Berg Publishers, 1999.

Umurangi, no. 14, December 10, 1992.

Vansina, J. *Le Rwanda ancien: le royaume nyiginya*. Paris: Karthala, 2001.

CHAPTER 17

RELIGIOUS TERRORISM AS PERFORMANCE VIOLENCE

MARK JUERGENSMEYER

ANY incident of terrorism is a kind of performance violence—a dramatic act meant to achieve an impact on those who witness it—but the performative character is heightened when it is associated with religion. Since its rise to power in 2014, the Islamic State of Iraq and Syria has used public beheadings as a political spectacle. The spectacular assaults of September 11, 2001 are another case in point. They were not only acts of violence; but also spectacular violence, conducted in a ritualistic way. The "Last Instructions" found among the possessions of Mohammad Attah, one of the hijackers on those tragic planes, provides a guide to conduct that clearly links the act with religious discipline (Lincoln).

The adjectives used to describe acts of religious terrorism—*symbolic, dramatic, theatrical*—suggest that we look at them not only as a tactic to achieve a tangible goal but also as a way of performing an element of an imagined reality. By using the term *performance,* I am suggesting that such acts are undertaken not only to draw attention to a cause but also to draw those who witness them, even those who witness them vicariously through images projected by the news media, into an experience of reality that the perpetrators want to share. Like religious ritual or street theater, the acts are dramas designed to confront those who witness them with an alternative view of the world and to force them, for at least a few moments, to be drawn into the perpetrators' view of the world.

When I interviewed Mahmud Abouhalima, one of the activists convicted of the 1993 bombing of the World Trade Center, he expressed frustration with the inability of the American, European, and Middle Eastern public to see, in his words, "what was really going on." Behind the calm of ordinary appearances, he thought, was a great contest between the forces of good and evil in the world.[1] In his view, the American government was the Satanic power that was leading the evil side. We were kept in the dark, he surmised, because our news media were complicit with these evil forces and we were under the illusion that all was well. He indicated to me that the public needed to be shaken awake (Abouhalima 1997). When I asked him whether this was the purpose of such terrorist acts as bombing the Oklahoma City Federal Building or his own efforts in attempting to bring down the World Trade Center, he simply smiled and said, "Now you know."

After September 11, 2001, we all knew. There was no need for a verbal message to be sent to the news media informing them that these buildings had been attacked because they were symbols of the economic and military power of the United States or that some people regarded their destruction as a scene in a great war. The images showed all of this; the medium was the message. Abouhalima's bombing attempt on the World Trade Center in 1993 and the more successful and spectacular one in 2001 that brought down the Twin Towers in a cloud of dust were more than attempts to seize the public's imagination. As Abouhalima implied, they were also attempts to bring those who witnessed the events into the worldview of those who planned them.

The Scenario of Cosmic War

Abouhalima's world was a world at war and not just an ordinary war but a cosmic war—the ultimate struggle between good and evil, truth and untruth, God and the devil. By thrusting us into a view of horrific violence, he attempted to make us experience that warfare and enter into his bellicose world. The image of cosmic war is not limited to his thinking or even to a particular kind of jihadi Islamic thought, of course; it is a part of the religious imagination of virtually every religious tradition (see Chapter 15 in this volume).

Warfare is a dominant theme of most religious histories. The Muslim theme of jihad and the admonishments to battle in the Qur'an are echoed in other religious traditions' texts and ideas. Whole books of the Hebrew Bible are devoted to the military exploits of great kings, their contests related in gory detail. Though the New Testament does not take up the battle cry, the later history of the church does in a bloody series of crusades and religious wars. In India, warfare contributes to the grandeur of mythology. The great epics the *Ramayana* and the *Mahabharata* are tales of seemingly unending conflict and military intrigue, and, more than Vedic rituals, they define subsequent Hindu culture. The legendary name for India,

Bharata, comes from the epics, as does the name *Sri Lanka*. The epics continue to live in contemporary South Asia—a serialized version of the epics produced in the mid-1980s was the most popular television series ever aired in India (and, considering that country's vast population, perhaps the most widely watched television series in history). Even cultures without a strong emphasis on sacrifice have persistent images of religious war. In Sri Lanka, for example, the legendary history recorded in the Pali Chronicles, the *Dipavamsa* and the *Mahavamsa,* has assumed canonical status. It relates the triumphs of battles waged by Buddhist kings.

This grand scenario of warfare is available to be employed in every religious tradition by those who imagine contemporary conflicts in the world to have more than worldly importance. Through an association with cosmic war, social and political encounters are lifted into the high proscenium of religious drama. Few modern terrorist acts are directly about religion, in the narrow sense of fighting for or against religious beliefs; but they are often informed by images of sacred struggle. In the case of Abouhalima, the timeless image of religious struggle identified with the concept of jihad was applied to the sociopolitical situation of Western influences in the Middle East. Thus a rejection of what was thought to be a kind of cultural colonialism was infused with the ferocity of godly war, and this confrontation justified the most evil of militant acts, including those perceived by victims and observers as acts of terrorism.

Thus, if terrorism is always a kind of performance, the scenario that underlies the performance of religious terrorism is often one of cosmic war, an enduring battle that may be cast in Manichaean moral terms as being between good and evil or in metaphysical terms as the clash between order and disorder. For other forms of terrorism, other scenarios may be operative—leftwing terrorism might be conducted with the sense of historical inevitability of the triumph of the working class versus the oppression of the bourgeoisie; and rightwing terrorism might be animated by a transformative vision of state power versus anarchism. Some religious terrorism could also be propelled by scenarios other than cosmic war—such as the notion that a particular religious community had divinely granted inalienable rights to a particular territory to which no other religious or ethnic group could be imagined to have valid claims. But even these religious justifications are often also colored by the persistent images of great conflict, such as the contest between rightful ownership and the squatters' rights claimed by unblessed occupants of what is perceived to be sacred soil.

Images of warfare can be enormously powerful because they provide a template of order to a situation of confusion and an illusion of power. If a small band of dedicated activists can bring down the tallest buildings in the most important city of the most powerful nation in the world, that is an exhilarating expression of strength. It may be an illusory sensation, because the small band of activists cannot really control the affairs of the world's superpower; but for a few moments this grand terrorist act gives the perpetrators the giddy sense that they, not the US government, are in control.

It is the idea of cosmic war that gives a rationale and a moral justification to such acts of violence. Movements that use violence need cosmic war, because they need a frame of reference that will give justification to their acts. Ordinarily only the state can morally sanction violence—for defense, policing, and punishment— but if the group is an antiauthoritarian rebel band that is not approved by the state, it needs other ways to find moral legitimacy. This is where religious authority and religious images of cosmic warfare can be appropriated and provide a basis for moral legitimation.

One of the reasons why cosmic war is such a powerful scenario in the performing of terrorist incidents is that it enables the acts to be performative as well as performance. Acts of religious terrorism often do more than put on a display, they also perform changes by affecting the viewer and altering the viewers' perceptions of the world. The concept of performative acts is an idea developed by language philosophers such as J. L. Austin in regard to certain kinds of speech that are able to perform social functions: Their very utterance is a speech act that has a transformative impact (Austin 1962). Like vows recited during marriage rites, certain words not only represent reality but also shape it; they contain a certain power of their own. The same is true of some nonverbal symbolic actions, such as the gunshot that begins a race, the raising of a white flag to show defeat, or acts of terrorism.

Terrorist acts, then, can be both performance events, in that they make a symbolic statement, and performative acts, insofar as they try to change things. When Mohammad Attah piloted an American passenger plane directly into the World Trade Center towers; when Yigal Amir aimed his pistol at Israel's prime minister, Yitzhak Rabin; and when Sikh activists targeted Punjab's chief minister with a car bomb in front of the state's office buildings, the activists were aware that they were creating more than enormous spectacles. They probably also hoped that their actions would make a difference—if not in a direct, strategic sense, then in an indirect way as a dramatic show so powerful as to change people's perceptions of the world. In the case of 9/11 the perpetrators were successful beyond their wildest imaginations; their act of imagined war lured US policy makers and many of the general public into a view of war, a "War on Terror" that dominated US foreign policy for eight years and supported the US invasion and occupation of two Muslim countries.

The Israeli and Sikh cases had somewhat different results. The fact that the assassins of Prime Minister Rabin and Chief Minister Beant Singh hoped that their acts would make such a statement does not mean that they did. Public symbols mean different things to different people, and a symbolic performance may not achieve its intended effect. The way the act is perceived—by both the perpetrators and those who are affected by it—makes all the difference. The same is true of performative speech. One of the leading language philosophers has qualified the notion that some speech acts are performative by observing that the power of the act is related to the perception of it. Children, for example, playing at marriage are not wedded by merely reciting the vows and going through the motions, nor is a ship christened by just anyone who breaks a bottle against it and gives it a name (Austin, 4).

Pierre Bourdieu, carrying further the idea that statements are given credibility by their social context, has insisted that the power of performative speech—vows and christenings—is rooted in social reality and is given currency by the laws and social customs that stand behind it (Bourdieu 1991: 117). Similarly, an act of terrorism usually implies an underlying power and legitimizing ideology. But whether the power and legitimacy implicit in acts of terrorism are like play-acted marriage vows or are the real thing depends, in part, on how the acts are seen and on whether their significance is believed.

This brings us back to the realm of faith. Public ritual has traditionally been the province of religion, one of the reasons that performance violence comes so naturally to activists from a religious background. In a collection of essays on the connection between religion and terrorism published some years ago, one of the editors, David C. Rapoport, observed—accurately, I think—that the two topics fit together not only because there is a violent streak in the history of religion but also because terrorist acts have a symbolic side and, in that sense, mimic religious rites. The victims of terrorism are targeted not because they are threatening to the perpetrators, he said, but because they are "symbols, tools, animals or corrupt beings" that tie into "a special picture of the world, a specific consciousness" that the activist possesses (Rapoport 1982: xii). The street theater of performance violence forces those who witness it directly or indirectly into that "consciousness"—that alternative view of the world.

The idea of warfare implies more than an attitude; ultimately it is a worldview and an assertion of power. To live in a state of war is to live in a world in which individuals know who they are, why they have suffered, by whose hand they have been humiliated, and at what expense they have persevered. The concept of war provides cosmology, history, and eschatology and offers the reins of political control. Perhaps most important, it holds out the hope of victory and the means to achieve it. In the images of cosmic war, this victorious triumph is a grand moment of social and personal transformation, transcending all worldly limitations. One does not easily abandon such expectations. To be without such images of war is almost to be without hope.

Insofar as the scenario of cosmic war is a story, it carries a momentum toward its completion and contains the seeds of hope for its outcome. I use the term *hope* rather than *fear*, for no one wants to believe in a story that cannot produce a happy ending. Those who accept that their life struggles are part of a great struggle, a cosmic war, know that they are part of a grand tale that will ultimately end triumphantly, though not necessarily easily or quickly. The epic character of the story implies that the happy ending may be long delayed—perhaps until after one's lifetime or after the lifetimes of one's descendants. In the meantime, the story will involve sadness and travail—like the great passion narrative of Christianity in which Jesus triumphs over death only after being subjected to the gruesome and humiliating spectacle of public execution.

PLAYING THE ROLES

The scenario of cosmic war is one in which the heroes of the drama might have to suffer, even unto death. After all, overcoming defeat and humiliation is the point of war. The story of warfare explains why one feels for a time beaten and disgraced—that is part of the warrior's experience. In cases of cosmic war, however, the final battle has not been fought. Only when it has can one expect triumph and pride. Until that time, the warrior struggles on, often armed only with hope. Personal tales of woe gain meaning, then, when linked to these powerful stories. Their sagas of oppression and liberation lift the spirits of individuals and make their suffering explicable and noble. In some cases, suffering imparts the nobility of martyrdom, and the images of cosmic war forge failure—even death—into victory.

This notion of a heroic, transforming death is the message projected by the architecture of the shrine that, for a time, accompanied Dr. Baruch Goldstein's grave near Hebron—an elegant plaza surrounded by plaques set inside boxes accompanied by votive candles that looked not unlike the stations of the cross in a Catholic sanctuary. It was clearly a shrine, for someone the young man guarding it described as both a martyr and a "hero in war" (Ron 1995). A similar attitude attended the funeral celebrations for the young Muslim men who gave up their lives in acts of "self-martyrdom," as the Hamas leaders called them. These celebrations were remarkable events recorded on the videotapes of the men when they gave their ardent last statements the night before their deaths. The tapes were then clandestinely circulated throughout Gaza and the West Bank as a sort of recruitment device for likeminded young men. These events were not really funerals, a fact symbolized by the drinking of sweetened rather than bitter coffee, the distribution of sweets, and the singing of wedding songs. A cross between a marriage and a religious festival, these affairs were a modern example of an ancient religious ritual: the sanctification of martyrs (see Oliver and Steinberg 2006).

Similar events have attended the memorials for martyrs in other religious movements. Activist Sikhs have proudly displayed pictures of the fallen leader Sant Jarnail Singh Bhindranwale, who died as a result of the military operation ordered by India's prime minister Indira Gandhi in 1984. His image has been displayed as prominently as those of the founding gurus of the tradition, and he has been remembered on both his birthday and his martyrdom day. Years after the end of the Khalistani uprising, his revolutionary image achieved a kind of Che Guevara iconic status within some quarters of the Sikh community both in the Punjab and abroad.

This attribute of martyrdom has also been conveyed to violent activists within other religious traditions, including Protestant Christianity in the United States. Many right-wing Christians have applauded the vicious acts of killing medical staff involved in performing abortions. When a Presbyterian pastor, Paul Hill, was executed by the state of Florida for killing John Britton and his voluntary escort in front of a Florida clinic that proformed abortions, another right-wing clergyman, the Lutheran pastor Michael Bray, lashed out at the brutality of a government that would take such a noble person's life (Bray 1997: 1). In 2010, when another friend of Bray, Scott Roeder, killed George Tiller in the vestibule of the church where he was worshiping in Wichita, Kansas, Bray declared that he had acted in "righteousness and mercy" in his savage attack on Tiller. In an open letter to Roeder published in his newsletter, Bray went on to praise the assassin as following the commandments of God as he "sought to deliver the innocents from the knife of a baby murderer."

Absent from Bray's sense of outrage was any respect for the lives of Britton and Tiller, which the assassins Hill and Roeder terminated—or "aborted," as Bray put it—in brutal acts of murder. In a curious twist of logic, Bray had imagined the killers to be the victims rather than the murderers that most of the American public regarded them to be. In this way, Bray was like those who mourned the deaths of Baruch Goldstein, Sant Jarnail Singh Bhindranwale, and the Hamas suicide bombers—each of whom sent scores of innocent people to early graves. Billy Wright, who had been convicted for his role in the terrorist acts conducted by the Protestant Ulster Volunteer Force paramilitary group, said that "there's no doubt" that within "every terrorist" there is the conviction that "he is the victim." According to Wright, this allows the terrorist to justify his action "morally within his own mind" (Dillon 1998: 65).

In the scenario of cosmic war—a scenario in which the activists see themselves on the righteous side—the enemies are, by definition, evil. Their deaths mean nothing. The only killing worth being concerned about is the slaughter of the innocents, which by definition are the ones on the righteous side, even if they were the ones who initiated the violence. If they were killed in the process they were martyrs. If they were not, they were heroes, content in the smug satisfaction that they were doing the will of God. The perpetrators of terrorism have thus achieved a kind of celebrity status and their actions an illusion of importance among their supporters. The novelist Don DeLillo goes so far as to say that "only the lethal believer, the person who kills and dies for faith," is taken seriously in modern society (DeLillo 1991: 157). When those who observe these acts take them seriously—either to applaud them or to be disgusted and repelled by them—their roles have been fulfilled.

THE STAGE FOR VIOLENCE

In most instances of religious terrorism in recent years, the place where the assault occurred has had symbolic significance. In some cases, the symbolism of the locale was specific to places that demonstrated the forces of evil as defined by the opponents who attacted them: clinics in the United States where abortions were performed, hotels in Bali occupied by foreigners with loose morals, military bases, boats, and diplomatic embassies in the Middle East, and of course the towers of the World Trade Center in New York City and the Pentagon in Washington, D.C. By revealing the vulnerability of a nation's most stable and powerful entities, movements that have undertaken these acts of sabotage have touched everyone in the nation's society. Any person in the United States could have been riding the elevator in the World Trade Center, for instance, and everyone in the United States will look differently at the stability of public buildings, transportation networks, and communication systems as a result of these violent incidents.

Why is the location of terrorist events—of performance violence—so important? David Rapoport has observed that the control of territory defines public authority, and ethnic-religious groups have historically gained their identity through association with control over particular places (Rapoport 1982). Ronald Hassner has argued that some of the most vicious of inter-religious warfare is over sacred ground (Hassner 2009). One of the most famous of these contested locations is on Temple Mount in Jerusalem, site of the ancient Jewish temple and also the location of the third-most-important shrine in Islam. Another example is the Indian town of Ayodhya, which is the site of an old mosque important to Muslims and a similarly ancient temple that is revered by Hindus. Roger Friedland and Richard Hecht point out that such religious conflicts are often not only about space but about the centrality of religious histories (Friedland and Hecht 1998).

Such central places—even if they exist only in cyberspace—are symbols of power, and acts of terrorism claim them in a symbolic way. They express for a moment the power of terrorist groups to control central locations—by damaging, terrorizing, and assaulting them—even when most of the time they do not control them at all. Days after the destruction of the World Trade Center towers in 2001, most businesses headquartered in the buildings were back to work, operating from backup information systems located elsewhere. In Oklahoma City, soon after the Alfred P. Murrah Federal Building was destroyed the governmental functions that had been conducted there continued unabated. Yet during those brief dramatic moments after a terrorist act levels a building or damages some entity that a society regards as central to its existence, the perpetrators of the act have asserted that they—and not the secular government—have had ultimate control over that entity and its centrality.

The act, however, is sometimes more than symbolic: By demonstrating the vulnerability of governmental power, to some degree it weakens that power, and the prophecy is fulfilled. Because power is largely a matter of perception, symbolic statements can lead to real results. On the whole, however, the small degree to which a government's authority is discredited by a terrorist act does not warrant its massive destructiveness. More significant is the impression—mostly an illusion—that the movements that perpetrate the acts have enormous power and that the ideologies behind them have cosmic importance. In the imagined war between religious and secular authority, the loss of a secular government's ability to control and secure public spaces, even for a terrible moment, is ground gained for religion's side.

DRAMATIC TIMING

Much the same can be said about the dramatic time—the date, season, or hour of day that a terrorist act takes place. There are, after all, centralities in time as well as in space. Anniversaries and birthdays mark such special days for individuals; public holidays demarcate hallowed dates for societies as a whole. To capture the public's attention through an act of performance violence on a date deemed important to the group perpetrating the act, therefore, is to force the group's sense of what is temporally important on everyone else.

On July 22, 2011, when Norwegian Anders Breivik allegedly ignited a truck bomb of explosives in downtown Oslo and took a boat to an island camp where he coldly slaughtered scores of young political activists, he also posted a collection of his writings on the Internet. The manifesto was titled "2083: A European Declaration of Independence." The dates of the attack and the title of his manifesto were significant clues to Breivik's ideology. July 22 was the day in 1099 that the Kingdom of Jerusalem was established during the First Crusade. The year 2083 would be the four hundredth anniversary of the Battle of Vienna, which occurred in the year 1683. On that date, the armies of the Ottoman Empire were defeated in a protracted struggle, thereby insuring that most of Europe would not become part of the Muslim Empire. In Breivik's mind, he was not a terrorist but a soldier who was part of that great struggle that he saw continuing into the present day. Behind Breivik's imagined earthly conflict was a cosmic war, a battle for Christendom. As the title of his manifesto indicates, he thought he was re-creating that historical moment when Christianity was defended against the hordes, and Islam was purged from what he imagined to be the purity of European society.

Breivik's vision of a purified Christendom in Europe was strikingly similar to Timothy McVeigh's notions of saving the United States for Christianity, an idea that was behind his attack on the Oklahoma City federal building in 1995. As in Breivik's case, the dates were significant. When Timothy McVeigh and his colleagues chose the date of their explosion at the Oklahoma City federal building, they were essentially imposing a public holiday—a dramatic public recognition—as a memorial to several events. April 19, 1995, was a special day for McVeigh and other Christian Identity activists for a number of reasons. It was Patriot's Day in New England, the day the American Revolution had begun in 1775; it was the day in 1943 that the Nazis moved on the Warsaw ghetto to destroy the Jewish population on what in that year was the Day of Passover; and it was the day in 1993 when the Branch Davidian compound in Waco, Texas, burned to the ground. It was also the day in 1995 when a Christian Identity activist, Richard Wayne Snell, was due to be executed in prison for murder charges.

In some cases, the days that are held sacred by an activist group are known only to that group or to a certain segment of society. With regard to the April 19 date of the Oklahoma City bombing, it was widely known in Christian Identity circles that this was Snell's execution date. In other instances, public religious holidays have created times of heightened sensitivities and have held the potential for violent reprisals. One of the most notorious incidents in recent Jewish history—Goldstein's massacre of Muslims praying at the shrine of the Tomb of the Patriarchs at Hebron—occurred during a religious holiday. Goldstein chose Purim as the time for his assault, a day that is revered by Jews as the celebration of vengeance against Amalek. The scroll of Esther notes that Haman was a direct descendant of the Amalekite king Agag, and it is likely that Goldstein associated his own killing with the biblical act of sanctifying God's name by avenging the killing of Amalek. In a sense, Goldstein was calling on Jews everywhere to reclaim their tradition, redress the humiliation of Jews, and give an immediate political meaning to the ideas they professed to honor on their sacred days.

In all of these cases, a certain time or timing was critical to the terrorist act. It provided a proscenium for the event. A special aura was imparted to the day or moment in history in which the act occurred. By locating themselves within a transcendent temporal dimension, the perpetrators declared their missions to be of sacred importance as well. Ultimately they were attempting to capture and reshape what society regarded as central in time as well as in space. What was significant about such symbolically central times and places—and for that matter, central things, including subways and airplanes—is that they represented power. They were *centers,* in Clifford Geertz's use of the term: "concentrated loci of serious acts" (Geertz 1983: 121). Such places and times constituted the "arenas" of society "where its leading ideas come together with its leading institutions" and where "momentous events" were thought to occur. When activists attacked such a place, during one of those momentous times, they challenged the power and legitimacy of society.

THE AUDIENCE FOR PERFORMANCE VIOLENCE

As the novelist Don DeLillo once said, terrorism is "the language of being noticed" (DeLillo 1991: 157). If terrorism was not noticed, it would not exist. The sheer act of killing does not create a terrorist act: Murders and willful assaults occur with such frequency in most societies that they are scarcely reported in the news media. What makes an act terrorism is that large numbers of people are terrified by it. The acts to which we assign that label are deliberate events, bombings and attacks performed at such places and times that they are calculated to be observed. Terrorism without its horrified witnesses would be as pointless as a play without an audience.

For many who have been involved in plotting terrorist attacks, the largest audience is the one that witnesses the acts indirectly as media events. It is their way of seizing control of the news media that they think misrepresents the reality of the world as they see it. Mahmud Abouhalima told me that the greatest threat to Islam was media misrepresentation (Abouhalima). He told me that secularism held a virtual lock on media control and that Islam did not have news sources to present its side of contemporary history. By implication, acts of terrorism, such as the one for which he was convicted, laid claim to the images and headlines of the world's media and portrayed his view of the world at war.

In a collection of essays on contemporary culture, Jean Baudrillard described the terrorism of the late twentieth century as "a peculiarly modern form" because of the impact that it has on public consciousness through electronic media. According to Baudrillard, terrorist acts have emerged "less from passion than from the screen: a violence in the nature of the image" (Baudrillard 1993: 75). Baudrillard went so far as to advise his readers "not to be in a public place where television is operating, considering the high probability that its very presence will precipitate a violent event." His advice was hyperbolic, of course, but it points to the reality that terrorist events are aimed at attracting news media exposure and perhaps would not happen as frequently, or in the same way, if the enormous resources of the news media were not readily at hand to promote them.

The worldwide media coverage of Breivik's massacre in Norway, the attacks on the World Trade Center, the London subway and Madrid train bombings, and the explosions in Bali and at the Oklahoma City federal building illustrates a new development in terrorism: the extraordinary widening of terror's audience. Throughout most of history the audiences for acts of terrorism have been limited largely to government officials and their supporters, or members of rival groups. What makes the terrorism of recent years significant is the breadth of its audience, a scope that is in many cases virtually global.

When television does not adequately report the ideas and motivations behind the actions of many activist groups, they have found the Internet and the World Wide Web to be effective alternatives. Others use social networks such as Facebook and cell phone texting and Twitter. Movements such as Hamas and Aryan Nations have well-established websites. An antiabortion site, "The Nuremberg Files," which advocated the killing of abortion clinic doctors and maintained a list of potential targets, was removed by its Internet service provider in February 1999 after a red line was drawn through the name of Barnett Slepian on the day after he was killed by an assassin. But sites like it returned, many of them including George Tiller as a target; Tiller was killed in Wichita, Kansas, in 2010. Other groups, including many Muslim jihadi groups and Christian militia activists, have protected their sites with passwords that allow only their members to gain access. Thus, even when the audience is selective, the message has been projected through a public medium.

In some cases, an act of violence sends two messages at the same time: a broad message aimed at the general public and a specific communication targeted at a narrower audience. In cases of Islamic violence in Palestine and Sikh terrorism in India, for instance, one of the purposes of the assaults was to prove to movement members that the leadership was still strong enough to engender the life-and-death dedication of their commandos. In other cases, the point was to intimidate followers of the movement and to force them to follow a hardline position rather than a conciliatory one.

Motives such as these help to explain one of the most puzzling forms of contemporary violence: silent terror. These intriguing acts of terrorism are ones in which the audience is not immediately apparent. The public is often mystified by an explosion accompanied only by an eerie silence, with no group claiming responsibility or explaining the purpose of its act. As days passed after bombs ripped through the American embassies in Kenya and Tanzania on August 7, 1998, and no person or group took credit for the actions, questions arose as to why no group had owned up to the attacks in order to publicize its cause. Similarly, no one, including members of Osama bin Ladin's al Qaeda network, claimed responsibility for the spectacular assault on September 11, 2001. If one assumes that the attack was conducted, in part, to advertise the group's cause, why would members of the group not take credit for it?

In a world in which information is a form of power, public demonstrations of violence are the messages, and they are potent messages. When groups are able to demonstrate their capacity for destruction simultaneously in different parts of the world, as in the case of the US embassy bombings in 1998, this is an even more impressive display than single-target events. It is no less so if the only audiences who know who did it, who can appreciate the perpetrators' accomplishment and who can admire their command over life and death, are within the group. The act demonstrates their ability to perform a powerful event with virtually global impact.

The forms of religious terrorism that have emerged at the beginning of the twenty-first century have been global in at least two senses. Both the choices of their targets and the character of their conspiratorial networks have often been transnational. The very name of the World Trade Center indicated its role in transnational global commerce. The attack on the building complex in such a spectacular fashion was terrorism meant not just for television but for CNN, a global English-speaking audience, and for al Jezeera, the global network based in Qatar whose Arabic channel broadcasts throughout the Middle East.

Increasingly, terrorism has been performed for a television audience around the world. In that sense, it has been as real a global event as the transnational events of the global economy. Ironically, terrorism has become a more potent global political force than the organized political efforts to control and contain it. The United Nations lacks the military capability and intelligence-gathering capacity to deal with worldwide terrorism. Instead, consortia of nations have been forced to come together to handle the information sharing and joint operations required to deal with forces of violence on an international scale.

This global dimension of terrorism's organization and audience and the transnational responses to it gives special significance to the understanding of terrorism as a public performance of violence—as a social event with both real and symbolic aspects. As Bourdieu has observed, our public life is shaped as much by symbols as by institutions. For this reason, symbolic acts—the "rites of institution"—help to demarcate public space and indicate what is meaningful in the social world (Bourdieu 1991: 117). In a striking imitation of such rites, terrorism has provided its own dramatic events. These rites of violence have brought an alternative view of public reality—not just of a single society in transition but a world challenged by strident religious visions of transforming change.

NOTE

1. Parts of this chapter are based on sections of my book, *Terror in the Mind of God.*

BIBLIOGRAPHY

Abouhalima, Mahmud. Interview with the author. Federal Penitentiary, Lompoc, California, September 30, 1997.

Austin, J. L. *How to Do Things with Words.* Oxford, UK: Clarendon Press, 1962.

Baudrillard, Jean. *The Transparency of Evil: Essays on the Extreme Phenomena.* Translated by James Benedict. London: Verso, 1993.

Bin Laden, Osama. "Fatweh." Translated by James Howarth in Bruce Lawrence, ed., *Messages to the World: The Statements of Osama bin Laden.* London: Verso Publications, 2005.

Bourdieu, Pierre. *Language and Symbolic Power.* Translated by Gino Raymond and Matthew Adamson. Cambridge, MA: Harvard University Press, 1991.

Bray, Michael. *A Time to Kill: A Study Concerning the Use of Force and Abortion.* Portland, OR: Advocates for Life, 1994.

Bray, Michael. "The Impending Execution of Paul Hill," *Capitol Area Christian News* 25, 1997.

DeLillo, Don. *Mao II.* New York: Penguin Books, 1991.

Dillon, Martin. *God and the Gun: The Church and Irish Terrorism.* London: Routledge, 1998.

Friedland, Roger and Richard Hecht. "The Bodies of Nations: A Comparative Study of the Violence at Ayodhya and Jerusalem." *History of Religions* 38.2 (Nov. 1998) 101–149.

Geertz, Clifford. *Local Knowledge: Further Essays in Interpretive Anthropology.* New York: Basic Books, 1983.

Hassner, Ron. *War on Sacred Grounds.* Ithaca, NY: Cornell University Press, 2009.

Juergensmeyer, Mark. *Terror in the Mind of God: The Global Rise of Religious Violence.* Berkeley: University of California Press, revised edition, 2003.

Lincoln, Bruce. *Holy Terrors: Thinking about Religion after September 11.* Chicago: University of Chicago Press, 2006.

Noble, Kerry. *Tabernacle of Hate: Why They Bombed Oklahoma City.* Prescott, Ontario: Voyageur Press, 1998.

Oliver, Anne Marie and Paul Steinberg. *The Road to Martyrs Square: A Journey into the World of the Suicide Bomber.* New York: Oxford University Press, 2006.

Rantisi, Abdul Aziz. Interview with the author. Khan Yunis, Gaza, March 2, 1998.

Rapoport, David and Yonah Alexander, eds. *The Morality of Terrorism: Religious and Secular Justifications.* New York: Pergamon Press, 1982.

Ron, Yochay. Interview with the author. Kiryat Arba settlement, Hebron, Palestinian territories, August 18, 1995.

CHAPTER 18

CHRISTIANITY AND TORTURE

KAREN L. KING

LINKING torture with religion frequently invokes contrary positions, either that properly religious people passionately and compassionately oppose torture or, alternatively, that religions, being violent (or at least intolerant) by nature, unsurprisingly offer religiously based support for torture. Such generalizations, however, are insufficient to illuminate the extraordinarily wide range of religious persons' behaviors or the diverse operations of religious ideology in regard to practices of torture.

For the purposes of this chapter, torture is defined following the United Nations Convention against Torture and Other Cruel, Inhuman, or Degrading Treatment and Punishment:

> Any act by which severe pain or suffering, whether physical or mental, is intentionally inflicted on a person for such purposes as obtaining from him or a third person, information or a confession, punishing him for an act he or a third person has committed or is suspected of having committed, or intimidating or coercing him or a third person, or for any reason based on discrimination of any kind, when such pain or suffering is inflicted by or at the instigation of or with the consent or acquiescence of a public official or other person acting in an official capacity. It does not include pain or suffering arising only from, inherent in or incidental to lawful sanctions. (1984: Article 1.1; see also Peters 1999: 141–148)

I am not engaging here in more recent debate over what constitutes torture (e.g., vs. "harsh" or "enhanced interrogation tactics"), not because such distinctions are irrelevant to how people are actually treated but insofar as such debates can be distractions from or serve as justifications for practices of torture (Physicians for Human Rights 2004; for additional problems in defining torture, especially its vague and sentimental uses, see Peters 1999: 148–155).

Torture focuses attention directly and immediately on human bodies in pain, and it poignantly points to questions of justice, power, and politics in ways that illness, natural disaster, or even crime and sadism do not, presented as the latter often are as the acts of nonhuman forces or attributed to base or mentally unstable individuals rather than public social institutions or ideologies. While all religious traditions address the realities of human suffering, they do so in widely varying manners. In order to probe such diversity more deeply, this chapter will focus on the case of Christianity.

Like other religious traditions, Christianity offers not a single, exclusive position on suffering and torture but a repertoire of stories, images, ideas and ideologies, exempla, strategies, and discourses that believers use to think with and that contribute to shaping their actions, attitudes, and feelings. Although rationalized arguments have been offered both for and against torture, behind the culture of terror and practices of torture "lie intricately construed long-standing cultural logics of meaning—structures of feeling—whose basis lies in a symbolic world and not in one of rationalism" (Taussig 1984: 471). Christianity in the modern West is deeply enmeshed in such tenacious "logics," which continue to form and inform a wide array of ideological positions and emotive attitudes in the most recent discussions of torture. This essay, however, will not ask, What is the (proper) Christian attitude toward torture? or even, How do Christians variously think and feel about torture? but rather, How are Christian theological perspectives and symbolic systems implicated in attitudes toward torture, and what difference does that make?

Christian tradition is no stranger to torture. A central image of Christian theological imagination and epic is the tortured body of Jesus, hanging in excruciating torment on a Roman cross outside Jerusalem. Not one, but four narratives of Jesus's suffering were included in the New Testament canon of Christianity, with countless citations over two millennia in sermons, literature, passion plays, and visual media, ancient and modern—as with the now iconic figure of a hooded man on a box, his arms outstretched, tortured and photographed at Abu Ghraib by US military personnel (Mirzoeff 2006). In the early centuries, Christians drew heavily on the figure of the crucified Christ to respond to the torture and execution of believers. It is not too much to say that torture from a Christian perspective is always ineluctably tied to rhetorical discourses of martyrdom formed under conditions of imperial Roman rule.

In accounting theologically not only for the torture of Jesus but also for that of his followers in the early centuries, Christians devised a wide range of stories and attitudes about what constitutes martyrdom; who a true martyr is; what kind of God allows, desires, or abhors this violence; and how believers should respond. The term *martyr* derives from Greek in which it literally means "witness," and for many early Christians that meant testifying in Roman law courts and arenas to the truth of Christian faith and practice. Their suffering was ascribed spiritual value as martyrs were said to take part in Christ's saving mission. Some early Christian stories portrayed martyrs in mystical communion with God, their brutalized and degraded bodies integrated into the glorious, immortal body of Christ, the true church. Martyrdom could also be portrayed as a test of one's loyalty to God or as a trial that would strengthen faith as well as prove it through adversity. Some emphasized that torture was a just punishment that purified believers and healed the spiritual wounds of their sin. They argued that suffering served as instruction in humility and gratitude before God by teaching believers to weigh the superior value of spiritual rewards over earthly things and to cast off the veil of the world to expose the presence of God. Perkins has argued that Christians promoted themselves as a community of sufferers and, in the process, redefined what it meant to be human and how to establish one's most intimate relationship to God through pain (Perkins 1995: 104–123). Scars and disfigurement marked survivors as "like Christ," signifying their purity, piety, and righteousness. In situations in which the overwhelming majority of Christians had apostatized, fled, or bought their way out, many churches conferred authority on confessors superior to that of priests and bishops. Throughout the persecutions, many Christians affirmed the power and justice of God, believing that it was God who grants all sovereignty to worldly rulers, even when they act unjustly and work on the side of demonic forces; in the end God would punish the unjust with eternal torture. All this, it was said, showed God as the only true ruler and just judge, a beneficent teacher and physician even in torture.

Others, however, rejected the notion that God desired the torture and brutal execution of his Son and believers. It is only false demigods and demons who satisfy their sadistic pleasure and lust for domination through sacrifice, torture, and murder, they argued. Jesus came to free humanity *from* suffering and death. He sent his disciples out to teach and heal, and it is through these activities that Christians properly take an active role in God's creative power to transform the world. Christian suffering and death at the hands of unjust powers is a consequence of speaking the truth in a world dominated by evil forces (King 2010). Based on an interpretation of Jesus's prayer for his torturers: "Forgive them for they know not what they do" (Luke 23:34), some humanized their oppressors (see, e.g., Kolbet 2008), and a few even suggested that the death of Jesus and his followers was a kind of accident, a mistake people ignorant of the truth make when misled by demons (James 29–30 in Kasser et al. 2007: 158–161). These Christians advocated a variety of postures, from fearless preaching of the gospel message to quietism, nonviolence, or passivism. Although those views which could ascribe no violence to God were largely marginalized or condemned and the dominant Christian perspective came to represent the torture of believers as God's will, nonetheless in the end, Christian tradition came to encompass a complex variety of theologically informed attitudes and positions.

Martyr ideologies did not lose their currency after the persecutions ended, but their deployments shifted as martyr stories proliferated, shrines were built, annual liturgies marked the "birth" of the martyrs into eternal life, and warring theological factions sought to claim martyrs for their side (Grig 2004). Violence became institutionalized at the core of Christian creed, canon, and artistic and ritual practice (especially Eucharist), all of which afforded a central place to the tortured body of the Christ.

Crucially, no biblical text explicitly condemns torture. To the contrary, early Christian visions of the end times, such as the book of Revelation, include graphic descriptions of God judging sinners and inflicting torments like those the Romans had used on them—only now escalated to cosmic proportions and lasting eternally. Later literature depicts Christians rejoicing, even gloating, over the suffering of their enemies (Stratton 2010). Such scenarios did not, however, remain merely imaginary or futuristic but were enacted sporadically in later centuries by Christians who practiced torture against criminals, heretics, blacks, Jews or other non-Christians, justifying it as just punishment for sin, rejecting God, or as a tool to provoke repentance for the salvation of souls (Gaddis 2005; Mathews 2008). Retribution, too, was a stated motive, most clearly in cases where the long-lived calumny that "the Jews killed Jesus"—initially invented largely to deflect blame from the powerful Romans whose governor executed the Jew Jesus—came to justify Christian hatred, persecutions, and pogroms against Jews.

Yet at the same time, the potent image of the suffering Jesus could be invoked as a strong deterrent against using torture and violence with impunity against the weak and the innocent. As Gushee insists, "for Christians a proper understanding of our ultimate loyalty—to Jesus the tortured one—makes any support of torture unthinkable" (2008: 91). Cavanaugh has argued that the solidarity of a Catholic Christian community centered around the Eucharist can offer a real social alternative to that of authoritarian regimes who use torture in the name of the public good. "Creat(ing) spaces to live inside God's imagination" makes justice and truth—and action—possible in a world where torture occurs. It also lends spiritual value to torture that restores honor and dignity to those who suffer the humiliations and evacuations torturers seek (2008: esp. 112). Cone, too, emphasizes that African American Christian communities, suffering lynching and other atrocities under the racism of white supremacy in the United States, "found in the cross the spiritual power to resist what was happening to them. Just as Jesus did not deserve his suffering, black suffering, too, was unjust. Their faith opened their eyes to the truth about their humanity and gave them strength and courage to fight against their humiliation…. The cross is God's critique of power—white power or any power of evil" (Cone 2011). The final word about the torture of black bodies is not death on a lynching tree but redemption in the cross—a miraculously transformed life found in the God of the gallows. It has the redemptive potential for white lynchers as well, Cone argues, but "not without profound cost, not without the revelation of the wrath and justice of God, which executes divine judgement, with the demand for repentance and reparation, as a presupposition of divine mercy and forgiveness" (Cone 2007: 53). Importantly, such a perspective requires not the torture of evildoers but their public admission of guilt, moral reformation, and action to rectify wrongs done.

What links these seemingly contradictory positions—Christian condemnation of torture and God's use of torture to punish—is the portrayal of Christians as the agents of God. On the one hand, martyrdom literature portrayed Christian subjectivity as surrender of the believers' will to that of God, transforming them into instrumental agents of God. Martyrs were represented as tools through whom God worked for the salvation of humanity. As victors who would reign with God in the eternal world to come, they would serve as witnesses and judges with Christ against those who tortured them and their fellow believers, sentencing them to eternal punishment and death. In a context in which overwhelming imperial force was brought to bear against any defiance,[1] this strategy of resistance transformed victimhood into power.

On the other hand, after the persecutions ended, the logic of instrumental agency enabled those who understood themselves as God's agents to enact that role from new positionalities in earthly administrative orders (such as bishops, judges, or kings). From this position, they could oppose the abuse of the innocent, but by representing torture as a tool God rightly uses to punish the wicked, it becomes discursively possible, perhaps even necessary, in situations in which Christians are in charge of "administering justice," to legitimize those who punish the wicked by representing them as God's agents. Like martyrs, they were to follow not their own desires but God's will. In this way, the judiciary logic of divine justice could be used both to oppose torture (of the innocent) and to legitimize torture (of the guilty).

In contrast to divine perdition, however, human use of judicial torture was rarely understood as punishment per se. Christians followed more closely the judicial practices of Greeks and Romans, who widely used physical coercion ostensibly to establish the facts or elicit confessions of guilt and who claimed that only torture would produce incontrovertible truth (duBois 1991; de Ste Croix 2006: 127–128). In practice, however, the ancients occasionally did recognize that torture would not produce reliable testimony (or reliable conversions) since people would say anything to stop the pain. As Langbein puts it, "History's most important lesson is that it has not been possible to make coercion compatible with truth" (2004: 101).

But if torture is not reliable, why do it? Scarry has argued that tortured bodies are "only brought forward when there is a crisis of substantiation" (Scarry 1985: 127). Torture operates in the absence of the facts or against the facts. Public torture and execution were used not merely to display power and justice but to create it; torture is one means to produce the reality of the state (Cavanaugh 1998; 2006). How does this work? As Scarry notes, weapons "can refer equally to pain or power"; the "incontestable reality" of physical bodies in pain can be lifted away from human beings, "attached instead to the regime," and used to substantiate that which "at that moment has no independent reality of its own" (Scarry 1985: 56, 125). This seems patently the case with ancient Christians: They were not tortured to get them to confess their crimes—they had already done that by declaring themselves Christian. The Romans' purpose was something else—to use bodily harm to convert power into truth.

Rather than resolve such situations, however, the indeterminacy and contingency that torture produces constantly threaten attempts to secure "truth" (and its concomitant conferral of legitimacy) incontrovertibly for one's side. This crisis exposes the power dynamics of torture: Who gets to say what truth—or, better, whose truth—these tortured bodies tell? Do the photos from Abu Ghraib show the just humiliation of cowardly terrorists, eliciting information to save lives; do they show Americans acting as barbaric torturers of helpless men and women; or do they attest to some other "truth" of power? When the answer is contested, social imaginaries, sacred stories, and symbolic frameworks of feeling and interpretation are brought into play in attempts to make meaning clear—with real effects.

Christians learned this lesson in contested representation early. The Romans, feeling secure in their overwhelming power, set the stage and scripted the contest in public law courts and arenas to demonstrate to their subjects the power of Roman justice to keep the civilized world safe by executing allegedly criminal, cowardly, and impious fanatics and barbarians—the torture and execution of Jesus and, subsequently, his followers being only the most infamous examples. How were Christians to testify to the power of their God in such a setting? Christians fully exploited the Roman rhetoric that pain produces truth. They sought to declare that the real truth displayed by their bodies under extreme and sustained pain was the piety of their beliefs and the reality of their God. When Christians told their stories, they represented Jesus and themselves neither as passive victims nor as suicidal heroes but as agents assenting freely to God's will. As such, they physically embodied the presence of God, indomitable, righteous, and just and proved that God's power vastly transcends not only pain but even death. Their bodies made God visible and real, a notion most strongly conveyed in Christian incarnation theology but also supplied in the representation of martyrs such as the female slave Blandina, whose entire body—broken, torn, scorched, and hanging on a post waiting for wild beasts to devour her—was seen by her contemporaries as the physical embodiment of Christ (Musurillo 1972: 75). In Scarry's terms, Christians were claiming that the regime to which their torture referred was the Kingdom of God, not the Roman Empire and its (false) deities. Through such discursively strategic narratives, they not only claimed moral righteousness, dignity, and honor while contesting Roman legitimacy and power, but in the end the empire eventually became officially Christian. In this way, Roman practices of judicial torture and public execution provided Christians not only with the provocations but also the opportunities and the tools for forging alternative narratives of resistance and survival. Christians rescripted the dramas of law court and arena as skirmishes between the cosmic forces of good and evil, God and Satan, in a battle they were providently destined to win (cp. Juergensmeyer 2003).

This representational triumph of the abject did not, however, lead ineluctably to the abolition of torture under later Christian regimes. When Constantine converted, the legal practice of judicial torture continued and, although it receded for a time, was revived in the thirteenth century. From then until the end of the eighteenth century, the ordinary criminal procedure of the Latin church and most European states allowed torture, most notoriously associated in Christianity with the Inquisition (Peters 1999 9–73). It was not widely challenged until, in a brief period of about fifty years, from 1750 to 1800, legislative revisions effectively ended judicial torture, condemning it on both legal and moral grounds (Peters 1999: 74–102). Recent scholars have suggested that, although usually credited as the consequence of Enlightenment sensibilities of humanitarianism, civilization, and reason, it was the development of alternative methods of establishing the facts in judicial proceedings (Langbein 1977) or other styles of social (bodily) disciplining (Foucault 1995) that made torture unnecessary—thus allowing a discursive rhetoric of human dignity and rights to flourish. These legal and discursive changes did not, however, end or even necessarily diminish torture but merely moved practices offstage where they became less subject to judicial limits and the surveillance of public opinion (Dershowitz 2004). While notorious public occasions continued, notably torture-lynching in the United States (Brundage 1997; Dray 2002; Apel 2004; Garland 2005), more commonly such practices moved to less public ("secret"), extrajudicial settings and became covert or disavowed, as in police or military "interrogations" (Peters 1985: 103–140). The examples are unfortunately many in which Christian moral teachings or institutions have offered implicit or active support to regimes that torture. In Argentina's "dirty war," for example, military chaplains not only were present during torture to urge confession and collaboration but comforted the torturers by reciting biblical parables (Osiel 2004: esp. 132–134). Scholars have pointed as well to cases in the twentieth century, such as Algeria (Lazreg 2008), Chile (Cavanaugh 1998), and Germany (Heschel 2008).

As these and other examples show, despite legal censure, torture and claims of torture are ubiquitous. Amnesty International recorded that, in 2009, "human rights abusers enjoyed impunity for torture in at least 61 countries" and that people were "tortured or otherwise ill-treated in at least 111 countries" (Amnesty International 2010). As public awareness of the military and colonial horrors rose, so did public protest. In 1984, the United Nations had promulgated a "Convention on Torture and Other Cruel, Inhuman, or Degrading Treatment and Punishment" (signed by 146 countries), which prohibits torture under any circumstance and aimed at ending such practices, but it has had only limited successes. In his massive study *Torture and Democracy*, Rejali argued that the increase in human rights monitoring has led governments and other agents of torture to develop "stealth" torture (practices that optimize pain without leaving evidence marked on the bodies of victims), secret prisons, and "outsourcing" to foreign soil, on the one hand, and on the other, to formulate ethical justifications, rationalizations, or offer outright denials (Rejali 2007).

How are we to understand this interplay of visibility and invisibility, affirmation and denial? If torture is about the display of pain to objectify claims to power, justice, and truth, is its effectiveness not undermined when covert? Not necessarily. Stealth torture and denials, as well as partial exposures and public justifications, all work to keep the facts unclear. This interplay of secrecy and palpability, Cavanaugh argues, serves the state: "The drama of torture must never be played out on a fully public stage. At the same time, the widespread imagination of torture is important for fostering both the dire sense of emergency and exception in which we live and the sense that the state will do whatever is necessary to protect us from the threat it helped create" (Cavanaugh 2008: 109–110; see also Taussig 1984). Mirzoeff argues that regimes of contemporary visual culture can operate analogously as state apparatuses attempt to discipline how and what people are allowed to see, while simultaneously instilling the belief that much is happening that is not being shown (2006). By building a contrast between themselves and tortured others, photos and narratives that cultivate the visualization of torture reaffirm the integrity and unity of the social body and allow viewers to feel themselves safe and "not torturable." All this points not to fundamentally new or different ends and effects but to shifts in strategies, discourses, and technologies.

Where, if anywhere, does the legacy of Christian ideology come into play? Do Christian theological-cultural "logics" play a role in such secular practices and discourses? If so, what and where are they operating? One site to explore these questions is afforded by the so-called ticking bomb scenario, a contemporary utilitarian argument for the limited use of torture in which a terrorist or some other criminal is tortured to gain information necessary to save innocent lives (Luban 2005; for earlier forms of this kind of argument, see Peters 1999: 176–187). Just as Christians could position themselves as agents of God, either as advocates on the side of righteous victims or as just agents using torture to elicit facts and save lives, so, too, this scenario works analogously by dichotomizing the actors as good or evil, innocent or guilty and by justifying torture only on the side of those who are just and who torture for the right motives. Its reasoning requires that the victim be represented as complicit in terrorist acts and the torturer as acting solely to save lives.

In Christian imagination, since God is the only one who is fully just and acts from entirely pure motives, he is scripted to play both roles: the crucified God-Christ who suffers torture for humanity's sake and the just ruler who condemns the unrighteous to eternal torture. God alone can judge; God alone is the righteous tortured one. Since no human being stands without guilt before God, only those who have surrendered their wills and being to God can legitimately stand as God's agents, notably martyrs whose deaths demonstrate their total commitment. Analogously in the ticking bomb scenario, those who order or perform torture may not do so for personal benefit, desire for revenge, or sadistic pleasure but only as a duty to a greater entity, such as God, nation, home, or history. "Make no mistake," writes Dorfman, "every regime that tortures does so in the name of salvation, some superior goal, some promise of paradise. So we must face this truth: torturers do not generally think of themselves as evil but rather as guardians of the common good, dedicated patriots who get their hands dirty and endure perhaps some sleepless nights in order to deliver the blind ignorant majority from violence and anxiety" (2004:16). Utilitarian ethicists often acknowledge explicitly that those who torture—even good men and women acting in the line of duty—have overstepped moral boundaries and cannot be held entirely innocent. Their "hands are dirty." The biblical Gospel of John offers a complex use of utilitarian argument in teaching that God's purpose is for one individual (Jesus) to be sacrificed to save not only the nation (as Jesus's opponents argue) but to save the whole world (John 11:47–53). It condemns those who kill Jesus but ultimately portrays their action as God's will.

A variety of strategies attempt to resolve or deny the paradoxes and ambiguities of this situation. Insofar as torturers (or leaders such as government or military officials who order or allow torture) are seen to be acting legitimately in the interests or as agents of God or the state, their image is revisioned, as when Walzer calls them "suffering servants" (a well-known title for the crucified Jesus). Their guilt is "expiated only if they are punished" (Walzer 1973: esp. 178–179). The call for their punishment comes, however, not only from the "despotic regimes" they are (rightly) fighting, but it may also come from those in whose name they are acting, for example, citizens who require a scapegoat for their collective expiation.

Another example that resonates with Christian martyr stories is the strategy of scripting role reversals. Early Christians had scripted martyrs as innocent victims, not criminals deserving of punishment as the Romans claimed, but now the group that tortures is represented as the innocent victims of persecution. Oddly this latter position results in an ironic kind of competition between the torturer and the tortured for the role of victim, since whoever wins this title claims the moral high ground. To profess victimhood, however, can produce significant repercussions by stoking fears of helplessness and anger, which may arouse a need to refuse the role of the victim, largely through engaging in active defense and offense. In this way, to claim the victim position for one's own group can operatively serve to justify the torture of others.

Dichotomizing strategies, such as one sees when Christians represent the situation of torture as a battle between God and Satan, are prevalent as well in demonizing and dehumanizing "the enemy," by making "torturable" those who are so identified, not least through hypermasculinized sexual and representational strategies. The violence of torture relies on sex/ gender differentiation for much of its public communication. In systems in which domination is coded masculine and submission feminine, defeat and humiliation implicitly require remasculinization, often through displays of hypermasculinity. Sexual humiliation and violence (though mutilation, the rape of men and women, or shaming them through naked exposure or forced homoerotic poses) deploy the ideological rhetoric of (heterosexual) male superiority to (re)inscribe relations of domination; victims are emasculated while torturers are represented as hypermasculine (e.g., Mathews 2008). Just so, the Romans had performed a hypermasculinity characterized by honor, dispassionate reason, and extreme violence through public "entertainments" that included torture and execution.

Arguably, ancient Christian discourse interrupted the Roman performances, in part, by recrafting masculinity. By elevating endurance from a largely female to a masculine virtue and by repositioning self-control, rather than control of others, as the primary moral virtue, their own suffering and refusal to surrender rhetorically affirmed their masculinity—and even women martyrs were declared to have become "male." In these ways, the martyr texts point both to the malleability of sex/gender difference and to the multiplicity of possible deployments of gender discourses (Barton 1994; Shaw 1996; Castelli 2004: 134–171). The virtues of endurance and self-control, however, operate against displays of hypermasculinity that are overtly violent; they do not lend themselves to support attacks on enemies but point to Jesus's injunction not to resist evildoers but to love one's enemies (Matthew 6:39, 44). This strategy does not seem to have wide modern application in public discussions, even by those who oppose torture on Christian theological grounds.

Two thousand years of history show that Christian narratives and images can be appropriated in complex ways for various, even opposing, ends and evoke many and contradictory logics and feelings either to support or to oppose torture. Narratives that were developed to resist Roman torture of Christians display strategies that in shifting contexts have served other ends. The logic of instrumental agency provides the possibility of one potentially powerful strategy of resistance to injustice but it can also give theological support to justify claims to torture or kill others as a "good." Christian theology has emphasized human fallibility but also empowered the desire for justice and revenge. The story of Jesus's death places the violence of torture at the center of Christian imagination and practice; with it comes the potential to assert the full humanity of those who are tortured, as well as to form communities of solidarity and resistance.

Some might wonder why I, as a Christian who opposes torture, go to such lengths to expose the possibilities within Christian tradition for supporting torture, if not to cast aspersion on religion generally and Christianity in particular. One reason is that claims that Christian tradition is absolutely or essentially against torture are historically inaccurate and therefore not persuasive. Opposition to torture on religious grounds will not be effective without acknowledging and addressing the fact that enculturated ways of thinking and structures of feeling cultivated in Christian stories, images, and theological discourses are implicated in a wide variety of attitudes and behaviors, both for and against torture. At the same time, exposing something of the genealogy and operations of powerful discourses and the emotions they evoke may open spaces for secularists as well as believers to disrupt their power to operate surreptitiously. How do religious communities, human rights advocates, or other voices effectively engage this tradition without enabling its potential for violence? This is a dilemma not only for believers but for all whose heritage includes these and similar cultural "logics" of feeling and thought.

NOTES

I wish to acknowledge here with gratitude my debt to the members of the Seminar on Christianity and Torture that convened at Harvard University's Radcliffe Institute, June 6 through 9, 2010: Elizabeth Castelli, James Cone, Rosalind Hackett, Susannah

Heschel, Katie Ford, Stephen Moore, Erin Runions, and especially to Sarah Sentilles, the co-convener, who also offered substantive criticism to this chapter. Their responses to an earlier version of this chapter, as well as their own contributions to the discussion, have been invaluable to me. All the remaining deficiencies are my own. My special thanks to the Radcliffe Institute for Advanced Study for their support through an Exploratory Seminar grant.

1. Pliny, the governor of Asia under the Roman emperor Trajan, for example, used torture to elicit testimony from Christian slaves, but upon finding no crime, he still advocated punishing the Christians with death because of their obstinacy in refusing to recant (Letter 96 in Radice 1969: 284–291).

Bibliography

Amnesty International. "Amnesty International 2010: The State of the World's Human Rights." http://thereport.amnesty.org/facts-and-figures (accessed August 18, 2010).

Apel, Dora. *Imagery of Lynching: Black Men, White Women, and the Mob.* New Brunswick, NJ, and London: Rutgers University Press, 2004.

Barton, Carlin. "Savage Miracles: The Redemption of Lost Honor in Roman Society and the Sacrament of the Gladiator and the Martyr." *Representations* 45 (1994): 41–71.

Brundage, W. Fitzhugh ed. *Under Sentence of Death: Lynching in the South.* Chapel Hill: University of North Carolina Press, 1997.

Bush, George W. Press Conference, October 18, 2007, accessed at www.whitehouse.gov/news/releases/20071017.html.

Castelli, Elizabeth A. *Martyrdom and Memory: Early Christian Culture Making.* New York: Columbia University Press, 2004.

Cavanaugh, William T. *Torture and Eucharist: Theology, Politics, and the Body of Christ.* Oxford, UK: Blackwell Publishing, 1988.

Cavanaugh, William T. "Making Enemies. The Imagination of Torture in Chile and the United States." *Theology Today* 63 (2006): 307–323.

Cavanaugh, William T. "Torture and Eucharist: A Regretful Update." In *Torture Is a Moral Issue: Christians, Jews, Muslims, and People of Conscience Speak Out.* Ed. George Hunsinger, 92–112. Cambridge, UK: Eerdmans.

Cone, James H. "Strange Fruit." *Harvard Divinity Bulletin* (2007): 47–55.

Cone, James H. *The Cross and the Lynching Tree.* Maryknoll, NY: Orbis Books, 2011.

de Ste. Croix, G. E. M. *Christian Persecution, Martyrdom, and Orthodoxy.* Oxford, UK: Oxford University Press, 2006.

Dershowitz, Alan. "Tortured Reasoning." In *Torture: A Collection.* Ed. Sanford Levinson, 257–280. Oxford, UK: Oxford University Press, 2004.

Dorfman, Ariel. "The Tyranny of Terror: Is Torture Inevitable in Our Century and Beyond?" In *Torture: A Collection.* Ed. Sanford Levinson, 3–18. Oxford, UK: Oxford University Press, 2004.

Dray, Philip. *At the Hands of Persons Unknown: The Lynching of Black America.* New York: Modern Library, 2002.

duBois, Page. *Torture and Truth.* New York and London: Routledge, 1991.

Foucault, Michel. *Discipline and Punish: The Birth of the Prison.* Trans. Alan Sheridan. New York: Vintage Books, 1995.

Gaddis, Michael. *There Is No Crime for Those Who Have Christ: Religious Violence in the Christian Roman Empire.* Berkeley: University of California Press, 2005.

Garland, David. "Penal Excess and Surplus Meaning: Public Torture Lynchings in Twentieth-Century America." *Law and Society Review* 39.4 (2005): 793–833.

Grig, Lucy. *Making Martyrs in Late Antiquity.* London: Duckworth, 2004.

Gushee, David P. "Six Reasons Why Torture Is Always Wrong." In *Torture Is a Moral Issue: Christians, Jews, Muslims, and People of Conscience Speak Out.* Ed. George Hunsinger, 73–91. Grand Rapids, MI: Eerdmans, 2008.

Heschel, Susannah. *The Aryan Jesus: Christian Theologians and the Bible in Nazi Germany.* Princeton, NJ: Princeton University Press, 2008.

Juergensmeyer, Mark. *Terror in the Mind of God: The Global Rise of Religious Violence.* Berkeley: University of California Press, 2003.

Kasser, Rudolphe, Gregor Wurst, Marvin Meyer, and François Gaudard, eds. *The Gospel of Judas Together with the Letter of Peter to Philip, James, and Book of Allogenes from Codex Tchacos.* Washington, DC: National Geographic, 2007.

King, Karen L. "Toward a Discussion of the Category 'Gnosis/Gnosticism': The Case of the *Epistle of Peter to Philip*." In *Jesus in apokryphen Evangelienüberlieferungen. Beiträge zu außerkanonischen Jesusüberlieferungen aus verschiedenen Sprach- und Kulturtraditionen.* Eds. Jörg Frey and Jens Schröder, 445–465. Wissenschaftliche Untersuchungen zum Neuen Testament. Tübingen, Germany: Mohr Siebeck, 2010.

Kolbet, Paul R. "Torture and Origen's Hermeneutics of Nonviolence." *Journal of the American Academy of Religion* 76.3 (2008): 545–572.

Langbein, John H. *Torture and the Law of Proof: Europe and England in the Ancient Régime.* Chicago: University of Chicago Press, 2006.

Langbein, John H. "The Legal History of Torture." In *Torture: A Collection.* Ed. Sanford Levinson, 93–103. Oxford, UK: Oxford University Press, 2004.

Lazreg, Marnia. *Torture and the Twilight of Empire. From Algiers to Baghdad.* Princeton, NJ: Princeton University Press, 2008.

Luban, David. "Liberalism, Torture, and the Ticking Bomb." *Virginia Law Review* 91.6 (2005): 1425–1461.

Mathews, Donald G. "The Southern Rite of Human Sacrifice: Lynching in the American South." *Mississippi Quarterly* 62 (2008): 27–70.

Mirzoeff, Nicholas. "Invisible Empire: Visual Culture, Embodied Spectacle, and Abu Ghraib." *Radical History Review* 95 (2006): 21–44.

Musurillo, Herbert. *The Acts of the Christian Martyrs: Introduction, Texts and Translations.* Oxford, UK: Clarendon Press, 1972.

Osiel, Mark. "The Mental State of Torturers: Argentina's Dirty War." In *Torture: A Collection.* Ed. Sanford Levinson, 129–141. Oxford, UK: Oxford University Press, 2004.

Perkins, Judith. *The Suffering Self: Pain and Narrative Representation in the Early Christian Era.* New York and London: Routledge, 1995.

Peters, Edward. *Torture.* Expanded edn. Philadelphia: University of Pennsylvania Press, 1999.

Physicians for Human Rights. "Aiding Torture: Health Professionals' Ethics and Human Rights Violations Revealed in the May 2004 CIA Inspector General's Report." http://physiciansforhumanrights.org/library/documents/reports/aiding-torture.pdf, accessed August 15, 2010).

Radice, Betty. *Pliny: Letters, Books VIII-X Panegyricus.* Cambridge, MA: Harvard University Press, 1969.

Rejali, Darius. *Torture and Democracy.* Princeton, NJ: Princeton University Press, 2007.

Scarry, Elaine. *The Body in Pain: The Making and Unmaking of the World.* Oxford, UK: Oxford University Press, 1985.

Shaw, Brent D. "Body/Power/Identity: Passions of the Martyrs." *Journal of Early Christian Studies* 4.3 (1996): 269–312.

Stratton, Kimberly B. "The Eschatological Arena: Reinscribing Roman Violence in Fantasies of the End Times." In *Violence, Scripture, and Textual Practice in Early Judaism and Christianity.* Eds. Ra'anan S. Boustan, Alex P. Jassen, and Calvin J. Roetzel, 45–76. Leiden, Netherlands, and Boston: Brill, 2010.

Taussig, Michael. "Culture of Terror—Face of Death: Roger Casement's Putumayo Report and the Explanation of Torture." *Comparative Studies in Society and History* 26.3 (1984): 467–497.

United Nations General Assembly. "Convention against Torture and Other Cruel, Inhuman, or Degrading Treatment and Punishment." Resolution 39/46, UN GAOR, Supp. 51, 1984. www2.ohchr.org/english/law/cat.htm.

Walzer, Michael. "Political Action: The Problem of Dirty Hands." *Philosophy and Public Affairs* 2.2 (1973): 160–180.

CHAPTER 19

....

JUST WAR AND LEGAL RESTRAINTS

....

JOHN KELSAY

IN 390 CE, the bishop of Milan wrote a letter rebuking the Roman emperor Theodosius. In the attempt to quell a public uprising in Thessaloniki, imperial forces had killed some 7,000 people, and Bishop Ambrose held Theodosius accountable. As the letter put it, such behavior would be inappropriate for any ruler, but as a faithful son of the church, Theodosius possessed a greater responsibility to avoid injustice. Ambrose declared that he would not celebrate the Eucharist in the presence of the Emperor apart from public demonstrations of the ruler's penitence.

In May 1999, the United Nation's International Tribunal for the Former Yugoslavia indicted President Slobodan Milosevic for crimes against humanity. By the time the trial began in 2002, the tribunal added charges of violating the laws or customs of war, grave violations of the Geneva Conventions, and genocide. For two years, the prosecution presented its evidence; Milosevic then argued his own defense. The trial ended without a verdict when prison officials found Milosevic dead in his cell on March 11, 2006.

Military historians remind us that technological restraints are a constant reality for those who would make war. Distance, difficult terrain, extreme heat or cold, and securing basic supplies present serious challenges and, in their own way, impose restraints on fighting. Yet the two examples cited, separated by considerable historical and cultural differences, point to the fact that most, if not all, human communities also attempt to limit fighting by means of religious, moral, and legal norms. The story of Ambrose's rebuke and Theodosius's repentance represents an important development in one set of norms, which we may characterize broadly as the just war idea. Despite its intimate link with Latin-speaking, "Western" Christians, the idea resonates in a number of religious and cultural settings: Jews and Muslims developed ways of distinguishing just from unjust wars, as did the traditions that grew up in South and East Asia. The reach of the just war idea is thus global, inviting comparative as well as more strictly historical inquiry.

The trial of Slobodan Milosevic points to another, more recent development: the attempt to build a system of positive international law. The relationship between just war and positive international law makes for an interesting story, not least with respect to comparative studies of religion, and the chapter concludes with some discussion of that matter. It begins, however, with the older notion of just war, particularly as it developed in relation to the changing place of Christianity in Europe and North America.

THE JUST WAR IDEA

Early Development

The phrase "just war" is the translation of the Latin *bellum iustum*. As this suggests, the origins of the idea rest in Rome. Cicero (106–43 BCE) traced the idea to the fetial laws, by which a class of religious specialists oversaw the initiation and conduct of wars in the interests of maintaining honor in Rome's public life. Sparing the innocent, magnanimity in victory, and avoidance of treachery are central to the notion, as are attempts to avoid war through diplomacy and public declarations of war. (Reichberg et al. 2006: 5–59)

When Christian authors such as Ambrose (339–397) and Augustine (354–430) wrote about war in the new context created by Constantine's (272–337) adoption of the faith, they drew on Cicero's discussion. For Ambrose, the son of a Roman official, a close identification of Roman virtue with biblical religion seemed natural, and his accounts of the duty to protect the innocent by means of the sword present stories of Moses and other heroes of faith as exemplary practitioners of the *bellum iustum* (Reichberg et al. 2006: 67–69). Augustine's position vis-à-vis Rome is more complicated, but he, too, found a way to weave biblical religion and Ciceronian virtue into an account of political life. For Augustine, the Divine Warrior depicted in Scripture uses war as a means to accomplish His will in a world affected by sin. According to Romans 13, the use of the sword to punish evildoers is assigned to public authorities; these hold power by a divine mandate. While Christians must not give in to hatred and other dispositions that constitute the true evils present in war, they are obligated to participate in the preservation of the "peace of a sort" represented in "earthly" political communities. For some, this implies a military vocation; for others (for example, clergy), it implies the "more excellent way" of religious and moral oversight of public life. Thus, the just war idea represents a way of thinking in which war itself is a kind of restraint. In particular, fighting authorized by public officials for the preservation of a political community and conducted in the right spirit serves to restrain those who would practice *violence*—a term designating various kinds of fighting that involve transgressions against public order and that thus raise the specter of anarchy. At the same time, those fighting in a just war must take care, or the energies created by battle might lead them into injustice. As Augustine put it, one should let necessity, rather than one's own will, slay the enemy (Reichberg et al. 2006: 70–90).

THE JUST WAR AND CHRISTENDOM

Augustine directed those words at Boniface, a great general charged with preserving the western portion of the empire from the incursions of various Germanic tribes in the late fourth and early fifth centuries. Perhaps the general and those with him succeeded in avoiding evil dispositions, but they did not succeed in protecting Rome. In 410, Alaric and his Visigoth tribesmen sacked Rome. In 430, Augustine died during Alaric's siege of Hippo in northern Africa. In a sense, one might say that the just war idea died with him—or at least entered a period of dormancy. Several centuries passed before a set of enterprising churchmen forged alliances with political and military leaders in ways that reconstituted the old notion.

When they did so, for example in the "peace of God" proclaimed at Charroux in 989 and in various declarations of the "truce of God" in the eleventh century, the results pointed to a desire to protect the social system forged by the western church following the collapse of the empire. Groups of bishops and other clergy published lists of persons and properties classed as protected from direct military action. As well, these proclamations limited fighting to certain days and seasons. By the time of the Second Lateran Council (1123), restrictions on the use of fire and the bow and arrow were included—the latter indicating an alliance between the church and the knightly class, with its interest in limiting the numbers and kinds of persons eligible to fight in just wars. In all cases, the sanction of excommunication—here, meaning not only lack of access to the church's religious goods (sacraments) but also a prohibition of trade and other social goods—was put in the service of restraining war.

At the same time, legally minded scholars poured energies into recovering Roman statutes that served as precedents for the development of canons or standards intended to guide judgments regarding decisions about war. The *Decretum Gratiani*, a set of judgments attributed to an otherwise obscure figure named Gratian, appeared in 1140. The *Decretum* provided a systematic statement on a variety of questions; over the next century, a series of commentators provided elaborations and clarifications that made possible Thomas Aquinas's (1225–1274) succinct and influential statement of the criteria for a just war:

> In order for a war to be just, three things are required. First, the authority of the prince by whose command the war is to be waged.... Secondly, a just cause is required.... Thirdly, it is necessary that those waging war should have a rightful

intention, so that they intend the advancement of good, or the avoidance of evil. (Reichberg et al. 2006: 177)

Thomas's exposition, like those of Ambrose and Augustine, situates the notion of just war in the context of the Christian account of a world created and judged by God as good yet affected profoundly by humanity's fall or turning away from God. In such a world, the wise use of military force is an aspect of good politics. Princes who authorize just wars serve the common good, as do soldiers who fight at the order of their sovereign. All must be wary of the temptations posed by fighting however. "For it may happen that the war is declared by the legitimate authority, and for a just cause, and yet be rendered illicit through a vile intention" (Reichberg et al. 2006: 177). Citing Augustine's delineation of envy, hatred, and other negative dispositions as the true evils of war, Thomas ties right intention to the maintenance of a properly ordered soul, in which reason regulates emotion and places it in the service of the will. At the same time, his discussions of the relationship between war, strife, and sedition indicate a concern for limits on fighting, as do texts addressing questions about tactics such as ambushes (these are allowed), the role of clerics in warfare (primarily to serve as moral guides), fighting on holy days (allowed under conditions of necessity), and the use of force against unbelievers (never to bring about faith but allowed when such people defame the faith or hinder its preaching; on this point, Thomas was ambivalent in regard to the Crusades.) The proper goal of just wars is the protection of the common good of a political community, understood as the means by which human beings might enjoy a modicum of the "natural" goods associated with family life and friendships, as well as to receive divine grace through the sacraments administered by the church in association with their ultimate destiny (Reichberg et al. 2006: 168–198).

The Emergence of Europe

Thomas's statement provided a platform for the subsequent development of an *ius ad bellum* fit for a world of states. The Spanish Catholics Vitoria (1492–1546), Molina (1535–1600), and Suarez (1548–1617) formed their arguments largely as commentaries on Thomas. Changing political contexts required these scholars to make revisions to their predecessor however. In particular, the emergence of large and powerful states with interests in the New World did away with any presumption of a unified Christendom. Instead, Spain, England, and other European states would become competitors in a contest for power. The encounter with Native American tribes also raised questions about the universal scope of Christian norms.

Competition extended to the just war idea itself. As the Jesuits articulated their case, Protestant scholars such as Gentili (1552–1645) and Grotius (1583–1645) developed an alternative, in which Thomas Aquinas proved less important than precedents from the Bible and ancient Rome. Despite the differences, however, Protestants and Catholics converged on a number of points. In doing so, they constituted a version of the just war idea reflected in modern, including twentieth- and twenty-first-century, discussion.

Thus, these authors presumed that authority or "competence of war" rested with sovereign states. They participated in an international order governed in some sense by longstanding customs: safe passage for diplomats, respect for treaties, and the idea of just conduct in war. From one point of view, the antiquity of these practices established their authority, particularly for the Protestants. From another angle, their authority rested on the notion that these customs could be regarded as laws and thus as obligations for states. In this latter sense, Protestants and Catholics alike spoke of the "law of nations" as grounded in natural law and thus having the status of norms that could bind all human beings, despite religious and cultural differences. While the Protestant versions of natural law drew from Stoic philosophy and the Catholics from Aristotle, both converged on the judgment that the norms governing states are universally valid. For example, Vitoria applied the law of nations to conflicts in the Americas. Allowing that the indigenous peoples might feel threatened by the presence of Spaniards and arguing that the latter ought to conduct themselves in ways that would minimize fear, Vitoria nonetheless judged the Indians responsible to allow safe passage for trade and missionary activity. Any who did not presented Spain with a just cause for war.

In arguing the case, Vitoria actually undercut a number of other justifications offered by Spain for military action in the New World. The fact of the natives' adherence to false religion did not constitute a just cause of war, for example. As well, the Spanish monarch could not command a war of conquest based on a papal grant of rights to territory. Finally, even the just cause associated with the Indians' failure to grant safe passage was to be handled with care; since difficulties in communication might lead the natives to misconstrue Spanish actions, it might be possible for Indian acts of war to take place in a condition of "simultaneous ostensible justice." In this case, the natives' ignorance might lead them to construe their cause as just. The true measure of right would then be the extent to which the warring parties' adhered to standards of right conduct in war. Indian wrongs or mistakes in initiating fighting would not, in other words, justify Spanish excesses or other violations of requirements such as those obligating soldiers to distinguish between civilian and military targets or to avoid causing damage beyond that which could be considered proportionate to a given strategic goal (Reichberg et al. 2006: 288–332).

THE DEVELOPMENT OF POSITIVE INTERNATIONAL LAW

By developing the notion of a universally valid law of nations, Vitoria and others moved the just war idea in directions fit for a world of states. The issue of sanctions remained. As indicated, in earlier periods, just war norms were attached to religious sanctions. Violators faced the threat of ecclesiastical authorities' refusal to administer sacraments or, ultimately, of excommunication. At one level, such threats relied on the pressure of conscience; at another, since excommunication, in effect, meant that other Christians were under pressure to cut off relations with a wrongdoer, such sanctions also called on important social pressures. In the new context, however, there was no universal ecclesiastical authority. Such sanctions as might exist relied on the decisions of rulers of sovereign states. Thus, if the natives in the Americas violated the law of nations, the Spanish ruler's authorization of military force imposed the sanction of just war—certainly a reflection of the old idea, but what if the wrongful behavior occurred on the Spanish side? In such a case, the rulers of other sovereign states might intervene and thus wield the sword of justice, but would their wrongs also be judged and punished?

It was in part the resulting pressure of this state of affairs that led to a variety of attempts to constitute a truly international legal order, with institutions fitted to reduce the extent to which the competition between states might be characterized as unregulated or even anarchic. In his essay on *Perpetual Peace*, Immanuel Kant (1724–1804) foresaw the development of a league of democratic republics, in which shared values might be joined to ordinary citizens' reservations about the costs of war in ways that would lead to states' submitting differences to arbitration. As Kant had it, the league might be a long time in coming, but come it would, because of the imperatives of justice (Kant 2003).

A less morally intent author than Kant might have suggested that the real motive for the envisioned order would be to lower the various costs of war. In any case, the nineteenth-century Concert of Europe pointed in the direction of such an arrangement and laid the groundwork for efforts to codify the law of war in the Hague Conventions (1899 and 1907), the Geneva Convention (1949, supplemented by the additional protocols of 1977 and 2005), the Charter of the United Nations, and a number of other international agreements. In their statement of norms related to the protection of civilians, just treatment of prisoners of war, outlawing or otherwise regulating the use of specific weapons or tactics, and requiring international authorization for any use of military force other than national defense, these agreements bear a close relation to the just war tradition. Progress in the development of mechanisms for enforcement remains difficult however. The trial of Slobodan Milosevic remains the exception rather than the rule. In that instance, as with other notable cases (for example, the Nuremberg Trials of 1945–1946), the power of international organizations relied on the support (or acquiescence) of individual states. In this sense, the international system remains, as Hedley Bull famously put it, an "anarchical society" (Bull 1977).

It is perhaps for this reason that the second half of the twentieth century saw a renewed interest in the older tradition of just war as a specifically moral way of speaking about the use of armed force. Particularly in the United States (and to a somewhat lesser extent, in Britain), a number of scholars appealed to Augustine, Aquinas, and other historic authorities in connection with arguments concerning the morality of nuclear deterrence, counterinsurgency, humanitarian intervention, and counterterrorism. Many of these scholars had ecclesiastical connections. Thus, the Jesuit John Courtney Murray (1904–1967) and the Methodist layman Paul Ramsey (1913–1988) presented just war arguments in ways that bore more than formal resemblance to their predecessors (Murray 1959; Ramsey 1968). Many authors took a different tack, however. James Turner Johnson (1938–) argued for the just war idea as a constitutive aspect of Western cultural history, providing precedents by which contemporary political and military issues might be illumined (Johnson 1981; Johnson 2011). And Michael Walzer's (1933–) influential treatment in *Just and Unjust Wars* explained simply that the "war convention"—an amalgam of common morality and international law—provided form to the sort of vocabulary presented in popular argument about the war in Vietnam (Walzer 1977). Perhaps resting on a theory of human rights, the just war idea could, in principle, be extended to any number of contexts, including that of the late twentieth century.

In general, the authors contributing to this renewal of just war argument thought of their discussion as analogous or complementary to the development of international law. Nevertheless, certain tensions were already clear in discussions related to the Cold War and arguably have become even more so in connection with events during the 1990s (for example, in the conflicts in the former Yugoslavia and in Rwanda) and (since 9/11) the War on Terror. Not least among these is the question of right authority. Does authority for war rest with the governments of sovereign states—as, for example, in historic just war thinking? Or does such authority rest with international organizations, as indicated (with the exception of wars of defense) in the Charter of the United Nations? One might put it this way: Vitoria, Grotius, and other architects of the early modern notion of just war designed a set of judgments fit for an international or interstate order and in ways that suggest that recognized governments impose the sanction of war on those who violate customary practices designed to allow trade and other forms of exchange between sovereign states. The norms of positive international law, by contrast, are now identified with the hope that an appropriate set of institutions might transcend and thus govern the behavior of sovereign states, imposing the rule of law in cases in which sovereign states (and their rulers) violate those norms intended "to save succeeding generations from the scourge of war" (United Nations 1985).

CONCLUSION

The system of positive international law associated with the United Nations and other international organization grew up, in part, as a response to the question: Who enforces the norms of just war in an order defined by sovereign states? The enforcement issue does not stand alone however. Recall that Vitoria, Grotius, and other early modern authors described the law of nations as universal and thus valid for conflicts between Europeans and (for example) the American Indians.

The question of the authority or purchase of just war norms across cultural lines deserves scrutiny.

Advocates of positive international law give one sort of answer. Wherever sovereign states indicate an assent to treaties, they are bound as members of the international system. Thus, all states accepting membership in the United Nations are bound by its charter, and are expected at some point to sign on to the provisions of subsequent treaties approved by the organization. The Nuclear Non-Proliferation Treaty is a case in point. First proposed by Ireland in 1958, the agreement was presented to member states of the United Nations in 1968. To date, 189 states are committed to its provisions, which focus on nonproliferation, disarmament, and the development of peaceful uses of nuclear power. There are, of course, a number of states that have not signed as well; North Korea, which signed in 1985, withdrew in 2003, and Iran, which signed in 1968, was judged in violation of the provisions of the agreement in 2003. Difficulties notwithstanding, the argument of proponents of positive international law is that consent establishes obligation. The universality of norms is thus a project to be achieved by means of negotiation among sovereign states.

Others suggest a different course. Noting that agreement to treaties is largely a task confined to elite members of states, these scholars argue that the authority of positive international law fails to account for the influence of longstanding religious and cultural traditions. Assuming that these provide a more accurate indicator of popular opinion than the statements of professional diplomats, the idea is that the universality of just war norms must be found—if it can be established at all—through a careful study of a number of diverse traditions aimed at sorting the difference between just and unjust war. Thus, Judaism, with its historic distinction between obligatory and discretionary war and the delineation of norms appropriate to each, and Islam, with its centuries-long juridical discussion of "judgments pertaining to armed struggle," must be compared with the standards of just war outlined in this chapter (Wilkes 2003; Kelsay 2007; Johnson and Kelsay 1990; Kelsay and Johnson 1991). Similarly, the case for the universality of norms governing war must take account of Chinese, Hindu, and Buddhist traditions (Twiss 2011; Bartholomeusz 2002).

As one might expect, such inquiries are fraught with difficulties. The outline of just war presented in the chapter shows that the idea is a moving target, in which changes reflect the dynamic nature of social and political institutions. Similarly, Jewish, Muslim, and other war traditions have developed in ways that make it difficult to fix on a particular formulation by which comparison may proceed or agreement be identified. Nevertheless, it seems possible to identify a number of salient features shared by the various traditions mentioned. An interest in limiting the right of war to publicly established authorities, and thus of restraining more anarchic forms of violence, seems to be a consistent feature of just war traditions. Similarly, the notion that total war ought not to be the norm, so that some distinction between military and nonmilitary targets is required, or that force is to be limited by the measure of "that which is necessary to achieve a legitimate objective" runs through most war traditions.

Perhaps such comparative studies serve, in the end, as a rough guide for those who seek to strengthen the regime of positive international law. They may also serve, however, to guide the conduct of sovereign states in a world in which the power of international organizations (and thus of international law) is not always up to the task of regulating war. In any case, the old idea by which Ambrose, Augustine, and their successors thought of just war as a means by which anarchic violence might be restrained is very much with us, sometimes complemented by and other times in conflict with the more recent regime of positive international law.

Bibliography

Bartholomeusz, Tessa. *In Defense of Dharma*. New York: Routledge and Curzon, 2002.

Bull, Hedley. *The Anarchical Society*. New York: Columbia University Press, 1977.

Johnson, James T. *Just War Tradition and the Restraint of War*. Princeton, NJ: Princeton University Press, 1981.

Johnson, James T. and John Kelsay, eds. *Cross, Crescent, and Sword*. Westport, CT: Greenwood, 1990.

Johnson, James T. *Ethics and the Use of Force*. Burlington, VT: Ashgate, 2011.

Kant, Immanuel. *To Perpetual Peace: A Philosophical Sketch*. Trans. Ted Humphrey. Indianapolis: Hackett Publishing, 2003.

Kelsay, John. *Arguing the Just War in Islam*. Cambridge, MA: Harvard University Press, 2007.

Kelsay, John, and James T. Johnson, eds. *Just War and Jihad*. Westport, CT: Greenwood, 1991.

Murray, John Courtney, S. J. *Morality and Modern War*. New York: Council on Religion and International Affairs, 1959.

Ramsey, Paul. *The Just War*. New York: Charles Scribner's Sons, 1968.

Reichberg, Gregory M., Henrik Syse, and Endre Begby, eds. *The Ethics of War: Classic and Contemporary Readings*. Oxford, UK: Blackwell, 2006.

Twiss, Sumner B., and Jonathan Chan. "The Classical Confucian Position on the Legitimate Use of Military Force." *Journal of Religious Ethics*, 40.3 (September 2012): 447–472.

United Nations. *Charter of the United Nations and Statue of the International Court of Justice*. New York: United Nations, 1985.

Walzer, Michael. *Just and Unjust Wars*. New York: Basic Books, 1977.

Wilkes, George. "Judaism and Justice in War." In *Just War in Comparative Perspective*. Ed. Paul Robinson, 9–23. Surrey, UK: Ashgate, 2003.

CHAPTER 20

RELIGIOUSLY MOTIVATED VIOLENCE IN THE ABORTION DEBATE

JULIE INGERSOLL

THOUGH violence has characterized the contemporary religious debate over abortion within North American Christianity more than anywhere else, it is an issue of ethical discussion within almost every religious tradition. In India, for instance, many modern-day Hindus find it morally justifiable even though some ancient Hindu texts oppose abortion. The issue in contemporary India is complicated with the ethical issues involved in the practice of using abortion as a form of sex selection, in terminating the gestation of girls rather than boys. Some Hindu theologians argue that a soul (Sanskrit: *atman*) is present in a fetus three months after conception, which would restrict some but not all abortions. Some Buddhists are tolerant of abortion (and in the Japanese tradition, *mizuko kuyo* is a ritual for the death of a fetus including one that has been aborted). Some traditional Buddhists, however, hold that life begins at conception, and therefore they oppose the termination of pregnancies. Tibetan Buddhism's Fourteenth Dalai Lama has said that the appropriateness of abortion must be decided on a case-by-case basis.

Orthodox Jews generally prohibit abortion except to save a mother's life. Conservative Jews usually allow abortion in a few other circumstances, and Reform Jews often state that abortion should be a matter of personal choice. Within Islam, there has also been a divergence of opinions. Many Muslim jurists argue that abortion can be permitted only up to the fourth month, at which point the fetus is thought to have a soul, unless the procedure is done to preserve the mother's life.

As in these other traditions, Christianity also contains a variety of perspectives, ranging from not allowing abortion, even to save a mother's life, to understanding abortion to be at times a compassionate, though difficult, choice. Emerging from this diversity of viewpoints are social movements opposing and supporting a woman's right to choose whether or not to have an abortion. Often the differences between these movements are contentious. The use of violence to oppose or prevent abortion is unique to the Christian tradition and almost exclusively found in North American Christianity. For this reason, this chapter will focus on the North American Christian case in exploring the role of violence in the religious controversy about abortion.

In the debate about legal abortion, there are no neutral terms for the various factions. Those who are in favor of a woman's right to choose, the so-called prochoicers, argue that abortion opponents, the ones in favor of not terminating the life of the fetus and therefore prolifers, are not in fact prolife since some of them are in favor of killing abortion providers and many more favor capital punishment and the use of violence in police and military operations. That some prolifers would legitimate the use of violence and even assassination to stop abortion seems paradoxical at best. Critics question in what sense that position can said to be prolife and how it can be squared with any version of Christian ethical teachings. On the other side, prolifers argue that abortion rights advocates are not really prochoice as they consider only the mother's right to make a choice and ignore the "choices" of unborn babies. The closest one can get to neutrality is to use the labels the groups use for themselves, recognizing that each is trying to frame the debate in the very language they use.

This chapter will explore the religiously legitimated use of violence in the extreme wing of the American prolife movement. Drawing on the works of a handful of leaders who have made the argument for the legitimacy of the use of violence in public ways, I will show the degree to which this is an internally coherent and consistent framing of one particular form of Christianity and the relationship between abortion and violence. This chapter is not an abortion-related polemic but an effort to understand the logic of this point of view. If one only views the issues from the assumptions embedded in the prochoice position (be it secular or Christian), this line of reasoning may seem to be incomprehensible. But as an exercise in "making the strange familiar," from within the framework of the radical wing of the prolife movement, the arguments are strikingly rational.[1]

CHRISTIAN RECONSTRUCTION

While some who engage in violence to stop abortion arrive at their convictions through Roman Catholicism, behind the most broadly disseminated philosophical and theological argument in defense of the use of violence lies an obscure form of

Calvinist Protestantism known as Christian Reconstructionism. The movement's central spokesperson in defense of the use of violence and author of the book *A Time to Kill*, Mike Bray has drawn on this tradition extensively. Randall Terry, founder of Operation Rescue and author of *Operation Rescue* (1988) and *The Judgment of God* (1995), was much influenced by this line of reasoning before he converted to Roman Catholicism in 2006. Paul Hill, executed in Florida for the killing of John Britton, was trained in a reformed seminary under Reconstructionist Greg Bahnsen and served in the ministry in the most traditionally Calvinist of the Presbyterian denominations, the Orthodox Presbyterian Church and the Presbyterian Church in America. Hill's writings share with Reconstructionists an approach to the Bible and an interpretive schema. That Hill found Christian Reconstruction compatible with his understanding of Christianity is demonstrated by a written exchange between Hill and Reconstructionist Gary North, which will be explored later in the chapter. Hill cited Rushdoony in essays supporting the use of violence to stop abortion, and he sent those essays to Gary North, seeking comments and, presumably, support. Hill wrote the essays in support of violence in the aftermath of the assassination of Dr. David Gunn by Michael Griffin. Just weeks after Hill had acted on the views he had articulated, North replied to his arguments rejecting their legitimacy on the grounds that the punishment of "evildoers" is, under biblical law, the responsibility of duly appointed civil authorities, not individuals, and that Hill's strategy was ultimately futile.

Despite North's rejection, leading to the potential conclusion that the argument in favor of the use of violence is a misapplication of Christian Reconstruction, it remains clear that for those who see such actions as legitimate, Christian Reconstruction is one of the underlying influences.

This version of Christianity understands the Bible to be a coherent whole. The Old and New Testaments together form the record of God's revelation of himself in history. Reconstructionists explicitly reject a modern framing of the text in which the wrathful God of the Old Testament is supplanted by the loving, forgiving God revealed in the person of Jesus in the New Testament. Ancient Israel, and the Law God laid out for it in the Old Testament, are to be the model for the Christian life today. As postmillennialists, they believe that ultimately the entire world will be Christian or that, as the Bible says, "every knee shall bow, every tongue confess."[2] The character of God is understood in distinctly Calvinist terms in which God is both a wrathful judge and a loving savior. Judgment is necessary to reflect God's justice and is deserved by utterly depraved, fallen human beings. That some of those human beings are lifted from their depravity by God's grace to salvation that they can in no way earn is a testament to God's love.

The legitimation of the use of violence to stop abortion finds its most public expression in an organization known as the Army of God, a loose affiliation of activists who have taken credit for numerous acts of violence, maintain a website and a series of links defending those who have been convicted of abortion related violence and promoting their writings, and raise money to support those convicted and their families. But the arguments made by the Army of God are, in many ways, the logical conclusion of the arguments put forth by the explicitly (if paradoxically) nonviolent Operation Rescue a decade earlier.

ABORTION AS VIOLENCE

The foundation of the argument that the use of force to stop abortion is potentially legitimate is the assertion that abortion is violent. The comparisons made by prolifers to slavery and the Holocaust are not mere rhetoric, and they are not held by only the extreme wing of the Right to Life movement. They were made effectively by Francis Schaeffer and former surgeon general C. Everett Koop in the book and film *Whatever Happened to the Human Race* (1979). Mainstream Evangelicals were persuaded by Schaeffer and others that, when a society devalues the lives of a category of human beings, making them effectively less than human, they make room for atrocities such as the Holocaust, slavery, and abortion. Moreover, legalized abortion is understood as part of a larger cultural transformation that is labeled a "culture of death," which, in the context of increasing opportunities and life choices for women, changed notions of childbearing. Marriage and childbearing, once thought of as the only options for women, are increasingly understood in the context of many other legitimate, alternative choices. Many opponents of legal abortion also oppose the use of contraceptives and do so on the basis that many contraceptives work, in part, by preventing the implantation of a fertilized egg and are, effectively, very early abortions. More broadly, though, contraception is challenged on cultural grounds as contributing to a "Planned Parenthood mentality" in that children are to be planned rather than welcomed as blessings from God. This argument is rooted in mainstream Catholic thought, articulated in the papal encyclical *Humane Vitae* and also in the Protestant movement known as either the Quiverfull or Biblical Patriarchy movements (Joyce, 2009, Ingersoll forthcoming). This Protestant movement, again tied to Christian Reconstruction, promotes a social order where submissive wives live out their lives seeking to produce as many children as possible.

OPERATION RESCUE AND NONVIOLENT CIVIL DISOBEDIENCE

When Randall Terry launched Operation Rescue in the 1980s, the effort to prevent specific abortions by using the tactics of nonviolence such as civil disobedience to close down abortion clinics, by blocking access to clinic doors, the organization had pre-"rescue" training sessions in which rescuers were taught Martin Luther King's principles of nonviolence. Rescuers were taught to passively resist arrest by "going limp" to delay the efforts of police to remove rescuers from the premises and reopen the clinic. All participants were required to sign a pledge, which read, in part:

> I understand the critical importance of Operation Rescue being unified, peaceful and free of any actions or words that would appear violent or hateful... I understand *for the children's sake* each Rescue must be orderly and above reproach. I commit to be peaceful and non-violent in both word and deed. Should I be arrested, I will not struggle with police in any way (whether deed or tongue), but remain polite and passively limp, remembering that mercy triumphs over judgment. (Italics in original, Terry, 1988, 228)

Intended to both prevent specific abortions and create social tension that Terry believed could bring about an end to legalized abortion, Operation Rescue was, perhaps contradictorily, explicitly nonviolent. Member training also included role-playing activities designed to help rescuers live up to their pledges.

In keeping with King's views on civil disobedience, rescuers often pled guilty and often accepted sentences, sometimes choosing jail time over fines to further "clog the system." In his book *Operation Rescue*, Terry explains that the civil disobedience effort to end abortion developed from his own repentance when he realized that he and other prolife Christians had been calling abortion murder but "not acting like it."

> Pro-lifers were saying that abortion was murder, and yet all we were doing about it was writing a letter now and then. If my little girl was about to be murdered, I certainly would not write a letter to the editor! I would dive in with both hands and feet to do whatever was necessary to save her life. (Terry 1988: 22)

But as a growing number of prolifers (many of whom had been leaders in Operation Rescue) came to see the command to "act like abortion is murder" as inconsistent with nonviolent civil disobedience, the numbers of violent incidents in opposition to abortion rose.

Even more, Terry argues that the United States is in a state of war; it is a defensive war against "philosophies and lifestyles that are destroying the nation," but, he says, "we need to 'declare war' on the child killing industry" (Terry 1988: 182–184).

> The most crucial need in the war against abortion is for *front line soldiers* who are willing to place their bodies where the battle rages. Rescuers who have been motivated Higher Laws and a burning desire to save children who are scheduled to die *today* are answering the call to the trenches. (Terry 1988: 184)

Terry, now director of Insurrecta Nex, maintains that he is committed to nonviolence and "the rule of law," yet he perpetuates ambiguity in regard to his position on the legitimacy of the use of violence. In statement at Scott Roeder's 2010 trial for killing Dr. George Tiller, Terry asserted that Tiller deserved to be killed and that Roeder had not been given a fair trial:

> The worst that can be said is that George Tiller was a mass murderer, and he reaped what he sowed: A murderer was murdered. Beyond that—after days of sitting in the trial—it became clear to me that Mr. Roeder was not being given a fair trial. In my opinion, he should have been given the chance to present what he knew about Tiller to the jury; how their bodies were torn limb from limb; how they were decapitated; how their mangled lifeless bodies were disposed of. (Terry's press release)

THE USE OF VIOLENCE TO STOP ABORTION

At the center of violent wing of the prolife movement is the Army of God, and the architect of the argument that violence can be legitimately used to stop abortion is Mike Bray. Bray is a graduate of Denver Seminary and a former pastor of Reformation Lutheran Church in Bowie, Maryland. In the 1980s, he was convicted and served time for arson in the destruction of seven abortion clinics. The actions for which he was convicted occurred at night when the clinics were closed and, according to Bray, the goal was limited to property destruction. He has never been implicated in actions to kill abortion providers but has been the primary advocate for the legitimacy of the actions on the part of people "who are so called."

Bray is reputed to be the author of the anonymous *Army of God Manual,* an apologia and tactical manual. While not claiming responsibility for the work, Bray refuses, in "solidarity with one who is being maligned for writing such a book," to disclaim it as well (Juergensmeyer 2003: 21). He is, however, the acknowledged author of *A Time to Kill* (Bray 1994) in which he marshals historical, theological, and biblical examples in which the faithful have legitimately violated civil law and even used violence to protect the innocent. In Bray's framing, the legitimate use of violence is not a political strategy to end legalized abortion or a vigilante action to avenge an act of abortion but a direct action to prevent specific abortions and thereby save specific lives. In that sense, they are "defensive."

Bray begins by drawing a distinction between "the use of force" and "violence," making the case that Scripture and Christian history consistently support the use of force under specified circumstances (Bray 1994; 34).

> Force, even lethal force, is not only commanded by God and performed by Him on innumerable occasions in the older scriptures, it is also prescribed in the Law for citizen's participation. When a man sacrificed his own children to a false God, the whole community was obligated in an execution by stoning (cf Lev. 20: 2–4). The use of lethal force is not only commanded as a judicial act, but granted to the individual in cases of self defense and defense of others. (Bray 1994: 41)

He engages anticipated objections from those who see the New Testament as distinctly separate from and a replacement of the Old and from those who argue that the ministry of Jesus (in the Sermon on the Mount, for example) might require a pacifism on the part of those who would follow him (Bray 1994: 37–52). He cites examples in which Jesus told his disciples to take up swords and examples in which Jesus used force against injustice (Bray 1994: 43). "Neither the life of Christ, nor his teachings, abolish the Law regarding godly force. Jesus of Nazareth came in humiliation to die. Yet even in that role, He had occasion to act forcefully" (Bray 42). Bray invokes the notion of role distinction to explain what others might see as contradictions in the ministry of Jesus:

> There is a time to kill to protect oneself and others, and there is a time to suffer and die voluntarily. In another passage, the account of Jesus commanding His

disciples to take swords with them illumines both the continuity of the biblical teaching on legitimate force and the principle of role distinction. (Bray 1994: 43)

In response to the criticism that biblical law limits the use of force to civil authorities operating in their God-ordained sphere of authority and that individuals usurp that authority when acting on their own, such as in Gary North's argument previously discussed, Bray acknowledges that the "distinct role of the state is to punish evildoers" but then asserts that the "duty to defend an innocent person rests with anyone who is standing by" (Bray 1994: 46).

In like fashion, Bray addresses each of the texts that seemingly prohibit the use of force and asserts that there is a "gross inconsistency" on the part of right to lifers who call abortion murder and then deny the "preborn child...the defense afforded any other person" (Bray 1994: 78). So a violent act against abortion, whether it be against property or against the person of an abortion provider, is legitimate, in Bray's terms, in that its goal is not to protest abortions but to prevent one or more from taking place. Bray has thus argued that there is a difference between killing a retired abortion doctor and one who continues to practice (Juergensmeyer 2003: 24).

Bray takes the argument a step further, though, in exploring the legitimacy of revolution. He begins by correcting what he sees as a misreading of the Bible on the character of God. God is a "God of War" and a "God who slays His apostate people," who "commands the slaughter of idol worship(ers)" (Bray 1994: 153). While much of it is drawn from the Old Testament, Bray asserts that this is the revelation of the character of the "pre-incarnate" Christ (Bray 1994: 153). The Bible, he argues, includes plenty of examples of God's involvement in war. And while Christians are admonished to obey civil authorities, "[t]he principle is qualified from the beginning. The people of God are never enjoined to unconditional submission. When tyrants ruled, God sent deliverers to the people. The Scriptures are full of examples of righteous disobedience and revolution" (Bray 1994: 158). Citing examples from Scripture and from history, he asserts, "There are times for resistance, times for revolution and times for assassination of heads of state." He gives the examples of Hitler and Pol Pot (Bray 1994: 171). Yet, Bray says, this is not such a time; not because revolution cannot be justified but because it is impractical in the context of an "emasculated Church" that cannot even see the legitimacy of the use of godly force (Bray 1994: 172).

ANTICIPATED VIOLENCE BY GOD IN JUDGMENT FOR THE SIN OF ABORTION

Another dimension of the relationship between abortion and violence is the inherent violence in the understanding of the character of God held by the activists who argue that violence to stop abortion is legitimate. The God envisioned by these Christians is a wrathful, vengeful God. The God who commanded the genocide against the Canaanites in the Old Testament, a God whose greatest act of love is the violent execution of his son (himself?) as the only adequate resolution to sin, a God who promised to bring vengeance to bear on a disobedient nation that allows the continued slaughter of babies in the womb (and a host of other social ills, the most significant of which is homosexuality).

Bray and Terry are each critical of contemporary Christianity, which sees God as a "jolly old perennial gift giver," a "semi-senile heavenly grandfather," or a "Cosmic Watchmaker." According to Terry, God is the awesome, fearful, dreaded sovereign Lord of the universe to whom all men will give an account. "It matters not to Him whether we acknowledge Him… He is our judge" (Terry 1995: 3–4). In *The Judgment of God: Terrorism, Floods…Droughts…Disasters,* Terry argues that the travails facing the United States are God's judgment on our nation and that the only way to avoid destruction is through repentance. While, in 1995, Terry warned of Islamic terrorism, at that point the greater threat was the AIDS epidemic:

> In light of the Holy Bible and in view of our nation's state of moral anarchy, I have come to the conclusion that A.I.D.S. is the judgment of God. I could be wrong, but I believe this horrifying plague is the chastening of the Lord against our nation as a whole and against the homosexual lifestyle in particular.
>
> The thought of A.I.D.S. being a judgment from the Almighty might violate every concept of God you have ever had. You might ask, how could a God of love send such a disease? The answer is because He is also just. And holy. And righteous. (Terry 1995: 25)

From the beginning, Terry urged fellow Christians to participate in Operation Rescue, in part, to forestall God's judgment on our society. He writes:

> The question is *not*, will America be judged? Judgment is inevitable because the blood of the children already killed must be avenged. Even if abortion were outlawed today, our nation will still pay for the blood of the past. The real question is, will we be judged and then restored, or will we be wiped out never to be restored? What form will God's judgment take? (Terry 1988: 161)

Conclusion

While contemporary scholars and many believers see the religiously justified use of violence by Christians to stop abortion as somehow inherently at odds with Christianity, such an argument can only be made by presuming a contemporary, modern version of Christianity as normative. Christians in the larger prolife movement, who believe abortion to be murder, embrace within their worldview the necessary components to arrive at the same conclusion as Mike Bray, Randall Terry, and Paul Hill, including the convictions that abortion is violent, a religious worldview that has at its core the violence of the Crucifixion, and the worship of a wrathful, vengeful deity.

NOTES

1. Scholars have sometimes described the field of Religious Studies as an effort to make the strange familiar and the familiar strange.
2. Isaiah 45:22–23 and repeated in the New Testament in Romans 14:10 and Philippians 2:9.

BIBLIOGRAPHY

Bray, Michael. *A Time to Kill.* Portland, OR: Advocates for Life Publications, 1994.

Ingersoll, Julie. *Building God's Kingdom: Christian Reconstruction in America.* New York: Oxford University Press, forthcoming.

Joyce, Kathryn. *Quiverful: Inside the Biblical Patriarch Movement.* Boston: Beacon Press, 2009.

Juergensmeyer, Mark. *Terror in the Mind of God.* Berkeley: UC Press, 2003 [2000].

Terry, Randall. *Operation Rescue.* Springdale, PA: Whitaker House, 1988.

Terry, Randall. *The Judgment of God: Terrorism, Floods...Droughts...Disasters.* Windsor, NY: The Reformed Library, 1995. www.christiannewswire.com/news/5621612924.html, 1 February 2010, accessed 1/3/2011.

CHAPTER 21

CONFLICTS OVER SACRED GROUND

RON E. HASSNER

NOT far from the Grand Canyon, in the Arizona Navajo Reservation, lie lands contested since 1934 by three Native American tribes, the Hopi, Navajo, and Paiute. This territorial dispute is particularly intractable because of the presence of the Echo Cliffs in the heart of the reservation. The cliffs are sacred to all three tribes, particularly to the Hopi and Paiute who worship the eagles that nest in these cliffs. Their shared devotion has led to considerable friction. The Paiute consider the eagles to be their special guardians so they seek to protect their aeries from harm. The Hopi, on the other hand, regard the eagles as messengers to the gods. At the climax of the midsummer *niman* ceremony, the Hopi facilitate the eagles' return to the gods by smothering them. It is easy to see how these competing practices have strained relations between the two groups.

The Arizona dispute is instructive for several reasons. First and foremost, it illustrates the prevalence of disputes over sacred sites even outside the Middle East, the Balkans, or South Asia, regions usually associated with religious strife. Disputes over sacred sites occur around the globe, from conflicts between Mormon churches over the site of the End of Times in Independence, Missouri, to disputes between Aboriginal tribes and Australian mining companies and clashes between Spanish authorities and Muslim worshipers, who have recently sought to reclaim the Mezquita Cathedral in Cordoba for Islam. Second, the Hopi-Paiute dispute demonstrates the tightly knit relationship between secular territorial disputes and conflicts over holy places. As in Jerusalem, the latter often stand at the center of the former, posing barriers to resolution by introducing religious and ideological motivations into disputes over territory, security, or resources. Finally, disputes such as these serve to sound a note of caution for scholars who, in the post-Huntington age, set high hopes on the natural harmony between religious movements as a recipe for conflict prevention or resolution. Contested sacred sites pose indivisibility challenges that can drive even natural religious allies into violent conflict.

In the following pages, I trace the multiple roots of conflicts over sacred sites based on the type of objective at stake: legitimacy, security, or profit. In the second part of the chapter, I move to explore several aspects that characterize these disputes, regardless of cause. The most important of these attributes is indivisibility: sacred sites cannot be shared to the satisfaction of all parties involved because partition deprives these sites of their value to religious communities. Indivisibility is the primary obstacle that dispute resolution efforts have tried, in vain, to overcome. I examine several of these strategies in the third part of the chapter.

CAUSES OF DISPUTE

Disputes over sacred places are endemic, spanning the globe and encompassing all religious persuasions, from Sri Lanka, where Tamil separatists have targeted Buddhist shrines, to Mexico City, where pre-Columbian shrines coincide with crucifixion reenactment sites, to Kosovo, where Albanian mobs recently demolished the scriptures, icons, records, and structures of 150 Orthodox churches. These disputes vary in scale and intensity, but most can be traced to one of three root causes: a contest over legitimacy, security, or profit.

Legitimacy disputes arise when religious movements bifurcate. As religions split, initially into competing sects and subsequently into rival movements, each of the resulting groups stakes claim to the sacred sites of the parent movement in order to establish its position as the rightful heir. A foothold at a foundational sacred site provides more than just legitimacy, it allows the claimants to monitor access by worshipers, such as pilgrims, and enforce rules that privilege their idiosyncratic preferences. Such competition occurs between Christian denominations in the Church of the Holy Sepulcher in Jerusalem and the Church of the Nativity in Bethlehem; between Shi'a and Sunni Muslims in Mecca and Medina, and between Sepharadi and Ashkenazi Jews vying over the tomb of Rabbi Shimon bar Yohai in the Galilee. In each of these cases, the competing parties wish to assert their primacy by controlling a significant sacred site while striving to exclude rivals whose followers might desecrate the site with their deviant practices.

More complex legitimacy disputes occur where imperial expansion and conquest bring alien religious traditions into conflict. Conquerors who have sought to impose their religion on a local population have learned that demolishing local shrines does little to diminish their influence: Manmade structures that embellish sacred places can be destroyed, but the underlying sacred space cannot be erased. Instead, crafty rulers have sought to repurpose existing shrines by weaving them into their own religious traditions. Just as Christian rulers have striven to neutralize pagan winter rituals by incorporating them into Christmas traditions, so have Christian and Muslim conquerors employed syncretism to defuse the sacred sites of rival religions. The result is a virtual palimpsest as each new occupier seeks to impose its own shrines and accompanying accounts atop its predecessors'. The Temple Mount or Noble Sanctuary in Jerusalem, where Muslim shrines are superimposed on the ruins of the Jewish Temple, exemplifies this type of conflict. Other examples abound at the periphery of empires: in Latin America, where conquistadors located Catholic shrines on indigenous sacred sites; on the Iberian Peninsula, where mosques and churches replaced one another in rapid succession; or in India, where Muslim shrines were often constructed on top of and out of the ruins of demolished Hindu temples.

A second category of disputes arises at times of war when vulnerable combatants, usually insurgents, seek to level the playing field by establishing strongholds in sacred shrines. This exploits both the physical attributes of sacred sites, often the most sturdy, crowded, and centrally located public structures in an urban environment, as well as the local population's bias toward maintaining the physical and spiritual integrity of these shrines. Insurgents who share religious affiliation with the community that worships at a sacred site can enjoy a freedom of movement and access that their adversaries do not benefit from. They may also rely on ancient sanctuary customs that grant the persecuted a safe haven in sacred space. Moreover, if insurgents can persuade worshipers that they are acting in defense of the faith, they may be able to flaunt taboos banning weapons or prohibiting the use of force, a luxury unavailable to their rivals. They may also escape responsibility for damage to the shrine, which will rest primarily with counterinsurgency forces positioned outside the structure.

Such calculations have led Shi'a fighters in Iraq to flee into the great mosques of Najaf and Karbala time and again; prompted Salafi rebels to initiate a hostage crisis in the Grand Mosque in Mecca in 1979; led Sikh insurgents to base their activities in the Harimandir in Amritsar, India, in the 1980s; encouraged Kashmiri insurgents to take over mosques in 1993 and 1995; induced Palestinian gunmen to seek refuge from Israeli forces in the Church of the Nativity in Bethlehem in 2002; impelled Muslim rebels to fight Thai government forces from the safety of the Krue Se Mosque in 2004; and driven Pakistani insurgents into the Lal Masjid in Islamabad in 2007. In all these cases, conflicts involved not claims to ownership of a contested site but unrelated violence centered on a sacred site. The sacred setting acts as a force multiplier for the insurgents inside the shrine while constraining the ability of the besiegers to use force at will.

When the land on which a sacred space is located holds material value for secular forces, a third type of dispute can emerge that has religious repercussions for only one of the parties. The same geological and topographical features that draw religious actors to natural sites, such as caves, lakes, or volcanoes, also draw secular actors to these places. Whereas the secular party to the dispute seeks financial profit from access to the site, the religious party to the dispute struggles to keep the threat of desecration at bay. These disputes rarely involve majority religious movements, who tend to enjoy state protection from predatory business interests. Instead, the targets in these disputes tend to be disenfranchised religious groups, most often indigenous movements. In Canada, the United States, and Australia, natives have been called on time and again to protect their holy sites from tourists, vendors, and developers.

For example, the Anaganu in Australia, the Wintu and Yurok in California, and the Lakota Sioux, Cheyenne, and Kiowa in Wyoming have sought to keep rock climbers off their sacred mountains, the Uluru monolith, Mount Shasta, and Mato Tipila ("Devil's Tower") respectively. The latter dispute has its roots in the 1870s when conflict between the Lakota Sioux and gold prospectors over the sacred Black Hills culminated in the Indian Wars and Custer's "Last Stand." More recently, the Pit River tribe in Northern California has protested plans by an energy company to sap Medicine Lake of the geothermal energy that is believed to underpin its healing powers. Since most of these conflicts are motivated by financial gain, they are usually resolved below the threshold of violence, often by means of side payments.

CHARACTERISTICS OF DISPUTES

Despite the variation in causes, locations, and participants across contested sites, most of these disputes share fundamental characteristics that emerge from the basic nature of sacred space. The most critical of these is the indivisibility of sacred sites that arises from the cohesion, boundaries, and value of sacred space. Most disputes over territory that has no religious value are resolved in one of three ways: partition, sharing, or side payment. These solutions are possible because secular territory is always divisible or fungible. Sacred sites are indivisible because believers perceive the sanctity of these sites to be dependent on their integrity, because believers perceive these sites to have clearly defined and inflexible boundaries and because believers will not relinquish a site in exchange for material substitutes.

Cohesion

The first of these characteristics, cohesion, emerges from the role of sacred space as a representation of the believers' spiritual cosmos. Though sacred shrines are often complex structures consisting of multiple components that can vary in material and design, these different parts serve the combined purpose of conveying a unified message of religious order to believers. Removing or destroying any part of a sacred site is tantamount to dissecting the spiritual universe and thus deprives the place of its meaning. In other words, the division of sacred space amounts to desecration.

Boundaries

The second attribute that renders sacred places indivisible is the rigidity of their boundaries. Because believers can expect to communicate directly with the divine at a sacred site and because the divine is both powerful and dangerous, the site must be distinguished from the surrounding secular space by means of precisely delimited boundaries. Any act that transgresses or blurs those thresholds is an act of desecration that endangers both the violator and the community. To guard against potential outrage, religious communities demarcate the boundaries of their sacred sites in an unambiguous manner, leaving no doubt as to the precise location and dimensions of the site.

Value

Finally, sacred places are indivisible because the religious events that occur there render them irreplaceable in the eyes of believers. By worshipping at the actual place at which a revelation or miracle took place, pilgrims can expect a more immediate interaction with the gods. Consequently, it is impossible for believers to place a value on these sites.

The cohesion, boundaries, and value of sacred space create an indivisibility challenge at each and every sacred site. Once contests over legitimacy, security, and profit provoke conflict over a holy place, this indivisibility precludes the possibility of compromise: Disputes over sacred places become all-or-nothing contests in which parties are willing to go to great (and violent) lengths to secure their sacred rights.

The severity of these conflicts is determined by the religious significance of the site and by its political vulnerability. Though some religious movements provide a clear and explicit ranking of sacred places, most do not. Estimating the relative importance of a sacred place requires assessing its ability to provide key functions to believers: for example, direct access to the divine, insight into religious meanings, the promise of blessing or healing. Reports of a revelation, significant relics, physical evidence of a holy presence (such as various footprints of Vishnu, Jesus, Muhammad, or Buddha), a record of miracles or prayers fulfilled, all these indicate the primacy of a sacred site. Truly central shrines attract pilgrims not only from a single country or region but from across the globe, as Bodh Gaya, Haifa, and Karbala do, for example, for Buddhist, Baha'i, and Shi'a worshipers respectively. When disputes over major shrines erupt, it is not merely a communal duty that compels believers to take action but a sense of obligation to ancestors, future generations, and even the gods. Such stakes leave practitioners with few incentives to make concessions.

A second determinant of conflict intensity is the political vulnerability of a sacred site. Even the most marginal shrines can take on a political significance if they are located in a sectarian conflict zone or near an ethnic fault line. As visible and imposing symbols of a religious group, often teeming with worshipers, such shrines can become targets of sectarian strife, as was the case in the war in Yugoslavia and as continues to be the case in Iraq or the Israeli-Palestinian conflict. Fear about harm to a sacred site can lead a community to elevate the value of the site, as can patriotic, emotional, or economic calculations. Local actors may wish to enhance the salience of a sacred place in order to fulfill political aspirations and mobilize followers by reinforcing political motivations with religious incentives. Political calculations thus complicate any attempt at assessing the likelihood and severity of conflicts over contested sites.

DISPUTE RESOLUTION AND MANAGEMENT

Are conflicts over sacred sites inevitable? Examples of peaceful coexistence at sacred sites are few and far between. Concord is possible at folk sites that have not undergone complete institutionalization and that remain at the margins of a religious landscape. At minor sites that are too insignificant to confer legitimacy on one group or another, the rules that delimit access or behavior may not have been implemented. Should sites like these grow in importance, due to a sudden rise in their popularity or increased sectarian tensions, their vulnerability to conflict is certain to increase as well. Sharing sacred space is only possible where it matters least: At important sacred sites, conflict is inescapable.

In seeking to avoid bloodshed, leaders have pursued three primary strategies: partition, scheduling, and exclusion. The first seeks to impose a division of the physical space to allow two or more groups to worship side by side. Drawing on its physical or legal superiority over the parties to the conflict, the peacemaker either forcibly excludes groups from accessing respective spheres of jurisdiction or merely indicates such spheres on legal documents and maps. The governments of India and Israel, for example, maintain an armed presence in several disputed shrines in order to enforce the partitioning of sacred space into Muslim and Hindu sectors, in the former case, and into Muslim and Jewish sectors, in the latter. In the Church of the Holy Sepulcher in Jerusalem, on the other hand, all rival Christian sects are free to use common space but are keenly aware of a jurisdictional division that assigns exclusive rights and functions to particular sects in particular corners of the church.

The second approach adopted by leaders who seek to mitigate conflict at sacred sites involves scheduling. Here time, rather than space, is divided so that contenders enjoy rights to parts of the site at different times based on an elaborate schedule, designed to keep the parties at bay. Often, as in the Tomb of the Patriarchs in Hebron, partition and scheduling are combined so that particular segments of the shrine are reserved for certain groups at various dates of significance. Finally, exclusion seeks to prevent conflict at a sacred site by barring all religious groups from access.

All three strategies require a third party, usually a government, that enjoys power preponderance over disputants and is willing to decree a solution to the dispute by fiat. Such solutions are inherently unstable. In fact, they are not solutions at all, since they fail to resolve the underlying dispute to the satisfaction of all parties involved. These approaches do not address the need of all groups to control access to and behavior in the entire space, indeed they deprive each party to the dispute of its ability to prevent sacrilege in half of the space all of the time or in all of the space half of the time. Rather than mitigate the conflict, these approaches create incentives for competition over more space and more time as a means for establishing relative legitimacy. By repressing the conflict and antagonizing all parties to the dispute, they create tensions that threaten to erupt as soon as one of the claimants perceives a change in the balance of power.

CONCLUSION

The failure of Israeli, Palestinian, and American negotiators to resolve the conflict over the Temple Mount in Jerusalem in 2000 led to the outbreak of the Al Aqsa Intifada, the collapse of the peace process and the resurgence of violence. The inability of the Indian government to prevent Hindu-Muslim friction in Ayodhya, where Hindu extremists believe a mosque to have been constructed on a Hindu sacred site, led to the violent demolition of the mosque in 1992 and the outbreak of vicious ethnic riots across India and Pakistan. Time and again decision makers, who have insisted on treating conflicts over contested sites like disputes over real estate, have deployed strictly political solutions such as partition, scheduling, and exclusion and have aggravated rather than ameliorated these disputes.

Due to the inherent indivisibility of these conflicts, they defy resolution. Actors can nonetheless manage these conflicts if they are sensitive to the ways in which religion and politics intertwine at sacred sites. Sacred sites translate religious beliefs into political strife but they also convert political preferences into religious convictions. The critical need for precise information about the boundaries and meaning of sacred places during negotiations, and the ability of religious leaders to block compromises when they are excluded from the bargaining table underscore the urgency of involving these elites in negotiations. Religious authorities face the risk of censure if they deviate too much from positions acceptable to their followers, so inducing their cooperation in the administering of holy places can be difficult. Yet under the right circumstances, religious leaders can introduce flexibility into the rules governing holy places and contribute a measure of harmony to contests over holy sites.

BIBLIOGRAPHY

Brereton, Joel P. "Sacred Space." *The Encyclopedia of Religion*. Vol. 12. Ed. Mircea Eliade, 526–535. New York: Macmillan, 1987.

Eliade, Mircea. *Patterns in Comparative Religion*. New York: New American Library, 1974.

Fair, C. Christine and Sumit Ganguly, eds. *Treading on Hallowed Ground: Counterinsurgency Operations in Sacred Spaces*. New York: Oxford University Press, 2008.

Franklin, Robert and Pamela Bunte. "When Sacred Land Is Sacred to Three Tribes: San Juan Paiute Sacred Sites and the Hopi-Navajo-Paiute Suit to Partition the Arizona Navajo Reservation." *Sacred Sites, Sacred Places*. Ed. David Carmichael, Jane Hulbert, Brian Reeves, and Audhild Schanche, 245–258. London: Routledge, 1994.

Friedland, Roger and Richard Hecht. "The Bodies of Nations: A Comparative Study of Religious Violence in Jerusalem and Ayodhya." *History of Religions* 38. 2 (November 1998): 101–149.

Hammer, Leonard, Yitzchak Reiter, and Marshall Breger, eds. *Confrontation and Co-Existence in Holy Places: Religion, Political and Legal Aspects in the Israeli-Palestinian Context*. London: Routledge, 2010.

Hassner, Ron E. *War on Sacred Grounds*. Ithaca, NY: Cornell University Press, 2009.

Holm, Jean and John Bowker, eds. *Sacred Place*. London: Pinter, 1994.

CHAPTER 22

RELIGION AND POLITICAL VIOLENCE

MONICA DUFFY TOFT

RELIGION is resurging the world over and with that resurgence comes renewed concern about the impact of religion and religious actors in relation to political violence. In some places, religious belief and practice are no longer part of people's daily routines, yet in most parts of the world religion remains a vital part of how people live their lives. Religion provides a set of beliefs and ideas about how the world works, along with a set of rituals and practices for acting properly in the world. Those who share these beliefs and practices become members of a community, and often this community demands supreme allegiance from practicing individuals.

This resurgence is so important because religious belief, practice, and allegiance were widely predicted to cease to exist or become obsolete in the modern era. Secularization theory predicted that as societies modernized, religion would die away (see Berger 1967; Casanova 1994; Norris and Inglehart 2011). No longer would there be a demand for religious expression in public life, and even in private life, religious beliefs and ideas would fade away. Religion would also no longer maintain its close interrelationship with the political fabric of societies. Yet this, too, did not happen. On the contrary, today 80 percent of the world's population believes that a god (or gods) exists and this number has increased since the 1980s (Grim and Finke 2010: chapter 7). Moreover, if we look at population trends, the number of those who identify with the major religious traditions increased from about 58 percent of the world's population in 1900 to about 70 percent in 2000 (World Christian Encyclopedia 2001). It is imperative to understand that, although there has been a decline in the level of religious belief and behavior in some places (for example, some states in western Europe), in most of the world religion remains a powerful social, political, and economic force. Furthermore, in many places this resurgence of religion has led to an increase in political violence both within and among communities.

The remainder of this chapter explains why religion is resurging in the political sphere and the conditions under which religion is most likely to cause troubling violence. It locates the source of the problem at the intersection of local politics and three global trends: modernization, democratization, and globalization.[1]

Modernization

Modernization can be understood as the movement from traditional, agrarian society to urban, industrial society. According to a 2007 United Nations Population Fund report, more than half of the world's population—3.3 billion—lives in urban areas. Over the course of the twentieth century, the world's urban population grew from 220 million to 2.8 billion, and by 2030, urban areas are expected to contain 81 percent of the world's population (UNPFA 2007). No longer are most of the world's citizens directly dependent on the land for sustenance. Instead, "modern" industry now supplies most of the world's employment, and wages from industrial labor are then exchanged for subsistence goods. Unfortunately, many of these offer such insufficient wages, these new urbanites live in relative poverty.

Of course, the urbanization that accompanied modernization was largely an artifact of the industrialization of production, including especially agricultural production. Having abandoned their fields for cities, newly urbanized workers lost their connection with the land and also their attachment to the rhythms of day and night and the four seasons. In premodern society, one's identity was contingent on what tribe or linguistic, ethnic, or religious group into which one was born. These were, in turn, often attached to locale. One had little or no control over one's fate, and choosing to engage or disengage from the group was not an option. Modernization was expected to shift this basis of identity, replacing the loss of group attachments and identities with the promise of choice over one's fate. The group would matter less, and the individual would matter more (Chadwick 1975).

As with secularization, most predictions of modernization did not come to fruition. First, the movement from rural to urban was uneven, and even where it did happen, it did not deliver on the promises of individual choice, wealth, and achievement. Second, even in the most modernized societies, group identities remained strong. Increasingly atomized and often working under difficult conditions, first-generation urbanites longed to find meaning attached to their labors and, in wartime, to their considerable sacrifices. Nationalism and religion each served this purpose well. Religious, cultural, and linguistic traditions and customs did not diminish in importance and secularization (the separation of church and state, private and public faith) did not expand as a norm. Even in those states where there was a strong tendency toward a strict separation of church and state, religious belief and practice did not necessarily diminish.

Part of the explanation for the lack of a "fading away" of religion as a meaningful part of people's lives has to do with a misunderstanding of what *secularization* means: religion should not determine government policy and vice versa. It does not mean that people in general will be less religious, rather that even for deeply religious persons, faith will be private. In this sense, secularization has failed because more and more populations worldwide believe religion should play a more public role; and with increasing levels of democratization, the second trend, this preference has had important political consequences. Why?

DEMOCRATIZATION

Part of the reason stems from the process of modernization itself. In the postcolonial period, modernization promised much but appeared to deliver little. In some cases, modernism demanded secularism—for example, Kemalism in Turkey—in others, such as communism and socialism, modernization demanded atheism. Populations in postcolonial regimes afforded their indigenous leaders some time to bring about change. However, their patience wore thin as these regimes displayed high levels of corruption and repression. Alternative forms of political expression and organization were sought. Although many religious actors and institutions fell victims to these regimes, most survived. By the late 1960s they felt ready to challenge existing authorities. For example, aided by Vatican II and its emphasis on freedom and dignity, Roman Catholics challenged political authorities across Latin America. In the 1970s, the tireless criticism and religious reflection of Muslim students and scholars in Iran and elsewhere culminated in the Iranian revolution of 1979. In the 1980s, Pope John Paul II helped delegitimize the communist regimes in Eastern Europe.

Today, people are seeking to integrate religion, religious actors, and politics in unprecedented ways. Consider the adoption of sharia by a number states in Nigeria; the popularity of the National Islamic Front in Algeria (which was denied an electoral victory in the 1989 elections); the 2007 electoral success of the Justice and Development Party, with its roots in political Islam, in secular Turkey; and finally, the Bharatiya Janata Party in India, which has a Hindu nationalist orientation and swiftly gained a substantial following in India in the 1980s and 1990s, creating deep divisions among India's multireligious population and challenging the notion of India as a secular state (Tambiah 1998: chapter 13).

This movement toward a greater voice for religion and religious actors was aided by the global movement for democratization, a trend that started in the

1970s and continues today. Consider data from Freedom House, which, since 1973 has provided a comparative assessment of political rights and civil liberties in the countries of the world.[2] In 1973, 46 percent of the countries surveyed were coded as "not free": These countries imposed severe restrictions on their populations both in terms of political rights and civil liberties. The proportion of these regimes was more than halved to 22 percent by the end of 2008. Today, far more countries —46 percent—are "free," with few or no restrictions on political rights and civil liberties. The remaining 32 percent are partly free. Whereas 43 percent of the world's population lived under "not free" systems in 1980, by mid-2008 that number had dropped to 34 percent. Much of the difference was due to an increase in the world's population living under "free" systems, which increased from 36 percent in mid-1980 to 46 percent in mid-2008.

Because religious actors and institutions tended to remain above the fray (or beneath it), their ideas and networks retained their legitimacy and capacity for mobilization against existing political authority. The failure of modernization and secular ideologies (which were often seen as forces of Western corruptiom), coupled with decreasing levels of repression, allowed for religious voices to be heard and facilitated the religious challenge to the existing political order.

GLOBALIZATION

The intensification of globalization was the final trend that aided this larger political role for religious actors and institutions beginning in the late 1960s and into the 1970s. Although globalization is not a new concept—late nineteenth-century Europe was a highly globalized arena—trends accelerated in the 1970s (World Development Report 2009: chapter 6). In some ways, this acceleration represented a qualitative shift in how relations were ordered in the international arena. The flow of ideas, people, and goods was facilitated by way of technological innovations in transportation (e.g., the container ship) and communications (e.g., cable, satellite, and the Internet). The costs have dropped every year since 1945 as illustrated in figure 22.1 (Frankel 2006).

As with increasing democratization, religious actors could easily capitalize on this increasingly globalizing world. Where lack of legitimacy of existing domestic regimes allowed religious actors to offer themselves as alternative sources of authority, the transnational nature of religious actors allowed them to mobilize and grow support for their cause relatively unhindered. Vatican II was powerful precisely because it globally encouraged the recognition that all humans deserve human rights protections. The reach of the Roman Catholic Church always extended beyond Rome, just as the existence of Islam is not contingent on a particular place but on people. But the costs of projecting influence—especially for

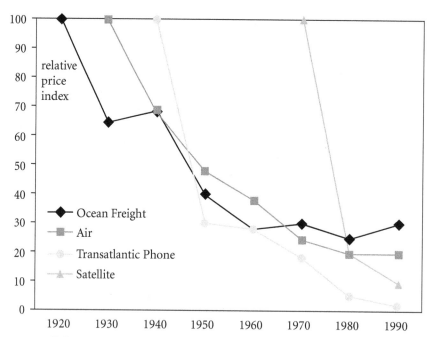

Figure 22.1 Relative transportation and communication costs. (*Source*: The World Bank)

religious groups whose influence depends less on material factors and more on ideational factors—have continued to drop. Thus, when globalization accelerated, religious actors were equipped to harness its associated technologies. Most often it was domestic religious actors challenging the local political order such as in Latin America, but sometimes, as with Pope John Paul II and his critique of the communist regimes in Eastern Europe, the challenge was external.

The transnational nature of religion and religious actors allowed them to become vocal and formidable to existing political authorities in ways that were difficult for local authorities to counter. The low costs of communication enabled passionate, vocal minorities and majorities the ability to set agendas and aggregate efforts to expand.

GLOBAL TRENDS IN RELATION TO RELIGIOUS VIOLENCE

Given the combined impact of modernization, democratization, and globalization, we should perhaps be unsurprised by a recent increase in religion-based or religious violence, including both terrorism and civil wars.

According to Bruce Hoffman, before the 1980s—religiously inspired terrorist organizations simply did not exist in the twentieth century. After the 1980s and well into the 1990s, the number of religious terrorist groups increased exponentially (Hoffman 2006: 81–82). The same trends could be seen in the nature of civil wars,[3] in which the proportion of civil wars with a religious basis has increased each decade: From about 22 percent of all conflicts started in the 1960s, 36 percent in the 1970s, 41 percent in the 1980s, 45 percent in the 1990s, increasing to 50 percent in the last decade. So, while there has been a decrease in the number of civil war onsets and a fair number of wars have been settled since the end of the Cold War, those wars that are active or might emerge are more likely to have a religious basis; and by "religious basis," I mean the conflict features religion as either central or peripheral to the fight.

In wars in which religion is central, the combatants had to be fighting over whether the state or a region of the state would be ruled according to a specific religious tradition, as in the cases of Afghanistan, Chad, and Sudan, all of which witnessed wars over whether Islamic law (sharia) would be supreme. In wars in which religion is peripheral, combatants were forced or compelled to identify with a specific religious tradition (e.g., former Yugoslavia involving Bosnian Muslims-Islam, Croats-Catholicism, and Serbs-Orthodox Christianity) and group themselves accordingly. The key to these wars was that the rule or dominance of a specific religious tradition mattered but was not the object of contention. From 1940 to 2010, there were a total of forty-four religious civil wars: Twenty-seven featured religion centrally, and seventeen featured religion peripherally.

Although religiously based civil wars have constituted only about one-third of all civil wars since 1940, there are a number of worrisome aspects to them: They tend to last longer than secular civil wars (about two years longer), are more deadly to noncombatants, are less amenable to settlement by negotiation, and are more likely to recur than nonreligious wars (Toft 2007: 97–131).

Religion in civil wars has had these effects for two reasons. First, religion often leads to uncompromising positions. Even given some liberty in translation and interpretation over time, the texts of the First Testament, Second Testament, and Qu'ran, for example, limit the conduct of followers in important ways (see Fish 2002).[4] Each of these three texts serves as a guide to conduct approved or mandated by a supreme being. Conduct departing from these guidelines puts a follower at risk of losing God's favor (the risks and penalties vary depending on the nature of the breach of conduct). Thus, when followers believe they are being asked to violate the key tenets of their faith as dictated or outlined in holy scripture, they are less likely to do so even when it might result in what most would consider a better outcome, such as peace.

Second, as a rule, religion encourages followers to discount their physical survival. The logic is simple. The physical self is mortal and thus temporary, but the religious self is potentially immortal and eternal. If belief is strong enough, it can therefore become rational to sacrifice the temporary and mortal to obtain the eternal and immortal (see Anderson 2006: 9–12; Toft 2003).[5] In the Christian and

Muslim traditions, it is believed that self-sacrifice in religiously prescribed conduct will be rewarded by eternal, superphysical existence in a heaven or paradise (see Juergensmeyer 2000).

Taken together, each aspect of religion as it relates to violence diminishes the desire for bargaining and self-preservation, two key pillars of the state system as established at the Peace of Westphalia in 1648. A rational person is expected to assess the tangible costs and benefits of action or inaction and then maximize his or her utility by choosing the course of action that will result in the highest likelihood of benefit with the lowest risk or cost. But zealots and fanatics (secular labels for dedicated followers of religion) will often diverge from this system, choosing instead to sacrifice tangible benefits for intangible ones, often to the point of sacrificing their own lives. Thus a secular actor (or state) can be coerced or deterred by the threat of destruction; whereas a religious believer (or theocracy) may be impossible to coerce or deter in the same way (see Toft 2006).

This is why the states system—a system, it must be observed, that had its birth in Europe following thirty years of religious wars of the utmost brutality—is so inimical to theocracy, or the idea that religious and secular authority should be combined (see Krasner 1999; Philpott 2001; Philpott 2002). States must act rationally and predictably on the basis of tangible costs and benefits; this is why European states sought to purge religion from governing affairs after 1648 (see Toulmin 1990; Hirschman 1977).[6] It is also for this reason that religious civil wars (and theocratic states such as Iran) are of concern to contemporary state policymakers disproportionate to their numbers. If the twin pillars of interstate stability and predictability weaken or collapse, the possibility of the interstate system entering a new era of instability is a great concern (see Huntington 1996).

A final trend worth considering is the disproportionately large presence of Islam in religious civil wars: Islam has been centrally or peripherally involved in more than 80 percent of civil wars since 1940. Of the ten civil wars that occurred among combatants with the same faith, nine of them involved Islam. Of those that engaged combatants from different faith traditions, Islam was involved in two-thirds of them. Why is Islam overrepresented in civil wars?

The first reason is the failure of the modernization of economies and the lack of secularization in most Muslim states. In a number of Muslim-majority states, secular elites failed to deliver on their promises of development, equity, and accountability. Often educated in the West and promulgating secular ideologies of socialism and communism, these elites failed to bring prosperity and equality. The Shah of Iran is a prime case. Bolstered by Western governments and ideas, the political system under his control developed a reputation as inept, corrupt, and disconnected from the people. After years of hardship, demonstrations gave way to revolutions and eventually an Islamic republic. Iran is not alone here. A number of countries experienced civil discord and war as part of the democratization trends since the 1970s with religious actors playing a central role: the National Islamic Front in Algeria, the Muslim Brotherhood in Egypt, and the Islamic Renaissance Party in Tajikistan are just a few examples.

Each of these involved Muslims competing with fellow Muslims over the proper role of Islamic values vis-à-vis the state. Although these were local conflicts, they had global resonance, especially after the revolution in Iran and then the emergence civil war in Afghanistan and the Soviet invasion in 1979. The invasion was viewed as an opportunity for Muslims "to defend a Muslim country from an attack by 'godless' Russian soldiers" (Moghadam 2008: 117). The defeat of the Soviet Union unified moderate and radical Muslims by legitimating the efforts of those who traveled great distances to defend the broader Islamic community against what was perceived as corrupt external forces.

The movement from a local to a broader global, transnational fight also calls to mind Sudan and the Islamist coup that led to the outbreak of the second civil war. Sudan has suffered two civil wars between the North and South, from 1956 to 1972 and from 1983 to 2005. The first civil war was largely fought over autonomy for the southern part of Sudan. Religion was only peripheral in the first war, resulting from the fact that the North was largely Muslim and viewed as dominant and the South was largely non-Muslim (animist and Christian) and subordinate. Southerners wanted more autonomy over their affairs and secured them after the war with the signing of the Addis Ababa Accords in 1972. The North, however, abrogated the treaty in 1983, unilaterally dividing southern Sudan into three regions with diminished and limited powers, and implementing an Arab and Islamist campaign that imposed Islamist values and codes throughout all of Sudan, including in the non-Muslim South (Johnson 2003: 79–80). The government's policies stemmed in part from its alliance with the National Islamic Front, which supported the regime so long as it imposed an Islamic constitution. Legitimacy and financial support came from outside Sudan's borders from fellow Muslim and Arab states. Yet, owing to its own internally strong Islamist political agenda, Sudan managed during the 1980s and 1990s to become a major player in the global Islamist terrorist movement, eventually leading to a 1991 invitation to Osama bin Laden that allowed him to operate his terrorist network from there until he was forced to leave in 1996 under international pressure (Collins 2008: 196–197).

The transnational dimensions of religion and, in particular, Islam in the current era thus explains why religious civil wars tend to begin local and become more global. A key factor, then, is the dissemination of ideas. The literature on Islam and terrorism has established the link between violent conflict and faith as embodied in the concept of jihad. A bid for increased religious legitimacy in this context means increased access to arms, cash, and fighters; who will, as part of a religious obligation, travel to the site of conflict and support whichever leader has done the best job of establishing his religious credentials. This is what happened in Afghanistan and Sudan. By contrast, one could hardly expect a similar appeal, in a current or modern Christian religious context, since the Thirty Years War intercedes between the Crusades (when Christians were able to increase their chances of going to heaven or at least expiate guilt for past sins by participating in an overtly religious struggle) and the present. We can make this example concrete by imagining that Sudanese Christian leaders, under siege in southern Sudan, wanted to gain the support of Britain, France, or the United States.

What should be the ideal content of that appeal? Would young men from France, Russia, and the United States stir themselves to go to Sudan to fight in response to a Christian appeal (Phares 1998)?[7] Nor would we expect the United States or United Kingdom, for example, to send military support to southern Sudan due to the religious persecution of Christians by Muslims.[8] But because Islam had no Thirty Years War, the Islamic world did not inherit the West's now instinctive rejection of the idea that violence in the name of religion enhances one's religious credibility (or more formally, has a positive utility), and church and state should be the same. If this is correct, then it helps to explain the account of why Islam today is more often involved in civil wars and in other forms of violence (such as terrorism) than are other religions. First, globalization has been intensifying. Second, the emergence of a new doctrine or interpretation of jihad has managed to capture the imaginations of adherents who are prepared to fight to defend their fellow Muslims.

Yet the global traction of a particular meaning of jihad should not diminish the importance of local grievances to explain why some corners of the world are more susceptible than others to external or transnational ideas and resources. Consider the conflicts and civil wars that emerged in the Caucasus after the dissolution of the Soviet Union in the 1990s. Yes, fighters from the Caucasus aided one another in their fights in Abkhazia and Chechnya, and some made their way as far as Kosovo (and then Iraq and Afghanistan). However, the first Chechen War (1994–1996), like the first war in Sudan, was largely a fight over national autonomy and self-determination. Chechens wanted control over what they perceived to be Chechen territory. Religion was a factor but only peripherally in that ethnic Russians are largely Orthodox Christians, while ethnic Chechens are predominantly Muslim. Religion did not play a significant role in the first war.

The role of religion in the second war (1999–) is more debatable given the alliance of Chechen commander Shamil Basayev with Omar ibn al-Khattab, a foreign-born guerrilla fighter who had fought in Afghanistan and Tajikstan. In this case, Khattab's invitation seemed to be one more of expediency and resources rather than the formation of an additional front in the global jihadist struggle. Three bits of evidence support this. First, it is not clear how dedicated Basayev was to the Islamist cause. Interviews with those close to him indicated that he was more interested in political power and challenging the political leadership in Chechnya (then president Aslan Maskhadov) and in preparing for another possible confrontation with Russia.[9] Second, the Chechens themselves follow a form of Islam that is more local, tribal, and based in Sufi traditions. The notion of adopting a unified, externally defined set of ideas (e.g., Wahhabism and Salafism) by the Chechen population writ large is somewhat fanciful. As a people, Chechens have time and again fought to be free of external control (and this might explain why Basayev and Khattab moved north to Dagestan where there seemed to be more sentiment in support of Wahhabism). Third, data on violence in the region reveals that religion has played only a modest role in the second war. From 2000 to 2008, the proportion of attacks that can be identified as Islamist has ranged from 0 to 0.15 over the entire period, while the remainder—including separatist attacks, ethnic clashes, government operations, and the activities of criminal gangs—has not been explicitly religious (see Toft and Zhukov 2010).[10] Only 4 percent of the violent attacks that took place on Russian soil in the Caucasus could be tied directly to those connected with Islam. Ninety-six percent were driven by factors having little to do with an Islamist agenda. Further analysis of the data reveals that a good portion of it results from the Russian government's acts of repression: Grievance over government policy seems to be driving the violence.[11]

Thus, despite the efforts of such global jihadists as Khattab (who was killed in March 2002 in Doha) and the pronouncements of the Russian government that it is fighting one of the fronts of the global war on terror, the war in Chechnya has remained largely a local affair and one rooted in local concern.

CONCLUSION

Two of the most important trends of our times involve religion. Globalization (consider the impact of the container ship on social and economic life in the developed world since 1980) has dramatically lowered the costs of shaping and disseminating ideas and resources. As a result, groups whose power resides primarily in the realm of ideas have been greatly empowered by access to the Internet and by the reduced costs of moving people and goods long distances. Religious groups—in particular minority religious groups—have benefited most of all.

Second, religion-inspired violence is on the rise, and given the centuries long investment in killing technology as a way to both enhance and protect against state coercion, it becomes clearer why states are ill positioned to respond. Responding effectively to religiously inspired violence demands mastery of the power of ideas, which in most Western states has been an extragovernmental power: In the United States it is Hollywood and Madison Avenue, for example, that have specialized in framing ideas and shaping beliefs (generally for profit). States have always relied on a monopoly of legitimate violence within a bounded territory. But globalization and the power of persuasion have caused this authority to be discounted: The power to kill remains an important foundation of state power, but when directed against persons of strong faith, it is unlikely to axiomatically cause compliance. A person of faith may actually seek out death as a religious obligation or as an act of defiance of a state's authority.

The solution to religiously inspired violence is simple but not easy. It demands the combination of religious authority with a better idea—a counterinterpretation of the legitimacy of acts of violence in defense of faith. Understanding the nature of that authority and the content of the countermessage cannot happen until the world's established state governments abandon their attempts to confront religious violence with state violence and turn toward countering religious violence with a more refined message and nuanced strategy.

NOTES

1. This article draws heavily on arguments made previously in Timothy Samuel Shah and Monica Duffy Toft, "Why God Is Winning," *Foreign Policy* (July–August 2006) and Monica Duffy Toft, Daniel Philpott, and Timothy Samuel Shah, *God's Century: Resurgent Religion and Global Politics* (New York: W. W. Norton, 2011).
2. Data are available online at: http://www.freedomhouse.org.
3. A civil war is defined as large-scale violence that occurs within the border of a state (at the start of the war) between at least two sets of organized combatants, resulting in at least 1,000 casualties on average per year of the war, and the possibility that the stronger side will suffer casualties.
4. Logically, we should therefore expect theocracies to be much more authoritarian than nontheocracies, because when church and state are fused, opposition to state policy becomes tantamount to opposition to god. On the other hand, a recent study of the alleged relationship between Islam, in particular, and "authoritarianism," found only one causal link between the antidemocratic character of Islamic states and Islam as a religion: the subordination of women.
5. Religion is not the only system of beliefs that can have this effect. Nationalism shares some of this in promising that one's sacrifice will help to guarantee the survival of the nation or group. However, while both promise the perpetuation of the group, nationalism does not promise individual salvation, whereas religion does.
6. Of course the transition was not complete in all corners of Europe, with some states establishing national churches and others allowing sectarian political parties to emerge in the nineteenth century. Nevertheless, the general trend was toward limiting, if not eliminating, the influence of religion in state policy.
7. Some of these calls have been made, but fellow Christians in the United States, for instance, have resorted to little more than shaming: Violence is not part of the struggle.
8. On the contrary, the most useful type of argument for a beleaguered combatant seeking support from the West to make today—be it an incumbent government or rebel group—is "ally in the war against [Islamic fundamentalist] terror."
9. Interviews by author with prominent Chechens and scholars of the region in Moscow, June 2008.
10. Out of nearly 28,000 violent incidents, only 1,200 of them had a religious basis, either involving religious actors or displaying religious motivation as evidenced by stated objectives of the fighters or the chosen targets.
11. The analysis confirmed that the use of repression by the government is associated with a significant increase in the probability of Islamist violence.

BIBLIOGRAPHY

Anderson, Benedict. *Imagined Communities: Reflections on the Origin and Spread of Nationalism.* London and New York: Verso Books, 2006.

Barrett, David B., George T. Kurian, and Todd M. Johnson, eds. *World Christian Encyclopedia: A Comparative Survey of Churches and Religions in the Modern World.* 2nd ed. New York: Oxford University Press, 2001.

Berger, Peter L. *The Sacred Canopy: Elements of a Sociological Theory of Religion.* New York: Anchor, 1967.

Casanova, José. *Public Religions in the Modern World*. Chicago: University of Chicago Press, 1994.

Chadwick, Owen. *The Secularization of the European Mind in the Nineteenth Century*. Cambridge, UK: Cambridge University Press, 1975.

Chechens and Scholars of the Region. Interviews by author in Moscow. June 2008.

Collins, Robert O. *A History of Modern Sudan*. Cambridge: Cambridge University Press, 2008.

Fish, M. Steven. "Islam and Authoritarianism." *World Politics* 55.1 (2002): 4–37.

Frankel, Jeffrey. "What Do Economists Mean by Globalization? Implications for Inflation and Monetary Policy." Academic Consultants Meeting, September. Vol. 28 (2006).

Freedom House. "Freedom in the World Comparative and Historical Data." *Freedom House*. Accessed at http://www.freedomhouse.org/sites/default/files/inline_images/FIW%202012%20Booklet – Final.pdf.

Grim, Brian J., and Roger Finke. *The Price of Freedom Denied: Religious Persecution and Conflict in the Twenty-First Century*. Cambridge, UK: Cambridge University Press, 2010.

Hirschman, Albert O. *Passions and Interests: Political Party Concepts of American Democracy*. Westport, CT: Greenwood Publishing Group, 2002.

Hoffman, Bruce. *Inside Terrorism*. New York: Columbia University Press, 2006.

Huntington, Samuel P. *The Clash of Civilizations and the Remaking of World Order*. New York: Simon and Schuster, 1996.

Johnson, Douglas Hamilton. *The Root Causes of Sudan's Civil Wars*. Bloomington: Indiana University Press, 2003.

Juergensmeyer, Mark. *Terror in the Mind of God: The Global Rise of Religious Violence,* 3rd ed. Berkeley: University of California Press, 2003.

Krasner, Stephen D. *Sovereignty: Organized Hypocrisy*. Princeton, NJ: Princeton University Press, 1999.

Moghadam, Assaf. *The Globalization of Martyrdom: Al Qaeda, Salafi Jihad, and the Diffusion of Suicide Attacks*. Baltimore, MD: Johns Hopkins University Press, 2011.

Norris, Pippa, and Ronald Inglehart. *Sacred and Secular: Religion and Politics Worldwide*. Cambridge, UK: Cambridge University Press, 2011.

Phares, Walid. "The Sudanese Battle for American Opinion." *Middle East Quarterly* 5.1 (1998): n. pag. Web. 18 January 2012.

Philpott, Daniel. *Revolutions in Sovereignty: How Ideas Shaped Modern International Relations*. Princeton, NJ: Princeton University Press, 2001.

Philpott, Daniel. "The Challenge of September 11 to Secularism in International Relations." *World Politics* 55.1 (2002): 66–95.

Rigg, Jonathan et al. "The World Development Report 2009 'Reshapes Economic Geography': Geographical Reflections." *Transactions of the Institute of British Geographers* 34.2 (2009): 128–136. Web. 18 January 2012.

Shah, Timothy Samuel, and Monica Duffy Toft. "Why God Is Winning." *Foreign Policy* 155 (2006): 38–43.

Tambiah, Stanley J. "The Crisis of Secularism in India." *Secularism and Its Critics*. Ed. Rajeev Bhargava, chapter 14. New Delhi: Oxford University Press, 1998.

Toft, Monica Duffy, Daniel Philpott, and Timothy Samuel Shah. *God's Century: Resurgent Religion and Global Politics*. W. W. Norton & Company, 2011.

Toft, Monica Duffy and Yuri Zhukov. "Violence in the Caucasus: Global Jihad or Local Politics?" A paper prepared for presentation at the annual International Studies Association Conference. New Orleans, February 2010.

Toft, Monica Duffy. "Getting Religion? The Puzzling Case of Islam and Civil War."
    International Security 31.4 (2007): 97–171.
Toft, Monica Duffy. "Issue Indivisibility and Time Horizons as Rationalist
    Explanations for War." Security Studies 15.1 (January 2006): 34–69.
Toft, Monica Duffy. *The Geography of Ethnic Violence: Identity, Interests, and the
    Indivisibility of Territory.* Princeton, NJ: Princeton University Press, 2003.
Toulmin, Stephen. *Cosmopolis: The Hidden Agenda of Modernity.* Chicago:
    University of Chicago Press, 1990.
United Nations Population Fund (UNPFA). "State of World Population 2007—
    Online Report: United Nations Population Fund." Web. 18 January 2012.

CHAPTER 23

RITUALS OF DEATH AND REMEMBRANCE

SUSUMU SHIMAZONO AND MARGO KITTS

DEATH is more than a biological condition. From the perspectives of religious studies, it is rather a socially constructed condition and a nexus for cultural themes that emerge at the site of the corpse and burial. These vary, of course, as do conceptions about when death occurs. In some societies death is reached in an instant, whereas for others it is a process that persists for years after the end of brain activity. The religious implications are so vast that historian William Pinch defines religion as the way through death (Pinch 2006: 15). This chapter will survey death rituals from ancient times to the present. Although death rituals are invariably shaped by ideologies of afterlives or heavenly rewards, historical records for these are often scant. Thus, the survey will be restricted to corpse treatments across traditions. These will be shown to range from secondary burials (e.g., after collecting bones from high altars) to cremations to complete interments to elaborate ceremonies replete with animal and/or human sacrifices.

First, as mentioned, the interval between the last breath and definitive death varies from culture to culture. For instance, the Dayak of Borneo shelter corpses in their homes or in temporary burial sites for intervals of six months to two years, after which a final ceremony and burial are conducted (Hertz 1960, 31). Melanesian and Madagascar communities see the soul as remaining weak while the body decays and, thus, perceive this period as an intermediate stage prior to the soul's eventual departure (Hertz, 1960, 47). In Thailand, the more important or wealthy bodies may be held in Buddhist temples for as long as a year to allow time to ritually dedicate sufficient merit to the deceased. In similar fashion, Hindus in Andhra Pradesh, India, perceive cremation as part of this intermediate stage and perform the *musivayanam* ritual on behalf of the deceased for ten days after the cremation (Knipe 2003). Among Tibetan Buddhists, rituals are held for forty-nine days while the deceased person travels through *bardo,* the intermediate state of existence. From these examples, we see that death may be a drawn-out process, wherein several death rituals precede the final one.

In contrast to these fairly elaborate rituals, our material evidence suggests that death rituals were unusual for ordinary people in ancient times. The pyramids in Egypt and the tombs of ancient kings in East Asia are spectacular, while ordinary graves are not, nor are they even marked. Corpse treatments for ordinary people in western and central Asia might have included exposing bodies on platforms for defleshing by carnivorous birds, a practice commonly referred to as sky burial and still practiced by some Zoroastrians and Tibetan Buddhists. Corpse interment under floors is evident in Mesopotamian excavations (Zorn, n.d.), whereas in the Mediterranean milieu we have evidence for cremations, shaft burials, and grave site processions, gifts, and meals, as well as animal sacrifices. But rarely do we find, as in the royal cemeteries at Ur or Jiangxi, significant precious artworks and multitudes of corpses reputedly belonging to the attendants of royalty. The Ur and Jiangxi cemeteries provide, of course, well-known examples of human sacrifices, or as such they are usually conceived.

Not surprisingly, the archeology of human sacrifice at graves is hugely controversial. Some evidence is hotly contested—as in the reputed child sacrifices at the Tophet in Carthage. Yet in the Mediterranean region, provocative finds have been invoked to support the reported sacrifice of twelve Trojan boys on the pyre of Patroklos in the Iliad (see, e.g., Hughes 1991, Coldstream 2003, Antonaccio 1995). Hypothetical motives for human sacrifice vary, from service in the afterlife to ritualistic displays of revenge (Hughes 1991, Kitts 2008). Classical tragedy represents human sacrifice at graves (e.g., the sacrifice of Polyxena, ostensibly a bride for Achilles [Eur. Hecuba 35–45]), and the Bible reports, if not explicit grave site sacrifices, at least the passing of children through the fires of Molech, a reputed Canaanite god of death (see, e.g., Levenson 1993, Niditch 1993)—as if the children were gifts. Since reports of child sacrifice also serve propagandistic purposes when attributed to aberrant kings (2 Kings 23:10) or when the prophets lambast the practice (e.g., Is. 57, Ez. 20:27–31, Jer. 30), literary evidence for human sacrifice is rarely deemed sufficient historical support. Strangely, the controversy is reversed in the evidence from Zhou-period China, since literature denies the practice, while archeology attests to it (Minford and Lau 2000: 173).

As may be suggested by the massive tombs at Ur, Jiangxi, and the terracotta army buried with the first emperor of Qin, tombs for the dead frequently come to transcend the commemoration of the buried individuals, spurring instead a variety of cultural sentiments. The tendency for grave monuments to become rallying points for religious, ethnic, and national sentiment is evident from early times. Martyr tales are still recounted at grave sites associated with suffering saints in the Christian and Muslim spheres (see, e.g., Brown 1981), and sites commemorating contemporary carnage—monuments in Cambodia, Rwanda, Kosovo, Bosnia-Herzegovina, Nazi-occupied Poland, and the World Trade Center—continue to attract pilgrimages, to incite reflection, or to inflame ethnic memories and calls for revenge. From the tomb of the unknown soldier to various walls of martyrs, shrines to national war dead have been erected on virtually every major continent. Clearly, grave monuments serve more purposes than simply the salutation of the dead.

Asian burial practices show a unique trajectory of development. Cremation appears primordial in India. Holy locales along the Ganges riverbank, such as Varanasi (Benares), are well known to be gathering places for persons waiting to die. Typically today, the corpse is burned together with wood picked up from the riverbanks, and its ashes are poured directly into the river. There is no urn. This is said to reflect the Hindu belief that a return to the source of life, or at least emancipation from earthly materiality, can be achieved through this treatment. Elsewhere in Asia, such as Thailand, Buddhist monks ritually separate the spirit from the body at the time of death.

However, over time Asian traditions have come to include the practice of entombing corpses, or relics of corpses, belonging to persons of high social or religious status. Hindu and Buddhist communities have erected pagodas, *cettiyas,* and stupas, raised mounds that are claimed to contain the relics of deceased monks or venerated individuals. As in Christian and Islamic cultures, the tombs of saints are thronged as sites for pilgrimage. Buddhist stupas, in particular, are felt to preserve the lives of saints. As long as a stupa is not demolished, the saint whose bones lie within "remains alive and—importantly—his community has a continuing shelter and refuge" (Schopen 2003: 133). Relic veneration in Asia continues into the present time, as it does at some Christian sites in Europe and the Middle East.

Broadly speaking, over the process of modernization, the practice of individual burial has come to prevail across continents. Personal graves, family plots, and large-scale cemeteries dot countrysides on all continents, and burial has become a major business. The right to use the space is prearranged. In some cases, mausoleums announce the wealth and status of a family. Much of this is probably due to Western influence, an indirect consequence of an emphasis on individualism. In Sri Lanka, for instance, the regular practice of burying corpses in unmarked graves has changed over the last forty years. In the 1970s, a few wealthy villagers began to erect grave markers in memory of their deceased. This practice spread to the middle and lower classes in the 1980s and 1990s (Walters 2003: 122). Today tombs for individuals and families are increasingly widespread.

The most common forms of corpse disposal in the world today are earth burial and cremation. After a person's death, the body is purified and adorned with a special costume. Then the corpse is either buried or cremated.

Earth burial tends to be associated with a hope for eternal life and a fear that the person's essence may be destroyed. Christians and Muslims expect the body to go to their god after posthumous judgment, and it is the norm for them to leave corpses as they are. In Islamic regions, the body is dressed in white and laid with the head directed toward Mecca. In some areas, Muslims place tree branches on each side of the corpse with the expectation that these will help the deceased stand up after the judgment. The grandeur of Islamic burial varies from one place to another. Stately tombs are common in Egypt, while in Saudi Arabia burials are marked often by simple stones on the ground.

In the traditional Chinese societies in which earth burials prevail, the respect given to the corpses reflects Confucian philosophy and ancestor worship. In Taiwan, Confucian or Daoist priests and Buddhist monks may be involved in funerals, and their rituals are seen to console the spirit of the deceased. In Korea, kin organizations build tombs and conduct respectful funeral services. Rituals for mourning and consoling the soul and visits to the tomb are conducted for many years. In Japan, where Buddhism has deeply permeated the culture, cremation and burial remain parallel practices. Even when bodies are cremated, fine graves may be built for the ashes. The traditions of visiting graves and holding memorial services have been ongoing for a long time.

In modern times, the traditional expression of social status through elaborate funeral ceremonies and the erection of large tombs is giving way in some countries to a movement toward simplification. This is probably due to the weakening of traditional beliefs as well as a mounting resistance to conspicuous displays of wealth in times of sorrow. In the Western Christian sphere, the simplification of funerals and tombs is notable among Protestant communities in particular. The Catholic communities, on the other hand, perhaps because of their ethnic pluralities, exhibit a variety of funerary behaviors, from gathering at wakes to the performative displays of professional mourners.

The most notable modern change is the spread of cremation. For spatial and practical reasons, North Americans and Europeans have advocated cremation since the nineteenth century. At the end of the twentieth century, the ratio of cremation to interment exceeded 50 percent in Britain, Germany, and the Scandinavian countries. A variety of forms of cremation occur now. Some people put ashes in an urn and bury it in the ground, while others store urns in columbariums. Occasionally, the ashes of more than one person are laid together. Alternatively, ashes may be scattered in special places.

In Korea, Taiwan, and expatriated Chinese communities, where cremation was infrequent in the past, cremation has rapidly increased since the end of the twentieth century. During the latter half of the twentieth century in Japan, almost all families chose to cremate their dead. Japanese urns traditionally are buried underground in family grave sites marked by stone monuments. The most recent styles of burial in Japan include ash scattering in the sea, laying ashes in a joint repository along with the ashes of family members, and tree funerals, wherein ashes are scattered in a forest and a memorial tree is planted. These trends imply a substantial shift from more elaborate Asian burial practices and a fluid adaptability to new situations. In Buddhist societies throughout Southeast Asia, cremation continues to be the preferred death ritual.

In surprising contrast, eastern European, Russian, and mainland Chinese funerals, which were simplified during the period under socialist governments, have grown increasingly elaborate since the collapse of the Union of Soviet Socialist Republics (USSR) and the move toward capitalism in China. A groundswell of sentiment to revive traditional funerals and graves shows that burial rituals reflect more than individual reactions to loss and choices about commemoration. They also reflect a variety of themes unique to particular histories and social pressures.

From ancient times to the current day, conceptions of death and the etiquette of remembrance converge in ceremonies associated with corpse disposal. Death rituals remain the locus for expression of a variety of cultural themes unique to particular historical, religious, and social exigencies. Into the future, doubtlessly, death rituals will continue to mark religious dispositions and sacred spaces.

ACKNOWLEDGMENT

Our gratitude to Michael Jerryson for his assistance with the research for this chapter.

BIBLIOGRAPHY

Antonaccio, Carla M. *An Archaeology of Ancestors.* London: Rowman and Littlefield Publishers, 1995.

Brown, Peter. *The Cult of the Saints: Its Rise and Function in Latin Christianity.* Chicago: University of Chicago Press, 1981.

Coldstream, J. N. *Geometric Greece 900–700 BC*, 2nd ed. London: Routledge, 2003.

Davies, Douglas J. and Lewis H. Mates, eds. *Encyclopedia of Cremation.* Farnham, UK: Ashgate, 2005.

Glennys Howarth and Oliver Leaman, eds. *Encyclopedia of Death and Dying,* New York: Routledge, 2001.

Hertz, Robert. *Death and the Right Hand.* Translated by Rodney and Claudia Needham. Glencoe, IL: The Free Press, 1960.

Hughes, Dennis. *Human Sacrifice in Ancient Greece.* New York:Routledge, 1991.

Kitts, Margo. "Funeral Sacrifices and Ritual Leitmotifs in Iliad 23." *Transformations in Sacrificial Practices.* Eds. E. Stavrianopoulou, Cl. Ambos and A. Michaels, 217–240. Performanzen Band 15. Berlin: LIT-Verlag, 2008, 217–240.

Knipe, David. "When a Wife Dies First: The *Musivayanam* and a Female Brahman Ritualist in Coastal Andhra." In *The Living and the Dead: Social Dimensions in South Asian Religions.* Ed. Liz Wilson, 51–94. New York: State University of New York Press, 2003.

Levinson, Jon. *The Death and Resurrection of the Beloved Son.* New Haven, CT: Yale University Press, 1993.

Minford, John and Joseph S. M. Lau, eds. *Classical Chinese Literature: An Anthology of Translations, Volume 1: From Antiquity to the Tang Dynasty.* New York: Columbia University Press, 2000.

Niditch, Susan. *War in the Hebrew Bible.* New York: Oxford University Press, 1993.

Pinch, William. *Warrior Ascetics and Indian Empires*. New Delhi: Cambridge University Press, 2006.

Schopen, Gregory. "The Suppression of Nuns and the Ritual Murder of Their Special Dead in Two Buddhist Monastic Texts." In *The Living and the Dead: Social Dimensions in South Asian Religions*. Ed. Liz Wilson, 127–158. New York: State University of New York Press, 2003.

Walters, Jonathan S. "Deanimating and Reanimating the Dead in Rural Sri Lanka." In *The Living and the Dead: Social Dimensions in South Asian Religions*. Ed. Liz Wilson, 113–126. New York: State University of New York Press, 2003.

Zorn, Jeff. "More on Mesopotamian Burial Practices in Ancient Israel." Retrieved May 22, 2011 from http://www.arts.cornell.edu/jrz3/More_on_MesopotamianHQ.pdf.

CHAPTER 24

VIOLENT DEATH IN RELIGIOUS IMAGINATION

MARGO KITTS

FREUD once pondered our deep suspicion that death is not natural, but rather derives from a crime; famously he traced this to the Oedipal complex and to the unconscious origins of religion. Whatever the true origins of religion, our intuition that death is unnaturally violent is supported by numerous aetiological myths, some of which identify death as what is wrong with life on earth—for example, primordial errors and homicides—while others make death what is right, for example, cosmogonic sacrifices, *Chaoskampf*s, redemptive death and rebirth. On top of these, across the world we find martyr legends and narratives of suicide that do more than salute the dead. They strike a deep chord, sometimes inspiring holy acts of lethal violence that target self or others. All of this impels us to ask: Why the recurrent theme of violent death in religious imagination?

This short chapter will survey selected religious myths of violent death under three rubrics: when death is primordially wrong; when violent death is cosmically right; and when violent death, particularly in the form of suicide, is enshrined as martyrdom. It will conclude with a brief reflection on religious imagination and its peculiar obsessions. There are few themes in religious studies that justify a sweeping overview, but violent death is recurrent enough to be one of them.

WHEN DEATH IS WRONG

The motif of death as a consequence of human error is hard to miss in biblical literature. Whether created last (Gen. 1) or first (Gen. 2) of creatures, humans by the end of Genesis 3 have won alienation from their creator, one another, and the earth to which they shall return (3:17–24). In Genesis and some apocryphal books, death comes into the world quite simply as punishment for a crime. Despite no explicit statement about primeval immortality (at least in Genesis), its loss is inferred when Adam and Eve are driven out of Eden so that they do not reach out and eat from the tree of life and live forever (3:22). Their disobedience and expulsion are followed by further discord: The first death, a murder, is followed by the exile and anguish of Cain (4:1–15). Next watchers fall from heaven, mate with human women, and populate the earth with giants—divine retaliation is a restricted human lifespan of 120 years (6:1–4). Finally, all of the first generations, except Noah and his animal pairs, are punished by death in a deluge, followed by this promise: "Never again will I curse the ground because of humans, even though every inclination of the human heart is evil from childhood. And never again will I destroy all living creatures, as I have done" (8.21).

A more pessimistic opening to life on earth is barely conceivable. While some may hear redemption in the biblical promise to the ground and creatures and in the upcoming blessing on Noah's descendants (9.1), notice here (8.21) that our intrinsic evil is not abated. Even without Paul and original sin (e.g., Rom. 5:12–22), and without those later, complex motivations for devaluing earthly experience and preferring heaven, the overt biblical legacy is to view death as an undestined but now irrevocable end to precious human life. It is in utter despair that Job longs for death (Job 3:11–19); only Enoch and Elijah escape it (Gen. 5:24; 2 Kings 2:11).

Then there are those stories that deemphasize human error but explain death as a by-product of adversarial relationships among gods. For instance, divine conflict penetrates human destiny in the Mesopotamian Atrahasis epic. There a strike among worker gods results in the decision to slaughter one god whose flesh and personality are mixed with divine saliva to create a race of apparently immortal worker humans, all due to the machinations of trickster-god Ea and the incantations of birth goddesses. Yet these new humans grow so populous, noisy, and offensive that chief god Enlil plans to destroy them. The first attempt is a plague, the second a famine, and the final one a deluge. Ea connives to save the Mesopotamian Noah figure, after which death by various means—disease, accident, starvation, and so on—is devised for subsequent human generations. Notably, violence is implicated both in the birth of humans (in the slaughter of a god, part of our flesh) and in the contrived means of our deaths. Divine plots to exterminate humans by flood, famine, or war may be found from Mesopotamia west to Greece. Such stories seem to extend heavenly spite and discord into the fabric of human life and death.

Curiously, many Asian religious classics portray the fact of death less as a fortuitous blight on human existence than as a background feature of incremental spiritual myopia. These texts problematize illusion over death. Yes, karma and samsara shape personal destiny in Hindu thinking, but the ancient Indian scheme of ages makes death less a violent penalty than a reflection of our dimming spiritual vision, which will be restored after the eventual dissolution and rebirth of the world. A similar myopia is implied in the scheme of ages underlying the Japanese Heike Monogatari. Our current loss of virtue manifests not only in discord but in our inability to attain enlightenment on our own; so we cling to savior figures in this third, *mappo*, age of Buddhist dharma. Daoist cosmology, or at least Zhuanzi (a.k.a. Chuang Tzu), attributes the loss of pristine consciousness to the introduction of formalistic behaviors, the coveting of knowledge and the lapse into pluralistic awareness; it is not death but rather various psychic estrangements that signal corruption of the natural mind (Girardot 1988: 71–76; 113–17). None of this is to say that Asian religious imaginations, in the way of imaginations everywhere, have not relished specters of hell, hungry ghosts, polluted corpses, and fearsome gods of death. Rather, it is to observe that Asian cosmic schemes, largely speaking, do not seem to approach death as an affliction based on primordial human error.

WHEN DEATH IS RIGHT

Alongside stories of primordial error, and sometimes intersecting with them, are stories that make violent death confer a boon on the world and its inhabitants. Such violent deaths are creative in that they generate new forms of order or somehow promote the defeat of disorder. Two motifs that illustrate this are the dema and the *Chaoskampf*. The first focalizes the victim, the other the victor.

The Dema and Its Lookalikes

More than half a century ago, Adolf Jensen coined the term dema-hypothesis to describe a mythologem he saw embedded in the east Indonesian cult of Hainuwele, a primeval woman violently slain and dismembered and whose buried body parts generated root crops and other useful stocks on which the culture depended. The slain dema-deity was not worshipped per se, but her original slaughter was commemorated as an event with ongoing, life-giving repercussions. She continued to pervade the cosmos (e.g., the moon and the underworld to which she descended) as well as agricultural products, particularly legumes; she was eaten in a rite with cannibalistic undertones (Jensen 1963:92, 167–168). Observing similar thinking among other traditions, Jensen contemplated the peculiar fixation of mythic imagination on violence. He saw such aetiological myths as reflecting radical insights (following Frobenius's *Ergriffenheit*, or imaginative plunge) about the links among violent death, diet, and cultural nascence (1963:65–66).

Similar myths appear elsewhere. A Laotian tale describes the angry retreat and murder of the rice goddess Nan Kosop. Her reluctance to end a famine provokes a hermit, worried about the extinction of Buddhism along with the human race, to slice her body into pieces, each generating different rices and rice-related spirits. A Japanese tale preserved in the Kojiki and Nihon-shoki describes kami Susanowo's exile from the sky to earth, where he murders Ohogetsu-hime in disgust over her offerings of food from her body—he sees them as polluted. From pieces of her slaughtered corpse, silkworms, rice seeds, millet, red beans, wheat and soybeans grow. In the Chinese Shanhaijing, it is from the Douguang plain, the field in which agricultural god Hou-ji was buried, that emerge a hundred delicious grains (Obayashi n.d.). Jensen's dema-hypothesis, therefore, resonates into a variety of agricultural environments.

It is not a huge leap from the dema-hypothesis to the spiritualized sacrifice associated with the Christ and other dying gods of the ancient world. Sometimes viewed as suffering servants or scapegoats for sin, such divinities famously are deemed to die violently in order to reform, restore, or create aspects of human life. Since Frazer and the *Golden Bough,* popular thinking has construed dying gods as a single type, but their stories vary in mythic disposition. We already have touched on the Mesopotamian slain god whose corpse becomes the stuff of humanity—not a salvific story, but one that alludes to our violent origins. A salvific variant may be seen in Christ's sacrifice—the seed for eternal life, says John (3.16); the antidote to original sin, says Paul (1 Cor. 15). Restricted in blessing but structurally parallel is the Mesopotamian myth of Inanna's boyfriend Dumuzi (biblical Tammuz), whose descent to the realm of death corresponds to the freeing of the love goddess whose presence we may enjoy on earth. The same motif may be seen in the slain and dismembered child-god Dionysos, or alternatively Zagreus (Diodorus 5.75.4, Nonnus, Dionysiaca 24.43). Zeus rescues the heart from the Titans and either eats it or feeds it to his paramour, who conceives the dangerous but oh-so-necessary god of wine, at least as Teiresias sees Dionysos (Eur. Ba. 275–285). No doubt serving a variety of cultural themes, these myths, like dema-myths, have the common feature of converting a violent death into a blessing for humans.

Chaoskampf and Cosmogony

Violent death is cosmically right also in mythic feats of supernatural strength that devastate chaos figures and refashion life on earth. Arguments abound about the historical origin for the Bible's *Chaoskampf* motif: is it Ugaritic, Babylonian, or Hebrew? (Fitzpatrick 2004) About its literary purpose,—is it mythopoeic, mythopoetic, or just metaphorical (Ortland 2010)? And what exactly does it celebrate—saving acts in history, world creation, divine enthronement festivals (Day 1985; Wyatt 2005)? Yet reports of an extraordinary act of destructive violence that sets the world right are not only biblical, but common in religious lore from West to East. Regional theologies aside, its appeal is not hard to appreciate.

Whether as longing, art, or simply entertainment, the biblical *Chaoskampf* theme involves death, rescue, and restoration. For instance, Revelation makes the slaughtered lamb (Jesus) a conquering hero coming to inflict wrathful punishment on enemies of the Christians (e.g., Rev. 6) and then to refashion reality, making "new heavens and new earth" (Rev. 21:1). Both Greek and Hebrew scriptures often make salvational acts lethal - for example, when Leviathan is destroyed to create the world (Is. 27)—but also beneficent—by killing the dragon God split open the sea, fed the deserts, and established the day and the night, the sun and the moon, the seasons, and the boundaries on earth (Ps. 74:13–17), it is almost dema-like. Poetic allusions convey a peculiar mix of dread and celebration: God will punish the earth for her sins (Is. 26:21) but, in defeating death, will restore the dead to life:

> [H]e will swallow up death forever, / ... But your dead will live; / their bodies will rise. / You who dwell in the dust, / wake up and shout for joy. / ... / the earth shall give birth to her dead. (Is. 26:8–19)

The destruction of the world is terrifying in Isaiah 24—heaven's floodgates will open, and the earth will shake, split asunder, and "reel like a drunkard...never to rise again" (24:19–21); yet in Daniel similar destruction is followed by new life:

> There will be a time of distress such as has not happened from the beginning of nations until then. But at that time...[m]ultitudes who sleep in the dust of the earth will awake: some to everlasting life, others to shame and everlasting contempt. (Dan. 12:1–2)

Chaoskampf themes echo into Matthew's crucifixion narrative (Matt. 27:51–52) and other New Testament end-of-time inferences (e.g., Mk.9:1, 13:2; Mat.13:37ff, 24:27). Whatever else they may express, such narratives display a relish for the violent spectacle that restores peace.

That relish was not born in the Bible. Perhaps the most famous parallel is Babylonian, wherein the cosmos is created by a primeval rebellion: Storm god Marduk slices the corpse of sea-monster Tiamat to make heaven and earth and slaughters her divine lover to make humans from his blood. Divine struggles that result in stability on earth often involve mutilation of the loser, as when Marduk slices Tiamat, Greek Cronos severs the testicles of Uranos, Ugaritic Baal dismembers Yam (Day 1985:8–9; Smith et al. 1997:102–105), or his sister Anat splits, winnows, and grinds Mot (Death), somehow returning her slain brother, Baal, to life. The divine warrior motif, wherein a god violently disposes of a foe to impose order on chaos, is replicated in royal spectacles and annals from Assyria, Egypt, and elsewhere in the ancient Near East (Noegel 2007). While no doubt serving a variety of theological purposes (Wyatt 2005:18–37; 205–237), this frequent motif must have thrilled ancient audiences.

Chaos-subduing violence is both cosmogonic and ontological in Asian classical literature, such as the Indian Sauptikaparvan, the Battle by Night (book 10) of the Mahabharata. Layers of caste dharma—especially warrior and priest—and cosmic dharma—Shiva possesses the body of Asvattaman—penetrate this narrative, which reads like a kaleidoscope of supernatural mayhem, with legions of demonic figures feasting on the flesh of the Pandava allies slaughtered in their sleep. Yet its mythic purpose, we are told, is to replicate the dissolution of the universe at the end of the Kali yuga; so the destruction, leading to rebirth, is ultimately cosmogonic (Johnson 1998: xxiii–xxxix). A strange parallel, but with subdued violence, is the cosmogonic sacrifice of the Vedic figure Puruṣa Sukta. The sacrifice and dismemberment of this human-figured god once generated the universe, as well as the natural and social order. Whatever historical perceptions about the carnage of war and actual human sacrifice reverberate through these ancient stories, their themes now serve the spiritual order of things. So, for instance, like Hainuwele, Puruṣa too continues to pervade the world, but as pure consciousness (puruṣa) entangled with matter (prakṛti), according to the third-century Sāṃkhya school. Humans replicate the same entanglement. The Battle by Night, like the entire Mahabharata, reads also as an internal struggle between the lower and higher aspects of human consciousness (Johnson 1998; Flood 1996: 106).

One ghoulish subtheme in the lore relating to *Chaoskampf* and cosmogony appears to be that of divine feast. Just as Asvattaman-Shiva is described as being drunk on his uncontained sacrifice in Mahabharata book 10 (Johnson 1998: xxxix), where joyfully bellowing *rākṣasas* also devour human entrails (Johnson 1998: 41), supernatural devastations frequently take on feasting innuendos in other religious literatures. Isaiah 34, for instance, provides a striking metonym for the Lord as bloodthirsty land:

> The Lord has a sword steeped in blood,
> it is gorged with fat,
> the fat of rams' kidneys and the blood of lambs and goats
> for he has a sacrifice in Bozrah,
> a great slaughter in Edom.
> Wild oxen shall come down and buffaloes with them, bull and bison together,
> and the land shall drink deep of blood
> and the soil be sated with fat. (34:6–8)

The trope of a post-victory banquet is robust in Near Eastern stories, evident in the Enuma Elish after Marduk defeats Tiamat, in the Ugaritic epic cycle featuring Baal after he defeats Yam (Smith et al. 1997: 106), and it appears to penetrate Exodus, when Moses and others dine at God's table (24:9–11) and metonymically to penetrate Ezekiel, when birds and beasts dine on Gog (39:4). What the biblical examples may infer, according to Susan Niditch, is that after defeating Israel's enemies, Yahweh dines on them (1993:38–40). The astonishing notion across these literatures is that supernatural acts of warfare culminate in feasting on the slain, as if the bodies of the conquered were to vitalize the conqueror. The sacrificial innuendos are obvious. (See also Carrasco, this volume.)

WHEN VIOLENT DEATH IS INSPIRATIONAL

Most contemporary mammals walk away from the spectacle of death, whereas humans build theologies about it, especially when the death is remembered to be brave, violent, or unfair. Beyond witnessing to truth—however conceived—the memory of individuals who died violently and courageously galvanizes groups set on retaliatory violence and occasionally consecrates look-alike deaths in the form of suicides. The spectacle of violent death has riveted individuals and mobs across traditions. Alongside the various aetiological myths, martyrs and suicides too evince the peculiar grip of violent death on religious imagination.

Remarkably, unless embedded within the commandment not to kill, there is no explicit prohibition on suicide in the Hebrew Bible. Individual stories may even commend it. Samson's suicide is applauded when, in an act of revenge, he pulls down the pillars of a house full of Philistines, thereby killing along with himself "more [Philistines] than those he had killed during his life" (Judges 16:30). The willing sufferings of the mother of Maccabees and her sons, martyrs tortured under the Greeks, are painstakingly described (2 Macc. 7). Saul's suicide is not martyr-like, but nor is it condemned when, to avoid a worse death at the hands of his captors, he falls on his own sword (1 Sam. 31:4), and there is no biblical chastisement when Job, stripped bare of all hope, curses his own birth (Job 3:11–17). Despite rabbinical laws proscribing suicide, these biblical traditions show appreciation for the despair as well as the courage that inspires it. It is not surprising that Masada is a pilgrimage destination.

The Greek scriptures continue the theme. The heart and soul of the Gospels is the punishing death of Jesus, who refuses to give Pilate an excuse to save him in the gospels of Luke (23:3–25), John (18:33–19:12), Matthew (27:11–14); and Mark (15:2–15). His intention, according to Luke, is explicitly to die (9:21–22). Resurrection narratives aside, the willing and courageous death of Jesus ("to lay down one's life for one's friends," John 15:13) was imitated by Christians from at least the time of Domitian forward. Their gruesome sufferings are lovingly recounted in martyr-narratives such as Perpetua's. Although the end game was salvation—when "God will wipe away every tear" (Rev. 7:17)—and despite the disapproval of suicide by some church fathers, the mass appeal of the suicidal hero seems based on the ancient perception that martyrs are brave. After all, Achilles too chose to die for love (Il. 18:80–100).

As in Christianity, martyrs in Islamic scriptures were promised heavenly blessings if they died testifying for the faith, which usually meant in defensive battle (e.g., Sura 4.95–99, 9.111). Suicide is forbidden in the Qur'an (e.g., at Sura 4.29), so martyrdom traditionally was gauged by the hard-to-win measure of fighting and dying selflessly, without intention to die ('Abdallah b. al-Mubarak, d. 797; cited in Cook n.d.88). Military struggle was constrained by precise Quranic strictures (e.g., Suras 2.191–192, 2.216–217, 4.90, 8.60–61, 9.6, 9.29, 9.36) but nonetheless, as in the Bible, was spiritualized by reports of heavenly assistance during battles (3.124–126, 8.9–19, 8.65, 9.25–26; cf. Josh 10:10–22; 2 Sam. 5:22–25; Ex. 15:14–15). These reports succeeded in glamorizing death in battle, a glamour preserved in stories of the early companions of the prophet (e.g., 'Awf b. Harith) and especially in the tragic and redemptive death of the Shiite hero, Imam Hussein.

Indian religious lore too is resplendent with the approved deaths of heroes, from Sikh martyrs back to the selfless practitioners of dharmic war in the great epics. Suicide per se may be prohibited—except when spiritualized by dharma, as in satí—but deliberate martyrdom is most exquisitely exalted by the Liberation

Tigers of Tamil Eelam, or what is left of it. Adhering to a reputedly Dravidian concept of selfless death for no heavenly reward, the altruistic *tiyāki* (martyr-hero) trains for spectacular suicide aimed at promoting a Tamil state (Schalk 2010). Through ascetic pursuits, the tiyāki learns to regard his or her life as a weapon. Still today, obligate memorial rituals and hagiographic recitations preserve the inexorable sting of the martyr's death and inspire new recruits. Ascetic suicides with less violent repercussions are of course familiar in the traditions of Buddhism, Jainism, and Hinduism, discussed elsewhere in this volume (see chapters by Jerryson and Wilson, within).

Heroic suicide in Japanese traditions harks back at least to the Heike Monogatari and gets ritualized in bushido recipes for self-demise during the Tokugawa era (King 1993: 123–156). Admiration for the dedicated warrior whose loyalty to *daimyo* or state overwhelms self-love and the love of family is enshrined in founding myths, monuments, imperial documents, and later tales by authors such as Mishima and Hearn. *Seppaku* actually served a variety of political purposes in Japanese history (see, e.g., Atkins 2010), but the associated values of facelessness and self-abnegation were supported in different ways by Confucian, Shinto, and Zen Buddhist strains of ideology from the eighth century into the twentieth.

Thus, perhaps we should not be astonished when suicide bombers win international attention and admiration by different religious groups. This sweep of suicidal traditions shows that suicide, construed as martyrdom, tugs at something deep in human imagination. The suicidal hero has been enshrined in religious legends for a very long time.

Conclusion: The Peculiar Obsessions of Religious Imagination

Although the preceding examples address the mythology of violent death, the ritualistic display of violent death—for example, in sacrifices or revenge rituals—could have been treated in equal breadth (Kitts 2010a, 2010b). For half a century, at least, ritual sacrifice has been a scholarly preoccupation (see, e.g., Carrasco and Burkert, in this volume). But in either sphere—myth or the ritual stage—violent death is apparently a rivet for religious imagination. Why?

Big theories abound. Some argue that sinister ideological manipulation lurks behind this emphasis on death; thus the fearsome spectacle of violent death encourages implicit respect for and obedience to supernatural authority. Others see in this death fixation the preservation of ethnic identities and memories of persecution (e.g., Volkan et al., 2002), which stoke flames of revenge. Still others argue, with Freud, that the subject of death speaks to our deep suspicion of its criminality, with Girard, that the violent exercise of power over life is seen as an index of true "being," with Burkert, that violent death arouses ancient ambivalences stemming from the hunt, or, with Otto, that it evokes a specter of power, a *numen* that conjures fascinating feelings of utter contingency. Or maybe it is simply self-love and the awareness of loss that makes violent death a riveting subject. Dozens of theories are plausible.

While no one theory is entirely satisfactory, this book is testament to the array of possible approaches to understanding the religious fascination with violence and with death.

Bibliography

Angel, Andrew. *Chaos and the Son of Man: The Hebrew* Chaoskampf *Tradition in the Period 515 BCE to 200 CE.* London: T&T Clark, 2006.

Atkins, Paul S. "The Stages of *Seppaku*: Performing Self-Execution in Premodern Japan." *Grammars and Morphologies of Ritual Practices in Asia,* vol. 1 of *Ritual Dynamics and the Science of Ritual,* 523–533. Ed. Axel Michaels et al. Weisbaden, Germany: Harrassowtiz, 2010.

Cook, David. "Suicide Attacks or 'Martydom Operations' in Contemporary Jihad Literature." http://www.ozlanka.com/commentary/jihad.htm. n.d. Retrieved August 2009.

Day, John. *God's Conflict with the Dragon and the Sea.* Cambridge, UK: Cambridge University Press, 1985.

Fitzpatrick, Paul E., S.M. *The Disarmament of God: Ezekiel 38–39 in Its Mythic Context.* Washington, DC: The Catholic Biblical Association of America, 2004.

Flood, Gavin. *An Introduction to Hinduism.* Cambridge, UK: Cambridge University Press, 1996.

Girardot, N. J. *Myth and Meaning in Early Taoism.* Berkeley: University of California Press, 1988.

Jensen, Adolf. *Myth and Cult among Primitive Peoples.* Transl. Marianna Tax Choldin and Wolfgang Weissleder. Chicago: University of Chicago Press, 1963.

Johnson, W. J. *The Sauptikaparvan of the Mahābhārata.* Oxford, UK: Oxford University Press, 1998.

King, Winston. *Zen and the Way of the Sword.* New York: Oxford University Press, 1993.

Kitts, Margo. "The Last Night: Ritualized Violence and the Last Instructions of 9/11." *Journal of Religion* 20:3 (July 2010a) 283–312.

Kitts, Margo. "*Poinē* as a Ritual Leitmotif in the Iliad." *State, Power, and Violence.* Vol. 3 of *Ritual Dynamics and the Science of Ritual.* Edited by Margo Kitts et al. Weisbaden, Germany: Harrassowitz, 2010b. 7–32.

Kövecses, Zoltán. *Metaphor and Emotion: Language, Culture and the Body in Human Feeling.* Cambridge, UK: Cambridge University Press, 2000.

Levenson, Jon D. *The Death and Resurrection of the Beloved Son.* New Haven, CT: Yale University Press, 1993.

Niditch, Susan. *War in the Hebrew Bible.* Oxford: Oxford University Press, 1993.

Noegel, Scott B. "Divine Violence in the Ancient Near East." *Belief and Bloodshed: Religion and Violence across Time and Tradition,* 13–28. Ed. James Wellington. Lanham, MD: Rowman and Littlefield, 2007.

Obayashi, Taryo. "The Kyushu Myths Explicate Japan and Asia." Asian Mythology Seminar. http://www.asianmonth.com/prize/english/lecture/pdf/10_03.pdf, retrieved May 21, 2010.

Ortland, Eric Nels. *Theophany and Chaoskampf: The Interpretation of Theophanic Imagery in the Baal Epic, Isaiah, and the Twelve.* Piscataway, NJ: Gorgias Press, 2010.

Schalk, Peter. "Memorialisation of Martyrs in the Tamil Resistance Movement of Tiam/Larnkä." *State, Power, and Violence.* Vol. 3 of *Ritual Dynamics and the Science of Ritual.* Ed. Margo Kitts et al. Weisbaden, Germany: Harrassowitz, 2010. 55–74.

Smith, Mark S, Simon B. Parker, Edward L. Greenstein, Theodore J. Lewis, and David Marcus. *Ugaritic Narrative Poetry.* Atlanta: Scholars Press, 1997.

Volkan, Vamik D., Gabriele Ast, and William F. Greer, Jr. *The Third Reich in the Unconscious.* New York: Routledge, 2002.

Wyatt, Nicholas. *The Mythic Mind.* London: Equinox, 2005.

PART III

ANALYTIC
APPROACHES

CHAPTER 25

RELIGION AND VIOLENCE FROM A SOCIOLOGICAL PERSPECTIVE

JOHN R. HALL

A strong but I think fair generalization: Before the beginning of the third millennium of the modern era, a good deal of historical and case-study research documented instances in which religion has been connected with violence (Candland 1992). However, up through the 1970s, sociological theory seldom focused on the nature of such relationships. The reasons are at least threefold. First, high-modern general social theories—structural-functionalism, Parsonian system theory and associated theories of modernization and secularization, Marxism, and world-systems theory—all either posited that religion is causally insignificant in general or that it had become increasingly subordinated to nonreligious social institutions under the auspices of modernization. Second, more narrowly, scholars studying violence—typically Marxists or other structuralists—gave short shrift to culture, including religious culture. Third, sociological and other scholars interested in religion generally concerned themselves with a variety of other topics—such as secularization, congregations and religious communities, fundamentalism, and religious identities. Among scholars of religion in the United States and Europe, concern with violence was largely limited to the study of religious movements such as Peoples Temple, the Branch Davidians, or Aum Shinryko.

Fortunately, in recent years the human sciences have become better positioned to move beyond our inherited limitations. Rational-choice analysts and others have found new routes beyond limits of the high-modern secularization model (Warner 1993), and sociologists of religion have increasingly demonstrated the independent causal significance of religion (Smilde and May 2010). To be sure, issues concerning secularization continue to be debated, but with the potential for considerably more comparative and historical sophistication (Gorski 2000). On the back of these developments, beginning in the 1980s and concertedly after 9/11, scholars from a variety of disciplines have become far more interested in connections between religion and violence. It is thus now worth attempting a provisional synthetic *theoretical* account. Because that is my project here, I will not review the many substantive analyses of religion and violence, nor will I attempt a compendium of the many cases that might be considered (for a review, see Hall 2003).

In sketching a synthetic theoretical account under the flag of sociology, I make no special claims for that discipline's scholarship. However, sociology as an intellectual arena offers three distinct advantages. First, it straddles, sometimes uncomfortably, the divide between causally oriented social-science methodologies and interpretive methodologies employed in more qualitatively oriented social-science research and the humanities; thus, it is especially open to considerations that draw on diverse sources. Second, relative to other social-science disciplines, sociology leaves a good deal of room for comparative structural analysis, while relative to scholarship in the humanities, it leaves more room for domain-specific (and sometimes wider) generalizations. Third, following Georg Simmel, sociologists are especially attuned to the possibility that relatively similar processes may take place at different scales of social complexity. Taken together, these characteristics allow for the consideration of multiple factors, processes, explanations, and interpretations, rather than the pursuit of any reductionist account.

In order to avoid either essentializing religion or neglecting diversity in its institutional and noninstitutionalized forms, I use as a initial theoretical point of orientation Martin Riesebrodt's general, nonfunctionalist sociological definition of religion as "a complex of practices that are based on the premise of the existence of superhuman powers, whether personal or impersonal, that are generally invisible" (Riesebrodt 2010: 75).

A separate problem concerns how to bring violence within the orb of social analysis. Clearly, not all violence is physical or material; some is symbolic. Just as clearly, definitions advanced from within social formations are notoriously uneven (usually downplaying their own violence, while being quick to find it in others and their cultural practices). In order to avoid such cultural relativism, Jackman has formulated an expansive but neutral definition, characterizing violence as encompassing "actions that inflict, threaten, or cause injury" and asserting that injury may be "corporal, written, or verbal" (Jackman 2001: 443). The very inclusiveness of this definition forces a broader analysis at the outset and opens out onto a recognition that extreme violence is not isolated either from other kinds of violence or from nonviolent types of action that can give rise to it.

Two general yet contrasting principles inform my theorization. First, there is no firewall between specifically religious actions and processes and the wider social world. Religions face many of the same organizational dilemmas as other social groups; religious movements are not immune to the dynamics that affect social movements more widely; socialization in religion is not inherently different from socialization elsewhere; and so on. But second, and in contrast, as a long line of scholars—Riesebrodt among the most recent—has emphasized, religious phenomena are distinctive relative to other social phenomena in the efforts that practitioners make to interact with the divine. Thus, a central question concerns whether, under what conditions, and how religious meanings, actions, and organizations per se become concatenated with violence.

That a potential for violence lies in specific religious structures is a point now well established in lines of analysis derived from the foundational work of Emile Durkheim, who famously argued that, for a community of participants, religion differentiates the sacred from the profane. Crucially, the sacred and profane are culturally defined, and thus, it is well within the realm of religious possibility that violence—whether extreme asceticism, martyrdom, war, or some other act—can become sacred duty. Pursuing such a line of analysis, René Girard has argued that scapegoating—the killing of a "surrogate victim" standing in for wider evils—is a primordial religious act intended to sustain the sacred in the face of pollution. In this theorization, violence is inherently fused within the sacred. Moreover, although some political theorists consider nationalist and ethnic conflicts to be "secular," diverse analyses point to the threads connecting religion, nationalism, and ethnic community, and other studies point to the origins of modern "secular" revolutionary and nationalist movements in religious apocalypticism (Hall 2009: 108–118, 132–147). In other words, the "sacred" bears a distinctly religious provenance, but religion cannot monopolize the sacred, and the relationships between ostensibly religious and nonreligious social formations and the sacred are variable, complex, and important subjects of inquiry in their own right.

Overall, Girard's theorization concerned with the sacred demonstrates one potential lineage of violence deriving from religion. Yet two sociological caveats bear emphasis. First, identifying one potential connection does not inherently rule out other possible relationships. Rather, the highly variable cultural content of religion virtually assures that depending on how religious actors formulate meanings of violence relative to their relationships with the supernatural, they will vary in how they assign cultural valences to even the "same" act of violence, however defined "objectively" (e.g., murder, suicide). Thus, social theorists concerned with violence will be well served by remaining open to the specification of processes and dynamics involving religion beyond those centering on the sacred-profane binary and scapegoating of the Other.

Second, to argue that religion offers a seedbed for violence is not to say that all religion is inherently violent. Even casual comparative observation suggests wide variation in religious practices—from the committed pacifism of Quakers, to everyday practices of religion relatively removed from either pursuit of or opposition to violence, to the "nonviolent resistance" championed by Mohandas Gandhi and Martin Luther King, Jr., and on to inquisitions, crusades, and holy wars. In relation to the shared features of religions that Reisebrodt describes as centered on interaction with superhuman powers, particulars of ritual, salvation, practice, organization, and so on are highly variable. Moreover, it is important to reaffirm that religious meanings are culturally specified and historically situated rather than ontologically given, or even socially determined solely by sacred texts. Thus, insofar as specifically social, cultural, and historical features of religions matter, there is no compelling basis for asking whether one or another religion (Christianity, Islam, Buddhism, etc.) is instrinsically violent or nonviolent. This is the wrong question. As Weber demonstrated in his path-breaking sociology of religion a century ago, major religions can give rise to a variety of salvation orientations and diverse forms of organization and practice, to both withdrawal from the world and engagement with it, and to quests for either perfectionist self-discipline or ecstatic enlightenment (Weber 1978 [1922]: part 2, chapter 6).

Thus, notwithstanding the thesis that religion is inherently violent, sociological theory must come to terms with variations in incidence and character of connections between religion and violence. Here, I pursue this challenge comparatively and typologically, by exploring the circumstances of violence in a way that identifies alternative "domains" in which religious concatenations of violence arise. On this approach, it becomes possible to ask whether some religious formations (not religious traditions) or religious or broader social circumstances are especially likely to involve violence, on what basis, and under what conditions. My core thesis is that manifestations of violence in relation to religion are diverse. They hinge on alternative circumstances wrought by different historical moments, institutional formations, and cultural meanings. In other words, violence is situational.

Analytically, the complex array of possible developments will be conditioned by—and, in turn, shape—specific kinds of religious organizations involved. For example, on average, a church—in Weber's and Durkheim's sense of an inclusive community of ritual oriented to a broad population—will engender different possibilities of violence than groups that I have identified (in *The Ways Out*) as "warring sects" and "other-worldly sects." In addition, the arena in which actions play out is an important demarcator among types of religious involvement with violence. Two general arenas of action seem important: (1) those in which the key dynamics of phenomena unfold within a given religious group and among its participants (and, as well, in relation to the group's wider potential audience); and (2) situations in which religious groups engage in actions connected to broader social processes. In the latter arenas, the key diacritical consideration turns on relationships between religious groups, "political" power, and hegemonic culture.

All these distinctions are analytic: In unfolding events of violence, issues of legitimacy, both of a religious group and of a social order, may be very much in play, and historical circumstances and, thus, trajectories of groups and their collective actions may shift (on this point, see, for example, Hobsbawm 1959; 58–59). Therefore, where a process is located in relation to an established order sometimes remains ambiguous, and it can shift over time. Moreover, with Max Weber, any particular concrete phenomenon may approximate more than one alternative typological model of situation in different ways or degrees or for different social actors (Weber 1978 [1922]: 20). On occasion, different meaningful structures of violence intersect with one another, notably, when individuals acting within a religious group become caught up in violence that involves the group in a wider social domain. In such cases, distinct mechanisms of violence can become interlocked in ways that reinforce one another. However, despite the fluidity of empirical trajectories and theoretical transitions among analytic types, diverse situations are not so idiosyncratically historicist as to prevent theorization of alternative patterns.

VIOLENCE WITHIN A RELIGIOUS DOMAIN

Within the arena of a given religion, its participants, and audience, four kinds of violence seem sociologically significant. First, implicitly in Durkheim and explicitly in Girard, the identification of the sacred with the religious community involves conditions in which ritual purification of the group may be achieved through scapegoating, witch hunts, discipline and punishment, or other kinds of boundary maintenance. Violation of the targeted individual is taken to affirm the sacred, even as it legitimates the capacity of the religious group to exercise power in the affirmation of the sacred and to chart the boundaries of group allegiance.

Second, and in turn, the very charting of boundaries, especially in strict or encompassing sectarian organizations, can create conflicts over identity and the allegiances of individuals. Individuals within encompassing groups who seek to leave sometimes find themselves subject to extreme psychological violence, physical violence, and what may amount to physical house arrest. By the opposite token, distraught family members may try to rescue a relative from a sect, even against the sect member's will. Boundary conflicts over individual loyalties may become consolidated into class actions that embroil a group in conflict with a wider array of opponents who seek to control religious groups (Hall, Schuyler, and Trinh).

Third, because religions traffic in possibilities of salvation, they can exercise de facto hierocratic domination over participants, in part by offering or withdrawing the blessings of the group. The individual, in order to obtain the boons of salvation, may engage in self-directed violence, ranging from mild asceticism such as occasional fasting to more extreme asceticism, and on to the pursuit of martyrdom by one or another means, including the possibility of directing violence toward others through altruistic suicide committed in the course of a crusade or holy war.

Fourth, religion is what O'Neill calls a "skin trade": The success of interactions between religious functionaries and their clientele both depends on and fosters a relatively low social distance compared to that which people usually maintain in social interaction outside their intimate primary groups (O'Neill 1972; 6). Charismatic figures, of course, can command a degree of hero worship, but even in relatively routinized roles, religious functionaries can receive an exceptional amount of trust. Such trust opens up possibilities of the violation of individuals submitting to pastoral care, as recent sexual-abuse scandals testify.

All these four types of violence occurring within religion may arise in other social formations as well. Thus, scapegoating can unfold as an expression of nationalism; boundary conflicts may surface in marital and custody disputes; self-destructive asceticism under commitment to a doctrine is hardly a monopoly of religion; and there are other "skin trades" than religion (psychiatry, for example) known for their abusive potential. However, especially in scapegoating, boundary conflicts, and asceticism, the basic logic that makes violence possible centers on the sacred, and that logic is religious at its core. Although pastoral abuse stems from religion's relationship to a larger class—of skin trades, the potential for abuse may be greater within religious groups because they traffic in the sacred. Religious claims made in relation to the sacred generate or accentuate certain manifestations of violence.

RELIGIOUS GROUPS AND POLITICAL POWER

The significance of violence that takes place within religious arenas is not necessarily limited to those arenas. Scapegoating, boundary conflicts, and asceticism, in particular, have the potential to become interlocked with wider social processes of conflict that can result in violence. However, such wider processes have distinctive mechanisms of their own, broadly bound up with the relationship between religion and power, especially power exercised by a state claiming a monopoly on the legitimate exercise of physical force within a fixed territory (the definition by Weber, 54). Given that religious groups asserting authority based on claims to interact with the divine may come into conflict with competing groups (religious or otherwise), the very existence and character of a social order are potentially contested. Nevertheless, in general terms, it is possible to differentiate alternative types of relatively institutionalized established social orders that are the products of tensions between religious and other powers—as well as their modalities of violence—from alternative types of violence that transpire under conditions in which hegemonic order is contested.

Established Orders of Religion and Power

In the 1960s, at the high-water mark of modernity, Western observers, especially in the United States, largely ignored issues of religion-polity conflict because the democratic nation-state that permits freedom of religious belief and expression seemed like the end point of modernization. However, the 1979 Islamic Revolution in Iran demonstrated an alternative trajectory, and by the 1990s, Juergensmeyer was bringing into question scholarly self-assurance about the modern trajectory of religion and the state. Today, possibilities remain open and often contested.

It is thus useful to note Weber's identification of alternative relationships between religion and polity. At the "hierocratic" extreme of theocracy, a religious organization exercises state power within a territory (or in a less hierocratic way, the religious organization legitimates a ruler as a manifestation or representative of the divine) (Weber 1978 [1922]: 1159–1169). At the other extreme, in caesaropapism, a secular ruler claims authority in all religious matters. A third range of possibilities depends on some relative degree of autonomy of religion and polity from each other. "Modern" resolutions of the religion-polity tension have varied in the degree to which they affirm divine legitimacy. On the one hand, regimes may continue to invoke divine legitimation but assert powers that are effectively autonomous from any claim of authority over them by a religious group, for example, in American "civil religion" (described in Bellah 1967). Alternatively, the modern state may center its legitimacy in "secular-sacred" claims, for example, the rights of mankind or the dictatorship of the proletariat.

The alternative formations just described to some extent condition different pathways, but one way or another, religion serves as a basis for legitimizing the violence. The theocracy may legitimate violence in its name as the exercise of the sacred power of the community, as Girard would expect. In the extreme, it pursues expansion through subordination of secular powers with which it contends or by conquest of new territory through a crusade or jihad. On the other hand, the caesaropapist may cynically invoke religious mission as the basis for wars of conquest directed to the building of an empire that uses religion simply to provide a veneer of legitimation (Lincoln). For their parts, modern secular states in effect have appropriated religious legitimations of sacred mission, bending them to the purposes of war, colonial expansion, and the building of empires. In such developments, not only will religion be called on to provide legitimation, but also, in many cases, religious organizations and their ideologies directly facilitate the spread of colonizing settlers or the pacification of conquered populations (Hall 2009: 87–94).

At the extreme of either theocracy or casaeropapism—or indeed, in the case of a single religious organization that is established and sanctioned by the state (a "church" in Weber's typological terms), a religion can engage in violence in order to maintain its monopolistic position or, further, to try to purge society of infidels. At the extreme, genocide, even as undertaken by a "secular" state, may have a religious or sacred cast to it, sometimes marked by rule that approximates caesaropapism.

In contrast, liberal, secular modern societies are marked by religious pluralism that involves tolerance of diverse religious groups, so long as those groups operate within the rule of law. In such societies, the state typically takes over the otherwise religious functions of defining boundaries of acceptable practice and policing religious deviance. So long as religion is not deemed to exceed those boundaries or directly challenge state authority, beyond the forms of violence internal to a religious group, the potential for violence emerges only occasionally, sometimes from conflict between religious groups for clientele, such as claims that a competing group is seeking to proselytize among a given group's traditional audience or from cultural opponents who seek to counter particular religious movements

(Hall, Schuyler, and Trinh 2000). Or, religiously inspired people may engage in self- or other-directed violence to protest or alter public policies in relation to proclaimed religious precepts.

Hegemonic Legitimation under Contestation

In turn, the "policing" of boundaries of religion inevitably points to the dialectically counterposed frame: violence in connection with contestations of hegemony. The late twentieth-century claim of Francis Fukuyama about the "end of history" notwithstanding, social formations are never completely free from the potential emergence of charismatic figures whose apocalyptic visions (that is, "revelations," or as the original Greek *apokalyptein* suggests, "disclosures") exceed the boundaries of the established order (Roth 1975). Moreover, religious communities "contained" by a state may nevertheless nurture countercultural ideologies. Such ideologies, under circumstances of widely experienced "apocalyptic" social crisis, give narrative structure to religious movements that contest hegemony, either passively or actively. Finally, the effective rule of political power and its cultural hegemony may themselves be in doubt.

A rich and complex set of possibilities is evidenced by studies of historical and contemporary religious movements (e.g., Cohn 1970; Lanternari 1960; Lewy 1974; Wilson 1973; Juergensmeyer 2003; Hall 2009). Of greatest significance will be the (potentially shifting) degree of symmetry versus asymmetry of legitimacy between parties to the conflict. Typically, either within the boundaries of an established social order or in its colonizing expansion or consolidated empire, the polity will assert and receive widespread acknowledgement of an asymmetric legitimacy, and it will bring inordinate physical power to bear in the pursuit of its claims. Yet occasionally, a movement will become broadly popular and assert a de facto symmetric claim of legitimacy, or two polities, each with its own territorial base and symmetric claims of legitimacy, may contest predominance in conflicts that bear a sacred character.

In theory, under hegemonic rule, a demarcation separates "contained" subcultural religious groups from countercultural movements. The latter, whether or not explicitly religious, in their break with (or challenge to) an established social order, tend to assert a sacred and charismatic legitimacy. However, many such groups ultimately seek accommodation with an established order, they seize on legal means of pursuing their objectives (for example, as social movements oriented to policy change), or they pursue alternative pathways of salvation (such as ecstatic transcendence via meditation) that are not directly threatening to an established order. In such cases, violence, if it occurs, takes forms within an established order.

By contrast, various kinds of "apocalyptic" movements draw together participants who see themselves on the cusp of dramatic social and historical upheaval and, on this basis, undertake one or another sacred course of action relative to what they tend to regard as "the end of the world as we know it." The differences among such groups depend on where they position themselves in time in relation to the end of the old order and the arrival of the new dispensation. At the sub-cultural end of the spectrum, conversion movements use the occasion of the pro-claimed apocalypse to supercharge their efforts at prosyletizing, a strategy that has by now become routinized. However, the most significant developments occur when countercultural movements emerge within an established order but in oppo-sition to it or, alternatively, when an external power asserts its jurisdiction in an act of territorial and societal colonization.

In circumstances "within" an established order, when intense apocalyptic anxieties and interests take hold, individuals may feel called to one or another extraordinary, charismatic action that breaks with their previous lives. Under these conditions, "postapocalyptic" countercultural movements seek to estab-lish utopian colonies "beyond" the old order. Such groups will vary considerably according to the specifics of the apocalypse they envision, with more utopian move-ments working to establish the "heaven on earth" or "Zion in the wilderness" of an "other-worldly sect" (Hall 1978), whereas those envisioning dystopian challenges may seek to establish an "ark of survival" in the midst of chaos. Either trajectory may generate conflicts and violence at its boundaries, especially if its formation comes to be regarded by nonparticipants as a "state within a state." In such condi-tions, dystopian survivalists are especially likely to adopt a siege mentality within a defended compound, and the potential for conflict and violence with a wider social order is thereby exacerbated. However, if either utopianists or dystopianists seek to "escape Babylon" through collective "religious migration," they reduce (but do not eliminate) the potential for conflict with the established social order. In turn, their future prospects are dictated by their potential to relocate in relatively unsettled lands or to reach accommodation with polities in territories to which they migrate. In either case, whether postapocalyptic groups stay within the territory of a home state or migrate outside it, if and when such groups become "pulled back" into the unfolding apocalypse, if they come to regard their chances of collective survival as limited, they may engage in violence toward their perceived opponents, undertake collective suicide, or both (Hall, Schuyler, and Trinh 2000).

Under conditions of colonization by an external power, possibilities of uto-pian flight or dystopian survivalism tend to be diminished or limited to flight to a "region of refuge." In such cases, as Lanternari and others have shown, a colonized group that holds to the sacredness of its community may ritually mark the demise of its culture. Alternatively, participants in cargo cults may ritually seek to gain the benefits displayed by colonizers (Worsley 1968).

The radical alternative to the postapocalyptic sect, whether utopian or dysto-pian, is the preapocalyptic "warring sect." Such a group undertakes what Weber described as "holy war" (Weber 1978 [1922]: 473–474) and what Juergensmeyer more recently has called "cosmic war" (Juergensmeyer 2003). Whether a war-ring sect operates under asymmetric conditions or attains a degree of symmetric equivalence in power, territory, and legitimacy are open questions in an unfolding conflict: Almost inherently, such movements begin as small primary groups, but successful movements can grow to the level of fielding full-scale military forces.

The ideological bases of warring sects are variable, as are their scale, goals, and constructions of mission. Historically, for example, in the case of Thomas Müntzer during the sixteenth-century Peasants' War in Germany, and still on occasion, leaders of a warring sect may construe its power in mystical terms, assuring adherents to the cause that they operate under divine protection. However, beginning with the sixteenth-century Puritan Revolution in England and especially in the wake of the French Revolution, apocalyptic war increasingly has fused with highly strategic and disciplined action, and what was once the province of religious messiahship has become secularized, and replicated on scale rarely seen since the Crusades—that of civilizational conflict.

Social scientists sometimes downplay the "religious" provenance of apocalyptic warring sects by suggesting that religion simply masks deeper forces—poverty, ethnic strife, or nationalism, or that religion may operate symbolically to mobilize other interests and create coalitions of solidarity, thereby sacralizing violence. Marx and Engels made similar assertions concerning class interests in early Christianity and the Peasants' War in Germany (Marx and Engels 1964).

However, an alternative thesis suggests that the sacred violence of apocalyptic war cannot be understood simply as a surrogate for deeper material interests, any more than it can be understood solely in cultural and ideological terms. Rather, apocalyptic war alters the structural circumstances of violence in important ways. In *Apocalypse*, I argue that the character of apocalyptic conflict shifted under conditions of emergent modern society in the West. Overall, on the one hand, states took over the "religious" functions of determining the legitimate boundaries of religion and "containing" the religious Other, especially in any apocalyptic dispensation. On the other hand, apocalyptic movements, typically abandoning mysticism, have increasingly organized their activities on a basis of strong self-discipline and strategic action. Under these conditions, apocalyptic violence shifted from a religious to a secular or secular-sacred venue. In the modern situation, the apocalyptic sect not only bears a distinctive sacred ideology. In addition, the structure of its organization tends toward that of a "charismatic community," and compared to conventional military forces, it benefits from support from sympathetic individuals who participate in a broader "apocalyptic milieu" (Hall 2009: 174–191).

CONCLUSION

Violence involving religion no doubt differs according to the kind of action involved, in Weber's terms—instrumentally rational, value-rational, traditional, and so forth (Weber 1978 [1922]: 24–26). However, those who undertake even the most value-rational action of symbolic violence (e.g., destroying sacred objects) will nevertheless engage in instrumental action, and conversely even instrumental action (e.g., seeking salvation) will be conditioned by the context of values in which it occurs and the cultural meanings that inscribe it. For this reason, in this chapter, I have proposed a phenomenological and cultural approach that theorizes multiple kinds of relationships between religion and violence according to structural situations. Not religious traditions but religious formations and their contextual circumstances shape their potential instantiations with violence.

Within arenas dominated by a particular religious group, violence may result from counterposing the Other to the sacred, from conflicts at the boundaries of the group, from individuals pursuing salvation through extreme asceticism, and from abuse of the intimate relationship made possible by the status of religion as a "skin trade." In wider social processes, the relationship of religion to political power differentiates a variety of hegemonic and counterhegemonic conditions in which religion and violence become concatenated. Although in some circumstances, religion simply partakes of wider social dynamics, in other situations, religion specifically structures the "sacred" meaning of action, thereby not only legitimating violence but also actually shaping its character as well as the patterns of social organization and processes in which violence occurs. Thus, theorizing relationships between religion and violence should not be an exercise in differentiating "ideal" and "material" causes but rather an effort to understand their complex interplay in social processes.

BIBLIOGRAPHY

Bellah, Robert. "Civil religion in America," *Daedalus* 96 (1967): 1–21.

Candland, Christopher. *The Spirit of Violence: An Interdisciplinary Bibliography of Violence and Religion.* New York: Guggenheim Foundation, 1992.

Cohn, Norman. 1957. *The Pursuit of the Millennium.* New York: Oxford University Press, 1970.

Girard, René. 1972. *Violence and the Sacred.* Baltimore: Johns Hopkins University Press, 1977.

Gorski, Philip. "Historicizing the Secularization Debate: Church, State, and Society in Late Medieval and Early Modern Europe, ca. 1300–1700." *American Sociological Review* 65 (2000): 138–167.

Hall, John R. *The Ways Out: Utopian Communal Groups in an Age of Babylon.* London: Routledge & Kegan Paul, 1978.

Hall, John R. "Religion and violence: social processes in comparative perspective." In *Handbook for the Sociology of Religion.* Ed. Michele Dillon, 359–381. Cambridge, UK: Cambridge University Press, 2003.

Hall, John R. *Apocalypse: From Antiquity to the Empire of Modernity.* Cambridge: Polity, 2009.

Hall, John R., Philip D. Schuyler, and Sylvaine Trinh. *Apocalypse Observed: Religion and Violence in North America, Europe, and Japan.* London: Routledge, 2000.

Hobsbawm, Eric, *Primitive Rebels.* New York: Norton, 1959.

Jackman, Mary R. "License to Kill: Violence and Legitimacy in Expropriative Social Relations." In *The Psychology of Legitimacy: Emerging Perspectives on Ideology,*

Justice, and Intergroup Relations. Eds. John T. Jost and Brenda Major, 437–467. New York: Cambridge University Press, 2001.

Juergensmeyer, Mark. "The New Religious State." *Comparative Politics* 27.4 (1995): 379–391.

Juergensmeyer, Mark. *Terror in the Mind of God*, updated ed. Berkeley: University of California Press, 2003.

Lanternari, Vittorio. *The Religions of the Oppressed.* New York: Knopf, 1963 [1960].

Lewy, Gunter. *Religion and Revolution.* New York: Oxford University Press, 1974.

Lincoln, Bruce. *Religion, Empire, and Torture.* Chicago: University of Chicago Press, 2007.

Marx, Karl, and Frederick Engels. *Marx and Engels on Religion.* New York: Schocken, 1964.

O'Neill, John. *Sociology as a Skin Trade.* New York: Harper & Row, 1972.

Riesebrodt, Martin. *The Promise of Salvation: A Theory of Religion.* Chicago: University of Chicago Press, 2010.

Roth, Guenther. "Sociohistorical Model and Developmental Theory: Charismatic Community, Charisma of Reason, and the Counterculture." *American Sociological Review* 40 (1975): 148–157.

Smilde, David, and Matthew May. "The Emerging Strong Program in the Sociology of Religion," *The Immanent Frame*, website. February 2010. http://blogs.ssrc.org/tif/wp-content/uploads/2010/02/Emerging-Strong-Program-TIF.pdf.

Warner, Stephen. "Work in Progress toward a New Paradigm for the Sociological Study of Religion in the United States." *American Journal of Sociology* 98 (1993): 1044–1093.

Weber, Max. 1922. *Economy and Society.* Eds. Guenther Roth and Claus Wittch. Berkeley: University of California Press, 1978.

Wilson Bryan R. *Magic and the Millennium.* London: Heinemann, 1973.

Worsley, Peter. *The Trumpet Shall Sound.* New York: Schocken, 1968.

CHAPTER 26

RELIGION AND VIOLENCE FROM AN ANTHROPOLOGICAL PERSPECTIVE

PAMELA J. STEWART AND ANDREW STRATHERN

A Scottish relative of ours, with an enquiring mind, once posed to us a blunt question as we sat waiting for a family homemade video to begin: Why would people of one religious faith attack those of another? The question reveals both the power and the trap of categorization. Religious identity, like ethnic or national identities, tends to be salient. If people practice Christianity, they can be described as Christian, although they may be other things, too, which are separate from their Christianity. Our answer to the question was that when violence occurs between people it is usually overdetermined by multiple factors and reasons, in which religion may be only one element or even may pull against violence as such. It remains the case, however, that when religion plays a focal role for people in their lives, it can be deployed as an ideological justification for any act, including violence, unless the religion absolutely forbids this. In some instances, religious postulates may enjoin aspects of violence in the name of a cause, although often divergent ideological strands within its adherents may negate this.

The discussion is complicated because of definitional difficulties with both religion and violence as descriptive or analytical terms. In either case, it is a question of broad or narrow definitions. For religion, Benson Saler has examined the consequences of such definitions (Saler 1993). On violence, the benchmark work of David Riches, with its concentration on physical action that causes harm (Riches 1986), has served as a guideline (see also Stewart and Strathern 2002); but broader extensions into what Pierre Bourdieu called "symbolic violence" tend to come to mind (Bourdieu 1977). For our purposes, minimalist definitions suffice. Religion can be seen as an engagement with spirit worlds and violence as harmful acts whose legitimacy is contested or ambivalent. The element of contested legitimacy is crucial (cf. Riches 1986: 11).

For our purposes we can also distinguish between anthropological theories of religion, anthropological theories of violence, and arenas of overlap that display conjunctions or disjunctures of religion and violent actions. It is this third arena that is most pertinent to the overall theme of this book, but the topics can usefully be separated in order to see how the conjunctures of religion with activity spheres such as violence come about. Rituals also pay a notable role in either supporting or opposing violence, whether or not the rituals have explicitly to do with spirit worlds.

Anthropological theories of religion have changed in their emphases and aims over times. Nineteenth-century and early twentieth-century writers, dubbed later on as "armchair" theorists, wanted to produce universal definitions and also to place different religious ideas on an evolutionary scale. Among these writers, Tylor's definition of religion as a "belief in spiritual beings" (cited in Morris 1987: 115) can be taken as a kernel of the intellectualist or mentalist approaches to definitions, concentrated on ideas and statements rather than social practices. Tylor's views were supported much later by Robin Horton (e.g., Horton and Finnegan 1973) and stretch forward to latter-day phenomenological approaches (e.g., Jackson ed. 1996). Needham, however, cogently questioned the category of belief (Needham 1972). All of these approaches are emic, in the sense that they take their cues from an interpretation of the meanings that people attribute to the worlds they live in. Tylor's original definition can also be applied across the board to many, if not all, religious systems, beginning with animism and supposedly culminating in monotheism. Frazer explicitly took a social evolutionary viewpoint in seeing magic as a primitive form of science, evolving over time into religious practices in which people sensed a dependence on spirits or deities and prayed to them for help rather than manipulating substances to attain their aims (e.g., Frazer, *The Golden Bough* 1935[1890]). Frazer's discussions were also mentalist, since they postulated that magic depended on the two principles of sympathy and contagion (like produces like, and things brought into contact can influence each other when separated).

Emile Durkheim took a different approach, which became foundational for much subsequent theorizing. He argued that religion was fundamentally social and founded on the expression of community values, the images of society itself (Durkheim 1965 [1915]). All religions were therefore "true" in a sense, because their "true" object was society. Durkheim used as a prime example the supposedly elementary case of Australian Aboriginal totemism, in which the totem is the sacred emblem of the group; but he insisted that his definition would apply to all cases (see

Morris 1987: 111–122). He insisted, too, that explanations should be founded on the sociology of groups and not on individual psychological traits. Magic, for him, was an individual activity and therefore not a part of religion as a collective practice centered on a "church." He did argue that religious practice was centered on an idea of the sacred (as against profane), and this might be seen as a mentalist proposition; but for Durkeim the sacred was society itself. Latter-day theorists have questioned too rigid a distinction between either the sacred and the profane or the domains of sociology and psychology.

Durkheim's views fed directly into the thinking of social anthropologists in Britain in the first and middle parts of the twentieth century and find their most immediate influence in the work of A. R. Radcliffe-Brown, beginning with his writings on the Andaman islanders of the Indian Ocean (Radcliffe-Brown 1964 [1922]). Radcliffe-Brown's view was that religion supported social structure (Durkheim's community, group, etc.) by underpinning it with values and sentiments to which people would adhere over time and transmit between generations (see, e.g., Morris 1987: 127; Radcliffe-Brown 1952). Religious taboos, instituted to mark out certain items or persons against disrespect, were analyzed in this vein. Since religion was seen as a primary force supporting solidarity, issues of religion and group identity were clearly represented as closely tied. Radcliffe-Brown's ideas were sedimented by later commentators into "structural-functionalism" and criticized for their stress on continuity rather than change. Meyer Fortes, as a major exponent of Radcliffe-Brown's ideas and a major ethnographer and theorist in his own right, added depth to functionalist theories by postulating the importance of psychological syndromes such as expressions of the hostility between generations (e.g., Fortes 1987). Fortes was influenced by Bronislaw Malinowski, the ethnographer of Trobriands society in New Guinea (e.g., Malinowski 1922), and Malinowski had developed his own overall theory of human society, building it from biological needs to the institutional practices that meet them and then to the "integrative imperatives" of holding groups together, which would include religious and ritual practices (Malinowski 1944; see discussion in Sörensen 2007).

Sentiments, integrative imperatives, psychological syndromes: All these ultimately focus on mechanisms of social reproduction and adaptation. They converge further on the significance of symbols in social life and how symbols work to motivate people or how people work to activate symbols. Clifford Geertz's formulation of religion as a unique domain in which symbols are deployed to establish long-lasting and valued motivations in people belongs to this thread of theorizing (Geertz 1975: 90; cf. Morris 1987: 313). Symbols for Geertz are both models of and models for reality, and he combines interpretive, phenomenological, and sociological analysis while making a distinction between cultural meanings and social (viz. also historical) causes (Morris, 315–316, our reformulation). It is clear overall that, for Geertz, religion is a powerful factor in collective life, just as it was for Durkheim. Roy Rappaport's work (Rappaport 1999) extended the theory of symbols further, drawing deeply on linguistic theory and on distinctions between words and embodied actions. Rappaport saw religion as an adaptive system, helping to coordinate a great range of activities in society. He also noted that certain embodied actions carry ritual power and significance beyond words, as when a man among the Maring people of Papua New Guinea attended a dance and by so doing signaled his willingness to act as an ally in warfare, with ancestor spirits as witnesses (Rappaport 1999: 57–58; 1967: 195). Finally, he postulated that religious liturgies preserve variant *degrees* of sacredness.

Rappaport distinguishes between Ultimate Sacred Postulates, cosmological axioms about the spirit world which sanctify and certify practices, and rules of conduct deriving from the higher-level axioms which may change over time while the sacred postulates do not (Rappaport 1999: 263ff.). Since rules of conduct may change, it is clear that Rappaport does not suggest that religion is entirely stable, but his theory is well adapted to the idea of continuity and indeed is premised on it. Theory may also have to take into account what happens when rules are broken, whether as a prelude to changing them or not.

A further brand of theorizing that also lends itself to broad generalizations is the cognitive theory of religion. There are several exponents and viewpoints here. Notable work has been done by, e.g. Boyer 1990, Lawson and McCauley 1990, Pyysiäinen 2001, and Sperber 1975, 1985; and the whole arena has been summarized by Tremlin 2006 and innovatively worked on by Harvey Whitehouse and James Laidlaw (Whitehouse and Laidlaw eds. 2007). Basically, this approach aims to explain religion as a phenomenon that emerges from perduring characteristics of the human mind. The approach hypothesizes that humans operate with a theory of mind (ToM) attributing agency and intention to living categories of things in the world outside of humans themselves (e.g., Guthrie 2007: 48–52). It is a short step from this proposition to an understanding that such forms of agency can be imaged as spirits or deities. Cognitive theory further suggests that ideas about spirits are only minimally counterintuitive and are therefore easy to accept and to develop, since spirits can be seen as like persons (and persons, perhaps, as like deities [e.g. Barrett 2007: 186–188]). One could comment that such ideas might not be counterintuitive at all but based on the experiences of particular individuals such as shamans and ritual experts who are thought to be hypersensitive to the spirit world. Consciousness of dangers and hazards in the world is a further component of the theory, leading its exponents ad hoc to hypothesize a hyperactive agency detection device (HADD), which is brought into play especially (but surely not exclusively) in ritual contexts as a means of warning against misfortunes or mistakes. Religious taboos may be seen as a result of the capacity for HADD. Lanman, for example, suggests that ritual contexts make people highly sensitive to dangers thought to come from supernatural forces, so reinforcing the belief in the spirit categories (Lanman 2007: 125–126). Feedback loops are thus posited in this theory, which seems to take the same circular form as the reasoning attributed to ritual practitioners.

While this approach, like others, is not intrinsically connected to any ideas about violence, it is clear that it can be linked. This becomes more obvious when cognitive theories are applied to "mystical" ideas, such as witchcraft, sorcery, and divination. Emma Cohen argues that these ideas are akin to ones that appear in contexts outside witchcraft (Cohen 2007: 137), as in the notion that misfortunes are due to the undisclosed agency of others (rather than being one's own fault), which may then require divinatory practices by specialists to uncover and deal with them. (Cohen, pp. 142–3). In turn, attributions of blame are often tied to stereotypical schemata about people, regarding them as essences that exhibit categories, such as the categories of witch and sorcerer (p. 144). Essences may in turn be seen as inherited between kin (p. 147). Since witchcraft and sorcery actions are generally held to be hostile, the response to them may also be violent.

Cohen's cognitivist propositions are a straightforward distillation of paradigmatic ethnographic sources, notably Evans-Pritchard's classic study of the Azande people of the Sudan in Africa (Evans-Pritchard 1937). Cohen contrasts her account with ones based on what she calls "conventional anthropological treatments" (137); but her propositions fall clearly in line with those either implicit or explicit in ethnographic discussions and may have been derived from these. In any case, as she notes, accounts of local processes may be combined with accounts of putatively pervasive mental processes. However, what the "conventional" approaches do is to exemplify the social, rather than purely mental, genesis of ideas in contexts of social life involving conflict, competition, jealousy, anxiety, and so on (see Stewart and Strathern 2004 for numerous illustrations of this point).

Within the subcategories Cohen recognizes as generated out of theories of secret agency and essentialist attributions, divination is of particular interest (Cohen: 140). We have emphasized this in our writings (e.g., Stewart and Strathern 2004: 125–126). Divination is used as an ostensibly objective technique to reveal what is otherwise opaque, either the will of spirits, fate, or what happened before and was unexplained such as a sickness or death. It can be used as a springboard for either violent actions (e.g., when it reveals an accused sorcerer who is said to have killed a victim by magic) or healing actions, such as when it reveals the violence of ancestors in sending sickness to their descendants and prescribes pigs for sacrificing to appease these ancestors. Divination was used in warfare to determine when to engage in battle or what the outcome of an impending battle would be (in ancient Greece and Rome, see Marcus Tullius Cicero, *On Divination*, trans. by C. D. Yonge, 148–149 and 222–223, 1853; Plutarch's *Lives*, trans. by J. and W. Langhorne, 217, 1836; Eidinow 2007 on Greek oracles; and Agamben 1998 on *homo sacer* in Rome: and also among the Maring people of Papua New Guinea studied by Rappaport [Rappaport 1967]). The result of a divination could be the means of legitimizing the hunting down and killing of a sorcerer held responsible for the death of kin among the Gebusi of Papua New Guinea (Knauft 1985). Divination, as a way of finding out "truth," is thus a crucial mediator between mental processes and their sociopolitical outcomes. The point can be carried further. Wider processes of social life may also be subject to divinatory scrutiny because they are held to be contingent on spirit actions and attitudes. For example, in the Mount Hagen area of Papua New Guinea, if at a dance marking a prestigious or peace-making event the decorations of the dancers fail to appear resplendent but instead are shabby in appearance or if rain sweeps over and covers the dancing ground, these events are attributed to the displeasure of ancestor spirits, on whom ultimately all success in life's activities is thought to depend. The whole ritual dance event, and the work to bring it into being, thus becomes a cosmic act of divination. The same can be said of a political complex such as a war or the interpretation of a natural disaster or an epidemic of sickness.

Reformulating the idea of cognition as presented in cognitivist theories, we may note that another way of looking at religion, ritual, magic, witchcraft, and sorcery is that they are products of the human imaginative capacity. By invoking imagination, we enlarge cognition to include the emotions and creativity (cf., e.g., Hallam and Ingold eds. 2007). Imagination, in turn, can leap to contexts of revenge and violence. If it is thought that a death is due to the actions of hostile spirits or sorcerers, retaliatory action may be taken. Gebusi spirit mediumship provides a dramatic illustration of this point (Knauft 1985). Dreaming may be involved (Stephen 1989a; Stewart and Strathern 2003a). Visions and prophesies may be at work. Michele Stephen calls this the domain of "autonomous imagining" that lends itself to the construction of "sacred worlds" (Stephen 1989b: 211ff.). René Girard explores this world of imagining in terms of his theory of sacrifice, scapegoating, and violence, arguing that, inter alia, there is a "double nature" in "all primitive divinities, the blending of beneficent and maleficent that characterizes all mythical figures who involve themselves in mortal affairs" (Girard 1993: 251, see also Burkert 2001). So the Roman god Janus, he says, "turns to his worshippers a countenance alternately warlike and peaceful" (ibid.). If he comes to stand also for war against foreigners, "that is because foreign war is merely another form of sacrificial violence" (ibid). For Girard, with his meditations on parricide and its expiation, the Oedipus complex, and Freud, forms of violence lie at the heart of the sacred. Other theorists do not make so close a connection. While the sacred may be conceived of as powerful, dangerous, and hedged with taboos, it may also be seen as the archetypal source of blessings and prosperity, peace building and reconciliation. Scott Appleby has explored both the violent and the peaceful aspects of potentialities of religion (Appleby 2000), using as his leitmotif the concept of ambivalence, as reflected in his title, "*The Ambivalence of the Sacred*," a phrase that jibes well enough with Girard's formulations.

Other works that chime in with the idea of connections between religion and violence, often tied in with sacrifice as a theme implying violence, include Peggy Sanday's "Divine Hunger: Cannibalism as a Cultural System" (Sanday 1986). Her approach is well illustrated in her treatment of Aztec sacrifice (see David Carrasco's chapter, 11, in this volume).

Aztec cannibalism was sacrificial and involved especially the offering to the gods of human hearts taken from captive victims, other parts of the victim's body being consumed by the sacrificers and their king. The hearts were consecrated to the sun god, to nourish him and presumably gain the continued blessings of sunlight. These hearts were described as precious eagle-cactus fruit, and the whole ritual complex of cannibalistic sacrifice is described by Sanday as a "part of a cosmo-magical-biological schema for social, physical, and sacred being" (Sanday 1986: 174). The Aztec case reminds us of the human suffering that often forms a part of ritual sequences in which extreme demonstrations of power and its renewal are enacted. The idea of suffering here points us to the corner of the victims in David Riches's (1986) triangle of violence, adding to Riches's model the point that the infliction of suffering may be underpinned, in the broadest of senses, by religious postulates.

In a further twist on this theme, we may note that religiously sanctioned or enjoined practices of inflicting harm on one's own body also depend on cosmology. Self-mortification in Christian and other traditions must depend on the idea that by punishing or harming the body one can attain a purification or higher state of the soul and thus, perhaps, a greater promise of attaining an honored place in the afterworld. In another version of this theme, it may be thought that one's sufferings on earth may be compensated for by bliss in the life after death. Acts of suicide may in some cases also be directed equally at the life left behind and at existence as a ghost in the future. In some parts of the New Guinea highlands, suicides, especially by females, can be seen as protests against mistreatment by their family and equally as threats that as ghosts they may enact revenge on those who have driven them to kill themselves (Stewart and Strathern 2003b). An "honor" suicide by a female in the face of a threatened violation may lead in some cultural contexts in Taiwan to the establishment of an arena of temple worship dedicated to the spirit of the dead person, as in the case of Wang Yulan in Jinmen where we carried out fieldwork in December 2012 (cf. Szonyi 2007). Loss of the physical body may be compensated here, too, by a commemoration of the spirit in a temple dedicated to the person's narrative of suffering.

This point, in turn, reminds us of ritual healing practices, which often aim at re-establishing balance and harmony within the individual, in this case implying holistic health and well-being (of body and soul, or of whatever cosmic components are thought to make up the person). Prayer, exorcism, shamanic "soul recovery," or diagnosis of possession, may all be involved in the pursuit of rebalancing the person, in some cases with the aim of perfecting the self as an aspect of the sacred in life. Here, the work of Thomas Csordas (e.g., 1994, 2002) can be cited as exemplifying the trends of analysis in a large body of work (see also Strathern and Stewart 2010 for a contextualization of healing within medical anthropological studies). Ritual healing stands as an opposite or counterpoint to the ritual infliction of suffering or sickness on others by torture or by sorcery. Meaning is clearly all, since ritual flagellation might seem like a violent or harmful act, yet it may be intended to lead to a kind of healing. The same may be said of initiation rituals that involve painful bodily alterations or beatings. They may be designed to strengthen the person for adult life, especially if the aim of the initiation is to produce (usually) male warriors. Initiation into warriorhood often tends to be violent. Among the Baktaman, as discussed by Fredrik Barth, novices in third-degree initiations underwent a number of procedures, including whipping over the face by bunches of nettles, carried out by senior males of the group. Barth notes that this would cause the boys considerable pain (Barth 1975: 68). They were also required to eat unpalatable food and were kept awake for four days, pushed up against fires (ibid.). Barth categorizes these events as "torture" (66). Ideas about spirits are involved because the rituals are intended to drive out harmful and polluting spirits (67) and to ensure successful hunting of wild pigs as well as strength for battle when needed.

Our examples have led us to cite materials widely from different ethnographic contexts, all indicating complex relationships among religion, violence, and social norms and ideals. Religion can be given broad or narrow definitions, but in either case it covers a great diversity of ideas and practice about the cosmos, including humans and spirit beings. As with humans, so with spirits: Tendencies to violence are counterposed to tendencies to benevolence. Returning, then, to our Scottish relative's question, religious ideologies can be invoked in cases of conflict, but a great complex of causes is encapsulated in every act of this kind. Religious identities and ritual practices may be called on in these cases simply because these identities and practices carry great potential salience and can be made the theoretical focus of political agendas. Yet the same salient identities may be summoned on other occasions to produce healing. Perhaps it was this kind of complexity that prompted the Greek dictum attributed to Heracleitus that "the road up and down is one and the same." Latter-day philosophers also struggled with this theme (see de Vries 2002).

BIBLIOGRAPHY

Agamben, Giorgio. *Homo Sacer. Sovereign Power and Bare Life*. Palo Alto, CA: Stanford University Press, 1998.

Appleby, R. Scott. *The Ambivalence of the Sacred. Religion, Violence, and Reconciliation*. Lanham, MD: Rowman and Littlefield, 2000.

Barrett, Justin L. "Ancestors and the Afterlife." In H. Whitehouse and J. Laidlaw, eds. *Religion, Anthropology,and Cognitive Science*, 179–207. Durham, NC: Carolina Academic Press, 2007.

Barth, Fredrik. *Ritual and Knowledge among the Baktaman of New Guinea*. New Haven, CT: Yale University Press, 1975.

Bourdieu, Pierre. *Outline of a Theory of Practice*. Translated by Richard Nice. Cambridge, UK: Cambridge University Press, 1977.

Boyer, Pascal. *Tradition as Truth and Communication: A Cognitive Description of Traditional Discourse*. Cambridge, UK: Cambridge University Press, 1990.

Burkert, Walter. *Savage Energies. Lessons of Myth and Ritual in Ancient Greece*. Translated by Peter Bing. Chicago: University of Chicago Press, 2001.

Cicero, Marcus Tullius. *On the Nature of the Gods, On Divination*. Translated by C. D. Yonge. London: Henry Bohn, 1853.

Cohen, Emma. "Witchcraft and Sorcery." In *Religion, Anthropology, and Cognitive Science*. Eds. H. Whitehouse and J. Laidlaw, 135–160. Durham, NC: Carolina Academic Press, 2007.

Csordas, Thomas. *The Sacred Self: A Cultural Phenomenology of Charismatic Healing*. Berkeley: University of California Press, 1994.

Csordas, Thomas. *Body / Meaning / Healing.* New York: Palgrave Macmillan, 2002.

Durkheim, Émile. 1912. *The Elementary Forms of the Religious Life.* Translated by J. W. Swain. New York: Free Press, 1965.

Eidinow, Esther. *Oracles, Curses, and Risk among the Ancient Greeks.* Oxford, UK: Oxford University Press, 2007.

Evans-Pritchard, E. E. *Witchcraft, Oracles, and Magic among the Azande.* Oxford, UK: Clarendon Press, 1937.

Fortes, Meyer. *Religion, Morality and the Person: Essays on Tallensi Religion.* Edited by Jack Goody. Cambridge, UK: Cambridge University Press, 1987.

Frazer, James G. 1890. *The Golden Bough*, 3rd ed. London: Macmillan, 1935.

Geertz, Clifford. *The Interpretation of Cultures.* London: Hutchinson, 1975.

Girard, René. *Violence and the Sacred.* Translated by Patrick Gregory. Baltimore: Johns Hopkins University Press, 1993.

Guthrie, Stewart Elliott. "Anthropology and Anthropomorphism in Religion." In *Religion, Anthropology, and Cognitive Science.* Eds. H. Whitehouse and J. Laidlaw, 37–62. Durham, NC: Carolina Academic Press, 2007.

Hallam, Elizabeth and Tim Ingold, eds. *Creativity and Cultural Improvisation.* Oxford, UK: Berg, 2007.

Horton, R. and R. Finnegan, eds. *Modes of Thought.* London: Faber and Faber, 1973.

Jackson, Michael, ed. *Things as They Are: New Directions in Phenomenological Anthropology.* Bloomington: Indiana University Press, 1996.

Knauft, Bruce M. *Good Company and Violence: Sorcery and Social Action in a Lowland New Guinea Society.* Berkeley: University of California, 1985.

Lanman, Jonathan A. "How 'Natives' Don't Think: The Apotheosis of Overinterpreation." In *Religion, Anthropology, and Cognitive Science.* Eds. H. Whitehouse and J. Laidlaw, 105–132. Durham, NC: Carolina Academic Press, 2007.

Lawson, E. T. and R. N. McCauley. *Rethinking Religion. Connecting Cognition and Culture* Cambridge, UK: Cambridge University Press, 1990.

Malinowski, Bronislaw. *Argonauts of the Western Pacific.* London: Routledge and Kegan Paul, 1922.

Malinowski, Bronislaw. *A Scientific Theory of Culture and Other Essays.* Chapel Hill: University of North Carolina Press, 1944.

Morris, Brian. *Anthropological Studies of Religion: An Introductory Text.* Cambridge, UK: Cambridge University Press, 1987.

Needham, Rodney. *Belief, Language, and Experience.* Chicago: University of Chicago Press, 1972.

Plutarch. *Plutarch's Lives.* Translated by John Langhorne and William Langhorne. Baltimore: William and Joseph Neal, 1836.

Pyysiäinen, I. *How Religion Works: Towards a New Cognitive Science of Religion.* Leiden, Netherlands: Brill, 2001.

Radcliffe-Brown, Alfred Reginald. *Structure and Function in Primitive Society.* London: Cohen and West, 1952.

Radcliffe-Brown, Alfred Reginald. 1922. *The Andaman Islanders.* Glencoe, IL: Free Press, 1964.

Rappaport, Roy A. *Pigs for the Ancestors: Ritual in the Ecology of a New Guinea People.* New Haven, CT: Yale University Press, 1967.

Rappaport, Roy A. *Ritual and Religion in the Making of Humanity.* Cambridge, UK: Cambridge University Press, 1999.

Riches, David. "The Phenomenon of Violence." In *The Anthropology of Violence*. Ed. D. Riches, 1–27. Oxford, UK: Basil Blackwell, 1986.

Saler, Benson. *Conceptualizing Religion: Immanent Anthropologists, Transcendent Natives, and Unbounded Categories*. New York and Oxford, UK: Berghahn Books, 1993.

Sanday, Peggy Reeves. *Divine Hunger: Cannibalism as a Cultural System*. Cambridge, UK: Cambridge University Press, 1986.

Sörensen, Jesper. "Malinowski and Magical Ritual." In *Religion, Anthropology, and Cognitive Science*. Eds. H. Whitehouse and J. Laidlaw, 81–104. Durham, NC: Carolina Academic Press, 2007.

Sperber, D. *Rethinking Symbolism*. Cambridge, UK: Cambridge University Press, 1975.

Sperber, D. *On Anthropological Knowledge*. Cambridge, UK: Cambridge University Press, 1985.

Stephen, Michele. "Self, the Sacred Other, and Autonomous Imagination." In *The Religious Imagination in New Guinea*. Eds. G. Herdt and M. Stephen, 41–64. New Brunswick, NJ: Rutgers University Press, 1989.

Stephen, Michele. "Constructing Sacred Worlds and Autonomous Imagining in New Guinea. In*The Religious Imagination in New Guinea*. Eds. G. Herdt and M. Stephen, 211–223. New Brunswick, NJ: Rutgers University Press, 1989.

Stewart, Pamela J. and Andrew Strathern. *Violence: Theory and Ethnography*. London and New York: Continuum, 2002.

Stewart, Pamela J. and Andrew Strathern. "Dreaming and Ghosts among the Hagen and Duna of the Southern Highlands, Papua New Guinea." In *Dream Travelers: Sleep Experiences and Culture in the Western Pacific*. Ed. Roger Ivar Lohmann, 42–59. New York: Palgrave Macmillan, 2003a.

Stewart, Pamela J. and Andrew Strathern. "The Ultimate Protest Statement: Suicide as a Means of Defining Self-Worth among the Duna of the Southern Highlands Province, PNG." *Journal of Ritual Studies* 17.1 (2003b): 79–88.

Stewart, Pamela J. and Andrew Strathern. *Witchcraft, Sorcery, Rumors, and Gossip*. Cambridge, UK: Cambridge University Press, 2004.

Strathern, Andrew and Pamela J. Stewart. *Curing and Healing: Medical Anthropology in Global Perspective*, 2nd ed. Durham, NC: Carolina Academic Press, 2010.

Szonyi, Michael. "The Virgin and the Chinese State: The Cult of Wang Yulan and the Politics of Local Identity on Jinmen (Quemoy)." In *Asian Ritual Systems. Syncretisms and Ruptures*. Eds. P. J. Stewart and A. Strathern, 183–208. New Brunswick, NJ: Rutgers University Press, 2007.

Tremlin, Todd. *Minds and Gods. The Cognitive Foundations of Religion*. Oxford, UK: Oxford University Press, 2006.

de Vries, Hent. *Religion and Violence: Philosophical Perspectives from Kant to Derrida*. Baltimore: Johns Hopkins Universitiy Press, 2002.

Whitehouse, Harvey and James Laidlaw, eds. *Religion, Anthropology, and Cognitive Science*. Durham, NC: Carolina Academic Press, 2007.

....

CHAPTER 27

RELIGION AND VIOLENCE FROM A PSYCHOLOGICAL PERSPECTIVE

....

JAMES W. JONES

RECENT studies in the discipline of the psychology of religion have focused on three general areas: the motivations, personality correlates, and psychosocial effects of various religious beliefs and practices (Pargament, Exline, Jones, Schafranske, Mahoney, in press; Wulff 1991). Such studies have been carried out within a wide range of psychological paradigms—personality psychologists, social psychologists, neuropsychologists, clinicians, and many others have investigated various aspects of the religious life, including the psychological dimensions of religion's role in promoting and (to a lesser extent) restraining violence (Jones, in press). This chapter will briefly review some of the methods and findings in this area.

PSYCHOPATHOLOGY?

....

No serious contemporary study has found any evidence for diagnosable psychopathology in those who commit acts of religiously motivated violence and terror (see, for example, the review in Horgan 2005). After reviewing all the literature on the perpetrators of genocide, the social psychologist James Waller concludes that he could find no evidence that the actual perpetrators of large scale atrocities, taken as a whole, displayed any particular psychopathology or character disorder (Waller 2002; see also Atran 2003; Horgan 2005; Post 1984; Reich 1998; and Victoroff 2005 for a similar conclusion).

PSYCHOLOGICAL STUDIES
OF ETHNOPOLITICAL VIOLENCE

Analyzing "religious extremist terrorism," the psychiatrist Jerrold Post insists that such violence is a group activity arising from a "collective identity" (Post 2007; Post, Ruby, Shaw 2002). This is because those who commit violence in the name of a religious ideology "have subordinated their individual identity to the collective identity, so that what serves the group, organization, or network is of primary importance" (Post 2007: 8). Such subordination to the group gives leaders almost limitless powers to shape the behavior of members. For Post, the psychology of the leader is the key to understanding the motivations of the group. Post finds a pattern of little or no relationship with fathers in many of the "charismatic" leaders of violent groups; for example Osama bin Laden (Post 2007: 193), Abdullah Ocalan of the Kurdistan Workers Party (PKK) (Post 2007: 70–71) or Abimael Guzman of the Shining Path (2007: 131). Such a childhood history, Post contends, produces "an intensely narcissistic personality" (Post, Ruby, Shaw 2002: 85–86; Post 2007: 75), externally confident and inspiring but vulnerable at the core. For Post, this dynamic of narcissistic leaders and needy followers is the key to the psychology of violent religious movements (Post, Ruby, Shaw 2002: 87; Robins, Post, 1997).

Such charismatic leadership, which Post takes as an essential characteristic of violence-prone political and religious groups, is "a property of a social system, a fit between leaders with particular characteristics and a wounded fellowship at a moment of crisis" (Post, Ruby, Shaw 2002: 87). Followers give charismatic leaders absolute allegiance and accept uncritically the leader's teachings and instructions (Post 2007: 195). Since the leader sets the tone and direction for the group, whether or not a political or religious movement turns violent "depends on the disposition of the leader" (Post, Ruby, Shaw 2002: 88). If the leader endorses and preaches violence, there is every likelihood that the movement will engage in murder and terror.

Like Post, Vamik Volkan has spent decades studying violence (Volkan 1997). Also like Post, he focuses on the centrality of group behavior in campaigns of violence. Volkan suggests that individuals susceptible to being recruited into violent campaigns had a personal experience of victimization or trauma. They become mobilized as they identify with injury to the larger ethnic or religious group. Such vulnerable individuals regress to a position of almost total dependency on the group and its leader. For Volkan, too, understanding this relationship of the member to the group and to the leader is key to understanding the psychology of group violence. Volkan suggests that leaders of religious groups come from troubled families, often with missing or unavailable parents. Such leaders seek to create a "family" in which they become the parent and so attempt to make up for a deficiency in their early experience. Such leaders and groups attract people without secure identities who regressively depend on the leader and the group for their identity.

These leaders, however, soon begin to abuse their "family members" as they were abused as children. In addition, such total dependence breeds a rage that may be masochistically turned on the self (committing suicide as Heaven's Gate and the Solar Temple or martyrdom operations did) or sadistically turned against outsiders (unrestricted warfare). Furthermore, violent tendencies are exacerbated when the group on which the individual depends appears threatened. Threats to the group are easily translated into threats against the self, which depends on the group for its psychological existence (Volkan 2004).

Volkan also points to the reciprocal, interaction effects between a violent group and those outside it. Even before they turn violent, such groups often evoke fear and anger in those around them. Sometimes this is the result of the group's deviant activities and sometimes it is simply the result of the outsider's fear of those who are different. This cycle of mutually increasing suspicion and mistrust almost always ends in catastrophe as it feeds the group's incipient paranoia about the outside world. This clearly happened with Aum Shinrykio in Japan (Jones 2008; Reader 2000), the Branch Dividians in Waco, Texas, (Wessinger 2000), and the People's Temple in Guyana (Kimball 2002).

Paralleling D. W. Winnicott's theory of transitional objects (Jones 1997), Volkan says that people require "moments of rest" (like Winnicott's "transitional space") where they can let go of a compulsive reality testing and indulge in creativity and fantasy through art, literature, music, and religion (Volkan 2004). For Volkan, like Winnicott, this function of religion is perfectly normal. However, Volkan says, individuals whose parent-child bond was not secure or who were raised in an excessively religious environment use religion in a regressive way. They use religion to blot out and deny rationality and reality rather than as a means of imaginatively transforming reality while remaining in touch with it. Denying reality in this way leaves the person vulnerable to group leaders who magnify and reinforce his or her fears and anxieties.

The two most widely cited social-psychological experiments in the literature of violent group behavior—Milgram's obedience to authority and Zimbardo's prison experiment—support this focus on group psychology. In the early 1960s, Stanley Milgram recruited a cohort of forty ordinary men from New Haven and found that the majority of them were willing to inflict what they thought were increasingly severe shocks on a subject as a punishment for wrong answers to questions. Even when the subject portrayed signs of severe distress or cried out, 65 percent of the participants were willing to inflict what they were told was a near fatal shock to the subject in obedience to the experimenter's commands. Significantly less than half the participants were willing to defy the experimenter at all. Over the years,

Milgram's findings have been replicated time and time again in a variety of different settings and countries (Blass 1999; Milgram 1974).

In 1971 at Stanford University, Philip Zimbardo recruited a cohort of typical college male undergraduates and randomly assigned one group to play the role of prisoners and the other to play the role of prison guards. He set them up in a mock prison setting. Anyone with noticeable psychological problems was screened out; only those most mature and stable participated. Given the random assignments, both groups were basically similar. Within days, a third of those assigned to be guards became increasingly cruel, sadistic, and tyrannical toward the prisoners, who they knew were really just fellow undergraduates like them, thus demonstrating how easy it is to elicit cruel and sadistic behavior even from those not otherwise inclined or socialized in that direction. In the mock prison, this brutality escalated so rapidly that the two-week-long experiment was stopped after six days (Zimbardo et. al. 2000). Both sets of experiments strongly suggest that ordinary people, with no particular history of violence, can be relatively easily recruited into roles in which they are willing and able to inflict severe pain on their fellow human beings.

On the same line, in a 2008 article titled "Who Becomes a Terrorist Today?" Scott Atran concludes that contemporary terror "networks are also built up around friendship and kinship but members are more marginal relative to surrounding society" (Atran 2008). Looking at the formation of terrorist networks from an evolutionary perspective, Atran concludes that current terrorists "kill and die for faith and friendship, which is the foundation of all social and political union, that is, all enduring human associations of non-kin: shared faith reigns in self-interest and makes social life possible; friendship allows genetically unrelated individuals to cooperate to compete" (Atran 2002; Atran 2008). The implication is that terrorist groups are no different psychologically from any other human group. The same inherited traits that drive other forms of social bonding also drive religiously motivated terror cells. They can be understood with the the same tools of analysis used for all human communities.

THE LIMITS OF SOCIAL INFLUENCE THEORIES

Most recently published, psychologically oriented articles on violence and terrorism focus primarily on the group processes and induction procedures by which individuals are recruited to perform such actions (Atran 2003; Moghaddam 2005; Moghaddam,

Marsella, 2004; Post, Sprinzak & Denny 2003). The stated assumption of this literature is that group dynamics alone can explain the transformation of a normal individual into one who kills for a cause (Zimbardo 2004). Milgram's and

Zimbardo's classic experiments and the commonly asserted finding that there does not seem to be any common personality or psychopathological traits exhibited by terrorists appear to point in that direction.

However, while often cited as analogues for intergroup violence and terrorism, there are significant differences between Milgrim's and Zimbardo's experimental conditions and contemporary campaigns of religious terrorism. There is more to such acts of religious violence than obedience (Miller 2004). Many other factors such as the demonizing of the opponent, the fascination with violence, and the sacralizing of one's cause play crucial roles in religious terrorism. There are also almost always economic, political, or cultural conflicts associated with religiously sponsored killing. In addition, such social influence models alone are not sufficient to explain why these groups possess significant common religious and moral characteristics, regardless of tradition, that shape the behavior of their members and increase their likelihood of turning violent: for example, their absolutist approach to a sacred text, idealized leaders, need to demonize their opponents, and strict boundaries around the group (Eidelson, Eidelson 2003; Jones 2008; Kimball 2002). Such models do not explicate the factors that make an individual vulnerable to the messages of violence prone groups (Jones 2008; Jones 2006).

In addition, not every member of a society from which terrorism arises joins a violent group and not every member of a violent cell actually engages in a violent operation, nor did every subject in Milgram's experiments comply with the experimenter's demands. So it seems most prudent to conclude with Victoroff, who writes after an extensive review of the literature, that "terrorist behavior is probably *always* determined by a combination of…factors…the much-cited claim that no individual factors identify those at risk for becoming terrorists is based on completely inadequate research" (Victoroff 2005, 4; see also Tobena 2004).

These social influence and social process models also apply best to tightly knit groups where there is a structured process of recruitment, initiation, training, and eventual deployment (this is the kind of process described by Horgan and most of the essays in Reich's collection and that of Moghaddam, Marsella). Here the type of group dynamics that Bandura, Milgram, Zimbardo, Horgan, and others emphasize are strong factors. While this certainly applies to the Irish Republican Army, the Red Brigades, and other such groups, contemporary religious terrorism is more likely the result of rapidly evolving "leaderless groups" or "self-starters" in which there is little overt recruitment and much of the training is done over the Internet or in small cliques (Atran 2008; Sageman 2008). Current examples such as radical jihadist cliques in Europe or the Army of God in the United States suggest commitment to a violent group happening without the heavy hand of a group leader or trainer but rather through reading religious literature on one's own, listening to sermons on tape or over the Internet, and discussions with friends (for examples see Atran 2008; Khosrokhavar 2005; Sageman 2008). In such loose confederations of the likeminded, classical models of top-down social influence may lose some of their explanatory power.

Psychodynamic Theories

Such social-psychological analyses are necessary for understanding religious violence, but are they sufficient for a full understanding? They say nothing about individual motivations beyond the common human needs for belonging, adventure, and a meaningful life. I certainly agree with Horgan that "explanations of terrorism in terms of personality traits are insufficient alone in trying to understand why some people become terrorists and others do not" (Horgan 2005, 76). No explanation is sufficient alone to explain that, but that does not entail that individual factors play no role. There remains the fact that some people have "a greater openness to increased engagement than others" with terrorist groups (Horgan 2005: 101). Hafez raises precisely this question when he asks, "[W]hy do some religious frames resonate with people whereas others fail to gain adherents?" (Hafez 2006: 169).

Heinz Kohut's theory of the origins of violence emphasizes the role of a person's sense of self and any threats to it. An important aspect of Kohut's theorizing for the psychology of religion is the way he shows that beliefs, institutions, and ideals can become a part of our sense of self. Then we become dependent on them to maintain that sense of self. A threat to a cherished belief, ideal, or institution can feel like as much (if not more) of a threat than a direct physical threat. Kohut suggests that "destructive rage, in particular, is always motivated by an injury to the self" (Kohut 1977: 117). The injury that evokes this destructive rage can be a direct threat, or, more commonly, it can be a threat to some ideal, ideology, or institution on which the individual depends for his or her identity and self-esteem. If one's identity and sense of self-worth are inextricably bound to an identification with a religious, political, ethnic, or professional community and its beliefs, when they are threatened, Kohut says, one feels threatened at his or her most basic level as a human person. Then one responds with what he calls "narcissistic rage" (Kohut 1973: 379). The main characteristic of such rage is that "those who are in the grip of narcissistic rage show total lack of empathy toward the offender" (Kohut 1973: 386). Such total lack of empathy is one of the most striking traits frequently seen in those who commit violence in the name of some ideal.

Kohut distinguishes such narcissistic rage from ordinary aggression by its totalistic qualities and complete lack of empathy. Here there is a limitless, insatiable quality to the desire for revenge, like that seen in the apocalyptic fanatics who want to purge the world of all evildoers, sinners, and nonbelievers. In contrast to normal aggression or even a normal desire for revenge, narcissistic rage "in its typical forms is an utter disregard for reasonable limitations and a boundless wish to redress an injury and to obtain revenge" (Kohut 1973: 382). While some religiously motivated terrorists may employ violence purely tactically in the pursuit of limited and achievable political goals, others dream of complete purification and the apocalyptic eradication of all unholy people. Such totalistic schemes of divine vengeance reek of narcissistic rage born of threats to cherished beliefs and institutions. Such totalistic dreams of vengeance on the unrighteous do not necessarily coincide with a loss of cognitive functioning. Devotees motivated by narcissistic rage can still fly planes, make sophisticated bombs, and author brilliantly rhetorical texts in the service of their visions of terror.

Religions almost always idealize and sanctify some ideas, beliefs, institutions, books, codes of conduct, or various leaders (Jones 2002). The idealized, sanctified religious objects become parts of their senses of self. Ken Pargament and his group have conducted a series of studies on the psychological impact of considering an activity sacred or sanctified (reviewed in Pargament, Mahoney 2005). Studying such common activities as being married (Mahoney et al. 2003), parenting, having a sexual relationship (Murray-Swank, Pargament, Mahoney 2000), or engaging in environmental activism (Tarakeshwar et al. 2001), they found that those who designate a facet of life as sacred place a higher priority on that aspect of life, invest more energy in it, and derive more meaning from it than happens with things not denoted as sacred. So denoting something as sacred appears to have significant emotional and behavioral consequences, even if that something is the jihad, ending abortion and turning the United States into a biblical theocracy, restoring the boundaries of biblical Israel, purifying the Hindu homeland, or converting the Tamils to Buddhism.

But this process of sanctification can set us up for narcissistic rage. Pargament and his group investigated exactly that possibility in a study of what they call "desecration" (the opposite of sanctification), which involves the perceived violation of something held sacred (Pargament et al. 2005). Such desecration most likely leads to rage. The desecration of something held sacred is experienced as a significant trauma bringing with it intense emotional distress. Desecration is usually associated with decreased mental health and increased anger. In another study, Pargament and his colleagues (Pargament et al. 2007) found that Christians who believed that Jews were responsible for Jesus's Crucifixion and other desecrations of Christian values displayed higher-than-average levels of anti-Semitism. Even when all other predictors of anti-Semitism were controlled for, belief that Jews desecrated Christian values was a robust predictor of anti-Semitism. Such results fit neatly with Kohut's model of narcissistic rage.

RELIGIOUS TERRORISM

A careful study of writings, websites, speeches, interviews of, and videos produced by religiously motivated terrorists reveals that certain themes seem common to most religiously sponsored terrorists: teachings and texts that evoke shame and humiliation; the demand for submission to an overly idealized but humiliating institution, text, leader, or deity; a patriarchal religious milieu; an impatience with ambiguity and an inability to tolerate ambivalence that lead to a splitting of the world into polarized all-good and all-evil camps and the demonizing of the other; a drive for total purification and perfection; narcissistic rage and a fascination with violence and violent imagery; doctrines that link violence and purification; and the repression of sexuality (Jones 2008; Silberman, Higgins, Dweck 2005). These constructs and images, embodied in the narratives of religious terrorists, regardless of tradition, are full of psychological content.

From a clinical, psychodynamic perspective, it is not coincidence that such themes often occur together. Something within certain individuals may predispose them to be attracted to and to accept a religion characterized by an apocalyptic view of the world and the splitting of humanity into all-good and all-evil camps, leading to prejudice and crusades against outsiders (Jones 2008, 2006). For example, psychoanalytic theory provides an account—grounded in clinical experience—of the genesis of the need to divide the world into rigidly polarized, warring camps that many commentators find at the heart of religious fanaticism. One solution to overpowering guilt or shame appears in the pursuit of perfection and absolute purity that pacifies a demanding conscience and/or rids the individual of self-hatred and self-loathing. In both cases, the pure cannot tolerate the impure, the holy cannot tolerate the unholy. Thus the apocalyptic scenarios of Asahara (Lifton 2000) and the *Left Behind* series so popular in American apocalyptic Christian circles (Jones 2010, 2008), as well as bin Laden's pronouncements, conclude with a vision of the future in which all the impure and unrighteous have been eliminated and the pure and holy can return to a paradise without complication or ambiguity or any sign remaining of the unrighteous and impure ones. Purification of oneself and the world comes to mean destroying impurity rather than transforming it, creating a perfectly clean, antiseptic, sterilized existence.

In addition, terrorist religions are "totalizing" religions, they make absolute claims on their devotees. Here, too, there is a psychology—the psychology of the need for something absolute, certain, infallible. This partly reflects the psychological need to overly idealize the objects of one's commitments and devotion. A devotee may demonstrate his or her devotion to an overly idealized object by committing extreme acts of violence and murder. Such totalistic visions erase all doubt and ambiguity and provide a claim of absolute certainty. The themes of splitting the world into completely pure and totally evil groups and the inability to tolerate ambivalence and ambiguity are connected. Totalistic visions promise the eradication of all ambivalence and ambiguity.

Research suggests, at least for religiously committed populations, that punitive and wrathful images of God are associated with external locus of control, anxiety and depression, lack of empathy, and less mature interpersonal relations (Brokaw, Edwards 1994; Spear 1994; Tisdale 1997). Thus it makes theoretical as well as empirical sense that a person who envisions God as wrathful and punitive—as those who hold the kind of apocalyptic vision affirmed by many religious terrorists do—would be inclined toward a more rigid dichotomizing of the world and less capacity for empathy, traits that characterize many religiously motivated terrorists.

Conclusion

While researchers often attend primarily either to group process theories and network analysis or to individual-focused models that look at personal motivations, traits, and vulnerabilities, most agree that studying both individual and group dynamics is necessary for a comprehensive understanding. There are other points of agreement: that individual psychopathology is rarely an explanation; that the experience of humiliation is often a precursor to violence; that religiously motivated terrorist groups share common themes regardless of tradition; that previously the leader-follower dynamic appeared crucial for turning a group violent, but understanding contemporary, "leaderless" groups may require different models; that understanding the psychology of apocalyptic theologies is important.

In addition, I would suggest (Jones 2008) that universal religious themes such as purification, the search for reunion with the source of life, or the longing for personal meaning and transformation—the classic instigators of spiritual search and religious conversion—can become subsumed into destructive psychological motivations such as evoking shame and humiliation, splitting the world into warring camps of the all-good against the all-evil, projecting rage onto those with whom they disagree and fomenting crusades against them, advocating violence and blood sacrifice as the primary means of purification, and idealizing a figure or instution that is punitive and humiliating. (Jones 2008). The result is the psychological preconditions for religiously sponsored terrorism and violence. This combination of powerful psychological motivations with profound spiritual desires gives the rhetoric of religious violence its appeal and power.

Bibliography

Altemeyer, Bob and Bruce Hunsberger. "Fundamentalism and Authoritarianism." In *Handbook of the Psychology of Religion and Spirituality*. Eds. Raymond Paloutzian and Crystal Park, 378–393. New York: Guilford Press, 2005.

Atran, Scott. *In Gods We Trust*. New York: Oxford University Press, 2002.

Atran, Scott. "Genesis of Suicide Terrorism." *Science* 229.5612 (2003): 1534–1539.

Atran, Scott. "The Moral Logic and Growth of Suicide Terrorism." *Washington Quarterly* 29.2 (2006): 127–147.

Atran, Scott. "Who Becomes a Terrorist Today?" *Perspectives on Terrorism*, II/5 at www.terrorismanalysis.com, 2008.

Bandura, Albert. "Mechanisms of Moral Disengagement." In *Origins of Terrorism*. Ed. Walter Reich, 161–191. Washington, DC: Woodrow Wilson Center Press, 1998.

Bandura, Albert. "The Role of Selective Moral Disengagement in Terrorism and Counterterrorism." In *Understanding Terrorism*. Eds. Fathali Moghaddam and Anthony Marsella, 121–150. Washington, DC: American Psychological Association Press, 2004.

Blass. Thomas, ed. *Obedience to Authority*. Mahwah, NJ: Erlbaum, 1999.

Baumeister, Roy and Kathleen Vohs. "Four Roots of Evil." In *The Social Psychology of Good and Evil*. Ed. Arthur Miller, 85–101. New York: Guilford Press, 2004.

Brokaw, Beth. and Keith Edwards. "There Is a Relationship of God Image to Level of Object Relations Development." *Journal of Psychology and Theology* 22.4 (1994): 352–371.

Eidelson, Roy and Judy Eidelson. "Dangerous Ideas: Five Beliefs That Propel Groups Towards Conflict." *American Psychologist* 58.3 (2003): 182–192.

Eisenberg, Nancy, Carlos Valiente, and Claire Champion. "Empathy-Related Responding." In *The Social Psychology of Good and Evil*. Ed. Arthur Miller, 386–415. New York: Guilford Press, 2004.

Gilligan, James. *Violence*. New York: Random House, 1996.

Hafez. Mohammed. "Rationality, Culture, and Structure in the Making of Suicide Bombers." *Studies in Conflict and Terrorism* 29.2 (2006): 165–185.

Hoffman, Bruce. *Inside Terrorism*. New York: Columbia University Press, 2006.

Horgan, John. *The Psychology of Terrorism*. London: Routledge Press, 2005.

Jones, James. "Playing and Believing: The Uses of D. W. Winnicott in the Psychology of Religion." In *Religion, Society and Psychoanalysis*. Eds. Janet Jacobs and Don Capps, 106–126. New York: Westview Press, 1997.

Jones, James. *Terror and Transformation: The Ambiguity of Religion in Psychoanalytic Perspective*. London and New York: Routledge, 2002

Jones, James. "Why Does Religion Turn Violent? A Psychoanalytic Exploration of Religious Terrorism." *The Psychoanalytic Review* 93.2 (2006): 167–190.

Jones, James. *Blood That Cries out from the Earth: The Psychology of Religious Terrorism*. New York: Oxford University Press, 2008.

Jones, James. "Eternal Warfare: Violence on the Mind of American Apocalyptic Christianity." In *The Fundamentalist Mindset: Psychological Perspectives on Religion, Violence, and History*. Eds. Charles Strozier, David Terman, James Jones, and Kathy Boyd, 91–103. New York: Oxford University Press, 2010.

Jones, James. "Religious Violence and Terrorism." *Handbook of Psychology of Religion and Spirituality*, vol. I. Eds. Pargament, Kenneth, Julie Exline, and James Jones.Washington, DC: American Psychological Association, (forthcoming).

Juergensmeyer, Mark. *Terror in the Mind of God*. Berkeley: University of California Press, 2002.

Khosrokhavar, Farhad. *Suicide Bombers: Allah's New Martyrs*. Translated by D. Macey. London: Pluto Press, 2005.

Kimball, Charles. *When Religion Becomes Evil*. San Francisco: Harper San Francisco, 2002.

Kohut, Heinz. "Thoughts on Narcissism and Narcissistic Rage." In *The Psychoanalytic Study of the Child*, 360–400. New York: Quadrangle Books, 1973.

Kohut, Heinz. *The Restoration of the Self*. Madison, CT: International Universities Press, 1977.

Lifton, Robert. *Destroying the World to Save It*. New York: Henry Holt-Owl Books, 2000.

Mahoney, Annette, Kenneth Pargament, Aaron Murray-Swank, and Nichole Murray-Swank. "Religion and the Sanctification of Family Relationships." *Review of Religious Research* 40 (2003): 220–236.

McCauley, Clark. "Jujitsu Politics: Terrorism and Responses to Terrorism." In *Collateral Damage*. Eds. Paul Kimmel and Chris Stout, 45–65. Westport, CT: Praeger, 2006.

Milgram, Stanley. *Obedience to Authority.* New York: Harper & Row, 1974.

Miller, Arthur. "What Can the Milgram Obedience Experiments Tell Us about the Holocaust?" In *The Social Psychology of Good and Evil.* Ed. Arthur Miller, 193–239. New York: Guilford Press, 2004.

Milller, Arthur, ed. *The Social Psychology of Good and Evil.* New York: Guilford Press, 2004.

Miller, Willaim. *Humiliation and Other Essays on Honor, Social Discomfort, and Violence.* Ithaca, NY: Cornell University Press, 1993.

Moghaddam, Fathali. "The Staircase to Terrorism: A Psychological Exploration." *American Psychologist* 60.2 (2005): 161–169.

Moghaddam, Fathali and Anthony Marsella. *Understanding Terrorism.* Washington, DC: American Psychological Association Press, 2004.

Pargament, Kenneth, Gina Magyar, Ethan Benore, and Annette Mahoney. "Sacrilege: A Study of Loss and Desecration." *Journal for the Scientific Study of Religion* 44.1 (2005): 59–78.

Pargament, Kenneth, Kelly Trevino, Annette Mahoney, and Israela Silberman. "They Killed Our Lord: The Persecution of Jews as Desecrators of Christianity as a Predictor of Anti-Semitism." *Journal for the Scientific Study of Religion* 46.2 (2007): 143–148.

Murray-Swank, Nichole, Kenneth Pargament and Annette Mahoney. "The Sanctification of Sexuality in Loving Relationships." Paper presented at the annual meeting of the American Psychological Association, Washington, DC, 2000.

Pargament, Kenneth, Julie Exline, James Jones, Edward Schafransk, and Annette Mahoney. *Handbook of Psychology of Religion and Spirituality.* Washington, DC: American Psychological Association, (forthcoming).

Pargament, Kenneth and Annette Mahoney. "Sacred Matters: Sanctification as a Vital Topic for the Psychology of Religion." *International Journal for the Psychology of Religion* 15.4 (2005): 179–198.

Post, Jerrold. "Notes on a Psychodynamic Theory of Terrorist Behavior." *Terrorism* 7.3 (1984): 241–256.

Post, Jerrold. "Terrorist Psycho-Logic." In *Origins of Terrorism.* Ed. Walter Reich, 25–40. Washington, DC: Woodrow Wilson Center Press, 1998.

Post, Jerrold, Keven Ruby, and Erik Shaw. "The Radical Group in Context." *Studies in Conflict and Terrorism* 25.2 (2002): 73–126.

Post, Jerrold, Ehud Sprinzak, and Laurita Denny. "The Terrorists in Their Own Words: Interviews with 35 Incarcerated Middle Eastern Terrorists." *Terrorism and Political Violence* 15.1 (2003): 171–184.

Post, Jerrold. *The Mind of the Terrorist.* New York: Palgrave Macmillan, 2007.

Reader, Ian. *Religious Violence in Contemporary Japan: The Case of Aum Shinrikyo.* London: Curzon Press, 2000.

Reich, Walter, ed. *Origins of Terrorism.* Washington, DC: Woodrow Wilson Center Press, 1998.

Robins, Robert and Jerrold Post. *Political Paranoia: The Psychopolitics of Hatred.* New Haven, CT: Yale University Press, 1997.

Sageman, Marc. *Leaderless Jihad.* Philadelphia: University of Pennsylvania Press, 2008.

Silberman, Israela. "Religious Violence, Terrorism, and Peace." In *Handbook of the Psychology of Religion and Spirituality.* Eds. Raymond Paloutzian and Crystal Park, 529–549. New York: Guilford Press, 2005.

Silberman, Israela, E. Tory Higgins, and Carol Dweck. "Religion and World Change: Violence, Terrorism versus Peace." *Journal of Social Issues* 61.4 (2005): 761–784.

Spear, Kathy. "Conscious and Pre-Conscious God Representations: An Object Relations Perspective." Unpublished doctoral dissertation. Fuller Theological Seminary, Pasadena, CA, 1994.

Stern, Jessica. *Terror in the Name of God*. New York: Ecco Press, 2003.

Strenski, Ivan. "Sacrifice, Gift, and the Social Logic of Muslim 'Human Bombers.'" *Terrorism and Political Violence* 15.3 (2003): 1–34.

Strozier, Charles. *Apocalypse: On the Psychology of Fundamentalism in America.* Boston: Beacon, 1994.

Strozier, Charles, David Terman, James Jones, and Kathy Boyd, eds. *The Fundamentalist Mindset: Psychological Perspectives on Religion, Violence, and History.* New York: Oxford University Press, 2010.

Tarakeshwar, Nalini, Aaron Swank, Aaron, Kenneth Pargament, and Annette Mahoney. "The Sanctification of Nature and Theological Conservatism." *Review of Religious Research* 42.4 (2001): 387–404.

Tisdale, Theresa. "A Comparison of Jewish, Muslim, and Protestant Faith Groups on the Relationship between Level of Object Relations Development and Experience of God and Self." Unpublished doctoral dissertation, Rosemead Graduate School, La Mirada, CA, 1997.

Tobena, Adolf. "Individual Factors in Suicide Terrorists: A Reply to S. Atran." *Science, 2004, 304/5667*: 47–49.

Victoroff, Jeff. "The Mind of the Terrorist: A Review and Critique of Psychological Approaches." *Journal of Conflict Resolution, 2005, 49/1*:3–42.

Volkan, Vamik. *Bloodlines: From Ethnic Pride to Ethnic Terrorism*, New York: Farrar, Straus and Giroux, 1997.

Volkan, Vamik. *Blind Trust: Large Groups and Their Leaders in Times of Crises and Terror.* Charlottesville, VA: Pitchstone Publishing, 2004.

Waller, James. *Becoming Evil*. New York: Oxford University Press, 2002.

Wessinger, Catherine. *How the Millennium Comes Violently*. New York: Seven Bridges Press, 2000.

Wulff, David. *Psychology of Religion*. New York: John Wiley, 1991.

Zimbardo, Philip, Christina Maslach, and Craig Haney. "Reflections on the Stanford Prison Experiment." In *Obedience to Authority*. Ed. Edited by Thomas Blass, 193–237. Mahwah, NJ: Erlbaum, 2000.

Zimbardo, Philip. "A Situationalist Perspective on the Psychology of Evil." In *The Social Psychology of Good and Evil*. Ed. Arthur Miller, 21–50. New York: Guilford Press, 2004.

CHAPTER 28

RELIGION AND VIOLENCE FROM A POLITICAL SCIENCE PERSPECTIVE

DANIEL PHILPOTT

RELIGION is "the most prolific source of violence in our history," writes author Sam Harris (Harris 2005: 27). Like other contemporary "neoatheists," including the famous essayist Christopher Hitchens, Harris claims not just that religion has been violent historically but that it is violent inherently. This charge against religion is not limited to today's polemicists but is rather a tenet of the secularization thesis, which all but dominated the thinking of Western intellectuals until only recently. The charge has three component claims, according to theologian William T. Cavanaugh: Religion is absolutist, divisive, and insufficiently rational (Cavanaugh 2009: 17–18). Again and again these claims show up in scholarly writings on religion's influence on social life.

Other recent studies, however, make the matter more complex, noting that, in the past generation alone, religion has furthered democratization, peace settlements, reconciliation initiatives, and human rights as well as terrorism and civil war (see, for instance, Appleby 2000). This is my own approach, which I have developed in my own writings and in collaboration with Monica Duffy Toft and Timothy Samuel Shah.[1] Observing that religion is violent in some instances but not in others, we ask: Under what conditions are religious groups likely to be violent? This is the approach that I adopt here. Why do some religious actors promote democracy, peace, reconciliation, women's rights, economic development, and international norms and organizations while others advance repression, terrorism, and civil war?

Scholars have proffered a wide array of answers to this question, including economic factors, demographic factors, colonial histories, grievances over perceived injustices, national and ethnic identities, competition with other religions, modernity, and theological beliefs. All of these influences are surely important in various combinations and circumstances. Two factors, though, prove particularly powerful for explanation: institutional independence and political theology. It is these factors to which I turn to account for religious violence in this chapter. In the next section, I look at institutional independence and political theology more carefully. A section that utilizes these two factors to explain one form of religious violence—communal conflict—follows. The final section does the same for another form of religious violence—terrorism.

Institutional Independence and Political Theology

Institutional independence is the degree of mutual autonomy between religious communities and state institutions in their foundational authority and deals with prerogatives in holding office, choosing officials, setting policies, and carrying out functions. In short, to what extent does each entity allow the other to govern itself? Independence can be high, or it can be low, in which case the relationship between religion and state can be called integrated. Institutional independence, though, varies not only in degree but also in kind, namely in respect to the level of consent that it involves. When both religion and state are content with the degree of independence that each enjoy, then independence is "consensual." When at least one party contests the arrangement, the relationship may be called "conflictual." Consensual independence is the condition of most constitutional liberal democracies. Consensual integration, in which both religion and state are content with a deeply intermeshed relationship—that is, one of low independence—obtains in such countries as Iran and Sri Lanka, at least with respect to dominant religious actors. Often in the same countries, though, other religious communities, usually minority ones, will be severely repressed, a condition that can be called conflictually integrated; for example, the oppressed minority is forcibly "integrated" into the state's laws, policies, and purview. A final possibility is conflictual independence, in which a religious community maintains significant de facto independence from the state but only by resisting the state's efforts to suppress it. The Catholic Church in communist Poland, Chile under Augusto Pinochet, and Indonesian Islamic movements under the dictatorship of Suharto fit the description.

Political theology is simpler. It is the set of ideas that a religious body holds on legitimate political authority. Who possesses it? The people? A sultan? A monarch? To what extent and in what way ought state authorities promote faith? Does a religious community maintain that it ought to be "established" or otherwise have a privileged relationship with the state? Does it hold that members of other religious faiths ought to have freedom to practice? What obligations do religious believers have toward the political order? What is the content of justice? Under what circumstances, for instance, may a state justly fight war or otherwise use force? A political theology may be shared widely within a given religion but can also vary among its component communities. In every religion, political theology evolves over time through both intellectual discourse and the influence of historical circumstances.

Propositions about the behavior of religious actors arise from institutional independence and political theology. Broadly speaking, for instance, religious actors will be most effective in promoting democratization and peace settlements when they enjoy substantial institutional independence from the state and when they carry a political theology that derives religious freedom and other tenets of democracy from the core teachings of their faith. What about violence? The opposite explanation applies. Religious communities and leaders take up violence and repression when their political theology favors an integrated state that gives them official status and that restricts the practice and expression of other faiths. Sometimes their political theologies actually sanction violence, either out of a doctrine of "emergency" or a claim of divine command. They also favor violence when they enjoy institutional integration—a friendly partnership—with a state that empowers them to assert dominance. Reciprocally, religious groups tend toward violence when they are disempowered—restricted in their practice and expression—by a state that privileges a rival faith.

Again, political theology and institutional independence are far from the only factors that explain religious violence. But they can account for broad patterns of two forms of religious violence: communal conflict and terrorism.

COMMUNAL CONFLICT

Communal conflict is violence on a large scale, usually focused in a single state but often spilling across borders, examples of which are popular insurrections, rebel militia offensives, and the suppression of both by the armed forces of the state. Sometimes religious communities take up such conflict, justifying it and sanctifying it according to their honor and their ideals. Every religious tradition in the world involves such conflict. Political scientist Monica Duffy Toft renders it as "religious civil war." Civil war, she avers, involves at least two combatant factions, the state being one of these, a dispute over the governance of the state, and at least

1,000 battle deaths. Civil war is religious when at least one of the warring communities is a religious one (Toft 2007: 112–113). In the work of another political scientist, Jonathan Fox, who drew from the Minorities at Risk dataset, communal conflicts are rendered as "ethnoreligious conflicts," defined as a subset of ethnic conflicts in which the conflicting groups are of different religions (Fox 2002: 70–71).

Together, the work of Toft and Fox paint a portrait of the place of religion in the world's communal conflicts of the past seventy years or so. Almost one-third of civil wars between 1940 and 2000 have involved religion, Toft reports—forty-four out of 135, or 33 percent (Toft 2007: 97). Fox's data delivers a broadly similar result, showing that 39 percent (105 out of 268) of disputes among ethnic minorities are ethnoreligious (Fox 2002: 71). Over the decades, religious communal conflicts have only increased in proportion. According to Toft, they made up 19 percent of civil wars in the 1940s, then rose to 30 percent in the 1950s, dipped to 22 percent in the 1960s, then climbed again to 36 percent in the 1970s, increased to 41 percent in the 1980s, rose further to 45 percent in the 1990s, and became 50 percent, or half, of all civil wars between 2000 and 2010.[2] Among the religions, who fights these civil wars? Both Toft and Fox stress their finding that Islam shows up disproportionately in religious communal conflicts. In 71 percent of the civil wars that Toft describes as religious, the place of Islam in the laws of the state was a disputed issue (Toft 2006a). In thirty-six of these civil wars, or 82 percent, one or both parties were Muslim. By contrast, in only 52 percent of these wars was at least one party Christian, despite the fact that Christians make up a larger percentage of the world population than Muslims. Likewise, 58 percent of all states that have fought civil wars have majority Muslim populations (Toft, Philpott, and Shah 2011:153; Toft 2007: 113–114). Among the twelve of the forty-four civil wars that have been fought between groups of the same faith, eleven have involved Muslims (Toft, Philpott, and Shah 2011: 155; Toft 2006: 15). Corroboratively, Fox finds that conflict among Muslims rose during the 1990s (Fox 2004: 68).

These broad statistical patterns, though, leave open the question of what exactly it means for communal conflict to be religious. Is a war between religiously defined communities in Kashmir, Sri Lanka, Sudan, or Northern Ireland really religious, or is religion a veneer that covers other propellants of conflict—land disputes, economic resource competition, ethnicity, or historical grievances? It is possible, of course, for religion to be little more than a rationalization. In two ways, however, religion can cause violent communal conflict. First, it shapes and defines the communities that engage in combat, their identities and their loyalties—those of Serbs, Irish Republicans, and Sinhalese Buddhists. More and more, religion is playing this role, argues sociologist Mark Juergensmeyer, as religious nationalism has supplanted an earlier secular nationalism (Juergensmeyer 1993). In this dynamic, religion exerts influence apart from its theological content. Sociologist Michael Sells documents how, over decades, religion in Yugoslavia became "folk religion"— shorn of theology but strong in ritual, lore, and custom and thus ripe for nationalist leaders to incite adherents to violence through language and symbols (Sells 1996). Political theology plays little role here; propositions about justice or right authority are not involved. Once religion has defined a community, it is other motives and forces that send it into combat—the desire for national self-determination, revenge for historical injustices, or economic motives. Toft categorizes seventeen, or 40 percent, of her forty-two post-1940 civil wars as ones where religion shapes identity (Toft 2007: 103).

There is a second dynamic, though, by which religion propels communal conflict, one in which it defines not only the identities but also the ends of combatant communities. True, in a few conflicts religion shapes ends but not communities—for instance, disputes between Islamic theological factions in Iran. Usually, though, when religion shapes ends it also shapes communities. Conflicts in which religion shapes both communities and ends make up twenty-five out of forty-two, or 60 percent, of the religious civil wars, Toft reports (Toft 2007: 103). It is where religion shapes ends and not merely identities that political theology exerts influence. What elicits an armed clash is often the integrationist character of these ends. The state, the opposition, or both espouses a political theology that demands a regime that denies institutional independence to a separate religious group, usually a minority one. In eighteen of these twenty-five conflicts, or 72 percent, at least one combatant party proclaimed integrationist goals. The prominence of integrationist political theology corresponds to the prominence of Islam in religious civil wars, a religion in which integrationist thought is comparatively widespread. In religious civil wars involving Islam, Toft shows, religion was a key disputed issue in eighteen out of thirty-four, or 53 percent of instances; whereas in civil wars involving other religions, religion was a central bone of contention in only three out of eleven, or 27 percent of instances (Toft 2006a). Fox's research finds similarly that over the years 1965 to 2001, the role of religious issues in armed conflicts between Muslims increased sharply (Fox 2004: 69).

It is important to remember when considering the proportion of various religions involved in conflict or of the different dynamics through which religion affects conflict that none of these numbers alone proves the causal role of religion vis-à-vis other hypothesized causes of conflict. For instance, a potential explanation for the disproportionate role of Islam in communal violence is poverty, which exists disproportionately in the Muslim world. A full test would have to incorporate these other potential causes, but a correlation of religion with communal violence is a first step in explanation. Deeper confidence in the causal role of religion arises from a look at the dynamics through which institutional independence and political theology affect the behavior of religious actors.

When religious groups with an integrationist political theology succeed in their quest to control the state, they often reshape the state's institutions in the image of their ideas. They impose integrated laws and institutions on their population, often discriminating against rival religious groups. Marginalized, these rival groups come to fear for their ability to practice their faith and even for their own security and, thus, become violent. Reasoning similarly, religious studies scholar Bruce Lincoln calls integrationist ruling groups "religions of the status quo" and characterizes them as seeking a partnership between a state that promotes the dominant faith and religious authorities who hold political powers (Lincoln 2003: 79–83). A total of twelve out of the twenty-five conflicts that Toft describes as taking place over religious ends involved states who practiced integrated relationships with the dominant faith community, according to my own analysis. In Sudan, for instance, an authoritarian Islamist state's efforts to impose a harsh version of sharia law on the Christian south was a major cause of twenty-one years of civil war, ending in 2005 (though other conflicts in Sudan continued after 2005). Similarly, civil war in Sri Lanka arose from an integrated Sinhalese Buddhist state, which discriminated against minority Tamil Hindus (as well as other religious minorities) in an effort to sustain and strengthen a Buddhist national homeland, as well as from a political theology carried by the Buddhist *sangha* that called for significant political powers for clerics. The separatism of the Liberation Tamil Tigers of Eelam (LTTE) in turn, though it is largely secular, was bred in good part by discrimination against Tamils in a Buddhist state (Tambiah 1993).

In a variant of the argument, factions and parties that are not associated with a religious institution can control a state, impose an integrated relationship between the state and religion, marginalize at least some religious groups, and thus beget violence. Their doctrine of religion and state is a secular one that calls for the sharp control of religion by the state, just as a political theology that espouses low and conflictual institutional independence does. Fitting the description are communist regimes. A communist coup in Afghanistan, for instance, sustained by an invasion by the Soviet Union in 1979, provoked an eleven-year insurrection in which Afghan Islamic leaders united with radical jihadis from all over the Muslim world (Roy 1993: 492). In like fashion, China's harshly secular communist regime's suppression of Tibetan Buddhists begat civil war in the early 1950s.

Other forms of regimes governed by a secular, integrationist ideology are not communist but spur a similar dynamic. The socialist authoritarian National Liberation Front of postcolonial Algeria, for instance, replicated a pattern of religion-state relationship that was common in the post–World War II Arab world by which the state sought to control Islam by allying with, promoting, and regulating a moderate reformist school while marginalizing more conservative factions. Reacting to this suppression as well as to economic stagnation and political corruption, Islamist movements arose and gained strong popular support in the 1970s and 1980s. In 1991, when the government finally conducted national elections, the Islamic Salvation Front won the first round only to see the government, backed by its army, cancel the second round, sparking a civil war that cost more than 100,000 lives in the 1990s (Malley 1996). Following the same pattern, the secular authoritarian government of Iran under its Shah suppressed conservative Islam in the name of modernization and social liberalization and provoked the rise of a Shia movement that brought on the 1979 revolution.

It is not only religious groups that govern the state that hold integrationist political theologies in conflicts over religious ends. Opposition groups can also be driven by integrationist ideas. Lincoln calls them "religions of resistance" and holds that they can then become "religions of revolution" (Lincoln 2003: 82–91).

These groups can be seen in the previously mentioned conflicts in Algeria, Iran, and Afghanistan, as well as in central Asian republics and in Chechnya. It is not always, either, that these groups conduct war against a state that enjoys an integrated relationship with a dominant religion—the Islamic Moro Islamic Liberation Front, for instance, wars against a Philippine government whose relationship with religious authority is broadly consensually independent. Sometimes other grievances propel opposition groups. My analysis of Toft's cases reveals that nine of the twenty-one religious civil wars in which religion has shaped ends have involved opposition groups with an integrationist political theology, all of them Muslim.

TERRORISM

Though the definition of terrorism is notoriously fraught, in my view terrorism is distinguished by its killing of civilians for political purposes (Hoffman 1998: 13–44). Terrorism may take place within a larger communal conflict or may be altogether separate from it. Usually it is more episodic and focused than communal violence, though it can also be repeated and directed at large and widespread targets. Governments may practice terrorism, though here my focus is on opposition groups. Religious terrorists are simply those whose primary aims and identities are religious. Terrorism expert Jessica Stern rightly cautions that the ends of these terrorists are rarely solely religious ones but also involve temporal, spiritual, ideological, profit-driven, instrumental, and expressive purposes (Stern 2003: 6–8). Still, if their motives are mixed, religious terrorists always proclaim religious purposes.

Religious terrorists were virtually the only terrorists until the nineteenth century. Religious terrorism expert David Rapaport relates that the modern English terms *assassin, thug,* and *zealot* derive respectively from Islamic, Hindu, and Jewish terrorists of ancient and medieval times (Rapaport 1984). By 1968, though, following the global trajectory of secularization, all of the world's then eleven known terrorist groups pursued solely secular ends. Religious terrorists began to show up again in 1980, when they amounted to two out of sixty-four terrorist groups in the entire world. But then, following the global resurgence of the political influence of religion of the past four decades, religious terrorists expanded rapidly (see Toft, Philpott, and Shah 2011: chapter 3). In 1992, eleven religious terrorist groups could be found; in 1994 sixteen of forty-nine, or 33 percent of terrorist groups, were religious; and in 1995 the number of these groups had climbed to twenty-six out of fifty-six, or 46 percent of all terrorist groups (Hoffman 1998: 90–94). In 2005, according to my own analysis of the Terrorism Knowledge Base, ninety-five out of 262, or 36 percent of known terrorist groups, were identifiably religious.[3]

Not only has religious terrorism become more common, it is also comparatively more deadly than secular terrorism. Between 1981 and 2007, Salafi-jihadists have been responsible for most of the largest proportion of terrorist deaths.

Their attacks killed an average of seventeen people and wounded an average of thirty-nine. In comparison, terrorists motivated by secular ideologies killed an average of three to four people and wounded another eight to sixteen per attack (Moghadam 2008: 50–54; Toft, Philpott, and Shah 2011: 122).

Scholars have put forth a range of motivations why religious terrorists engage in violence, including being on the loser's end of globalization, the instability created by urbanization and economic progress, colonialism and Western imperialism, oppressive regimes that suppress religious and political expression and participation, adventure, profit, opposition to foreign military occupation, the erosion of secular nationalism, the loss of masculinity, and heavenly rewards. (See variously Stern 2003; Ranstorp 1996, 41–60; Juergensmeyer 2003: 183–185; Pape 2003, 343–361; Almond, Appleby, and Sivan 2003.) Almost none of these analyses, though, claims that these motivations account sufficiently for religious terrorism. Poverty and various forms of oppression apply to entire populations, only a tiny portion of whom become religious terrorists. Common political, economic, and demographic environments also host diverse militant movements and cannot alone account for their diversity. Separatist movements in Kashmir, for instance, range from secular nationalist to radical Islamist and sprout from common soil.

Most all of these analyses also emphasize the crucial importance of the beliefs of religious terrorists. They show how religious terrorists understand their scriptures and their traditions so as to justify their urgent resort to violence. Common themes in these beliefs include divine sanction for indiscriminate killing, violence as a sacramental or divine duty, opposition not just to a regime but to an entire corrupted social order, an apocalyptic vision, and appeals to their own followers as an audience (Hoffman 1998: 94–95). "Whereas secular terrorists generally consider indiscriminate violence to be immoral and counterproductive," writes terrorism expert Bruce Hoffman, "religious terrorists regard such violence not only as morally justified but as a necessary expedient for the attainment of their goals" (Hoffman 1995: 272). What might also be given central status is the religious terrorists' political theology. Nearly all such groups believe that a given regime has lost its legitimacy for having violated or failed to advance authentic religious faith and should be overthrown for one that tightly integrates religious and political authority and that actively fosters true religious faith.

Nearly all religious terrorist groups espouse an integrationist political theology. Whatever other motivations spur them, they hold and act on such religiopolitical beliefs. In one description of Iranian-backed Shia terrorists: "[They] do not believe in the legitimate authority of secular governments.... Since Iran is the only state to have begun to implement 'true' Islam, however, it is thought to be the world's only legitimate state with a unique obligation of facilitating the worldwide implementation of Islamic law. Force and violence are not only acceptable but necessary means of doing so" (Hoffman 1998, quoting Zonis and Brumberg 1984). As recently as 2005, 91 percent of all religious terrorist groups were what can be called radical Islamic revivalist, calling for a caliphate or for an Islamic regime that contains a strongly integrated version of sharia law. Islamic terrorism is dominated by one school of thought in particular: Salafi jihadism, the ideology that guided al-Qaeda. Roughly equivalent notions are held by Christian white supremacist movements in the United States as well as Jewish extremist movements such as the Kach movement of Rabbi Meir Kahane.

In addition to pernicious political theology, a lack of institutional independence between religion and state is also behind religious terrorism. Gabriel Almond, Scott Appleby, Emmanuel Sivan have made this argument, claiming that when states hinder religious groups from expressing their beliefs, increasing their numbers, raising money, and the like, these groups are more likely to become violent. On some occasions, states may succeed in quashing them but like phoenixes they often arise again. The obverse dimension of Almond, Appleby, and Sivan's argument is that under independent institutions—such as democracies—religious terrorism will be far rarer. Under a democratic regime, religious groups can worship, practice, and speak openly, but they are also forced to debate, face challenges from, and ally with other groups, activities that tend to temper, moderate, and even factionalize these groups. Integrated religion-state relationships do not alone spawn religious terrorists while democracies do not alone dispel them. Under both sorts of regimes, religious people and groups make diverse and plural choices, not just choices for terrorism (Almond, Appleby, and Sivan 2003, 218). But on balance, all else being equal, religion-state relationships incubate or stifle religious terrorists.

Not all scholars agree, though, that democracy diffuses terrorism. Some argue the opposite. Political scientist Robert Pape, who focuses on suicide terrorist attacks, finds democracies are more likely to be the object of such attacks than authoritarian regimes and shows that since 1980 all suicide terrorism campaigns have aimed at democracies. Pape does not argue, though, that it is democratic regime structures or independent religion-state relationships that encourage terrorists but rather that terrorists attack those states they believe wrongfully occupy their lands and that all of these states turn out to be democracies. That he focuses only on suicide terrorists also circumscribes the generalizability of his findings (Pape 2003: 343–361). Other scholars also find a positive link between terrorism and democracy. Leonard Weinberg and William L. Eubank discovered that terrorism occurred more frequently in democracies than elsewhere in 1994 and 1995 (Weinberg and Eubank 1998). Political scientist Gregory Gause argues similarly, drawing from a State Department report revealing that, between 2000 and 2003, 269 major terrorist incidents occurred in "free" countries (using Freedom House rankings), whereas 199 took place in "partly free" countries and 138 in "not free" countries (Gause 2005).

Still other scholars, though, reach findings that support Almond, Appleby, and Sivan's argument. Alberto Abadie, for instance, shows that the risk of terrorism and authoritarianism are strongly correlated, that terrorism and political freedom are inversely correlated, and that terrorism and poverty are not correlated once regime type is factored into the equation. He warns, though, that the risk of terrorism is higher in countries in the zone between authoritarian and free, warranting caution toward the transition to democracy (Abadie 2004). All in all, the link between terrorism and democracy is uncertain, a conclusion that Gause explicitly reaches.

While most of these studies examine where terrorists operate, a different approach—one more directly relevant to the argument here—would focus on where terrorists incubate. Even if terrorists attack democracies they may well emerge under dictatorships. Offering support for this claim is a Freedom House study that shows a connection between the lack of political and civil rights and the formation of terrorist movements. Between 1999 and 2003 terrorists originating from "not free" countries caused 70 percent of all deaths attributable to terrorism. Only 8 percent of terrorist deaths during the same period were inflicted by groups with origins in "free" countries (Freedom House 2005).

Even more relevant to the argument at hand would be a focus on religious terrorists in particular, who make up 36 percent of all terrorists. My analysis of the Terrorism Knowledge Base reveals a positive connection between authoritarian regimes and the site where religious terrorists operate. Only thirty-one out of ninety-five, or 32 percent of religious terrorist groups, conduct their operations in "free" countries, whereas forty-two, or 43 percent of, religious terrorists operate in "not free" countries, while twenty, or 21 percent of, religious terrorists operate in "partly free" countries. Another database, the International Religion Indexes of Grim and Finke, helps to show that religious groups operate in settings that are not simply authoritarian but also integrationist (Grim and Finke 2006). Their Government Regulation Index, which assesses government interference in religion on a scale of 0 to 10, averages to 5.75 for countries where terrorists operate, in contrast to an average of 3.07 for the entire set of 196 countries that they study. Similarly, their Government Favoritism Index, which assesses direct government support for religions, averages 6.92 for countries where terrorists operate as compared to 4.34 for the entire dataset.

Unfortunately, data that show where religious terrorists originate rather than operate are scarce. One way to establish a connection between integrated regimes and the formation of religious terrorists, though, is the perceptions of religious terrorists. Such perceptions constitute less direct and more subjective evidence, but they do contribute to the case. Consider again that 91 percent of religious terrorists are radical Islamic revivalists, who maintain that Islam is being attacked and eroded by outside influences (as well as internal influences). Revivalists commonly trace their lineage to early and mid-twentieth-century intellectuals who believed all of Islam to be in a condition of defensive struggle—Abu al-A`la Maududi of Pakistan and Hasan al-Banna and Sayyid Qutb of Egypt. They also agree that religiously repressive state institutions prevent the flourishing of Islamic law and morality. Among these integrated institutions have been colonial regimes imposed by the West; nationalist, authoritarian, and secular Arab regimes; and communist regimes. It is in reaction to what revivalists regard as these attempts to marginalize them that they came to wage terroristic jihad.

Both religious terrorism and communal violence, then, are arguably propelled by political theology and religion-state relationships of an integrated kind.

Communal violence is fomented by groups that espouse integrationist political theologies and sometimes secular doctrines of integration and that, when they capture control of the state, impose integrationist institutions on members of other faiths or dissenting members of the same religion, thus creating a dynamic of violence. Violence also results from religious groups who take up opposition to states out of integrationist political theologies. Religious terrorism arises from groups with integrationist political theologies and the marginalization of religious groups by integrated authoritarian regimes.

The key lesson of these findings is that religious violence is least likely to originate—though it will sometimes operate—in settings of consensual independence, which are, in turn, found most commonly in religion-friendly liberal democracies. These practice what political scientist Alfred Stepan has called "the twin tolerations"—the state's toleration of religion and religion's relinquishment of political monopoly (Stepan 2001). Contrary to secularization theory, religion is not always violent and ideologies that portray it as so are only likely to make it so. It is rather what Pope Benedict XVI has called "positive secularism"—something much like Stepan's twin tolerations—that is likely to bring peace.

NOTES

1. The current essay is adapted from Daniel Philpott, from "Explaining the Political Ambivalence of Religion" by Daniel Philpott *American Political Society Review*, Volume 101, Issue 3 (2007): 505–525. Copyright © 2007 by the American Political Science Association. Reprinted with the permission of Cambridge University Press. The thinking from this piece was further developed in Monica Duffy Toft, Daniel Philpott, and Timothy Samuel Shah, *God's Century: Resurgent Religion in Global Politics* (New York, NY: W.W. Norton, 2011).
2. Again. numbers are updated and slightly changed according to Toft, Philpott, and Shah 2011: 153.
3. The Terrorism Knowledge Base no longer exists under the same name. The data that I collected from it do not necessarily correspond to the data from which Bruce Hoffman derived his numbers and thus should not be taken as a side-by-side comparison with the data from previous years.

BIBLIOGRAPHY

Abadie, Alberto. *Poverty, Political Freedom, and the Roots of Terrorism.* Cambridge, MA: Harvard University and NBER, 2004.

Almond, Gabriel, R. Scott Appleby, and Emmanuel Sivan. *Strong Religion: The Rise of Fundamentalisms around the World.* Chicago: University of Chicago Press, 2003.

Appleby, R. Scott. *The Ambivalence of the Sacred: Religion, Violence, and Reconciliation.* Lanham, MD: Rowman and Littlefield Publishers, 2000.

Cavanaugh, William T. *The Myth of Religious Violence: Secular Ideology and the Roots of Modern Conflict.* Oxford, UK: Oxford University Press, 2009.

Fox, Jonathan. *Ethnoreligious Conflict in the Late 20th Century: A General Theory.* Lanham, MD: Lexington Books, 2002.

Fox, Jonathan. *Religion, Civilization, and Civil War.* Lanham, MD: Lexington Books, 2004.

Freedom House. *Freedom in the World 2005: Civic Power and Electoral Politics: A Report From Freedom House,* 2005.

Gause, Gregory F. III, "Can Democracy Stop Terrorism?" *Foreign Affairs* 84.5 (September/October 2005): 62–76.

Grim, Brian J. and Roger Finke. "International Religion Indexes: Government Regulation, Governmental Favoritism, and Social Regulation of Religion." *Interdisciplinary Journal of Research on Religion* 2.1 (2006): 3–40.

Harris, Sam. *The End of Faith: Religion, Terror, and the Future of Reason.* New York: W. W. Norton, 2005.

Hoffman, Bruce. "'Holy Terror': The Implications of Terrorism Motivated by a Religious Imperative." *Studies in Conflict and Terrorism* 18 (1995): 271–284.

Hoffman, Bruce. *Inside Terrorism.* New York: Columbia University Press, 1998.

Juergensmeyer, Mark. *The New Cold War? Religious Nationalism Confronts the Secular State.* Berkeley: University of California Press, 1993.

Juergensmeyer, Mark. *Terror in the Mind of God: The Global Rise of Religious Violence,* 3rd ed. Berkeley: University of California Press, 2003.

Lincoln, Bruce. *Holy Terrors: Thinking about Religion after September 11th.* Chicago: University of Chicago Press, 2003.

Malley, Robert. *The Call from Algeria: Third Worldism, Revolution, and the Turn to Islam.* Berkeley: University of California Press, 1996.

Moghadam, Assaf. *The Globalization of Martyrdom: Al Qaeda, Salafi Jihad, and the Diffusion of Suicide Attacks.* Baltimore: Johns Hopkins University Press, 2008.

Pape, Robert. "The Strategic Logic of Suicide Terrorism." *American Political Science Review* 97, no. 3 (2003): 343–361.

Philpott, Daniel. "Explaining the Political Ambivalence of Religion." *American Political Science Review* 103.3 (2007): 505–525.

Ranstorp, Magnus. "Terrorism in the Name of Religion." *Journal of International Affairs* 50.1 (1996): 41–60.

Rapaport, David. "Fear and Trembling: Terrorism in Three Religious Traditions." *American Political Science Review* 78.3 (1984): 658–677.

Roy, Olivier. "Afghanistan: An Islamic War of Resistance." In *Fundamentalisms and the State.* Eds. Martin E. Marty and R. Scott Appleby, 491–510. Chicago,: University of Chicago Press, 1993.

Sells, Michael A. *The Bridge Betrayed: Religions and Genocide in Bosnia.* Berkeley: University of California Press, 1996.

Stepan, Alfred. "The World's Religious Systems and Democracy: Crafting the 'Twin Tolerations,'" in *Arguing Comparative Politics,* 213–253. Oxford, UK: Oxford University Press, 2001.

Stern, Jessica. *Terror in the Name of God: Why Religious Militants Kill.* New York: HarperCollins, 2003.

Tambiah, Stanley J. "Buddhism, Politics, and Violence in Sri Lanka." In *Fundamentalisms and the State: Remaking Polities, Economies, and Militance.* Eds. Martin E. Marty and R. Scott Appleby, 589–619. Chicago: University of Chicago Press, 1993.

Toft, Monica Duffy. "Religion, Civil War, and International Order," BCSIA discussion paper, 2006–03, Belfer Center for Science and International Affairs, July 2006, 9.

Toft, Monica Duffy. Personal communication. 2006(a).

Toft, Monica Duffy. "Getting Religion? The Puzzling Case of Islam and Civil War." *International Security* 31.4 (2007): 97–131.

Toft, Monica Duffy, Daniel Philpott, and Timothy Samuel Shah. *God's Century: Resurgent Religion in Global Politics.* New York: W.W. Norton, 2011.

Weinberg, Leonard and William L. Eubank, "Terrorism and Democracy." *Terrorism and Political Violence* 10.1 (1998): 108–118.

Zonis, Marvin, and Daniel Brumberg. "Behind Beirut Terrorism." *New York Times*, October 8, 1984.

CHAPTER 29

....

RELIGION AND VIOLENCE FROM LITERARY PERSPECTIVES

....

MARGO KITTS

Destroyer of enemy lands—
you, Inanna, empowered the storm
Beloved of Enlil,
you let terror reign over the land of Sumer.
    Enheduanna, first known poetess of Mesopotamia[1]

As Enheduanna's praise poem to Inanna attests, the splendor of divine terror is at least as old as Western literature, from the third millennium BCE. The theme is not limited to Mesopotamia. Hundreds of samples might be listed. Representations of divine violence are profuse in classical religious texts, as are reports of human violence sanctioned by divine sources and often mimicking them. This chapter addresses, first, some theories that account for the crystallization of violence into religious texts and, second, some theories that account for the "violent imaginaries" (Schmidt and Schröder 2001: 9–13) derived from such texts. In short, it will explore how violence gets into religious texts and how it gets out of them, into action.

A work of literature is defined as an artifact of verbal art, usually established in writing but not restricted to it, thus including oral literature and inscriptions in other media, such as mystical texts. Examples are drawn primarily from the West.

How Violence Gets into Religious Texts

A distinctive feature of our earliest Western representations of religious violence is its association with natural power. From the onset of religious poetry, natural power has inspired paeans of awe and fear. Tracing the poetry and iconography of the ancient Near Eastern storm deity, Alberto Green has observed its double-edged personality as a god of fertility and violence (2003: 76). Especially in flood-prone Mesopotamia, the storm god, personified early on as a thunder-brandishing figure astride or flanked by a fire-spitting dragon, came to embody a complex of ideas that were beneficent and terrifying, life giving but also life destroying. Different attributes were attached to regional storm gods from Mesopotamia to Greece, but a legacy of storm-based violence persisted and came to manifest the power of a number of gods. This is evident in glyptic depictions (thunder-wielding figures), in divine epithets (the probably pan–Near Eastern "rider on clouds"; Weinfeld 1973) and in mythopoetic elaborations, wherein natural models for cosmic power are not just aqueous but also involve fire or wind or thunderous noise: "When you [Inanna] roar at the earth like thunder, no vegetation can stand up to you" (Weinfeld 1973: 423); "[w]hen the [biblical] Lord roars from Zion and thunders from Jerusalem, the shepherds' pastures are scorched and the top of Carmel is dried up" (Amos 1:2; Weinfeld 1973: 423).[2] Natural catastrophe would seem an obvious correlate for divine violence. Epiphanies of natural power presumably aroused an imaginative reflex in which terror and catastrophe became associated with celestial deities, or even with chthonic ones.[3]

But environmental explanations fail to capture the continued appeal of divine violence and fall short in explaining the capacity of religious literature to motivate violent acts. Building on Mary Douglas's approach, others have explored the cosmic ordering spectacle of ritualized warfare as represented in poetry and art. For instance, divine violence and conceptions of cosmic order are entwined in the Babylonian creation poem named the *Enuma Elish*. The poem recounts the might of god Marduk, who slaughters sea goddess Tiamat, dismembers her body, and tramples various body parts in order to create the world. He also terrifies and tames her loyal army, depicted as a chaotic horde. His cosmogonic feats are celebrated yearly by a performed reading of the poem and by royal rituals wherein the king, resplendent with divine symbols (e.g., radiating *melammu* from his head), mimics the god's subduing of chaos by manipulating iconic codes for disorder (Noegel 2007). In Assyrian art, the king is depicted as having killed and beheaded barbarian foes and slaughtered lions, both representing liminal creatures that threaten the civilized world. Assyrian royal annals boast of similar feats, wherein kingly power mirrors divine (Ponchia 1987). The chaos-subduing motif is so common in Near Eastern art and poetry as to constitute a veritable type scene for cosmic war.

Feats of cosmic war comprise a distinctive theme in biblical literature especially, in the motif of the *Chaoskampf*. In ancient mythopoesis, the biblical god is imagined not only as establishing national boundaries and dominion over sea serpents and chaos demons (e.g., Isa. 24, 27; Ps. 74:12–17; Ez. 38–39; Dan. 2) but also as eradicating death and bringing new life (e.g., Isa. 26; Dan. 12; Rev. 21:1 [Fishbane 2004; Ortlund 2010]). Its Mesopotamian or Ugaritic roots notwithstanding (Fishbane 2004; Ortlund 2010; Day 1985), the *Chaoskampf* motif is often linked historically to the first Diaspora and Jewish hopes for national renewal (Fitzpatrick 2004). Yet clearly it riveted Christian imagination too. Triumphalist, even blood-thirsty, hopes pepper Christian apocalyptic literature (e.g., Rev. 7–19), and end time reveries flavor Gospel reports (e.g., Matt. 13, 24; Mk. 9, 13, 14; John 5:28–29) and the letters of Paul (1 Cor. 7:29–31; 15:51–57; 1 Thess. 4; 2 Thess. 2; Rom. 16:20).[4] For that matter, such hopes are alive and well in Christian Reconstructionist fantasies and discernible in the fringes of contemporary Zionism (Aho 1990; Juergensmeyer 2000; Sells, this volume). Nearly all world religions have entertained eschatological visions in which waves of violence culminate in peace. A quest for cosmic order would seem ubiquitous in religious imagination.

More intricate issues underlie the process of inscribing violence into texts. One trend, pursued by anthropologists as well as Near Eastern and Mediterranean historians, is the study of the capacity of words, intoned and inscribed, to generate violence by themselves (e.g., Tambiah 1968; Noegel 2010; Bottéro 2001). When ritually intoned—as in oaths, curses, and spells—or when inscribed in special media—as in lead—some words and word strings are seen as sensuously connected to the objects they name, both in ancient times and in many cultural pockets today. Thus, words not only signify objects, they manipulate them. Curses in Homeric and Hittite treaties were expected to harness cosmic forces to their tasks (Kitts 2005: 93–100) and studies of Near Eastern word magic reveal how stylistic enhancements—special rhythms and dialects, rhyming, punning (Faraone 1993; Noegel 2010)—were thought to amplify the performative and often lethal power of ritual speech. In the Bible, the practice of inscribing, effacing, and smashing texts (e.g., Ex. 34, 32:19–33; Job 19:23–24; Isa. 30:8; Jer. 36:22–23) was intended to alter destiny (Noegel 2010), despite risking cosmic reprisals.[5] According to Jean Bottéro, Mesopotamian scribes saw the act of writing words as profoundly analogous to the act of creation (2001: 178)—parallel to etching fate into a cosmic text. Creating and destroying such etchings were sensed to exert supernatural power over all of reality, conceived as a text. A poetic representation of the same conception penetrates Isaiah's vision of the heavens rolling up like a scroll:

> He will totally destroy them,
> he will give them over to slaughter.
> Their slain will be thrown out,
> their dead bodies will stink;
> the mountains will be soaked with their blood.
> All the stars in the sky will be dissolved
> and the heavens rolled up like a scroll;
> all the starry host will fall
> like withered leaves from the vine,

like shriveled figs from the fig tree.
(Isaiah 34:2–4, New International Translation)

The potential violence in verbal manipulations is not restricted to the sphere of ancient word magic. It extends into contemporary speech act theory. Philosophers and anthropologists observe how speech acts may forge new awarenesses and seal commitments, and thereby wield perlocutionary force (Austin 1975; Rappaport 1999). Thus, vows, knighting ceremonies, war declarations, and other performatives in high communicational registers manipulate social realities, as ritually charged texts do cosmic realities. A latent violence may be perceived in either kind of formal illocution, in that its commissive force stymies the free play of possibility.

A related trend is to study how poetic articulations, etched into fixed texts, may displace religious epiphanies and serve imperialist propaganda, clinching a battle for hearts and minds. Competition for theological authority is discernible at the origins of many religious literatures,[6] conceivably spawning them. For instance, an apparent struggle for theological authority is captured in the rancor between the prophets of Yahweh and Baal reported in First Kings 18, a struggle thought by some scholars to evoke prophecy's more ancient oracular mission of sanctioning holy wars.[7] The Sturm und Drang of prophetic ranting saturated nascent biblical religion. Discord between guilds of prophets, between prophets and other kinds of ecstatics, even internally within individual prophets (e.g., Jeremiah's despair arising from suspicions of divine misguidance, as well as from stubborn audiences) likely was one impulse for the commission of oral texts to writing in the first place (Geller 2007), instantiating an ideological coup in the form of a fixed text. Oralists no longer see a hard divide between oral and literate cultures in the way they manipulate imaginations, but a certain literary imperialism is implicit in this ancient privileging of texts, tied to their capacity to seal cosmological visions and behavioral codes into time.

At the same time, social friction in any era may inspire new strategies of violence by the parties forced to yield, leading to subversive inscriptions in new media, as in bodies. While not comprising written texts, assault sorceries—traditional performances of ritualized chants, spells, and bodily manipulations—have been noted of late to articulate a competing cosmology resistant to hegemonic control among populations in Papua New Guinea and Amazonia.[8] Thus they encrypt subversive "texts" on individual and social bodies, aiming for lethal intent. In some Papua New Guinean traditional societies, it is the colonial suppression of traditional modes of justice, such as revenge and vendetta, and the imposition of European-based modes that have spurred expansions and mutations of assault sorcery (Stewart and Strathern 1999, 2002): Older forms of warfare being futile or nearly so, new syntheses of mystical ideas and ritual practices, intending deadly assault, emerge from the interstices of the old and the newly encountered systems. Curiously, Christian evangelizing seems to have augmented shamanic warfare in Amazonia, inspiring alleluia prophets with distinct mystical codes and practices to battle more traditional shamans in numinous warfare (Whitehead 2002: 128ff). Resonating with Michael

Taussig's explorations, recent research on assault sorcery reveals a flourishing discourse of violence with symbolic and mystical features at cultural margins. Rumors of preternatural violence may inspire fears of ritualized cruelty and enchantments within the hegemonic societies. Whitehead has called such cultural formations a "poetics of violence" (2002: 191–194), read differently by the various sides.[9]

A similar discourse, also based in ritual performance, may be discerned in the last instructions of the suicide activists of 9/11, in their jihad hymns (Seidensticker 2006), in the taped last words of many suicide activists, and on the bodies and instruments of those who commit to fighting unto death. For instance, what are we to make of instruction 12 of the 9/11 last instructions, which enjoined reciting verses of the Qur'an and then expectorating them onto knives, clothing, passports, and papers (Kitts 2010a: 306–307)? In its apparent holy contagion, might spitting verses onto carry-on items compare to wearing crosses on clothing or even branding them onto one's skin for Pope Urban's Christian crusaders (Riley-Smith 1997: 68; Kitts 2010a: 293–299)? Both groups swore to fight unto death. From these examples, we see that religious incantations and symbols may inscribe violence into texts beyond the page.[10]

Manipulating religious rhetoric and symbols to serve violent ends is not new, obviously. For instance, in the 1990s a calculated poetics of persecution and revenge was strategically employed to ignite violence in the Balkans, in the revival of epic songs and legends recounting Serbian (Christian Orthodox) loss to Turkish (Muslim) forces at the fourteenth-century Field of Blackbirds in Kosovo. Oralists have long looked to Yugoslavia to explore the dynamics of a thriving bardic tradition built around this battle. Pondering Radovan Karadzic's propensity to represent himself as one of these traditional Slavic bards, Žižek sardonically questions the war support offered by a "poetic-military complex" (2009). Karadzic did not shy from proclaiming himself the new Hades:

> This fateful hour stiffened and reached the sky
> Like a tree it now binds all existence in its branches
> I am the cause of universal distress[11]

Inveigling "inclemency and wine" and a "godhead [who] forbids you nothing" (Žižek 2009: 504), Karadzic's poems offered an ecstasy of vengeance. Such poetry does more than distill resentments; it intends to trigger violent response.

HOW VIOLENCE GETS FROM RELIGIOUS TEXTS INTO ACTION

On the one hand, the power of religious literature to incite violent imaginings is apparent on its face. Religious and classical literatures proclaim glorious spectacles of warfare by gods and heroes. Gods even model combat for heroes. Just as deities

Poseidon, Ares, Athena, Ishtar, Ashur, and Yahweh march in front, leading troops in battle, perpetrating terror and vengeance, so, too, do ancient heroes Odysseus, Hector, Achilles, Mursilis, Assurbanipal, and biblical figures Joshua and Barak, described frequently in language identical to that of the gods. Battlefield narratives are riddled with angels and saints. Angels fought alongside Muslims in early battles (Q. Sura 8), one led the Israelites through the enemy lands into Canaan (Ex. 33:2), and Christ and the Virgin Mary marched with the first crusaders into Syria (Riley-Smith 1997: 78–80; Partner 1997: 70). As religious imagination would have it, gods, angels, saints, and heroes support the good fight.

On the other hand, it is equally apparent that religious literature can commemorate loss and inflame anguish. Loss is mourned in countless stories of primordial rupture wherein present-day dissonance clashes with distant harmony. Fallen ages, forfeited Edens, stubborn hearts, and strained relationships with gods, one another, and the natural world are the subjects of popular stories, and martyrs and villains populate them. Rumors of betrayal make martyr tales particularly incendiary, for example, Huseyn at Karbala, Jesus in Jerusalem, Prince Lazar at Kosovo. But all of it—rupture, betrayal, prophetic chastisement, genocide—stirs salt in deep wounds kept raw by these stories. Reading them, penitents and revolutionaries mount restorative campaigns on all kinds of battlefields—moral, social, political, and geographical.

Besides posing as artifacts of civilizations, then, religious literatures clearly help to construct them, by providing archives of cosmologies, memories, personalities, and symbols for collective imagination. Elaine Scarry has explored biblical narratives of torture and pain and their profound impact on Western conceptions of God and civilization (1994), but other literatures—such as the *Iliad, Mahabharata*, and classical Japanese war tales—may be argued similarly to construct and also to lay bare the cultural psyches of those who produce them. Note that wars and violence exert a peculiar fascination in such stories, beyond the fascination with ethnic blessings or divine providence. Yet each of the above national literatures is undergirded by religious assumptions. It is the persistent marriage of war and religion in classical literatures that has led some scholars to ponder universalizing theories of religious violence as emergent in literature.

Hence, René Girard's theories have struck a chord. In Girard's view, violence, perceived as an index of true "being,"[12] fascinates but also terrifies us because of its destructive consequences and implicit anarchism. It is therefore a widespread cultic and literary preoccupation, which he illustrates by drawing on disparate evidence, from Dinka ritual to Greek tragedy to Disney's *Lion King*. As is well known, Girard also claims that sacrificial violence lies at the heart of religious institutions and is foundational for their stability, due to an inexorable tendency for generative scapegoating based on mimetic rivalry.[13] Ignoring the merits and demerits of the scapegoating and mimesis theses, we may observe that Girard's point about the fascination of violence falls in the wake of a number of other prominent theories that likewise fixate on primal violence: Robertson-Smith's totemic hypothesis, Freud's Oedipal hypothesis, Jensen's *dema* hypothesis, and the hunting hypothesis of Walter Burkert, who is contemporary with Girard. All address to some degree what Jensen refers to as the moment of imaginative seizure (*Ergriffenheit*) created by the shock of ritualized killing. This shock, it is argued, penetrates religious literature, particularly sacrificial narratives.

But others deny this universal human fascination with violence. First, war historians and anthropologists do not see a correlation of violence, religious or otherwise, with the emergence of human societies. Brian Ferguson points to the ambiguity and scarcity of evidence for warfare or symbolic violence of any kind before the Neolithic period (2008). As for gathering authentic evidence about innately violent tendencies from simple tribes, Neil Whitehead explained the inherent contamination of the evidence by quizzical anthropologists and encroaching colonial powers. Similar problems infect studies of the violence of other primates, who are already impacted by human encounters and loss of habitats (Whitehead 2007). Second, in contrast to Girard, Freud, and Burkert and based on case studies, Jonathan Z. Smith comments on the improbability of nonagrarian societies' sacrificial rituals ever being rooted in an "ontic" seizure or primal event and looks instead to the "exegetical ingenuity" of a society's "imagination and intellection of culture" and to societal concepts of process and work (2004: 148–150). All of this skepticism, part of a larger critique of metanarratives, favors the autonomy of particular traditions in any discussion of violence.

Emphasis on the autonomy of particular traditions has fueled a discussion of classical Greek sacrifice in recent decades, under the conceptual umbrella of cuisine. Problematizing the rubric of sacrifice because of its Christian connotations, Vernant and Detienne restricted their investigation to Greek *thysia*, or commensal sacrifice, in its literary and artistic representations. They saw it as unique. Unlike Vedic sacrifice as described by Hubert and Mauss, Greek thysia never promoted a transmigration of human beneficiaries to the divine world and back again to the mundane but instead rooted its participants firmly in a complex of dietary codes that defined the human plane against that of the Olympian immortals. Violence, an overt theme in Christianity's core sacrificial narrative, was in Greek cuisine either absent or muffled; the few sacrificial myths that betrayed homophagic associations played warning roles in support of the normative dietary code. Yet, perhaps ironically, Vernant claimed that Western scholars were in a unique position to ascertain such a code, because Western was an extension of Greek tradition and thus less likely to misconstrue it.[14] That dietary code was discernible in multiple texts or, rather, a very broad text. Expanding the scope of a "text"—by inference a textile or a weaving of a "bundle of relations" (per Claude Lévi-Strauss)—into a larger tradition spanning from 800 BCE to 200 CE, the French school explored the broad sweep of Greek dietary semantics, wherein no one ingredient might divulge its themes out of connection with the others, despite the amplification of different themes at different sites.

Critics of the French school point to the problems with reading one thousand years of Greek dietary semantics as a single, dechronologized text; with the classicists' presumption that we have relatively smooth access to a two-thousand-year-old imagination (Grottanelli 1988); and with the model of culture as text, given the surface dissimilarity between what goes on in daily social interaction and "the solid composure of lines on a page" (Geertz, 1983: 31). But the most radical critique pertains to the underlying notion that religious and classical literatures represent a closed imaginative circuit. As Ricoeur pointed out years ago, "If reading is possible, it is indeed because the text is not closed in on itself but opens out onto other things" (1981: 158). Ricoeur's point is rooted in two others, discussion of which will lead us to contemplate the "violent imaginaries" that stem from religious literatures.

The first point from Ricoeur is far reaching, harking back to hermeneutics and existential phenomenology. As Ricoeur (1981) and Gadamer (1976: 9) taught us, we never read texts with the extralinguistic world suspended. At one level, this ability to comprehend is simply preverbal. Regardless of what we suppose to be motivating our stance toward a text, it is embodiment that grounds our comprehension of at least some of it (Jackson 1983; Kövecses 2000). For example, our contemporary grasp of ancient fury or shame may be imperfect, but we can grasp ancient metaphors based on gravity, verticality, and virtuality (e.g., three-dimensionality, vitality, and the desire to thrive; Kövecses 2000: 139–163).

But on another level, a vaster range of extralinguistic experience is implicated in our ability to respond to narratives of terror, a fairly recent preoccupation. Our ability to comprehend other people's terror seems to be rooted in a sense of contingency, unpredictability, and potential rupture within our own customary worlds (Strathern and Stewart 2006: 7, 13). Although one might argue that these are part of bodily virtuality (or at least Bourdieu's *hexis*), the discussion has stimulated forays into other experiences that are slippery to cognitive grasp. In addition to terror, both trauma and torture are argued to intrude into awareness at a level beyond signification (Crapanzano 2004: 91).[15] Also pain, noted since Nietzsche to be a powerful mnemonic device and a forceful creator of context, nonetheless resists integration into personal narratives (Crapanzano 2004: 90–91), while riveting national ones (Scarry 1994). To this list of discursively elusive but sensed experiences, suspense and the uncanny, fairly traditional items of poetic analysis, can be added. Without an intrinsic sense of those elements, how would we comprehend a passage such as this?

> Like one that on a lonesome road
> Doth walk in fear and dread,
> And having once turned round walks on,
> And turns no more his head;
> Because he knows a frightful fiend
> Doth close behind him tread.
> (Coleridge, *The Rime of the Ancient Mariner*).

Or this?

> And I will make those of you who are left in the lands of your enemies so ridden with fear that, when a leaf flutters behind them in the wind, they shall run as if it were a sword behind them; they shall fall with no one in pursuit (Lev. 26:36–37).[16]

Both speak to a chilling, paranormal presence. All of these experiences—trauma, terror, pain, suspense, and the uncanny—reach beneath discursive analysis and challenge the postmodernist trend to see human experience as entirely socially constructed. Poetic simulations of trauma, terror, the uncanny, and the like represent a peculiar and traditional feature of the literature we associate with religion, which seems to be the capacity to reach deeply into human nature and to yank at the core of it.

This brings us to our second point drawn from Ricoeuer. In reading, says Ricoeur, we conjoin our own discourses to the one inscribed in texts (1981: 158), so that, however perspectival our own discourse, that conjoining elicits novel ways of seeing the world. Conjuring new ways of seeing is also the intention of oral poetry, which is ostensibly at the origin of Western religious literatures. Our best example is Homeric poetry, performed for a century or more before diverse audiences, from whom it presumably elicited recognition of the diachronically oldest themes— the most universal—while integrating regional imaginations about them, at least in part (Cf. Nagy 1990). The resulting blend of ancient theme and contemporary imagination became encrypted in poetic art, which, because of its deep reach, still resonates millennia later. The most profound elements of religious literature ought to persist similarly, continually resonating because of their reach into the deepest recesses of what humans can imagine. Trauma, terror, pain, and the like are among these profound elements of religious literature and conjure a violent imaginary.

An imaginary has been defined variously but, generally speaking, refers to the dimension of imagination that spurs action and makes it meaningful. Charles Taylor sees a social imaginary as background understanding—"that largely unstructured and inarticulate understanding of our whole situation, within which particular features of our world become evident, … which makes practice possible" and for which "practice largely carries the understanding" (2002: 107). Strathern and Stewart see violent imaginaries as shaped by the cosmological themes, gods, and emotions that figure in meaningful actions (2006: 6). There are three orders in Aijmer's schematic of the imaginary: the discursive—a multifaceted range of social inquiries and intentional performative acts addressing people's conversation about themselves and their world; the iconic—by which he seems to mean a network of images elusive to discourse but instrumental, even motivating, in the visionary building of possible worlds; and the ethological—which entails the biological/genetic realities of human activities and our susceptibility to pain and death (2000: 3–5). These overlap, of course. Death and pain are ethological facts but in iconic representation educe the brute reality of violence and can assume socio-symbolical significance in launching revenge and a discourse about martyrdom, all at the same time. The crucifixion theme evoked by the famous photo of the hooded prisoner on a box at Abu Graib is a notable example (Binder 2010), wherein the iconic impact on American imagination immediately eclipsed the discursive and ethological dimensions (we were speechless) but eventually spurred a discussion about martyrdom, torture, and aberrant art. As is well known, that photo has motivated retaliation, not just angst.

Each of the poems discussed in this chapter might exemplify violent imagination, but a violent imaginary, by definition, takes shape in violent acts. It would be remarkable if religious literatures, conveying a mesh of icons, legends, symbols, theological notions, and ritual practices involving violence, did not shape outright expressions of violence as well as the significance attributed to them. Violent imaginaries certainly inform wartime actions represented within ancient literature, in some cases saturating warlike acts with sacrificial themes, as in biblical *hērem* and the military feats of Joshua (see Niditch 1993, cf. Homeric *poinē*; Kitts 2010b). Whole tomes now describe the contemporary appeal of holy terror, ostensibly based in scripture, in the minds of religious activists across oceans and web browsers (Juergensmeyer 2000, most notably). Religious warriors from all ages of history have basked in the sanction of scripture. If there were ever doubt, there is no question now that religious ideology is a material force.

WHENCE RELIGIOUS VIOLENCE?

Baudrillard once supposed that the rapid fire of media-based imagery shooting across oceans and continents had saturated human consciousness so far as to numb us to sensuous connection with "the real" and to generate a palpable nostalgia for it. Some see this nostalgia as motivating a flood of dystopic novels, horror films, and also trauma art, which "transubstantiates" ordinary objects into arenas of intense focus, endows them with an excess of meaning usually tied to death or disaster, and stages the viewing of them as affective rituals (Siebers 2003: 15), akin to sacred dramas. By this thinking, modernity is consumed by *memento mori*: We stare at spectacles of death and violence because we crave an intensity of experience we reputedly have lost. Does this mean that our fascination with religious violence is just contemporary and books like this one merely a sign of our time?

On the one hand, contemporary imagination is clearly in flux and on fire, particularly online. Rumors attract and inflame virtual communities whose members are drawn from every continent. Traditional literatures are increasingly denationalized and deterritorialized, and generate an amalgam of arcane models and rationales for behavior, including violent behavior. Diasporic communities are forging new idioms and genres of literature for which cultural disruption—a modern fact of life—is a major theme. Various media help to promote legends about terror and terrorists (Prestholdt 2009).

On the other hand, violence, it should be remembered, was a preoccupation of authors at the start of Western tradition and is inscribed into our earliest texts. Religious violence may not necessarily precede texts or be endemic to human nature, but it cannot be denied that Western religious texts present, among other things, an almost continuous stream of both human and divine violence and destruction. While we cannot simply blame religion for violence, its unambiguous plenitude in Western religious traditions speaks to our enduring obsession with it. It is hard to imagine that any conscious being, on reading, hearing, or seeing, would not be riveted by a spectacle of violent destruction, grasping immediately the specter of his or her own demise.

NOTES

1. German translation by Dr. Annete Zgoll; English translation (from German) at http://www.angelfire.com/mi/enheduanna/Ninmesara.html
2. Similar tropes describe divine destruction elsewhere in the Mediterranean, for example, the fiery blast of Hephaestus in Homer's *Iliad*:
   Hephaestus extended his prodigious fire.
   First the fire blazed in the plain and burned the many corpses
   which covered it, those whom Achilles killed.
   The entire plain was scorched and the shining waters checked,
   . . .
   burned were the elms, willows, and tamarisks,
   burned were the clover, rushes, and marsh grass
   which grew all around the lovely streams of the river.
   Within the eddies the eels and fish were distressed
   and tumbled hither and thither through the fine streams,
   being oppressed by the blast of resourceful Hephaestus. (21.343–355)
3. See, for example, Psalms 18 and 144.
4. On Paul's cosmic war myth, see Mackey 1998.
5. For the match with Mesopotamian practice, see the Code of Hammurabi, epilogue 19: "If that man has not paid attention to the commandments that I have inscribed on this stone and if he has forgotten my threatened curses and has shown no fear for the curses threatened by god, and if he has destroyed the rules I ordained and changed my commandments and emended what I have written, and if he has removed my name from the inscription and inscribed his own...almighty Anu, father of the gods,...will smash his staff and curse his destiny" (Noegel 2010: 45, note 8).
6. See Ruth Finnegan's thoughtful overview in *Oral Tradition* (2010).
7. "Elijah, like his God, was full of 'zeal' (*quin'a*), militant passion. Elisha actually instigated a war of extermination against the Baalists. Prophecy and violence entered a permanent symbiosis" and thus "[t]he ancient prophetic function of sanctioning holy war by providing rulers with oracles was immensely expanded by the religious warfare of the ninth century" (Geller 2007: 49).
8. In Neil Whitehead's words, this constitutes "a distinct poetic of violence within a cosmological theater of predatory death at the hands of divine forces" (2002: 208).
9. "[D]ark shamans are not simply vilified and hunted down, but can become, as with the kainamá, the source and symbol of a potent indigenous society and culture that is capable of defending itself against the depredations of the outside world.... Its current florescence is an aspect of native self-affirmation in the face of colonizing modernity" (Whitehead 2002: 204–209).
10. Cf. Talal Asad 1983: 287–327.
11. http://www.pbs.org/wgbh/pages/frontline/shows/karadzic/radovan/poems.html.

12. Either a metonym for the abundance of confidence and menacing power exuded by a model, as seen by his rival (Girard 1977: 146–147), or equivalent to divine power (Girard1977: 152).

13. Note that one act of altruism by one person unexposed to Christ deflates the hypothesis of inexorable mimetic rivalry without Christ (Kitts 2002: 20–21).

14. "The Greeks are not as foreign to us as others are. They are transmitted to us without a loss of continuity. They are still living in our cultural tradition to which we continue to remain attached" (Vernant, 1991: 7).

15. "[Trauma] is autonomous, a chance event: it bursts through the symbolically structured (and defended) world of the individual; it is beyond his or her control, desire, will, or comprehension. Therein lies its power" (Crapanzano: 91); "[Torture] creates uncertainty and unpredictability—a sense of the fully contingent that lies neither with a god nor destiny but squarely in human hands" (Crapanzano 2004: 88).

16. Cf., "Terror spread through the army in the field and through the whole people; the men at the post and the raiding parties were terrified; the very earth quaked, and there was panic" (1 Sam. 14:15). See also Isaiah 13:6–8.

BIBLIOGRAPHY

(All citations describe printed sources, unless otherwise noted.)

Aho, James. *The Politics of Righteousness: Idaho Christian Patriotism.* Seattle: University of Washington Press, 1990.

Aijmer, Göran. "Introduction: The Idiom of Violence in Imagery and Discourse." *Meanings of Violence: A Cross-Cultural Perspective.* Edited by Göran Aijmer and Jon Abbink, 1–21. Oxford, UK: Berg, 2000.

Asad, Talal. "Notes on Body Pain and Truth in Medieval Christian Ritual." *Economy and Society* 12.3 (August 1983): 287–327.

Austin, J. L. *How to Do Things with Words.* 1962. Cambridge, MA: Harvard University Press, 1975.

Binder, Werner. "Ritual Dynamics and Torture: The Performance of Violence and Humiliation at the Abu Ghraib Prison." *Ritual Dynamics and the Science of Ritual.* Vol. 3. Edited by Margo Kitts, et. al., 75–104. Wiesbaden, Germany: Harrassowitz Verlag, 2010.

Bottéro, Jean. *Religion in Mesopotamia.* Trans. Teresa Lavender Fagan. Chicago: University of Chicago Press, 2001.

Burkert, Walter. *Homo Necans.* Berkeley: University of California Press, 1983.

Cook, David. "Martyrdom Operations in Contemporary Jihad Literature." *Novo Religio* 6.1 (2002): 7–44.

Crapanzano, Vincent. *Imaginative Horizons: An Essay in Literary-Philosophical Anthropology.* Chicago: University of Chicago Press, 2004.

Day, John. *God's Conflict with the Dragon and the Sea.* Cambridge, UK: Cambridge University Press, 1985.

Derrida, Jacques. *Of Grammatology.* Baltimore: Johns Hopkins University Press, 1976.

Detienne, Marcel and Jean-Pierre Vernant. *The Cuisine of Sacrifice among the Greeks.* Translated by Paul Wissing. Chicago: University of Chicago Press, 1989.

Faraone, Christopher. "Molten Wax, Spilt Wine and Mutilated Animals: Sympathetic Magic in Near Eastern and Early Greek Oath Ceremonies." *Journal of Hellenic Studies* cxiii (1993): 60–80.

Ferguson, R. Brian. "War before History." *The Ancient World at War.* Edited by Philip deSouza. Thames and Hudson, 2008. http://andromeda.rutgers.edu/~socant/War BeforeHistory.pdf

Finnegan, Ruth. "Response from an Africanist Scholar." *Oral Tradition* 25.1 (2010). http://journal.oraltradition.org/issues/25i/finnegan

Fishbane, Michael. *Biblical Myth and Rabbinic Mythmaking.* Oxford, UK: Oxford University Press, 2004.

Fitzpatrick, Paul E., S.M. *The Disarmament of God: Ezekiel 38–39 in Its Mythic Context.* Washington, DC: Catholic Biblical Association of America, 2004.

Gadamer. Hans-Georg. *Philosophical Hermeneutics.* Berkeley: University of California Press, 1976.

Geertz, Clifford. *Local Knowledge: Further Essays on Interpretive Anthropology.* New York: Basic Books, 1983.

Geller, Stephen A. "The Prophetic Roots of Religious Violence in Western Religions." *Religion and Violence: The Biblical Heritage.* Edited by David A. Bernat and Jonathan Klawans, 47–56. Sheffield, UK: Sheffield Phoenix Press, 2007.

Girard, René. *Violence and the Sacred.* Translated by Patrick Gregory. Baltimore: Johns Hopkins Press, 1977.

Green, Alberto R.W. *The Storm-God in the Ancient Near East.* Winona Lake, IN: Eisebrauns, 2003.

Grottanelli, Cristiano. "Uccidere, donare, mangiare. Problematiche attuali dei sacrificio antico." *Sacrificio nel mondo antico.* Edited by C. Grottanelli and N. G. Parese, 3–52. Rome-Bari: Laterza, 1988.

Jackson, Michael. "Knowledge of the Body." *Man* 18.2 (June 1983): 327–345.

Jensen, Adolf E. *Myth and Cult among Primitive Peoples.* Translated by Choldin and Weissleder. Chicago: University of Chicago Press, 1973.

Juergensmeyer, Mark. *Terror in the Mind of God.* Berkeley: University of California Press, 2000.

Kitts, Margo. "Sacrificial Violence in the Iliad." *Journal of Ritual Studies* 16.1 (2002): 19–39.

Kitts, Margo. 2005. *Sanctified Violence in Homeric Society.* Cambridge, UK: Cambridge University Press, 2012.

Kitts, Margo. "The Last Night: Ritualized Violence and the Last Instructions of 9/11." *Journal of Religion* 20:3 (July 2010a): 283–312.

Kitts, Margo. "*Poinē* as a Ritual Leitmotif in the Iliad." *State, Power, and Violence.* Vol. 3 of *Ritual Dynamics and the Science of Ritual.* Edited by Margo Kitts, et. al., 7-32. Weisbaden, Germany: Harrassowitz, 2010b.

Kövecses, Zoltán. *Metaphor and Emotion: Language, Culture and the Body in Human Feeling.* Cambridge, UK: Cambridge University Press, 2000.

Mackey, Peter W. *St. Paul's Cosmic War Myth.* New York: Peter Lang, 1998.

Nagy, Gregory. *Greek Mythology and Poetics.* Ithaca, NY: Cornell University Press, 1990.

Niditch, Susan. *War in the Hebrew Bible.* Oxford, UK: Oxford University Press, 1993.

Noegel, Scott B. "Divine Violence in the Ancient Near East." *Belief and Bloodshed: Religion and Violence across Time and Tradition.* Edited by James Wellington, 13–28. Lanham, MD: Rowman and Littlefield, 2007.

Noegel, Scott B. "The Ritual Use of Linguistic and Textual Violence in the Hebrew Bible and Ancient Near East." *State, Power, and Violence.* Vol. 3 of *Ritual Dynamics and the Science of Ritual.* Edited by Margo Kitts, et. al., 33–46. Weisbaden, Germany: Harrassowitz, 2010.

Ortlund, Eric Nels. *Theophany and Chaoskampf: The Interpretation of Theophanic Imagery in the Baal Epic, Isaiah, and the Twelve.* Piscataway, NJ: Gorgias Press, 2010.

Partner, Peter. *God of Battles.* Princeton, NJ: Princeton University Press, 1997.

Ponchia, Simonetta. "Analogie, metafore, e similitudini nelle iscrizioni reali assire: semantica e ideologia." *Oriens antiquus.* XXVI.3–4 (1987): 223–255.

Prestholdt, Jeremy. "Phantom of the Forever War: Fazul Abdullah Muhammad and the Terrorist Imaginary." *Public Culture* 21:3 (2009): 451–464.

Rappaport, Roy A. *Ritual and Religion in the Making of Humanity.* Cambridge, UK: Cambridge University Press, 1999.

Ricoeur, Paul. *Hermeneutics and the Social Sciences.* Cambridge, UK: Cambridge University Press, 1981.

Riley-Smith, Jonathan. "The State of Mind of Crusaders to the East." *The Oxford Illustrated History of the Crusades.* Ed. Jonathan Riley-Smith, 66–90. New York: Oxford University Press, 1997.

Scarry, Elaine. *The Body in Pain.* New York: Oxford University Press, 1994.

Schmidt, Bettina E. and Ingo Schröder. "Introduction: Violent Imaginaries and Violent Practices." *Anthropology of Violence and Conflict.* Edited by Bettina Schmidt and Ingo Schröder, 1–24. London: Routledge, 2001.

Seidensticker, Tilman. "Jihad Hymns (*Nashīds*) as a Means of Self-Motivation in the HamburgGroup." *9/11 Handbook.* Edited by Hans G. Kippenberg and Tilman Seidensticker, 71–78. London: Equinox, 2006.

Siebers, Tobin. "The Return to Ritual: Violence and Art in the Media Age." *Journal for Cultural and Religious Theory* 5.1 (December 2003): 9–33. http://www.jcrt.org/archives/05.1/siebers.pdf.

Smith, Jonathan Z. *Relating Religion: Essays in the Study of Religion.* Chicago: University of Chicago Press, 2004.

Stewart, Pamela and Andrew Strathern. "Feasting on My Enemy: Images of Violence and Change in the New Guinea Highlands." *Ethnohistory* 46.4 (1999): 645–669. http://muse.jhu.edu/journals/ethnohistory/v046/46.4stewart01.html

Stewart, Pamela and Andrew Strathern. "Revenge." *Violence: Theory and Ethnography.* 108–139. London: Continuum International Publishing Group, 2002.

Strathern, Andrew and Pamela J. Stewart. "Introduction: Terror, the Imagination, and Cosmology." *Terror and Violence: Imagination and the Unimaginable.* Eds. Andrew Strathern, Pamela Stewart, and Neil Whitehead, 1–39. Ann Arbor, MI: Pluto Press, 2006.

Tambiah, Stanley J. "The Magic Power of Words." *Man* 3.2 (1968): 175–208.

Taylor, Charles. "Modern Social Imaginaries." *Public Culture* 14.1 (2002): 91–124.

Vernant, Jean-Pierre. *Mortals and Immortals: Collected Essays by Jean-Pierre Vernant.* Edited by Froma Zietlin. Princeton, NJ: Princeton University Press, 1991.

Weinfeld, Moshe. "'Rider of the Clouds' and 'Gatherer of the Clouds.'" *Journal of Ancient Near Eastern Studies* 5 (1973): 421–426.

Whitehead, Neil L. "Violence & the Cultural Order." *Daedalus* (Winter 2007): 1–10. JSTOR database.

Whitehead, Neil L. *Dark Shamans: Kanaima and the Poetics of Violent Death.* Duke University Press, 2002.

Žižek, Slavoj. "Notes on a Poetic-Military Complex." *Third Text* 22.5 (September 2009): 503–509. Taylor and Francis Social Sciences database.

CHAPTER 30

RELIGION AND VIOLENCE FROM CHRISTIAN THEOLOGICAL PERSPECTIVES

CHARLES KIMBALL

A survey of Christian history reveals three distinct attitudes and approaches to the use of violence by those who claim to follow Jesus: pacifism, the just war, and the crusade. A brief consideration of these three approaches illustrates the connection between temporal political power and a theological justification for violence among adherents in what is now the world's largest religious tradition. While these models emerged primarily in relation to real or perceived external threats, the theological frameworks have also been employed to justify the use of violence within the Christian communities over many centuries. This chapter outlines the movement from pacifism to just war and crusade, illustrates ways prominent Catholic and Protestant leaders have advocated and employed harshly violent measures within their communities, and identifies contemporary manifestations of these three approaches among twenty-first-century Christians.

From Pacifism to the Just War Doctrine and Crusades

Many New Testament texts present an image of Jesus proclaiming and embodying a gospel of love. Jesus rejected the mantle of a military savior many zealots were anticipating and some urged on him. Jesus's teachings and behavior focused instead on a distinctly different approach to conflict and injustice. The Sermon on the Mount begins with the Beatitudes, teachings that include a promised blessing for the peacemakers, those who work earnestly to make peace will be called "children of God" (Matthew 5:9, NRSV). Jesus turned conventional wisdom upside down by telling his disciples to "love your enemies, and pray for those who persecute you. (Matthew 5:43). As he was arrested in the garden of Gethsemane, one of Jesus's followers drew a sword and struck the servant of the high priest. Jesus immediately said to him, "Put your sword back into its place; for all who take the sword will perish by the sword" (Matthew 26:52).

The book of Acts records stories of the earliest Christian communities, including major points of tension and disagreement alongside an experiment in communal living in which people gave up private ownership so that everyone's needs could be met. The letters of Paul speak frequently about the centrality of love and the call to a ministry of reconciliation. Writing to the Christians at Rome, Paul underscored their responsibility: "Do not repay anyone evil for evil, but take thought for what is noble in the sight of all. If it is possible, so far as it depends on you, live peaceably with all.... Do not be overcome by evil, but overcome evil with good." (Romans 12:17–18, 21) Paul also speaks directly to the relationship between religion and governing authorities as he presents the theological framework that guided the Christian communities for the first three centuries. In Romans 13, Paul insists on submission to government authorities:

> Let every person be subject to the governing authorities; for there are no authorities that exist except from God, and those that exist have been instituted by God. Therefore whoever resists authority resists what God has appointed, and those who resist will incur judgment...for the same reason you also pay taxes, for the authorities are God's servants, busy with this very thing [*i.e., punishing bad conduct*]. Pay to all what is due them—taxes to whom taxes are due, revenue to whom revenue is due. (Romans 13:1–2, 6–7)

The later pastoral letter of 1 Timothy, which purports to be written by Paul, urges followers of Jesus to pray for those in positions of authority:

> First of all, then, I urge that supplications, prayers, intercessions, and thanksgivings be made for everyone, for kings and all who are in high positions, so that we may lead a quiet and peaceable life in all godliness and dignity. (1 Timothy 2:1–2)

The followers of Jesus were pacifists for the first three centuries (Cadoux, 1982). Numerous early church leaders and documents underscore the unwavering commitment to nonviolence. It appears that only a handful of Christians were soldiers prior to the fourth century. John Ferguson puts it succintly:

> Christianity and war were incompatible. Christians were charged with undermining the Roman Empire by refusing military service and public office: they answered that human life was sacred to them, that they were…given over to peace, that God prohibits killing even in a just cause, without exception, that the weapons of the Christian were prayer, justice and suffering. (Ferguson 1978: 103)

Constantine's rise to power early in the fourth century was the decisive turning point. Engaged in a multisided contest for leadership in the Roman Empire, he prevailed in a decisive battle the day after reportedly having had a vision of a white cross with the Greek inscription "In this sign you will conquer." Shortly after two of the worst waves of Roman government persecution, Christianity was now on the way to becoming the official religion of the Roman Empire. Constantine was able to consolidate his rule over a period of two decades (Carroll 2001: 165–207). From this point forward, Christianity in Europe became linked with state power. Threats to the state now became threats to the church. While the pacifist tradition did not disappear, it was marginalized as most church leaders sought to redefine the responsibilities of Christians within the state.

Some prominent religious leaders began to distinguish between clergy, whose vocation required total dedication, and laity, whose duty as citizens included military service. Late in the fourth century, Ambrose (c. 340–397 CE) furnished the first ingredients of what would develop into the Christian doctrine of the just war: the conduct of war must be just and monks and priests should abstain (Bainton 1960: 88–91). Augustine (354–430 CE), the highly influential thinker and theologian, then developed elements of the code of war. Augustine's writings reflect his views on sin and punishment, the challenge of living in this world and not yet in the city of God, and the threat posed by barbarians storming the gate. Church historian Roland Bainton summarized Augustine's views in this way:

> The war must be just in its intent—which is to restore peace…. Those wars may be defined as just which avenge injuries…. The war must be just in its disposition, which is Christian love…. Love does not preclude a benevolent severity, nor that correction which compassion itself dictates…. (War) is to be waged only under the authority of the ruler…. The conduct of the war must be just…. Faith must be kept with the enemy. There should be no wanton violence, profanation of temples, looting, massacres, or conflagration. Vengeance, atrocities, and reprisals were excluded, though ambush was allowed. (Bainton 1960: 95–98)

Various Christian approaches to war and peace during the following centuries are visible in numerous texts, edicts, and oaths reflecting the conflicting influences. The dominant themes, however, reveal a chaotic era when diverse religious views and military campaigns were intertwined among groups within and on the fringes of the empire: Visigoths, Vandals, Franks, Saxons, Norsemen, Slavs, Berbers, and others. For centuries, Europe was beset with major wars and local conflicts. A well-known story of Clovis, a ruthless military hero who converted the Franks to Christianity, illustrates the reversal from early church understandings and practices. Clovis offered this response to the crucifixion of Jesus: "If I and my Franks had been there, it never would have happened!" The Saxons were converted by force during a long series of wars against Charlemagne (c. 742–814 CE), the king of the Franks and emperor of the Romans. Charlemagne fought against "pagans and infidels" with the papal blessing (Ferguson 1978: 106–107).

The convoluted story of church history includes efforts to redefine the criteria for Christians' participation in war. We now find many instances of clergy engaging in battle. Roland Bainton reports, for example, that ten German bishops fell in battle between 886 and 908 and quotes the archbishop of Mainz who claimed he had personally dispatched nine men in battle using a mace (Bainton 1960: 104). A monk named Gratian is credited with introducing the concept of the just war into legal discourse during the middle of the twelfth century. Many people developed and refined criteria depending on the nature of the war and the status of the combatants. The doctrine of the just war was finalized in the sixteenth century:

> There were four basic criteria: (i) it must be proclaimed by lawful authority; (ii) the cause must be just; (iii) the belligerents should have a rightful intention, to advance good or avoid evil; (iv) the war must be fought by proper means. Additional criteria are sometimes found: (v) action should be against the guilty; (vi) the innocent should not suffer; (vii) war must be undertaken as a last resort; (viii) there must be a reasonable chance of success. (Ferguson 1978: 111)

Woven into the many positions put forward between the fourth and eleventh centuries, one finds arguments suggesting that pagans, heretics, and infidels were guilty of opposing the law of God. This view was widely held during the centuries when the behavior of many European Christians was arguably furthest removed from the teachings and example of Jesus: the era of the Crusades.

The first Crusade was instigated by Pope Urban II in November 1095. At a meeting in Clermont, France, Pope Urban II delivered an impassioned sermon in which he called on the Franks to march to the East with the dual purposes of helping the Byzantines and then liberating Jerusalem from Muslim control: "You are obligated to succor your brethren in the East, menaced by an accursed race, utterly alienated from God. The Holy Sepulcher of our Lord is polluted by the filthiness of an unclean nation.... Start upon the road to the Holy Sepulcher to wrest that land from the wicked race and subject it to yourselves" (Bainton 1960: 111–112).

The appeal produced a powerful response that day with the crowd reportedly shouting, "God wills it!" In the next few months, the message spread through sermons, papal letters, and word of mouth in France, Italy, and parts of Germany. Far from being a just war declared by a king, volunteers now came forward to fight in a war instigated by the church. With little preparation or adequate provisions, many began marching toward Jerusalem under the banner of the cross. The first was launched with several organized groups taking different routes toward Constantinople and eventually Jerusalem. From the outset, the righteous zeal of these soldiers for God produced horrific behavior. Before leaving Germany, some crusaders massacred more than 1,500 Jews at Speier, Worms, Mainz, and Metz, considering them also to be "enemies of Christ" (Johnson 1980: 245). The vast majority of those in this first wave of crusading pilgrims died of hunger, exposure, disease, and in battle far from Jerusalem.

In a 1995 British Broadcasting Corporation documentary titled *The Crusades*, historian Christopher Tyerman stresses how this new approach to war reflected a dramatic theological reorientation: "Whereas in 1066 soldiers who fought at Hastings had to do penance for their slaughter, on the first Crusade the slaughter itself was considered a penitential act." Many of the crusaders became savage extremists. Crusaders often returned to camp carrying the heads of Muslims on spears or forcing prisoners to carry the heads of their comrades on spears. Near Antioch, Radulf of Caen described cannibalism as "[o]ur troops boiled pagan adults in cooking pots. They impaled children on spits and devoured them grilled." All along the routes to Jerusalem, crusaders terrorized and massacred Jews and many Orthodox Christians as well.

The first Crusade was instigated ostensibly to expel the Turks from Jerusalem. By the time the crusaders reached the sacred city, however, the Turks were no longer in control. Egyptians ruled the city of 100,000 where Jews, Christians, and Muslims were functioning well in a multicultural setting. Nevertheless, on July 15, 1099, the crusaders breached the defenses of Jerusalem and began slaughtering wantonly. They set fire to the Great Synagogue where the Jews had gathered for safety, burning them alive. They stormed the Noble Sanctuary (or Temple Mount) where thousands of Muslims had gathered that Friday for prayers. Fleeing into the al-Aqsa mosque, the Muslims paid a huge ransom in return for worthless guarantees of their safety. The next day they were all slaughtered. Raymond of Agiles summarized the gruesome scene:

> Some of our men (and this was more merciful) cut off the heads of their enemies; others shot them with arrows, so that they fell from the towers; others tortured them longer by casting them into flames. Piles of heads, hands and feet were to be seen in the streets of the city. It was necessary to pick one's way over the bodies of men and horses. But these were small matters compared to what happened at the temple of Solomon, a place where religious services are ordinarily chanted. What happened there? If I tell the truth, it will exceed your powers of belief. So let it suffice to say this much at least, that in the temple and portico of Solomon, men rode in blood up to their knees and the bridle reins. Indeed, it was a just and splendid judgment of God, that this place should be filled with the blood of unbelievers, when it had suffered so long from their blasphemies. Now that the city was taken it was worth all our previous labors and hardships to see the devotion of the pilgrims at the Holy Sepulcher. How they rejoiced and exulted and sang the ninth chant to the Lord. (Bainton 1960: 112–113)

The marches toward and capture of Jerusalem set in motion a series of counter-crusades and new crusades that continued for some five centuries. In addition to the organized initiatives focused on the Holy Land, various lesser crusades were mounted with other destinations as the clashes with Muslims played out from

Spain to central Europe to the eastern end of the Mediterranean. The leadership of the Catholic Church was intimately involved in this dynamic process, organizing and often motivating crusaders with the promise of an indulgence or forgiveness for the temporal penalties of sin for a penitent person who performed some arduous or virtuous task designated by the church. The abuse of indulgences was one of the major factors sparking the Protestant Reformation led by Martin Luther and others.

The Crusades represent the third type of response to war and peace among Christians, joining the ongoing just war and pacifist traditions. The just war doctrine evolved between the fourth and seventeenth centuries. During the same time period, the pacifist tradition that defined the early church was suppressed but not eliminated. It continued through the centuries, particularly among some monastic groups, the most notable being Saint Francis of Assisi (c. 1181–1226 CE) and the Franciscans. Francis was a pacifist, and his movement rejected the view that the Crusades were an appropriate way to spread the Gospel. In the later Middle Ages, a number of pacifist groups surfaced among the Waldensians, the Hussites, and some followers of John Wycliffe. In the sixteenth, seventeenth, and eighteenth centuries, we find prominent individuals advocating a pacifist stance and the rise of the historic peace churches: the Anabaptists (mostly today known as the Mennonites), the Brethren, and the Quakers.

There is another major part of the wider Christian community that is often overlooked, especially among Christians in Europe and the West, namely, the Oriental Orthodox churches. The Coptic, Armenian, and Syrian Orthodox churches are among the oldest Christian communities. Declared heretical in the mid-fifth century by Catholic and Eastern (Greek) Orthodox Christians presumably for overemphasizing the divinity of Christ rather than affirming Jesus as fully God and fully human, these churches—along with the Assyrian Church of the East (Nestorians)—have always comprised the large majority of Christians in Egypt, Syria, Iraq, and Iran. (Precise demographic information is often not available for these Middle Eastern Christian communities. Most estimates put their total number at between 12 and 14 million in the first decade of the twenty-first century.) Dominated by the Byzantine Empire and, for the last fourteen centuries, by various forms of Muslim rule, these self-standing churches have highly developed organizational structures and have remained largely independent of the political systems in which they function. These Middle Eastern Christian communities parallel somewhat the experiences of minority Jewish communities living in the Diaspora. They have maintained and perpetuated strong religious communities while continually negotiating space for their churches while others held political power over them. Rather than engage in just wars or Crusades, these Christians have nurtured their communities for almost 2,000 years following the guidance of the Apostle Paul: "If it is possible, so far as it depends upon you, live peaceably with all." (For an extended treatment of the overview in this section, see Kimball 2008: 169–182 and Kimball 2011: 58–83.)

THE INQUISITION AND CALVIN'S GENEVA

The theological justifications for the use of violence against external threats to the Holy Roman Empire paved the way for theological arguments and actions deemed necessary to stifle dissent and preserve the religious and political status quo. Two prominent examples—the Inquisition within the Catholic Church and the city-state of Geneva under John Calvin's leadership within the emerging Protestant movement—illustrate how pervasive the use of violence in the name of religion had become by time many Western Christians embraced the idea of the Crusades or holy war.

The Catholic Church established the Office of the Inquisition in 1215. Under the rubric of protecting the doctrines of the church from error and saving errant Christians from the fires of hell, inquisitors secretly gathered information about possible heretics in a given region. If substantive proof was not available, hearsay evidence was sufficient. Charges were brought against suspects—who may or may not even know why they were on trial—and they were given an opportunity to confess. Various forms of torture were sanctioned—the rack, water torture, and leg screws were frequently employed—to extract confessions. The rate of confession was about 90 percent. Severe physical and financial penalties were meted out for those who confessed. Those found guilty were often burned slowly at the stake.

The Inquisition was primarily concentrated in Italy, France, Germany, Spain, and Portugal. Initially, such Christian groups as the Waldensians and Cathars in France were a primary target. For several centuries, inquisitors were engaged literally in witch hunts. Targeted attacks on Protestants and creative thinkers such as Galileo reflect another phase of the Inquisition over the centuries. By the nineteenth century, most of the gruesome practices had ceased. However, the Office of the Inquisition remained until 1965 when it was reshaped into the Office of the Congregation for the Doctrine of the Faith during the Second Vatican Council. In 1998, Pope John Paul II called on the church for an examination of conscience and advocated an exploration of the Inquisition, which he called "a tormented phase in the history of the Church." He then ordered the opening of centuries of previously secret Vatican archives for scholarly scrutiny (Kimball 2008: 159–161).

The deadly use of church-state powers directed at presumed heretics was one of many types of abuse that fueled the Protestant Reformation. The two most prominent names associated with the reform movements of the sixteenth century were Martin Luther in Germany and John Calvin in Switzerland. Just twenty-four years after Luther launched the Reformation when he issued his Ninety-Five Theses in 1517, John Calvin implemented his vision for the church and state in Protestant Geneva.

A lawyer and theologian, Calvin in 1541 promulaged his *Ecclesiastical Ordinances,* which provided the structure to discipline individuals in the city-state. Pastors and elders formed a disciplinary institution called a consistory.

Severe punishments were inflicted on anyone expressing opinions contrary to the doctrines of the church, for not attending church, or for failing to master the catechism. Men or women convicted of adultry were subject to the death penalty. In one of the most notorious cases, Michael Servetus, who directly challenged Calvin's theology, was convicted of heresy in Geneva and then executed by fire in 1553. Historian Francois Wendel reports that Calvin's attitude and behavior was not unusual among the reformers:

> Servetus suffered the fate that hundreds of heretics and Anabaptists suffered at the hands of Protestant authorities.... Calvin was convinced, and all the reformers shared this conviction, that is it was the duty of a Christian magistrate to put to death blasphemers who kill the soul, just as they punished murderers who kill the body. (Wendel 1963: 97)

The justification for violence in the name of the Christianity can be observed among Protestants in many settings throughout Europe and North America during the last five centuries. Multiple religious wars raged for more than one hundred years following the Protestant Reformation. Harsh forms of corporal punishment—including the death penalty for various offenses—were meted out in England under the Anglican rule initiated by Henry VIII in the sixteenth century and by Puritans in America within the Massachusetts Bay Colony during the seventeenth and eighteenth centuries. At the same time, revival of the pacfist tradition gained ground in Europe and took root in America through William Penn and the Quakers who settled in Pennslyvania.

Violence and Christian Theology in the Twentieth and Twenty-First Centuries

During the twentieth and twenty-first centuries, a wide variety of theological approaches to religiously sanctioned violence can be seen among those who identify as followers of Jesus. A few selected examples from predominantly Christian countries illustrate the continuing role of pacficism, just war theory, and holy war or Crusade in various churches and church-related groups.

With ominous signs on the horizon, an international conference of Christians gathered in Switzerland in 1914 in an effort to prevent the outbreak of war in Europe. The war, however, began during the conference. Two of the participants—an English Quaker and a German Lutheran—pledged that they would find a way to work for peace even though their countries were now at war. This pledge was the foundation for an international and ecumenical Christian organization committed to nonviolent conflict resolution: the Fellowship of Reconciliation (FOR). The US branch of the FOR was formed one year later in 1915. In the century since its formation, the FOR has become an interfaith movement with branches and groups in more than forty countries with active participation by Christians, Jews, Muslims, Buddhists, Hindus, and others. The FOR encouraged nonviolent resistance to World War II, led the opposition to internment of Japanese Americans, and endeavored to rescue Jews and others fleeing Naziism. The organization grew in prominence in conjunction with two of its most highly visible members—Martin Luther King, Jr. and the Vietnamese Buddhist monk and author Thich Nhat Hanh—who embodied pacifism in the civil rights movement and in oppostion to the war in Vietnam. (See www.forusa.org.)

The FOR, which enjoys strong support among Catholics, Methodists, Presbyterians, Lutherans, and most other Christian communions, has worked closely with numerous Christian organizations seeking to reclaim what they understand to be Jesus's message of nonviolence. These groups include Pax Christi (Catholic), the American Friends Service Committee (Quaker), the Mennonite Central Committee (Mennonite), and Sojourners (a Washington, DC–based evangelical Christian organization founded in the 1970s that draws support equally from evangelical and mainline Protestants as well as Catholics), and organized peace fellowships within most major denominations.

Serious and thoughtful reflection on the just war criteria surfaces among many Christian leaders when major international conflicts arise. In the aftermath of Iraq's invasion of Kuwait in 1990, the United States and various European and Middle Eastern countries began gearing up for war. In the United States, many Protestant leaders and the US Conference of Catholic Bishops released statements underscoring how the proposed war with Iraq failed to meet several of the just war criteria. Had all the options been exhausted? What of the "right intention"? If the reason for mobilization and war centered on the naked aggression of Saddam Hussein toward the hapless people of Kuwait, why did the United States and others not respond militarily to the desparate pleas for assistance from Iraqi Kurds and Iraqi Shi'ites when Saddam Hussein's government was crushing them? Many Christian leaders raised serious questions about the proportionality of the response, a point that turned out to be especially well founded. Although casualities on the Allied side were far below initial Pentagon estimates, more than 150,000 Iraqis and several thousand Kuwaitis were killed in the war. The number of civilian casualties in the decade following the war was almost certainly much higher.

The overwhelming majority of indigenous Middle Eastern Christians urged Christians in the West to oppose the war and work actively for peace. In late 1990 and early 1991, the Middle East Council of Churches—a body comprised of all the major Orthodox, Catholic, and Protestant communions in the region—issued a number of statements and documents reflecting the strong concensus among Middle Eastern Christians. Many American Christian leaders, including Edmond Browning, the presiding bishop of the Episcopal Church—the head of the church in which both President George H. W. Bush and then Secretary of State James Baker were members—embraced the call of the Middle Eastern Christian leaders and made their views known publicly. Browning was a member of an ecumenical delegation whose visit to Iraq included a meeting with then President Saddam Hussein.

The group issued a public statement titled "War Is Not the Answer: A Message to the American People" (Delegation to the Middle East, *Sojourners* 1991).

At the same time, there were many highly visible Christian leaders who strongly supported the march toward war with Saddam Hussein. Many prominent evangelical Christians with television ministries in the United States framed the impending conflict as a modern day holy war. Among those who promulgated a premillennial, dispensational theology, many boldly connected the coming Gulf War as the prelude to their much anticipated battle of Armegeddon. In this view, human history was about to end and the call to support the United States and others was linked to support for Israel in what were presumed to be the end times.

Another manifestion of holy war/Crusade theology moved front and center in the first decade of the twenty-first century. In the years following the horrific attacks on New York and the Pentagon on September 11, 2001, a number of vocal and visible evangelical and fundamentalist Protestant leaders presented Islam as the focus of evil in the world and an imminent threat to Christianity. As with some Islamic extremists such as Osama bin Laden, the former leader of al-Qaeda, some American Christian leaders portrayed the challenges facing God's people quite starkly as nothing less than the struggle of good versus evil, Christianity versus Islam (or vice versa).

As has always been the case, these three Christian theological approaches to religion and violence have real-world consequences. For Christians who might be inclined toward the just war theory, new global realities now challenge that worldview. The efficacy of limiting war by the merits of carefully considered criteria is ever more dubious. Arguments about the failure to meet the church's requirements have rarely prevented political and military leaders from pursuing war. In addition, the haunting presence of many types of weapons of mass destruction—not only chemical, biological, and nuclear weapons but also readily available chemical fertilizer and commercial airplanes—in an increasingly interconnected and interdependent world community cannot be casually set aside. In the context of the twenty-first century, a growing number of Christian thinkers have been examining the traditional models and considering new approaches.

Over the past two decades, a number of Christian ethicists, theologians, and experts in conflict resolution have produced an alternative to pacifism and just war theory: the just peacemaking paradigm. This effort seeks to shift the focus to initiatives that can help prevent war and foster peace. These Christian scholars and activists developed ten key practices and detailed guidelines for peacemaking:

1. Support nonviolent direct action.
2. Take independent initiatives to reduce threat.
3. Use cooperative conflict resolution.
4. Acknowledge responsibility for conflict and injustice and seek repentance and forgiveness.
5. Advance democracy, human rights, and religious liberty.
6. Foster just and sustainable economic development.

7. Work with emerging cooperative forces in the international system.
8. Strengthen the United Nations and international efforts for cooperation and human rights.
9. Reduce offensive weapons and weapons trade.
10. Encourage grassroots peacemaking groups and voluntary associations. (Stassen 1998)

For 2,000 years, Christians have wrestled with questions about their religion and the role of violence. For more than 1,700 years, followers of Jesus have embraced vastly different approaches to what the earliest community understood to be Jesus's teachings. The unprecedented circumstances of multireligious societies in an economically and ecologically interconnected world of nation-states have spurred a new generation of theologians and ethicists to fashion contemporary responses by asking once again with a clear sense of urgency, "What would Jesus do?"

BIBLIOGRAPHY

Bainton, Roland H. *Christian Attitudes toward War and Peace.* Nashville: Abingdon Press, 1960.

Cadoux, C. John. *The Early Christian Attitude toward War.* New York: Seabury Press, 2nd ed., 1982.

Carroll, James. *Constantine's Sword: The Church and the Jews.* Boston: Houghton Mifflin Company, 2001.

Delegation to the Middle East."War Is Not the Answer: A Message to the American People" *Sojourners* (February–March 1991): 5.

Ferguson, John. *War and Peace in the World's Religions.* New York: Oxford University Press, 1978.

Johnson, Paul. *A History of Christianity.* New York: Atheneum, 1980.

Kimball, Charles. *When Religion Becomes Evil: Five Warning Signs.* San Francisco: HarperOne, 2nd ed., 2008.

Kimball, Charles. *When Religion Becomes Lethal: The Explosive Mix of Politics and Religion in Judaism, Christianity, and Islam.* San Francisco: Jossey-Bass, 2011.

Stassen, Glen, ed. *Just Peacemaking: Ten Practices for Abolishing War.* New York: Pilgrim Press, 1998.

Wendel, Francois. *Calvin.* London: Collins, 1963.

PART IV

NEW DIRECTIONS

CHAPTER 31

SACRIFICIAL VIOLENCE

A PROBLEM IN ANCIENT RELIGIONS

WALTER BURKERT

THE suicide attackers of September 11, 2001, left a text which has been titled "Spiritual Guidance," that is, preparation for death (Kippenberg 2004). There we read: "Purify your heart and clean it from stains, forget or ignore anything called 'world.'…Be joyous, because there are just a few moments between yourself and your marriage, when the happiness, blessed by god, and eternal grace…will start." This sounds strikingly similar to Christian texts of consolation in view of death, including martyrdom. Everything normal, rational, personal, or just human becomes irrelevant in the face of an otherworldly relation to "god." Religion at its best, one might be tempted to say; religion's worst perversion would be the normal judgment. The project is mass murder through suicide, envisaged as the direct way to paradise. The suicidal murderer presents himself as *homo religiosus*.

Islamic suicidal terrorism is a recent development, dependent, among other things, on the availability of explosives. But it has opened our eyes to much more general problems: It may be the case that religion does not prevent but rather motivates mass killings. Horror scenarios are neither new nor rare within religious practice, in both suicidal and murderous variants: saints starving to death, mass suicide in sects (Krause 1978), and mass murder between Hindus and Muslims in India in 1945, when the prospect of independence gave way to old religious antagonisms.

The conflict of Jews and Palestinians is still far from a solution, based on the Bible's promise of the land to Israel. The oldest story of suicidal mass murder has its place right in the Bible: At the festival of Dagon, the god of the Philistines, Samson, captured and blinded by them, breaks the central column of the meetinghouse and kills himself and 3,000 Philistines (Judges 16:23–31).

In the public view today, there is strong opposition to all forms of violence. In consequence, religion is drawn into the focus of criticism more than before. Religion claims and is generally thought to promote sense, order, and peace in our world; but it is seen to explode into violence again and again. Accusations against Christianity on these lines have a long history already: burnings of heretics, crusades, religious wars in Europe, and as to the more modern situation, what about complicity with colonialism, alliances with nationalism, and entanglements of capitalism?

The prominent religions that monopolize the scene today, Judaism, Christianity, and Islam, have all three been classified as "secondary religions" (Wagner 2006). Zoroastrianism belongs to the same group, possibly as the oldest among them. They are classified as secondary because these religions define themselves in opposition to other, "wrong" forms of religion, which generally are the older ones. This makes aggression enter the fundamentals of the creed: Secondary religions are bound to provoke and to perform religious persecution. The Hebrew Bible is full of atrocities committed against the other tribes and cults in the name of Yahweh. Christianity has taken strength and enormous propaganda from the persecutions by pagan Rome but started its own persecutions of pagans and more still of heretics and Jews as soon as it came to power. Islam postulated "fervor in advancing the cause of Islam"—this is the meaning of jihad—and called for the expansion of an Islamic world by battling nonbelievers. A Zoroastrian priest boasted how "the communities of Jews, Buddhists, Brahmins, Nazarenes, Christians, Baptists, and Manichaeans were crushed in the kingdom" (Stausberg 2002: I 225f).[1]

The older religions we know, from the ancient Near East to Greece and Rome, lack such an aggressive missionary zeal in self-definition and practice. It is these older, "primary" religions that shall be in focus here: Even in the oldest recognizable forms of religious activity, acts and fantasies of violence seem to be contained. The term that obtrudes itself in this context is *sacrifice*. In its original Latin form, *sacrificium* means "doing the sacred." Some concept of the sacred or holy is normally taken to be a characteristic of religion, even if sacrifice seems to lose its meaning in our modern world. In the ancient world, however, sacrifice denotes the slaughter of animals, with human slaughter as a possibility in the background. Religion is perpetrated in an arena of death, of killing. This is ubiquitous, common, and problematic.[2]

There are multiple levels of describing and explaining religious phenomena. To mention at least four of them: The ancient Greeks used the terms *dromena* and *legomena*, "what is done" and "what is said," a distinction that has remained useful. What is done, according to ritual prescriptions, should be obvious, apart from intentional occultation and secrecy. What is said by the practitioners and especially by officiating priests is equally important. It makes for religious lore, but it may contain misunderstandings as well as intentional disclaimers. On a third and fourth level, there are explanations from modern scholarship through interpretative psychology and sociological constructs. Uncertainties arise from the fact that traditional psychology is currently in a process of transformation, developing more and more penetrating natural science, while psychology and social theory are definitely destroying traditional mythologies. Yet they cannot claim a final triumph, given the complexity of the human brain. A basic fact of religious history remains. Since its beginnings, religion was never the invention of a single human; everyone has learned religion from the elders, from generation to generation, in a way somehow similar and parallel to the learning of language. Even religious innovators were following pre-existing tracks, albeit in protest.

A current and still strange phenomenon in ancient religions is the prominence of animal sacrifice. It seems to occur worldwide in varying forms. This chapter is not aiming at a general theory or a comprehensive overview of sacrifice; it concentrates only on those civilizations that form the basis of our own Near Eastern-European tradition.

The fundamental role of sacrifice in ancient societies has been studied intensively. Along with vows and prayers, it has its place in communal life, including economy and politics. There is no authority without the leading person performing sacrifice, be it in a family, city, or tribe; no treaty, no change of status, no initiation is able to proceed without it. Coalitions, in general, are concluded in the form of sacrifice. It functions as a collective act that establishes and reconfirms group solidarity. Hierarchy is constituted and demonstrated in the distribution of meat. Greek *geras* means "honor" but also, in a concrete sense, the piece of meat that the high-ranking participant is to receive. Greek words used to translate "fate," *moira, aisa*, are, in a literary sense, just the "portions" that are being distributed in a feast. In Latin, he who is first in rank is *princeps*, "he who gets first." Animals are slaughtered to honor the gods and to make meat available to humans. As animal sacrifice accompanies important decisions, it also comes to dominate divination: Liver inspection, mostly of slaughtered sheep, became the primary practice of seers. Sacrifice also is prominent in ceremonial iconography. In Greek pictures of sanctuaries, the blood-stained altars are a prominent feature. In plastic decoration, cattle skulls with fillets and garlands are the adornment of altars and of architecture in general. One of the finest artistic monuments from the time of Augustus is the Altar of Peace (*Ara Pacis*) in Rome; it shows the emperor Augustus surveying "sacrifice," as in animal slaughter. Slaughter is the essence of "peace"; slaughter is piety.

Sacrifice to the ancient gods was forbidden by Christian legislation. Yet sacred slaughter was not abolished by Christianity; it could now be performed to honor the saints (Trombley 2001:131f). There are offshoots extending to modern folklore; to slaughter animals on Sunday in front of the church, as an individual's donation to god or to some saint, has remained common in Eastern Christianity, especially in Armenia but also in Greece where it is degenerating nowadays into a touristic attraction. Yet note how the Christian prescriptions for fasting concentrate on abstinence from meat, which thus remains the center of attention.

In the Muslim world—Indonesia excluded—there remains, parallel to the hajj to Mecca, a day of slaughter once a year, the festival *el eid*, when each family is expected to slaughter an animal, and the refuse ends up blocking the streets. People feast on the animal, inviting neighbors and relatives and giving part of the meat to the poor. In the background, there is an interpretation of Abraham's sacrifice (Gen. 23). Islam began more than one thousand years after the original writing of the Abraham text; yet its interpretation follows an old track. By offering and accepting the ram instead of the son, Allah was allowing, establishing, animal sacrifice; "in the name of Allah," the butcher says. At Mecca the pilgrim, toward the end of the various rituals, is presumed to cut an animal's throat—today, with millions of participants, the sanitary problems require other forms of piety.

Only two aspects of sacred animal slaughter will be discussed here. One aspect is intimately linked to the eating, the feasting, of the community constituted by the sacrificial act. The other aspect is the killing of the sacrificial victim, which makes for an abiding problem. Feelings of happiness, horror, and triumph emerge and mix. An irrevocable seriousness remains.

The role of eating has not so much caught the attention of historians of religion (cf. Detienne and Vernant); eating seems banal, "worldly" behavior, out of touch with the divine. Yet such eating is anything but negligible. In the Hebrew Bible, there is the prescription: "Any Israelite who slaughters an ox, a sheep, or a goat...and does not bring it to the entrance of the Tent of Revelation to present it as an offering to the Lord...shall be guilty of bloodshed: that man has shed blood" (Lev. 17:3). Shedding blood means to become "guilty." "Offering to the Lord" is a transformation that turns bloodshed into a demonstration of piety. There are further restrictions, both for Israelites and Greeks: Blood must be poured out at the altar, and Jews must not consume kidneys; on these conditions, "sweet smoke" will go to heaven, while the meat remains for humans to eat. This means that every dish of meat presupposes sacrifice. This has been a widespread rule. Early Christians had difficulties in their cities to get meat that did not come from pagan sacrifice (1 Cor. 10:25–28). Biblical Hebrew calls normal sacrifice *zäbah*, which means "slaughter"; the more religious designation is *ʿolah*, "burnt offering," deriving from "to ascend."

The combination of piety and eating was paradoxical even for the ancients. "How they sacrifice, these rascals," the misanthrope disdainfully says in Menander's comedy, "not for the gods but for themselves!"; they deposit for the gods the tip of the loin and the gallbladder, because these are inedible and "swallow down the rest" (Men. Dyskolos 447–453). The famous myth presented by Hesiod makes this a deliberate deceit of Zeus, perpetrated by cunning Prometheus for the sake of humans (Hes. Theog. 535–557). Myth indicates and solves the problem by the Trickster figure. Prometheus was duly punished; but there has remained the accepted sacred practice.

A much earlier text has been published recently that describes the installation of sacrifice on somewhat similar lines but without a Trickster: Killing animals for the purpose of human food was invented with the guidance and participation of the gods. This is a Sumerian text that comes from the end of the third millennium BCE. In this story, the hero Lugalbanda has become sick and is abandoned by his companions to die alone in the wilderness. But Lugalbanda recovers, and he finds himself without any food. What to do? Lugalbanda reinvents fire with a flint stone, and he turns to hunting: Using traps, he catches a bovid and two goats. The gods then intervene through a dream. They give advice on how to slaughter the animals, an axe on the bovid and a knife on the goats so that the blood will flow into a pit. Lugalbanda awakens and follows the directions. Blood is flowing, meat is roasted, and with the rise of day Lugalbanda invites the great Sumerian gods, Anu, Enlil, Enki, and Ninhursag, to share the feast beside the pit. Lugalbanda offers libations, prepares the meat, and "from the meal prepared by Lugalbanda Anu, Enlil, Enki and Ninhursag received the best parts" (Hallo 1983: 165–180). The gods have given decisive advice as to how humans get food from animals; it is an act of gratitude to invite the gods to partake in the festival. At the start, there is human hunger, but it is the community with the gods that gives the act its ceremonial form.

Karl Meuli gave the most penetrating explanation of animal sacrifice in its complexity: the killing, the feast, and the gods (1975: 907–1022). The question is not why people eat meat but why they need gods for the purpose. The use, the need, for human food, for high-value proteins, is obvious. The problem is killing, shedding blood as a prerequisite of a substantial meal. This is experienced as culpable, as worthy of "bad conscience." Rituals are introduced to mark and to circumvent the problems; the language invokes superior partners in order to justify and to control what is being done. Sacrificial ritual secures its divine justification.

Karl Meuli collected comparative material from "primitive" tribes, in particular from Siberian hunters (Meuli 1975: 947ff). Their rituals, he found, express respect toward the game along with feelings of hesitation and bad conscience. The rituals also show scrupulous preparations to ensure the "purity" of the hunter and, after the kill, attempts at restoration to reset the balance of life. There is especially— and this is a striking parallel to Greek sacrifice—the preservation of the bones, the deposition of thigh bones and skulls at special sacred places (1975: 958–963; 985–987).[3] In the verbalizations that go with the ritual, Meuli found excuses and declarations of "guilt" toward the animal; the guilt is sometimes playfully dispelled in a half-serious way, for which Meuli coined the impressive term *comedy of innocence*. They claim that the animal had agreed to be killed by its own free will, was guilty in some way, or even that the killing had been done by other evil people (Meuli 1975: 952ff). They start to lament the animal they have slain (Meuli 1975: 955ff). By depositing the bones at some sacred spot, at a stone or in a tree, they indicate sacred order and even some form of restoration. Sacrificial rituals, Meuli found, are so similar in details to these hunters' practices that one should conclude that they derive from preagrarian civilization, continuing the same psychological attitudes.

If Karl Meuli thus found, as the basis of animal sacrifice, "a memorable manifestation of pity," of the "consciousness of the unity of life,... the sacredness of life,... [the] great powers, which nature and life themselves have installed to fight egotism and cruelty" (in short, "veneration for life" in the footsteps of Albert Schweitzer), this might be dismissed as too romantic by others; does the investigator fall victim to his own projections?[4] It may be hazardous to make guesses about the psychology of prehistoric man. It seems easy to find contrasting examples in "primitive" societies that survive, wherein we see an apparent lack of any emotion at the killing of animals. Anyhow, one has to reckon with wide diversity among humans and cannot expect to meet with one simple explanation.

On the other hand, psychologists have been studying the evolution of empathy in humans, especially in children, in comparison with chimpanzees; they found parallels and distinctions. In humans, empathy appears to be much more developed; it makes the understanding and manipulation of partners much more effective. This would be a problem in hunting and would render the victim a partner from the start. Hunting victims are usually mammals with eyes, limbs, corresponding motions, and flowing blood; the same may be said of the objects of sacrifice. Notice that carnivores do not care about butchery. It is humans who seek to learn about the inner organs and who realize, also through wars and wounding, that the same organs exist in humans. *Heart* is a common Indoeuropean word. Humans know about it; you can feel it in yourself and notice its stop at death—but can you eat it?[5]

It is true that one of Meuli's central pieces of evidence, the supposed depositions of skulls and bones of bears by Palaeolithic hunters, has been exploded (Bächler 1940; Burkert 1992a). Yet the main idea of Paleolithic hunting as the background of ancient rituals dealing with animals remains persuasive. It opens up breathtaking historical dimensions: The hunting of large animals was decisive in hominization. Only by hunting and thus consuming larger quantities of meat could humans get out of Africa more than a million years ago. This presented the possibility for *Homo erectus* to conquer, finally, the whole of the world. The construct of "man the hunter" has come under attack from feminist perspectives; hunting, wherever observed, is still predominantly a male affair. The importance of hunting for the first phases of human evolution cannot be denied. The first biological success of primates, their primary adaptation, depended on the grip of hands and feet, in order to climb trees, to reach for fruit and to escape predators. Hunting was the "new" behavior that allowed our ancestors to get beyond leaves and fruit. Humans spread by hunting, on a scale far beyond the traces of hunting that have been observed in chimpanzees. The oldest exemplar of a hunting spear found in Germany is about 400,000 years old; it is made of wood hardened by fire, the weapon Odysseus reinvents to blind the eye of the Cyclops (Burkert 1967: 281–299). Neanderthalers, we are told, lived on a nearly exclusive diet of animal meat.[6]

Most will agree that killing for food is the only form of killing that makes biological sense; it is a predominant element in the struggle for existence, in the whole sphere of life. It remains an unavoidable paradox: Life must be destroyed for the sake of life. "God has made it impossible to get preserved without damaging another being" (Plutarch, *Sept. sap conv.* 159c).

Cries of opposition have been raised in various times and locations from an early date. The oldest outcry may be Zarathustra's *gatha* 29 "against slaughtering the cow" (West 2010: 44–49), even if Zoroastrianism did not lead to complete vegetarianism. More consistent was Buddhism: There is a touching proclamation by King Ashoka (about 300 BCE) in a Greek inscription from Kandahar: "The king pointed out piety to the humans; and everything thrives on the whole earth; and the king abstains from food in which there is soul, and the other humans too; and hunters or fishermen of the king have stopped hunting" (Donner and Röllig 1966–1969, nr. 279). Even earlier, in Greece, Empedocles (fifth century BCE) produced powerful propaganda against eating meat. Souls, he taught, after Pythagoras, are migrating from humans to animals and vice versa. Were we to sacrifice, the consequence might be that "his own son, who has changed shape, the father lifts up and slaughters with a prayer, the fool!" (Diels/Kranz 1951:31 B 137). Food that has a "soul" must be avoided; this formula seems to have won out especially among sectarians who claimed to have been taught by the mythical Orpheus. Possibly older is the rule that hunters at least must abstain from meat[7]—the animals would smell the odor of a carnivore and flee. Note that such abstinence is not an advance to more "humane" behavior, its purpose is to make the kill effective.

Vegetarians have remained a minority. More than a million years of consuming meat have left their evolutionary mark: Most humans enjoy meat as the essence of a good meal. It seems the first settlers of Japan did not bring animal husbandry with them; they relied on fish, a primarily marine diet. So there is no ancient tradition of raising domestic animals for food in Japan. The Japanese may perform a "memorial service" instead for the souls of fish and shellfish consumed by humans. Yet with rising wealth in the course of modernization and globalization, McDonalds are multiplying in every Japanese city. Eating animals remains common especially in wealthy societies. We do it without religious ado, avoiding the spectacle of the butcher's shop.

Success does not quell anxieties. Hunters know that their existence depends on the ongoing availability of the game. Annihilation of life brings the worst anxiety. Yet preservation of life requires death. Humans always killed animals to preserve their own lives. This they made a basis of celebrations; this, according to Meuli, is the root of sacrificial ritual. One might try to develop from this a theory of the evolution of religion in general. At any rate, religious ritual addressing these themes has been preserved right through the invention of agriculture and continues to dominate ancient high cultures. Humans recognize death, which chimpanzees do not. Thus an authority beyond death has been introduced to control anxieties. The consequence remains: As slaughter becomes sacrifice, the specter of death begins to accompany piety.

Yet such a history on Meulian lines seems insufficient to explain the full scope and effectiveness of sacrifice as we find it in ancient civilizations. The shadow of death seems most obtrusive when sacrifice comes to its violent peak in human sacrifice. In the view of an irreligious observer, this appears to be the most abominable fusion of religion and crime; it is senseless in its essence but exerts a strange fascination. Human sacrifice is normally separated from cannibalism though. That historically documented societies practiced human sacrifice is a thesis under attack nowadays, at least in the two best known cases, Phoenician child sacrifice—attributed to the sway of the god "Moloch," based on unclear passages in the Hebrew Bible[8]—and the Aztec civilization in Mesoamerica (Hassler 1992). Other examples of human sacrifice from the ancient world are rare and less well attested, except for killings at funerals (Hughes 1991, Bonnechere 1994). There is a tendency to attribute human sacrifice to the others, to strangers, far-away barbarians, or to a distant past.[9] Mythical fantasies abound however. Lucretius, in his fight against *religio*, makes human sacrifice his most dashing argument; but he has to take his example from classical mythology, from tragedies of Aeschylus and Euripides: Iphigeneia, sacrificed by her father, Agamemnon, at the start of the Trojan War. "So much evil religion could put forth," *tantum religio potuit suadere malorum* (Lucr. 1.101).

"Our" present religions, Judaism, Christianity, and Islam, sometimes called Abrahamic religions, have the theme of human sacrifice right at their inception, with the founding father, Abraham. We are accustomed to the story, which remains a text of "terror and trembling," as Kierkegaard put it. Abraham is commanded by god to "sacrifice" his only son Isaac, and he is willing to do so (Gen. 22). The Hebrew term for this sacrifice is ʿolah, "make to rise upwards," as fire and smoke rise to heaven;[10] the action is to cut the throat with a knife and to burn the corpse on wood—the knife and wood expressly mentioned in the text. The human victim must be fettered in order to receive the deadly cut. Abraham does obey his god's command, without even an attempt at protest. The text enjoys the paradox: "the son that you love"; "and the two walked together" (Gen. 22.1–19: 2; 8). In Muslim tradition, the place where Abraham "bound" his son is the rock on the temple hill of Jerusalem, which, since Khalif Omar, is covered by the "temple dome" with its golden cupola. Of course, an angel stops Abraham's action at the last moment, pointing to an animal for sacrifice. The text says God was "testing" (*nissah*) Abraham, and his submissive obedience is highly rewarded. The text also states that god accepted the ram "instead of" (*tachath*) Isaac.

One way to discard the terror of the story is to introduce a perspective of historical progress: God was replacing human sacrifice by animal sacrifice. This could be termed an advance in civilization. The Islamic interpretation comes close to this interpretation, as it makes this a founding myth for el eid. Real reforms to stop human sacrifice have occurred sometimes (Paul 2009, 310), but as to historical facts, one has to admit that eating animals has been common ever since the beginnings of hominization or even before.[11] In history, human sacrifice must be secondary. There was slaughter for food, first, which later led to animal slaughter without eating the remains, just for a message, which is basically killing for killing's sake. This would include the killing of humans as intensification. Such phenomena usually occur in a context of aversion, substitution, or purification—even if these termini are questionable by themselves.

It is cruel fantasy that the text of the Bible enjoys. Slaughter is to raise the absolute authority of god. Everything personal or human is disappearing from view. The fully developed form of Jewish religion, in the Second Temple period, opted for a radical separation of sacrifice and eating. This makes the Promethean paradox disappear but also eliminates the basic biological sense of animal sacrifice. It is mandated that the fire should burn on the altar incessantly and two sheep are to be slaughtered and burned every day. This is killing for killing's sake, a distant observer would note, with fire that points to heaven and makes corpses disappear in the form of a "sweet smell" for Yahweh (Lev. 6:2, 6.8).[12] An older text, preserved in Leviticus (17:3–5), had made every slaughter a sacrifice. Henceforth sacred slaughter became profane, provided the blood ritual was observed. Still, eating the sacrificed meat was allowed for priests even in the special cases of sin sacrifice (*hattat*) and guilt sacrifice (*asham*) (Lev. 6.18–7.7). Ritualized eating of sacrificed meat perseveres in the quintessential ritual of Passover but also in Jewish family religion: For the day of purification (*Yom Kippur*), one should cut the throat of a fowl or a goose, which may then go into the refrigerator to serve as a meal later on. But the central sacrifice at the only temple was what the Greeks called "total burning," holocaust. This seems characteristic of a secondary religion. It makes for both the distinction and the isolation of the Jewish religion in the eyes of others, especially the Greek observers: We might admire it, but "we would give up the practice."[13]

Back to Abraham: The text indicates that the murder of humans by humans lurks in the background of the slaughter of animals. The logic is simple: One action is done "instead of" (*tachat*) the other (Gen. 22:13). Sacrifice means to kill by the command of god, as an honor to god; "instead of" implies that animal sacrifice presumes human sacrifice as its background.

If animal sacrifice without eating the meat is a secondary development in the case of Judaism, its seriousness all the more derives from violence. The performance required is death. But there is an escape through substitution. Such forms of sacrifice, killing to honor a god and to save humans, to prevent death through substitution, are widely attested in ancient civilizations, in Mesopotamian, Greek, and Roman sanguinary sacrifice—and also far beyond.

The idea of substitution seems to be basic. Yet there are divergent contexts and verbalizations. A term commonly adopted is *giving*, that is, giving and giving back. Giving, no doubt, is a basic human activity in order to establish relations of common benefit; yet it has its variations. It vacillates between free and personal giving and "giving up in panic," for the sake of escape (Mauss 1923; Burkert 1996). A gift may mean to pay honor and thus to acknowledge superiors; it may mean to pay amends, including self-punishment, to mitigate the wrath of superiors; it may also be used in despair for the sake of flight, as in leaving some possession or even some part of the body in order to divert or partially satisfy a pursuer—which has avatars in animal behavior (Burkert 1996: 40–47). Even amid panic, some kind of rationality is at work, judgments about values, strategies of investment and benefit, and manipulations. Substitution means an act of trade and includes the possibility of deception.

In the case of sacrifice, the recipients may be unclear or changing shapes; one may name god or gods but wicked and greedy demons as well. A "substitute sacrifice" may imply dangerous, demanding superiors who must be satisfied, controlled, or kept away by giving or "throwing" something to them, valuables or even living beings. Greeks spoke of sacrifices of "aversion," *apotropaia*. The question how a "gift" reaches those powers is superfluous curiosity; the consequences are felt.

What is generally presupposed in premonetarian societies is, of course, the availability of animals, without the uncertainties of the hunt. Domestication has made animals important pieces of countable possession, indeed units of currency.

"Giving" may be performed by abandoning or "sending away" an animal: The most famous case is the proverbial scapegoat in the Hebrew Bible (Lev. 16; Burkert 1979: 59–77). But normally those animals are killed. The apparent motive is to divert mortal danger by another's death. Situations of danger and debasement, passive sufferings, are turned into success by reclaiming the activist's role, by killing the substitute. In the background there is agitated anxiety; but the killing side is the winning side. This does not exclude an accompanying feast.

Sallust, a Platonic philosopher close to Julian the Apostate (fourth cent. CE), wrote: "Since we have everything from the gods, and it is just to give the givers a tithe of what has been given, we present such tithings from possessions by dedications, from the body by hair, from life by sacrifices" (16.1). This is a philosopher's attempt to make sense even of curiosities such as offerings of hair; as to "life," it is edifying nonsense: We cannot "give" life, as if it were a transferable possession. Life can only be destroyed. Yet the ideology of substitution is felt to be convincing or at least reassuring. Let others die so that we might be saved. It is tempting to include human sacrifice in such a concept of substitution.

The underlying motive for such rituals ultimately goes back to the experience of animals threatened by predators, a normal situation in biological reality: As one member of the flock falls victim to the hungry carnivores, the others may feel relief; for the moment the danger will recede, they may feel safe (Burkert 1996: 42ff). For a long time, humans have been able to feel safe within their civilization, ever since the mastery of fire and the construction of weapons; but old anxieties do not disappear. Experiences of dread take shape as if carnivores were around. Religious imagination, in particular, invents "demons" that, in myth and in art and even in ritual, take the shape of predators. "Your enemy the devil prowls round like a roaring lion looking for someone to devour," we read in the Bible (1 Peter 5:8). To depict the terror of hell, Christians invented the picture of a huge devouring mouth with yawning jaws. Aversion, to use a term derived from Greek,, is performed through animal sacrifice, in accordance with religious institutions.

To give a few examples of substitution sacrifice in rituals and legends: Disease is experienced as an assault of some "hateful demon" (Od. 5.396). Thus healing will ensue through killing an animal as a substitute. An Akkadian text gives guidance toward "substitution of a man for Ereshkigal," the Sumerian-Akkadian goddess of the underworld: Put a goat to bed with the sick person, cut its throat, but then tend it "as if it were a dead man," while the patient leaves the house. When the animal has been decently buried, the patient should be healed (Ebeling 1931: nr. 15, 65–69, cf. nr. 16; Burkert 1992b: 74). Greeks use various apotropaic rituals to "turn away" evil powers, be it worms, evil winds that destroy the crops, or demons of sickness; this usually requires animal sacrifice: "The *Erinys* (a mighty pursuing power) leaves the house, when the gods accept the sacrifices," proclaims Aeschylus (Sept. 699f.). Ovid has a recipe for how to get rid of demoniac birds that allegedly threaten babies at night. It is a ritual of butchery: The entrails of an animal are laid out in the house as an offering of "soul for soul" (Ov. Fast. 6158–6167). *Animam pro anima*, soul for soul, is also a well-known formula in votive inscriptions to Saturnus from North Africa (Leglay 1996). A dangerous god, Saturnus-Kronos, is connected in ancient tradition with Phoenician and especially Carthaginian sacrifices of children. Diodorus says these had been replaced by animal sacrifice or by holocausts of the more normal form, but in a situation of disaster, during the siege by Agathocles in 310 BCE, the Carthaginians switched to human sacrifice again, as the more efficacious means to move the gods (Diod. 20, 14, 4–7), and as "ransom for avenging demons," as Philo of Byblos declared later (FGrHist. 790 F 3b).

How to escape the avenger by sacrifice, this is impressively taught in the founding story of Israel: To make the pharaoh dismiss the Israelites from Egypt, the Lord is going to kill the firstborn in every house at midnight; the Israelites, however, are ordered to eat the Pesach lamb that night and to smear some of its blood at their doorposts. This is a "sign of protection," to make God the killer pass by (Ex. 12:6–30). It is a feast of a special character; the meat must be consumed before the break of day. But it is the blood of the victims that turns away the killer, proof that killing has already been performed in the house. The mark makes the "sign of protection."

The violence in animal sacrifice is not hidden; it may be proudly visible. Sacrifice can be used widely as a metaphor, a description, even as justification, especially when the word refers to a form of violence that is still accepted and deemed necessary in contemporary civilizations: capital punishment and war. Both are under rigorous attack today but still far from extinction. Whatever we may think about capital punishment and war, it is a fact that strong opposition against both hardly comes from Christianity and less from Islam; it has come from European humanism and enlightenment.

Execution has some analogies to sanguinary sacrifice. In ancient Rome, a Law of Romulus ordered that a traitor should be killed as a "sacrifice" (*thyma*) to underworld gods (Dion. Hal. *Ant.* 2,10). There are unmistakable elements of a "comedy of innocence" in several steps in the execution: feeding the culprit well, masking the henchman, making the performance a collective action. Plutarch describes how, in 63 BCE, the Catalinarians, who had planned some form of revolution, were led to death at Rome: "People shivered and let them pass in silence, especially the young ones, as if they were initiated into certain traditional sacraments of aristocratic power" (Plut. Cic. 22,2; Burkert 1986:46). Dostoevky's *Brothers Karamasov* has a devastating description of how pious Geneva celebrated the execution of a murderer who had proclaimed his "conversion" to Christianity (book V:IV).

It even seems to be a characteristic of "secondary religions" such as Judaism, Christianity, and Islam to define or invent new crimes that should be met with capital punishment, such as the practices of foreign cults but also homosexuality in Judaism, heresy in Christianity, and apostasy in Islam. See the inscription of King Herod at the "Holiest of Holies" in the Temple of Jerusalem: "Access forbidden. Who violates this law shall blame himself: There is capital punishment" (RE IX 948 s.v. Jerusalem). Greeks, too, were prone to invent similar prohibitions at least in mythical tales.[14] But even in classical Athens an Eleusinian priest could postulate capital punishment for an act nobody else would understand as an offence; and some Aetolians who had entered the mystery hall of Eleusis by accident were actually put to death.[15]

War has accompanied human evolution probably from the start. Even a chimpanzee "war" has been observed. Since earliest times and nearly everywhere, the worst shedding of blood has been accepted as the highest form of virtue. Old forms of war were ceremonial and integrated in religious ceremonies, especially in sacrificial rituals. Still today we speak of victims of war and violence. Christianity, despite the solemn declaration of "peace on Earth" at the birth of Christ, came to acknowledge war and to tolerate the soldiers' profession, as soon as it came to power and civil responsibility (Burkert 1996:184–199). In Classical times, Pindar's poetry transformed the battle cry (*Alala*) into a goddess of sacrifice: "Listen, Alala, daughter of War, to the prelude of spears, you, to whom sacrifice is made, men for the sake of the city, death by holy sacrifice" (Fr. 78). Sacrificial rituals accompanied war in antiquity from beginning to end (Burkert 1986: 47ff; 2007: VII, 195–207). Greeks introduce battle by slaughtering animals, *sphagia*, but peacemaking is also confirmed by sacrifice—see the Ara Pacis once more. Victory is taken to be the most glorious manifestation of a god's power. This goes from cuneiform Samsuiluna to *"Nun danket alle Gott"* ("now we all thank our God") in the German tradition (Borger 1979: I 5ff; Burkert 1986b69ff).[16] After the victory at Marathon in 490, the Athenians decreed to sacrifice, for each Persian slain in the battle, one goat to the gods; they sacrificed five hundred animals a year and had not yet come to an end ninety years later (Xen. Anab. 3,2,12).

There is the famous case of Roman *devotio*. It means to arrange for a substitute killing on one's own side in advance, in order to ensure the defeat and death of the adversaries on the other side. The main text is in Livy. Historicity may be questioned, but the sequence of anxieties, expectations, and rituals is telling (Liv. 8,6,9–8,10; Wissowa RE V 277–280).[17] As war is going on with the Latini, a dream indicates to both consuls that the general from one side and the troops from the other were "owed" to infernal powers, to the subterranean *Manes* and to Mother Earth. There is no debate about the impending necessity, but there is clear calculation of loss and gain: one life against common success.[18] The action of war is dominated by substitute sacrifice. First "one decreed to slaughter victims in order to avert the anger of the gods" (Liv. 8,6,11). But these are just preliminaries. The seers' extispicy with the slaughtered animals confirms what had been known before: One Roman general was to "devote" himself by seeking his own death in battle. This act will gain the favor of the gods, and victory will fall to the Romans. Anxieties are overcome by voluntary self-sacrifice: The substitute's death means that the sacrifice has been accepted by the gods.

The most sublime transformation of sacrificial violence in ancient civilization is found in Greek tragedy (Burkert 1966). *Tragoidoi*, the singers performing onstage, are explained by the ancients as the "singers at the goat sacrifice." Whether this identification is accepted or not, it should be noted that several tragedies directly deal with human sacrifice—Euripides' *Iphigeneia at Aulis, Iphigeneia at Tauris, The Bacchae*—and that human sacrifice is introduced as a secondary motif in numerous others—Euripides' *Heracles, Erechtheus, Hecuba, The Phoenician Women*. Just as important, metaphors of sacrifice are found in nearly all the texts of the surviving tragedies. Each act of violent killing can be termed sacrifice. The themes of violence and killing make tragedy. Even Medea, at the verge of killing her own children, resorts to the language of sacrifice (1053 ff.): "Who is not allowed to be present at my sacrifices, shall care for himself."[19] There are vase paintings that show Medea slaying her children on an altar. In his *Electra*, Euripides invents a genre to show how Aegisthus is slain by Orestes at a rural festival (774 ff.): Aegisthus invites a stranger, Orestes in disguise, to the feast and asks him to cut up the bull that has already been killed; while Aegisthus is looking at the bull's liver to detect ominous signs, Orestes hits him from behind with the sacrificial axe. Sacrificial bull slaughter and murder: the same gesture, the same utensil. If tragedy is about paradoxes of death, animal sacrifice presents the most pertinent patterns and verbalizations.

Further remarks must be made on the Christian theology of sacrifice, especially in the Roman Catholic version. Pilate, the procurator of Judaea, would hardly have had qualms to pass sentence and to execute a potential rebel who had accepted the acclamation as King of the Jews; see the inscription on the cross, as well as the beginning of the hearing in Mark (15:2). Yet in order to give religious sense to a routine execution, Jesus's adherents introduced the ideology of sacrifice: This was a substitute sacrifice, a willing self-sacrifice of highest rank, in order to reestablish the relations with an almighty god, to make good for the sins of all humans. Texts from the Hebrew Bible came forth: "Punishment rests on him, in order that we have peace; by his wounds we are healed…like a lamb led to slaughter…he gave his life as sacrifice for sin [*asham*]" (Is. 53:5,7; quoted in Acts 8:32–35). This message tied in with the sacrificial feast of Pesach, the communal eating of a sheep. If some people think that Jesus cannot but have been a vegetarian, the Gospel is clear. "I very much wanted to eat this Pesach with you" (Luke 22:15). Then there are the famous words of Christ about eating his flesh and drinking his blood. Sacrifice is still a feast. The saying of John the Baptist about "the Lamb of God who carries the sins of the world," *agnus dei, qui tollis peccata mundi* (John 1:29), combines both the scapegoat and Pesach. Real animals, henceforth, fall out of the theological construct and become free for unlimited human use.

In sum, ancient religions are characterized by the practice of killing for sacrifice. Such rituals are age old and routine; while expanding and developing, they remain central pillars of the sacred. The tradition seems to come from the most remote beginnings of hominization, from situations in which humans were being hunted by as well as hunting animals. Exposed to the enduring precariousness of life, living beings experience a dangerous world. Religion enters and addresses not so much illusions of peace and paradise but confirmations of optimism within dangerous realities: There is a promise of life, even if others are going to be destroyed; and there is the sustenance of life by feasting, while animals are killed in the process. There is the affirmation of superiority by giving animals, or killing them as a substitute for one's own survival. Superiors are introduced, they are necessary and ordering constructs for both the dangers and the success. Religion is in touch with the natural world insofar as it deals with a "struggle for existence," but it also creates a superworld with its promise of averting evil and sanctifying access to what is "good," including, at the simplest level, the necessary food. Anxieties and fears that are inseparable from life are not made to disappear, rather they are displaced. This makes for ultimate seriousness: Outdo one terror by a stronger one, "The fear of god is the highest fear" (Aesch. Suppl. 479). Christian Hieronymus was to agree: "The fear of god annihilates the fear of men" (Chronicon, *praefatio*). Religion acknowledges danger, fear, and violence, while presenting rules concerning how to deal with them, one of which includes the risk and the triumph of killing.

The violent, sanguinary side of animal sacrifice may be suppressed in modern reports or even in the practitioners' explanations; various local rituals at least make the blood disappear. But slaughter remains a problem. Interesting examples, not surprisingly, come from outside classical antiquity, from India.

In 1975, American sponsors organized and financed a Vedic fire festival at Panjal (Kerala, India), in accordance with the Vedic texts that brahmins still know by heart. It took twelve days, it was filmed and documented in a huge book titled *Agni* or "fire" (Staal 1983: I:303). Present-day brahmins eagerly participated in the rituals and evidently enjoyed their protracted recitals. Several times there should have been "sacrifice" in the form of the killing of goats; yet the Vedic specialists decided not to use animals and invented a vegetarian substitute instead. Was this abhorrence of killing? Was it to thwart the media interest? Or was it a strategy to demonstrate that the performance was a theater rehearsal rather than worship? Would only real killing have made the ritual serious? At any rate, animal sacrifice was the critical step that had to be evaded.

In an Arabic version of the Buddha legend (Gimaret 1971: 81ff) that was to become a popular Christian text,[20] an adolescent Buddha is told by his parents, in the course of a festival, to cut the throat of a sheep. This is to prove that he is a normal man. Buddha, as if by awkwardness, thrusts the knife into his own left hand. In this society, killing an animal, shedding blood, was taken to be the mark of manliness; it is at this point that Buddha refuses to partake in the accepted custom. He will never kill animals. This makes for a new way of life, a new "secondary" religion.

The most consequential attempt to transcend our world of fighting and killing, by virtue of "knowledge" of higher realities, is to be found in Manichaeism. This religion was founded by the Syrian Mani (217–275 CE), for whom it was a radical form of Christianity; he possibly had connections with Buddhist India too.[21] The cosmogony he taught is of Gnostic character, dualistic, with antithetic principles of light and darkness, good and evil. There is nothing in between. So when the realm of darkness launches an attack on the realm of light, there is no means of defense. "In the world of light there is no devouring fire, which could be poured out to oppose the Evil, there is no steel that cuts, nor waters that suffocate, nothing evil at all of this kind. On the contrary, everything is light and noble space, and there is no possibility to do harm to the Evil" (Boehlig 1980:136).[22] The radical negation of aggression becomes a poignant paradox: "God lacks the Evil with which he could wield punishment." The pagan philosopher Simplicius finds this blasphemy: "They introduce god as a coward, who is afraid of Evil, when it comes close to his borders.... On account of this cowardice he has thrown souls...into Evil..."[23] For Mani, the good has just one possibility to react: giving up, which is to say, sacrifice. "In the manner of a shepherd who sees a lion coming to destroy his flock: he cunningly takes a lamb and makes it a trap in order to catch the lion; through one lamb he saves his whole flock of sheep. Afterwards he heals the lamb that has been wounded by the lion" (Alex. Lyk., 55, Adam.). This is the text of a Coptic psalm, with a flight from reality to fantasy: Wounds may be lethal. In Mani's system, three divine persons are put to action, the Father, the Mother of Life, and the Son, who is Adam and Christ in one person. He is the one who is sent out to meet the evil. Then, what is bound to happen occurs: The Son is overwhelmed, torn to pieces, devoured by the evil. Since this aboriginal catastrophe, souls, sparks of light, or, in other words, suffering Christ, has been enclosed in evil, which is matter. Yet this was intelligent planning by the good: Evil matter has in itself something it cannot comprehend nor hold forever. Souls will be freed again and return to their perfect origin. In the meantime, a Manichaean will lead a life of utmost caution. Encircled by a world of desires and sufferings, every activity means to hurt, to add to the existent grief. Even every kind of work is an act of violence against animated beings by which we are surrounded. "The fig cries, when it is plucked from the tree, and her mother, the tree, sheds milky tears" (Augustine conf. 3.10,18). The rule "thou shalt not kill" is obeyed without exception. It is impossible for a Manichean to be a hunter, butcher, or soldier; he tries not even to do harm to the smallest living being, a fly, wasp, or ant; he should not even frighten an animal. He can only use donated food. He says to the bread: "I did not mow thee, I did not grind thee, I did not knead thee nor throw thee into the stove: somebody else has done this and brought thee here. I ate without guilt." The comedy of innocence is played out in seriousness. A world without violence is in view.

Persecuted by Christians and by Islam, the Manicheans found shelter in the Uigur kingdom in inner Asia; they disappeared with the impact of Genghis Khan.

NOTES

1. Kerdir, third century CE.
2. There is a huge secondary literature on sacrifice. For recent surveys, see V. Mehl and P. Brulé (2008), and S. Paul (2009).

3. Note *euthetisas*, "setting the bones in right order" in the Prometheus tale, Hes. Theog. 541.

4. "uralte, höchst denkwürdige Erscheinungsform des Mitleides" (Meuli 1975: 978); "Gefühl der Schuld, das Bewusstsein der Lebenseinheit" (Meuli 1975: 979); "Glaube an die Heiligkeit und an die Ganzheit des Lebens" (Meuli 1975:1012) "ahnungsvolle Ehrfurcht vor jenen grossen Mächten, die Natur und Leben selbst gegen Egoismus und Grausamkeit eingesetzt haben" (Meuli 1975: 979; cf. 980).

5. "Not to eat heart" was a special prohibition for Pythagoreans (Burkert 1972: 181f).

6. Modern man may have survived in South Africa around 120,000 BCE by a marine diet (Marean 2010: 59–65). Still, in ancient sacrifice the role of fish is minimal, and crabs and snails do not appear.

7. Greek testimony in Euripides, Hipp. 952–955, with reference to Orpheus.

8. Leviticus 18:21; 2 Kings 23:10 (cf. 2 Kings 21–27; Jer. 7:30; Micah 6). The Greek evidence is massive as to child sacrifice at Carthage, for example, Plat. *Minos* 315bc; Demon FGrHist 327 F 18 (Sardinia); Theophrastus in Porph. abst. 2,27,2; especially Diod. 20,14,4–7; legal counteractions by Dareios (Iustin 19,1,10), Gelon (Theophrastus Fr. 586 Fortenbaugh = *Schol.* Pind. Pyth. 2,2; Plut. *Reg. et imp. apophth.* 175a; *De Sera* 552 a), finally Tiberius (Tert. *Apol.* 9,2). Child burials, called Tophets by historians, have been identified in Carthage, in Motye-Mozia (Sicily), and in Sardinia (Stager 1978/79: 56–69). But the evidence has been called into question by various scholars since S. Moscati (1987). The children buried in the Tophet of Carthage seem to have died a natural death. There is high political interest in the question from the side of modern Algeria.

9. Porphyry, *On Abstinence*, based largely on a lost book of Theophrastus, *On Piety*, derives normal sacrifice from "original" human sacrifice.

10. *cl* is a common Semitic root.

11. Chimpanzee hunting has been discovered by J. Goodall (1971).

12. Quite similar is Homer, *Iliad* 1:317, at the sacrifice which is to stop the plague: "The savor of fat reached heaven, whirling around the smoke."

13. Theophrastus in Porphyry, *abst.* 2,26.

14. Precinct "not to be entered" at the Arcadian Lykaion (Burkert 1986: 91).

15. "Depositing a suppliant's branch" at Eleusis (Andocides 1, 110–116); Aetolians at Eleusis (Liv. 31,14,6, following Polybius). There were heavy political tensions between Athens and Aetolia at the time; war ensued.

16. Battle of Leuthen, Prussians versus Austrians, 1757.

17. 340 BCE.

18. This principle is formulated even in John 11:50 (Burkert, 1996: 51).

19. Cf. the proscription of Herod.

20. cf. Barlaam and Joasaph. A tick of Arabic writing has transformed boddhisatva into Ioasaph in the Christian version.

21. There is a huge bibliography on Manicheism, for example, Adam, Boehlig, Koenen and Römer, Burkert (1996b).

22. Cf. Adam p. 14.

23. Simplicius, *Commentaire sur le manuel d'Épictète*, ed. I. Hadot, Leiden, Netherlands, 1996: 322–326.

BIBLIOGRAPHY

Adam, A. *Texte zum Manichäismus.* 2nd ed., Berlin: De Gruyter, 1969.

Bächler, E. *Das alpine Paläolithicum der Schweiz.* Basel: Birkhäuser, 1940.

Baumann, P. *Neandertaler-Vermächtnis*. Basel: Johannes Petri, 2010.

Boehlig, A. *Die Gnosis III: Der Manichäismus*, Zurich: Artemis, 1980.

Bonnechere, P. *Le sacrifice humain en Grèce ancienne*. Athènes-Liège: Centre International d' Étude de la Religion Grecque Antique, 1994.

Borger, R. *Babylonisch-assyrische Lesestücke*, 2nd ed. Rome: Pontificium Institutum Biblicum, 1979.

Burkert, W. "Greek Tragedy and Sacrificial Ritual," *Greek, Roman and Byzantine Studies* 7, 1966, 87–121.

Burkert, W. "Urgeschichte der Technik im Spiegel antiker Religion." *Technikgeschichte* 34 (1967): 281–299.

Burkert, W. *Lore and Science in Ancient Pythagoreanism*. Cambridge, MA: Harvard University Press, 1972.

Burkert, W. *Structure and History in Greek Mythology and Ritual*. Berkeley: University of California Press, 1979.

Burkert, W. *Homo Necans*. Berkeley: University of California Press, 1986 (Burkert 1986a).

Burkert, W. "Krieg, Sieg und die Olympischen Götter der Griechen." In F. Stolz, ed., *Religion zu Krieg und Frieden*. Zurich: Theologischer Verlag, 1986, 67–87 (Burkert 1986b).

Burkert, W. *Opfer als Tötungsritual: Eine Konstante der menschlichen Kulturgeschichte?* In F. Graf, ed., *Klassische Antike und neue Wege der Kulturwissenschaften*. Basel: Verlag der Schweizerischen Geslllschaft für Volkskunde, 1992, 169–189 (Burkert 1992a).

Burkert, W. *The Orientalizing Revolution*. Cambridge, MA: Harvard University Press, 1992 (Burkert 1992b).

Burkert, W. *Creation of the Sacred*. Cambridge, MA: Harvard University Press, 1996 (Burkert 1996a).

Burkert, W. "Zum Umgang der Religionen mit Gewalt: Das Experiment des Manichäismus." *Berliner Theologische Zeitschrift* 13 (1996): 184–199 (Burkert 1996b).

Burkert, W. *Kleine Schriften* VII, Göttingen: Vandenhoeck & Ruprecht 2007.

Detienne, M. and J.-P. Vernant. *La cuisine du sacrifice en pays grecque*. Paris: Gallimard, 1979.

Diels, H. and W. Kranz. *Die Fragmente der Vorsokratiker*. Berlin: Weidmann, 1951.

Donner, H. Röllig, W. *Kanaanäische und aramäische Inschriften* I–III. Wiesbaden: Harrasowitz, 1966–1969.

Ebeling, E. *Tod und Leben nach den Vorstellungen der Babylonier*. Berlin: De Gruyter, 1931.

Gimaret, D. *Le livre de Bilawhar et Budasf*. Geneva: Librairie Droz, 1971.

Goodall, J. *In the Shadow of Man*. London: William Collins Sons, 1971.

Hallo, W. W. "Lugalbanda Excavated." *Journal of the American Oriental Society* 103 (1983): 165–180.

Hallo, W. W. *Origins. The Ancient Near Eastern Background of Some Modern Western Institutions*. Leiden: Brill 1996, 212–221.

Hassler, P. *Menschenopfer bei den Azteken?* Bern: Lang, 1992.

Hughes, D. *Human Sacrifice in Ancient Greece*, London: Routledge, 1991.

Kippenberg, H. and T. Seidensticker. *Terror in Namen Gottes*. Frankfurt: Campus, 2004.

Koenen, L. and C. Römer. *Der Kölner Mani-Codex. Kritische Edition*. Opladen: Westdeutscher Verlag, 1988.

Krause, C. A. *Guyana Massacre*. New York: Berkley Publishing Corporation, 1978.

Leglay, M. *Saturne Africain*. Paris: de Boccard, 1966.

Marean, C. W. "Als die Menschen fast ausstarben." *Spektrum der Wissenschaft* 12 (2010): 59–65.

Mauss, M. "Essai sur le don." *Année sociologique II* 1 (1923/4).

Mehl. V. and P. Brulé (eds.), *Le sacrifice antique*. Rennes: Presses Univeritaires de Rennes, 2008.

Meuli, K. *Griechische Opferbräuche*, in *Gesammelte Schriften* I/II. Basel: Schwabe, 1975, 907–1021.

Moscati, S. "Il sacrifico punico dei fanciulli: realtà o invenzione?" *Quaderni dell' Accademia Nazionale dei Lincei* 261, Rome, 1987.

Paul, S. "Le Sacrifice en question." *Kernos* 22 (2009): 303–311.

Staal, F. *Agni: The Vedic Ritual of the Fire Altar*. Berkeley: Asian Humanities Press, 1983.

Stager, L. E. *Oriental Institute. Annual Report* 1978/1979, Chicago, 56–59.

Stausberg, M. *De Religion Zarathushtras*. Stuttgart: Kohlhammer, 2002.

Trombley, F. R. *Hellenic Religion and Christianization c. 370–525*. Leiden: Brill, 2001.

Wagner, A. S., ed. *Primäre und sekundäre Religion als Kategorie der Religionsgeschichte des Alten Testaments*. Berlin: De Gruyter, 2006.

West, M. L. *The Hymns of Zoroaster*. London: I. B. Tauris, 2010.

Wunn, I. *Die Religionen in vorgeschichtlicher Zeit*. Stuttgart Kohlhammer, 2005.

CHAPTER 32

CITIES AS ONE SITE FOR RELIGION AND VIOLENCE

SASKIA SASSEN

CITIES have long been sites for conflicts arising out of the hatred of those who are different from us—racism, religious hatreds, expulsions of the poor. At the same time, cities have historically evinced a capacity to triage conflict through commerce and civic activity; this contrasts with the modern national state, which historically has tended to militarize conflict. But major developments in the current global era signal that cities are losing this capacity and becoming sites for a whole range of new types of conflicts, such as asymmetric war and urban violence.

Religion has emerged as one critical vector for these conflicts in cities—both as a "cause" and as a consequence. Religious conflicts are not urban conflicts per se, even though the city is a key site for the materializing of religious sentiment into actual conflict. Large cities at the intersection of vast migrations and expulsions often were the spaces that could accommodate enormous diversity of religious groups. Such cities at various historical times actually enabled a kind of peaceful coexistence for long stretches of times. These periods of peaceful coexistence demonstrate that conflict does not necessarily inhere in the condition of religious difference. And it is not only the famous cases of Augsburg and Moorish Spain, where a genuinely enlightened leadership secured a prosperous coexistence, in good part because this strengthened what was anyhow the preference of the citizenry—and so often is, if given a chance. Old Jerusalem's bazaar was a space of commercial and religious coexistence for long periods of time. Baghdad was a flourishing polyreligious city under the Abbasid caliphs, around 800; and even under Saddam Hussein's extremely brutal leadership was a city where religious minorities, such as Christian and Jewish communities, often centuries old, lived in relative peace—a sharp contrast with today's situation in which ethnic cleansing and intolerance are the de facto "regime," one that was catapulted by the disastrous and unwarranted US invasion. These and so many other historical cases show that a particular exogenous event can suddenly reposition religious or ethnic difference as an agent for conflict. The same individuals can experience and enact that switch. Saddam Hussein's Baghdad had a systemic logic that was indifferent to minorities such as Christians and Jews; it was not simply a question of tolerance, let alone an enlightened leadership.

Different systemic logics can mark religious or ethnic identities very differently.

The role of systemic logics in marking or not marking religion as a source of religious conflicts suggests that such conflict does not inhere in religion as such but rather in a larger systemic condition. Within that larger condition the city can then switch from a space that enables and furthers fruitful coexistence to a space that enables and furthers conflict and hatreds (see Hassner, "Conflicts over Sacred Ground," chapter 21, and Hall, "Sociological: Theorizing Religion and Violence from a Sociological Perspective," chapter 25). In each case, specific capabilities of the city get mobilized: Being neighbors can go in both directions and so can the fact of neighborhood life. Dense urban spaces can deliver a sort of collective learning about diversity, or they can become the occasion for murderous attacks. The city as a complex system can transform a disease into an epidemic, but it can also produce what we might call "positive epidemics" as became evident in the so-called 2011 Arab Spring.

Here I explore these questions through an examination of current urban sites for conflicts dressed in the clothing of religious difference, even as this might not be the actual source. This unsettling of the urban order and its differences with the order of national states is part of a larger disassembling of existing organizing system logics (Sassen 2008). It is happening even as national states and cities continue to be major factors of the geopolitical landscape and the material organization of territory. The type of urban order that gave us the open city is still there, but increasingly as mere visual order and less so as social order.

In this chapter I, first, briefly introduce the question of organized religions in our complex global modernity. I examine the shift from an epoch dominated by secularizing forces to one in which the rise of organized religions is not an anomaly but structurally part of our global modernity, even when their doctrines are not modern. Next, I examine a range of interactions between, on the one hand, the rise of cities as key global spaces for economic, political, and cultural conditions and, on the other, the rise of religion as a major force in settings where it was not quite so for much of the twentieth century that saw the rise of the secularizing state. I develop one of these interactions, the urbanizing of war, because it feeds a particularly acute and violent bridging of cities with religious conflicts. Then I take two specific instances of asymmetric war, one in Mumbai and one in Gaza, to examine the variable and contradictory elements in this bridging.

The Rise of Organized Religions in Today's Global Modernity

The rising power of organized religions over the last three decades is, in my reading (2008), part of a larger process that takes off in the post-1980s: the partial and often specialized disassembling of the nation-state as historically constructed in the West. I argue that the critical aspect of this larger process for the rise of organized religions is that this disassembling produces structural holes, or blank spaces, in the older, mostly secular fabric of most nation-states. A key outcome of these tendencies is that the center, as constructed in modern history, no longer holds the way it did in the twentieth century. That center found its most complex instantiation in the modern state and the legitimizing of its power to secularize.

This disassembling and the resultant "structural holes" enabled the rise of older, complex assemblages that had been pushed out of diverse spheres of the polity and of social life by the expanded power of the secularizing modern state. Organized religions are a major example of these assemblages—an array of elements from diverse institutions and worlds of practice in both political and social life. They are also heuristic in that their high visibility helps us understand how old formations can resurface as part of new global organizing logics and thereby become part of our global modernity, notwithstanding age-old doctrines. I make a similar argument about a range of diverse contemporary trends that we experience as regressive or as belonging to the past.

Whether it is good or bad is a separate matter.

The partial disassembling of the national as the dominant condition of our global modernity also enables the emergence of novel types of assemblages at the global and the subnational scales. Among these are global financial networks that have little resemblance to traditional nation-state-centered banking. A different example is the complex organizational architecture of global civil-society struggles, such as the causes engaged by Oxfam, Amnesty International, and Forest Watch. The key organizational feature of these struggles is the linking together of multiple local (noncosmopolitan) efforts and their global projection through a major organization with worldwide recognition. The rise or global expansion of old and new organized religions also follows this pattern. The current multiplication of partial, specialized, and applied orders is unsettling the grip of the center—the state—and producing distinct challenges in the context of a still prevalent world of nation-states.

From this perspective, today's major organized religions have undergone a reassembling of the critical components that historically have constituted them as an operational system—a feature to be distinguished from their status as belief systems. This would mean that the old doctrines *can* be part of our new modernity because they have shifted to novel organizing logics (Sassen 2008: chapters 1 and 9). One way of describing this shift is that they are now part of a different assemblage of elements that can include the old but also the new, as for instance in the debate within the Anglican Church about having gay bishops. These assemblages are partly embedded in specific situations—thus the Anglican Church in Africa is constituted through a somewhat different assemblage of elements than the one in the United States. Similarly, Islam's doctrines today are distributed across a range of such assemblages—across countries, across diverse communities within a given country, onto new types of settings, as is the case with the black Muslims in the Southside of Chicago.

ASYMMETRIC WAR: A VIOLENT BRIDGING OF RELIGION AND CITIES

The current period makes legible the variability of the spaces (institutional, ideational, tactical) of organized religions. It also makes visible that the secularization of states is not an inevitable outcome of modernity—the role of organized religions is not confined to narrower and narrower domains as modernity proceeds. New types of globalities and cosmopolitanisms in several religions are becoming visible in our current modernity.

These diverse trends unsettle the meaning of *modernity* associated with the secularizing state of the twentieth century, and they unsettle the meaning of organized religions associated with that epoch. Several major and growing organized religions now occupy a place, and have a potential in liberal democracies not foreseen in the major theories and models of the last century.

It is in this context of the ascent of organized religions and their entry into institutional spaces once confined to the state that asymmetric war becomes the dominant form of war. Asymmetric war—between a conventional army and armed insurgents—has made cities a strategic site in the map for warring. Asymmetric war found one of its sharpest enactments in the US war on Iraq. The US conventional military aerial bombing took only six weeks to destroy the Iraqi Army and take over. But then asymmetric war set in, with Baghdad, Mosul, Basra, and other Iraqi cities becoming the sites of conflict. And it has not stopped since. Further, the entry of a conventional army into cities with pre-existent divisions, such as the Shia-Sunni division in Iraq, is generating yet another variant of urbanized war, one in which both sides are so-called unconventional armed forces (Kaldor 2007). And it can activate conflicts between different religious groups that have coexisted in relative calm for centuries. Cities worldwide are becoming a key theater for asymmetric war, regardless of what side of the divide they are on—allies or enemies.[1]

Organized religions and asymmetric war are two ascendant complex assemblages of actors, capabilities, and projects. It is an interaction marked by a wide range of possibilities—conflict, overlap, mutual advantage, utilities, and irrelevance. At one end of this variable, the city is the kind of space where their interaction can become incendiary, with violence feeding more violence, in a destructive process of cumulative causation that can engender new genealogies for future con-flicts. This is still a minor trend—the vast majority of cities are not part of the map of asymmetric war. But cities are one key space where both organized religions and asymmetric war are increasingly present and easily lead to mutually strengthened escalations. Insofar as the standard explanation for much of asymmetric war holds that it has little to do with religion per se, we can allow for the possibility that religious conflicts are activated by asymmetric war but not necessarily caused by them. However, even if it is mere activation of old or underlying conflicts or gen-eration of new divisions, the fact that asymmetric wars are proliferating may well feed more religious conflict and violence.

While asymmetric wars can be diverse, they share a few features. These wars are partial, intermittent, and lack clear endings. There is no armistice to mark their end. They are one indication of how the center's power to organize hierarchically, even though never absolute, has weakened—whether the center is the type of impe-rial power we saw in the 1800s or the national state in the twentieth century.

The urbanizing of war evinces highly variable features.[2] Here I want to dis-tinguish four types of asymmetric war, not necessarily mutually exclusive but still different. One of these is the actual encounter between conventional and unconven-tional forces on urban terrain, with post-2003 Iraqi cities as prominent instances. A second is the extension of the space for war beyond the actual "theater of war," as might be the case with the bombings in London, Madrid, Bali, and other cities after the war on Iraq was launched. A third is the embedding of conventional state conflicts in an act of asymmetric war, as might be the case for the recent Mumbai attacks. And the fourth is the activating by asymmetric war of older conflicts that evolve into armed conflict between two unconventional forces, as is the case with the Shia-Sunni conflicts in Iraqi cities.[3]

Religious and ethnic "cleansing" in their diverse variants are present in most asymmetric wars today. Killings and persecution can lead to mass expulsions or mass voluntary flight, as has been the case in post-2001 Baghdad, with the flight of Sunnis, Christians, and others. Secondly, in many diverse contemporary armed conflicts, the warring forces avoid battle or direct military confrontation, a feature described by Mary Kaldor (2007) in her work on the new wars. Their main strat-egy is to control territory through the expulsion of "the others" as defined in terms of ethnicity, religion, tribal membership, or political affiliation. The main tactic is terror—conspicuous massacres and atrocities pushing people to flee.

These types of displacements and evictions have a profound impact on the cosmopolitan character of cities. Cities have long had the capacity to bring together people of different classes, ethnicities, and religions through commerce, politics, and civic practices. Contemporary conflicts unsettle and weaken this cultural diversity of cities when they lead to forced urbanization or internal displacement. Cities as diverse as Belfast, Baghdad, or Mosul, each was or is at risk of becoming an assemblage of separate urban ghettoes due to religious and ethnic cleansing. This in turn leads to the destruction of their civic character, one key source of resistance to urban armed conflict. Baghdad has undergone a deep process of such "cleansing," which produced a relative peace in the late 2000s—but a type of peace that cannot last.

The new urban map of war is expansive: It goes far beyond the actual countries involved. The bombings in Madrid, London, Casablanca, Bali, Mumbai, Lahore, Jakarta, and so on are all part of this expansive map—they are not part of the theater of war narrowly defined in military terms. Further, each of these bombings has its specifics and can be explained in terms of particular grievances and aims. As material practices, they are localized actions by armed groups, acting independently of each other. Yet they also clearly are part of a new kind of multisited war—a distributed and variable set of actions that gain larger meaning from a particular conflict with global projection.

Religion has emerged as one key organizing and legitimating passion, even as it is often not the cause. It has long had the power to turn around a condition of relative peace and to mobilize and justify brutality against those who may have been your friendly neighbors. In the context of this global, multisited map of asymmetric wars and skirmishes, it can become an easy and lethal source for action that is mostly self-destructive—both in the short and in the long run.

Yet, there are contradictions in this global map of asymmetric conflicts. The next section examines some of these particularities and contradictions.

The Physics of the City

Elsewhere (Sassen 2010) I have explored in greater detail whether and, if so, in what ways the urbanizing of war makes visible the limits of superior military power and generally of armed attacks to overcome the physics of the city. By "physics of the city," I mean the mix of buildings and people, processes and urban civic practices. I find that together these are a built-in capability of cities that can contest and thwart superior armed force, the latter understood as a nonurban actor—in other words, not the typical urban gang or average murderer, of which there are plenty in quite a few cities.[4] Here I limit myself to examine the kinds of contradictions that arise from urban physics and that become visible in the specifics of recent asymmetric conflict. I focus on the 2010 attacks in Mumbai and the 2009 attack on Gaza. These contradictions bring to the fore the capabilities arising from civic action and the physics of the city.

Both these places have long histories of conflict but represent sharply different trajectories and assemblages of elements. In this regard, they help illuminate the multiple particularities of asymmetric conflict. A question both these cases raise is whether they represent some of the future shapes of war. Mumbai is caught up in the older India-Pakistan conflict, with sharp fluctuations in its role as one site for asymmetric war. Gaza is marked by a continuously live and open conflict with a modern state, Israel, a conflict that eventually fed a conflict with another asymmetric force, the Palestinian Authority. Both cases are enormously complex, and here I merely isolate a few particular aspects.

Mumbai: The City Talks Back and Neutralizes Religious Differences

The Mumbai attacks succeeded in pulling a conventional interstate conflict into the specifics and momentary event that was that attack. The available evidence thus far suggests that the masterminds of the attack exploited the fact of a long-standing, mostly low-intensity conventional conflict to achieve their own, perhaps separate concerns.[5] Quite a few analysts warned that one purpose of the attacks was to draw India and Pakistan into conventional border warfare and, therefore, distract from Pakistani efforts at containing terrorism.

Veena Das, among others, complicates this analysis, wondering if the "new form of warfare" these attacks represent rely "less on actual damage to life and property and more on the effects that it hopes to generate."[6] These effects could range from "communal riots, more suspicion between Muslims and Hindus, further weakening of the recently elected government in Pakistan, and, ultimately, a war between India and Pakistan" (see Veena Das, "Violence and Nonviolence at the Heart of Hindu Ethics," chapter 1). All of these effects comprise the means and implications of warfare in cities. Meanwhile, where does the most effective response to these effects originate? Sidestepping the engagement of "failed and weak states," Das focuses on how "civil action succeeded in thwarting the effects that the brutal violence had surely hoped to provoke." She explains the various ways civic ideals contributed to avoiding the possible intended effect of exacerbating the interstate conflict (and, I would add, the religious conflict that fed the separation of these two states). The characterization of the attacks as a war on the city itself furthered this civic effort and overwhelmed old religious conflicts.

Some observers point to the larger web of local interests within which this attack should be understood. Devji sees a successful swallowing of an international terrorist network by its local protector, obsessed with totally local concerns: "[T]he global has disappeared into the local to animate it from within." The aims of the group responsible for the attacks are neither "military nor political advantage for Pakistan, nor a global Islamic caliphate" but some sort of factional, localized priority for Muslim communities against their local oppression. This type of program, Devji explains, transcends the political, even if it originates in political grievances. Older genealogies of religious conflict, which can indeed localize in multicultural cities, are also one of the activators of that interstate conflict. And the city's physics evince a capacity to override religious difference.

Arvind Rajagopal finds that the urban geography of this attack, as with the 1993 bombings in Mumbai, marks a departure from "previous episodes of a more domestic violence": Not only did both attacks target rich areas in retribution for violence mostly concentrated on the poor, but "violence in media-dark ghettos has been followed by violence in the most public and media-bright parts of the city."[7] While the usual response is to assert that such "senseless" violence reveals the limits of the political, Rajagopal explains that terrorism and other new technologies of publicity disclose the presence of those denied legality, albeit through criminal acts (see also on this issue Body-Gendrot 2011). If outlaws once laid the basis for law, today the challenge before the law is to respond not only to the terrorist but as well to the migrant, the slum dweller, the uprooted peasant and other victims of industrial development, and the religious and ethnic minority.

Sankaran asserts that while "the ordinary Indian is unperturbed by terror," accustomed to other forms of persistent urban violence, this does not hold for elite India. The degree of carnage is not remarkable when compared to the casualties of sectarian riots or even past terrorist attacks. Even the tactics are familiar, recognizable to anyone familiar with the Lashkar-e-Taiba, which has been carrying out these *fedayeen* (literally, "death-defying") suicidal frontal attacks (therefore unlike most "suicide attacks") against Indian government targets in Kashmir for years. Sumantra Bose calls fedayeen "a rudimentary form of 'shock and awe' warfare" and observes that its perpetrators have now "brought the 'war'—as they see it—to India's elite class, and to affluent Westerners living in or visiting India's most cosmopolitan city." This is what urban insecurity represents in global cities, signaling the important connection it has to national security and the national interest, in the form of the global commercial and political value of the city that these sites represent. Dipesh Chakrabarty also connects the attacks to India's experience with globalization: He argues that "diverse global tensions" such as "terrorism, economic-environmental crises, and civil wars that dislocate populations" will raise the question of whether "democratic states" need to become "security-states" to cope with these new challenges.[8]

The physics of the city can be a critical factor even if the attackers are not familiar with the city. Appadurai describes geographies of power and identity that received the attack on different terms, reflecting the city's other circuits and geographies, such as the "struggle between the Indian Ocean commercial/criminal nexus and the land-based nexus that stretches from Mumbai to Delhi to Kashmir...the struggle between political and commercial interests now located in Maharashtra and Gujarat for control over Mumbai," and a more subtle struggle between the plebian Hindu nationalism of north and greater Mumbai who care little for wealthy south Mumbai and "the more slick, market-oriented face of the Bharatiya Janata Party, whose elite supporters know that South Mumbai is crucial to the mediation of global capital to India."[9] Even if the enactors of the violence had no idea of these particularities, they are seen as resulting from the consequences of warfare in a city that has its own history of religion and identity, aside from globalized narratives of terrorism that threaten to flatten these qualities.

Gaza: When Religious Difference Is Used to Fight a Territorial Battle

As a space for asymmetric war, Gaza is in a different category from most other pertinent cases. There is an asymmetry there, but ironically, it may well be of a more advanced sort than the other cases that are usually mentioned. Here I want to explore whether what we are witnessing is part of a larger emergent dynamic, one with vastly diverse manifestations and normative valences. This means seeing Gaza not just in its present condition of helplessness confronted with a vastly superior military force, but as a moment, an epoch in a trajectory that moves into the future. The increasingly acute asymmetry marking the Israel-Gaza "interaction" may be pointing to a breaking point in the geometry of the current period. Importantly, this is a case in which religion feeds and gives extreme intensity to an old-fashioned struggle for territory.

The 2009 one-way Israeli bombing of Gaza was reminiscent of the six-week one-way bombing of Iraq in the 2003 US-led invasion. But the asymmetric war that followed in Iraq's cities once the US-led forces were on the ground did not take off; it was a continuation of a long history of regular incursions and assaults by Israeli armed forces and mostly the regular stone throwing by Palestinian youths. Hamas fired mostly ineffective rockets on civilian populations, which terrorized but did not inflict the deaths of civilians and military seen in Iraqi cities. Gaza has become an extreme site for the unilateral developing and enacting of the instruments of war in urban settings on the part of Israel's conventional military force. It is a site where Israeli forces can experiment with modes of urban warfare (see Weizman 2007 for some instances), given the fact of its occupation and control over most of the means of survival of the Gaza people. In the process, it terrorizes a whole population, but it cannot win a clear victory over that population and it cannot effectively occupy Gaza for reasons that go well beyond military capacity.

In this process, Gaza has become a site that makes visible the limits of power in a condition of absolute military superiority (Sassen 2010). Even in such an unbalanced military situation, the superior force can hit a point at which it has to switch to obstructionism rather than pulverizing its enemy. Particular conditions need to come together to produce such constraints on the superior military force, and those conditions can be highly variable. In Israel's case, it did not have the Dresden or Hiroshima option partly because launching its most powerful bomb would have become self-destructive, but also partly because it is caught in a web of international interdependencies, none of which could actually restrain a country. These interdependencies derive their power from *non*military capacities.

Gaza shows us the limits of power and the limits of war. Gaza is part of an asymmetry so extreme that it cannot even accommodate the kinds of asymmetric war we saw in Iraqi cities once the on-the-ground occupation started. In this regard, it shows us the limits not only of power but also of war. Israel's active making of Gaza's vulnerability to conventional military attack and control has had the ironic effect of raising the importance of Hamas as the main provider of services and goods to the civilian population, thereby raising the importance of Hamas in Gaza. And all along, Israel cannot use its most powerful weapon and is reduced to an obstructionist force, whose tasks include stopping food and construction materials sent to Gaza by international aid agencies. Israel has destroyed thousands of homes, bombed schools and hospitals and the economic infrastructure. It has carried out targeted assassinations of Hamas leaders. It has basically razed vast parts of the built environment of Gaza, attacked the water and electricity supplies, and dismembered its territory. It has done just about all that is conceivable to destroy Gaza and demoralize a people. Yet it is still not a victor according to its own definition of victory. And we can sense that it is not the end of Gaza—Gaza is not going away.

Haroub observes that the real effect of "terror" has been to assure Palestinian trust in the everyday ability of Hamas to resist Israeli militancy (Open Democracy 2009).[10] This is built into the asymmetric nature of modern warfare in urban settings.[11] In my reading, there is a temporal dimension in this type of urban war that is critical to the unconventional side, in this case Hamas. It makes legible not only the limits of military superiority but also the fact that, under certain conditions, powerlessness can become complex (Sassen 2008: chapter 6); in this complexity lies the possibility of making the political, of making history.[12] But this entails a far longer temporality than that of military superiority.

There is, in all of this, a conflation of military, political, and religious vision that may be one of the systemic dynamics of asymmetric war in our epoch. Juan Cole describes this type of warfare as microwar, to distinguish it from conventional macrowar (Informed Comment 2009).[13] He outlines its specific strategies, notably ties to regional support, provision of civic/social services, and media exposure. Israel, on the other side, seeks to challenge the ability of Hamas to support the Gaza public, "denying it enough food, fuel, electricity and services to function healthily, in hopes that it could be made to turn against Hamas." What is remarkable here, in my view, is to what extent this violent encounter of two different religions that at various times have lived in peace with each other is ultimately a territorial war.

CONCLUSION

The urbanizing of war and its consequences are part of a larger disassembling of traditional all-encompassing formats, notably the nation-state and the interstate system. The consequences of this disassembling are partial but evident in a large number of domains, well beyond the questions discussed in this short chapter (see Sassen 2008: parts 2 and 3).

The changed systemic position of cities beginning in the 1980s with economic globalization and emerging in a very different way with the ascendance of asymmetric war in the 2000s is part of that disassembling. So is the rise and growing structural power of organized religions. Cities and organized religions are complex and ambiguous instances of this dis- and reassembling. They play variable roles in developments such as asymmetric war and make visible the diverse ways in which a long history of religious conflict is part of this epoch. Gaza makes visible the territorial conflict driving some of the current religious conflict even as both sides make use of this long history to justify their actions. The attacks in Mumbai make visible the multiple elements in a long genealogy of religious conflict and how this conflict can be used for nonreligious aims such as a decades old interstate conventional conflict. Further, in each case, the city enables and makes visible embedded resistances to armed force—the social physics of the city obstruct superior military force in Gaza and activate civic action across religious differences in Mumbai rather than falling prey to old histories of religious conflict.

Notes

1. Since 1998 most asymmetric attacks have been in cities. This produces a disturbing map. The US Department of State's Annual Report on Global Terrorism allows us to establish that today cities are the key targets for what the report defines as terror attacks—attacks by nonconventional combatants. This trend began before the September 2001 attacks on New York and the Pentagon. The report finds that, from 1993 to 2000, cities accounted for 94 percent of the injuries resulting from all terrorist attacks and for 61 percent of the deaths. Secondly, in this period the number of incidents doubled, rising especially sharply after 1998. In contrast, in the 1980s hijacked airplanes accounted for a larger share of terrorist deaths and destruction than they did in the 1990s. Access to urban targets is far easier than access to planes for terrorist hijacking or to military installations. The report does not include conventional military action in and on cities; I consider this also part of the urbanizing of war.
2. Today's urbanizing of war differs from past histories of cities and war in modern times. In older wars, such as the two so-called world wars, large armies needed large open fields or oceans to meet and fight and to carry out invasions. These were the frontline spaces of war. In World War II, the city entered the war theater not as a site for war making but as a technology for instilling fear: the full destruction of cities as a way of terrorizing a whole nation, with Dresden and Hiroshima the iconic cases.
3. Elsewhere I have examined how today's civil wars generate a specific type of the urbanizing of war: As control over territory becomes acute and evicting people is critical, refugees flow into cities, the last refuge in many cases, and bring the conflict with them.
4. A very general background condition is that the countries with the most powerful conventional armies today cannot afford to repeat Dresden with firebombs or Hiroshima with an atomic bomb—whether in Baghdad, Gaza, or the Swat Valley. They can engage in all kinds of activities, including severe violations of the law: rendition, torture, assassinations of leaders they do not like, excessive bombing of civilian areas, and so on, in a history of brutality that can no longer be hidden and seems to have escalated the violence against civilian populations. But superior military powers today stop short of pulverizing a city, even when they have the weapons to do so. The United States could have pulverized Baghdad, and Israel could have pulverized Gaza. But

they did not. It seems to me that the reason was not respect for life or the fact that a certain kind of mass killing is illegal according to international law—since they do this frequently.

5. See generally http://news.bbc.co.uk/2/hi/south_asia/7764475.stm; http://www.guardian.co.uk/commentisfree/2008/nov/29/india-pakistan-terrorism; Faisal Devji, *Landscapes of the Jihad: Militancy, Morality, and Modernity* (Ithaca, NY: Cornell University Press 2005); Veena Das, *Mirrors of Violence: Communities, Riots and Survivors* (Delhi: Oxford University Press 1990).

6. http://blogs.ssrc.org/tif/2008/12/09/jihad-fitna-and-muslims-in-mumbai/

7. http://blogs.ssrc.org/tif/2008/12/15/violence-publicity-and-sovereignty/

8. http://blogs.ssrc.org/tif/2008/12/04/reflections-on-the-future-of-indian-democracy/

9. http://blogs.ssrc.org/tif/2008/12/07/is-mumbais-resilience-endlessly-renewable/; see also Appadurai, *Fear of Small Numbers* (Durham, NC: Duke University Press, 2006).

10. Haroub http://www.opendemocracy.net/article/hamas-after-the-gaza-war

11. See Larison on Israeli strategies of asymmetric warfare, though not explicitly in urban contexts (American Conservative, 2009). Larison http://www.amconmag.com/larison/2009/01/02/proportionality-and-deterrence-again/ and http://www.amconmag.com/larison/2009/01/14/wrong-and-ineffective/

12. My argument is that we need to open up powerlessness into a variable: At one end, it is elementary and can be understood simply as the absence of power. But at the other end, powerlessness becomes complex and thus a far more ambiguous condition. Israel's military superiority has made legible the complexity of the powerlessness of Hamas and Gaza insofar as it has made the people of Gaza even more dependent on Hamas beyond war, for daily life.

13. http://www.juancole.com/2009/01/gaza-2008-micro-wars-and-macro-wars.html.

Bibliography

Kaldor, Mary. *New and Old Wars: Organized Violence in a Global Era*, 2nd ed. Palo Alto, CA: Stanford University Press, 2007.

Sassen, Saskia. *Territory, Authority, Rights: From Medieval to Global Assemblages.* Princeton, NJ: Princeton University Press, 2008.

CHAPTER 33

ARMAGEDDON IN CHRISTIAN, SUNNI, AND SHIA TRADITIONS

MICHAEL A. SELLS

> This is not a clash of two powers or two races, but a clash of two promises.
>
> —*Safar al-Hawali* (1994: 18)

In 2006, alarms sounded through American media in regard to the religious beliefs of Iranian president Mahmud Ahmedinejad and other members of Iran's ruling elite. Robert Spencer, the director of Jihad Watch, fired the first salvo in a July 27 article of the conservative magazine *Human Events*. The Iranian president was driven by nuclear apocalypticism, Spencer warned. Ahmadinejad had announced August 22 as the date he would respond to United Nations (UN) demands in regard to Iran's nuclear program. Citing as his authority Farid Ghadry, a Syrian-American entrepeneur, former defense contractor and activist who aligns himself with American neoconservative circles, Spencer stated that August 22 fell on the annual commemoration of the Mi'raj or heavenly ascent of Muhammad. The date held ominous significance for Ahmedinejad, Spencer claimed. The Iranian president might "respond" to UN demands on that date by launching a nuclear attack, not with any conventional military objective but in order to hasten the return of the

Twelver Shiite Imam, who will reenter history as the Mahdi, defeat unbelievers, and usher in an Islamic utopia. Spencer did not indicate how Ghadry, who had no stated background in the study of Iranian Shiism, would be in a position to analyze the apocalyptic implications of the Mi'raj in Iran or would be privy to Ahmedinejad's personal commitment to using nuclear weapons to bring about the return of the Mahdi on that date.

The same claim appeared in an August 8 *Wall Street Journal* article by Bernard Lewis, an emeritus professor of history at Princeton and influential adviser to the Bush administration. Lewis made no reference to either Ghadry or Spencer, thus implying that the likelihood of a nuclear Iranian Mi'raj commemoration was something he knew independently. Francis Poole, described as an "anti-terrorism consultant to law enforcement and the military," published a third warning on August 17. Poole asserted that Ahmedinejad "believes that a great cataclysm of bloodshed anticipates the return of the Twelfth Imam, in particular the destruction of infidels—Jews and Christians—that will usher in a new dawn of Islamic worldwide dominance," thus reinforcing Spencer and Lewis's arguments regarding the ominous import of the impending Mi'raj anniversary. Although the date for the nuclear Mi'raj attack passed without incident, American military and security consultants, cable television and talk radio commentators, and some prominent Israelis continued to raise the alarm (Esfendiari 2005). Iran is governed by a "messianic cult of death, the idea that millions have to die in order for their particular Islamic messiah to come," said Israeli prime minister Benjamin Netanyahu of the Iranian rulers during a November 17, 2006 interview on CNN's *Glenn Beck* show. "Millions have to die," he repeated, "and the sooner the better, in their view."

Hopes for the advent of a messianic champion have waxed and waned in all three Abrahamic traditions and have taken a variety of forms. The messianic advent can be viewed as a distant or imminent event, as taking place in a far-off future or as already beginning to unfold. Expectations for it can constitute one element within a complex mosaic of motivation and judgment, or they can become the focal point of a community's expectations or an individual's sense of meaning in life. It can be viewed as the culmination of progress toward a more peaceful and pious world or, by contrast, as coming about only when the world has reached a nadir of wickedness and after a devastating period of natural calamities and war.

It is rare for a prophesier to claim that any specific human action can bring on the return of the messianic figure—such a claim would challenge the priority of God's will and timing—but longing for an imminent return and for the global violence that in some visions is at once the herald and the necessary condition for that return can become a self-fulfilling expectation, in regard to the violence if not necessarily the messianic advent. If a nation with the capability or on the verge of attaining the capability of constructing nuclear weapons and their delivery systems were governed by those with such longings and expectations, it would be a matter of genuine security concern. And if it were governed by a ruling elite that actually believed it could bring on the return by plunging the world into a nuclear holocaust, that concern would clearly be urgent.

In this chapter, I examine actual or alleged cases of apocalypticism within contemporary Iranian Shiite, Saudi Sunni, and American Christian circles. Apocalypticism burgeoned during and after 1979. That was the year that saw the Islamic revolution in Iran and subsequent Irano-American hostage crisis, the violent takeover of the Grand Mosque in Mecca by a militant Sunni group proclaiming the arrival of the Mahdi, and the formation of the Moral Majority under the leadership of militant Christian messianist leaders, including Jerry Falwell, Robert McAteer, and Tim LaHaye. The following year saw the establishment of the International Christian Embassy in Jerusalem, an institution guided by an apocalyptic vision that had developed largely in the United States.

Qur'anic depictions of the end times and the day of judgment focus on a sudden, even instantaneous transformation in which the earth and heaven are rent, scattered, or melted away, and each human soul stands to hear the judgment on its eternal destiny. In contrast to the Christian Bible, the Qur'an offers few passages describing or alluding to a messianic return. It is in the hadith collections that messianic predictions take form. Some hadith recount the coming of a Mahdi who will abolish unbelief and establish a rule of justice on Earth. Others elaborate the return of 'Isa (Jesus), the *Masih* (Messiah), who will vindicate his true nature as the nondivine but divinely sent messenger, embrace Muslims as his true followers, and vanquish an anti-Messiah known as *al-Dajjal* (e.g., Sahih Muslim 41). The Twelver Shiite tradition of Iran views the Mahdi as the Twelfth Imam who will return from the occultation he entered during the rule of Abbasid Caliphs. Sunni traditions view the Mahdi not as returning but as appearing for the first time. In both Shiite and Sunni traditions, Jesus and the Mahdi appear during the same period and work together to defeat the forces of al-Dajjal.

The American messianic tradition represented by Falwell, McAteer, and LaHaye is known as dispensationalism. It was brought to North American by the British missionary John Darby in the 1860s, came to dominate American fundamentalist circles, and was institutionalized in the Scofield Reference Bible (1909, 1919), which became the core text at American Bible colleges for decades. Dispensationalism taught that when the world reached the most advanced stage of wickedness and apostasy, a series of biblically predicted catastrophes would unfold, Christians would be taken up from the earth in an event known as the Rapture, and the rest of humanity would suffer through seven years of natural catastrophe and war, culminating in the battle of Armageddon, the triumphant return of Jesus, the slaying of the Antichrist, and the establishment of Jesus's millennial or thousand-year-long rule from his world capital in Jerusalem. Before Jesus would return, however, the world's Jews would have to return to the biblical lands of Israel, reestablish their state, and rebuild their temple. Dispensationalists viewed such events as imminent, and many expected to live to experience the Rapture. Under the leadership of William E. Blackstone, the dispensationalist movement brought dozens of American leaders from Congress, the courts, state and local governments, business, and science together to demand that the world's powers give persecuted Russian Jews a homeland in Palestine. After World War I, however, the dispensationalist movement retreated from political activity until the social tensions over abortion and school prayer and the excitement over Israel's victory in the 1967 Arab-Israeli War powered the emergence of a new wave of activist dispensationalism (Boyer 1992, Sizer 2004, Weber 2004, Marsden 2006, and Clark 2007).

Forty-two percent of respondents in the 1996 Angus Reid Group Cross-Border Survey of religion and political beliefs in Canada and the United States agreed that "[t]he world will end in a battle in Armageddon between Jesus and the Antichrist" (Boyer 2000). Polls, however, offer only a crude measurement of beliefs and convictions. An individual may affirm belief in the battle of Armageddon without using that belief to anchor his or her spiritual life, political commitments, or attitudes toward unbelievers. Some might be inclined to express such beliefs in some situations and dismiss them in others, and fascination with end times prophecy can operate as an undercurrent among congregations that do not stress it in their formal ministry. Many Americans who may not view themselves as religious have been influenced by dispensationalist apocalypticism through novels and films. The appeal of apocalyptic messianism in countries such as Iran and Saudi Arabia is even more difficult to poll and just as difficult to evaluate.

In addressing contemporary militant apocalypticism, I pay special attention to the competition between its American Christian and Islamic versions. My analysis of apocalypticism is part of a larger study of religion and violence, and before proceeding with that analysis, I would like to mention the principles on which that wider study is based: 1) Religious militancy reads the sacred texts and traditions of its own tradition or that of the traditions of others as proof that the religious other is not only wrong but also an enemy of God and a threat to the true faith, and it reads contemporary conflicts as a confirmation of that ideology. 2) Religious militancy exacerbates conflicts over seemingly mundane issues such as resources, political power, territory, and nation, even as such conflicts increase the appeal of religious militancy. 3) Religious militancy is not confined to those who present themselves as religious or who are particularly observant or even observant at all. 4) Several paradigms from sacred texts and prophetic models can be interpreted in inclusive or exclusive, militant or nonmilitant manners, including martyrdom and its commemoration, reenactment, or imitation; purity; holy war based on passages in scripture where a sacred, transcendent power demands warfare or engages in it; pilgrimage and sacred space; heaven and hell; and the apocalyptic appearance of a messianic champion. 5) These paradigms are intertwined and presuppose one another, even when one of them, as in the case at hand, predominates. 6) A person can make a militant statement or adopt a militant position and then change; and many traditions have undergone periods of militancy only to become less militant when circumstances changed. However, as is the case with the examples discussed ahead, a given tradition can become locked in militancy for a time, sometimes in competition with a similar, rival militant tradition. 7) Each entity—be it a person, nation, or tradition—is (or becomes) what it is and simultaneously is (or becomes) what it is in relation to others. I return to the last principle at the end of the chapter.

With these points in mind, I turn to recent cases of apocalypticism, real or alleged, in Iran, the United States, and Saudi Arabia.

AMERICA, IRAN, AND NUCLEAR APOCALYPSE

Those warning of Iranian nuclear apocalypticism cite several alleged examples. Ahmadinejad claimed that, as he was speaking before the UN, a light descended and held his audience in thrall; he expressed his belief in the emergence of a "perfect man"—a concept that surfaces in Islamic thought in both messianic and nonmessianic contexts. He granted a government subsidy to a mosque viewed in local tradition as a place to which the Shiite Twelfth Imam is expect to return as Mahdi. He maintains ties with the militant cleric Ayatollah Mesbah-Yazdi whose movement, known as the Hojjatia, reportedly believes that by sowing chaos in Iran they can hasten the Mahdi's return. Finally, the Islamic Republic of Iran Broadcasting network (IRIB) produced a television show and accompanying website, *The World toward Illumination* (*WTI*), that discussed Islamic traditions of end times battles and, in doing so, demonstrated that Iranian leaders would use nuclear weapons to bring on the Mahdi. None of these examples indicates how the beliefs of Iranian leaders differ from the messianic beliefs of earlier Iranian rulers, let alone any convincing evidence of violent, proactive messianism—with the one exception of *WTI*. While not comforting, that exception shows something other than what has been claimed.

WTI provides an overview of utopian and messianic horizons in differing religions, civilizations, and historical epochs. The segment on contemporary Iran describes the hopes of many Iranians for a return of the Shiite Twelfth Imam as Mahdi, and expounds on traditions regarding the signs that will herald his coming and the battles that he will wage.[1] It addresses current speculations about the end times in Iran and reviews various accounts of the signs of the imminent arrival of the Mahdi, the battles he will fight, and his establishment of Kufa (in today's Iraq) as the capital of his realm, from where he will send "ten thousand of his forces to the east and west to uproot the oppressors and set up a society in which no one encroaches upon the rights of others, a world in which there will be no deceit, wars, or discrimination." It makes no claim that the Mahdi's arrival is imminent, although it includes prayers to God to hasten his arrival, a commonplace of Shiite piety in Iran.

An earlier *WTI* segment reviewed utopian and dystopian visions, nightmares, and expectations, including Augustine's *City of God*, Thomas Moore's *Utopia*, Francis Bacon's *The New Atlantis*, Plato's *The Republic*, Al-Farabi's *The Virtuous City*, Marxist proletariat utopias, Aldous Huxley's *Brave New World*, Alvin Toffler's *The Third Wave*, Samuel P. Huntington's *The Clash of Civilizations and the Remaking of the World*, and Francis Fukuyama's *The End of History and the Last Man*, the theories of Marshall McCluhan on the global village and Neil Postman on the transformations brought about by television technology, as well as the disturbing questions the two authors raised concerning power, truth, media, and the production of images. A third segment surveyed the American apocalyptic messianism exemplified by William E. Blackstone, John Walvoord, Pat Robertson, and Hal Lindsey. It characterized these men as "extremist Christians" and offered a reasonably accurate account of their theological doctrines: the restoration of the state of Israel will bring the imminent return of the Christian messiah, the Islamic sanctuary of the Haram al-Sharif will be destroyed and Jews will reconstruct their ancient temple on its site, Christians in some version of this belief will be taken to heaven (by spaceship, according to the program, which in this case inaccurately imputes an outlier variant within the Rapture literature to the larger dispensationalist movement as a whole), and Jesus will lead his forces to victory in end-times battles.

Just as some Americans have cited Mahmoud Ahmadinejad's statements on the Mahdi and his claims to have seen the audiences he was addressing held in thrall by a mysterious light as proof that Iran intends a nuclear Armageddon, *WTI* finds evidence of American nuclear apocalypticism in a remark attributed to Ronald Reagan: "When I look at the ancient prophets, the holy book, and the signs that predict Armageddon, I ask myself will we be the generation that will witness this war? Believe me, these predictions are in accordance with the era we live in" (Halsell 1986: 48–50).[2] *WTI* adds that apocalypticist Christians gained further influence with the election of George W. Bush, and cited as evidence Bush's 2003 announcement that the United States had a God-given mission to bring freedom to the world. Bible colleges and televangelist media networks, it warns, are "placing the issue of the end of the world as the axis of many of their products and insinuate that Armageddon is near." *WTI* showed equal concern with seemingly secular American scenarios of Armageddon such as the films *Armageddon* (1998), in which "U.S. technicians and oil companies come to save the earth"; *The Matrix* (1999), in which "the only utopia in the world and the way for man's salvation is the city of Zion that is under the ground"; and *Independence Day* (1996), which used powerful special effects to depict the American defense of earth from an attack by space aliens. "Finally on July 4, that is Independence Day in the United States, the Americans manage to destroy the extraterrestrial enemy. The movie's message is that the United States and the cultural system ruling the West is the only system that protects the world from the dangers," *WTI* adds, suggesting that it might even have a date—to paraphrase Lewis—for unleashing what it has in store.[3] In contrast to such violence-satured religious and nonreligious visions, *WTI* puts forward what it views as a peaceful Twelver Shiite alternative. Whether Iranian leaders hold to a more benign messianic belief than the American preachers, politicians, and film producers *WTI* criticizes remains to be seen, but *WTI* certainly does not indicate any proactive nuclear apocalypticism or hold out global violence as a precondition for messianic return.

In his warning regarding Iranian nuclear apocalypticism, Francis Poole asserted that, in contrast to the biblical model "where the return of Jesus is preceded by waves of divinely decreed natural disasters," the contemporary Iranian model of messianic return puts inordinate emphasis on human agency and violence (2006). Poole gave no details on Ahmedinejad's beliefs on the matter (beyond stating, without documentation, that Ahmedinejad has confided a belief in an imminent, violent apocalypse to friends), and thus Poole's allegations regarding Ahmedinejad remain beyond rational scrutiny. His claim regarding biblical apocalypticism, however, can be tested by looking at the more influential American works in that genre.

American Apocalypticism and
God's Promise to Israel

"Messiah Jesus will first strike those who have ravaged His city, Jerusalem," wrote Hal Lindsey. "Then he will strike the armies amassed in the valley of Megiddo. No wonder blood will stand to the horses' bridles for a distance of two hundred miles from Jerusalem!" (1973: 215). The ocean of blood marks the final stage of the Tribulation, the seven-year period of violence that will end with the return of Jesus. Christians do not suffer the Tribulation but are taken up in the Rapture and then return to earth seven years later as Jesus defeats the Antichrist at the battle of Armageddon and inaugurates the Millennium, a thousand-year kingdom of God on Earth.

Hal Lindsey came to prominence with *The Late Great Planet Earth* (1970). The book went on to sell more than 35 million copies, the *New York Times* declared it the best-selling nonfiction book of the 1970s, and it was translated into more than fifty languages (Weber 2004: 191). *Late Great* was just the first in a series of Lindsey best sellers. Lindsey also constructed a sprawling media and publishing enterprise; founded and directed several institutes devoted to issues of Middle East policy, national security, and military strategy; and served as the host of television and Internet news programs that take the form of network and cable news analysis but blend that analysis with biblical prophesying. The end times thriller he pioneered offers readers a double spectacle. Readers can preview the events by reading the graphic depictions Lindsey and other writers conjure and then, either through belief or imagination, put themselves in the position of raptured believers watching the apocalyptic drama unfold live and in real time. The blurb on Lindsey's *Planet Earth: The Final Chapter* beckons the reader to take "a chilling tour of the world's future battlefields, as the Great Tribulation, foretold more than two thousand years ago by Old and New Testament prophets, begins to unfold" (1998, back cover).

Lindsey's books are categorized by best seller lists as nonfiction and yet are written in a manner that might appeal to those who would approach them as a good read, as fantasy, an escape. With the successive advent of television, ratings, television remote control and, and finally, satellite and cable competition, news and political commentary programs found themselves competing directly with entertainment programs. Religious broadcasters felt the same challenge. As teleministries expanded, the standard gospel hour expanded also to include breaking news, political commentary, and end times prophesy, as well as appropriating the production, format, and video techniques of the nonreligious news and entertainment. Lindsey and his successors continually improved the end times thriller genre with techniques adapted from the popular genres of written and televised romance; action-adventure; science fiction; what has been called "breaking news," "headline news," "action news" and documentary. The end times fiction-nonfiction thriller emerged from a society that claimed to maintain at least some distance between the secular and the religious, between actual events as presented in the news and dramatic fiction, between news and entertainment but that, at the same time, was invested in the breaking down of those same distinctions.

Revelation 14:20 provides a key verse for the dispensationalist version of end times prophecies: "And the wine press was trodden outside the city, and blood flowed from the wine press, as high as a horse's bridle, for a distance of about two hundred miles." Dispensationalists align the winepress verse with the Armageddon verse of Revelation 16:16: "And they assembled them at the place that in Hebrew is called Harmagedon." In 1973, Lindsey wrote that he traveled to Israel to view the area of the coming battle of Armageddon. The distance from Jezreel to the Gulf of Aqaba measured 200 miles—the equivalent, he writes, of the 1,600 biblical furlongs mentioned. "Apparently," he exclaimed, "this whole valley will be filled with war materials, animals, bodies of men, and blood!" He then considers the means by which the majority of the earth's population will be wiped out. "The earth could be shaken either by a literal earthquake or by a full-scale nuclear exchange of all remaining missiles," he writes. "I lean toward the nuclear conflict; I believe that when these powers lock forces here, there will be a full-scale exchange of nuclear weapons, and it's at this time that the cities of the nations fall. Just think of the great cities of the world, London, Rome, Paris, Berlin, New York, San Francisco, Los Angeles, Mexico City, and Tokyo—all these great cities are going to be judged at that time!" (1973: 237).[4] Lindsey has retuned his scenario with the latest developments in science, technology, and strategic warfare. He bolstered his account with charts and statistics on US and Soviet arsenals, broken down into numbers of missiles and strategic bombers, numbers of warheads, "total deliverable megatonnage," and stockpiles of defensive weapons (1981: 67–96). He responded to a scientific question concerning the predicted 200 mile sea of blood. "Some have asked," he wrote (1995: 251–252), "wouldn't the blood coagulate and not flow?" Not if the cataclysm was nuclear, he replied. "Blood exposed to intense radiation doesn't coagulate." Three years later, he cited scientific studies of radiation to calculate the depth of the blood sea (1998: 284–285): "Because of the intense radiation, blood will not coagulate. It will literally become a sea of blood five feet deep."

Since 1979, dispensationalism has dominated the Christian Zionist movement in the United States. The expression *Christian Zionism,* as it has been defined by both proponents and critics since 1979, goes beyond political and moral support on the part of Christian groups or individuals for a Jewish homeland in the Middle East or for Israel as a Jewish state. It refers instead to an ideology with a highly specific set of assumptions, expectations, and positions. Alain Epp Weaver, a Mennonite Christian theologian and Middle East peace activist, defines it as "the belief among some Christians that the return of the Jews to their ancestral lands, and the establishment of the state of Israel, is in accordance with biblical prophecy and a necessary component for Jesus' second coming" (2007: 169). The Third International Christian Zionist Conference, which was sponsored by the International Christian Embassy in Jerusalem, convened for three days in February 1996 and was attended by more than 1,500 delegates and participants from more than forty nations. It adopted a proclamation of principles (ICEJ 1996) that included the following: The Messiah will return at the appointed time to sit on the throne of David in Jerusalem and rule the world; according to "God's distribution of nations," the Jewish people "have the absolute right to dwell in and possess" the Land of Israel, "including Judea, Samaria, Gaza, and the Golan"; without the Jewish nation, "God's redemptive purposes for the world will not be completed"; Jerusalem must remain undivided and under Israeli sovereignty, and no part of the land promised by God to Israel can be partitioned; and Christians should support and encourage the ingathering of Jews from all other nations to Israel.

Peacemaking in this perspective is a demonic ruse: "Yitzhak Rabin was a fine gentleman and a good soldier, but the peace agreement he set in place will not last because it is not God's peace in God's timing," Zola Levitt, a Jewish Christian who became a leading television personality on religious broadcasting networks, wrote of the former prime minister of Israel who worked for a negotiated peace in the Middle East (1996). "Ultimately," Levitt added, drawing on the biblical book of Daniel (8:25), "all the world's peacemaking will be done by that 'Dark Prince,' of whom Daniel, the clear-eyed forecaster of the endtimes, remarks, 'He shall magnify himself in his heart, and by peace shall destroy many.'"

Jewish Christians such as Levitt broadened the appeal of apocalyptic Christian Zionism. Born into Jewish families, they embrace Jesus as their savior and adopt the theologies of Rapture and Tribulation. By referencing their own Jewish heritage, they work to assure the wider Christian community that the movement has the best interests of Jews and Israel in mind and that the Christian Zionist movement is grounded in a correct understanding of Jewish history and tradition. As a movement that is both religious and political, Christian Zionism also includes non-Christian Jewish Americans. Activists such as Esther Levens, Rabbi Yechiel Eckstein, and David Brog have joined Christian Zionist organizations and worked to assure the American Jewish community as well as nonmessianic Christian and secularist supporters of Israel that the Christian Zionist agenda will benefit Jews and will serve the cause of Israel. Since 1978, when Israeli prime minister Menachem Begin invited Jerry Falwell on his first tour of Israel, Israeli leaders have also contributed to the movement by inviting its leaders to Israel; briefing them on international security, nuclear threats, and strategic planning; taking them on tours of battlefields and Israeli military installations; attending their conferences and rallies in the United States; appearing on their television news and prophecy programs; and addressing their congregations.

By 2005, San Antonio pastor John Hagee had emerged as end times Christian Zionism's most powerful American advocate. In 2010, according to the group Ministry Watch, John Hagee Ministries' television broadcasts were available in 92 million homes on 120 television stations throughout the United States, and the *John Hagee Today* radio program was broadcast on 110 stations.[5] In 2006 Hagee spearheaded the formation of Christians United for Israel (CUFI), an organization dedicated to "communicating the need to defend Israel, in light of biblically-based matters, with members of the United States Congress." Hagee's position was clear. "For those of you in Washington," he warned, "Jerusalem is not up for negotiation at any time, for any reason, in the future, no matter what your Road Map calls for. There are still people in this nation who believe the Bible takes precedence over Washington, D.C." (Interview with Terry Gross, *Fresh Air,* September 18, 2006).[6]

Hagee's books combine end times theology with geopolitical and military strategy, and Hagee bolsters his security and geopolitical expertise by detailing his connections with important political and military leaders, claiming to have visited with every Israeli prime minister since Menachem Begin. A sentence from Hagee's *The Battle for Jerusalem* begins, "When I recently had dinner with former Prime Minister Netanyahu." Hagee then describes a security briefing Netanyahu gave him in regard to a program by Russian scientists to help Iran develop the capability of striking New York City and other coastal American cities with long-range missiles (2001: 146).[7] Hagee later claimed that Netanyahu had revealed that American intelligence officials had dismissed the findings of Israeli intelligence on the Russian-Iranian long-range missile program (2006: 39–40).

In *The Battle for Jerusalem,* Hagee writes of Iranian president Ahmadinejad that "[a] twenty-first-century Hitler has put in place a plan to exterminate the Jews with nuclear warfare." He then states that that nuclear war between the United States and Iran is inevitable as predicted in the book of Jeremiah, that America must support a preemptive Israeli strike against Iran or risk the wrath of God, and that Iran has in place a secret plan to use dirty bombs to annihilate seven US cities simultaneously. Like Lindsey, Hagee views nuclear Armageddon with undisguised excitement. *The Battle for Jerusalem* includes a chapter built on hymnic refrains and repeated incantations of the words "we are the terminal generation" (2001: 103–119). In the same book, he comments on Isaiah 63, the inspiration for the "grapes of wrath" verse in "The Battle Hymn of the Republic" (184). "This is no weak-wristed, smiling Jesus come to pay the earth a condolence call," he declares. "This is a furious Christ, ready to confront the gathered armies of the world on a plain called Armageddon. The first time He came to earth, He was the Lamb of God, led in silence to the slaughter. The next time He comes, He will be the Lion of the tribe of Judah, who will trample His enemies until their blood stains His garments, and He shall rule an age of peace with a rod of iron."[8]

For expertise on Islam, Hagee turned to Ramon Bennett, an Israeli Jewish proclaimer of the messiah-hood of Jesus who describes himself as "a Bible teacher whose field of expertise is the prophetic role of Israel in the end times." Hagee placed the following words of Bennett at the center of his own chapter on Islam: "*Islam is the antithesis of Christianity.* Christianity advocates love and compassion toward God and one's neighbor. Islam promotes cruelty, diabolical cruelty. Execution, crucifixion, the severing of hands, feet and tongues, the gouging out of eyes are all part of Islam's 'submission to the will of Allah'" (emphasis Hagee's; Bennett 1995: 42; Hagee 2001: 184). Hagee offers a similar definition of Islam in explaining the motives of the 9/11 terrorists. "They were all Islamics who practice the teachings of the Qur'an," he writes (2007: 68). "Islam not only *condones* violence, it *commands* it" (emphasis Hagee's).[9]

Hagee has found support with influential members of Congress. "I would describe Pastor Hagee with the words the Torah uses to describe Moses," exclaimed Senator Joe Lieberman at Hagee's Christians United for Israel conference in July 2007. "He is an 'Eesh Elo Kim,' [Elohim] a man of God, because those words fit him; and like Moses he has become the leader of a mighty multitude in pursuit of and defense of Israel." Hagee, Lieberman continued, understands the difference "between good and evil, between eternal and temporal, between Israel and other nations."

"Dear friends," Lieberman concluded, "you Christians United for Israel clearly follow in the footsteps of Joshua and Caleb. Your faith is strong, and so is your confidence. And so great will be your effect. I thank you and pray that God will bless you and all that you do." Hagee reciprocated in kind: "Therefore it is time for America to embrace the words of Senator Joseph Lieberman and consider a military preemptive strike against Iran to prevent a nuclear holocaust in Israel," he declared. When asked if he knew the teachings of Christians United for Israel on the Middle East, Lieberman replied that all he needed to know was that they, like he, supported Israel, supported the war in Iraq, and were "very agitated about this particular Iranian regime"; the other question was, he said, "a private theological matter" (Greenwald 2007).

A former football player, Hagee posts the following analogy on his *Rapture Ready* website: "I believe that we have arrived at the 'two-minute warning' on God's clock. Unlike the players in a professional football game, we do not know how much time we have left. What we do with the time remaining will make all the difference in the world…and in eternity. It is vital we live every day for Him." Hagee's team funds Israeli settlements and warns that whoever proposes peace in the Middle East may be the Antichrist. It proclaims Israel's inalienable, nonnegotiable possession of the West Bank, the Golan Heights, Gaza, and all areas of the "royal grant" of Genesis 15:12. It asserts that Jerusalem is Israel's one, eternal, and indivisible capital. It supports efforts to breed the red heifer that would remove a major obstacle to rebuilding the temple, and invites American Christians to work on temple restoration planning. It declares Islam an evil religion, proclaims a biblically mandated Judeo-Christian alliance against Islam and urges American and Israeli leaders to carry the war to Lebanon, Syria, and Iran.

Apocalyptic Christian Zionist support for Israel is not unconditional, however. After Israeli prime minister Ariel Sharon suffered a stroke in 2005, Pat Robertson declared that God was punishing Sharon for giving away God's land in Gaza and for breaking God's covenant with Israel. After Sharon announced the Gaza withdrawal, the International Christian Embassy in Jerusalem issued a warning to all nations:

> The Bible is clear about the fact that those nations that divide the Land of Israel will incur the disfavor of God. So, the conflict now unfolding in Gaza has serious implications for all the world. The Land of Canaan belongs to God! He has bequeathed it to the Jewish people as an everlasting possession as part of His plan for world redemption. To meddle with that which God has given is a grave oversight. The nations must be warned and even though they happily discount the reality of the God of Heaven, they will soon hear from Him. (ICEJ 2005)

The statement also addressed Israel—"The prophets have always spoken to Israel about her spiritual condition"—and then elaborated: "Her departure from serving the God of her forefathers has always led to judgment, anguish and trouble within her borders. In addition, the God of the Bible has always warned Israel about making alliances with foreign nations that in the end bring her to a place of compromise and land forfeiture. Israel is called upon to trust God fully" (ICEJ 2005). It then called on Israel to atone for the abandonment of the Gaza portion of the land that belongs to God by proclaiming "a Day of Humility and Repentance." In any case, it added, "God is dealing with Israel and in the end He will have His way with her."

In *Philistine: The Great Deception*, the work mined by Hagee as an authoritative source on Islam, Ramon Bennett wrote that "[t]he current government led by Prime Minister Yitzhaq Rabin and Foreign Minister Shimon Peres is a humanist government—perhaps even the most ungodly government ever to be in power during Israel's entire 4000 years of history" (1995: 200). Bennett added that Rabin had been a coward in battle, and that Rabin and Peres had betrayed Israel to Godless humanism (215–230). The book appeared a few months before Rabin's assassination at the hands of a Jewish extremist who shared Bennett's views on Rabin. A few years later, Bennett looked back on Rabin's fate with unconcealed satisfaction; claimed that Rabin and Peres had come to power as part of a plot by the administration of George H. W. Bush to give away God's lands of Samaria, Judea, Gaza, and the Golan; and charged them for "sedition before God" (2000: 29, 45–49, 63, 70–71). Dispensationalist end times prophesiers have stated that the Tribulation will fall with special severity on all Jews, Christianized or not. Lindsey's mentor, John Walvoord, had written that the sufferings of the Jews throughout history would be but a "prelude" to what would befall them during the Tribulation (1962: 111–112).[10]

End times writers differ over how many Jews will perish, when and how the various judgments will fall, and how many Jews will convert. Most agree that at the end of the Tribulation, Jesus will enfold Israel—once purified from its iniquities and of Jews who refuse to recognize Jesus as their savior—into his thousand-year kingdom.[11]

During Netanyahu's November 2006 appearance on his show, Glenn Beck aired the film *Exposed* for his viewers and asked Netanyahu to comment on the film. The film was one of three produced in that period (the others being *Obsession* and *Islam: What the West Needs to Know*) that presented similar warnings about Islam. All three used film and web resources of two organizations dedicated to showing Islamic extremism and antisemitism, MEMRI and Palestinian Media Watch, as a platform. All three featured Walid Shoebat, a self-declared former Palestine Liberation Organization terrorist and Islam expert, who compared Islam (unfavorably) to Nazism and who has stated that 73 percent of all Muslims are suicidal jihadists bent on annihilating the United States and Israel (cf. Hagee, 2001: 73). What the film bios did not mention was that Shoebat is a Christian end times prophesier who has declared that Islam is in league with the Antichrist and offers vivid scenarios for its imminent annihilation in the battles accompanying the return of Jesus.[12] After viewing *Exposed* with Beck, Netanyahu stated, as his own conviction, one of the film's claims. "Iran is Germany and it's 1938," he declared. "It wants to dominate the world, annihilate the Jews, annihilate America." Deterrence will not work with an Iran possessing nuclear weapons. Iran is not a normal power or regime: "It's a messianic cult. It's a religious messianic cult that believes in the Apocalypse, and they believe they have to expedite the apocalypse by bringing about the collapse of the West.... Do we let this fanatic regime, this messianic cult of the Apocalypse, get their hands on atomic weapons?"

There are indications that even those warnings about Iran that appeared in nonreligious vehicles such as the *Wall Street Journal* and the *National Review* were composed with the messianic Christian audience in mind. Thus Bernard Lewis presented Ahmedinejad as using an end times code common to writers such as Shoebat, Lindsey, and Hagee in order to "respond" to the nuclear issue but did not supply any context for showing that the Iranian leader was using such a code. Joel Rosenberg's January 3, 2007, column in the *National Review*, which cited *WTI* as evidence of Iranian nuclear apocalypticism, was blatant in this regard. Iranian leaders are determined to bring about the conditions needed for the return of the Mahdi, and to do that, Rosenberg warned, they will instigate a nuclear attack. Rosenberg cited a passage in *WTI* that gave various theories of when the Mahdi would return:

> Some say it would be Friday and the date will be Ashura or the 10th of Moharram, the heart-rending martyrdom anniversary of his illustrious ancestor, Imam Husain. Others say the date will be the 25th of the month of Zil-Qa'dah and may coincide with the Spring Equinox or Nowrooz as the Iranians call it. A saying attributed to the Prophet's 6th infallible heir, Imam Ja'far Sadeq (PBUH) says the Mahdi will appear on the Spring Equinox and God will make him defeat Dajjal

the Impostor or the anti-Christ as the Christians say, who will be hanged near the dump of Kufa.

That was enough for Rosenberg to claim that Iran, which was to celebrate its nuclear program at the beginning of the new year, which fell on March 20, might be planning its attack for that specific date. Evidently, when Spencer, Lewis, and Poole's August 22 Mi'raj anniversary failed to live up to predictions (and *WTI* did not even mention the Islamic calendar date for the Mi'raj as among those viewed as possible occasions for the Mahdi's return), Rosenberg chose another date.

Rosenberg is the former public relations advisor to Benjamin Netanyahu who at some point embraced the dispensationalist Christian vision preached by Tim LaHaye and Jerry Jenkins, the authors of the best-selling Left Behind series of novels. In *The Ezekiel Option*, an Armageddon thriller he wrote in emulation of the Left Behind novels, Rosenberg anticipates the destruction of Islam at the hands of Jesus (Rosenberg 2005: 410):

> Live coverage from Al-Jazeera showed fireballs hitting Mecca and Medina. In a millisecond, hundreds of thousands gathered to pray for the destruction of Israel were incinerated on live television. Local coverage from Istanbul showed the seventeenth-century Blue Mosque now smoldering wreckage.... Within minutes it seemed as if the whole of Lebanon, Syria, and Saudi Arabia was a blazing inferno.

Most dramatic is the fate of Jerusalem. "Burning sulfur and massive meteorites rained down on the Temple Mount," Rosenberg writes. "One after another, seven balls of fire smashed into the Dome of the Rock, the al-Aksa Mosque, and everything around them, shattering rocks and melting anything that would not burn. It was as if God Himself was cleansing the holy site" (2005: 411). After the area is cleansed of Muslims and Muslim heritage, Jesus turns to the leaders of the Antichrist coalition: a Russian named Golgolov and the Islamic Antichrist, to whom Rosenberg gives the name Jibril, Arabic for the angel Gabriel. According to Islamic traditions, Jibril transmitted the Qur'anic revelation from God to Muhammad. Jesus turns first to Jibril: "The man's flesh crackled and slit open, melting from his bones as his eyes turn to liquid in their sockets." As for Golgolov, "[h]e cried for mercy he would never see. He felt the searing heat from the demons ripping at his eyes and face with claws like razors. And then, in a terrifying flash of clarity, he realized it would never end" (410–412).[13]

Rosenberg composes nonfiction as well. His best seller, *Epicenter* (2006), includes strategic security analysis along with a commentary on Gog and Magog, the mysterious figures that appear in the biblical books of Ezekiel (chapters 38–39) and Revelation (chapter 20). Rosenberg writes that a joint attack by Russia (Gog) and an Arab-Iranian alliance (Magog) against Israel will set the stage for Armageddon.[14] There is nothing in *WTI* remotely as violent or as intoxicated with violent apocalyptic scenarios as Rosenberg's fiction and nonfiction works.

Historians may one day look back on the dispensationalist militancy of today as a phase in the movement's evolving history. A complaint by Zola Levitt reveals the possibility of change. At the time of his death in 2006, Levitt's television and Internet presence had made him one of the most watched and influential forces in militant Christian Zionism. By 2001, however, Levitt was worried that some of the most important dispensationalist institutions no longer taught that "Israel is the timepiece by which we can estimate world events and the fulfillment of End Times prophecies." Institutions such as the Moody Bible Institute, Dallas Theological Seminary, Talbot Seminary, and Biola College that were formerly "on track with God's workings in Israel," Levitt lamented, "had de-emphasized that nation in recent times" and had sacrificed core truths in favor of an unauthentic doctrine Levitt referred to as "Progressive Dispensationalism." When influential, self-professed adherents to a given tradition denounce their contemporaries for abandoning its true vision, they reveal the contestation—latent or actual—that is at the heart of any interpretive tradition.

Yet the market for apocalyptic violence remains strong. Tim LaHaye, Rosenberg's role model in composing *The Ezekiel Option,* heralded Rosenberg's work as an "exciting, action-packed thriller based on one of the most important end-times prophecies" (Rosenberg 2005, front cover). Ralph Peters, the security analyst for Fox News and the *New York Post,* praised Rosenberg's *The Ezekiel Option*—with no detectable irony—as "another direct hit on the dangers of a troubled world." In that book, writes Peters, Rosenberg "displays an uncanny eye for global realities along with his powerful storytelling ability—and a sense of the spiritual challenges of our time" (Rosenberg 2005, front matter). In a note at the beginning of the book, Ron Beers, the publisher of *The Ezekiel Option,* describes it as a "thrill ride bringing to life the prophecies leading up to the events of Revelation."

"So turn the page, and enjoy the ride of your life," Beers adds. "Where you're going, there's no turning back."

A Saudi Salafi Armageddon

The allegations of violent apocalyptic expectations in Iran are so lacking in information or sources that it becomes impossible, on the basis of such allegations, to determine the nature of such expectations, the traditions and texts in which they are grounded, and the identity of those who hold them. What might a contemporary militant Islamic messianism look like? The clearest examples I have found stem from the Saudi religious scholar Safar al-Hawali and an American Sunni activist, Ali al-Timimi (aka Ali al-Tamimi), who came under Hawali's influence.

In a 1996 speech at an Islamic center in London, Timimi declared that world peace will be achieved "only when the Christians and Jews are eradicated from the face of the earth." Timimi spoke in the wake of the March 13 "Global Summit of the Peacemakers" at the Egyptian resort of Sharm al-Sheikh, which brought together Egyptian president Hosni Mubarak, American president Bill Clinton, and twenty-six other government leaders to "enhance the peace process, promote security, and combat terror" (Bassiouni and Ben-Ami 2009: 183).[15] For Timimi, the summit sought nothing less than the "annihilation of Islam from the face of the earth." His response was categorical; the Middle East would not be the land of peace envisioned by the "Global Summit of the Peacemakers" but "a land of tribulation, and warfare, and bloodshed until the Day of Judgment."

A son of well-educated Iraqi immigrants, Timimi had grown up in a suburb of Washington, DC, and had attended a largely Jewish private school. He had Jewish friends, attended one friend's bar mitzvah, and he flourished academically. He proceeded to gain a bachelors degree in biology, work in high-tech computational fields, attain a PhD in computational biology at George Mason University, and publish scientific papers in the area of genetics and cancer research. At the same time, he was also immersed in the study of Islam as it was taught in Saudi Arabia, where he had lived for a year as a teenager and to which he returned for intensive study. He enrolled at the Islamic University in Medina in 1987, taking advantage of the Saudi offer to provide Muslim students with scholarships and stipends at Islamic institutions in the kingdom. There, the gifted young scholar came under the influence of Shaykh Abdulaziz bin Baz, the chancellor of the Islamic University and the future grand mufti of Saudi Arabia.

Bin Baz had come to prominence in the 1960s under the rule of King Feisal, who led the Saudi kingdom in what has been called the Arab cold war against the socialist and secularist regimes in Egypt, Syria, and Iraq, and formed a strong partnership with the United States based on opposition to socialism and communism worldwide. Feisal also launched educational initiatives and opened Saudi Arabia to new forms of media and technology long distrusted by Saudi *ulema* (religious scholars). To do so, he made a grand bargain by promoting ulema like Bin Baz, who were allowed to propound a worldview at odds with the policies of the kingdom as long as they supported the legitimacy of the monarchy. Bin Baz offered a stark reading of the teachings of Muhammad ibn abd al-Wahhab, the founder of Saudi Salafism or Wahhabism. Salafism is a revival of the vision of the fourteenth-century jurist Ibn Taymiyya, who called on Muslims to return to the Islam of the first generations, *salaf* ("select"), by purifying their beliefs and practices of all later accretions and of influences from other traditions. Bin Baz called on Muslims to reject such influences and portrayed Christians and Jews as unbelievers, enemies of the faith, and deserving of the contempt of Muslims. Muslims and Muslim states should under no circumstances take them as patrons or allies. Bin Baz also exceeded Ibn Taymiyya in his demands for purification. He taught that musical instruments of any kind (except the use of tambourine in a nonrhythmical manner to announce a wedding) are forbidden; that it is forbidden for men outside a woman's immediate family to hear that woman's voice; that all images of living beings are forbidden except for photographs used for passports and other identification purposes. He branded practices of most of the world's Muslims, especially those practices associated with Sufism and Shiism, as unacceptable innovation or downright infidelity, *kufr*; and Muslims guilty of *kufr* deserved execution as apostates. The more the Saudi monarchy violated these teachings or allowed them to be violated, the more severely Bin Baz and his colleagues would reaffirm them in their courses at the Islamic University of Medina and elsewhere. As part of its worldwide campaign to fight communism, Sufism, and Shiism, Saudi Arabia sponsored a massive propagation of Salafi Sunni Islam as taught by Bin Baz and other Saudi scholars as well as works by Pakistani Islamist Abul A'la Mawdudi and the Egyptian Islamist Muhammad Qutb, the brother of Sayyid Qutb who was executed in Egypt.

In the 1980s two Salafi scholars based at the Islamic University of Medina and working under the supervision of Bin Baz, Taqi al-Din al-Hilali and Muhsin Khan, institutionalized an interpretation of Islam that portrayed Jews and Christians as enemies of the faith through their influential work, *Translation of the Meanings of the Noble Qur'an in the English* (1985). In it, they used sustained interpolations to insert the interpretations of the Bin Baz school directly into the English rendition of the Qur'an. It was distributed worldwide by the King Fahd Center for the Study of the Qur'an, in both print and electronic format, and used to inculcate Muslims and potential Muslims with militant interpretations of Islam artfully disguised, through parenthesis, as teachings of the Qur'an pure and simple.

Timimi recommended works by Bin Baz, Muhammad ibn Salih al-'Uthaymin, Khan, and Hilali to those wishing to learn about Islam, and his general positions on Jews, Christians, and non-Salafi Muslims were grounded in the worldview propounded by those authors. For his apocalyptic vision, however, Timimi turned to a Saudi scholar mentioned neither in his 1996 talk nor on his list of recommended authorities on Islam, Safar al-Hawali.

Hawali was one of the two leaders, along with Salman al-'Awda, of the Saudi Sahwa (awakening) movement. The two publicly rebuked the king for allowing non-Muslim U.S. troops to be stationed on Saudi territory and for allowing Western and other decadent influences to pervade Saudi society. They also rebuked their former mentor Bin Baz for going against his own long-time teachings by agreeing to the king's policy. Their stance found favor with Osama bin Laden, and when the two were detained by Saudi authorities, Bin Laden issued his 1994 public rebuke to Bin Baz:

> When the regime decided to attack Sheikhs Salman al-'Awda and Safar al-Hawali, who had stood up for the truth and risked much harm, you [Bin Baz] issued a juridical decree condoning everything suffered by the two Sheikhs as well as justifying the attacks and punishments suffered by the two preachers, [other] sheikhs, and [the] youth of our umma who were with them. May God break their fetters and relieve them of their oppressors' injustice. (Lawrence 2005: 95–99)[16]

The first major outbreak of messianism in Saudi Arabia occurred with the 1979 seizure of the Kaaba by a group led by Juhayman al-'Utaybi. 'Utaybi's group had been influenced by Bin Baz and denounced Saudi society as filled with what Bin Baz's group taught was apostasy and wickedness. It then crossed the line to denouncing the monarchy for failing in its duty to preserve the Islamic character of the nation and for making alliances with Christian powers. After seizing the Kaaba along with thousands of Muslim pilgrims whom he took hostage,

'Utaybi declared one of his co-rebels to be the Mahdi and called on all Muslims to join the battle (Kechickian 1986 and 1990; Hegghammer and Lacroix 2007; Trofimov, 2007). Yet 'Utaybi's pronouncements do not appear to have had a strong influence on the specific messianic vision advanced by Timimi in 1996. Timimi tied his messianic teaching to hadith that associated the final days with a great battle between Muslims and Jews, denounced Middle East peace efforts as a demonic ploy, and summoned the ultimate annihilation of Jews and Christians from the face of the earth. The hadith collections offer contradictory reports in regard to the end time struggle between the Messiah Jesus and Dajjal. According to one, the Dajjal will lead an army of people with small eyes, red faces, and flat noses; or with faces that will look like shields coated with leather; or with shoes made of hair. Of the hundreds of hadith accounts of end time occurrences, Timimi mentions only those offering the starkest vision of the conflict between Muslims, on the one hand, and Christians and Jews, on the other. One particular hadith has emerged in recent years at the heart of anti-Jewish polemics surrounding the Israeli-Palestinian conflict, and Timimi feels secure in assuming that the Salafi British audience for his speech on the Middle East conflict would need no help in recalling the substance of what he called "the hadith of the rock and the tree you all know." The hadith states that Abu Hurayra, a companion of the Prophet Muhammad, heard Muhammad say that the final hour would not arrive until Muslims fight and kill the Jews, to the point that Jews seek shelter behind the rocks and trees. But the rocks and stones would speak up, saying: "O Muslim, O servant of God, there is a Jew behind me. Come and kill him!" Only the Gharqad tree would remain quiet, Abu Hurayra's hadith added, because that is the tree of the Jews (Sahih Muslim 041: 6985).

Over the decades of Israeli-Palestinian conflict, the hadith of the rock and the Gharqad tree—at least in the version that specifies those hiding behind the stones and trees as Jews—assumed increasing prominence in the sermons and writings of militant Islam (see Cook 2005: 36). It appears, for example, in the 1988 charter of Hamas, a group formed by radical members of the Muslim Brotherhood and dedicated to the destruction of Israel as a Jewish state in the Middle East. The hadith is often evoked more as a gesture of anti-Jewish belligerence than as an element in a fully developed messianic vision. Yet rather than turning to classical Islamic traditions to develop his messianic narrative, Timimi offers instead a a refutation of American dispensationalist messianism in order to advance what he views as the more authentic, messianic promise. He explains that Christian Zionism predated Jewish Zionism and outlines the messianic Christian convictions of the British leaders who crafted the November 2, 1917, Balfour Declaration committing Britain to the establishment of a national home for the Jewish people in Palestine. He explains the role of American Christian messianism in helping shape the Zionist movement and, in more recent times, advancing the cause of a greater Israel. He discusses William E. Blackstone, whose 1878 book *Jesus Is Coming* "was translated into 48 languages, including Hebrew, and sold over a million copies," and that called Christians to gather all the children of Israel in Palestine to prepare for the Messiah, and introduces Blackstone's historic 1891 petition to President

Benjamin Harrison, known as the "Blackstone Memorial," that called for Palestine to be set aside for a Jewish state. He then addresses the resurgence of such ideas in the post–World War II United States; around a platform expressed by the televangelist Jimmy Swaggart in regard to the "spiritual umbilical cord" between the United States and the "Judeo-Christian" concept that "goes all the way back to Abraham," and in God's twin promises "to bless Israel and to bless those who bless Israel." Timimi affirms the historical, even cosmic importance of Jews but reverses the moral: Every nation that has supported "the Jews" has declined, he tells his London audience, and that decline explains the misery that they see around them every day. He also elucidates the claims of Jerry Falwell that the United States is a "Judeo-Christian republic," that opposition to Israel is opposition to God, that Arabs bear the curse of the Canaanites, and that God promised Israel all the land from the Euphrates to the Nile.

Timimi takes care to inform his audience not only of the doctrines but also of the reach of messianic Christian Zionism.[17] "We know that in 1982 Americans donated $60 billion to the church," he adds, while "most Muslim countries don't have $60 billion as their gross national product. He cites a report in the *International Bulletin of Missionary Research* estimating missionary donations in 1989 at $151 billion, and states that American evangelists have also extended their mission throughout the world of Islam through thirty-eight television stations, sixty-six cable networks, 1,480 radio stations, four telesatellites, and the *The Jesus Film*, which had been produced in fifty languages worldwide.[18] By warning of what he calls the Christian *da'wa*, Timimi touches on a nonviolent but deeply serious competition between Sunni Muslim da'wa programs and Christian missions that stretches across every continent. According to Timimi, the number of American schools, at various levels of study, controlled by conservative evangelical Christians—or fundamentalists, as Timimi calls them—has increased from fewer than two hundred in 1954 to more than one hundred times that number in 1996. "Today Christian fundamentalists have more than 20,000 schools [in the United States] where millions of students study. However, the Islamic University of Medina, probably one of the few Islamic institutions we have in the Islamic world, has no more than 1000 or 2000 students in the student body."

Timimi's speech drew deeply from the lectures and writings of Safar al-Hawali. In a 1994 lecture in Jedda, Saudi Arabia, Hawali outlined the coming global clash. That clash, he stated, would not be fought between two nations or races but between two messianic promises. In both promises, the Messiah will appear in the Holy Land claimed by Israelis and Palestinians, and in both he will slay the unbelievers. It was in this 1994 lecture that Hawali tied together interpretations of Armageddon, the Middle East peace process, the Israel-Palestine dispute, and the Fatiha, which is the opening passage of the Qur'an and the invocation used in Muslim daily prayers. The Bin Baz–supervised *Meanings of the Noble Qur'an in the English Language* reads the Fatiha as a declaration of Muslim enmity toward Christians and Jews, even though neither group is mentioned by name in the Fatiha. Both Timimi and Hawali tied that reading of the Fatiha to the violence of the end times.[19]

A book compiled from Hawali's 1994 Jedda lecture opens with a facsimile of a page of the Qur'an beginning with verse 5:51: "O you who believe, do not take the Jews and the Christians as patrons [or allies, *awliya'*]. They are patrons to each other. He who turns to them is one of them." It includes two major illustrations: a full-page reproduction of an Arabic translation of the biblical book of Revelation with the caption "The Millennium and the Battle of Armageddon," and an Arabic version of the passage from the First Epistle of Paul to the Thessalonians assuring Christians that they will be "taken up" to heaven, with a caption reading "The Source for the Evangelicals' Doctrine of the Rapture" (1994: 35–36).[20]

Hawali expresses respect for socially conservative apocalypse-centered Christians in the United States for sharing his commitment to faithful religious observance; the protection of heterosexual marriage; and opposition to birth control, pornography, sexual promiscuity, popular music, television, film, and other evils of secularist modernity. Both groups of fundamentalists reject the Middle East peace process and believe that the Middle East is destined for a great war during which the Messiah Jesus will return to champion his people and slay the unbelievers. Both believe that God promised them Jerusalem and the adjacent Holy Land and that the world is entering into a clash pitting "the Antichrist Messiah (in Arabic *Masih Dajjal*) against the true Messiah Jesus." At the great battle, which Christians call Armageddon, the true Messiah will proclaim the one, true God and slay the Antichrist and all those who follow him; only then will there be peace on earth, Hawali concludes.

Hawali also reviews the teachings of apocalyptic Christian Zionists (Pat Robertson, Jerry Falwell, Jimmy Swaggart, and George Otis). He explains that American fundamentalists view the Madrid and Oslo peace process as an effort to compromise the God-given territory of Israel in defiance of the divine plan and thereby as interference in the timing of the Messiah's return, and he offers an overview of their publishing, radio, and television enterprises. He then presents statements by American Christian leaders denouncing the peace process and compares it to what he calls the Islamic position: "Everyone who believes or who goes along with the project to create a safe and secure Israel is, willingly or unwillingly, knowingly or unknowingly, working for the establishment of the Kingdom of the Masih Dajjal;" and working "willingly or despite themselves, knowingly or unknowingly, for the sake of Zionism." Islam's position toward the peace process, Hawali emphasizes, is one of unwavering, categorical, definitive, rejection "rooted not in stubbornness or obstinacy, but in inviolable religious doctrine" (1994: 55–69).

In a chapter titled "Shared Rejection," Hawali explains what might seem to be a puzzling agreement between the position of American Christian fundamentalists and their Muslim counterparts and archenemies. He traces the agreement to the shared belief that peace will come only when Jesus the Messiah leads his followers to victory in the Armageddon-like final battle. "Questions have been raised among Arabs and in the West concerning the agreement of the two fundamentalisms, here and there, in rejecting the peace project. We believe in the true promise of God and they believe in the fabricated promise, a slander against Almighty God. And the two promises will not come together, ever." He also points to the last two verses of the Fatiha to demonstrate that it is Islam that holds the true promise. For Hawali, as for Bin Baz, Khan, and Hilali, those mentioned in the Fatiha as having incurred God's wrath are the Jews, and those who have gone astray are the Christians. "In every movement of prayer, we read the Fatiha; in reading it, we are reading the words of God Almighty," Hawali adds. He then explains that those divine words rebuke the Messiah of the Christians and Jews as false and promise that Jesus will emerge to vindicate Islam and slay the Jewish and Christian Dajjal at the end time battle. The Middle East will not be a place of peace as envisioned by the advocates of the new world order but "a land of tribulation, and warfare, and bloodshed" until the final day (1994: 68–74), a scenario Timimi would revisit in almost identical terms during his 1996 London talk.[21]

Hawali expanded his apocalyptic theology in his book *The Day of Wrath*, which appeared on the Internet in a full English translation in 2003. Instead of resting with a simple Islamic counter-Armageddon as a response to end times Christian Zionists, *The Day of Wrath* features a three-hundred-page study of the Christian Bible, with special attention to Daniel, Ezekiel, and Revelation, and employs many of the same interpretive methods and comes to many of the same conclusions as his messianic Christian rivals. Just as his Christian rivals present alternate possibilities for interpreting certain highly charged biblical verses, so does Hawali but with his own twist. The two-horned beast of Revelation, for example, is "Zionism with its two faces, one Jewish, the other Christian" or "Jews in general and Zionists in particular." The United States, he adds, has become the new Babylon that will be destroyed as a prelude to Jesus's final annihilation of all infidels. The armies that "shall come from the North or from the East" will be that of the Muslim mujahidin, he adds. American end time prophesiers have also identified the armies from the north or east with the Islamic mujahidin, though for them Jesus will be engaged not in leading the mujahidin but in destroying them.[22]

CONCLUSION: ARMAGEDDON IN THE MIRROR

The two groups of Christian and Sunni Muslim apocalyptics examined here can be seen as creating, separately and in tandem with one another, the conditions they believe are needed for the return of the end times champion. They portray the religious other as evil, human peace efforts as demonic, and hail a war that is complete, global, and ending only in the annihilation of the other. They sanctify those who, once the end-times conflict is viewed as underway, kill the peacemakers; and in the name of their particular religious tradition, present religious others as enemies of God and, once the conflict begins, as no more human than the Orc mutants that perish by the thousands in the *Lord of the Rings* Trilogy. Under the influence of such apocalyptic teachings, Jewish, Christian, and Muslim individuals and groups have repeatedly stoked confrontations in Jerusalem over issues of archeological digs, shrine construction, and shrine destruction. Although such teachers do not call for overt acts of violence, some are led to draw what they view as the logical next step. Christian and Jewish messianists have attempted to blow up the Islamic shrines at the Haram al-Sharif (Gorenberg 2000: 107–137) in order to bring on a wider war and pave the way for the reconstruction of the temple of Solomon. In 2005 Timimi was convicted for his involvement in a 2002 plot, known as the Paintball Jihad, during which he encouraged several Salafi Muslims based in Virginia to travel to Pakistan in order to fight with the Taliban, al-Qaeda, or the LeT (Lashkar-e Taiba) terror and jihadist group against the United States.

I attempt here to locate specific sites and formations of religious militancy, at the same time refraining from essentializing individuals or traditions. To the latter end, I need to qualify the expression "the Christian and Sunni Muslim apocalyptics." The noun "apocalyptics" refers to the authors or speakers of particular statements in specific times or circumstances. The same individuals may well have offered a different perspective at other times and, if they are still living, may do so in the future. Similarly, the adjectives "Christian" and "Sunni Muslim" need to be de-essentialized. American evangelical Christianity is (becomes) what it is and also (becomes) what it is in its relations to its others—to return to the last of the principles stated at the outset of this essay. The American evangelical tradition has a core of accepted texts and authorities and continuity over time: it is what it is. But what it is is also shaped by conversation and debates from within, debates that include the centrality of the apocalyptic vision to religious life and the nature of the messianic return, the place of work for social justice in the premillennial world, and the modes of engagement with non-evangelical Christian and non-Christian perspectives. One of the voices in that conversation, dispensationalism, also shapes itself through interior conversation, as noted above in Zola Levitt's criticism of progressive dispensationalist teachings. At the same time, dispensationalism is becoming what it is, that is shaping how it defines itself and its core teachings, in relation to its others: nondispensationalist forms of millennialism, nonmillemnialist forms of evangelical Christianity, Catholicism, Judaism, and of course what its exponents view as secular or secular humanist society. Dispensationalist apocalypticism is shaping itself as well in relation to popular, secular apocalyptic literature and films, and in relation to international others: Islam has replaced the Soviet Union as the most powerful geopolitical actor on the side of the Antichrist, for example, at least for those dispensationalists discussed here.

Similarly, Sunni Islam is and is becoming what it is through its interior conversations (between modernist or progressive Salafists and the antimodernist clerics discussed above, for example). Saudi Islam, in particular, has been shaping itself in part through the symbiotic relationship between relatively accommodationist monarchy and fiercely anti-accommodationist Wahhabi ulema. And the teachings propounded by those ulema over the past three decades have shaped themselves in relationship to their religious others within Islam, secular and socialist forms of Islam which may be viewed as religious or nonreligious, religious non-Muslims, and through their proclaimed struggle against communism, western cultural influences, and Israel—and in the case of Safar al-Hawali – in mimetic rivalry with American dispensationalists.

There are three Abrahamic religions, but militant apocalypticism, like other forms of religious militancy, is ultimately dualistic. In the final analysis, there is only us and them, the good and the evil. For the past several decades, both secular and religious militants who associate themselves with the Christian, Jewish, and Muslim traditions (all three of which have rich heritages of both conflict and cooperation with one another and of mutual interpermeation) have declared a permanent and inherent clash between the Judeo-Christian world or, in Bin Laden's terms, the Jews and the Crusaders, and Islam.

In a July 2008 opinion piece in the *New York Times*, the Israeli historian Benny Morris wrote that "Israel will almost surely attack Iran's nuclear sites in the next four to seven months," and if the attack were to fail to destroy or significantly stall the Iranian nuclear program, "the Middle East will almost certainly face a nuclear war—either through a subsequent pre-emptive Israeli nuclear strike or a nuclear exchange shortly after Iran gets the bomb." Morris added that "Given the fundamentalist, self-sacrificial mindset of the mullahs who run Iran, Israel knows that deterrence may not work as well as it did with the comparatively rational men who ran the Kremlin and White House during the cold war." Unless the United States launched a pre-emptive attack first, Morris argued, Israeli leaders were determined to launch their own attack, even though it would bring incalculable destruction to the entire Middle East, Israel included. (Morris 2008: A19).

The scenario was eerily familiar. According to Hal Lindsey, an Israeli general had told him in 1974 that the Israeli military was guided no more by the Masada principle, in which Israeli soldiers pledge to fight to the death protecting Israel. It now followed the "Samson Complex" (1981: 37–38). When Samson chose death over slavery, Lindsey explained, "he destroyed his enemies as well. It doesn't take a vivid imagination to see how this applies to the Middle East." The intent of the Morris warning was to prod the United States, weary of wars in Iraq and Afghanistan, to strike Iran before Israel did in a manner that, although Morris did not label is as such, would be self-sacrificial, befitting the Samson scenario. Did Morris know Israeli leaders and security experts agreed on such actions or was he using the specter of self-sacrificial Israeli leadership to frighten the United States into acting against an Iran that, whether guided by a desire for self-destruction or not, was a self-proclaimed enemy of Israel?

Spencer, Lewis, Poole, and Netanyahu made a more direct appeal to the American public, with vivid claims about the apocalyptic nature of the self-sacrificial ideology of Iranian leaders. They couched their warnings in language that would be particularly persuasive to dispensationalists, who proclaimed an in-our-lifetime violent return of a messianic champion and would be therefore be likely to believe that Iranian leaders would be driven by a similar, albeit false, expectation, and who would be prone to accept whatever violent consequences might result from a war with Iran as fitting into their own messianic scenario. Do those secularists who address warnings of nuclear Armageddon with language that would appeal to religious messianists do so in the belief that they can control the messianic activists they help to empower, as Americans who supported the Afghan mujahidin believed they could control the jihadist ideology of the more radical of the groups they supported, or former Serbian president Slobodan Milosevic believed he could control the Serbian religious nationalists he helped unleash? Or are they driven in some part by a sacrificially apocalyptic impulse of their own? In offering these observations and questions I make no assumptions about proper security policy for the United States or Israel vis-à-vis an Iran or vice-versa. After decades of conflict, both sides have ample reason to distrust, fear, and expect the worse from one another.

We are what we are and become. Like a religious tradition a person is neither a static nor a monotonic entity. A person may have a number of voices at the interior governing table: some voices may argue for the value of life on earth, for the person in question, his children and descendents, and for his others; others may evoke the longing for closure, for a settling of accounts, for the climactic end of the story; and some of this latter group may consciously or unconsciously advocate measures that that would hastened the desired end. When speaking of "them," I do not mean only the named individuals who have preached or attempted to exploit the militant apocalypticism discussed in this chapter, but all insofar as they/we speak or act on the impulse to bring the story to an imminent, violent finale.

NOTES

1. The *WTI* transcripts posted at http://english.irib.ir/ were divided into eighteen segments, only a few of which were dated: November 20, November 27, December 11, and December 25, 2006, and January 1, 2007. However, the signing off on January 1, 2007, was worded: "That was the end of the 25th and last edition of our programme The World Towards Illumination. Thank you for keeping us company and goodbye, with an earnest prayer to God to speed up the reappearance of the Savior of Humanity. Amen." Accessed in 2007.
2. Reagan made the remarks to Tom Dine of the American Israel Public Affairs Committee in October 1983.
3. Although quite detailed, *WTI*'s program omits telling details. In *Independence Day*, for example, the last American nuclear weapon jams inside the jet that was to deliver it, so the pilot employs his missile-laden aircraft as a flying bomb. As he hurtles toward death, he comes to grips with his past failures in life and atones for them. He is shown piloting his aircraft into the massive alien command center, a science fiction flying Babylon, hovering above the doomed planet, gliding into the heart of evil, serene in the hope that, even if the suicide bombing does not defeat the enemy, it may at least allow him to be cleansed of his past sins. The film's epilogue shows the American suicide bomber striking the fatal blow to the evil force, saving the world and winning a glorified new life in the memory of humanity and in the hearts of millions. American film critics have disagreed over the role of satire in *Independence Day*. Even films that are self-knowingly satirical can perpetuate the themes they knowingly parody; and

satire is not readily apparent across cultures. At any rate, if satire was present in the film, the producers of the Iranian program and the experts interviewed for it did not perceive it or find it worth mentioning.

4. John Walvoord, president of the Dallas Theological Seminary and Lindsey's mentor, wrote of the fate of non-Christians left behind by the rapture: "According to Revelation 6:7, the judgments attending to the opening of the fourth seal involve the death with sword, famine, and wild beasts of one fourth of the earth's population." "If this were applied to the present world population now approaching three billion, it would mean that 750,000,000 people would perish." The judgment of the fourth seal, Walvoord wrote, will form only one in a cascading crescendo of Revelation "judgments"; another will consume one-third of those still surviving, and the judgment of the "seventh bowl" will exceed all previous judgments in devastation (1962:111).

5. According to Hagee's *Rapture Ready* website, his 1996 *The Beginning of the End* was a runaway best seller on the *New York Times* Best Sellers list and the number one book in 1996 in the Christian Book Association nonfiction division; his *Final Dawn over Jerusalem*, released in February 1998, had become a number one best seller by April the same year.

6. The CUFI board of directors has included Jerry Falwell and Gary Bauer. David Brog, the organization's executive director, describes the group as the Christian equivalent of AIPAC, the American Israel Public Affairs Committee. Thousands of evangelical activists joined senators Rick Santorum and Sam Brownback at CUFI's 2006 inaugural event, held as Israel commenced a ground and air assault on Hezbollah positions in Lebanon and the strategic bombing of Lebanese infrastructure. In his address to CUFI, Falwell threatened to "rebuke" the State Department each time it urged Israel to show restraint.

7. For other accounts of Israeli military and intelligence cooperation with end times prophesiers, see Evans and Corsi 2006: 202–203, and Chuck Missler's description of one of his "End of the World" tours to Israel, in which Missler lists the following experts as scheduled to provide talks and briefings to the tour group: Avigdor Kahalani, Brigadier General of the IDF; Aviv Oreg, former Shin Bet leader and counterterrorism consultant; Uzi Dayan, former national security advisor; Uzi Arad, former director of intelligence for the Mossad; Benny Elon, Knesset member and head of the Judeo/Christian Alliance; and representatives of the Ramat David Valley Squadron, IDF airbase in the Valley of Armageddon. http://www.endoftheworldbustour.com/speakers.html.

8. An earlier book by Hagee focused on developments in biological warfare, disease control, and computer chip technology (to be used by the Antichrist to control humanity through required identification cards), as well as radiation and breakthroughs in weapons technology (1999: 187). "Incredible! one-fourth of the Earth's population will die as the rider on the pale horse goes forth," exclaims Hagee of the punishment of the fourth seal, which will include biological and chemical attacks as well as the widespread slaughter of humans by wild animals. While most of a city's population could be destroyed in an atomic attack, the entire population could be eliminated by a biological attack within a single week, Hagee adds, citing a study by Frank Holtman, the chairman of the University of Tennessee bacteriology department.

9. "Those who live by the Qur'an have a scriptural mandate to kill Christians and Jews." http://www.npr.org/templates/story/story.php?storyId=6097362.

10. John Walvoord cited a passage in the book of Zechariah to predict the doom that would befall Jews at the end time (1962:111): "And it shall pass, that in all the land, saith the Lord, two parts therein shall be cut off and die; but the third shall be left

therein. And I will bring the third part into the fire, and will refine them as silver is refined, and will try them as gold is tried" (King James version, Zechariah 13:8–9).

11. Of the Jews who do not accept Jesus, Lindsey wrote in 1979, those who are not "cut to pieces" by the armies of the Antichrist will perish when Jesus judges, condemns, and destroys all nonbelievers left alive after the battle of Armageddon (*Apocalypse Code*).

12. Shoebat's teachings on such matters appeared in the book he cowrote, titled *This Is Our Eden, This Is Our End*, some of the chapters of which read as follows: Mystery Babylon: Does it fit Mecca or the Vatican? Satan's master plan to use Islam to deceive the world; Who is the Gog of Ezekiel and how does he fit Islam? Is the Messiah coming back to rescue Israel and annihilate Islamic forces? The Binding of Satan and the entire Muslim world – Is this true? The Destruction of Mecca the Harlot City. What is going to happen in the Rapture? http://www.abrahamic-faith.com. Accessed August 18, 2007.

13. The fate of Jibril and Golgolov appears to be modeled on a vignette from the Left Behind Series (LaHaye and Jenkins 1999:143), which appears to imitate the depiction of the fate suffered by Nazis attempting to steal the Ark of the Covenant in Stephen Spielberg's 1981 film *Raiders of the Lost Ark*.

14. Rosenberg outlined *Epicenter* on CNN Headline News, "Honest Questions about the End of Days," *Glenn Beck,* March 30, 2007, during an interview that featured him along with LaHaye and Jenkins.

15. Deutsche Presse-Agentur, "Declaration of Sharm el-Sheikh Conference," March 13, 1996, in Final Statement, Summit of the Peacemakers at Sharm al-Sheikh (March 13, 1996) [U.N. GAOR, 51st Sess., U.N. Doc. A/51/91 (1996)] (Doc. 448 in Bassiouni and Ben-Ami (2009: 183).

16. In response to protests over the American military presence near the holiest sites of Islam, Bin Baz had issued a fatwa justifying their presence and also composed a treatise titled "On How Peace (*sulh*) with Jews and Christians Does Not Constitute Affection toward Them or Taking Them as Patrons." For the role of al-Hawali and al-'Awda in Saudi Arabian politics, see Fandy (1999).

17. Timimi was wrong about one point. Falwell did not claim all the land "from the Euphrates to the Nile" for Israel. According to Falwell and other American Christian Zionists, the biblical "river of Egypt" lies to the east of the Nile: The Land of Israel extends from the Euphrates through much of Iraq, Lebanon, Syria, and Jordan and through all the territories taken by Israel in the 1967 war but stops west and south of Gaza.

18. By 2008, *The Jesus Film,* originally financed and produced by the Campus Crusade for Christ in 1979, was available in 1,044 languages, had been accessed in online form more than eight billion times, and ostensibly had inspired the conversion of 200 million people. http://www.jesusfilm.org/.

19. The online edition of Hilali and Khan's work at some point omitted the interpolations of Jews and Christians from the Fatiha but left the dozens of other similar interpolations in the English rendition of the Qur'an in place. By removing the interpolations from the Fatiha, the King Fahd Center that sponsored Hilali and Khan's work may have been responding to complaints about the injection of an anti-Jewish and anti-Christian meaning into the English text, but it did not change the overall effect of the translation, because the same meaning was interpolated into the entire Qur'an. In any case, the original Hilali and Khan version is widely disseminated on websites, referenced by search engines and in print form, and has become the default choice of numerous mosques and Islamic studies centers throughout the Anglophone world.

20. The term *al-Quds* in the title can refer to Jerusalem or, more generally, the Holy Land; both meanings are evoked by the title and in the text.

21. The Arabic phrases used in Hawali and rendered by Timimi as "land of peace" and "land of tribulation and warfare and bloodshed" are "*mantiqa amn wa salam*" and "*mantiqa fitn, malahim wa dima',*" 72–73.

22. For examples from the Egyptian writers Said Ayyub and Bashir Abdullah, see Cook (2005: 39, 43). For a more detailed discussion of Timimi's background, his study under Bin Baz, and the ideology of Bin Baz, Hilali, and Khan, see Sells 2006. At the time I wrote that essay, I had not yet accessed the transcripts from Timimi's 2005 terrorism trial that revealed that, after 9/11, Timimi had stayed in urgent, close telephone contact with al-Hawali during the period he was allegedly involved in the Paintball Jihad plot.

BIBLIOGRAPHY

Al-Hawali, Safar ibn 'Abd al-Rahman. *Al-Quds bayn al-wa'd al-haqq wa al-wa'd al-batil al-muftara* [Al-Quds between the Real Promise and the False, Fabricated Promise]. Cairo: Maktaba al-Sunna al-Salafiyya, 1994.

Al-Hawali, Safar ibn 'Abd al-Rahman. *Yawm al-ghada: hal nada'a bi-intifadat rajab: qira'a tafsiriyya li-nubuwwat al-tawra 'an nihayat dawlat isra'il* [The Day of Wrath: Did It Begin with the Intifadeh of Rajab? An Exegetical Reading of Torah Prophecy Concerning the End of the Nation of Israel]. Mecca, 2002. n.p.

Al-Hawali, Safar ibn 'Abd al-Rahman. *Day of Wrath,* 2003 [English translation of Hawali, 2002]. http://www.witness-pioneer.org/vil/Books/AH_DOW/default.htm.

Al-Hilali, Taqi al-Din and Muhsin Khan. *Translation of the Meanings of the Noble Qur'an in the English Language.* Maktabat al-Salam, 1985. Online edition, King Fahd Complex for Printing the Holy Qur'an. http://www.qurancomplex.org.

Al-Timimi, Ali. "The Muslim World—Where Is It Heading?" Audio recording of an undated speech in London, 1996. http://www.uponsunnah.com/tamimi.php. Accessed July 17, 2006.

Altaf, Muhammad and Walid Shoebat. n.d. *This Is Our Eden, This Is Our End.* http://www.abrahamic-faith.com. Accessed August 18, 2007.

Bassiouni, M. Cherif and Shlomo Ben-Ami. *A Guide to Documents on the Arab-Palestinian/Israeli Conflict: 1897–2008.* Leiden, Netherlands: Brill, 2009.

Bennett, Ramon. *Philistine: The Great Deception.* Jerusalem: Arm of Salvation, 1995.

Bennett, Ramon. *The Wall: Prophecy, Politics, and Middle East "Peace."* Citrus Heights, CA: Shekina Books, 2000.

Bin Baz. 'Abd al-'Aziz, Muhammad bin al-'Uthaymin and 'Abdullah bin Jibrin. *Fatawa.* 3 volumes. Edited by Qasim al-Rifa'i. Beirut: Dar al-Qalam, 1998.

Boyer, Paul. "666 and All That: Prophetic Belief in America from the Puritans to the Present." Ed. Loren Johns. *Apocalypticism and Millennialism: Shaping a Believers Church Eschatology for the Twenty-First Century.* Kitchener, Ontario: Pandora Press, 2000, 236–256.

Boyer, Paul. *When Time Shall Be No More: Prophecy Belief in Modern American Culture.* Cambridge, MA: Belknap Press, 1992.

Clark, Victoria. *Allies for Armageddon: The Rise of Christian Zionism.* New Haven, CT: Yale University Press, 2007.

Cook, David. *Contemporary Muslim Apocalyptic Literature.* Syracuse, NY: Syracuse University Press, 2005.

Corsi, Jerome R. *Showdown with Nuclear Iran: Radical Islam's Messianic Mission to Destroy Israel and Cripple the United States.* Nashville: Nelson Current, 2006.

Daly, Bryan and Gregory M. Davis, producers. 2006. *Islam: What the West Needs to Know.* London: Quixotic Media.

Esfendiari, Goinaz. "Iran: President Says Light Surrounded Him During UN Speech." Radio Free Europe, November 29, 2005. http://www.rferl.org/content/article/1063353.html/

Exposed: The Extremist Agenda. Glenn Beck on CNN. No production information given, 2006. http://transcripts.cnn.com/TRANSCRIPTS/0611/15/gb.01.html.

Fandy, Mahmoun. *Saudi Arabia and the Politics of Dissent.* New York: St. Martins, 1999.

Ghadry, Farid. "Understanding the Importance of Laylat al-Sira'a [sic] and al-Mira'aj [sic]." http://www.apfn.net/MESSAGEBOARD/08-10-06/discussion.cgi.42.html. July 24, 2006.

Gorenberg, Gershom. *The End of Days: Fundamentalism and the Struggle for the Temple Mount.* Oxford, UK: Oxford University Press, 2000.

Greenwald, Glenn. "The Mainstream, Sane, Serious Joe Lieberman." *Salon,* July 26, 2007. http://www.commondreams.org/archive/2007/07/26/2786. Accessed June 22, 2012.

Hagee, John. *From Daniel to Doomsday: The Countdown Has Begun.* Nashville: Thomas Nelson, 1999.

Hagee, John. *The Battle for Jerusalem.* Nashville: Thomas Nelson, 2001.

Hagee, John. *Jerusalem Countdown: A Warning to the World.* Lake Mary, FL: Frontline, 2006.

John Hagee, "Jerusalem: Countdown to Crisis." In "Pastor John Hagee Discusses His Foundation Christians United for Israel and His Beliefs for the Last Days," Interview with Terry Gross, *Fresh Air,* National Public Radio, September 18, 2006.

Halsell, Grace. *Prophecy and Politics.* Westport, CT: Lawrence Hill & Company, 1986.

Hegghammer, Thomas and Stéphane Lacroix. "Rejectionist Islamism in Saudi Arabia: The Story of Juhayman al-Utaybi Revisited." *International Journal of Middle East Studies* 39.1 (2007): 103–122.

ICEJ (International Christian Embassy in Jerusalem), Malcolm Hedding, executive director. "Special ICEJ Release on Disengagement." July 21, 2005.

ICEJ (International Christian Embassy in Jerusalem). "Proclamation of the 3rd International Christian Zionist Conference," February 29, 1996, available at http://christianactionforisrael.org/congress.html. Accessed August 13, 2011.

Islamic Republic of Iran Broadcasting (IRIB). "The World toward Illumination." Tehran, 2006–2007.

Kechichian, Joseph A. "The Role of the Ulema in the Politics of an Islamic State: The Case of Saudi Arabia." *International Journal of Middle Eastern Studies* 18.1 (1986): 53–71.

Kechichian, Joseph A. "Islamic Revivalism and Change in Saudi Arabia: Juhayman al-Utaybi's 'Letters' to the Saudi People." *Muslim World* 86 (1990): 1–16.

LaHaye, Tim and Jerry B. Jenkins. *Apollyon.* Carol Stream, IL: Tyndale House, 1999.

LaHaye, Tim and Jerry B. Jenkins. *Glorious Appearing.* Carol Stream, IL: Tyndale House, 2004.

Lawrence, Bruce, Ed. *Messages to the World: The Statements of Osama bin Laden.* London: Verso, 2005.

Ledeen, Michael. "Iran with the Bomb, or Bomb Iran: The Need for Regime Change" (2007). Online Encyclopaedia Brittanica Blog.

Levitt, Zola. "Israel, Earth's Lightning Rod," part 3. *Levitt Letter*. November 1996, http://www.levit.com/essays/foreshocks.html. Accessed August 12, 2011.

Levitt, Zola. "Enter the Antichrist (Part II)." *Levitt Letter*. March 2001, http://www.levitt.com/newsletters/2001–03.html#FOURTH. Accessed August 12, 2011.

Lewis, Bernard. "Does Iran Have Something in Store?" *Wall Street Journal*, August 8, 2006.

Lindsey, Hal. *The Late Great Planet Earth*. London: Lakeland, 1970.

Lindsey, Hal. *There's a New World Coming*. Santa Ana, CA: Vision House, 1973.

Lindsey, Hal. *The 1980's: Countdown to Armageddon*. New York: Bantam, 1981.

Lindsey, Hal. *The Final Battle*. Palos Verdes, CA: Western Front, 1995.

Lindsey, Hal. *Planet Earth: The Final Chapter*. Beverly Hills, CA: Western Front, 1998.

Marsden, George M. *Fundamentalism and American Culture*. New York: Oxford University Press, 2006.

Ministry Watch, "John Hagee Ministries/Global Evangelism Television," http://www.ministrywatch.com/profile/John-Hagee-Ministries.aspx. Accessed April 26, 2010.

Missler, Chuck. Undated. "Sights and Speakers." In Chuck Missler, "BBC TWO—Wonderland 'The End of the World Bus Tour': The Real Story." http://www.endoftheworldbustour.com/speakers.html. Accessed August 12, 2011.

Morris, Benny. "Using Bombs to Stave Off War." *New York Times*, July 18, 2008.

Netanyahu, Benjamin. Interviewed by Glenn Beck. *Glenn Beck*, November 17, 2006.

Poole, Francis. "Ahmedinejad's Apocalyptic Beliefs." *FrontPageMag.com*. August 17, 2006.

Rosenberg, Joel. *The Ezekiel Option*. Carol Stream, IL: Tyndale House, 2005.

Rosenberg, Joel. *Epicenter: Why Current Rumblings in the Middle East Will Change Your Future*. Carol Stream, IL: Tyndale House, 2006.

Rosenberg, Joel. "Iran Sobered Us Up on New Years: A Message of Nuclear Proportions." *National Review Online*, January 3, 2007. http://www.nationalreview.com/articles/219632/iran-sobered-us-new-years/joel-c-rosenberg#.

Sahih Muslim, Kitab Al-Fitan, Book 41. http://www.cmje.org/religious-texts/hadith/muslim/041-smt.php

Sells, Michael A. "War as Worship, Worship as War," *Religion and Culture Forum*, University of Chicago Divinity School, December 2006. http://divinity.uchicago.edu/martycenter/publications/webforum/122006/commentary.shtml.

Shore, Raphael. Producer. *Obsession: Radical Islam's War Against the West*. New York: Honest Reporting, 2006.

Sizer, Stephen. *Christian Zionism: Road Map to Armageddon?* Leicester, UK: Inter-Varsity Press, 2004.

Spencer, Robert. "Iran's Day of Terror?" *FrontPageMag.com*.,July 27, 2006.

Trofimov, Jaroslav. *The Siege of Mecca: The Forgotten Uprising at Islam's Holiest Shrine and the Birth of Al Qaeda*. New York: Doubleday, 2007.

Walwoord, John. *Israel in Prophecy*. Grand Rapids, MI: Zondervan, 1962.

Weaver, Alain Epp, ed. *Under Vine and Fig Tree: Biblical Theologies of Land and the Palestinian-Israeli Conflict*. Telford, PA: Cascadia, 2007.

Weber, Timothy. *On the Road to Armageddon: How Evangelicals Became Israel's Best Friend*. Grand Rapids, MI: Baker Academic, 2007.

"World Toward Illumination," Islamic Republic of Iran Broadcasting network, http://english.irib.ir/.

CHAPTER 34

PHENOMENAL VIOLENCE AND THE PHILOSOPHY OF RELIGION

HENT DE VRIES

THERE is little doubt that recent decennia have seen a turn from the reflection on violence from its brute empirical (physical, psychological, and political) features and impact, via its more abstract and nonempirical ("transcendental") conditions, spelled out in metaphysical or ontological terms, to what I would like to call here its phenomenal concreteness, content, and form. Violence and notably religious violence as it manifests itself in the current day and age of global markets and media—as a surrounding element and an integral aspect of global religion, it turns out—stands out by its excessiveness, on the one hand, and by its novel, at times quite elusive, modes of manifestation, on the other. Phenomenologically speaking, violence now reveals different traits of religion or, in any case, shows them—and, thereby, global religion, religion as a "total social fact"—in an altogether unexpected, unprecedented, and different light.

Philosophical approaches, coming out of the tradition of the so-called phenomenological school of thought and drawing on—as well as critically distancing themselves from—the writings of Edmund Husserl, Martin Heidegger, and their most influential interpreters (Jean-Paul Sartre and Emmanuel Levinas among them), have provided the theoretical vocabulary to bring this striking aspect of violence into full view. And even where the presuppositions of this school of thought (phenomenology) are not shared per se, thinkers, among them philosophers of religion, have remained fascinated with the phenomenal aspect of religious violence as it manifests itself under current global conditions. By this, I mean the age of new technological media and ever-expanding economic markets, each developments that have dramatically altered the structure of communication and commerce and, thus, the nature—substance and form, in any case, the general perception and overall effect—of empirical and nonempirical violence, including religious violence as such.

All this is not to suggest that the current interest in and fascination with violence is primarily or exclusively oriented toward its most remarkable and extraordinary—phenomenal, in the sense of extreme—manifestations (for instance, suicide bombings and terror attacks, shock and awe, to say nothing of foreign assassinations via drone missiles perpetrated by individuals and groups as nonstate actors, on the one hand, or ordered and condoned by national states and international agreements, on the other). Nor am I claiming that the violence in question is phenomenal, meaning "deeply subjective," based on non- or counterexperiences of a strikingly immediate—affective and often traumatic—in any case, deeply impressive nature that eludes (present) thoughts, that is to say, concepts and knowledge, but can be intuited or sensed and testified to nonetheless. While these two aspects of fascination with extremes and subjective impressiveness may play a role in most discussed cases, I take the term *phenomenal* to indicate a radically new mode of manifestation (appearance, apparition, indeed, revelation) that has not found the attention in philosophy, notably the philosophy of religion, it so clearly deserves.

Finally, the theme and problem of violence has received some of its most innovative and rigorous analyses, if not explanations, in the philosophical accounts that we tend to associate with the phenomenological school of thought and the discourses that—mostly critically—built on it (philosophical hermeneutics, deconstruction, neopragmatism, among them). After all, one of the meanings of the adjective *phenomenal* is "relating to a phenomenon." And phenomena need not be excessive, nor are they limited to subjective perception alone.

What, then, does it mean to say that violence, including or perhaps a fortiori religious violence, is—or has (once again, perhaps, for the first time in the most original of ways) become—a phenomenon and quite some phenomenon, as we colloquially say? Moreover, in what respect do the present economic and technological, media-driven conditions under which global religion must operate (just as much as it—global religion—no doubt, also contributes to these driving historical and cultural factors, in turn), reflect or inflect this social and eminently political, theologico–political phenomenon under consideration? More precisely, what characterizes its at once saturated and negative aspects, each of which, as we will see, captures part of the meaning of *global* (as in global religion) that interests us here?

In the present contribution, I would like to provide one example of a philosophy— a philosophy of religion, on all counts—starting out from an author, namely Jacques Derrida, whose writings on metaphysics or religion and violence have occupied me in different contexts and to whose crucial type of questioning I keep returning. I would claim that ever since Derrida introduced the theme of violence in his reading of Claude Lévi-Strauss—the second pivotal thinker in the history of structuralism (after Ferdinand de Saussure), with whom he would take critical issue at a time this movement was still on the rise—this topic has not ceased to inspire and haunt his writing, even where it went unmentioned in explicit terms. Indeed, this very indirectness raises an important issue: Perhaps violence is mostly and best spoken of obliquely, as if bringing it directly in front of our eyes merely creates a false illusion of mastery, the vain hope of circumscribing, localizing, and, thus, containing it here and there? After all, violence, even where it manifests itself most extensively and intensively—expanding to global proportions, as it were—also has the tendency to retreat into the finest mazes of the web that makes up social relations, taking refuge in the vaguest and most common notions and sentiments, just as it can inflate into tragic and dramatic proportions whose measure we can still not fully fathom.

More consistently than any contemporary thinker, Derrida has taught us that while violence is not all (there is), it looms everywhere and at all moments without reprieve. And while the ethical and political perspective from which this is claimed has emphatic—that is, infinitizing, even messianic—aspirations (not unlike the thought of an Emmanuel Levinas with whom Derrida felt increasingly close), it is a messianic aspiration without hope, without eschatology (as Derrida, in his earlier reading of Levinas in "Violence and Metaphysics," did not fail to point out as a logical consequence of this author's affirmation that religion is the very relation to an other that does not close itself off in a totality). Such aspiration retains the "spirit" of messianic movements and critiques, not their content per se. Its "messianicity without messianism" (as the later Derrida would often phrase it) is the at once formal (i.e., structural, generic) and concrete (i.e., historical, pragmatic) index of a more general phenomenon, its formal indication, as it were (to use the technical jargon that Martin Heidegger introduces in *Phenomenology of Religious Life*, his famous lecture on "Phenomenology and Theology" and, most importantly, in *Being and Time*, but not much beyond this relatively early period of his teaching and writing).

Before drawing some general conclusions as to what Derrida contributes specifically to our understanding of the intimate relationship between religion and violence, testimony and sacrifice, and more specifically of, phenomenal violence—to be distinguished from the "performance" violence that scholars, notably Mark Juergensmeyer, have rightfully highlighted in recent years—let me begin with a broad outline of the genesis and structure of Derrida's overall thinking, writing, and interpretative praxis.[1]

FIDELITY AND VIOLENCE

We need to begin by asking what receiving a thought—Derrida's or any other—must necessarily assume, not so much in terms of some principle of interpretative charity, nor because of the inevitable selectiveness that any such interpretation brings with it, but in light of the sheer historical and more than simply historical—indeed, near-ontological—weight that these kind of questions assume. For it is here, already, that the theoretical problem and practical reality of violence announces itself, well before it phenomenologizes itself in the phenomenal manifestations (of mostly events, both salutary and averse) that interrupt and reshape—and, as it were, re-create and reorient—our contemporary world.

As Derrida said and wrote so often: To be faithful to an author's oeuvre, to a legacy, a tradition, a thought and practice inevitably requires one to be unfaithful to it as well. To follow in its footsteps, to respect the moves it made and continues to make, the traces it left and leaves, one must, precisely, go beyond its original formulation and, as it were, forget its historical location and situatedness, its genesis and thesis, its intended and accumulated meaning and audience, in short, its effective history, its *Wirkungsgeschichte*.

Such a reading, then, must be systematic and constructive, establishing new connections, discerning new affiliations where there seemed none (or merely other, known ones), not just exegetical or hermeneutic. The reading must explore and engage the archive of the work, author, and thought in question and not limit itself to a documentary retrospective alone.

To turn or return to an oeuvre and everything it inaugurates and condensates (Derrida goes on to meditate on the ways he has turned to authors that inspired, intrigued, or troubled him), one must also, inevitably and simultaneously, turn against it, displacing its original horizon and supplementing whatever sense, reference, and overall impact its author or authors may originally have had in mind. One can, must, and ought not mechanically reproduce or repeat its first form and strict content, let alone assign their future significance to the mere automatic execution of whatever programmatic outlines one falsely assumes it had.

Paradoxically, even to repeat or, as Derrida says, reiterate an oeuvre's singular idiom, fundamental concepts, and overall arguments, purpose, and style—in order to help it live on (*survivre*)—implies that one changes its putative intent and meaning, direction and reference, and, thereby, inevitably exposes it to distortion and misunderstanding, abuse and betrayal. Iterability—and no text, work, or act would extend and supplement itself without it—entails repetition plus change, an at least nonformal tautology, and does so at the risk of parody (insincerity, theatricality but also idolatry, blasphemy, profanity, and all their known analogues). In being right on target, as one explicates authors and texts, ideas and arguments, ideas and figures of speech, one is always already and ever so slightly off as well. This has profound philosophical and theological implications.

As Derrida often says with reference to Levinas, one of the teachers who inspired and influenced him in so many remarkable ways: the turn "to God" (in French, *à Dieu*)—and nothing less than quasidivine and religious infinity orients ethical responsibility, including the responsibility that comes with "reading" and receiving a text, an oeuvre—implies a no less decisive leavetaking or farewell (in French, *adieu*) from this singular name, general concept, and peculiar figure (i.e., God) as well as from everything else this name (concept, figure) historically and presently stands for or may still come to address and represent, evoke and symbolize in the near or distant future (de Vries 1999, 2000).

Derrida analyzed the inevitability of the betrayal inherent in even the most faithful pronunciation of a name or rendering of a thought nowhere more clearly than in his 1983 letter to a Japanese friend and translator, Izutsu, where he mused about the etymology, meaning, and fate as well as possible misunderstanding of the term and notion that organized his own oeuvre from beginning to end, namely *deconstruction* (Derrida 2008). The latter term, he noted, although it had imposed itself spontaneously and proved itself of good use in reorienting the Heideggerian conception of so-called *Destruktion*, just as it had been helpful in redirecting the more problematic assumptions and theoretical matrix of classical structuralism, was ultimately not a "satisfactory" name, word, or concept. No word or concept ever is. Yet, the difficulty the chosen term *deconstruction* (or, for that matter, any of its related terms, such as the *trace, Difference* with a capital *d, différance, pharmakon, pragrammatology,* etc.) imposed on translators and interpreters offered as many philosophical or semantic-pragmatic openings as it introduced risks, some of them fatal. The overhasty and thoughtless identification of deconstruction with some negative or skeptical operation or, worse, with, for example, postmodernism or even post- or neostructuralism being cases in point.[2]

Derrida also urged that we do not let ourselves be bogged down by these difficulties, which belong to the heart of the matter that *deconstruction* names. Instead, we should realize that we cannot but use the conceptual and metaphorical or rhetorical tools of tradition and modernity, including those of some of their failed overcomings, to dislodge these same tools' most stifling—dogmatic and unreflective, superstitious and dreamlike, in any case, unconscious—grip on our thoughts, judgments, and conduct. There would be no point in pretending that we could somehow leave them behind by one stroke (or should have that vain ambition in the first place). And to opt for altogether different terms and words, names and concepts, whether drawn from the age-old archives or from newly instituted ones, would merely reintroduce the same difficulty. Again, not even the most accurate and literal as well as genuine and subtle translation—into French, for example—escapes this predicament, which forms the element, exercise, and experimentation of language and thought. Its gesture toward getting it right, in the endless attempts that it takes, must also—still—get it wrong.

To conclude that such an infinite task of what is, at bottom, an impossible and interminable process of translation—of what Derrida, early on, called the work of "nonsynonymous substitution," "paleonymics"—has all the fateful reminiscences of "a type of negative theology," whose true inheritor and modern representative it may well be; to say that the translation of *deconstruction* (indeed, deconstruction as translation) is thus deeply steeped into the legacy of religious tradition and notably mysticism (Christian, Jewish, and, who knows, other), that is to say, of legacies, whose metaphysics of presence it must nonetheless seek to displace—all this is somewhat precipitous. This is not to say that such claim is false. On closer scrutiny, it would be neither true nor false.

But the historical and formal parallel between deconstruction and so-called apophatic of mystical theology is far from fortuitous and, in fact, extremely useful. Recent attempts to reclaim some form of atheism or radical atheism for Derrida's overall project are, in my view, as misguided as the earlier contrary attempts to domesticate his writings for confessional and apologetic purposes. They simply miss the point that his writings made time and again in the clearest of possible ways, namely the fact that neither classical theism nor modern atheism, neither metaphysical presentism nor even mystical apophatics, fully captures the overall aims and methods of reading and thinking that deconstruction both observes and formalizes.

As so often in these matters, things are far more complicated. Even if Derrida has not always chosen to change the traditional or contemporary terms of debate—drawing on the vocabularies the distinctive positions of theology and the critique of religion invent or invoke—he has definitely altered our way of identifying, opposing, or relating their regulating concepts and figures in the most productive of ways. His contribution to understanding violence, including religious violence—and, notably, the phenomenal violence that accompanies so-called global religions in an age of expanding markets and new technological media—is a case in point.

SOME MINIMAL BACKGROUND

Born in El Biar, Algeria, in 1930, Derrida received his academic education at the École Normale Supérieure, rue d'Ulm, in Paris, where in 1963 he took up a teaching position at the invitation of Louis Althusser. Over the years, Derrida further held positions as professor at several American universities (Johns Hopkins; Yale; Cornell; University of California, Irvine; New York University) as well as, from 1984 onward, as *directeur d'études* at the École des Hautes Études en Sciences Sociales in Paris. He was a founding director of the Collège International de Philosophie, in 1983, a cofounder of the Association Jan Hus (which supported intellectuals and offered clandestine seminars in Communist Prague), and received the Adorno Prize in 2001. He died in 2004.

As the most influential representative of the so-called deconstructive praxis of reading foundational Western philosophical and literary texts, introduced and exemplarily demonstrated by the simultaneous publication, in 1967, of *L'écriture et la différence*, *La voix et le phénomène*, and *De la grammatologie*, Derrida played an influential role as a groundbreaking thinker, on the one hand, and a patient and extremely devoted teacher and mentor, on the other. His many scholarly publications were often distilled from his widely attended public seminars (the manuscripts of which are now appearing in print posthumously in numerous volumes), whose themes and concerns were mostly prompted by specific occasions (the so-called Jerusalem lecture on apophatic, negative theology, titled "Comment ne pas parler. Dénégations"—but also his lectures on James Joyce, Paul Celan, as well as his dialogues with Jean-Luc Nancy and Jean-Luc Marion—being cases in point).

Only late in his career and more or less reluctantly did Derrida come to accept the role of a public French intellectual whose views, expressed in elaborate and meticulously edited interviews and rare signed petitions, were accompanied by repeated urges not to judge too hastily, to acknowledge and assess the complex and often contradictory injunctions imposed by historical, institutional, and especially juridical contexts as well as by ordinary no less than exceptional ethical and political decisions, their implications, unintended effects, and the like. A significant example is his dialogue and joint public intervention with Jürgen Habermas in the wake of the 9/11 attacks in the United States in 2001, with regard to the definition and consequences of international terrorism (first published in English under the title *Philosophy in a Time of Terror*; Derrida 2003), the fateful interventionist policies against so-called rogue states (*états voyous*) implemented in its wake, and the urgent need for a common European international and military policy that would allow Western democracies—perhaps, even "an other Europe," that is to say, a "Europe to come"—to move beyond economic protectionism, while continuing to counterbalance and refuse, at least, two models: "the politics of American hegemony" but also "an Arab-Islamic theocratism without Enlightenment and without political future" (Derrida 2007: 41). With regard to these two dominant models—and they are far from being the only troubling ones (as semibiological, familial-fraternalist invocations of a politics of "friendship" but also the regimes of Stalinist socialism, the state-capitalist venture of Chinese "communism," and the "disastrous and suicidal politics of Israel—and of a certain Zionism" (Derrida 2007, 39), all testify in singular ways)—Derrida hastens to add that we should "not minimize the contradictions, the processes underway" and "join forces with those who resist from within these two blocs" as well as, we might add, from within all others (Derrida 2007: 41).

In all this, the direction of Derrida's inquiry and engagement seem clear: When it comes to democracy, a variety of alternative models and examples must be explored, in addition to further strengthening our allegiance and fidelity to the principles, if not always practices, of the "good old *Aufklärung*." Likewise, "in certain situations," we must and ought to continue to be faithful to a certain "we"—as in "*nous les juifs*" and also "*nous les français*"—which, in the specific case of Israel, despite all expressed reservations, Derrida confesses, means also the fidelity towards a singular "judeity" (Derrida 2007: 35) that he, for his part, would never deny.

THREE AXES

Three major theoretical axes in Derrida's interrogation underlying and framing these more political—or should we say, theologicopolitical—issues as they relate to the specter of violence can be distinguished. They concern the "mystical foundation of authority" and the enforcement of the rule of law in legal decision and jurisprudence; the problem of sovereignty and the expansive interpretation of individual or human rights in the wake of globalization or (as Derrida writes with a telling neologism, underscoring a certain Christian, more precisely, Roman Catholic legacy) of "globalatinization (*mondialatinization*)"; and the nonregulative idea of a democracy always still to come (*démocratie-à-venir*), whose single or multiple origins and ultimate referent cannot and ought not be approached in a piecemeal way, step by step, that is to say, incrementally and asymptotically (as progressive liberalism and reform socialism tend to do). Rather, like the demand for infinite justice, the idea of democracy always still or forever to come imposes itself unconditionally and with the greatest urgency, regardless of time and place, even though it also calls for its immediate (rather than merely subsequent or secondary) mediation, negotiation, and limited distribution and, thus, painful compromise in matters of peace and fairness. All the elements and forms of betrayal that fidelity requires imply a pragmatics but one whose paradox—perhaps, aporia—only a "*programmatology*," as Derrida calls it playfully, enables us to study in all necessary rigor and detail.

Now, all these three axes touch on a quasireligious—and, when taken in isolation or when kept unchecked, potentially violent—motif as well as motivation of structural "messianicity," which Derrida, from *Spectres de Marx* (*Specters of Marx*) onward, takes great pains to distinguish from the all too concrete and idolatrous political messianisms and political theologies that have punctuated and structured the history of the West in its feudal and industrial, colonial as well as postcolonial phases. These messianisms have acquired renewed actuality in the age of global economic markets and new technological media that accompany and enable them (and that are perhaps inspired and produced as well as provoked and resisted, even used, by them in turn).

While these twentieth- and twenty-first-century global phenomena have empowered religious traditions and spiritual movements to reclaim a decidedly public—global—role, thus falsifying the modern assumption of a linear and unidirectional, increasing process of secularization, rationalization, and privatization, Derrida puts much effort into analyzing their deep ambiguity (i.e., their potential for the worst no less than the best). As to the role claimed by these "public religions of the modern world" (to use José Casanova's expression), Derrida stresses their fundamental paradox and aporetics, which reveals them to be at once exponents and opponents of the central features of what are, admittedly, increasingly differentiated societies in the West and inevitably elsewhere. It is this ambiguity, besides much else, that turns so-called global religions into symptoms and vehicles of both great promise and perennial danger.

THE CRITIQUE OF VIOLENCE

The first aforementioned axis finds its first full expression in Derrida's interpretation of Walter Benjamin's *Zur Kritik der Gewalt* (*Critique of Violence*) against the background of a dictum, drawn from Pascal and Montaigne, which stated that justice and force presuppose or require each other. Take one in isolation and the other reverts into its opposite (powerless idealism or moralism, on the one hand, sheer, brutal might without right, on the other). Refining his earlier, somewhat elliptical remarks on the performative structure of the American Declaration of Independence (but the appeal to the idea of, say, Europe or perestroika functions no differently), Derrida here resumes a central motif that traverses political thought from Rousseau through Michel de Certeau's studies of seventeenth-century mysticism all the way up to contemporary theories of political liberalism and radical democracy: the idea that the foundation and condition of legitimacy cannot itself be *legitimated* in the same (or any) juridical terms and modes of justification whose normative power and legal procedures it calls into being and sustain in its dynamics, its capacity for renewal. The function once taken by the mythical, foreign lawgiver is thus depersonalized—defamiliarized and disincarnated—and, from here on, ascribed to an empty place, signifier or, as Derrida, with reference to Pascal and Montaigne, says, "postulate," the "mystical foundation of authority."[3]

Derrida speaks of an unconditional affirmation, an absolute performative, whose contours—and success—are not established, much less warranted by any preexisting conditions and whose "act"—if we follow the theory of speech acts formulated by J. L. Austin and, at a distance, John Searle—is, literally or technically, no speech act at all. Neither speech nor acting, *stricto sensu*, is among its essential features. Instead, we are dealing with what is an always fallible, potentially self-contradictory and self-undermining, address or gesture—or, as Derrida proposes, "perverformative"—at most. Behind and well beyond the historical and systematic abyss of the infinite and indefinite that the postulation of the mystical foundation of all authority assumes, a profound lack of original or final justification opens up under any subsequent decision that refounds, that is to say reaffirms or reinvents, the polity (or so-called body politic) and thus protects and maintains its sovereignty. This abysmal lack of reasons at the inception and heart of Western (or any other) order and concept of reason is the source of its contestation, self-criticism, its democratic ideal and process. Needless to say, it is a standing possibility and perhaps necessary threat of its illegitimacy and abuse, terror and demise as well. That this is so is no small price to pay, but it is a risk we should and must freely wage. The possibility of the worst is the condition of the best.

Religion and Its Dual Source

The second axis of Derrida's work is introduced in *Foi et savoir: Les deux sources de la "religion" aux limites de la simple raison* ("Faith and Knowledge: The Two Sources of 'Religion' at the Limits of Reason Alone"), published in 1996, and condenses his related conviction that recent processes of internationalization and capitalization, induced by ever-faster modes of communication and their virtually omnipresent technological media, cannot be appropriately understood without taking into account a certain imaginative and iconic hegemony resulting directly from the history of religions. Derrida's reference is here, first of all, to the so-called Abrahamic religions and a question remains how other, for example, non-Western religions (such as Hinduism, Buddhism, Confucianism, etc.) alter the picture as they are likewise affected by expanse of markets and invasive media and construe— or reconstrue—alternative modernities that have not only much deeper historical roots but that may well come to compete with the self-image in which the West has sought to shape the world (and whose "de-Europeanization," to cite Levinas, may well be imminent).

Derrida associates this self-image's influence and fateful dominance first of all with Rome (hence, once again, the Latin in this most suggestive among his neologisms, namely *mondialatinisation,* "globalatinization"). Just as he had earlier, in *Specters of Marx,* detected a troubling neoevangelical tendency in the neoconservative views about the post-1989 "victories" of American-style capitalism and liberalism, so also his attention to the role of media in modern religion, in "Faith and Knowledge" and *Surtout pas des journalistes!* (Above All No Journalists!), invokes the *"nouvelles nouvelles"* of the globalized religion and its televised "miracles" as a deeply ambiguous "gospel" that curves social spaces and warps our sense of temporality in ways that are not always inspiring or liberating but also potentially threatening to the "living together" that democracy both requires and calls for.

These considerations—more urgent than ever—respond to what Derrida calls the "strange alliance of [Graeco-Roman, but especially Latin, HdV] Christianity, as the experience of the Death of God, and tele-technoscientific capitalism" (Derrida 1998 1998: 13). The term *mondialatinisation* captures the old-new and new-old taken as a total social phenomenon and one that is "at the same time hegemonic *and* finite, ultra-powerful *and* in the process of exhausting itself" (Derrida 1998: 13).

Yet, deconstructing this predominantly Christian legacy does not mean overcoming it for good or in toto, let alone by one stroke, but assigning it—therapeutically and in the spirit of an assertive, yet nondoctrinal "republicanism"—within certain limits, deflating its pretension, while affirming its "spirit" and perhaps the more genuine among its remaining aspirations. With the same gesture, "deconstructing Christianity" (to adopt the term for a project that Jean-Luc Nancy has made his own, in *La déclosion,* and that Derrida salutes in *Le toucher*), means to liberate the lasting potential of this religion's semantic and rhetorical, imaginative and affective archive, within the context of a liberal and parliamentary democracy as well as literary culture in which anyone should, in principle, be allowed to think and say or write just about anything and do so publicly, thus emancipating religion, together with its political theologies and supposed secular analogues, from dogmatism and obscurantism, authoritarianism and extremism.

Further, deconstructing Christianity means to relieve religion (or whatever comes to take its place) from *doxa,* if not necessarily from faith, even less from the faith that Derrida, following Kant, calls "reflective." On the contrary, the latter forms the dimension that—like "messianicity"—is irreducible to the historical "messianisms" and that resembles the "spirit of Marxism" (as *Specters of Marx* has it) that is, likewise, invulnerable to the withering away of its ontological and economic theses and historical predictions and, thus, keeps the political (*le politique*) and politics (*la politique*) open for the "always already and always still to come." This would hold true, first and foremost, for "democracy," but, mutatis mutandis, the same could also be claimed for the idea of "another Europe," of "America," and, we might add, for a secular "Zionism" not yet (or no longer) perverted by the oppressive practices unworthy of its original concept and practice.

Geo- and Theologicopolitics

The third axis is the topic of *Voyous* (*Rogues*), which attempts to dislodge the theological-political premises, the concept, of sovereignty and seeks a new figure beyond any appeal to a quasibiological notion of filiation, whether of the Christian, ecclesial *corpus mysticum* (whose genealogy was unearthed by Henri de Lubac and, in his footsteps, Ernst Kantorowicz) or of the modern revolutionary and postrevolutionary appeal to brotherhood (whose deconstruction forms an explicit theme in Derrida's own *Politiques de l'amitié*). The place and function of the body politic, as community and nation, is taken here by a reinterpreted *demos*, now no longer seen as the fuller expression of a distinct population, people, or even greater humanity but as "*at once* the incalculable singularity of anyone, before any 'subject,' ... beyond all citizenship, beyond every 'state,' indeed every 'people,' indeed even beyond the current state of the definition of a living being as living 'human' being, *and* the universality of rational calculation, of the equality of citizens before the law, the social bond of being together, with or without contract" (Derrida 2003: 120).

This composite—and deeply paradoxical, even aporetic—idea of a reinterpreted *demos* is tied to notions of power, force, and justification that are not so much identified with instinctual social pressure or formal legality but with a concept of justice whose infinity and urgency are distinguished from the supposed asymptotic approximations of regulative, if counterfactual, ideas adopted by political and procedural liberalism and exemplified, for instance, by the work of John Rawls and Jürgen Habermas. The far more emphatic notion of a never present— i.e., nonpresentable and never merely representational—"democracy to come" could, in full rigor, not even claim the designation of a *political regime,* in any of the classical and modern senses of that phrase. Instead, democracy and a fortiori "democracy to come" calls out for alternative forms of social and cultural, juridical and political alliance for which the appeal to a "new international" (*Specters Marx*) or to an emerging movement towards so-called alterglobalism—together with the old and new senses of a "hospitality" taken by its word—may not be such bad images after all.

NEITHER NATURAL NOR MADE UP

Along these three axes, Derrida not only insists on an indelible legacy of the metaphysical tradition of Western thought, imbued as it is with theology (political and other), he also pays minute attention to the ways in which concepts and discourses on laws and rights, subjects and citizens, duties and values remain shot through by a certain problematic fictionality or literariness that was never alien to the narrative structure of religion, myth, and mysticism. The "mystical foundation" of all authority is as much a "fable," as Michel de Certeau already knew, as it is a "postulate," that is to say, a theoretical proposition for which no proof or empirical warrant can be provided and whose noncriteriological status is that a of "passionate utterance" (Stanley Cavell) first and foremost. As such, the mystic fable and postulate of authority express the disturbing, yet also strangely liberating, circumstance and insight that the foundations of sovereignty and nation, people or community, law and jurisprudence, politics and policies are neither based on natural facts and simple givens nor simply made up.

The latter point is important to underscore. Derrida's position is neither that of Nietzsche's perspectivism nor of Hans Vaihinger's fictionalism nor, for that matter, does he accept the narrativist and fundamentally identitarian or communitarian accounts of cultural relativism. While at odds with the general tendencies of so-called postmodernism (or, for that matter, any other postism, *posthistoire*, posthumanism, poststructuralism, and the like), emphasizing instead his undiminished sympathy for the "good old *Aufklärung*" and the increasing need for a new one, Derrida's analyses instead call for a relentless interrogation of modern conceptions of citizenship and freedom, self-determination and human rights, the public and the private, all of them notions whose stability and historical demarcations he considers deeply questionable and in need of constant revaluation and reformulation.[4]

Yet their amelioration and perfectibility in view of a strong notion of justice and infinite responsibility, if not absolute hospitality, are the expression not of their obsolescence but merely of their provisional character, of their fallibility and pervertibility. The willingness and possibility to discuss such internal or even transcendental historicity, Derrida claims, characterizes the notion of a democracy, which remains forever "to come" and whose public self-criticism must be protected by laws making sure that its corrective and ameliorative process—again, its perfectibility—must be considered as open, and this ad infinitum. And while justice and infinite responsibility, unconditional hospitality, together with "democracy to come," do not constitute immediately applicable politicojuridical concepts—let alone down-to-earth practical policy directives—per se, no finite, conditional, empirical responsibilities concerning rights and laws, acts and decisions, administrative measures or common sense would be thinkable, responsible, or possible without them. Thinking the ethical and the political—and, more in particular, engaging oneself morally and pragmatically—thus entails the simultaneous

invocation of two heterogeneous, irreducible, yet indissociable aspects and realities whose relationship, Derrida insists, remains nonconclusive—paradoxical,
aporetic—to be decided in an infinite series (or *sériature*) of singular instances,
that is to say, case by case, time and again.

The Virtual Repository
of the Religious Archive

My central claim would be that for this relationship to be thought through but also
for it to be experienced and experimented with in its all its philosophical and spiritual, practical and aesthetic repercussions, we have to "turn to religion." No historical (and more than simply genealogical or merely documentary) archive offers
richer conceptual and argumentative (rhetorical and imaginative, motivational
and affective) resources than that of religion and theology, including apophatics
and mysticism whose shared legacy constitutes a virtual repository for the powerful expression and precise articulation of the greatest possible variety of questions
and problems, acts and affects.

For all his reservation as to their dogmatic content and institutional legacies,
tainted as they are (as all archives must be) by symbolical and empirical violence—
which, moreover, is a predicament from which not even the silence or counter-
discourses of mysticism and heterodoxy can fully escape—Derrida meditates
incessantly on religion's semantic, figural, and spiritual resilience to the often justified and fair, even fatal, objections that have been leveled against it by the most
lucid and vigilent among philosophers and critics and this nowhere more eloquently
and subtly than by the modern institutions or counterinstitutions called the university and literature. The writings of a James Joyce and Franz Kafka, Paul Celan
and Maurice Blanchot, Jean Genet and Antonin Artaud are invoked in this second
respect, whereas others are relatively or virtually absent: Marcel Proust and Samuel
Beckett come to mind. The first reference to the university, by contrast, bases itself,
first of all, on Kant, especially on his *Streit der fakultäten* (*Conflict of Faculties*),
although other signpostings of the same—earlier and later—problematic of academic learning and the concept of reason abound throughout Derrida's writings.

In retrospect, Derrida's remarkable relation not so much to metaphysics or
ontotheology generally (where he seems to be mostly on the side of Heidegger at
a certain stage of his career and consistently read against the grain), but to "religion" (a term he largely adopts in its Levinasian definition as epitomizing the
"relation to the Other and that does not close itself off in a totality") is thus anything but straightforward, but instead punctuated by an "originary affirmation"
and repeated "denials [*dénégations*]" that keep each other in and off balance in a
nuanced, if paradoxical, and, ultimately, aporetic way. This is not to say that this
rhythm of thinking, acting, and judging is aporetic as such or in its essence. As he

demonstrates in *Apories*, not even the notion of aporia can be thought consistently in its purity and is, therefore, itself "aporetic" of sorts.

What general lessons, then, could be drawn from this peculiar insight, which, we now know, is not so much an understanding of the nature of unintelligibility or the aporetic—of some nonformal variety of asserting *p* and ~*p*, per se—but the more modest awareness that there is principal and residual, marginal or sublimi-nal, minimal unintelligibility wherever we turn? How do these lessons affect the central themes (notably, religion and the theologico-political) that determine the concept of violence in so many ways?

Perhaps we should say this. More than anyone else of his generation, Derrida has taught us that the distinction and often opposition between tradition and moder-nity, between the thinking of infinity and of finitude, theism and atheism, orthodoxy and heterodoxy, theology and idolatry, prayer and blasphemy—in short, between our being either on the "inside" or the "outside" of the historical legacy and its contesta-tions—is, on closer scrutiny, no longer pertinent and perhaps never was. As oppo-sites, the terms that make up these conceptual pairs should no longer be seen as alternatives, as positions that could be held in isolation, at will or upon reflection.

As a matter of metaphysical no less than historical fact, archival layers from our past and present—and *a fortiori* those expressive or reminiscent of religion—are intimately interwoven, impossible to disentangle, even and especially in so-called secular and postsecular times and ages. Elements from the older strata well and surge up and recede again, just as in a world of global media the old and the new are more and more prompted and propelled, not only to intersect and change places, but to the point of becoming virtually indistinguishable from each other.

There is a remarkable consequence of this observation that we have only begun to slowly realize and live up to, namely that certain habitual patterns of temporal and spatial separation, of the now and then, here and there—perhaps even of cause and effect, of what comes supposedly first and what after—simply no longer obtain in full rigor, if ever they did. As Derrida rightly observes: "One can be the 'anach-ronistic' contemporary of a past or future 'generation'" (Derrida 2007: 27).

THE LAST AND THE LEAST

No better illustration of this far-ranging insight than Derrida's provocative claim, in the semiautobiographical text called "Circumfession," devoted to Saint Augustine, namely, that he considered, confessed himself to be—and follow ("*je suis*")—"*le dernier des juifs*," that is to say, the last and least of the Jews. He was thereby sug-gesting that, wherever the question of the historical or cultural archive and legacy is at issue (which is to say, virtually everywhere), one must and should affirm to be the latest in line, in the sense being the intellectually, ethically, even spiritually most astute and advanced of its witnesses, while at the same time assuming the risk of having, in one's reception of and borrowing from tradition, also misunderstood and perverted, what, in this same tradition, mattered more than anything else. We could call this the tradition's uniqueness, exemplarity, election, and perhaps universality, in short, everything that denies or resists iterability, repetition plus change, automatism, technicity, and the danger of parody and perversion (thus, idolatry, blasphemy, and profanization) that any legacy inevitably also entails.

Since Derrida affirms this necessity (or, with Freud, this *Ananke*), which is also a chance ("la Chance," as he writes), we can only be struck by the curious—appealing, perhaps even healing, salvaging—mixture of the unmistakable pathos and indifference, engagement and disengagement that characterizes several of his most challenging observations and figures of speech. I am thinking of his insistence on a "messianic act of faith" that could well be "irreligious and without messianism" (Derrida 2005: xiv); or, in the Christian, Pauline, and Kantian idiom that he adopts just as easily, his repeated reference to an irreducible "reflective faith" that "supposes, in its purity, that nothing is assured, probable, or believable" (Derrida 2001: 70). Such faith, therefore, while geared toward a notion or idea of infinity—justice, absolute hospitality, democracy still and forever to come—would thus seem directed towards the "absolute finitude" that such fallibility and pervertibility represents. In other words, it would be oriented toward a possible future that must remain without hope or redemption, eschatology, or apocalyptics.

Put differently, if all thought, not least Derrida's own, circles around the "divine name" (*Sauf le nom*), just as it aspires to be somehow "angelic" (as *La Carte postale* had already suggested), then this by no means excludes that the implied and addressed, invoked and implored God—in his or its concept or idea, existence and essence—also "already contradicts" himself/itself. "*Dieu déjà se contredit*," we read in *L'écriture et la différence*, in the essay on Edmond Jabès, and Derrida's whole subsequent oeuvre could be reconstructed as an indefatigable attempt to unpack this formula, yet another aporetics of sorts.

This self-contradiction, nothing else, is the logic of the *à-dieu/adieu*, of the simultaneous address and leavetaking, of turning oneself at once toward and away from the only reference that figures all that matters and, in a sense, regulates—or, rather, orients and disorients—all our thoughts and actions, namely God (and of everything that plausibly and rightfully comes to substitute for this "divine name"). It is with relentless consequence that Derrida will come to insist (with a catchy phrase that Levinas might not have accepted) that *tout autre est tout autre*, that is to say, that "every other is totally/every bit other" (*Donner la mort*). This dictum opens responsibility and responsiveness up to nonhuman—even nonliving—"others" that a Levinasian interpersonal ethics—epitomized by its *humanisme de l'autre homme* (humanism of the other human being)—would seem to have to disregard.

But then, it could also be argued that the phrase *tout autre est tout autre* not only restates the familiar, if often ill-understood, logic of *différance*—that is to say, of temporalization and displacement, of the trace and the supplement or *pharmakon*, of a repetition that cannot be but change, of a substitution that will always be nonsynonymous—but also respects the fundamentally Levinasian logic and gesture of the *à-dieu/adieu*, even though it pushes the latter to its logical and ethical extreme. On this reading, Levinas's thought may well reveal ethical implications it did not dare or care to consider.

Following Levinas in his reading of the Abrahamic sacrifice, Derrida would seem to suggest that this logic of address and of leavetaking, of a turning oneself at once toward and away from the only reference that matters—precisely because it founds, structures, and inspires all else as the possibility, if not reality or actuality, of the best and the just—cannot insulate itself from and is virtually cotemporaneous and coextensive with the possibility of the worst: the perhaps ungodly (indeed, *a-dieu*) par excellence.

If this suggestion can be claimed to be one of Derrida's radical, in the sense of latest and most profound, insights, then it also merely confirms a previous one, formulated early on in *De la grammatologie*. I mean his claim that the "theological," as it spans the whole spectrum of the worst, the better, and the best, "is a determined moment in the total movement of the trace." For this economic formula encapsulates what I take to be one of the most significant contributions of Derrida's thought, the fact that it enables a meditation on all the ins and outs, that is to say, on all the "from withins" and "from withouts" or, again, on all the deconstructed-deconstructable binaries to which I have been alluding so far (tradition and modernity, infinity and finitude, religion and the secular, messianicity and messianism, and faith and knowledge). All these binaries let themselves be summed up, condensed, and formalized, as many instances of the perturbation of philosophy in its encounter with its—now external, then internal, and, in the end, undecidable—other, including the other that the individual or collective self can become to itself.

All these motifs and motivations would require further investigation and exemplification. But their overall logic, if one can still say so, seems by now firmly established—even clear and distinct, irrefutable, implying a nonformal tautology and heterology, repetitions of the same and "inventions of the other" (as the subtitle of *Psyché* has it)—and revolves around a single conviction, which is that of the maximal import of minimal difference.

Conversely, the same conviction also implies the minimal effect of maximal—of all-totalizing, thetic, all too positive-affirmative—claims. Genuine thought and action steers clear of such extremes while once again acknowledging their standing possibility and, thus, permanent risk.

Near and Far

Having laid out these central axes of Derrida's project, let us, in conclusion, summarize a few lines of possible reception and future orientation in the philosophy of religion that his meditations on transcendental, empirical, and other forms of—as I have suggested, phenomenal—violence invite us to explore further.

If paying homage, instead of being an act of submission, an impossible promise of repetition without change, means to soberly take stock of what one hopes to have received or has freely taken—if not without some interpretative violence—from an author by way of study, listening, and conversation, then with respect to Derrida's teaching I would like to mention a few more lessons about the relationship between religion and violence whose instruction and ethos might safely stay with us.

To do so is not an easy task, not least since it is presumptuous to assume that one might know and state in full detail what one has effectively learned, registered, or failed to note. Following Derrida's suggestion, one may discover oneself to be at once close to and at the furthest remove from a tradition and legacy—or, for that matter, oeuvre—into which one wishes to insert oneself, seeking a belonging without belonging, a faithfulness without strict fidelity, a hermeneutic charity with critical distance. After all, this simultaneous proximity and distance, nothing else, forms the modality of any serious reception and translation of a work of philosophy.

To illustrate this, I should mention a puzzling observation made during my early studies of Levinas and the emerging scholarship devoted to his writing, to wit: the fact that the only essay that truly impressed me and radically challenged this philosopher's thought (not least by Levinas's own account), namely Derrida's 1961–1962 essay on *"Violence et métaphysique"*—republished as what is arguably the most beautiful and powerful chapter of *L'écriture et la différence*—at once pulled the carpet from under my hero's philosophical work and, strangely enough, also paid it the ultimate respect or homage it was due. How could Derrida force this author to reverse course—in a virtual turn or *Kehre*, not unlike Heidegger's, that would lead him from the methodic project and "ethical first philosophy" of *Totalité et infini* to that of more "an-archical" meditations of *Autrement qu'être ou au-delà de l'essence*—while claiming at the same time that there was "not a single thesis" written by Levinas with which he, Derrida, would disagree? In other words, how was this combination of ultimate respect and the apparent lack thereof possible and productive as a mode of doing philosophy?

Again, how could one be at once close to and at the furthest remove from the oeuvre one wished to make known and one's own and, at the same time, expose it to questions and domains it could perhaps not have foreseen and that, with benefit of hindsight, might well force us to make or let it shift grounds, rethink its major emphases (which, by the way, is precisely what happened in the development of Levinas's subsequent oeuvre)?

Finally, what did deconstruction, which is, after all, anything but a negative operation of destruction or skeptical doubt, but one of affirmation, even originary affirmation, more than anything else, have to do with this paradoxical—perhaps aporetic—situation and predicament of all understanding, of every engagement, each judgment? Was it, if not a method in the strict sense of the word, then at least a procedure and practice or technique of reading and argumentation, observation, and intervention, enabling one to register what goes on in all genuine—that is to say, responsible—reception and critique? But, if this was the case, in what situation would this leave the prospects for future philosophical and religious thought as it affects and inflects the political, including the theologico-political, and politics?

It is in the discussion of sacrifice and testimony, together with its institutional ramifications, that this situation and the task it imposes is assessed and, as it were, conceptually and rhetorically worked through. More in particular, it is in his reflections on the mystical postulate and notably Derrida's borrowings from Michel de Certeau's *La fable mystique* that this inquiry finds a provisional solution, albeit it one that leaves many questions unanswered while perhaps allowing to place them on a different footing and to reassign and reimagine their principal terms.

This I take to be Derrida's most profound and deeply sobering lesson: that there is no violence without (at least some) religion and no religion without (at least some) violence; that we cannot but mobilize the best of the Western metaphysical archive to combat the worst of its excesses and doctrinal fixations; and, finally, that we cannot but think and live and act on this contradictory given, whose tensions we must constantly negotiate and bring to a hypothetical resolution.

QUANTITATIVE AND QUALITATIVE REVERSALS

In more practical terms: As one of his most telling titles indicates, Derrida's entire analysis, in "Faith and Knowledge," is driven by a certain reticence about the central presupposition of the project of modernity and perhaps of the philosophical tradition in toto as it seeks to distinguish—on principled rather than empirical or pragmatic grounds—between *muthos* and *logos*, *phusis* and *nomos*, *doxa* and *episteme*, and faith and knowledge:

> one would blind oneself to the phenomenon called "of religion" or of the "return of the religious" *today* if one continued to oppose so naïvely Reason *and* Religion, Critique or Science *and* Religion, technoscientific Modernity *and* Religion. Supposing that what was at stake was to understand, would one understand anything about "what's-going-on-today-in-the-world-with-religion"?...Beyond this opposition and its determinate heritage (no less represented on the other side, that of religious authority), perhaps we might be able to try to "understand" how the imperturbable and interminable development of critical and technoscientific reason, far from opposing religion, bears, supports and supposes it. (Derrida 1998: 28)

Derrida maintains that there is a more than accidental or trivial relationship between the "mysticism" and "mechanicism" (to cite Henri Bergson's *Les deux sources de la morale et de la religion [The Two Sources of Morality and Religion]* which forms an important reference here) or, more broadly, between the religious and the technological (the artificial, mediatic, and digital), as we must now add. For one thing, they "make" common cause, even if they, strictly speaking, do not "have" one but refer to at least two sources—two aspects, two prospects—that we are aware of as their historical articulation and opposition has occupied and counterproductively influenced much of the Western theological and philosophical imagination, opposing reason and revelation as the sum—and summation—of all things human (and divine).

As Derrida suggests, the aforementioned conceptual oppositions block our sight on past and present phenomena—not least those of phenomenal violence—the understanding of which is crucial to address and engage future conflicts (which is not the same as successfully negotiating, resolving, let alone preventing them).

A crucial example of such unhelpful binaries in our day and age is the portrayal of so-called political Islam in what now turns out to be an unrealistic way, namely as the epitome of religious fundamentalism or, as the French say, of *intégrisme*. The latter is supposedly a more fateful version of the already suspect forms of communitarianism that supposedly oppose themselves to the putative enlightened stances of civic republicanism (itself not immune to the accusation of secular fundamentalism, as we now know). As Derrida notes:

> the surge of "Islam" [*le déferlement "islamique"*] will be neither understood nor answered as long as one settles for an internal explanation (interior to the history of faith, of religion, of languages or cultures as such), as long as one does not define the passageway between this interior and all the apparently exterior dimensions (technoscientific, tele-biotechnological, which is to say also political and socioeconomic etc.) (Derrida 1998: 20)

Derrida leaves no doubt that this apparent trespassing of the supposedly exterior on the presumably interior—to the point at which the distinction between the from-without and from-within collapses—must have held true at all times in every religion. After all, the technological as well as political and economic element is not merely added to religion but co-constitutes it from the onset even though it is and must remain also analytically distinct.

At no point in history was religion not exposed to a certain artificiality and technicity, to the kind of machinations and fabrications of old no less than those of late that have come to accompany it on its peregrinations throughout the vicissitudes of historical time and geographical as well as sociopolitical space. What is new is the fact that we have witnessed a generalization and intensification beyond measure of the modes of communication and mediatization that stir and frame all narratives and every practice. They affect the realm of the spiritual no less than that of the political and have done so at such massive scale and pace that this quantity of change has effected a virtual qualitative reversal of the ways we think and act, judge and feel, believe and know things and beings.

Never before has it been so evident that there can be no such thing as an ultimate—analytical (*de iure*), let alone empirical (de facto)—neutrality of the public and, a fortiori, global sphere. Never before has it been clearer that an indelible, now minimal, then again maximal, in this case, phenomenal violence affects the purest of ideals and the sincerest of intentions, together with the most faithful of rituals as well as authentic of practices, from the first of their utterance and performance onward.

Attention to this persistent—or renewed, in any case, newly framed, that is, phenomenal, technologically mediated, and ontologically virtual—prominence of religion dispels the phantom, the dangerous utopia of a culturally homogeneous society (without tension and conflict, without the changing of the guards of hegemonies, political, cultural, and other, that vie for our approval and nudge us subliminally). For if social space is now differently and more extensively as well as intensively curved, if the punctuated rhythm of its historical, collective, objective as well as subjective time is deeply warped, then at any given place and at each single moment, all (i.e., everything and everyone) can be in play, that is, to be gained or at risk, resolved or in jeopardy.

This simple and complex—nonempirical—observation, if at all plausible, would affect even the most universal of political declarations. The curious temporality and spatiality of foundational acts and the subsequent giving and maintaining of laws, of revolutions and reform, electoral strategy and political spin, demonstrate this fact—a total social and global fact, if ever there was one—each step along the way.

Wars of Religion

As Derrida shows, this fate and potential fatality of the political is nowhere more obvious than in the current ways in which contemporary "wars" (in this distinct from their traditional and modern counterparts) are often, unofficially, declared and, just as often, secretively waged or in which what is commonly called terror (often seen as the violence of nonstate actors, groups, and networks) is all too rashly defined and combated (at times, illegally, in blatant conflict with ratified standards of international law).

In an age of global media, these phenomena have become more and more pervasive even though their terminology and reference are, it seems, less and less clear. Not surprisingly, religious rhetoric and motivations assume an important justificatory function in this realignment of forces, perturbing nations and states, groups, and wider networks and creating new modalities of religious manifestation, with its accompanying phenomenal violence, along the way:

> Like others before, the new "wars of religion" are unleashed over the human earth and struggle even today to control the sky *with finger and eye*: digital systems and virtually immediate panoptical visualization, "air space," telecommunications satellites, information highways, concentration of capitalistic-mediatic power—in three words: *digital culture, jet,* and *TV* without which there could be no religious manifestation today, for example no voyage or discourse of the Pope, no organized emanation [*rayonnement*] of Jewish, Christian or Muslim cults, whether "fundamentalist" or not. (Derrida 1998: 24)

Derrida observes that if religion was ever dead and overcome, in its resurrected form it is much less localizable and predictable than ever before, most manifestly in the "cyberspatialized or cyberspaced wars of religion [*guerres de religion*]" or "war of religions [*guerre des religions*]" (Derrida 1998, 24, 30). These wars can take all the forms of radical evil and atrocity, even when they often mask themselves behind the most enlightened and universalistic intentions. Conversely, even when they draw on the most archaic and primitive of ancient sources, present affects, and future-oriented aspirations, they conceal and generate emancipatory processes as well. Where they are driven by sacred causes and the holiest of commitments or by secular humanist causes, their implementation in the world we know is not without some phenomenal violence of its own:

> [I]t is not certain that in addition to or in face of the most spectacular and most barbarous crimes of certain "fundamentalisms" (of the present or the past) *other* over-armed forces are not *also* leading "wars of religion," albeit unavowed. Wars or military "interventions," led by the Judaeo-Christian West in the name of the best causes (of international law, democracy, the sovereignty of peoples, of nations or of states, even of humanitarian imperatives), are they not also, from a certain side, wars of religion? The hypothesis would not necessary be defamatory, nor even very original, except in the eyes of those who hasten to believe that all these just causes are not only secular but *pure* of all religiosity. (Derrida 1998: 25)

The reasons why this is impossible are multiple. The reason, that is, that global politics is mirrored and mimicked by global religion and vice versa, the reason that both find in violence and war their element or horizon, unable to expunge this stain from their respective bodies (the body politic and international community, on the one hand, and the *corpus mysticum* or virtual Umma, on the other, to mention just a few of their ancient, modern, and contemporary configurations)—all this hinges on the complexity of identifying and defining a phenomenon, a phenomenal violence that is *global* in more one sense of this term. This circumstance affects the order of the political (the theologico-political) no less than that of the religious (in all the depth, width, and more than simply historical weight of its archive):

> To determine a war of religion *as such*, one would have to be certain that one can delimit the religious. One would have to be certain that one can distinguish all the predicates of the religious. One would have to dissociate the essential traits of the religious as such from those that establish, for example, the concepts of ethics, of the juridical, of the political or of the economic. And yet, nothing is more problematic than such a dissociation. The fundamental concepts that often permit us to isolate or to *pretend* to isolate the *political*—restricting ourselves to this particular circumscription—remain religious or in any case theologico-political. (Derrida 1998: 25)

Yet it would be false to identify and explain religion and its violence by reducing them to any of separate field of study. Nor is it correct to associate religion with particularistic and idiomatic or even idiosyncratic views alone. Religion has other, ecumenical, pluralistic, universalizing tendencies as well.

What is needed, therefore, is a conceptual and empirical analysis of the multiple ways in which religion and its phenomenal violence not only shape the experience of possible tensions and conflicts between collective and personal identities—and perhaps challenge the very concept of identity (De Vries and Weber 1997)—but also affect the conditions under which such tensions and conflict, empirical and symbolical violence and wars can be addressed, worked through, if not resolved.

CONCLUSION

Such diagnosis and its subsequent analysis may seem hopelessly abstract and global and, thus, unable to tackle the problems of real people in a through-and-through material—and, it appears, largely economically driven, "globalized"—world.

However, to counter such objections, authors such as Mark Juergensmeyer must be cited. In his *Terror in the Mind of God,* he addresses different instances in the modern world in which Christian, Jewish, Muslim, Hindu, Sikh, and Buddhist individuals and groups act out what would seem minimal differences through excessive—phenomenal—violence in what he terms the drama of "cosmic war." In this scenario and, literally, theater of war, an explicit or implicit notion of martyrdom of fallen heroes and demonization—"satanization," he writes—of the primary or secondary enemy go hand in hand.

The verbal expression *acting out* is used deliberately here. Juergensmeyer offers an interpretation of these instances of religious violence—of religiously motivated violence and of violence empowering and staging religion—in which the so-called performative moment and momentum are rightly seen as central. Just as Hannah Arendt had already insisted that violent acts and protests do not so much "promote causes, neither history nor revolution, neither progress nor reaction," and added that they "can serve to dramatize grievances and bring them public attention" (Arendt 1970: 79), so also Juergensmeyer—in critical engagement with the work of sociologists such as Pierre Bourdieu and comparativists such as René Girard—stresses that the violence of, for example, terrorist attacks should be understood not so much as part of an elaborate calculation or "*tactics* directed towards an immediate, earthly or strategic goal" but as "performance violence": They are the performance of "*dramatic events* intended to impress for their symbolic significance." As such, Juergensmeyer concludes, "they can be analyzed as one would analyze any other symbol, ritual, or sacred drama." (Juergensmeyer 2003: 123). Religious violence or the violence that takes on religious qualities (the difference matters little, phenomenologically speaking) present a *"performance violence"* (Juergensmeyer 2003: 124) whose paradoxical goal is a (posthistorical) peace and whose modality and motivation should not be confused with a political act or elaborate theory in disguise. As Juergensmeyer notes, the reason why "violence has accompanied religion's renewed political presence" has everything to do with the fact that

> the religious imagination…has always had the propensity to absolutize and to project images of cosmic war. It has also much to do with the social tensions of this moment of history that cry out for absolute solutions, and the sense of personal

humiliation experienced by men who long to restore an integrity they perceive as lost in the wake of virtually global social and political shifts. (Juergensmeyer 2003: 242)[5]

An alternative to the much debated and much decried "clash of civilizations" (Samuel Huntington) or more subtle "clash within" (Martha Nussbaum) would thus impose itself: The declared abysmal rift between separate(d) cultural systems does not explain the intensity and intractability of phenomenal violence on whose body religion leaves its signature, of which it feeds and against which it protests; it is, rather, the maximal effect of minimal differences, irreducible to communitarian or, more broadly, identitarian discourses of whatever nature that explains the surprise and horror of much conflict, war, and terror today.

This is not to deny the historical and cultural—that is, conceptual and normative, imaginary and affective—distinctions that religiously oriented civilizations may once have had (or by which they continue to define and assert themselves, increasingly desperately but, ultimately, in vain). It means to question that these traditional and modern metaphysical and theological, axiological, and perceptual differences have any real and decisive ontological—or otherwise substantial—resources at their disposal left. Paradoxically, their marketed and mediatized global expansion has turned them into largely global (as in vague and thinned out) phenomena as well.

Yet, it is precisely this minimum of difference that invites and provokes (or allows?) the maximal vehemence of these cultural differences' (and, by extension, global religions') response all the more and does so with a logic of inverse proportions that characterizes the worst of violence no less than the most miraculous of its endings.

Of course, one could call this a reactive response against, for example, modernity and its neutralizing, leveling tendency were it not for the fact that the theological minimum was itself, in a sense, theologically produced. The political religions and religious wars and terrorisms in the contemporary world protest their own—intrinsically, that is to say, autonomously produced—demise or rumors thereof. In vain, it would seem, they fend off the transformation of their putative miracles into mere special effects, effects that—under present conditions—have all the more impact to the extent that their theological backup is increasingly weakened.

More precisely, the observed or, in any case, much debated "turn to religion" would not be a protest against the "*verkehrte Welt*" that modern processes of rationalization in market and state (read capitalism and bureaucracy) have brought about but a revolt against this global turn to religion itself. The now celebrated, then decried turn to God or gods (*à dieu*, to again use Levinas's felicitous phrase, adopted by Derrida) would at the same time be a turn away from the same God or gods (*adieu*), a turn that would always come with the risk of conjuring or exposing oneself to the worst, the ungodly (*a-dieu*).

If religion thus produces its opposite effect—or the effects that oppose it— just as modernity produces its supposed opposite, religion, we can safely say that both religion and modernity, like religion and phenomenal violence, are each other's inevitable counterparts and, thus, follow and shadow each other incessantly. There would be a necessary distortion of autoaffection at the source of each, a reversal into heteroaffection, which ultimately affects much else besides. When this is the case, then the response to this self-engendered dynamic can be only that of "conjuring the effect," "repressing" it by means of an always counterbalancing tendency, namely that of "critique" (Deleuze 1991: 20–21), but a critique that now knows its limits.

NOTES

1. What *"sacrifice"* means for Derrida I discuss extensively in de Vries 2002, 123–210.
2. For a critique of the views of Manfred Frank, Peter Dews, and others in this respect, see de Vries 2005, appendix.
3. For an extensive discussion, see de Vries 2002, 211–292.
4. I have discussed this topic in the concluding chapter of de Vries 1999, entitled "Apocalyptics and Enlightenment."
5. For a somewhat different take on the origins, meaning, and import of religious and other terrorisms, see the informative studies by Stern (Stern 2003; Stern 1999). Based on extensive interviews around the world with religious extremists of all stripes, she concludes: "Religious extremists see themselves as under attack by the global spread of post-Enlightenment values such as secular humanism and the focus on individual liberties.... The point of religious terrorism is to purify the world of...corrupting influences" (Stern 2003, xviii–xix).A case in point would be Ayman Zawahiri, Osama bin Laden's deputy who "accuses Western forces of employing international institutions such as the United Nations, multinational corporations, and international news agencies as weapons in their new 'crusade' to dominate the Islamic world. The new world order is 'humiliating' to Muslims, he writes." (ibid., xviii). Yet underlying these "grievances," Stern continues, is a "deeper kind of angst and a deeper kind of fear. Fear of a godless universe, of chaos, of loose rules, and loneliness...[T]he slogans sometimes mask not only fear and humiliation, but also greed—greed for political power, land, or money. Often, the slogans seem to mask wounded masculinity" (ibid., xix).What would make religious terrorism such a dangerous brand, she suggests, echoing a motif Juergensmeyer develops more fully, is that "leaders deliberately intensify those feelings to ignite holy wars" and influence individual motivations to join extremist causes, by making use of "the challenges and opportunities posed by globalization and technological change" (ibid.).

BIBLIOGRAPHY

Arendt, Hannah. *On Violence.* San Diego, New York, London: Harcourt Brace Jovanovich, 1970.

Deleuze, Gilles. *Bergsonism.* Trans. Hugh Tomlinson and Barbara Habberjam. New York: Zone Books, 1991.

Derrida, Jacques. "Faith and Knowledge: The Two Sources of 'Religion' at the Limits of Reason Alone." Trans. Samuel Weber. In *Religion.* Eds. Derrida and Vattimo, 1–78. Palo Alto, CA: Stanford University Press, 1998.

Derrida, Jacques. "Above All No Journalists!"Ttrans. Samuel Weber. In *Religion and Media*. Eds. Hent de Vries and Samuel Weber, 56–93. Palo Alto, CA: Stanford University Press, 2001.

Derrida, Jacques. "Autoimmunity: Real and Symbolic Suicides: A Dialogue with Jacques Derrida." In *Philosophy in a Time of Terror: Dialogues with Jürgen Habermas and Jacques Derrida*, Ed. Giovanna Borradori, 85–136. Chicago and London: University of Chicago Press, 2003.

Derrida, Jacques. *Rogues: Two Essays on Reason*, trans. Pascale-Anne Brault and Michael Naas. Palo Alto, CA: Stanford University Press, 2005.

Derrida, Jacques. *Learning How to Live Finally: An Interview with Jean Birnbaum*, trans. Pascale-Anne Brault and Michael Naas. Hoboken, NJ: Melville House Publishing, 2007.

Derrida, Jacques. "Letter to a Japanese Friend." In idem, *Psyche: Inventions of the Other*. Eds. Peggy Kamuf and Elizabeth Rottenberg, 1–6. Palo Alto, CA: Stanford University Press, 2008.

de Vries, Hent. "Introduction." In *Violence, Identity, and Self-Determination*. Eds. Hent de Vries and Samuel Weber, 1–13. Palo Alto, CA: Stanford University Press, 1997.

de Vries, Hent. *Philosophy and the Turn to Religion*. Baltimore and London: Johns Hopkins University Press, 1999, 2000.

de Vries, Hent. 2002. *Religion and Violence: Philosophical Perspectives from Kant to Derrida*. Baltimore and London: Johns Hopkins University Press, 2006.

de Vries, Hent. *Minimal Theologies: Critiques of Secular Reason in Theodor W. Adorno and Emmanuel Levinas*. Baltimore and London: Johns Hopkins University Press, 2005.

de Vries, Hent. "'The Shibboleth Effect': On Reading Paul Celan." In *Judeities*. Ed. Bettina Bergo, 175–213. New York: Fordham University Press, 2007.

Juergensmeyer, Mark. *Terror in the Mind of God: The Global Rise of Religious Violence*. Berkeley: University of California Press, 2003.

Stern, Jessica. *Terror in the Name of God: Why Religious Militants Kill*. New York: HarperCollins, 2003.

Stern, Jessica. *The Ultimate Terrorists*. Cambridge, MA, and London: Harvard University Press, 1999.

CHAPTER 35

THE CONSTRUCTION OF EVIL AND THE VIOLENCE OF PURIFICATION

DAVID FRANKFURTER

IT has always been captivating to speculate about evil in the abstract: What deeds or events count as evil? When did evil enter the world, and why? Are we all prone to evil while in the world? These are the types of speculative topics that have inspired modernist intellectuals as much as ancient Jewish scribes. But for most people in history, the sense that evil might be lurking nearby—in the criminal, foreigner, demon, or witch—has demanded not speculation but action: preemptive or vengeful action, to obliterate or purify or to signify triumph. A local but "different" population's interest in our women or children, an individual seemingly dedicated to our (or our children's) suffering—such people appear to embody a monstrosity and danger that cannot be tolerated. Their presence threatens us; their efforts to live among us as equals must conceal a deep-seated, conspiratorial hunger for our destruction, our children, even our blood. We have no choice, then, but to eliminate these individuals or groups and at the same time to demonstrate somehow their malevolent, predatory nature—staging that elimination either preemptively or reactively. The most atrocious acts of violence—the kinds we moderns tend speculatively to label "evil"—invariably occur in the course of ridding communities and landscapes of evil: that is, of the impure, the monstrous, or the savage.

My own work has been on the images and myths—paradigmatic narratives—of evil that impel such preemptive, purificatory action, whether in the form of witch purges, anti-Jewish (or, in Roman times, anti-Christian) pogroms, ethnic cleansing, or moral panics with their ensuing riots or judicial prosecutions (Frankfurter 2000, 2001, 2005, 2006, 2008). While the precise strategies of violence in purification are culturally contingent (burning, drowning, dismembering, beheading, expulsion; see Davis 1975, Frankfurter 2004), the stories and images of the monstrous other that have historically mobilized violent response involve a consistent range of motifs, a common ambivalence (hatred and fascination) in response, and certain social catalysts for "realizing" a myth of evil in one's community.

MYTHS OF EVIL: IMAGES AND NARRATIVES THAT IMPEL VIOLENT RESPONSE

What kinds of stories and images call for violent response? What we find exciting to contemplate on the periphery of our world as the custom of the savage or the monster in his own domain becomes terrifying when it is imagined to occur in our domain—in our neighborhoods. Ancient notions of the savage as disorderly and brutal, nocturnal, sexually libertine (even voracious), and sometimes cannibalistic —all ideas recycled in classic American films about Africa, Haiti, and fictional places, as in the 1933 *King Kong*—came historically to be distilled as the alleged customs of witches, Christians, and Jews at different times, of Muslims in parts of India (see Kakar 1996), African Americans in the South and Midwest, and so on: All come to be imagined as "foreigners perpetrating their savage customs among us." With customs that both invert and pervert our own, the monstrous foreigner must regard us as prey (if he does not threaten our very institutions by his savagery). He seeks out our youth, our children, our women for his voracious impulses.

But a far more frightening aspect arose around the image of the foreign savage with the establishment of political and religious institutions: conspiracy. In this case, the predatory nature of the other is extended, on the one hand, to notions of dissimulation and concealment and, on the other hand, to an articulated system—a counterinstitution—formulated over history to infiltrate and destroy our culture. Disorderly monstrosity now manifests as cold bureaucracy. A voracious appetite for our children or our blood turns into controlled scenarios of ritual slaughter in secret chambers. The popular shopkeeper or midwife or police officer becomes, in secret, the high priest of some "cult," meticulously slaughtering an infant before a god we cannot comprehend according to some esoteric calendar. (See Moscovici 1987, Bromley 1994, and Frankfurter 2006: 101–128.)

In contemporary Africa, it is precisely such conspiracies that ignite the most violent lynchings and expulsions: rumors of people roving with syringes, shrinking penises with a handshake, grabbing children for *muti* (an indigenous term for some kind of ritual substance) or simply amassing commodities outside any recognizable system for accumulation and prestige and therefore, clearly, out of diabolical pacts. The most recent witch-cleansing movements have striven to prove to communities that local suspects are not just individual malefactors but part of a witch conspiracy, with secret identity and allegiance. In early modern Europe, of course, the small-scale lynchings of accused witches that had long occurred in local cultures shifted in many places to large-scale roundups and executions when the individual witch, enemy of local society, was constructed as a servant of Satan, part of a large-scale counterchurch that was ritually and organizationally dedicated to the subversion of all Christendom. (Of course, innovations in jurisprudence and torture often facilitated the expansion of the number of accused witches in any one region; but popular fear of the witch cult grew, whether ten people were executed or fifty.) That an elderly neighbor long avoided for the evil eye (or, alternately, visited for her charms) might participate in an infanticidal Sabbat and take her orders from demons rendered her entirely predatory—more dangerous in her dissimulation—and rendered her unmasking through torture, procession, and execution that much more vital for civic fortune. (See Ankarloo/Henningsen eds., 1990, Cohn 1993, Briggs 1996.)

Conspiracy likewise integrated eruptions of the blood libel among Jews in medieval and early modern Europe: that is, the perennial rumor that Jews required the blood of a child (or the Eucharist, or a child who appears miraculously in the Eucharist, as in some legends) to complete some mysterious ritual such as the Passover seder. Behind the quotidian familiarity of Jewish life and commerce in parts of England and Germany, there came to be understood a secret practice of kidnapping a Christian child and stabbing him to death, both to reenact the Crucifixion of Jesus and to collect the blood for ritual purposes. This practice was supposed to be derived from Jewish law, conducted not by deviants but by community elders and coordinated secretly across European Jewry. The horror, again, lay in the paradox between the overt—the everyday humanity and sociability of local Jews—and the covert—the transregional coordination and sacramental necessity of child sacrifice (Strack 1909, Hsia 1988, Langmuir 1990, Rubin 1999).

These kinds of stories of conspiracy, that integrate images of the other's monstrosity (child sacrifice, rape, cannibalism) across large areas and even through history, constitute myths of evil: narratives that draw in communities and individuals both for their recognizability (institutional coordination and ritual) and for their perverse horrors. Evil, in this case, signifies a tableau of practices not only antithetical to humanity and society (as culturally understood) but also demanding action, not just discussion and condemnation. Those imagined as evil must be purged, both physically (in the sense of material completeness) and ritually, involving a range of symbolic practices and declarations that render the postpurge environment supernaturally pure.

The repertoire or tableau of motifs that constitute the myth of evil, especially (but not exclusively) in Western cultures, does not dissipate as a result of secularism but rather is repeatedly reasserted, and not necessarily in new guises either. If conceptions of witchcraft and devil worship have assumed modern guises to incorporate experiences such as AIDS and medical discourse, in the United States and United Kingdom the most archaic notions of secret, infanticidal Satan worship cults gained credibility among feminists, law enforcement officers, and psychiatrists during the 1980s and 1990s, demonstrating the perennial nature and relevance of the tableaux of evil (Frankfurter 2003, 2006).

THE AMBIVALENCE OF MYTHS OF EVIL:
PRURIENCE AND REVULSION

The combination of institutional conspiracy and tableaus of perversion that so often underlies myths of evil creates a disturbing paradox for communities and for individuals. On the one hand, the often dispassionate framework of ritual tradition or institutional coordination—or, in modern allegations about Satanic cults, pseudo-Catholic liturgy (see Frankfurter 2006: 112–128)—frames a series of perverse and bloody acts as coldly premeditated in the extreme: an unambiguous evil. On the other hand, the recycled images of child cannibalism, rape and sexual perversions, as well as orgy, perverse uses of bodily fluids, parodies of legitimate liturgy, and oral and anal excess all have historically invited a mixture of revulsion and prurience in the communities that believe them to occur. These images constitute, in psychoanalytic terms, aspects of primary process fantasy. They are typical of small children's alternately pleasurable and frightening fantasies of psychic boundaries collapsing or inverting. In social terms, they constitute a perfect tableau of impropriety that can be "officially" repulsive and threatening but also liberating, erotic, and—as the 2005 American documentary film *The Aristocrats* demonstrated—anxiously hilarious. What allows these sensations of pleasure at some unconscious level, or (more often) simply the legitimate prurience of the "concerned," is the framing of the tableau itself: as the practices of witch, savage, or "cult"—that is, of those justly relegated to an inhuman status. The framing as evil virtually requires the public's attention, keeping atrocity and perversion and all they call forth at the center of community focus. (See Frankfurter 2006: 129–167, 2009; see also Cohn 1975: 258–263, Briggs 1996: 163–168, 384–388.)

Prurient fascination and righteous revulsion—these complementary responses embolden and repel each other, creating an anxiety of confusion that has led in many circumstances to community (and individual) efforts to purge the subject, the symbol, of that confusion. Perhaps no better example can be found than the circumstances that led to the lynching of African American men in the South and Midwest in the first half of the twentieth century. Newspapers and community leaders cast the victims in such monstrously phallic terms that the community responded to them as if to the antitheses of proper sexual relations. The bodies were invariably castrated and harvested for souvenir body parts over the course of the lynching—a meticulous and highly ritualized neutralizing of the monstrous body. (See Harris 1995, Frankfurter 2004: 525–530.)

We find similarly prurient mobilizations to violence against Jews in blood-libel pogroms and, in modern Europe, against "white slavery rings" (e.g., Morin 1971). The spectacle of child sacrifice has historically invited as much prurience as the alleged abduction, rape, and enslavement of (in this case), white women (Frankfurter 2006: 137–153).

Early modern witch-finding manuals and sermons likewise depicted the evil of witches in eroticized terms, sometimes reminiscent of carnival effervescence, other times inverting the magic that "we" need to protect our babies as the magic "they" derive from our babies. (See especially Lesourd 1973, Stephens 2002: 180–276.) Of course, such literature can gain a life of its own, inspiring unconscious erotic pleasure and overtly righteous condemnation in readers without mobilizing violent purges. Heresiography, for example, has a long history as a quasi-pornographic genre, leading from such early church fathers as Tertullian and Epiphanius up to the anticult literature of the late twentieth-century United States and United Kingdom. In the late 1980s, what began as an evangelical Christian literature migrated into new areas of feminist, psychotherapeutic, law enforcement, and victim-advocacy ideology, gaining hybrid legitimacy as Satanic ritual abuse literature. Beginning with the 1980 book *Michelle Remembers: The Story of a Year-Long Contest Between Innocence and Evil,* proponents of a conspiracy by Satanic cults to rape and impregnate young girls created a substantial print and broadcast media that revolved around frankly pornographic scenarios, framed as absolutely evil through their explicit association with devil-worship. (See Richardson/Best/Bromley, eds., 1991, Nathan/Snedeker 1995, La Fontaine 1998, Haaken 1998, Frankfurter 2006.) Community response varied, with draconian incarcerations levied in some areas, while in others the Satanic Ritual Abuse ("SRA") claims of clinicians and police "experts" were soundly rejected; and by the late 1990s the entire idea of SRA (and its corollary notion of "recovered memory") had been repudiated by the major psychological organizations. What this teaches us is that the shift from community anxiety about evil and erotic prurience to violent mobilization depends on many historical and social factors besides mere impulse. An erotic fascination with the nature and deeds of evil may persist as a living genre for centuries without lending itself to societies as legitimation for purge, as the next section will discuss. But it is a careful and ever-shifting balance: the sense of cultural safety that allows us to imagine horrific actions imputed to some monstrous other and the small eruptions of cultural anxiety that lead us to repel those images and destroy their embodiment—some neighbor or immigrant or cultural deviant.

LEADERSHIP AND THE REALIZATION OF EVIL

By what means do myths of evil gain reality and urgency in communities, motivating violent response? It is the expert in the identification of evil who situates such myths in local terms. Most small societies have one or another individual who claims—or is popularly credited with—the clairvoyant capacity to perceive the nefarious powers operating behind misfortunes—evil eye, particular demons, ill will. Sometimes such figures gain regional reputations—as "cunning men" or "wise women" in English tradition—and may be credited with the charismatic authority to unveil witches. That charismatic authority develops in relationship to the discerner's performative ability to lay out plausible local scenarios of supernatural maleficence and to provide strategies for their resolution, whether by private ritual offerings of some sort or through purging the actual malefactors—the witches. The expert in the identification of evil has the ability to show evil forces working in events or in people—to transform an ambiguous community member into a witch in the eyes of others. (See Favret-Saada 1980, Simpson 1996, Briggs 1996, Gaskill 2005, Frankfurter 2006: 31–72, 168–198.) Witch-cleansing movements in modern Africa function likewise, although the leaders are more often outsiders to the local world, trading on that social status to bring the most ostensibly "modern" technologies to bear on a common village crisis, rampant witch subversion (see, e.g., Auslander 1993). In neither the European nor the African cases do these figures represent institutions. Rather, their authority is a hybrid of their personal expressions of clairvoyance, their often peripheral or itinerant relationships to settled communities, and their intimations of modernity through the ostentatious use of books, scientific instruments, uniforms, bureaucracy, and such.

Another source of authority in the synthesis of popular charisma in the identification of evil is the religious institution, especially an institution with traditions of exorcism of evil forces, such as Christianity (although smaller-scale institutional ideologies of exorcism have historically arisen in China and the Near East as well). To the degree that this institution's influence on society involves the popularization of an official demonology (that is, a hierarchy and nomenclature of principal demons), representatives of that institution will be viewed as uniquely authoritative in the identification of malevolent powers and the discernment of demonic conspiracy. We see this social process in the literary records of many early Christian monks, on the one hand, and, on the other hand, in the activities of many late medieval and early modern friars in western Europe, who actively wove local traditions of malevolent witchcraft with official Christian demonology and heresiography in an effort to ramify the popular notion of the witch. (See Frankfurter 2006: 31–48.) It is not that these ecclesiastical authorities could independently direct violent purges but that they had the capacity to mobilize regional judicial processes, law enforcement, and popular terror through their institutional affiliation and their personal conviction in the discernment and immediacy of Satanic conspiracy (see, e.g., Mormando 1999: 52–108).

A similar combination of institutional (Christian) authority and personal conviction in the discernment of evil has developed among certain Pentecostal pastors in modern sub-Saharan Africa. The traditional demonological interests and exorcistic claims of Pentecostalism are now directed toward the articulation and resolution of traditional witch fears. As those witch fears have developed and ramified to reflect experiences of modernity, disease and the claims of biomedicine, the commodification of bodies, and the incoherence of new prestige systems, so these particular Pentecostal pastors articulate Pentecostalism as the distinctly modern and potent solution to a diabolical threat, battling a modern Satanic force that afflicts people in traditional ways but now with modern armaments.

In most cases—institutionally affiliated and maverick—the specialist in the discernment of evil gains charisma as a synthesizer of systems. He brings together the changing, often inchoate anxieties of his audience with various idioms and accoutrements of authority: ecclesiastical and scientific, theological and judicial, scholarly and clairvoyant, military and iconographic. Such figures articulate local fears and anxieties within grandiose frameworks that ramify the scale of crisis, situate it within a larger myth of evil conspiracy, and—most importantly—demonstrate evil's resolution through ritual, purge, and collective involvement, all under the leadership of the specialist.

In this respect the specialist in the identification of evil is comparable to the modern Western moral entrepreneur, who articulates inchoate social anxieties in the immediate terms of a singular moral threat: foreign or racial infiltration, political infiltration, new religions' (cults') infiltration, deviant youth styles, or the such. The discourse of the moral entrepreneur likewise revolves around conspiracy, allegedly identifiable behind some current moral threat, and likewise depends on motifs of savagery like infanticide and sexual deviance inherited from archaic images of the other. The moral entrepreneur in modern times invariably develops his charisma from some recognizable role of circumscribed authority—police officer, child welfare advocate, veteran, radio personality—and continues to depend on that status while seeking authority to identify and prosecute Evil (see Jenkins 1992, Goode/Ben-Yehuda 1994, Frankfurter 2006: 53–72).

In most cases of moral entrepreneurs during the later twentieth century in the United States and United Kingdom, prevailing legal systems restrained the wholesale expansion of their powers to cleanse society. However, the patterns of their claims, discourses of evil, and hybrid charismatic roles have much in common with the figures who successfully mobilized "ethnic cleansing" massacres in modern history. One feature of the moral entrepreneur in modern cultures is her or his creative distance from religious, especially ecclesiastical, discourse—drawing on it as needed to convey anxieties and strategies but usually independent of its hierarchy.

RELIGION, EVIL, VIOLENCE, AND THE PROBLEM OF CAUSALITY

When violence is mobilized through the realization of a myth of evil and the leadership of some expert in the identification of evil, it is invariably conducted as purification or as preemptive defense against a polluting, subversive, and imminently aggressive force of evil. Often, as in exorcisms, lynchings, and witch cleansings, the procedures can involve protracted rituals and processions whereby the victims are made to assume evil or monstrous identities before suffering public annihilation (see Frankfurter 2004: 522–525; 2006: 179–188). In one notable case, the extermination of the Jews of Jedwabne, Poland, by their neighbors in 1941, the Jews were forced to process through town and out to a barn while bearing objects that, to the villagers, symbolized the conspiracy of which they were supposedly a part. (See Gross 2001.) Likewise in early modern Europe, accused witches were paraded nude before inquisitors and in special garb on the way to the gibbet or pyre.

But the factors that allow myths of evil and the charismatic agency of experts in evil to ignite violence—judicial, large-scale "cleansing," lynching, exorcism, or pogrom—end up being quite complex. The stability of a political system, the nature and restraining capacity of a legal system, the direction of police and military powers, and the capacity of a leader or institution—whether friars in early modern Switzerland, Nazis in 1930s Germany, or Satanic abuse experts in the 1990s United Kingdom—to seek control over these central elements of mobilization have all dictated whether the application of violence would be extreme or limited. In the case of early modern European witch hunts, scholars have often debated how much the ecclesiastical or judicial inquisitions and executions involved popular participation or agency at all, beyond what emerged from victims under torture. Of course, the effectiveness of local and regional witch finders before and beyond the "official" inquisitions suggests that laity had a strong investment in security from witchcraft, whether that witchcraft was supposed to be small scale or large scale and Satanic. In most cases communities were not just passive victims of judicial savagery but were quite invested in the myth of evil, the expulsion of its nefarious agents, and the state's and church's authority to conduct that expulsion. That is to say, a population's propensity to realize evil in its midst and to seek its violent expulsion is not simply a function of "top-down" political manipulation but arises as a function of internal social dynamics. It is a propensity of what we might well call the religious sphere, in which social practice and social imagination interact.

It must be acknowledged that the perennial need to avoid and purge malevolent powers has long compelled communities to develop traditions of sublimating violence in the engagement with evil. Small and large-scale curse rituals (see Abusch 1989), apotropaic and evil eye practices (see Frankfurter 2007: 124–126, Bailliot 2010: 25–69), and exorcisms—even the elaborate spatial exorcisms of the contemporary Pentecostal "spiritual mapping" movement—have allowed gesture, speech act, and symbol to bring about protection, purification, or the expulsion of evil. Here, for example, ritual drama allows the performance of a kind of violence, but directed against toys, not people:

> COLORADO SPRINGS—A minister used a blowtorch and a sword during a church service this week to drive home his belief that Pokemon games and toys are only sugar-coated instruments of the occult and evil. At a church service Wednesday at Grace Fellowship Church, children's pastor Mark Juvera told 85 children ages 6 through 12 that Pokemon is evil. To make his point, Juvera burned Pokemon trading cards with a blowtorch and struck a plastic Pokemon

action figure with a 30-inch sword. Juvera's 9-year-old son then tore the limbs and head off a Pokemon doll. During the demonstration, the children chanted: "Burn it. Burn it," and "Chop it up. Chop it up." (Emery 1999)

The ritual drama here involves aggressive, violent gesture, of course, as well as audience participation; one might even call it mimetic (in the anthropological, not Girardian sense) of mob purges. But the victims, only vaguely anthropomorphic, are mere surrogates—and not for humans but for the inchoate assault of commodities on religious purity. One is reminded of the Protestant iconoclastic purges of the early Reform period discussed in Natalie Zemon Davis's famous essay "The Rites of Violence" (1975), in which the desecrating impurity that had to be obliterated from the world consisted of "idols"—statues, relics, and other Catholic sacra that interrupted pure Christianity. There is violence, to be sure, but not homicidal (in contrast, Davis points out, to Catholic efforts to purge Protestants).

Dramaturgy and procession, too, can bring brutal but cathartic narratives of saints and monsters, martyrs and their persecutors into the immediate festival lives of communities. (See Frankfurter 2009.) The expulsion of Moors from an Iberian town, the demise of some child at the hands of Romans or Jews and his salvific reappearance, the elimination of some heathen cult and the consecration of its space—such religious foundation myths, while predicated on stories of violence and social cleansing, are more likely reenacted at holidays with no compulsion to attack real people (see, e.g., M. Harris 2000; although Passion plays in Germany, it must be said, have often inspired vengeful purges against local Jews).

But the rich panoply of mimetic spectacles and antidemon traditions across cultures does not vitiate the horrendous violence committed to eliminate the forces of evil, protect the church, and restore the world. And this fact—Jews massacred to protect children, mass executions of accused "witches," and numerous other groups killed as incarnations of evil or pollution—invites a final question from the comparative history of religions. To what degree might Christianity itself, as a transregional ideology, be particularly responsible for religious violence as articulated in this chapter?

Most of the general observations in this chapter apply as well to Nazi, Stalinist, or Vietcong purges as to witch hunts, and in that sense the dynamics of the myth of evil and the charismatic expert in the identification of evil transcend religious ideology. Secular modernity and bureaucracy can create systems for mass purification from evil and social pollution in ways that could not be envisioned in early modern Europe or colonial Africa. One might today argue that especially dangerous circumstances occur when states or hegemonic institutions construct themselves as victims of persecution, such that dissidents or resident aliens represent a fifth column of some global threat, which the state or institution must then suppress with its full arsenal.

However, there are ways in which, historically, Christianity brought unique attention and articulation to the definition of evil in societies. Whereas most religious systems in history, including Buddhism, rabbinic Judaism, and Islam, have attributed an ambiguity, even (in Asia) a ritual flexibility to maleficent supernatural forces, Christianity's explicit attention to the absolute evil of the Satanic host preoccupies its earliest scriptures and pervades its historical negotiations with non-Christian cultures. (See Frankfurter 2006: 13–37.) It is no mystery that the image of a Satanic witch conspiracy and cannibalistic Sabbat arose in the fifteenth-century Western church and came to dictate its relationship with popular religion in many regions of Europe, for its learned exponents had a sizeable library of heresiography and demonology from which to draw that no other religious systems in history could claim. While some bishops and local churches might preserve an ambiguity or tolerance in the understanding of practice, belief, and the broader supernatural world—as we see, for example, in the syncretistic Christianities that evolved in Latin America—the force of canon and a tradition of supernatural polarization always lay historically close at hand. (See Frankfurter 2005, 2007, Verrips 1997, Bushman et al. 2007). Social and terrestrial purity, utopia, apocalyptic cleansing, combat with Satan in multiple arenas—these fundamental ideals of Christian scripture, practice, and community provided a latent ideological predisposition to a myth of evil of varying scale.

Of course, brutality and atrocity are perennial features of any culture, often exacerbated in situations of historical stress independent of religious system. But we have only to look at the readiness with which Pentecostal Christian pastors in Nigeria and Angola have led the identification of child witches or Catholic priests and nuns contributed to the extermination of Rwandan Tutsis in 1994 to see, in a more restricted scale, that essential Christian disposition to offer a religious framework for the identification and expulsion of pure evil. (See Longman 2001, 2010; LaFraniere 2007; "Nigeria 'Child Witch Killer'" Held; Behrend 2007; Daneel 2008).

BIBLIOGRAPHY

Abusch, Tzvi. "The Demonic Image of the Witch in Standard Babylonian Literature: The Reworking of Popular Conceptions by Learned Exorcists." In *Religion, Science, and Magic in Concert and in Conflict*. Eds. Jacob Neusner, Ernest S. Frerichs, and Paul Virgil McCracken Flesher, 27–58. New York: Oxford University Press, 1989.

Ankarloo, Bengt, and Henningsen, Gustav, eds. *Early Modern European Witchcraft: Centres and Peripheries*. Oxford, UK: Clarendon Press, 1990.

Auslander, Mark. "'Open the Wombs!' The Symbolic Politics of Modern Ngoni Witchfinding." In *Modernity and Its Malcontents: Ritual and Power in Postcolonial Africa*. Eds. Jean Comaroff and John Comaroff, 167–192. Chicago and London: University of Chicago Press, 1993.

Bailliot, Magali. *Magie et sortilèges dans l'Antiquité romaine: archéologie des rituels et des images*. Paris: Hermann, 2010.

Behrend, Hieke. "The Rise of Occult Powers, AIDS and the Roman Catholic Church in Western Uganda." *Journal of Religion in Africa* 37 (2007): 41-58.

Briggs, Robin. *Witches and Neighbors: The Social and Cultural Context of European Witchcraft*. New York: Viking, 1996.

Bromley, David G. "The Satanism Scare in the United States," *Le Défi magique 2: Satanisme, sorcellerie.* Ed. Jean-Baptiste Martin, 49–64. Lyon, France: Presses universitaires de Lyon, 1994.

Bushman, Brad J.; Ridge, Robert D.; Das, Enny; Key, Colin W.; and Busath, Gregory L. "When God Sanctions Killing: Effect of Scriptural Violence on Aggression," *Psychological Science* 18 (2007): 204–207.

Cohn, Norman. *Europe's Inner Demons.* New York: Basic Books, 1975.

Cohn, Norman. *Europe's Inner Demons.* Rev. ed. Chicago: University of Chicago Press, 1993.

Daneel, Marthinus L. "Coping with Wizardry in Zimbabwe in African Initiated Churches." In Coping with Evil in Religion and Culture: Case Studies, 51–70. Ed. Nelly van Doorn-Herder and Laurens Minnena. Amsterdam: Rodopi, 2008.

Davis, Natalie Zemon. "The Rites of Violence." In *Society and Culture in Early Modern France,* 152–187. Palo Alto, CA: Stanford University Press, 1975.

Emery, Erin. "Springs Minister Torches Pokemon, Tells Kids It's Evil." *The Denver Post* (14 August 1999), A1.

Favret-Saada, Jeanne. *Deadly Words: Witchcraft in the Bocage.* Tr. Catherine Cullen. Cambridge, UK: Cambridge University Press, 1980.

Frankfurter, David. "'Things Unbefitting Christians': Violence and Christianization in Fifth-Century Panopolis." *Journal of Early Christian Studies* 8.2 (2000): 273–295.

Frankfurter, David. "Ritual as Accusation and Atrocity: Satanic Ritual Abuse, Gnostic Libertinism, and Primal Murders." *History of Religions* 40.4 (2001): 352–380.

Frankfurter, David. "The Satanic Ritual Abuse Panic as Religious Studies Data." *Numen* 50.1 (2003): 108–117.

Frankfurter, David. "On Sacrifice and Residues: Processing the Potent Body." In *Religion in Cultural Discourse: Essays in Honor of Hans G. Kippenberg on the Occasion of his 65th Birthday.* Religionsgeschichtliche Versuche und Vorarbeiten 52. Eds. Brigitte Luchesi and Kocku von Stuckrad, 511–533. Berlin and New York: De Gruyter, 2004.

Frankfurter, David. "Violence and Religious Formation: An Afterword," in *Violence in the New Testament.* Eds. Shelly Matthews and E. Leigh Gibson, 140–152. Harrisburg, PA: T & T Clark, 2005.

Frankfurter, David. *Evil Incarnate: Rumors of Demonic Conspiracy and Satanic Abuse in History.* Princeton, NJ: Princeton University Press, 2006.

Frankfurter, David. "The Legacy of Sectarian Rage: Vengeance Fantasies in the New Testament." In *Religion and Violence: The Biblical Heritage..* Eds. David A. Bernat and Jonathan Klawans, 114–128. Sheffield, UK: Sheffield Phoenix Academic Press, 2007.

Frankfurter, David. "Le mal et ses complots imaginaires. Du cannibalisme des premiers chrétiens jusqu'aux abus rituels sataniques." *Le Terrain* 50 (2008): 14–31.

Frankfurter, David. "Martyrology and the Purient Gaze," *Journal of Early Christian Studies* 17.2 (2009): 215–245.

Gaskill, Malcolm. *Witchfinders: A Seventeenth-Century English Tragedy.* Cambridge, MA: Harvard University Press, 2005.

Goode, Erich, and Ben-Yehuda, Nachman. *Moral Panics: The Social Construction of Deviance.* Oxford, UK, and Cambridge, MA: Blackwell, 1994.

Gross, Jan T. *Neighbors: The Destruction of the Jewish Community in Jedwabne, Poland.* Princeton, NJ: Princeton University Press, 2001.

Haaken, Janice. *Pillar of Salt: Gender, Memory, and the Perils of Looking Back.*
   New Brunswick, NJ: Rutgers University Press, 1998.

Harris, J. William. "Etiquette, Lynching, and Racial Boundaries in Southern History:
   A Mississippi Example," *American Historical Review* 100.22 (1995): 387–410.

Harris, Max. *Aztecs, Moors, and Christians: Festivals of Reconquest in Mexico and
   Spain.* Austin: University of Texas Press, 2000.

Hsia, R. Po-chia. *The Myth of Ritual Murder: Jews and Magic in Reformation
   Germany.* New Haven, CT, and London: Yale University Press, 1988.

Jenkins, Philip. *Intimate Enemies: Moral Panics in Contemporary Great Britain.*
   New York: De Gruyter, 1992.

Kakar, Sudhir. *The Colors of Violence: Cultural Identities, Religion, and Conflict.*
   Chicago: University of Chicago Press, 1996.

La Fontaine, Jean S. *Speak of the Devil: Tales of Satanic Abuse in Contemporary
   England.* Cambridge, UK: Cambridge University Press, 1998.

LaFraniere, Sharon. "In Africa, Accusation of Witchcraft leads to Abuse," *New York
   Times* (15 November 2007).

Langmuir, Gavin I. *Toward a Definition of Antisemitism.* Berkeley: University of
   California Press, 1990.

Lesourd, Dominique. "Culture savante et culture populaire dans la mythologie de la
   sorcellerie." *Anagrom* 3/4 (1973): 63–79.

Longman, Timothy. "Church Politics and the Genocide in Rwanda." *Journal of
   Religion in Africa* 31.2 (2001): 163–186.

Longman, Timothy. *Christianity and Genocide in Rwanda.* Cambridge, UK:
   Cambridge University Press, 2010.

Moscovici, Serge. "The Conspiracy Mentality," *Changing Conceptions of Conspiracy.*
   Eds. Carl F. Graumann and Serge Moscovici, 151–169. New York: Springer-Verlag,
   1987.

Morin, Edgar. *Rumour in Orléans.* Tr. Peter Green. New York: Pantheon, 1971.

Mormando, Franco. *The Preacher's Demons: Bernardino of Siena and the Social
   Underworld of Early Renaissance Italy.* Chicago: University of Chicago Press, 1999.

Nathan, Debbie, and Snedeker, Michael. *Satan's Silence: Ritual Abuse and the Making
   of a Modern American Witch Hunt.* New York: Basic Books, 1995.

"Nigeria 'Child Witch Killer' Held," *BBC News* (4 December 2008).

Richardson, James T.; Best, Joel; and Bromley, David G., eds. *The Satanism Scare.*
   New York: De Gruyter, 1991.

Rubin, Miri. *Gentile Tales: The Narrative Assault on Late Medieval Jews.* New Haven,
   CT, and London: Yale University Press, 1999.

Simpson, Jacqueline. "Witches and Witchbusters," *Folklore* 107 (1996): 5–18

Stephens, Walter. *Demon Lovers: Witchcraft, Sex, and the Crisis of Belief.* Chicago:
   University of Chicago Press, 2002.

Strack, Hermann L. *The Jew and Human Sacrifice: Human Blood and Jewish Ritual.*
   8th ed., tr. Henry Blanchamp. London: Cope & Fenwick, 1909; repr. New York:
   Benjamin Blom, 1971.

Verrips, Jojada. "Killing in the Name of the Lord: Cases and Reflections Regarding
   Reli-Criminality in the Western World." *Ethnologia Europaea* (1997): 29–45.

CHAPTER 36

MIMETIC THEORIES OF RELIGION AND VIOLENCE

WOLFGANG PALAVER

RENÉ Girard, the French-American historian, literary critic, and anthropologist has developed one of the most fruitful and challenging approaches to understanding the multifarious and complex relationship between violence and religion. His mimetic theory does not give in to those popular and much too simple concepts that either scapegoat religion by declaring it as the main cause of human violence or exculpate it in general by overlooking its close relationship to violence. An example of the first mistake is Richard Dawkins's accusation of religion as the main cause of human violence. Dawkins opens his book *The God Delusion* with John Lennon's song "Imagine"—a hymn of the peace movement of the early 1970s—suggesting that the abolition of religion will automatically and easily lead to a peaceful world:

> Imagine, with John Lennon, a world with no religion. Imagine no suicide bombers, no 9/11, no 7/7, no Crusades, no witch-hunts, no Gunpowder Plot, no Indian partition, no Israeli/Palestinian wars, no Serb/Croat/Muslim massacres, no persecution of Jews as 'Christ-killers', no Northern Ireland 'troubles', no 'honour killings.'…Imagine no Taliban to blow up ancient statues, no public beheadings of blasphemers, no flogging of female skin for the crime of showing an inch of it. (Dawkins 2006: 1–2)

Dawkins represents a currently widespread view that only religious agitation causes conflicts, violence, and wars among a species that is peaceful by default. Girard rejects such naive anthropologies that overlook how easily human relations can take a negative turn. He criticizes the social sciences for their systematic neglect of the fragility of human relations:

> "Our social sciences should give due consideration to a phenomenon that must be considered *normal*, but they persist in seeing conflict as something accidental, and consequently so unforeseeable that researchers cannot and must not take it into account in their study of culture." (Girard 2001: 11)

According to Girard, conflictive human relations are not accidental but occur easily and normally. Does that mean that Girard assumes an aggressive human nature that is prone to violence and war? No, he distanced himself as clearly from ontologies of violence as he parted from naive anthropologies that evade the normality of human conflicts. This normality of the relationship between religion and violence is exactly the focus of his argument. As it will become clear in the following unfolding of mimetic theory, however, this relationship is not at all characterized by a linear causality but is quite complex.

COMPETITION OR MIMETIC RIVALRY
AS THE SOURCE OF VIOLENCE

According to Girard, not aggression but competition is the main source of human violence. By referring to competition, Girard is declaring that mimetic desire is a main cause of rivalries and violence. Whenever human beings imitate others and desire objects they cannot share or enjoy together, they easily turn against one another:

> We are *competitive* rather than aggressive. In addition to the appetites we share with animals, we have a more problematic yearning that lacks any instinctual object: *desire*. We literally do not know what to desire and, in order to find out, we watch the people we admire: we *imitate* their desires. Both models and imitators of the same desire inevitably desire the same object and become rivals. Their rival desires literally feed on one another: the imitator becomes the model of his model, and the model the imitator of his imitator. Unlike animal rivalries, these *imitative* or *mimetic* rivalries can become so intense and contagious that not only do they lead to murder but they also spread, mimetically, to entire communities. (Girard 2004b: 9–10)

Girard's explanation, that violence has its roots in competition or mimetic rivalry, brings him close to the English philosopher Thomas Hobbes, who also emphasized this cause of violence at the beginning of the modern era: "If any two men desire the same thing, which nevertheless they cannot both enjoy, they become enemies; and in the way to their End,...endeavour to destroy, or subdue one another" (Hobbes 87). But this affinity between Girard and Hobbes should not lead us to the assumption that they share a pessimistic anthropology or an ontology of violence. Whereas Hobbes assumes that human beings are necessarily prone to violence and war, Girard's starting point is positive because he emphasizes in the same book, in which he accuses many social scientists of neglecting the fragility of human relations, that "mimetic desire is intrinsically good" (Girard 2001: 15).

ARCHAIC RELIGION: PEACE BUILT ON VIOLENCE

As the long, preceding quotation makes clear, in Girard's view mimetic rivalries can lead whole communities into a deep crisis, resulting in a war of all against all. According to mimetic theory, exactly such crises triggered the emergence of archaic religion at the dawn of human cultures. Girard does not part from Dawkins's view of religion because of its evolutionary approach—Girard sees mimetic theory in basic agreement with Darwinism (Girard 2007b, Girard 2008b)—but because it does not understand properly the role of religion in the emergence of human culture. According to Girard, it was religion that helped archaic communities to overcome the communal crises created by recurrent mimetic rivalries.

To understand this claim, one has to focus on the rites and prohibitions that played an essential role in early religions. One must go beyond modern understandings, which reduce religion to merely cognitive concepts, and examine the anthropology of conflict. Girard clearly sides in this regard with thinkers such as the French sociologist Emile Durkheim, the anthropologist Arthur Maurice Hocart, and Walter Burkert, a scholar of Greek mythology and cult, and not with Richard Dawkins and others who do not understand the evolutionary role of early religions (Durkheim 1965: 463–466; Hocart 1936: 34–40; Burkert 1983; Hamerton-Kelly 1987; Palaver 2010e). Girard expressly rejects those who "believe that religion is primarily an intellectual explanation of the world," who neglect the importance of sacrifice and ritual (Girard and Palaver 2008; cf. Girard 2008b: 71–73):

> "I believe that the two great institutions of archaic religion, prohibitions and sacrifice, played an essential role in the ability of our still-animal ancestors to evolve into human beings without destroying themselves in the process." (Girard 2007b: 36)

This insight leads to a main pillar of mimetic theory: Girard's hypothesis that human culture is rooted in the scapegoat mechanism. According to Girard, early human communities had no cultural or social institutions to keep mimetic rivalry in check. The natural outcome was a general crisis because all were drawn into rivalries and violence. Hobbes's description of the state of nature is similar to Girard's account of this crisis at the dawn of human civilization: "During the time men live without a common Power to keep them all in awe, they are in that condition which is called Warre; and such a warre, as is of every man, against every man"

(Hobbes 88). Without a solution to this war of all against all, human communities would have disappeared entirely because, unlike other mammals, no instinctive brakes or dominance patterns prevent them from destroying themselves. But, according to Girard, mimesis—the source of the crisis—also helps to overcome violent chaos. At the height of the crisis when all are drawn into violent rivalries and all objects that initially triggered the conflicts are no longer at the center of the rivals' attention, mimesis can unify because all the objects that created disunity have been supplanted by hatred and violence between antagonists. Unlike exclusive objects, violence against a rival can be shared. Whereas mimetic desire in its acquisitive mode causes "disunity among those who cannot possess their common object *together*," it is its antagonistic mode—a highly increased form of mimetic rivalry in which violence between the opponents has been substituted for the desire for concrete objects—that creates "solidarity among those who can fight the same enemy *together*" (Girard 1991: 186; cf. Girard 1978: 26). The arbitrary blow of one of the rivals against another can fascinate others to such a degree that they imitate this deed and join in striking the momentarily weaker individual. The war of all against all suddenly becomes a war of all against one. The single victim is expelled or killed. Girard calls this unconscious, collective deed the scapegoat mechanism.

The expelled or killed scapegoat is seen by the persecutors in two ways. He is made fully responsible for the crisis; therefore, he is an absolute evil that had to be expelled. But the sudden peace and the reconciliation that result among the persecutors are also attributed to the scapegoat. He or she is seen as both an absolute evil and an absolute good at the same time. This strange experience of badness and goodness at the same time is the archaic religious experience. The Latin root of the word *sacred, sacer,* for instance, originally meant something that is both cursed and blessed at the same time. The victim is sacralized and deified. He or she becomes a god. Archaic religion is not an invention of priests to deceive their people but the result of an unconscious social mechanism to overcome a dangerous internal crisis. It is for this reason that Girard claims that "the peoples of the world do not invent their gods. They deify their victims" (Girard 2001: 70). According to Girard, the scapegoat mechanism is the origin of religion and culture that makes all the central elements of religion (myths, rites, prohibitions) intelligible.

In regard to the relationship between violence and religion, archaic religion is first of all an important cultural institution for overcoming a primordial crisis of violence without, however, being able to free itself from violence because the killing or expulsion of the scapegoat remains a highly violent act. According to Girard, the "paradox of archaic religion" is "that, in order to prevent violence, it resorted to substitute violence" (Girard 2004b: 13). Archaic religions are violent institutions that emerge to tame and control human violence. It is for this reason that Girard claimed in his famous book on archaic religions, *Violence and the Sacred,* that violence is the "heart and secret soul of the sacred" (Girard 1972: 31). But at the same time, he did not turn religion into a simple scapegoat in order to excuse humanity's violence, by overlooking how even archaic religions are always already aiming for peace. Early on in the unfolding of mimetic theory, he underlined the fact that these "religions of violence" were also "always in search of peace" (Girard 1978: 401).

Bloody sacrifices are traces of violence leading back to the founding murder that enabled a relative peace in archaic societies. Wilhelm Mühlmann, a German anthropologist, used the term *peace of God* to discuss forms of religiously facilitated times and spaces of peace in archaic societies (Mühlmann 1964: 313–319). Two examples taken from Tacitus's *Germania* clearly show how these forms of peace are predicated on bloody sacrifices. The first example tells about a religious cult of the Semnones, a Germanic people, that was practiced in a pacified holy wood. Peace is visible in the fact that all the participants enter the sacred grove "bound with a chain" preventing the use of weapons (Tacitus 1999: 39). The ceremony, however, contains quite open violence: "A human victim is slaughtered on behalf of all present to celebrate the gruesome opening of the barbarous ritual." Given the original Latin—*ritus horrenda primordia*—the most likely reference is a founding murder (Burkert 2010: 53–54). An even stronger example can be found in Tacitus's description of a feast celebrated by some nations of the Baltic Sea who worship the goddess Nerthus, identified with Mother Earth. During the days of the feast they experience "peace and quiet" (Tacitus 1999: 40): "No one goes to war, no one takes up arms, all objects of iron are locked away." But again this time of peace relies on human sacrifice. The slaves who were washing the equipment of the cult and maybe even the goddess afterwards were "swallowed up in the same lake."

The Biblical Difference

Girard's analysis of archaic religion, however, does not explain religion in general or especially the religions of the Bible. He maintains a "biblical 'difference'" where he compares these two types of religion more closely (Girard 2004b: 14). Girard was able to demonstrate that many myths and rituals of different cultures and epochs can easily be explained with his theory. When he turned to biblical texts, however, he discovered that the main passages are not like archaic myths telling the story of a collective murder from the perspective of the murderers, but rather they side with the victim and expose the violence of the persecutors. Already in very old texts—like in the book of Genesis—we can find passages expressing a movement away from a world that practices human sacrifice. The most important text in this regard is the story of Abraham (Gen. 22) who was going to sacrifice his son Isaac until God asked him to offer a ram instead (Girard 1978: 239; Girard 2014a: 28–29). Other texts challenge the mythic pattern of archaic religions more deeply by siding directly with victims of collective persecution. Penitential psalms, the dialogues in the book of Job, passages in the writing prophets—especially the Suffering Servant Song (Isa. 52–53)—tell us about the collective violence against an innocent victim. The most important passages in the Bible in this regard are the passion narratives in the New Testament. Like mythical texts, these narratives talk about collective violence against a single individual. For Girard, biblical narratives, unlike other myths, do not side with the persecutors but reveal the innocence of the scapegoat Jesus. In John's gospel, a quote from Psalms underlines clearly the innocence of Jesus: "They hated me without a cause" (Jn. 15:25; cf. Ps. 35:19). From a Girardian point of view, Judaism and even more so Christianity stand in opposition to archaic religion. The biblical religions are not rooted in the scapegoat mechanism but expose it.

ISLAM AS PART OF AN ABRAHAMIC REVOLUTION

More recently mimetic researchers have pondered whether Islamic traditions also expose the scapegoat mechanism (Girard 2010: 211–217; Palaver 2010c). The debate is still going on, but there is enough evidence to understand Islam as part of an Abrahamic tradition that is characterized by the overcoming of scapegoating. We justly can speak of an Abrahamic revolution that overcame the stage of archaic religions (Palaver 2009). Compared to the Bible, the Qur'an is not so much a narrative text but a collection of prophetic words addressed to different problems and situations facing the prophet Muhammad. Due to this, it is important to read not only the text of the Qur'an but also the biography of the prophet to come to a better understanding. A traditional perspective is given for instance in Martin Lings's *Muhammad: His Life Based on the Earliest Sources*. From a mimetic perspective, this biography includes a moving story about the grandfather of Muhammad, Abd al-Muttalib, who once vowed to sacrifice one of his sons if God would bless him with ten sons that would all grow to manhood. This vow forced him into deep troubles when he finally had ten grown-up sons. In the end, however, he did not sacrifice his son but a hundred camels instead, saving by this the life of 'Abd Allāh who became later the father of Muhammad.

This story is of course a biographical parallel to the biblical story about Abraham and Isaac that we can also find in the Qur'an in the narrative wherein Abraham sacrificed an animal instead of his son Ishmael (Sura 37:107: "And We ransomed him with a momentous sacrifice"). Bruce Chilton refers to Sura 37:106 ("this was obviously a trial") to show that the Qur'an refined the vision of God by detaching it even further from the violence. Muhammad's vision was that "violence is never God's requirement, but only an obvious trial" (Chilton 2008: 170). An important passage in the Qur'an in this regard is also Sura 12, which tells the story of Joseph, the lengthiest biblical narrative that is also included in the Qur'an. Like the biblical story, this story of Joseph represents the overcoming of scapegoating and the monotheistic rejection of the divinization of the victim, because Joseph is proved innocent. According to Girard, the story about Joseph is essential to understanding the overcoming of the scapegoat mechanism (Girard 2004a: 107–113; Girard 1987: 149–153; Girard 2014a: 28–29; Girard

2001: 107–117; cf. Williams 1991: 54–60; Goodhart 1996: 99–121). All these stories show us that Islam is part of the Abrahamic revolution breaking with the sacrificial culture rooted in the scapegoat mechanism. Like Judaism and Christianity, it sides with the victims of aggression and condemns the persecution of the innocent. Life is sacred, and the killing of innocents is not allowed: Sura 5:32 ("If any one slew a person…it would be as if he slew the whole people: and if any one saved a life, it would be as if he saved the life of the whole people") and Sura 17:33 ("Nor take life—which Allah has made sacred—except for just cause").

CHRISTIAN NONVIOLENCE AND SACRIFICE

The Second Testament especially opens a nonviolent way toward peace (Wink). The Sermon on the Mount (Mt. 5–7) makes people aware of how dangerous it is to succumb to mimetic rivalry in that it recommends a nonviolent response to all threats of violence. Because violence is such a contagious and mimetic force, Jesus warns his disciples not to give in to its attraction: "Put your sword back into its place; for all who take the sword will perish by the sword" (Mt. 26:52). The Gospel aims for peace without legitimating violence as a means to this goal. Such a thesis, however, needs further clarification because Christian nonviolence does not mean a stance beyond and completely outside violence. It is a dangerous illusion to think that such a neutral space outside violence is desirable or even possible.

In the early stage of the development of mimetic theory, Girard had given in to this temptation. Girard emphasized the difference between archaic sacrifice and biblical Christianity so much that he vehemently rejected the use of the term *sacrifice* to describe Jesus's laying down of his life on the cross in his earlier writings (Girard 1987: 240–243). To distance himself from the nineteenth-century identification of myth and the Bible, he avoided using the same term for the archaic sacrifice and for Jesus's suffering on the cross. Girard, however, did not continue his initial and radical rejection of the term *sacrifice*. His longtime collaboration with Raymund Schwager, a Jesuit who taught dogmatics in Innsbruck, led him to the conclusion that emphasizing the difference between archaic sacrifice and Christian self-giving love does not prevent him from accepting a humanistic and progressive illusion concerning his understanding of sacrifice. In an interview with Rebecca Adams, conducted in 1992, he openly criticizes his earlier position, admitting that at that time he was scapegoating the word *sacrifice,* really "trying to get rid of it" (Girard and Adams 1993: 29). The most extensive treatment of his new approach on sacrifice can be found in his contribution to the Festschrift that was published on the occasion of Schwager's sixtieth birthday in 1995 (Girard 1995; Girard 2014b: 33–45; cf. Schwager 1999). Since then, he again and again explained his changed attitude in regard to sacrifice (Girard 2014a: 4, 114–115; Girard 2007a: 28, 1001; Girard 2008b: 216–217; Vattimo and Girard 2010: 92–94). Most importantly, his new attitude can be found in the new French volume that came out in 2007 comprising Girard's first four books. In a long footnote he distances himself from his earlier position, and he deletes also a passage from *Things Hidden since the Foundation of the World* that became most questionable to him (Girard 2007a: 28, 998, 1001; cf. Girard 1987:243).

How can we summarize Girard's new position on sacrifice? First, Girard maintains, of course, that the difference between "archaic sacrifices" and the "sacrifice of Christ" is so great that hardly anything greater can be conceived (Girard 2014b: 41): "No greater difference can be found: on the one hand, sacrifice as murder; on the other hand, sacrifice as the readiness to die in order not to participate in sacrifice as murder" (Girard 2008b: 215). Girard holds to his view developed in his earlier work that there is a fundamental difference between myth and the Bible. But this important distinction does not have to be understood as a radical separation negating any connection between archaic religions and the Judeo-Christian revelation. According to Girard, a "paradoxical unity of religion in all its forms" exists if we take the whole of human history into account, referring with this expression indirectly to an ontology of peace that is rooted in creation and has a forming influence on the archaic religions too (Girard 2014b: 43). Whoever rejects this unity—we modern people are tempted to deny it—easily turns toward scapegoating, because by occupying a seemingly innocent and pure position one thinks one is legitimated in condemning all archaic attempts to make peace. Modern massacres—the slaughter of indigenous people in Latin America legitimated by the rejection of their reputed human sacrifice is one telling example—are the result of this moralistic and puritan attitude of a *corruptio optimi pessima*, a corruption of the best always leading to the worst (Palaver 2013: 234–236). Girard's emphasis on the paradoxical unity of all that is religious opens his theory to an interreligious perspective because it no longer relies on an unbridgeable gap between Christianity and all other religions. It is also systematically important to understand with Girard that we cannot easily put aside all violence that necessitates sacrifice. Violence—as long as it remains part of human relations—is either shifted on someone else (scapegoating) or it is overcome by someone ready to endure it (self-giving). It corresponds to this line of thinking that Simone Weil distinguishes the "false God" changing "suffering into violence" from the "true God" changing "violence into suffering" and that she explains the "redemptive suffering" of "a perfectly pure being" like the "just servant of Isaiah" or the "Lamb of God" as the transformation of sin into suffering (Weil 2002: 72).

The Ambiguous Cachet of Victimhood

This short reflection on the complex topic of sacrifice is a good illustration of the possible and dangerous distortions that came about with the Abrahamic revolution. The exposure of the scapegoat mechanism does not automatically lead to a

more peaceful world but rather may terribly increase violence when the scapegoat mechanism is distorted. To a certain degree, such fragmented and distorted
influences of the Abrahamic revelation help us to explain some of the temptations
toward violence in our contemporary world. Girard was clearly aware of this problem when he referred early on to misuses of the biblical perspective:

> If the revelation is to be used as a weapon of divisive power in mimetic rivalry
> it must first be divided. As long as it remains intact it will be a force for peace,
> and only if it is fragmented can it be used in service of war. Broken into pieces
> it provides the opposing doubles with weapons that are vastly superior to what
> would be available in its absence. (Girard 1986: 116)

The most intriguing example of such a distortion of the Abrahamic tradition is
connected to its siding with the victims. The Abrahamic concern for victims has
led to the best and worst in our world. On the one hand, it has led to a strong
emphasis on human rights. On the other hand, it has led to violent defenses of victims in the human rights struggle. The Abrahamic solidarity with the victim easily
turns into an aggressive weapon if taking the side of the victim is not connected
with forgiveness of persecutors.

We can underline both these tendencies by referring to Elias Canetti's concept
of the "religions of lament" (Palaver 2008; Palaver 2010a). Referring especially to
Christians and Shiite Muslims, Canetti pointed out that members may side with a
persecuted victim in order to expiate their own guilt as persecutors (1960: 143–145).
Canetti refers to two additional legacies of religions of lament. First, he mentions
the tremendous increase of the value of each individual who accompanies the
spread of Christianity (1960: 467). A second, much more indirect, consequence is
a certain tendency to legitimate violent and revengeful actions by siding with a
persecuted victim. Lament can easily turn into war. Canetti mentions a typical
transmutation: "A man is killed and the members of his tribe lament him. Then
they form into a troop and set out to avenge his death on the enemy; the lamenting
pack changes into a war pack" (1960: 127; cf. 38).

There are many examples of vengeful religious lament throughout history.
Canetti refers to the Shiite lament of Hussein helping us indirectly to understand
its impact on the Iranian war with Iraq, in which Ayatollah Khomeini motivated
his people in the eight-year-long war by mandating enhancement of their lament
for Hussein (Volkan 1988: 134–135; Bonney 2007: 246). The Christian tradition also
reflects this temptation connected to lament. The most striking examples are the
Crusades when Christians fought against Jews and Muslims, legitimating their violence by emphasizing their solidarity with the crucified Jesus (Bartlett 2001: 109).
The temptation of a vengeful religious lament has become a common dimension
of contemporary incidents of religiously—and also secular—motivated violence,
especially of terrorism. Muslim, Jewish, and Christian terrorists and even the Aum
Shinrikyo group that carried out a poison gas attack on the Tokyo subways in 1995
legitimate their violent acts as deeds in defence of persecuted victims (Hoffman
1998: 95–127; Juergensmeyer 2001: 12; Taylor 2004: 36). Osama bin Laden is a perfect
example of this tendency when he accuses America and Israel of "killing the weak

men, women, and children in the Muslim world and elsewhere" (Lawrence 1996:
40). He sides instead with the victims and refers to oppressed Muslims in Saudi
Arabia, persecuted Palestinians, 600,000 children suffering in Iraq because of
United Nations sanctions, killed Muslims in Bosnia-Herzegovina, and Japanese
victims who were killed by atomic bombs used by the United Stated in World
War II. Louise Richardson, one of the leading experts on terrorism, summarized
the way terrorists all over the world see themselves today as representing the perspective of the victim:

> Sociologist Mark Juergensmeyer asked Dr Abdul Aziz Rantisi, one of the founders
> of Hamas (assassinated by Israel in April 2004), in what way he thought Hamas
> was misunderstood. He said, 'You think we are aggressors. That is the number-
> one misunderstanding. We are not: we are victims.' Bin Laden, characteristically,
> phrased it more dramatically: 'The truth is the whole Muslim world is the victim
> of international terrorism, engineered by America and the United Nations.'
> A member of the IRA explained to Kevin Toolis why he joined the terrorist
> movement: 'I knew that the IRA were our defenders, looking after our interests,
> fighting for our rights. There was a great sense of anger.' On another occasion bin
> Laden used a homely analogy to explain his followers' behaviour: 'Let us look at a
> chicken, for example. If an armed person was to enter the chicken's home with the
> aim of inflicting harm on it, the chicken would automatically fight back.' Seeing
> oneself as a victim who is fighting defensively, of course, makes it altogether easier
> to justify one's action. (Richardson 2006: 65)

The temptation of vengeful lament has so much influenced our world that even fascism—including national socialism—is characterized by a violent exploitation of
the claim of being victimized (Paxton 2004: 30, 36; Taylor 2004: 36). It is therefore
no surprise that George Orwell remarked in his 1940 review of Hitler's *Mein Kampf*
that the appeal of the German Führer resulted largely from his self-stylization as
"Christ crucified," as a "martyr" and as a "victim." The Dutch writer Geert Mak
drew on Robert Paxton's description of fascism's violent exploitation of the sentiment of victimization to explain radical Islamism and right-wing populism in his
book reflecting on the murder of Theo van Gogh by a radical Muslim. According to
Mak, the emphasis on victimhood is central for the justification of violent actions
by extremists (Mak 2005: 81–83, 90). As soon as such people view themselves as
victims, the aggression against their enemies becomes limitless. Considering
Canetti's concept of religions of lament it is furthermore interesting to note that
suicide bombers first emerged among Shiite Muslims known for their lament of
Hussein, the murdered grandson of Mohammed. Only later did Sunni terrorists
begin to imitate them (Allam 2002: 139–140). Navid Kermani, a German Muslim
writer and Islamic scholar, summarizes how lamenting Hussein is connected to
contemporary wars and acts of terrorism: "During the Iran-Iraq War, the Shiite
cult of martyrdom prompted many Iranian soldiers, including children and teenagers, to rush headlong into the Iraqi minefields, with the cry 'Ya Hussein' on their
lips. It also led in 1983 to a member of the Lebanese Hizbollah being willing, for the
first time, to carry out a suicide bombing." Kermani, however, is also right to claim

that there is no direct connection between lamenting Hussein and terrorist acts such as 9/11: "The question of why people are prepared to transform themselves into living missiles cannot... be fully explained by telling the story of Hussein; but September 11 probably also cannot be explained without reference to this story" (Kermani 2002).

Far beyond Islam as such or specific developments in this religion, there is a general tendency toward a "cult of the victim" in our world that easily leads to violence (Lasch 1991: 67–68). Terrorism is closely connected to the vengeful instrument of victimhood. It is part of what psychiatrist Vamik Volkan called the "egoism of victimization" (Volkan 1988: 176). Volkan explains plausibly how a certain view of one's victimization, the inability to mourn properly, and one's own weakness may lead quickly to terrorism: "The individual who perceives his group as victimized and whose own sense of self is threatened by that perception may be drawn to terrorist activities in the same way that a nation that perceives itself to be victimized may go to war" (176–177). What makes our situation today even worse is the fact that counterterrorism, too—especially Bush's war against terror— has been strongly influenced by the temptation of a vengeful religious lament (Tönnies 2002: 46–49).

The temptation of vengeful religious lamenting has accompanied Abrahamic monotheism from its beginning. It has remained, of course, a permanent temptation throughout Jewish, Christian, and Muslim history. Many secularized versions of it contribute to our contemporary culture of radical victimology, often turning the concern for victims into an even more dangerous weapon. The Canadian philosopher Charles Taylor has taken up basic insights of Girard's mimetic theory to explain the dangers of our modern cult of the victim, which he calls the "powerful cachet of victimhood" (Taylor 2004: 36; cf. Palaver 2010d). With Girard, Taylor refers to the abuse of the concept of the innocent victim:

> [The Gospel] points toward the raising up of victims, of the despised and rejected. Various religious reforms involve taking the idea of reversal farther. The Reformation itself is one such example, as also is modern humanism, which defends ordinary human life against persecution in the name of 'higher' modes of spirituality. So this élan becomes part of the ethic of our time, the political ethic.... This becomes on one hand, a great force for battling against injustices. But it also becomes a way of drawing lines, denouncing enemies, the evil ones.... Because my being the victim means that you are the victimizer, I am pure. Claiming victimhood is an assertion of our purity; we are all right. Moreover, our cause is good, so we can fight, inflict a violence that is righteous: a holy violence. Hence we have a right to do terrible things, which others have not. Here is the logic of modern terrorism. (Taylor 2004: 36)

Girard has also addressed again and again the dangerous cult of the victim. According to him, we often "practice a hunt for scapegoats to the second degree, a hunt for hunters of scapegoats" (Girard 2001: 158). This perversion of the concern for victims is the reign of the Antichrist, in which fighting persecution leads to even more cruel acts of violence (Girard 2014a: 38; Girard 2001: 181).

THE ABRAHAMIC TRADITION
OF FORGIVENESS

The Abrahamic religions, however, do not automatically lead to violent abuses of victimhood. Only a distorted use of the biblical revelation is used as a weapon in the mimetic struggles of today. A quick look at the Second Testament shows how the concern for victims is accompanied by forgiveness. Contrary to all temptations of vengeful lament, the Second Testament's solidarity with the victims does not at all legitimate retribution. Jesus's heavenly father personifies the love for enemies and the rejection of revenge: "Love your enemies and pray for those who persecute you, so that you may be children of your Father in heaven; for he makes his sun rise on the evil and on the good, and sends rain on the righteous and on the unrighteous" (Mt. 5:44–45). In accordance with his father, Jesus forgave his enemies when he was murdered on the cross: "Father, forgive them; for they do not know what they are doing" (Lk. 23:34). And when he met his disciples again after his resurrection, he offered them his peace without blaming them for their weakness and cowardliness (Schwager 1999: 146, 52, 207): "Peace be with you" (Jn. 20:19). The true Christian spirit contradicts vengeful lamenting and is beyond all resentment.

In the other two Abrahamic religions, Judaism and Islam, we can also find important ways overcoming resentment and preventing the vengeful exploitation of victimhood. Derrida refers to an Abrahamic tradition of forgiveness (Derrida 2001: 28, 42). We are today so much in need of forgiveness that we should encourage all religions and worldviews to develop it as strongly as possible. Marc Gopin, for instance, emphasizes how important it is for a Jewish conflict resolution theory to overcome conceptions of enmity defining the enemy as the incarnation of evil (Gopin 2002: 41–42, 78–79). In Exodus 23:5 and in Proverbs 25:21–22, he sees important starting points in the Bible leading to the humanization of the enemy.

Forgiveness is most important to overcome the temptations of vengeful lament. It is not only recommended in the Bible in Judaism and Christianity but also in Islam. Just look to its version of the story of Joseph that represents the overcoming of scapegoating and the monotheistic rejection of the divinization of the victim. It is an important story concerning reconciliation because Joseph ultimately forgives his brothers (Gen. 50:20–21; Williams 1994: 82). This forgiveness is also powerfully expressed in the Qur'an: "Have no fear this day! May Allah forgive you, and He is the Most Merciful of those who show mercy" (Sura 12:92). In accordance with God who is seen as the "All-Merciful," the Muslim believers are called to overcome retaliation and repel evil with good (Suras 42:40–43, 16:126, 60:7, 4:34–35; Osman 2004: 58, 69–70). Islam emphasizes the need of forgiveness: "A requital for a wrong-doing is equal to it, but whoever forgives and makes peace [with the other], his [/her] reward rests with God; He, verily, does not love the transgressors" (42:40). Jawdat Said, a contemporary Muslim scholar who focuses especially on nonviolence in Islam, also emphasizes the importance of forgiveness and refers therefore to Jesus as an important example (Said 2000: 127). The Qur'an emphasizes the way of healing: "The good deed and the evil deed are not alike. Repel the evil deed with one which is better, then lo! he, between whom and thee there was enmity (will become) as though he was a bosom friend" (Sura 41:34; Said 2000: 126).

In his recent writings, Charles Taylor has focused on ways to overcome the deadlock of the cult of the victim. He recognizes a special danger in all attempts to seek a stance of purity, which easily results in scapegoating. Drawing on the work of Dostoyevsky, he contrasts the slogan "no one is to blame" and its dangerous consequences to an attitude that characterizes all the novelist's redemptive characters, "we are all to blame." According to Taylor, only those who do not exempt themselves from all evil are able to forgive others and find "a new footing of co-responsibility to the erstwhile enemy" (Taylor 2004: 39). Forgiveness is based on a "recognition of common, flawed humanity" (Taylor 2007: 709). By this, Taylor indirectly refers to the concept of original sin that, despite its many abuses and distortions throughout history, helps us to overcome attempts to blame all evil on the other by adopting a violent moralism typical of crusaders (Taylor 2007: 651–653, 698, 709). This liberating dimension of original sin is also highlighted in Girard's interpretation of Shakespeare's *The Winter's Tale*, which refers to humanity's inclination to purify oneself at the expense of scapegoats (Girard 1991: 284–287).

This applies also to our attitude toward the archaic past. The more we think we can completely break free from the bloody past, the more we are in danger of increasing our dependency on scapegoating. This problem was already addressed in relation to the difficult question of sacrifice. According to Taylor, the "recreation of scapegoating violence both in Christendom…and in the modern secular world" results from attempts of reform that try to break entirely with the past: "It is precisely these claims fully to supersede the problematic past which blinds us to the ways in which we are repeating some of its horrors in our own way" (Taylor 2007: 772). Also Girard's book on Clausewitz is fully aware of this danger, and therefore, in probably the most important chapter of this book, he follows Hölderlin's insight that there is not only a "fundamental discontinuity" but also a "continuity between the Passion and archaic religion" (Girard 2010: xv; cf. 129). Whereas the earlier Girard only emphasized the fundamental difference between Dionysus and the crucified in reversing Nietzsche, the mature Girard complements this important insight with Hölderlin's emphasis on the connection between Dionysus and Christ—"you are the brother also of Evius." That does not, however, hide the truth that "Dionysus is violence and Christ is peace" (Girard 2010: 127, 30). There is always the possibility of either slowly transforming the archaic world to the perspective of the kingdom of God or of cutting short a long and difficult path by violently eradicating the archaic past. Modern terrorism and many types of fundamentalism—including secular forms—represent attitudes that want to break completely free from the past. We are, however, in need of transformative attitudes that are ready to deal with our own involvement in violence and search for a common attempt to overcome it. Taylor refers to current examples of ways to side with the victims without giving in to revenge and counterviolence. He mentions such people as the Dalai Lama, Adam Michnik in Poland, and especially Nelson Mandela in South Africa:

> There was great political wisdom there. Because following the only too understandable path of revenge would have made it impossible to build a new, democratic society. It is this reflection which has pushed many leaders after periods in history to offer amnesties. But there was more than that here. Amnesties have the flaw that they usually involve suppressing the truth or at least consciousness of the terrible wrongs that have been done, which therefore fester in the body politic. Mandela's answer was the Truth and Reconciliation Commission, one which is meant to bring terrible deeds to light, but not necessarily in a context of retribution. Moreover, the deeds to be brought to light were not only those of the former ruling side. Here is the new ground of co-responsibility which this Commission offered. (Taylor 2007: 710)

The *Summum Bonum* and Creative Renunciation: Overcoming the Deadlocks of Mimetic Rivalry

Because mimetic rivalries are mainly responsible for human violence, we have to ask if religion provides us with a possible answer to the deadlock of mimetic rivalry. The traditional Christian answer referred to God as the highest good of our deep longings. If God is our *summum bonum,* we can imitate each other without becoming automatically enemies because God is not at all a good that is lessened if more people reach out for it. The longing for God can be shared and imitated without being driven into relationships of violence and war. The Christian tradition was fully aware of this important path to overcome violence. Both Girard and Taylor follow the tradition in this regard:

> The only way fully to escape the draw towards violence lies somewhere in the turn to transcendence, that is, through the full-hearted love of some good beyond life. Here we enter a terrain, that of religion and violence, which has been explored in a very interesting way by René Girard. (Taylor 2007: 639)

In this regard, we can find an important difference between Hobbes and Girard. Hobbes parted from the tradition of the *summum bonum* and became, therefore, a representative of an ontology of violence. For him, there was no way out of violence but only different forms to control it. It was Eric Voegelin who most clearly mentions this problem in his reflections on Hobbes:

> If there is no *summum bonum*... there is no point of orientation that can endow human action with rationality. Action, then, can only be represented as motivated by passions, above all, by the passion of aggression, the overcoming of one's fellow man. The 'natural' state of society must be understood as the war of all against all, if men do not in free love orient their actions to the highest good. (Voegelin 2000: 306; cf. 234–238)

The following focuses on the religious answer responding to the mimetic nature of human beings. We consciously broaden the perspective beyond Judaism, Christianity, and the Western world because it is exactly this broader perspective that scholars today justly demand from a further development of mimetic theory (Depoortere 2008: 147; Nordhofen 2008: 243–248; Kirwan 2009: 120–131). Even Girard has begun to open up mimetic theory by starting to take also the Vedic tradition, the Upanishads, Buddhism, and Jainism into account (Girard 2011; Girard 2008b: 211–214).

We can start this final section by emphasizing the universally recognized interdependence of imitation and religion. Human beings are mimetic and religious at the same time. *Homo mimeticus* and *homo religiosus* cannot be separated. In the Western world, we can point to Plato and Augustine who both emphasized that we always imitate what we admire (Plato 2000: 205 [Rep. 500b–c]; Augustine 2003: 324 [De civ. VIII.17]). This insight is also part of the Asian tradition if we turn, for instance, to the Bhagavad Gita: "Whatsoever a great man does, the same is done by others as well. Whatever standard he sets, the world follows" (Radhakrishnan 2003: 140 [III.21]). The modern world brings this connection even more strongly out into the open. The modern worship of celebrities characterizing our world of media is probably the most visible sign today how imitation and religion are still strongly connected to each other. Human beings are characterized by self-transcendence, a religious yearning to go beyond our natural given self (cf. Taylor 2007: 5–12, 638–639). Mimetic desire roots in this religious dimension of human life. Mimetic theory explains convincingly how easily mimetic desire turns into rivalry and violence. As soon as our basic needs are satisfied, mimetic desire is likely to turn us quickly into rivals fighting for recognition, exclusive objects and other worldly goods. Hölderlin summarized this tendency in a remarkable metaphor in his novel *Hyperion*: "Young lambs butt their heads together when they are sated with their mother's milk" (Hölderlin 1990: 69). A negative turn of mimetic desire, however, is not inevitable. Girard's mimetic theory is not an ontology of violence.

In the biblical traditions it is especially the tenth commandment of the Decalogue that speaks to the religious response to mimetic rivalry. Girard has strongly emphasized the importance of this biblical text (Girard 2001: 7–9; Girard 2008b: 62–63): "You shall not covet your neighbor's house; you shall not covet your neighbor's wife, or male or female slave, or ox, or donkey, or anything that belongs to your neighbor" (Ex. 20:17). Again it is not that difficult to find parallels in other world religions. In the Qur'an, we can read a similar commandment: "Covet not the thing in which Allah hath made some of you excel others" (Sura 4:32). Also in the first mantra of the Isha Upanishad, in which Mahatma Gandhi recognized a summary of the Bhagavad Gita and also the truth that can be found in all religions, we can find the prohibition of mimetic rivalry: "All this, whatsoever moves on earth, is to be hidden in the Lord (the Self). When thou hast surrendered all this, then thou mayest enjoy. Do not covet the wealth of any man!" (Upanishads 1962: 311; cf. Gandhi 1976: 258–260, 289–290).

In all the great religious traditions, we can find prohibitions of covetousness to prevent mimetic rivalry. These traditions, however, must not be reduced to prohibitions. Their core consists in allowing human beings a way of life that does not end up in the deadlock of mimetic rivalry. We have to take the Decalogue in its entirety to realize that it is the first commandment that addresses God who as our highest good enables us to reach mimetically out for him without being at the same time forced into envious destruction (Palaver 2005: 150–151). A saying of Muhammad also summarizes this positive side dedicated to the overcoming of mimetic rivalry: "None of you has faith until you love for your brother what you love for yourself" (Sahih Al-Bukhari, Kitab al-Iman, Hadith no. 13). The Christian tradition has also always emphasized the longing for God as our highest good— our *summum bonum*—as a way to overcome and avoid envious rivalry. It is along this way that Pope John Paul II emphasized in his speech to the General Assembly of the United Nations in 1979 the importance of the spiritual goods to build peace in the world. He understood it as the major task of Christianity and all the other religions in the world to focus on these spiritual or eternal goods (John Paul II). In regard to positive mimesis Girard emphasizes the imitation of Christ. It is the way Christians are told to lead a life beyond mimetic rivalry. Girard interprets the imitation of Christ in the context of rivalries prohibited in the tenth commandment of the First Testament:

> Jesus asks us to imitate him, rather than the neighbour, in order to protect us from the mimetic rivalry. The model that encourages mimetic rivalry isn't necessarily worse than we are, he is maybe much better, but he desires in the same we do, selfishly, avidly, therefore we imitate his selfishness, and he is a bad model for us, just as we will be a bad model for him in the process of doubling that is bound to take place as soon as the rivalry escalates. (Girard 2008b: 63)

An important biblical passage summarizing how a proper orientation of our mimetic longings enables us to overcome the deadlocks of mimetic desire can be found in Luke 12:13–34. This passage consists mainly in warnings against covetousness, which is mimetic desire turning into greed or miserliness: "Take care! Be on your guard against all kinds of greed; for one's life does not consist in the abundance of possessions" (Lk. 12:15). The parable of the rich fool (12:16–20) illustrates the futility of a life longing for nothing but worldly possessions. By using ravens and lilies as positive examples, Jesus explains to his disciples how a life of covetousness, of mimetic desire turning into insatiable runaway rivalries, ends up in a life full of worries. It is not by chance that Hölderlin, a hypermimetic person living in an age more and more governed by mimetic rivalries, writes all the time about a life threatened by worries, hopelessly seeking silence and peace. Walter Benjamin rightly calls worries a "mental illness characteristic of the age of capitalism" in his currently much discussed fragment "Capitalism as Religion" from 1921 (Benjamin 1996: 290; Palaver 2007: 221–223). How deeply this passage in the Gospel of Luke is aware of mimetic rivalry as the source of these problems becomes visible in the opening of it, which refers to two enemy brothers fighting over their inheritance.

One of them asks Jesus to solve their conflict: "Teacher, tell my brother to divide the family inheritance with me" (Lk. 12:13). Jesus's answer to this request makes clear that he is not willing to solve this conflict by those means of worldly justice that always rely to some degree on violence, by referring indirectly to the murder that Moses committed when he intervened in a conflict: "Friend, who set me to be a judge or arbitrator over you?" (Lk. 12:14; cf. Ex. 2:14). René Girard rightly remarks in his refection on Jesus's response that violence is no longer an option to create justice.

> It is no longer possible to separate the enemy brothers by a controlled violence that would put an end to their violence.... There are only enemy brothers, and they can only be warned against their mimetic desire in the hope they will renounce it. (Girard 1986: 129)

According to the teachings of Jesus, worldly justice has to give in to the justice of the kingdom of God that enters our world wherever we turn our hearts toward the highest good: "Strive for his kingdom.... For where your treasure is, there your heart will be also" (Lk. 12:31–34). Most encyclicals in the tradition of Catholic social thought since *Rerum novarum* in 1891 refer, for instance, to this call to seek the kingdom first or its parallel in the Gospel of Matthew (Mt. 6:33), in order to emphasize that only a true order of goods overcomes all ontologies of violence and enables a development towards a more peaceful world (Palaver 2005: 156–158).

Again, not only the Judeo-Christian tradition is aware how renunciation, the lifting up of your hearts to God, helps humankind to overcome the deadlocks of mimetic rivalries. Mahatma Gandhi's comment on the previously cited mantra shows that it comes close to the passage we just discussed from the Gospel of Luke. He again and again came back to this mantra recognizing in it a deep religious truth—beyond any particular religion—that is essential to create peace in the world. In a speech in 1937, he underlined how much this mantra contributes to a peaceful life:

> If you believe that God pervades everything that He has created, you must believe that you cannot enjoy anything that is not given by Him. And seeing that He is the Creator of His numberless children, it follows that you cannot covet anybody's possession. If you think that you are one of His numerous creatures, it behoves you to renounce everything and lay it at His feet. That means that the act of renunciation of everything is not a mere physical renunciation but represents a second or new birth. It is a deliberate act, not done in ignorance. It is therefore a regeneration. And then, since he who holds the body must eat and drink and clothe himself, he must naturally seek all that he needs from Him. And he gets it as a natural reward of that renunciation. As if this was not enough, the *mantra* closes with this magnificent thought: Do not covet anybody's possession. The moment you carry out these precepts you become a wise citizen of the world, living at peace with all that lives. (Gandhi 1976: 259–260)

What Gandhi summarized in this speech comes close to the deeper meaning of the Decalogue or the commandment of love in the Second Testament and goes well with Girard's understanding of a "creative renunciation"—a concept influenced by the writings of Simone Weil—in the last chapter of his first book *Deceit, Desire and the Novel* (1966: 307; Weil 2001: 99; cf. Palaver 2010b).

BIBLIOGRAPHY

Allam, Fouad. *Der Islam in einer globalen Welt*. Trans. Karl Pichler. Berlin: Verlag Klaus Wagenbach, 2002.

Augustine. *Concerning the City of God against the Pagans*. Trans. Henry Bettenson. London: Penguin Books, 2003.

Bartlett, Anthony W. *Cross Purposes: The Violent Grammar of Christian Atonement*. Harrisburg, PA: Trinity Press International, 2001.

Benjamin, Walter. "Capitalism as Religion." In *Selected Writings. Volume 1: 1913–1926*. Eds. Marcus Bullock and Michael W. Jennings, 288–291. Cambridge, MA: Belknap Press of Harvard University Press, 1996.

Bonney, Richard. *Jihad: From Qur'an to Bin Laden*. New York: Palgrave Macmillan, 2007.

Burkert, Walter. *Homo Necans: The Anthropology of Ancient Greek Sacrificial Ritual and Myth*. Trans. Peter Bing. Berkeley: University of California Press, 1983.

Burkert, Walter. "Horror Stories. Zur Begegnung von Biologie, Philologie und Religion." In *Gewalt und Opfer. Im Dialog mit Walter Burkert*. Eds. Anton Bierl and Wolfgang Braungart, 45–56. Berlin: De Gruyter, 2010.

Canetti, Elias. *Crowds and Power*. 1960. Trans. Carol Stewart. New York: Farrar Straus and Giroux, 1984.

Chilton, Bruce. *Abraham's Curse: Child Sacrifice in the Legacies of the West*. New York: Doubleday, 2008.

Dawkins, Richard. *The God Delusion*. Boston: Houghton Mifflin Company, 2006.

Depoortere, Frederiek. *Christ in Postmodern Philosophy: Gianni Vattimo, René Girard and Slavoj Zizek*. London: T & T Clark, 2008.

Derrida, Jacques. *On Cosmopolitanism and Forgiveness*. Trans. Mark Dooley and Michael Hughes. London: Routledge, 2001.

Durkheim, Emile. *The Elementary Forms of the Religious Life*. 1912. Trans. Joseph Ward Swain. New York: The Free Press, 1965.

Gandhi, Mohandas Karamchand. *The Collected Works of Mahatma Gandhi. Vol. 64: November 3, 1936–March 14, 1937*. New Delhi: The Publications Division, 1976.

Girard, René. *Deceit, Desire and the Novel: Self and Other in Literary Structure*. Trans. Yvonne Freccero. Baltimore: Johns Hopkins University Press, 1966.

Girard, René. *Violence and the Sacred*. Trans. Patrick Gregory. Baltimore: Johns Hopkins University Press, 1977.

Girard, René. *The Scapegoat*. Trans. Yvonne Freccero. Baltimore: Johns Hopkins University Press, 1986.

Girard, René. *When These Things Begin: Conversations with Michel Treguer*. Translated by Trevor Cribben Merrill. East Lansing: Michigan State University Press, 2014a.

Girard, René. *A Theater of Envy: William Shakespeare*. Oxford, UK: Oxford University Press, 1991.

Girard, René, and Rebecca Adams. "Violence, Difference, Sacrifice: A Conversation with René Girard." *Religion & Literature* 25.2 (1993): 11–33.

Girard, René. *When These Things Begin: Conversations with Michel Treguer*. Translated by Trevor Cribben Merrill. East Lansing: Michigan State University Press, 2014a.

Girard, René. *The One by Whom Scandal Comes*. Translated by M. B. DeBevoise. East Lansing: Michigan State University Press, 2014b.

Girard, René. *I See Satan Fall Like Lightning*. Trans. James G. Williams. Maryknoll, NY: Orbis Books, 2001.

Girard, René. *Oedipus Unbound: Selected Writings on Rivalry and Desire*. Palo Alto, CA: Stanford University Press, 2004a.

Girard, René. "Violence and Religion: Cause or Effect?" *The Hedgehog Review* 6.1 (2004b): 8–20.

Girard, René. *De La Violence À La Divinité*. Bibliothèque Grasset. Paris: Bernard Grasset, 2007a.

Girard, René. *Wissenschaft und Christlicher Glaube*. Trans. Shivaun Heath. Tübingen, Germany: Mohr Siebeck, 2007b.

Girard, René, and Wolfgang Palaver. "The Bloody Skin of the Victim." In *The New Visibility of Religion: Studies in Religion and Cultural Hermeneutics*. Eds. Michael Hoelzl and Graham Ward, 59–67. London: Continuum, 2008.

Girard, René. *Evolution and Conversion: Dialogues on the Origin of Culture*. London: Continuum, 2008b.

Girard, René. *Battling to the End: Conversations with Benoît Chantre*. Trans. Mary Baker. Studies in Violence, Mimesis, and Culture. East Lansing: Michigan State University Press, 2010.

Girard, René. *Sacrifice*. Trans. Matthew Pattillo and David Dawson. Breakthroughs in Mimetic Theory. East Lansing: Michigan State University Press, 2011.

Goodhart, Sandor. *Sacrificing Commentary: Reading the End of Literature*. Baltimore: Johns Hopkins University Press, 1996.

Gopin, Marc. *Between Eden and Armageddon: The Future of World Religions, Violence, and Peacemaking*. Oxford, UK: Oxford University Press, 2002.

Hamerton-Kelly, Robert G., ed. *Violent Origins: Walter Burkert, René Girard, and Jonathan Z. Smith on Ritual Killing and Cultural Formation*. Palo Alto, CA: Stanford University Press, 1987.

Hobbes, Thomas. *Leviathan*. 1651. Cambridge, UK: Cambridge University Press, 1991.

Hocart, Arthur Maurice. *Kings and Councillors: An Essay in the Comparative Anatomy of Human Society*. 1936. Chicago: University of Chicago Press, 1970.

Hoffman, Bruce. *Inside Terrorism*. London: Gollancz, 1998.

Hölderlin, Friedrich. *Hyperion and Selected Poems*. Trans. Eric L. Santner. The German Library. New York: Continuum, 1990.

John Paul II. "Address to the United Nations." (1979). <http://www.newadvent.org/library/docs_jp02u1.htm>.

Juergensmeyer, Mark. *Terror in the Mind of God: The Global Rise of Religious Violence*. 2001. Berkeley: University of California Press, 2001.

Kermani, Navid. "A Dynamite of the Spirit." *Times Literary Supplement*. 5165 (2002): 13–15.

Kirwan, Michael. *Girard and Theology*. Philosophy and Theology. London: T & T Clark, 2009.

Lasch, Christopher. "Liberalism and Civic Virtue." *Telos* 88 (1991): 57–68.

Lawrence, Bruce, ed. *Messages to the World: The Statements of Osama Bin Laden*. London: Verso, 2005.

Lings, Martin. *Muhammad: His Life Based on the Earliest Sources*. 1983. Rochester, VT: Inner Traditions, 2006.

Mak, Geert. *Der Mord an Theo Van Gogh. Geschichte einer moralischen Panik*. Trans. Marlene Müller-Haas. Frankfurt am Main: Suhrkamp, 2005.

Mühlmann, Wilhelm E. *Rassen, Ethnien, Kulturen. Moderne Ethnologie*. Neuwied, Germany: Luchterhand, 1964.

Müller, Friedrich Max, trans. Upanishads. *The Upanishads. Part I*. 1879. New York: Dover Publications, Inc., 1962.

Nordhofen, Jacob. *Durch das Opfer erlöst? Die Bedeutung der Rede vom Opfer Jesu Christi in der Bibel und bei René Girard*. Beiträge zur mimetischen Theorie. Vienna: LIT, 2008.

Orwell, George. "Review of *Mein Kampf* by Adolf Hitler." In *George Orwell: The Collected Essays, Journalism & Letters. Vol. 2: My Country Right or Left, 1940–1943*. 1940. Eds. Sonia Orwell and Ian Angus, 12–14. Boston: David R. Godine, 2000.

Osman, Mohamed Fathi. "God Is the All-Peace, the All-Merciful." *Beyond Violence: Religious Sources for Social Transformation in Judaism, Christianity and Islam*. Ed. James L. Ashland Heft, 57–73. New York: Fordham University Press, 2004.

Palaver, Wolfgang. "Envy or Emulation: A Christian Understanding of Economic Passions." *Passions in Economy, Politics, and the Media: In Discussion with Christian Theology*. Eds. Wolfgang Palaver and Petra Steinmair-Pösel, 139–162. Beiträge zur mimetischen Theorie. Münster, Germany: LIT, 2005.

Palaver, Wolfgang. "Challenging Capitalism as Religion: Hans G. Ulrich's Theological and Ethical Reflections on the Economy." *Studies in Christian Ethics* 20.2 (2007): 215–230.

Palaver, Wolfgang. "The Ambiguous Cachet of Victimhood: On Violence and Monotheism." In *The New Visibility of Religion: Studies in Religion and Cultural Hermeneutics*. Eds. Hoelzl, Michael and Graham Ward, 68–87. London: Continuum, 2008.

Palaver, Wolfgang. *René Girard's Mimetic Theory*. Translated by Gabriel Borrud. East Lansing: Michigan State University Press, 2013.

Palaver, Wolfgang. "Abrahamitische Revolution, politische Gewalt und positive Mimesis. Der Islam aus der Sicht der mimetischen Theorie." Im *Wettstreit um das Gute. Annäherungen an den Islam aus der Sicht der mimetischen Theorie*. Eds. Wilhelm Guggenberger and Wolfgang Palaver, 29–73. Beiträge zur mimetischen Theorie. Vienna: LIT, 2009.

Palaver, Wolfgang. "The Ambiguous Cachet of Victimhood: Elias Canetti's "Religions of Lament" and Abrahamic Monotheism." *Forum Bosnae* 49 (2010a): 19–31.

Palaver, Wolfgang. "Die Frage des Opfers im Spannungsfeld von West und Ost. René Girard, Simone Weil und Mahatma Gandhi über Gewalt und Gewaltfreiheit." *Zeitschrift für Katholische Theologie* 132.4 (2010b): 462–481.

Palaver, Wolfgang. "An Essay on Islam and the Return to the Archaic." *The Bulletin of the Colloquium on Violence & Religion* 37 (2010c): 6–10.

Palaver, Wolfgang. "Religion und Gewalt: René Girards und Charles Taylors komplementäre Beiträge zu einer zeitgemäßen Theorie." In *Kommunitarismus und Religion*. Ed. Michael Kühnlein, 319–328. Deutsche Zeitschrift für Philosophie. Sonderband. Berlin: Akademie Verlag, 2010d.

Palaver, Wolfgang. "Violence and Religion: Walter Burkert and René Girard in Comparison." *Contagion: Journal of Violence, Mimesis, and Culture* 17 (2010e): 121–137.

Paxton, Robert O. *The Anatomy of Fascism*. New York: Alfred A. Knopf, 2004.

Plato. *The Republic.* Trans. Tom Griffith. Cambridge, UK: Cambridge University Press, 2000.

Radhakrishnan, S. *The Bhagavadgita: With an Introductory Essay, Sanskrit Text.* New Delhi: HarperCollins Publishers India, 2003.

Richardson, Louise. *What Terrorists Want: Understanding the Terrorist Threat.* London: John Murray, 2006.

Said, Jawdat. "Law, Religion and the Prophetic Method of Social Change." *Journal of Law and Religion* 15.1/2 (2000): 83–150.

Schwager, Raymund. *Jesus in the Drama of Salvation: Toward a Biblical Doctrine of Redemption.* 1990. Trans. James G. Williams and Paul Haddon. New York: Crossroad Publishing Company, 1999.

Schwager, Raymund. *Must There Be Scapegoats? Violence and Redemption in the Bible.* 1978. Trans. Maria L. Assad. San Francisco: Harper & Row, 1987.

Tacitus, Cornelius. *Agricola and Germany.* Trans. Anthony Richard Birley. Oxford World's Classics. Oxford, UK: Oxford University Press, 1999.

Taylor, Charles. "Notes on the Sources of Violence: Perennial and Modern." In *Beyond Violence: Religious Sources for Social Transformation in Judaism, Christianity and Islam.* Ed. James L. Ashland Heft, 15–42. New York: Fordham University Press, 2004.

Taylor, Charles. *A Secular Age.* Cambridge, MA: Belknap Press, 2007.

Tönnies, Sybille. *Cosmopolis Now. Auf dem Weg zum Weltstaat.* Hamburg: Europäische Verlagsanstalt, 2002.

Vattimo, Gianni, and René Girard. *Christianity, Truth, and Weakening Faith: A Dialogue.* Trans. William McCuaig. New York: Columbia University Press, 2010.

Voegelin, Eric. *Modernity without Restraints: The Political Religions, the New Science of Politics, and Science, Politics, and Gnosticism.* The Collected Works of Eric Voegelin. Columbia: University of Missouri Press, 2000.

Volkan, Vamik D. *The Need to Have Enemies and Allies: From Clinical Practice to International Relationships.* Northvale, NJ: Jason Aronson, 1988.

Weil, Simone. *Gravity and Grace.* 1947. Trans. Emma Crawford and Mario von der Ruhr. London: Routledge, 2002.

Weil, Simone. *Waiting for God.* 1951. Trans. Emma Craufurd. New York: Perennial Classics, 2001.

Williams, James G. *The Bible, Violence, and the Sacred: Liberation from the Myth of Sanctioned Violence.* Foreword by René Girard. San Francisco: HarperSanFrancisco, 1991.

Williams, James G. "'Steadfast Love and Not Sacrifice': A Nonsacrificial Reading of the Hebrew Scriptures." In *Curing Violence.* Eds. Mark I. Wallace and Theophus H. Smith, 71–99. Sonoma, CA: Polebridge Press, 1994.

Wink, Walter. *Jesus and Nonviolence: A Third Way.* Minneapolis: Fortress Press, 2003.

CHAPTER 37

RELIGION AND SCARCITY

A NEW THEORY FOR THE ROLE OF RELIGION IN VIOLENCE

HECTOR AVALOS

I⊤ is no secret that September 11, 2001, renewed our attention to the relationship between religion and violence. That event certainly helped me to focus more on a topic that I had already discussed in academic venues (Avalos 2001). By the time I began work on my book, *Fighting Words: The Origins of Religious Violence* (2005), I had concluded that scarce resource theory offered a viable and wide-ranging framework to explain violence from the smallest units of human organization to the largest.

Scarce resource theory can be traced at least to the work of Thomas Malthus (1766–1834). Malthus analyzed how growing populations would create greater demand for scarce resources, especially food. The inability to meet this demand, in turn, could drive conflict. Modern variants of Malthusian analysis can be found in the work of Amartya Sen, winner of the 1998 Nobel Prize in Economic Sciences, and Jeffrey Sachs, director of the Earth Institute at Columbia University.

I found scarce resource theory particularly illuminating in explaining religious violence. Some of my thinking was influenced by a book by Regina Schwartz, *The Curse of Cain: The Violent Legacy of Monotheism* (1997). Therein, she argued that monotheism was inherently violent. Since monotheism advocates only one legitimate deity, then the worship of anything else is a violation of boundaries.

The creation of a group of outsiders then becomes the prime catalyst for violence. The life of outsiders may be devalued, and so killing them can be justified. But more intriguing was her allusion to the scarce resources created by monotheism.

I wondered if similar mechanisms were at work, not just in monotheism but in religion as a whole. I asked myself whether religion is inherently violent. If not, what are the mechanisms by which religion results in violence? Are those factors the same as the ones that cause other types of violence? Is there something special about religion that makes it prone to violence? Or are we misperceiving religion by focusing too much on its violent side?

The questions seemed particularly important because there is a definite stream of popular opinion and scholarship that denies that religion is the cause of some specific conflicts or of violence in general. One prominent representative is William T. Cavanaugh, author of *The Myth of Religious Violence* (2009), which argues that religion does not really exist, and so religious violence also does not exist. Similarly, Alan Jacobs has argued that "the whole notion of religion as a cause of violence is...a function of the desire to believe that religion is eliminable" (2003: 231).

In contrast to Cavanaugh and Jacobs, I conclude that religion does have a coherent and detectable referent in the real world and that religion, while not always causing violence, is inherently prone to violence (see also Wellman and Tokuno 2004). But more importantly, I came to wonder how and why religions can be prone to violence. After much thought and the comparison of many religions, I formulated the following thesis:

1) Most violence is due to scarce resources, real or perceived. Whenever people perceive that there is not enough of something they value, then conflict may ensue to maintain or acquire that resource. This can range from love in a family to oil on a global scale.
2) When religion causes violence, it often does so because it has created new scarce resources.

This chapter aims to illustrate the viability of this theory by applying it to cases ranging from the ancient to the modern world and to the three Abrahamic religions (Judaism, Islam, and Christianity).[1]

DEFINITIONS

Any claim that religion is inherently prone to violence must begin with definitions. The first pertains to *religion,* which I define as a mode of life and thought that presupposes the existence of and relationship with unverifiable forces and/ or beings. As such, our definition is squarely and unapologetically within the empirico-rationalist tradition.[2]

This definition encompasses religions focused on personal deities as well as those that focus on forces whose existence cannot be detected by empirico-rationalist means.

All definitions of violence are value laden insofar as we choose the type of suffering and violence we value (Casey 1981). Our definition is somatocentric insofar as it values the physical human body and regards any sort of "soul" or "spirit" as nonexistent. Religions often espouse a pneumatocentric justification for violence, in which the value of the entities called the "soul" or "spirit" is paramount to those of the body. Accordingly, we define *violence* as the act of modifying and/or inflicting pain on the human body in order to express or impose power differentials.[3]

By this definition, pain or bodily modification can be inflicted on a person by others, or it can be self-inflicted, as in the case of self-flagellation and martyrdom. There are degrees of violence; a haircut or a tattoo, both bodily modifications, are not always regarded as violent. At the same time, our definition allows for the fact that depilation and tattooing can be painful forms of torture (Mascia-Lees and Sharpe 1992). Likewise, circumcision could be subsumed under violence in that it modifies a body for the purpose of expressing power differentials. Circumcision also imposes a power differential on a child, as it is not the result of a mutual decision between parent and child. Killing, of course, is regarded as the ultimate imposition of a power differential on the body.

Under our concept of violence, we can also distinguish between justified and unjustified violence. Violence in self-defense or the defense of the physical well-being of others is acceptable. The surgical modification of the body for the purposes of saving a life or empowering an individual, especially if the individual so chooses to be modified, is justified violence. In contrast, any violence not based on verifiable causes and phenomena is senseless and immoral.

CAUSALITY AND HISTORICAL EXPLANATION

Since at least the time of David Hume (1711–1776), the notion of causality has undergone severe scrutiny (Howson 2000). In the realm of historical explanation, the notion of cause has produced a crisis that is still unfolding. For our purposes, we argue that religion causes violence if and when the perpetration of violence is a logical consequence of beliefs in unverifiable forces and/or beings. The expression "logical consequence" can be represented in a more formal manner: Religious Belief X, therefore Act of Violence Y (see also Kitts 2005; Ginges and Atran 2011).

Accordingly, attribution of religious causation requires demonstration that an act of violence had a necessary precedent in a religious belief. Without that causational belief, the specific act of violence would not have occurred. For example, suppose Person A really believes that God has commanded him or her to kill witches, and this person then kills a witch. In this case, we can say that Belief X

(God has commanded Person A to kill a witch) caused the killing of the witch. In such a case, we may say that the religious belief was necessary, if not sufficient, to perpetrate this act of violence. In the clearest cases, the perpetrators may themselves cite such beliefs.

To understand how scarce resource theory can help explain religious violence, it behooves us to examine how scarcity can be viewed as fundamental to nearly all violence. A resource is any entity that persons utilize in the enterprise of living. Not all resources are regarded as of equal value, and scarce resources may be considered some of the most valuable of all. A resource may be described as scarce when it meets one or both of the following requirements: It is not easily available, whether in reality or in perception, and maintenance or acquisition of that resource requires the expense of a significant amount of emotional or physical capital and labor.

The mechanism by which scarce resources cause violence is usually the same: the effort to maintain and/or acquire Scarce Resource X. Scarce resources can range from insufficient love within a family to energy on a global scale. Thus, if an older child receives more privileges than a younger one, this may cause conflict between them. The scarce resource there is privilege. If one partner in a couple does not feel he or she has enough respect from the other, then respect is the scarce resource that may cause conflict. If nations do not have enough oil, they may fight to acquire or protect oil supplies (e.g., the Gulf wars are often said to be about oil).

The creation of a scarce resource by religion occurs when belief in supernatural forces and/or beings generates the belief that a resource is scarce in some manner. These are really perceived scarcities rather than ones we can verify exist when we do not share the religious presuppositions of believers. The effort to maintain and/or acquire that resource will be the mechanism of violence, just as it is with nonreligious types of violence.

Accordingly, religion is not the cause of all violence. Poverty, politics, nationalism, and even neuropsychological factors may generate violence. Rather, when religion causes violence, it usually does so because it has created a scarce resource.

Demonstration of this thesis consists of at least two main types of evidence. The first centers on the words of perpetrators of violence. Too often, in debates about religion and conflict, the attribution of motives is based on secondary sources or faulty deductions. One example of a clear attribution of violence to religious reasons can be seen in the following hadith reported by Al-Bukhari, perhaps the most authoritative collector of traditions about Muhammad. Al-Bukhari (1:73) tells us:

> The prophet said, "Allah...assigns for a person who participates in (holy battles) in Allah's Cause and nothing causes him to do so except belief in Allah and in His Messengers, that he will be recompensed by Allah with a reward, or booty (if he survives) or will be admitted to Paradise (if he is killed in the battle as a martyr)."

Here is a clear attribution of the reason for violence from a Muslim. This sort of self-attribution by practitioners of a religion certainly would count as strong evidence that violence was due to religious beliefs.

Not every religion in the world needs to be studied in order to establish this thesis. While most religions may be prone to violence, not all religions have an equal impact on the quality or quantity of violence that we see in the world. Here we focus on the so-called Abrahamic religions: Judaism, Christianity, and Islam, which are related insofar as they see Abraham, the biblical patriarch, as an exemplar of righteousness and as a progenitor of monotheists. The chapter discusses how religion creates scarce resources and then focuses on the following: access to the divine will, particularly through inscripturation; sacred space; group privileging; and salvation.

INSCRIPTURATION

Inscripturation refers to the reduction to writing of what is believed to be uniquely authoritative information about or from supernatural forces and/or beings. William Schniedewind has recently written on the process of textualization, which may generally refer to the process of transitioning from oral to written media (2004). However, it is important to distinguish textualization from inscripturation, as the latter has more specific features beyond those borne by simply the production of a text. A sacred scripture is created when a text is believed to bear the authoritative thoughts and actions of a god (or gods) and/or supernatural forces.

All Abrahamic religions purport to have a record of supernatural revelations in some form of writing. For Jews, it is the Tanakh. In Exodus 34:1, God is said to have written at least part of the Bible: "The LORD said to Moses, 'Cut two tablets of stone like the former ones, and I will write on the tablets the words that were on the former tablets, which you broke.'" Muslims have the Qur'an as a basic document of revelation. Christians use both the Jewish Tanakh, reconceptualized and reorganized as the "Old Testament" as well as what they call a New Testament.

In terms of scarce resource theory, writing becomes a scarce resource when not everyone has access to the writings or lacks the ability to read those writings. In the ancient Near East, most people never mastered some of the more complicated writing systems of Mesopotamia (Vesicant 2000) and would not be able to read anything regarded as sacred scripture. If these books are the basis of authority, then they are a scarce resource to those who cannot read them. But by far the most conflictive aspect of inscripturation comes when it is claimed that only one particular book or set of books contains authoritative divine revelation.

Alternatively phrased, these scarce resources can be described as centering on interpretive authority or special access to revelation. The fact that violence can result from disagreements about who has the proper access to divine communication is clear in Deuteronomy 18:20: "But any prophet who speaks in the name of other gods, or who presumes to speak in my name a word that I have not commanded the prophet to speak—that prophet shall die." Divine communication is a scarce resource, and violence must be used to maintain access to what is perceived to be the right conduit.

Conflict due to inscripturation continues into the New Testament. Note, for example, Acts 19:19: "A number of those who practiced magic collected their books and burned them publicly; when the value of these books was calculated, it was found to come to fifty thousand silver coins." The premise of such burning is that the so-called magic books did not contain God's word, and joining Christianity meant destroying rival scriptures. In Galatians 1:6–8, Paul makes the following remarks:

> I am astonished that you are so quickly deserting the one who called you in the grace of Christ and are turning to a different gospel—not that there is another gospel, but there are some who are confusing you and want to pervert the gospel of Christ. But even if we or an angel from heaven should proclaim to you a gospel contrary to what we proclaimed to you, let that one be accursed!

A gospel, here, can simply mean an oral proclamation of beliefs. But we can reasonably infer that those following such proclamations would have written them down and so constituted rival written Gospels.

Some four hundred years later, Pope Leo I (440–461) is said to advocate destroying rival scriptures: "And the apocryphal scriptures, which under the names of the Apostles, form a nursery-ground for many falsehoods, are not only to be proscribed, but also taken away altogether and burnt to ashes in the fire" (NPNF 12:25). We have other tantalizing clues about inter-Christian conflict that may have involved rival scriptures.

An example of violence between Christianity and Judaism on the issue of holy scripture can be found in the Hebrew chronicles of anti-Jewish violence in 1096, during the movements associated with the Crusades. Emicho of Leinigen was the leader of the anti-Jewish mobs, which rampaged through a number of Jewish communities, including those in Cologne, Mainz, and Worms. The chronicle of Solomon bar Simson tells what happens when a Christian destroys the Torah of a Jewish household (Eidelberg 1977: 37):

> There was also a Torah Scroll in the room; the errant ones [Christians] came into the room, found it, and tore it to shreds. When the holy and pure women, daughters of kings, saw that the Torah had been torn, they called in a loud voice to their husbands: "Look, see, the Holy Torah—it being torn by the enemy!" ... "Alas, the Holy Torah, the perfection of beauty, the delight of our eyes, to which we used to bow in the synagogue, honoring it; our little children would kiss it. How has it now fallen into the hands of these impure uncircumcised ones?" When the men heard the words of the these pious women, they were moved with zeal for the Lord, our God, and for His holy and precious Torah.... They found one of the errant ones in the room, and all of them, men and women, threw stones at him till he fell dead.

It is seldom that we have such a detailed rationale for violence perpetrated because of the perceived holiness of a text. The example certainly can be reduced to the form: "Belief X, therefore Act of Violence Y. In this case, the belief that the Torah is holy and cannot be desecrated is explicitly stated to be the reason for the killing of the Christian who desecrated that text. At the same time, the Christian desecrated the Torah because he did not regard it as holy.

Attacks on sacred scriptures continue today. According to a report posted on the CNN website on April 1, 2002, a synagogue in Marseilles, France, was attacked: "'All the religious objects, books, the Torah, all of it burned,' Sydney Maimoun, the synagogue's president, told The Associated Press, adding there's 'really nothing left.'"[4] While most of the perpetrators in this case are thought to be Muslims, the truth is that violence against scriptures can involve all sorts of permutations within the Abrahamic traditions.

SACRED SPACE

All of the major world religions share the idea of sacred space. We may define sacred space as a bounded space whose value is placed above the surrounding space for religious reasons. Because not everyone has access to or can live in a sacred space, then it becomes a scarce resource; and because of this scarcity, then it becomes a potential center of conflict.

Some spaces may be sacralized because they possess economic and political value first. In the Abrahamic religions, the value of one sacred space, Jerusalem, is almost entirely the creation of religion. Jerusalem has no great economic or strategic value other than what is derived from the sacrality bestowed on it by the sacred scriptures of these religions. Ultimately, the sacrality of Jerusalem originates in the Hebrew Bible (see Zechariah 2: 12, Psalm 76: 1–2; Roberts 1982). Judaism, Christianity, and Islam all have had members willing to die for the supposed holiness of Jerusalem (and the broader space called the Holy Land).

In Christian history, some of the clearest examples of the relationship between violence and sacred space may be found in the First Crusade and the propaganda meant to incite Christians to join it. The speech that initiated this crusade was delivered by Urban II at Clermont in 1095. This speech has not been directly preserved, but we have various versions of it from supposed witnesses or recorders. These testimonies are all gathered in the monumental *Recueil des historiens des Croisades* (RHC), which still forms a basic source for all studies of the Crusades.[5]

We must be cautious in representing these testimonies as a stenographic record of the speech and thought of Urban II. Rather they are to be seen, in part, as retrospective narratives colored by regionalism and the success of the First Crusade (Mayer 1972: 10–11; Tyerman 1998: 8–29). Otherwise, these testimonies constitute evidence of what the authors understood to be the motives for the First Crusade. Urban's motivation for this Crusade is clear in the version of Robert the Monk: "Let the holy sepulchre of the Lord our Saviour, which is possessed by unclean nations, especially incite you, and the holy places which are now treated with ignominy and irreverently polluted with their filthiness."[6]

Another version of Urban II's speech begins by arguing that not all space is of equal value:

> If among the churches scattered about over the whole world some, because of persons or location, deserve reverence above others (for persons, I say, since greater privileges are accorded to apostolic sees; for places, indeed, since the same dignity which is accorded to persons is also shown to regal cities, such as Constantinople), we owe most to that church from which we received the grace of redemption and the source of all Christianity.[7]

The speech subsequently outlines the various reasons why Jerusalem is holy. Not one of the reasons is economic or even outwardly political. Instead, the speech harkens to scriptural warrants for declaring Jerusalem holy. Note the following argument:

> If this land is spoken of in the sacred writings of the prophets as the inheritance and the holy temple of God before ever the Lord walked about in it, or was revealed, what sanctity, what reverence has it not acquired since God in His majesty was there clothed in the flesh, nourished, grew up, and in bodily form there walked about, or was carried about; and, to compress in fitting brevity all that might be told in a long series of words, since there the blood of the Son of God, more holy than heaven and earth, was poured forth, and His body, its quivering members dead, rested in the tomb. What veneration do we think it deserves?[8]

If the city was holy before Jesus walked its streets, it should be even holier after that. Yet Jesus need not have lived or died in Jerusalem to render it holy. As the speech argues:

> "Let us suppose, for the moment, that Christ was not dead and buried, and had never lived any length of time in Jerusalem. Surely, if all this were lacking, this fact alone ought still to arouse you to go to the aid of the land and city—the fact that 'Out of Zion shall go forth the law and the word of the Lord from Jerusalem!'"[9]

Thus, the main reason is a scriptural warrant, at least as represented in this interpretation of Isaiah 2:3 (see also Micah 4:2).

Similar rationales are given on the Muslim side by 'Imad ad-Din, who says: "Islam wooed Jerusalem, ready to lay down lives for her as a bride-price...Saladin marched forth...to remove the heavy hand of unbelief with the right hands of Faith, to purify Jerusalem of the pollution of those races, of the filth of the dregs of humanity" (Gabrieli 1969:147). The fight over Jerusalem is consistent with the main mechanism outlined for the generation of violence: The effort to maintain and/or acquire Scarce Resource X.

Aside from Mecca, Medina, the first town to come under Muslim rule, is also an important sacred space. Al-Bukhari (3:68) reports that "Al-Madina is a sanctuary (*haramun*).... Its trees should not be cut and no heresy should be innovated nor any sin should be committed in it." Again, sacrality correlates with behaviors deemed correct by the Muslim masters of the sacred space. Freedom of religion does not seem to be allowed in this sacred space.

Today, the sacrality of Jerusalem and other spaces in the Middle East still fuels much violence in the world. Osama Bin Laden said as much in his infamous 1998 fatwah, which outlined some of his reasons for his jihad against the United States: "First, for over seven years the United States has been occupying the lands of Islam *in the holiest of places*, the Arabian Peninsula, plundering its riches, dictating to its rulers, humiliating its people, terrorizing its neighbors, and turning its bases in the Peninsula into a spearhead through which to fight the neighboring Muslim peoples."[10] Sacred space continues to be a generator of violence in Abrahamic religions. As long as people deem certain spaces sacred, the potential for violence will remain.

Group Privileging

Closely linked to inscripturation and sacred space is group privileging, which refers to the idea that certain groups have privileges and rights not granted to those outside the group. As such, those privileges become a scarce resource to outsiders (Lenski 1984).[11] In some cases, the privileges need not cause conflict if they are not valued by the outsider. For example, not all outsiders care that only priests can enter the Holy of Holies of the Temple of Solomon. If outsiders live far away, it may not matter to them.

However, if belonging to one religious group means that one receives certain economic benefits that others in proximity do not, then conflict may ensue. Those economic benefits are now unequally distributed and so constitute scarce resources. Violence may follow attempts to acquire those benefits or attempts to prevent the loss of those benefits.

At the most extreme level of violence, group privileging resulted in the extermination of at least some groups of people that were seen to threaten the privileged group in power. This is most clear in a number of passages, such as the following:

> When the LORD your God brings you into the land that you are about to enter and he clears away many nations before you—the Hittites, the Girgashites, the Amorites, the Canaanites, the Perizzites, the Hivites, and the Jebusites, seven nations mightier and more numerous than you—and when the LORD your God gives them over to you and you defeat them, then you must utterly destroy them. Make no covenant with them and show them no mercy. Do not intermarry with them, giving your daughters to their sons or taking their daughters for your sons, for that would turn away your children from following me, to serve other gods. Then the anger of the LORD would be kindled against you, and he would destroy you quickly. But this is how you must deal with them: break down their altars, smash their pillars, hew down their sacred poles, and burn their idols with fire. For you are a people holy to the LORD your God; the LORD

your God has chosen you out of all the peoples on earth to be his people, his treasured possession. (Deuteronomy 7:1–6)

Note that this passage links the "chosenness" of Israel with the destruction of the particular outsiders and that destruction of others is attributed to Israel's "holiness."

Likewise, the hadith, the traditions about Muhammad, are permeated by the feeling of superiority among Muslims. Thus, Al-Bukhari (2:250) records one tradition in which the religious status of a boy is at issue. The boy has a non-Muslim mother and a Muslim father. A group of Muslims state that custody must be given to the Muslim parent. The episode concludes with the statement that "Islam is always superior and never inferior." Such a view, in turn, has led to the subjugation and killing of non-Muslims throughout Islamic history (Friedmann 2003).

SALVATION

The ultimate supernatural prize in the Abrahamic religions is *salvation,* a term that is highly complex and often ambiguous. Salvation, for our purposes, refers to the idea that one receives a supernaturally favorable status or permanent benefit by belonging to a particular religion. It is closely allied with group privileging, except that the reward called salvation is ultimately not tangible or verifiable. Salvation is a commodity that exists only insofar as people believe in it.

In any event, salvation is a scarce resource insofar as it is not equally distributed. Within the Catholic tradition, the concept of *Extra Ecclesiam nulla salus* (Outside the Church there is no salvation) developed. As Hans Küng notes, the Council of Florence (1442) was unequivocal:

> The Holy Roman Church...firmly believes, confesses and proclaims that outside the Catholic Church no one, neither heathen nor Jew nor unbeliever nor schismatic will have a share in eternal life, but will, rather, be the subject to everlasting fire."
> (1986: 23)

René Girard has argued that the salvific sacrifice of Christ, the god man, could effect the complete overthrow of scapegoating violence. In reality, the notion that salvation of humankind had been achieved through such a trauma to the deity spawned a number of rationales for violence, whose consequences echoed in many forms. For example, a persistent rationale for violence used the violent death of Christ to justify forcing the conversion of others. Since God had made such a great sacrifice, it behooved human beings to be grateful. To not convert after knowing of the suffering of the Christ meant that one was ungrateful. That lack of gratefulness needs to be punished, as indicated in Hebrews 10:29: "How much worse punishment do you think will be deserved by those who have spurned the Son of God, profaned the blood of the covenant by which they were sanctified, and outraged the Spirit of grace?"

Thomas Aquinas, the most influential theologian of the Middle Ages, used rationales for violence that were linked to the maintenance and expansion of the scarce resource we call salvation. One main reason that Aquinas gives for waging war and imprisoning unbelievers is not so that those unbelievers will convert but rather so that those unbelievers do not hinder the salvation of others (*Summa Theologica* II-II, Q 10, A 8, Obj. 4). Here we can clearly see how salvation is a scarce resource, not available except through sanctioned means. Violence may be used in order to allow or maintain access to this scarce resource.

Aquinas (*Summa Theologica*, Part II-II, Q 10, A 8, Reply Obj. 3) likewise favored bodily compulsion for heretics who strayed from Christianity. One of the main biblical texts used by Aquinas, among others, to sanction such compulsion was Luke 14:23: "Then the master said to the slave, 'Go out into the roads and lanes, and compel people to come in, so that my house may be filled.'" This instruction is part of a parable given by Jesus, who is speaking of a rich man who gave a feast, but the invitees did not come. The master of the house told his servants to force people off the street into the banquet. By analogy, if Christians are the servants and Jesus is the Master of the House, then Christians must compel nonbelievers to enter the kingdom of God. Violence in order to preserve the salvation of the favored group can also be found in ancient Judaism and Islam.

Other violent rationales generated by the idea of Christ's sacrifice are less appreciated. In a magisterial study, Timothy Gorringe argued that Anselm's theory of atonement had wide influence on justice systems in Europe. He notes that the need to hang or torture criminals was never self-evident. Often there were debates about the necessity of such practices. However, when they were upheld it was often because of allusions to Anselm's theory or New Testament ideas of the atonement. As Gorringe phrases it, "the theology of satisfaction, I contend, provided one of the subtlest and most profound of such justifications, not only for hanging but for retributive punishment in general" (1996: 12).

An Ethical Critique
of Religious Violence

Although we focus on how scarce resources cause religious violence, an overarching theme of the thesis is that the lack of verifiability in religious belief differentiates ethically the violence attributed to religion from the violence attributed to nonreligious factors. The quality of any scarcity created by religion is fundamentally different from scarcities created by natural means.

Within a moral, relativistic frame that accepts empirico-rationalism as providing reliable data, our argument that religious violence is always immoral begins by positing the seemingly obvious proposition that what exists has more value than what does not exist. Only what exists can be said to have any value, if it has any value for us. If that is the case, then life, as an existent phenomenon, must have more value than what does not exist. We can schematize our rationale as follows:

1) What exists is worth more than what does not exist.
2) Life exists.
3) Therefore, life is worth more than what does not exist.

Accordingly, we may deem immoral any action that places the value of life as equal to, or below, the value of nothing. Therefore, it would always be immoral to kill for something that does not exist.

We can also extend this argument to what cannot be proven, on empirico-rationalist grounds, to exist. For example, if I were to say that I am killing because undetectable Martians have declared it obligatory to kill, the argument would be regarded rightly as absurd. But, the possibility of undetectable Martians existing is not what would declare such a statement absurd. It is perfectly possible that undetectable Martians exist and order people to kill other people.

The main reason that we do not accept this rationale as moral is that we, as observers, cannot verify that undetectable Martians exist, and so we would regard the perpetrator's claims as unjustified. Lack of evidence for the existence of invisible Martians, and not merely the possibility of their existence, provides the basis for our ethical judgment here.

This is not to deny that secular violence certainly may be immoral sometimes or even most of the time. Killing for something that is not necessary to human existence, for example, may be deemed immoral. Yet killing in self-defense is usually not considered immoral. Killing when there is no other way to survive is not considered immoral. As long as a person needs a basic resource (food, water) to survive, then it is usually deemed morally permissible to fight and kill for it.

In contrast, any violence for religious reasons is always immoral because bodily well-being is being traded for the acquisition or loss of a resource that does not exist or cannot be verified to exist. The fact that religious violence is always immoral and that nonreligious violence is not always immoral is the fundamental ethical distinction between religious and nonreligious violence.

SOLUTIONS AND CONCLUSIONS

If religious violence is always immoral, then how do we solve the problem of religious violence? Two obvious logical choices present themselves: Retain religion, but modify it so that scarcities are not created; or remove religion from human life. Each of these choices has its own advantages and disadvantages. First, note that "minimization" is the key, as violence cannot be eliminated for the simple reason that scarce resources will probably always exist. Competing interests will always exist. In some cases, violence should not be eliminated as self-defense is a legitimate use of violence. Minimization means that we concentrate on ridding ourselves of unnecessary violence.

Since religious violence is mainly caused by competition for resources that are actually not scarce at all, then part of the solution must involve making religious believers aware of how they have created belief in scarce resources. Non-believers must challenge believers to explain why they believe in such resources in the first place. We should challenge believers to explain why they believe a certain space is sacred. Nonbelievers should challenge believers to explain how their notion of salvation is any more verifiable than the notion offered by another religion. Of course, it is naive to expect believers automatically to examine their beliefs and abandon them. However, making believers aware of how religion can create scarce resources must be a starting point if there is a solution at all.

One can object that eliminating the notions of salvation, sacred space, divine revelation, and group privileging would eliminate religion itself. This is only the case if one judges religion to essentially consist of these elements. Of all of these elements, however, I can only think of divine revelation as the only essential feature of all religions. That is to say, a person who believes that there is some sort of god or even transcendent force must have some notion that he or she is able to perceive those entities. Sacred space, salvation, and group privileging are not so clearly "essential," though they certainly may seem so. The notion of the holy land had been redefined or abandoned by many Jews and Christians who could still call themselves religious at some level. Such redefinitions, in effect, made competition for a physical space irrelevant sometimes.

The second logical solution, removing religion from life, is of course much more complicated. But academic biblical scholars and scholars of religion, more often than not, maintain the value of religious texts that promote or endorse violence. This maintenance is accomplished by hermeneutic strategies that sanitize the violence, claim to espouse multivocality in readings, or claim aesthetic value to texts, even if historical aspects of the texts are minimized (Avalos 2005). In this regard, we are influenced by theories that see the academic study of literature as a locus and instrument of power (Guillory 1993).

Removing religion from human life need not involve violence, and education is the main strategy. One obstacle for this goal resides in the perceived mission of religious studies, particularly in secular institutions of higher learning. Noam Chomsky argued cogently during the Vietnam War that "it is the responsibility of intellectuals to speak truth and to expose lies" (1987: 60). However, since public universities are funded by taxpayers, the mission of religious studies is perceived to mean that scholars must be sympathetic or neutral toward religion. Religions must be understood but not criticized. Any research indicating that religion is injurious or that particular religions are injurious can bring a response that universities, as publicly funded institutions, cannot seek to undermine the faith of constituents.

Otherwise, the notion of academic responsibility has not been consistent from field to field. Professors in the sciences, for example, routinely are expected to help solve problems in society, ranging from finding a new medication for cancer to learning how to suppress odor produced by swine containment facilities. This is particularly the case in so-called land grant universities, which are expected to be involved directly in the betterment of the society around them. In the case of science, academics are encouraged to identify a "problem" and then help to solve it.

Within religious/biblical studies, John J. Collins, president of the Society of Biblical Literature in 2002, urged an activist stance when he concluded: "Perhaps the most constructive thing a biblical critic can do toward lessening the contribution of the Bible to violence in the world, is to show that certitude is an illusion" (Collins 2003: 21). I would go much further. As an academic scholar of religion, it is my responsibility to analyze, on the basis of verifiable facts and reason, how religion may contribute to the detriment or well-being of humanity (see also McCutcheon 2001).

If empirico-rationalism and methodological naturalism are held to be the proper approaches to truth, then it becomes feasible to argue that the best way to deal with religious violence is to undermine religion. Just as we undermined the religious belief that Genesis 1 is scientifically true or that witchcraft causes illness, academic biblical scholars should continue to undermine any religious belief that can result in violence. Even if it can never be achieved, the most ethical mission of academic religious studies may be to help humanity move beyond religious thinking.

NOTES

1. Unless noted otherwise, all scriptural quotations are from the *New Revised Standard Version* (New York: National Council of the Churches of Christ in the United States of America, 1989).I will not take the time here to defend my definition of religion or argue against the claim that *religion* is not a useful referent term. For a recent discussion of this issue, see Juergensmeyer (2009) and Smart.
2. There is now a vast literature on the social role of the body and embodiment. Among some these studies include Shilling, Stafford, Williams and Bendelow, Berquist, Martin, Eilberg-Schwartz, and Ashley.
3. See "French, Belgian Synagogues Burned," CNN World (April 1, 2002). Online: http://articles.cnn.com/2002–04–01/world/synagogue.attacks_1_synagogue-attacks-semitism-anti-semitism?_s=PM:WORLD. Last visited on February 16, 2011.
4. *Recueil des historiens des Croisades* (Paris: L'Académie impériale des inscriptions et Belles-Lettres, 1841–1906), from which all our Latin citations are drawn.
5. RHC 3:728: "Prasertim moveat vos sanctum Domini Salvatoris nostri Sepulcrum, quod ab immundis gentibus possidetur, et loca sancta, quae nunc inhoneste tractantur et
   irreverenter eorum immundiciis sordidantur."
6. RHC 4.137: "Si inter ecclesias toto orbe diffusas alieae prae aliis reverentiam pro personis locisque merentur; pro personis, inquam,dum apostolicis sedibus privilegia majora traduntur, uti est civitas Constantinopolitana, praebetur: illi potissimus ecclessiae deberemus ex qua gratiam redemptionis et totius originem Christianitatis accepimus."
7. RHC 4.137–138: "Si enim haec terra Dei haereditas et templum sanctum, antequam ibi obambularet ac pateretur Dominus, in sacris et propheticis paginis legitur, quid

sanctitatis, quid reverentiae obtinuisse tunc creditur, quum Deus majestatis ibidem incorporatur, nutritur, adolescit, corporali, vegetatione hac illacque perambulat aut gestatur; et, ut cuncta quae longo verborum gyro narrari possunt, digna brevitate constringam, ubi Filii Dei sanguis, coelo terraque sanctior, effusus est, ubi corpus, paventibus elementis mortuum, in sepulchro quievit? quid putamus venerationis emeruit?"

8. RHC 4.138: "Ponamus modo in Iherusalem Christum neque mortuum, nec sepultum, nec ibidem aliquando vixisse. Certe, si haec deessent omnia, solum illud ad subveniendum terrae et civitati vos excitare debuerat, quia de Syon exierit lex et verbum Domini de Iherusalem."

9. For this translation and the Arabic text, see http://www.library.cornell.edu/ colldev/ mideast/wif.htm. Emphasis mine.

10. Lenski (39), however, still sees Judaism and Christianity as providing a "basis for an ethical criticism of the existing order." Lenski, therefore, still has assimilated uncritically benign views of how Judaism and Christianity create and maintain privilege.

BIBLIOGRAPHY

Al-Bukhari. *Shahih Al-Bukhari.* Trans. Muhammad Muhsin Khan. 9 vols. Riyadh, Saudi Arabia: Darussalam Publishers and Distributors, 1997.

Aquinas, St. Thomas. *Summa Theologica.* 3 vols. New York: Benziger Brothers, 1947.

Ashley, Benedict. *Theologies of the Body: Humanist and Christian.* Braintree, MA: Pope John XXIII Medical-Moral Research and Education Center, 1985.

Avalos, Hector "Violence in the Bible and the *Bhagavad gita." Journal of Vaishnava Studies* 9 (2001): 67–83.

Avalos, Hector. *Fighting Words: The Origins of Religious Violence.* Amherst, NY: Prometheus Books, 2005.

Berquist, Jon L. *Controlling Corporeality: The Body and the Household in Ancient Israel.* New Brunswick, NJ: Rutgers University Press, 2002.

Casey, Stephen J. "Defining Violence." *Thought: A Review of Culture and Idea* 56: 5–16, 1981.

Cavanaugh, William T. *The Myth of Religious Violence.* New York: Oxford University Press, 2009.

Chase, Kenneth R. and Alan Jacobs, eds. *Must Christianity Be Violent? Reflections on History, Practice and Theology.* Grand Rapids, MI: Brazos Press, 2003.

Chomsky, Noam. "The Responsibility of Intellectuals." In *The Chomsky Reader.* Ed. James Peck, 59–82. New York: Pantheon Books, 1987.

CNN World. "French, Belgian Synagogues Burned." April 1, 2002. Accessed at http:// articles.cnn.com/2002–04–01/world/synagogue.attacks_1_synagogue-attacks-sem itism-anti-semitism?_s=PM:WORLD on February 16, 2011.

Collins, John J. "The Zeal of Phinehas: The Bible and the Legitimation of Violence." *Journal of Biblical Literature* 122 (2003): 3–21.

Eidelberg, Shlomo. *The Jews and the Crusaders: The Hebrew Chronicles of the First and Second Crusades.* Madison: University of Wisconsin Press, 1977.

Friedmann, Yohanan. *Tolerance and Coercion in Islam: Interfaith Relations in the Muslim Tradition.* Cambridge, UK: Cambridge University Press, 2003.

Fulcher of Chartres. *A History of the Expeditions to Jerusalem, 1095–1127.* Trans. Frances Rita Ryan, ed. Harold S. Fink. New York: W. W. Norton, 1969.

Eilberg-Schwartz, Howard. *People of the Body: Jews and Judaism from an Embodied Perspective*. Albany: State University of New York Press, 1992.

Gabrieli, Francesco. *Arab Historians of the Crusades*. Trans. E. J. Costello. New York: Barnes & Noble, 1969.

Gell, Alfred. *Wrapping in Images: Tattooing in Polynesia*. Oxford, UK: Clarendon, 1993.

Ginges, Jeremy and Scott Atran. "War as Moral Imperative (Not Just Practical Politics by Other Means)." Proceedings of the Royal Society B: Biological Sciences, 2011. http://rspb.royalsocietypublishing.org/content/early/2011/02/08/rspb.2010.2384.full?keytype=ref&ijkey=l6GCdRvBXiTDPQ6.

Girard, René. *Violence and the Sacred*. Trans. Patrick Gregory. Baltimore: Johns Hopkins University Press, 1977.

Gorringe, Timothy. *God's Just Vengeance: Crime, Violence, and the Rhetoric of Salvation*. Cambridge, UK: Cambridge University Press, 1996.

Guillory, John. *Cultural Capital: The Problem of Literary Canon Formation*. Chicago: University of Chicago Press, 1993.

Howson, Colin. *Hume's Problem: Induction and the Justification of Belief.* New York: Oxford University Press, 2000.

Jacobs, Alan. Afterward. *Must Christianity Be Violent?* Eds. Kenneth R. Chase and Alan Jacobs, 224–235. Grand Rapids, MI: Brazos Press, 2003.

Juergensmeyer, Mark. *Terror in the Mind of God: The Global Rise of Religious Violence*. Berkeley: University of California Press, 2001.

Juergensmeyer, Mark. "Presidential Address: Beyond Words and War: The Global Future of Religion." *Journal of the American Academy of Religion* 78: 882–895, 2009.

Kitts, Margo. *Sanctified Violence: Oath Making Rituals and Narratives in the Iliad*. Cambridge, UK: Cambridge University Press, 2005.

Küng, Hans. *Christianity and the World Religions: Paths to Dialogue with Islam, Hinduism, and Buddhism*. New York: Doubleday, 1986.

Lenski, Gerhard E. *Power and Privilege: A Theory of Social Stratification*. Chapel Hill: University of North Carolina Press, 1984.

Martin, Dale B. *The Corinthian Body*. New Haven, CT: Yale University Press, 1995.

Mascia-Lees, Frances E. and Patricia Sharpe, eds. *Tattoo, Torture, Mutilation, and Adornment: The Denaturalization of the Body in Culture and Text*. Albany: State University of New York Press, 1992.

Mayer, Hans Eberhard. *The Crusades*. Trans. John Gillingham. New York: Oxford University Press, 1972.

McCutcheon, Russell T. *Critics Not Caretakers: Redescribing the Public Study of Religion*. Albany: State University of New York Press, 2001.

New Revised Standard Version. New York: National Council of the Churches of Christ in the United States of America, 1989.

Recueil des historiens des Croisades. Paris: L'Académie impériale des inscriptions et Belles-Lettres, 1841–1906.

Roberts, J. J. M. "Zion in the Theology of the Davidid-Solomonic Empire." In *Studies in the Period of David and Solomon and other Essays*. Ed. Tomoo Ishida, 93–108. Winona Lake, IN: Eisenbrauns, 1982.

Sachs, Jeffrey. *Common Wealth: Economics for a Crowded Planet*. New York: Penguin, 2008.

Schaff, Philip and Henry Wace, eds. *The Nicene and Post-Nice Fathers*. Grand Rapids, MI: Eerdmans, 1997.

Schniedewind, William. *How the Bible Became a Book*. Cambridge, UK: Cambridge University Press, 2004.

Schwartz, Regina. *The Curse of Cain: The Violent Legacy of Monotheism*. Chicago: University of Chicago Press, 1997.

Sen, Amartya. *On Inquality*. New York: Oxford University Press, 1997.

Shilling, Chris. *The Body and Social Theory*. 2nd edition. London: Sage, 2003.

Smart, Ninian. "The Global Future of Religion." In *The Oxford Handbook of Global Religion*. Ed. Mark Juergensmeyer, 625–630. New York: Oxford University Press, 2006.

Stafford, Barbara Maria. *Body Criticism: Imaging the Unseen in Enlightenment Art and Medicine*. Cambridge, MA: MIT Press, 1997.

Tyerman, Christopher. *The Invention of the Crusades*. Toronto: University of Toronto Press, 1998.

Vesicant, Guise. *The Power and the Writing: The Early Scribes of Mesopotamia*. Bethesda, MD: CAL Press, 2000.

Wellman, James K., Jr. and Kyoto Tokuno. "Is Religious Violence Inevitable?" *Journal for the Scientific Study of Religion* 43 (2004): 291–296.

Williams, Simon J. and Gillian Bendelow. *The Lived Body: Sociological Themes, Embodied Issues*. New York: Routledge, 1998.

....

CHAPTER 38

RITUAL, RELIGION, AND VIOLENCE

AN EVOLUTIONARY PERSPECTIVE

....

CANDACE S. ALCORTA AND RICHARD SOSIS

Archaeological and ethnographic evidence suggests that violence and conflict with outsiders has been a central element of religion since its emergence in human evolution. While the recent rising global tide of religious violence has shocked and perplexed many observers, such violence is neither new nor exclusively directed at external foes. Anthropologists have recorded a wide array of torturous and terrifying ritual practices that are both self-inflicted and performed on other members of one's own religious group. Such practices occur in totemic, animistic, ancestral, polytheistic, and monotheistic religions alike. The adolescent rites of passage found in nearly three-quarters of traditional cultures throughout the world frequently include kidnapping, isolation, food and sleep deprivation, scarification, and other psychological and physical ordeals, including genital mutilation. In New Guinea, Ilahita Arapesh men dressed as frightening boars traditionally lacerated the penises of young boys with bamboo razors and pig incisors as part of initiation rites, and men publicly incised their own genitals after marriage (Tuzin 1982: 337–339). Male elders dressed as masked ancestral spirits kidnapped, tortured, and circumcised youth in the traditional Mukanda ceremony of the African Ndembu (Turner 1967: 151–279). Sticks and eagle claws were used to rip open the flesh of adolescent male initiates of many Native American plains cultures (Glucklich 2001: 147–149).

Such practices are not confined to traditional, non-Western societies. Religious violence and "sacred pain" have been important elements in the mythology and ritual of Western religious traditions since their inception. Terrible gods, hideous demons, and bloody sacrifice are all recurrent themes of the animistic and polytheistic religions of early Europe, Greece, and Rome. One observer described first-century rituals at the temple in Uppsala, Sweden:

> Of all the living beings that are male, nine head are offered; by whose blood it is the custom to appease the gods. Their bodies, however, are hung in a grove which is beside the temple. The grove is so sacred to the heathen that the individual trees in it are believed to be holy because of the death or putrefaction of the sacrificial victims. There, even dogs and horses dangle beside people, their bodies hanging jumbled together. (Ewing 2008: 5)

Violence has also typified monotheistic traditions (Armstrong 1993: 19). The god of early Judaism, Islam, and Christianity commanded Abraham to sacrifice his son in order to prove his faith. Sacrifice and trials by ordeal were commonplace throughout medieval Europe; the Spanish Inquisition refined torture and violence to a fine art. From the Crusades to the witch trials of the colonial United States to the recent bloodshed in Bosnia-Herzegovina, Western Christianity has been awash in sacrifice, blood, and holy terror.

The type, extent, and targets of violence perpetrated in the name of religion vary greatly both across and within religious traditions over space and time. Yet most religions require some sacrifice of adherents, and many mandate self-inflicted violence through acts of penitence, deprivation, and self-mutilation. For example, male circumcision is required in both Islam and Judaism. Fasting is common to all the world religions. Christian penance has historically included acts of self-mortification, including corporal punishment. During the annual Ashura festival, Shia Muslims commemorate the death of Muhammad's grandson Hussein through bloody rites of self-flagellation. Religiously inspired suicide bombers inflict violence and terror on infidels, but they also inflict such violence on themselves. Clearly, the relationship between religion and violence is complex (Purzycki and Gibson 2011: 24). Paradoxically, religions that at times inspire joy, love, and awe also inspire fear, pain, and terror.

Examining religion from an evolutionary perspective can offer insights into these paradoxes. This requires that we first deconstruct religion in order to identify its constituent components and then compare those components with the ritualized displays of nonhuman species. Such a comparison allows us to situate religion within a larger framework of signaling theory. It also highlights a critical difference between human and nonhuman signaling systems; while the ritualized displays of nonhuman species incorporate evolved motivational signals, human religious ritual creates motivational symbols by investing social abstractions with emotional meaning. Examining how religion creates such symbols and invests them with motivational force provides significant insights into the relationship between religion and violence.

Signaling theory also offers insights into the broader causal questions of why religion first emerged in human evolution and what functions it serves. Numerous researchers have argued that one of the primary functions of religion is the promotion of group solidarity (Durkheim 1969: 62–63; Rappaport 1999: 417; Wilson 2002: 45–46). More recently, costly signaling theorists have proposed that such solidarity facilitates intragroup cooperation and alliances (Sosis and Alcorta 2003: 266–268). For early human populations inhabiting rapidly changing environments, the ability to create large, cohesive, cooperative male-based groups would have provided a competitive advantage, particularly in relation to warfare. That same advantage is likely to explain the role of religion in the recruitment of contemporary suicide terrorists. To understand why suicide terrorists are willing to give their lives for their life-affirming religions, we must first understand religion itself.

What Is Religion?

There are almost as many definitions of religion as there are researchers who study it, but the definition offered by sociologist Emile Durkheim nearly a century ago is still valuable today. Durkheim proposed:

> "A religion is a unified system of beliefs and practices relative to sacred things, that is to say, things set apart and forbidden—beliefs and practices that unite into one single moral community called a Church, all those who adhere to them." (1969: 62)

Durkheim's definition encompasses universal elements of religion, including supernatural beliefs, communal ritual, and moral values. It is the sacred, however, that constitutes the heart of Durkheim's definition. Examining what constitutes the sacred and how it is created can tell us much about the paradoxical relationship between religion and violence and the functions served by each.

The Sacred: The Heart of Religion

At the heart of all religions is the separation of the sacred from the profane (Durkheim 1969: 462). In contrast to the profane, or ordinary, the sacred is both mystical and extraordinary. Sacred places, objects, symbols, and beliefs comprise the core of religion; it is the sacred that instills faith and inspires the devotion of the faithful (Alcorta and Sosis 2005: 332). Sacred things are powerful; they are charged with symbolic significance and moral meaning. It is not just inappropriate to treat sacred things profanely; it is viscerally repugnant. This strong autonomic response to the profanement of the sacred is apparent in American veterans' reactions to protest burnings of the American flag as well as in recent worldwide Muslim response to the proposed burning of the Qu'ran. In both instances the destruction, or even threatened destruction, of cloth and paper elicited intense emotional reactions far in excess of their material worth. For Americans and Muslims, respectively, Old Glory and the Qu'ran are not simply a flag and a book; they are sacred symbols that evoke deep emotional and social meaning. To profane them is not simply the destruction of a material object; it is the violation of a group's most sacred values and beliefs.

Sacred things do not exist in nature waiting to be discovered. There are no inherently sacred flags, books, or beliefs. Objects, places, and beliefs considered sacred by one individual may be deemed utterly worthless and profane by another. Since sacred things do not occur naturally, they must be created. The means for creating sacred things is communal ritual. It is through such ritual that people, places, objects, and beliefs are imbued with sacred meaning, rendering them powerful, awesome, and dangerous (Rappaport 1999: 279). Participation in communal ritual transforms myths into holy doctrine, channels self-reflection into prayer, and renders abstract objects as emotionally evocative symbols of shared communal values. Once sanctified, these beliefs, practices, and symbols become potent motivators and reinforcers for individual choices, judgments, and behaviors.

Communal Ritual and the Creation of the Sacred

How does ritual create the sacred and invest it with properties of awe, power, and danger? Ritual clearly does not conjure up sacred objects nor does it transform the object; holy water and tapwater share the same chemical formula and are, to the nonadherent, equally good to drink. What communal ritual changes are the perceptions and emotional valuations of participants in relation to that which is sanctified. Once this occurs, both the cognitive classification and emotional valuation of the sacred person, place, object, or belief is forever changed in the mind of the adherent (Alcorta and Sosis 2005: 332).

Anthropologist Roy Rappaport has described ritual as "the ground from which religion grows" (1999: 26). He notes "religion's major conceptual and experiential constituents, the sacred, the numinous, the occult and the divine, and their integration into the Holy, are creations of ritual" (1999: 3). How does religious ritual create the numinous, the occult, the divine, and the sacred?

Religious rituals differ widely across cultures. Some are as simple as the Mbuti *kumamolimo* in which adult males sing together around a campfire as a sacred trumpet sounds (Turnbull 1962: 87–89). Others are as elaborate as the Christian sacrament of Communion in which specially robed religious specialists perform the transubstantiation of wine and bread into blood and flesh for communal consumption. Regardless of the complexity of religious rituals, however, all share a common "deep" structure. All involve "the performance of more or less invariant sequences of formal acts and utterances not entirely encoded by the performers" (Rappaport 1999: 24). Communal religious rituals are formal, patterned, sequenced, and repetitive. These features clearly distinguish them from ordinary, mundane behaviors and move such rituals outside ordinary conceptions of time and meaning.

Simultaneously, the formality, patterning, sequencing, and repetition of ritual frame, exaggerate, and enhance the signals, symbols, and actions embedded within the ritual structure. These same structural elements of religious ritual are found in the structure of ritualized displays in nonhuman species as well. Understanding the purpose and impacts of these elements in the ritualized displays of nonhuman species can provide insights into the functions they serve in religious ritual.

The Roots of Ritual

Like religious ritual, the ritualized displays of nonhuman species constitute one end of a continuum of signals that communicate important information between conspecifics (Laughlin and McManus 1979: 82–84; Smith 1979: 54–55). This continuum includes signals as simple as body size and as complex as the colorful and elaborate nest constructions in the courtship behaviors of bowerbirds. The simplest signals are indexical, deriving directly from physical properties. The croaking pitch of frogs is an indexical signal that communicates the body size of the signaler since the laws of physics dictate that the larger the frog the deeper the pitch. Other signals convey information in regard to a signaler's state. The musth signature of bull elephants provides potential mates and competitors with important information about the reproductive state, testosterone levels, and potential aggression of the sender. Signals may also convey information about intent. Intent signals frequently involve the transference of behaviors from an originally evolved context to a ritualized one. The incorporation of these transferred behaviors, or releasers, is intended to elicit in the receiver the same autonomic and neurophysiological responses associated with the signal's original functions. Food begging displays in bird courtship rituals provide an example of such transference. The embedding of food begging behaviors in many courtship displays has evolved to elicit the same neurophysiological approach responses in potential mates as those evoked by dependent offspring (West-Eberhard 2003: 245).

In nonhuman species, ritualized displays are among the costliest of signals. The formalization, patterning, sequencing, and repetition of ritualized displays differentiate them from "ordinary" behaviors, setting them apart and dramatically framing both the embedded signals and the sender's message. The structural features of ritual are not arbitrary; laboratory experiments show that the formality, patterning, sequencing, and repetition of ritual have important neurophysiological effects on participants. These elements alert and focus attention, engage and enhance memory, and improve associational learning (Rowe 1999: 927–928). They prime the receiver to more effectively attend, analyze, and assess the signals embedded within the ritual display and they elicit neuroendocrine responses, as well (Wingfield et al. 1999: 255–284). Ritualized displays require significant expenditures of time, energy, and/or resources and often incur significant predation and aggression risks. It is, therefore, not surprising that they occur most frequently in contexts in which fitness stakes are high, such as courtship and competition.

Ritual and Symbolic Culture

Humans also employ a wide range of signals and ritualized behaviors for conspecific communication. Panhuman social signals of affiliation, dominance, and submission—including such behaviors as kissing, bowing, and prostration—occur worldwide and likely predate language. Many human rituals, like the rituals of our nonhuman kin, incorporate numerous signals and action releasers intended to convey important information and influence conspecific responses. In contrast to most nonhuman rituals, however, human ritual further amplifies and enhances the effects of embedded signals and innate releasers through the creation and use of cultural artifacts. Modern human courtship behaviors often include female use of lipstick to exaggerate and redden lips and provocative clothing to direct attention to breasts, hips, and other sexually arousing body parts. These cultural artifacts are used to exaggerate innate indexical signals and engage evolved neuroendocrine responses. Anthropologist Camille Power has argued that the South African red ochre comprising the earliest known evidence of human symbolic behavior served just such a function (1999: 92).

We will probably never know precisely how red ochre artifacts were used by our early ancestors or what they symbolized, but such crafted pieces, including body paint, art, and architecture, appear to have co-evolved with and been prominent elements of human symbolic ritual for more than 100,000 years (Henshilwood et al. 2001: 668). Similar to the use of lipstick in contemporary courtship, many of the artifacts that feature prominently in religious rituals throughout the world are intended to elicit autonomic and emotional states in participants by mimicking, exaggerating, or distorting natural stimuli that evoke innate evolved responses. Candlelight processions that cast flickering shadows, masks that distort and disfigure faces, and statues that bleed all engage innate responses to particular classes of stimuli that heighten, intensify, and enhance the emotions of ritual participants (Alcorta and Sosis 2005: 338). These cultural artifacts help to differentiate between an order, realm, mood, or state of being that is mundane, ordinary, or "natural" and one that is unusual, extraordinary, or "supernatural" (Dissanayake 2001: 49).

The cultural artifact likely to be of greatest significance for ritual's ability to differentiate the extraordinary from the ordinary is music. More than six centuries ago, Sufi mystic al-Gazzali observed:

> The heart of man has been so constituted by the Almighty that, like a flint, it
> contains a hidden fire which is evoked by music and harmony, and renders man

beside himself with ecstasy. These harmonies are echoes of that highest world of beauty which we call the world of spirits, they remind man of his relationship to that world, and produce in him an emotion so deep and strange that he himself is powerless to explain it. (qtd. in Becker 2001: 145)

Music, Ritual, and the Sacred

Music is a fundamental feature of religion in every culture known (Levitin 2008: 2). It is intimately interconnected with a sense of the sacred, the numinous, and the divine (Alcorta 2008: 231). Ethnomusicologist Judith Becker notes that "most, if not all, societies have some form of institutionalized, religious trance ceremonies that also include music" (2004: 1). Music has an inherent ability to evoke powerful emotional responses in listeners (Koelsch 2010: 131; Wendrich and Staudinger 2010: 144). Musically evoked emotions impact and enhance the subjective experience of other sensory stimuli as well (Baumgartner et al. 2006: 151).

Listening to music alters autonomic functions, including heart rate, blood pressure, respiration, immunological function, and neuroendocrine responses (Hirokawa and Ohira 2003: 189; Kuhn 2002: 30). Like food and sex, music has innate reward value for humans. Listening to music activates the brain's reward circuitry, releasing the neurotransmitter dopamine (Blood and Zatorre 2001: 11822; Menon and Levitin 2005: 175), a "feel good" chemical critical for reward processing, memory (Shohamy and Adcock 2010: 464), and reinforcement learning (Daw 2007: 1505; Hurlemann et al. 2010: 4999).

Humans are one of only a few species capable of synchronizing to the beat of music (Patel et al. 2009: 827). This ability to synchronize to music allows us to entrain our autonomic and emotional responses with others. Music also increases oxytocin release (Levitin 2008: 50–51; Nilsson 2009: 2153). Oxytocin is critical to interpersonal trust (Ross and Young 2009: 534) and affiliation (Israel et al. 2008: 435) and has been linked with altruistic behaviors (ibid.). Oxytocin reduces background anxiety (Missig et al. 2010: 2607), enhances the stress-buffering effects of social support (Pierrehumbert et al. 2010: 168), and suppresses the body's hypothalamic-pituitary-adrenal (HPA) "stress response" (Neumann 2008: 858; Pierrehumbert et al. 2010: 168).

Music has the ability to activate reward processes, evoke strong emotions, elicit and entrain autonomic responses, and enhance oxytocin production. These attributes render it an extremely powerful social tool. Musicologist Ian Cross has noted that "music is not only sonic, embodied, and interactive; it is bound to its contexts of occurrence in ways that enable it to derive meaning from, and interactively to confer meaning on, the experiential contexts in which it occurs" (2003: 108). Music takes us outside ourselves; it elicits inexplicable emotions of joy, awe, and ecstasy while increasing trust, empathy, and cooperation among participants. It also provides a symbolic mnemonic capable of readily evoking both cognitive and emotional memories. When music is embedded in religious ritual, these capacities of music heighten and intensify the ritual experience, transforming the ordinary into the extraordinary and laying the foundation for creation of the sacred.

Terror, Violence, and Sacred Pain

Music offers a portal to the sacred through its ability to evoke feelings of ecstasy and awe and to elicit powerful emotional and autonomic responses in listeners. There is, however, another side to religious ritual and another way to elicit powerful autonomic and emotional responses in participants. The counterpoint to the joy, ecstasy, and awe elicited by music-based communal ritual is the fear, terror, and sacred pain that are prominent elements of many religions, even as the music plays. Hideous masks, demonic statues, and other compelling "agent" representations are common elements across religions. The dissonant and malevolent faces of Bebuten witches in the trance festivals of Bali, the leering gargoyles of Roman Catholic cathedrals, and the fantastic demons that populate the artwork of numerous religious traditions throughout the world all seize our attention and evoke evolved neurophysiological responses of disgust, fear, and terror. Such stimuli are emotionally powerful and highly memorable, particularly when intensified by music and framed within the multisensory experience of ritual.

Fear and revulsion are not the only negative responses evoked by religious ritual. Pain is also a prominent component of religion. Prolonged kneeling, standing, and prostration; fasting; sleep deprivation; dancing to exhaustion; self-flagellation; and bodily mutilation are common practices across religious traditions. Pain alters body states and, in doing so, alters our perceptions of time, space, and self (Damasio 1999: 79). Glucklich views "sacred pain" as "the mediating force that makes the acquisition of third-level (spiritual) reality possible" (2001: 151). Drawing on the work of Lazarus (1991) and others, Glucklich asserts "strong feelings induced by pain affect our capacity to perceive and know reality" (2001: 150). Anthropologist T. O. Beidelman describes the pain in traditional East African Kaguru initiation ceremonies as "so incontestably real that it seems to confer its quality of 'incontestable reality' on that power that has brought it into being" (1997: 179). Self-inflicted suffering and pain are required of adherents by many faiths. There is, however, one category of religious ritual in which the use of violence to induce such "sacred pain" is particularly prevalent: adolescent rites of passage.

Adolescent Rites of Passage

Throughout human history and across the vast majority of cultures throughout the world, religion has been the preferred means of shaping our social and moral brains. Adolescence has been the preferred life stage for doing so (Alcorta 2006: 72–73). Children everywhere hear the narratives and witness the rituals of their culture's sacred beliefs, while childhood rites, such as infant baptism and eighth-day circumcision, effectively signal the individual's membership in the community. Such rites do little to initiate the child into the sacred, however, since there is neither individual choice nor understanding involved. Adults occasionally convert to new faiths, but it is adolescents who are regularly initiated into "the sacred." Nearly three-quarters of all cultures throughout the world conduct adolescent rites of passage. These rites have the explicit purpose of inculcating sacred values deemed necessary to transform children into socially responsible adults.

Adolescent rites of passage differ considerably from culture to culture. They may involve a single individual or an age-related group. Group rites are more commonly conducted for males, with approximately 30 percent of societies throughout the world conducting male group initiations as compared to about 10 percent for female group initiations. Conversely, individual rites are more frequently conducted for females; individual female initiation rites are found in 50 to 60 percent of societies throughout the world, compared to 30 to 40 percent for males (Lutkehaus and Roscoe 1995: xiv). The rites of some cultures are relatively simple, consisting of little more than the oral transmission of knowledge. Such simple rites are recorded for the Yamana and Halakwulup of Tierra del Fuego and are also prevalent in most contemporary Western religions. In other societies, however, rites were traditionally lengthy, intense, and often violent.

There is considerable variation in adolescent rites of passage across cultures, but all such rites exhibit a similar three-phase structure (van Gennep 1960). In the first phase, the initiate is separated from society and stripped of his previous identity. The second, or liminal, phase involves the ritual resocialization of the initiate into a new identity. In the last phase, the individual is reincorporated into a defined group bearing a new adult social identity with associated economic, political, and reproductive responsibilities and benefits.

The psychological and social transformation of the initiate occurs during the liminal phase. This phase may be as benign as memorizing and publicly reciting sacred texts or as intensely painful as undergoing food and sleep deprivation, torture, and genital mutilation. The use of violence and pain to transform the initiate during the liminal phase is not uncommon. Numerous researchers have examined the psychological and symbolic mechanisms by which such transformation occurs (Beidelman 1997; Glucklich 2001; McCauley 2001; Turner 1967; Whitehouse 2004). More recently, the neurophysiological impacts of such rituals have received increased attention. Cognitive scientist Robert McCauley's description of Baktaman initiation rituals notes the impacts of violent and painful rituals on initiates' emotional arousal:

> [T]he initiations bombard initiates' senses in order to arouse their emotions. They are routinely deprived of food, water and sleep. They are repeatedly beaten and tortured. They are forced to eat what are, in their own estimation, all sorts of disgusting concoctions. They are forced to dance to the point of utter exhaustion.... Stimulating ritual participants' senses is the most straightforward, surefire means available for arousing their emotions. The intuition is that the resulting levels of emotional excitement are often at least roughly proportional to the levels of sensory stimulation a ritual contains. These emotional responses are virtually always involuntary, and with particularly intense sensory stimulation, they are often difficult to control. (2001: 119)

Such emotional responses and changes in autonomic state are also apparent in the traditional sun dance rites of many Native American plains cultures. These rituals require initiates to fast, dehydrate, and dance to exhaustion. The chests of initiates are then pierced by elder males using sticks or eagle claws fastened to a central ritual pole. As the community watches, the adolescent males are required to break free of the pole by tearing their own flesh. Manny Twofeathers, a ritual initiate, describes the experience:

> I lay there on the ground, looking up into the sky. Then I handed Lessert my piercing bones. He got down on his knees next to me, and his father knelt by my left side. I felt both of them grab my chest and rub it with some dirt, because I was sweaty and slippery. This way their thumbs and fingers wouldn't slip. They pinched my skin, and I felt as the knife went into my flesh. I felt a sharp, intense pain in my chest, as if somebody had put a red-hot iron on my flesh. I lost all sense of time. I couldn't hear any sounds. I didn't feel the heat of the sun. I tried to grit my teeth, but I couldn't.... I prayed to the Creator to give me strength, to give me courage.... When I stood up, I did feel pain. I felt pain, but I also felt that closeness with the Creator.... The pain did not compare to what I was receiving from this sacred experience.... I was tied to the tree with that rope as securely as a child is tied to its mother by the umbilical cord. The only way off that cord was by ripping myself off. Every time I leaned back on my rope, I felt intense pain in my chest. It became a raw ache that reached all the way down to my toes.... It felt glorious and explosive. The energy was high and brilliant.... I went back, back. I looked at the tree and said silently, "Grandfather, please give me strength." I ran faster and faster and faster. I hit the end of the line. I heard my flesh tear, rip, and pop. I saw the rope bouncing way up in the tree. It dangled there for a second, then dropped. While this was going on, I fell backwards. I had broken loose.... I was so happy, I let out a big yell. (qtd. in Glucklich 2001: 147–148)

Violence was even more pronounced in the Mukanda rites of the Ndembu of Africa. Young adolescent males were kidnapped from their mothers and siblings and secluded and sequestered in the forest for months. During their seclusion, they were subjected to dietary restrictions, sleep deprivation, and numerous psychological and physical tortures. The final and central component of the rites was the circumcision of the initiates in a communal ceremony accompanied by incessant drumming and terrifying symbolism. Red-stained elders, the "killers" of the boys, performed the circumcision with knives as participants watched (Turner 1967: 181–182). Such painful, violent, and terrifying rites of passage sometimes result in physical mutilation or impairment or even death (Pinto and Baruzzi 1991: 821–822). Boys who successfully complete these initiations, however, are transformed physically, psychologically, and socially. They carry with them both the visible signal of circumcision as well as the invisible but equally powerful sacred symbols created through participation in this violent and painful ritual. Glucklich notes: "The sharp pain of the cut leads to a fairly strong psychological dissociation and triggers extremely powerful emotions.... There is also a strong cognitive learning process, which is enhanced by pain" (2001: 143).

The sacred pain and ritualized violence that occur in many adolescent rites of passage elicit strong autonomic responses and evoke intense emotions that may subsequently be suppressed but are nearly impossible to erase (LeDoux 1996: 124). Clinical, experimental, and neuroimaging findings independently demonstrate that emotions are critical to our daily behaviors and choices. Emotions do not simply influence our social judgments and personal choices; they are absolutely essential to them (Bechara, Damasio, and Damasio 2000: 305–306; LeDoux 2002: 253–254). Emotions learned through past experiences weight our present choices. In the absence of these emotional weights, we may be able to accurately solve problems in the abstract, but we are simply incapable of making appropriate personal choices (Damasio 1994: 52–82). This is true not only for social and moral choices but for "rational" economic decisions as well (Frank 1998: 254–259). Understanding this critical role of emotion in our judgments and behaviors provides important insights into the centrality of the sacred to religion and the role of violence in the creation of the sacred.

The use of violence and pain in communal ritual to evoke strong emotions and alter autonomic states provides an effective tool for investing symbols, beliefs, and other social abstractions with emotional significance. When these abstractions are also counterintuitive and supernatural, they are more arresting and memorable. Most significantly, they are also unfalsifiable (Rappaport 1999: 428). The reward value of music and the positive emotions evoked by participation in communal ritual provide opportunities to invest social symbols with positive emotional weighting through reinforcement learning. However, negative emotions are more salient than positive emotions and longer lasting (Vaish, Grossmann, and Woodward 2008: 384). As a result, the conditioned association of sacred symbols with violently evoked negative emotions and painful body states through terror, violence, and sacred pain is motivationally powerful and nearly impossible to extinguish. The costs associated with such violence are considerably greater than those incurred through participation in joyous rituals. No initiate has ever died from too much music, but food deprivation, torture, and genital mutilation can and do disable and kill. The greater longevity and motivational force of classic fear conditioning makes violence a powerful and effective tool when group values and sacred symbols require high personal sacrifice and risk.

Violent rites of initiation comprise one end of a spectrum of religious rituals. Such highly charged and emotionally intense ritual experiences not only transform initiates physically, psychologically, and socially; they also sculpt indelible neurophysiological changes.

Various researchers have noted a positive relationship between stress levels and the incidence of religious ritual. Victor Turner reported that among the Ndembu "there is a close connection between social conflict and ritual at the levels of village and 'vicinage'" (1969: 10), and Rappaport also observed that spacing of the ritual kaiko cycles of the Maring was contingent on interhousehold stress levels (1999: 154). Moreover, cross-cultural research shows that the degree to which painful and dangerous elements are incorporated in initiation rites is positively and significantly correlated with the incidence of warfare in preindustrial societies (Sosis, Kress and Boster 2007: 234).

Violent initiation rites invest group symbols and values with strong motivational force. They also prime initiates' response systems for threat, thereby producing higher levels of aggression (Niehoff 1998). When violent rites of initiation involve groups of initiates, they create bonded "brothers," as well. Recent research shows that individuals who have previously experienced a life-threatening situation during childhood or adolescence exhibit higher levels of oxytocin production in response to stressful events (Pierrehumbert et al. 2010: 168). Violent and painful initiation rites sanctify group values, increase levels of aggression, and neurophysiologically bond "brothers in arms." As a result, such rites are likely to produce the most cohesive groups and the most effective warriors. Military boot camps and paramilitary terrorist training camps effectively employ violence and pain to the same end (Nesser 2008: 234–256). Adolescents who participate in such rites are changed forever. Advances in our knowledge of the adolescent brain explain why this is so.

Changes that occur in the human brain during adolescence make this developmental period particularly receptive to the neurophysiological effects of religious ritual, in general, to rites of passage, in particular, and to violent and painful rites most specifically (Alcorta 2008: 111–116). Neuroimaging indicates "greater involvement of the amygdala in processing of emotional stimuli in human adolescents than adults" (Spear 2000: 445). During adolescence, the reward value of inherently pleasurable stimuli, such as food, sex, drugs, and music, peaks and the brain's dopaminergic systems undergo substantial reorganization. At the same time, the prefrontal cortex and the temporal cortex mature (Spear 2000: 439–445). The prefrontal cortex is the brain region responsible for impulse inhibition, social judgment, personal decision making, and abstract reasoning; the temporal cortex functions in face recognition, music, language, and the integration of other social stimuli. Neuroscientist Sarah-Jayne Blakemore notes that brain areas involved in social cognition, including the medial prefrontal cortex, the anterior cingulate cortex, the inferior frontal gyrus, the superior temporal sulcus, the amygdala, and the anterior insula experience considerable change during adolescence (2008: 267). She notes that medial prefrontal cortex and the superior temporal sulcus, involved in face recognition and mental state attribution, "undergo structural development, including synaptic reorganization during adolescence" (2008: 267). The shift in the adolescent brain's dopaminergic system occurs in tandem with the maturation of these cortices as reward and emotional processing structures more closely integrate with and increasingly come under control of the prefrontal cortex, the brain's "executive" processing center (Spear 2000: 440–441). This synaptic reorganization in social and executive processing regions of the brain occurs in tandem with heightened adolescent reward salience and emotional responsivity (Spear 2000: 440–441). These changes in the structures and circuitry of the adolescent brain provide a unique developmental window for linking social experiences with abstract, symbolic representations and investing those representations with emotional significance and reward value capable of influencing subsequent social judgments and behavioral choices (Dehaene and Changeux 2000: 219–230; Feenstra 2000: 133–164). Religious ritual appears to be optimally designed to do just that. Rappaport presciently described such effects of ritual:

> When that sign is carved on the body the abstract is not only made substantial but immediate…and if the mark is indelible, as in the case of the subincision, the excised canine, the lopped finger, the scarified face, chest or back, it is ever-present. As the abstract is made alive and concrete by the living substance of men and women, so are men and women predicated by the abstractions which they themselves realize. (1999: 149)

RELIGION AND SUICIDE TERRORISM

What can this tell us about suicide terrorists or religious violence in general? Many contemporary Western stereotypes cast religiously motivated terrorists as either desperate or deranged madmen. Substantial psychological research, however, indicates that suicide terrorists are neither psychopaths nor sociopaths. Terrorist expert Scott Atran reports that "study after study demonstrates that suicide terrorists and their supporters are not abjectly poor, illiterate, or socially estranged" (2004: 75). Nor is there a distinctive suicide terrorist psychological profile or personality. Sociologist Mark Juergensmeyer notes that the vast majority of recruits to extremist religious organizations are young, unmarried males who perceive themselves to be marginalized by the dominant culture (2003: 193–194). In his governmental report, *The Sociology and Psychology of Terrorism: Who Becomes a Terrorist and Why?*, Rex Hudson makes a similar observation: "Terrorists are generally people who feel alienated from society and have a grievance or regard themselves as victims of an injustice" (1999: 50). Maajid Nawaz, a former leader of the radical Islamic group Hizb ut-Tahrir, states that he originally joined the movement "out of disaffection with the racism and discrimination that poisoned his teenage years in southeast England" (qtd. in Rice-Oxley 2008). For Nawaz, the organization's secret meetings, conversion missions, and evangelistic forays to university campuses and foreign countries created a sense of importance, community, and purpose. Mamoun Fandy of the International Institute for Strategic Studies in London asserts: "There remains in London a problem of assimilation for outsiders. The society is closed. The city is open, but the people are not" (qtd. in Marquand and Quinn 2009). Such closure is likely to be felt particularly acutely by young unattached adolescent and young adult males who are actively seeking meaningful social relationships. These young men who have spent their childhood in traditional societies are literally caught between worlds that diverge sharply in social structure, intersexual relations, and the sacred values that intermediate between these and personal behaviors (Alcorta 2010). A Pakistani expert on militant Islam notes, "I've felt for a long time that if radical Sharia law comes to the rest of the world it will start on the streets of London.... Young Muslims are smart, raised as British citizens. If they come from abroad, many have great hope and are often disillusioned. They live between worlds, in the cracks. When they go home to their families they are often more radical than their friends" (qtd. in Marquand and Quinn 2009). According to Atran "more than 80 percent of known jihadis currently live in diaspora communities, which are often marginalized from the host society and physically disconnected from each other" (2006: 135).

For such individuals, membership in religious extremist groups is likely to be particularly appealing. These groups afford marginalized youth a sense of community within a larger alien culture. They provide a network of social support within a structure and value system that is familiar and "moral." For marginalized immigrants, religious extremist groups offer cultural familiarity and endorse the values and worldview instilled through early socialization. These groups provide a sense of order within the perceived chaos of the foreign culture and reaffirm personal worth and meaning through social identity. Their reaffirmation of the individual's indigenous values reduces the cognitive dissonance and sense of anomie experienced by many marginalized youth.

In contrast to secular social groups such as school clubs and athletic teams, religious groups provide marginalized youth with a sense of shared moral values, individual purpose, and existential meaning. Marginalized youth who join these congregations are no longer merely anonymous cogs in a global economic system; they are valued individuals in the eyes of both their fellow adherents and in the eyes of God. Extremist militant religious organizations offer adherents the additional promise of power (Juergensmeyer 2008: 175). Recruits are not only brothers but brothers in arms, many of whom receive training in isolated, rigorous, and physically demanding terrorist training camps (Nesser 2008: 234–256; Yousafzai and Moreau 2010: 30–37). Juergensmeyer notes, "The nineteen men who volunteered for the al Qaeda suicide mission on September 11, 2001 were... participants in semisecret male societies" (2003: 223). Like other adolescent rites of passage, these semisecret societies employ pain, violence, and ritual to reshape the psychological, political, and social identities of initiates.

RELIGION, SOCIAL GROUPS, AND THE SOCIAL CONTRACT

Humans are one of many social species that create and maintain large social groups. Such groups provide individual members with fitness benefits in relation to vigilance, reproduction, and defense. From an evolutionary perspective, however, social groups also introduce problems of competition, defection, and cooperation (Krebs and Davies 1993: 120–133). These inherent problems have been resolved in various ways by different species. In many species, group membership is based primarily on genetic relatedness. This ensures that the inclusive fitness of all group members is enhanced by cooperative behaviors. Other species, such as bats, live in large colonies of unrelated individuals and share resources with "friends." Such reciprocal altruism depends on a "tit-for-tat" approach to secure cooperation. Reciprocal altruism extends cooperation to unrelated individuals but necessarily confines the extent of cooperative interactions to those that can be remembered.

Human social groups rely on both kinship and reciprocal altruism to achieve and enhance cooperation. Although there is considerable variation across cultures, in most traditional human societies, as in the societies of our closest cousins, the chimpanzees and bonobos, kinship is male based (Wrangham and Peterson 1996: 24). Females leave the natal group upon reaching adolescence and join an unrelated group. Such fraternal societies are less common than female-related societies across species but are advantageous when intermale cooperation provides significant benefits. For chimpanzees, group hunts and intergroup raids are predominantly male enterprises that depend on intermale cooperation for success (Wrangham and Peterson 1996: 24–25). Male cooperation would have benefited early human groups in both hunting and intergroup raiding as well. Most significantly, cooperative male groups would have wielded a distinct advantage in pre-industrial intergroup warfare (Alexander 1987: 79–81). These large groups would have afforded early human populations additional advantages as well.

The major environmental shift that has been documented for early human environments certainly posed challenges in relation to both resource competition and exploitation (Marean 2010: 54). Environmental changes would have altered traditional resource bases and increased competition among groups for the resources remaining. Under such circumstances, larger groups would have realized a number of competitive advantages.

For the relatively small early human populations of Africa, one of the major advantages to larger group sizes was likely to be a demographic one. Larger groups represent a broader, deeper gene pool for dampening demographic fluctuations (Hammel 2005: 2251–2252) and avoiding genetic bottlenecks (Marean 2010: 55). Such groups also enjoy an information advantage in regard to widely spaced, clumped, and cyclical resources and an innovative advantage in regard to resource utilization and exploitation. Across primate species, including our own, it is predominantly older individuals that constitute the repository for group information, and it is predominantly younger members who engage in innovation. In traditional hunter-gatherer societies such as the Kung San, it was the group elders who provided critical information in regard to the location of scarce water holes and long-term cyclical resources (Moore 1998: 119). Alternately, across societies, it is primarily juveniles who engage in innovative "play," trying out novel resources and behaviors that may subsequently be adopted by the group (Diamond 1997: 118). Groups large enough to maintain wide demographic diversity during times of environmental stress are more likely to benefit from both the greater information of elders and the broader innovation of juveniles. In preindustrial societies, groups that also include large numbers of adolescent and young adult males realize significant competitive advantages in intergroup raiding and warfare.

Given all of the advantages of larger groups, it is reasonable to ask why all social groups are not large. The most obvious answer to this question is that resources limit the size that groups can grow. Yet even when the resource base is sufficient to sustain larger groups, increasing group sizes introduce new problems that must be solved.

THE COSTLY SIGNALING THEORY OF RELIGION

As human social groups increase in size, new problems of free riding, control, and cooperation emerge. Proponents of the costly signaling theory of religion view religion as an important human adaptation to solve these problems by facilitating intragroup cooperation (Irons 2001: 292; Sosis 2003: 92–94). Anthropologist William Irons views the primary adaptive benefit of religion to be its ability to promote cooperation and overcome problems of collective action, including food sharing, hunting, defense, and warfare (2001: 292–293). When social groups are small and closely related, collective action problems are relatively limited by the operation of kin selection and reciprocity. However, as group size increases and genetic relatedness decreases, there is increasing incentive for individuals to free ride on the efforts of others. Group members who can benefit from the cooperative efforts of others with no costs to themselves realize the greatest gains. This is particularly true in high risk, high cost endeavors such as hunting, defense, and, particularly, warfare. While everyone may gain if all group members invest in the cooperative goal, actually attaining such cooperation is often difficult without social mechanisms that limit the ability of some group members to free ride on the efforts of others. As the risks associated with cooperative endeavors increase, the greater incentive there is for individuals to defect and free ride. As a result, whenever an individual can falsely claim cooperation and then successfully defect, the most credible signals of cooperative intentions are those that entail costs and are difficult to fake.

Costly signaling theorists posit that religious behaviors and rituals have evolved in human groups as hard-to-fake signals that advertise an individual's level of commitment to the goals and ideals of the group, both to oneself and to others (Sosis and Alcorta 2003: 267). Participation in such rituals promotes ingroup cooperation through the neurophysiological mechanisms previously discussed, and it also signals group commitment to others. Observers of religion have long noted the costliness of religious obligations (Sosis 2006: 61–68). Even relatively simple, joyous religious rituals such as the *molimo* ceremony of the African Mbuti entail time, energy, and resource costs. Many religious rituals include joyous elements but also incorporate fearful elements as well. The costliest rituals add to this sacrifice, violence, and pain. Initiation rites are among the costliest of religious rituals and frequently include beatings; tattooing; isolation; food, water, and sleep deprivation; consumption of toxic substances; psychological and physical torture; genital mutilation; and risk of death. The performance of these costly behaviors has significant neurophysiolgoical effects on initiates, reinforcing the cognitive and emotional substrates of individual commitment to group ideals and values. Such performance also provides a powerful signal of commitment and loyalty to the group and the beliefs of its members. Enhanced trust and commitment among group members is essential to collective enterprises and enables groups to minimize costly monitoring mechanisms that are otherwise necessary to overcome the free rider problems that typically plague collective pursuits.

Empirical research conducted over the last decade has demonstrated that religious ritual is an effective tool for increasing group cooperation and cohesion. Cross-cultural research has shown a significant positive correlation between participation in religious ritual and group longevity (Sosis and Bressler 2003: 225–228). Experimental studies conducted on Israeli kibbutzim show a significant positive correlation between participation in religious ritual and cooperation as well (Sosis and Ruffle 2003: 718–719). Although overcoming challenges of cooperative production and consumption were undoubtedly important in human evolution, warfare and defense likely posed even greater challenges due to the life and death consequences of cooperation and defection. Cross-cultural studies suggest that violent and painful rites may serve to bond males in societies where warfare is most prevalent (Sosis, Kress, and Boster 2007: 243–245). Research further indicates that the costliest religious requirements in terms of pain, violence, and bodily harm occur in preindustrial societies that exhibit the highest rates of warfare (ibid.). Under such circumstances, individual incentive to defect and free ride is particularly great. Participation in costly initiation rites leaves indelible traces on both the minds and bodies of initiates, signaling both to themselves and one another their commitment to the group.

Origins of Religion

Early human populations inhabiting Africa 100,000 years ago faced significant challenges introduced by the major environmental shift occurring at that time (Marean 2010: 54). Climate change diminished traditional resources, thereby increasing competition over those remaining. For many early human populations, this meant extinction. Yet along the coastal regions of South Africa several early human groups appear to have successfully outcompeted their contemporaries and overcame the challenges brought about by climate change. These South African coastal dwellers used sophisticated tools to exploit new resources, including mussels and other marine life as well as hard-to-find and difficult-to-extract tubers. These populations lived in large, relatively sedentary groups at a time when their nomadic contemporaries were quickly disappearing (Marean 2010: 54–61).

The coastal populations were successful when most other early human populations were not. Larger group size and all the associated advantages such size confers was undoubtedly an important key to their success. The information of elders, the innovation of juveniles, and the aggression of adolescent and young adult males were all likely factors in the group's ability to explore and exploit new resources and outcompete their contemporaries. Sophisticated tool kits associated with these groups are evidence of technological innovation. Alongside these tools is evidence of another innovation that may have been equally fundamental to their success: red ochre.

In association with the sophisticated tool kits of the South African coastal populations, archaeologists have found ground red ochre and worked red ochre lumps incised with abstract etchings (Henshilwood et al. 2001: 668; Marean 2010: 58–59). Based on ethnographic analogies, archaeologists have concluded that these artifacts are evidence of symbolic ritual in these populations. If so, symbolic ritual—the roots of religion—emerged much earlier in human evolution than previously believed and may have been a critical factor in the ability of the South African coastal populations to overcome the problems of cooperation and free riding associated with increasing group size and sustain the large populations that contributed to their survival. Selective pressure for an adaptation that afforded early human groups a means of enhancing intermale cooperation would have been strong given the high levels of competition that were undoubtedly induced by environmental change at the time. The emergence of symbolic ritual coincides with both increasing sedentism and a significant increase in group size. For these populations, symbolic ritual may have constituted the solution to the large group problems of free riding, social control, and intermale cooperation.

Biological anthropologist Terrence Deacon has argued that communal religious ritual originated as a way to socially signal sexual exclusivity through marriage in multimale groups (1997: 405–407). Other researchers have proposed that music-based communal ritual evolved as a mechanism for creating intergroup alliances (Hayden 1987: 83–84). Combining these two hypotheses may offer the best model for understanding the origins of symbolic ritual. In many traditional cultures, the exchange of women between groups both creates and cements intergroup alliances that are consummated and signaled through ritual (Lévi-Strauss 1963: 22). Such ritual publicly acknowledges pair bonds and the sexual exclusivity of mates within multimale social groups while simultaneously forging flexible, cooperative intermale bonds both within and between groups.

Mounting evidence suggests that the evolution of religion is closely associated with the emergence of large social groups in early human populations. The oldest evidence of symbolic ritual occurs during a period of significant environmental change. Intergroup competition is likely to have been a potent selective force at this time. Adaptations that facilitated the creation of large social groups through cooperative intermale alliances would have been advantageous in both warfare and defense. Such groups would also have realized advantages in relation to technological innovation and a broader gene pool during demographic shifts. The evolution of symbolic ritual as a costly signaling system would have provided early human populations with a flexible mechanism for enhancing intermale cooperation, increasing group size and cohesion, and controlling problems of sexual exclusivity, social order, and free riding within the social group. The ability to alter the individual and social effectiveness of symbolic ritual through the incorporation of violent and painful practices makes this adaptation particularly advantageous under conditions of increasing intergroup competition, decreasing intragroup male relatedness, and escalating environmental stress. In early human environments, as in the globalizing world of today, violence is likely to have been both a component of and catalyst for religion.

Conclusion

The relatively recent emergence of the secular nation-state has been accompanied by the ongoing marginalization of religion across Western societies and in communist nations throughout the world. In these societies, the validation and inculcation of social behaviors are no longer religiously mandated and sanctioned but are instead monopolized by the legal and educational powers of the state. Enforcement is transferred from punishing moral gods and their divine warriors to specialized professionals trained and controlled by the secular state. As the power of the secular nation-state has risen, that of organized religion within these states has declined (Norris and Inglehart 2004: 25). While this decline has been state mandated and enforced in communist nations, it has been a gradual development in the democracies of western Europe and the United States. Church attendance in nearly all Western nations has steadily decreased over the past two decades (Norris and Inglehart 2004: 72). The United States constitutes an anomaly with some 43 percent of American respondents reporting regular weekly church attendance (Newport 2010a). Other surveys have found a consistently lower US church attendance figure, however, and a 2010 Gallup poll indicates that "Americans have become increasingly less tied to formal religion in recent decades, with the percentage saying they do not have a specific religious identity growing from near zero in the 1950s to 16 percent this year" (Newport 2010b). Nearly 20 percent of Americans consider religion as not very important in their lives, while close to 30 percent view religion as "largely old-fashioned" (ibid.).

This decline of organized religion in developed industrial nations has been accompanied by a growing incidence of suicide and depression (Miller 2006: 459; WHO 2001). Sociologist Phil Zuckerman notes that suicide rates are "the one indicator of societal health in which religious nations fare much better than secular nations" (2006: 59). At the same time, Pentecostalism and other charismatic religions have grown rapidly throughout the world and particularly in developing nations (Pew Research Center 2006). For many, these "renewalist" religions provide social support, purpose, and meaning as the institutions and values of traditional cultures are marginalized and eroded by globalization. For others, however, religion serves a different purpose. For many young, unattached males who perceive themselves to be marginalized by a dominant, hostile, foreign culture (Juergensmeyer 2008: 220–223), religion provides both a welcoming community and an effective tool for forging the cohesive, cooperative intermale alliances necessary to challenge the hegemony of the secular nation-state and its global impacts.

As in our nonhuman primate kin, adolescent males in human societies constitute both the periphery and the front guard of the social group. From a reproductive standpoint, they are the most expendable group members and from a neurophysiological perspective, they are the most vulnerable. Whether as migrants to foreign urban cities or military recruits, these young males most frequently constitute the "first wave" of intergroup contact (Alcorta 2010). From a proximate perspective, their greater propensity for novelty seeking and risk-taking behaviors predispose them to assume this role, while their social powerlessness relative to older group males may compel them to do so (Thayer 2008: 130–132). For many, however, the stress, cognitive dissonance, and culture shock they experience results in anxiety, depression, psychosis, and suicide. The incidence of adolescent depression and suicide throughout the world has escalated tremendously over the past several decades and is particularly pronounced among adolescent males in marginalized cultures such as American Samoa (McDade, Stallings, and Worthman 2000: 792), Micronesia (Ran 2007: 80; Rubinstein 2002: 33), and Native American populations (CDC 2007; Health Canada 2002; Inuit Tapiriit Kanatami 2009). Religious conversion to Mormonism, Pentecostalism, and other forms of Christianity has provided some of these individuals with the new purpose, values, and social support necessary to successfully assimilate within the dominant Western culture. For a growing number of marginalized young males throughout the world, however, religion is not a mechanism for integration within the larger global culture but rather an effective tool for violent confrontation against it. For the young male members of al Qaeda, Hezbollah, Aum Shinrikyo, the Christian Identity movement, and a score of other extremist groups, religion offers purpose, values, beliefs, and social support, but it also offers something more; for these adherents religion offers the promise of power through the justification and glorification of violence (Juergensmeyer 2008: 220–223).

Religious ritual appears to be an effective evolved mechanism for shaping the adolescent brain and creating cohesive, cooperative intermale groups. Violence is and has been an integral component of such ritual across widely diverse human cultures throughout human history. Advances in our understanding of the human brain help explain why this is so on a proximate level; advances in our understanding of religion as an evolved adaptation help explain why selection has favored religious violence under diverse conditions. Understanding both the proximate and evolutionary mechanisms that link religion and violence is an important first step in understanding and hopefully eradicating the religious violence that has become so prevalent in the modern world.

ACKNOWLEDGMENT

This work was supported by an ESRC Large Grant (REF RES-060-25-0085) entitled "Ritual, Community, and Conflict."

BIBLIOGRAPHY

Alcorta, Candace S. "Religion and the Life Course: Is Adolescence an 'Experience Expectant' Period for Religious Transmission?" *Where God and Science Meet: How Brain and Evolutionary Studies Alter Our Understanding of Religion, Vol. II, The Neurology of Religious Experience.* Ed. Patrick McNamara, 55–80. Westport, CT: Praeger Press, 2006.

Alcorta, Candace S. "Music and the Miraculous: The Neurophysiology of Music's Emotive Meaning." *Miracles: God, Science, and Psychology in the Paranormal, Vol. 3, Parapsychological Perspectives.* Ed. J. Harold Ellens, 230–252. Westport, CT: Praeger Press, 2008.

Alcorta, Candace S. "Religious Behavior and the Adolescent Brain." *The Biology of Religious Behavior.* Ed. Jay R. Feierman, 106–122. Santa Barbara, CA: Praeger Press, 2009.

Alcorta, Candace S. "Biology, Culture, and Religiously-Motivated Suicide Terrorism: An Evolutionary Perspective." *Politics and Culture* 2010.1, n. p. Accessed June 16, 2012 on http://www.politicsandculture.org/2010/04/29/biology-culture-and-religiously-motivated-suicide-terrorism-an-evolutionary-perspective/.

Alcorta, Candace S. and Richard Sosis. "Ritual, Emotion and Sacred Symbols: The Evolution of Religion as an Adaptive Complex." *Human Nature* 16.4 (2005): 323–359.

Alexander, Richard D. *Biology of Moral Systems.* New York: Aldine de Gruyter, 1987.

Armstrong, Karen. *A History of God.* New York: Ballantine Books, 1993.

Atran, Scott. "Mishandling Suicide Terrorism." *The Washington Quarterly* 27.3 (2004): 67–90.

Atran, Scott. "The Moral Logic and Growth of Suicide Terrorism." *The Washington Quarterly* 29.2 (2006): 127–147.

Baumgartner, T., K. Lutz, C. F. Schmidt, and L. Jancke. "The Emotional Power of Music: How Music Enhances the Feeling of Affective Pictures." *Brain Research* 1075 (2006): 151–164.

Bechara, Antoine, Hanna Damasio, and Antonio Damasio. "Emotion, Decision-Making and the Orbitofrontal Cortex." *Cerebral Cortex* 10 (2000): 295–307.

Becker, Judith. "Anthropological Perspectives on Music and Emotion." *Music and Emotion.* Eds. Patrick Juslin and R. Sloboda, 135–160. Oxford, UK: Oxford University Press, 2001.

Becker, Judith. *Deep Listeners*. Bloomington: Indiana University Press, 2004.

Beidelman, T. O. *The Cool Knife: Imagery of Gender, Sexuality, and Moral Education in Kaguru Initiation Ritual*. Washington, D.C.: Smithsonian Institution Press, 1997.

Blakemore, Sarah-Jayne. "The Social Brain in Adolescence." *Nature Reviews Neuroscience* 9.4 (2008): 267–277.

Blood, Anne J. and Robert A. Zatorre. "Intensely Pleasurable Responses to Music Correlate with Activity in Brain Regions Implicated in Reward and Emotion." *Proceedings of the National Academy of Sciences of the United States of America* 98.20 (2001): 11818–11823.

Centers for Disease Control. "Suicide Trends among Youths and Young Adults Aged 10–24 Years—United States, 1990–2004." United States Center for Disease Control, MMWR 56(35) (2007):905–908. Accessed February 22, 2011. http://www.cdc.gov/mmwr/preview/mmwrhtml/mm5635a2.htm.

Cross, Ian. "Music as a Biocultural Phenomenon." *The Neurosciences and Music. Annals of the New York Academy of Sciences, Vol. 999*. Eds. G. Avanzini, C. Faienza, D. Minciacchi, L. Lopez, and M. Majno, 106–111. New York: New York Academy of Sciences, 2003.

Damasio, Antonio R. *Descartes' Error*. New York: Avon Books, 1994.

Damasio, Antonio R. *The Feeling of What Happens*. New York: Harcourt Incorporated, 1999.

Daw, N. D. "Dopamine: At the Intersection of Reward and Action." *Nature Neuroscience* 10 (2007): 1505–1507.

Deacon, Terrence. *The Symbolic Species*. New York: W. W. Norton, 1997.

Dehaene, S. and J. P. Changeux. "Reward-Dependent Learning in Neuronal Networks for Planning and Decision-Making." *Cognition, Emotion and Autonomic Responses: The Integrative Role of the Prefrontal Cortex and Limbic Structures*. Eds. H.B.M. Uylings, C. G. van Eden, J.P.D. de Bruin, M.G.P. Feenstra, and C.M.A. Pennartz, 219–230. New York: Elsevier, 2000.

Diamond, Jared. *Guns, Germs and Steel: The Fates of Human Societies*. New York: W.W. Norton, 1997.

Dissanayake, Ellen. *Homo Aestheticus*. Seattle: University of Washington Press, 1992.

Durkheim, Emile. 1912. *The Elementary Forms of the Religious Life*. New York: The Free Press, 1969.

Ewing, T. *Gods and Worshippers in the Viking and Germanic World*. Stroud, Gloucestershire UK: Tempus Publishing Group, 2008.

Feenstra, M. G. P. "Dopamine and Noradrenaline Release in the Prefrontal Cortex in Relation to Unconditioned and Conditioned Stress and Reward." In *Cognition, Emotion and Autonomic Responses: The Integrative Role of the Prefrontal Cortex and Limbic Structures*. Eds. H. B. M. Uylings, C. G. van Eden, J. P. D. de Bruin, M. G. P. Feenstra, and C. M. A. Pennartz, 133–164. New York: Elsevier, 2000.

Frank, Robert H. *Passions within Reason: The Strategic Role of the Emotions*. New York: W. W. Norton, 1988.

Glucklich, Ariel. *Sacred Pain*. New York: Oxford University Press, 2001.

Hammel, E. A. "Demographic Dynamics and Kinship in Anthropological Populations." *Proceedings of the National Academy of Sciences* 102 (2005): 2248–2253.

Hayden, Brian. "Alliances and Ritual Ecstasy: Human Responses to Resource Stress." *Journal for the Scientific Study of Religion* 26 (1987): 81–91.

Health Canada. "Acting on What We Know: Preventing Youth Suicide in First Nations." *Report of the Suicide Prevention Advisory Group of Canada*, 2002. Accessed February 22, 2011 on http://www.hc-sc.gc.ca.

Henshilwood, C. S., F. d'Errico, C. W. Marean, R. G. Milo, and R. Yates "An Early Bone Tool Industry from the Middle Stone Age at Blombos Cave, South Africa: Implications for the Origins of Modern Human Behaviour, Symbolism and Language." *Journal of Human Evolution* 41 (2001): 631–678.

Hirokawa, E. and H. Ohira. "The Effects of Music Listening after a Stressful Task on Immune Functions, Neuroendocrine Responses, and Emotional States in College Students." *The Journal of Music Therapy* 40 (2003): 189–211.

Hudson, R. A. *The Sociology and Psychology of Terrorism: Who Becomes a Terrorist and Why?* A Report Prepared under an Interagency Agreement by the Federal Research Division, Library of Congress, September 1999. Accessed June 16, 2012 on http://www.loc.gov/rr/frd/pdf-files/Soc_Psych_of_Terrorism.pdf.

Hurlemann, R., A. Patin, O. A. Onur, M. X. Cohen, T. Baumgartner, S. Metzler, I. Dziobek, J. Gallinat, M. Wagner, W. Maier, and K. M. Kendrick. "Oxytocin Enhances Amygdala-Dependent, Socially Reinforced Learning and Emotional Empathy in Humans." *Journal of Neuroscience* 30 (2010): 4999–5007.

Inuit Tapiriit Kanatami. *Inuit Approaches to Suicide Prevention.* 2009. Accessed February 22, 2011 on www.itk.ca/Inuit-Approaches-to-Suicide-Prevention.

Irons, William. "Religion as a Hard-to-Fake Sign of Commitment." *Evolution and the Capacity for Commitment.* Ed. R. Nesse, 292–309. New York: Russell Sage Foundation, 2001.

Israel, S., E. Lerer, I. Shalev, F. Uzefovsky, M. Reibold, R. Bachner-Melman, R. Granot, G. Bornstein, A. Knafo, N. Yirmiya, and R. P. Ebstein. "Molecular Genetic Studies of the Arginine Vasopressin 1a Receptor (AVPR1a) and the Oxytocin Receptor (OXTR) in Human Behaviour: From Autism to Altruism with Some Notes in Between." In *Advances in Vasopressin and Oxytocin: From Genes to Behaviour to Disease.* Eds. I. D. Neumann and R. Landgraf, 435–449. Oxford, UK: Elsevier B.V., 2008.

Juergensmeyer, Mark. *Terror in the Mind of God: The Global Rise in Religious Violence.* 3rd ed. Berkeley: University of California Press, 2003.

Juergensmeyer, Mark. *Global Rebellion.* Berkeley: University of California Press, 2008.

Koelsch, Stefan. "Towards a Neural Basis of Music-Evoked Emotions." *Trends in Cognitive Science* 14 (2010): 131–137.

Krebs, J. R. and N. B. Davies. *An Introduction to Behavioural Ecology.* 3rd ed. Oxford, UK: Blackwell Science, 1993.

Kuhn, D. "The Effects of Active and Passive Participation in Musical Activity on the Immune System as Measured by Salivary Immunoglobulin A (SigA)." *The Journal of Music Therapy* 39.1 (2002): 30–39.

Laughlin, C. D., Jr. and J. McManus. "Mammalian Ritual." *The Spectrum of Ritual.* Eds. E. G. d'Aquili, C. D. Laughlin, Jr., and J. McManus, 80–116. New York: Columbia University Press, 1979.

Lazarus, R. S. *Emotion and Adaptation.* New York: Oxford University Press, 1991.

LeDoux, J. E. *The Emotional Brain.* New York: Simon and Schuster, 1996.

LeDoux, J. E. *Synaptic Self.* New York: Viking, 2002.

Lévi-Strauss, Claude. *Structural Anthropology.* New York: Basic Books, 1963.

Levitin, Daniel. *The World in Six Songs.* New York: Penguin Books, 2008.

Lutkehaus, N. C. and P. B. Roscoe. "Preface." *Gender Rituals: Female Initiation in Melanesia.* Eds. N. C. Lutkehaus and P. B. Roscoe, xiii-xix. New York: Routledge, 1995.

Marean, C. W. "When the Sea Saved Humanity." *Scientific American* 303 (2010): 54–61.

Marquand, R. and B. Quinn. "Was Umar Farouk Abdulmutallab Radicalized in London?" *The Christian Science Monitor*, December 28, 2009. Accessed February 22, 2011 on http://www.csmonitor.com/World/Europe/2009/1228/Was-Umar-Farouk-Abdulmutallab-radicalized-in-London.

McCauley, Robert. "Ritual, Memory and Emotion: Comparing Two Cognitive Hypotheses." *Religion in Mind*. Ed. J. Andresen, 115–140. Cambridge, UK: Cambridge University Press, 2001.

McDade, T. W., J. F. Stallings, and C. M. Worthman. "Culture Change and Stress in Western Samoan Youth: Methodological Issues in the Cross-Cultural Study of Stress and Immune Function." *American Journal of Human Biology* 12 (2000): 792–802.

Menon, V. and D. J. Levitin. "The Rewards of Music Listening: Response and Physiological Connectivity of the Mesolimbic System." *NeuroImage* 28 (2005): 175–184.

Miller, G. "The Unseen: Mental Illness' Global Toll." *Science* 311 (2006): 458–461.

Missig, G., L. W. Ayers, J. Schulkin, and J. B. Rosen. "Oxytocin Reduces Background Anxiety in a Fear-Potentiated Startle Paradigm." *Neuropsychopharmacology* 35 (2010): 2607–2616.

Moore, Alexander. *Cultural Anthropology: The Field Study of Human Beings*. 2nd ed. San Diego: Collegiate Press, 1998.

Nesser, P. "How Did Europe's Global Jihadis Obtain Training for Their Militant Causes?" *Terrorism and Political Violence* 20 (2008): 234–256.

Neumann, I. D. "Brain Oxytocin: A Key Regulator of Emotional and Social Behaviours in Both Females and Males." *Journal of Neuroendocrinology* 20 (2008): 858–865.

Newport, F. (a) "In U.S., Increasing Number Have No Religious Identity." Gallup Poll, May 21, 2010. Accessed February 22, 2011. <www.gallup.com/poll/128276/increasing-number-no-religious-identity.aspx.>

Newport, F. (b) "Americans' Church Attendance Inches Up in 2010." Gallup Poll, June 25, 2010. Accessed February 22, 2011. <www.gallup.com/poll/141044/americans-church-attendance-inches-2010.aspx.>

Niehoff, Debra. *The Biology of Violence: How Understanding the Brain, Behavior, and Environment Can Break the Vicious Cycle of Aggression*. New York: The Free Press, 1998.

Nilsson, U. "Soothing Music Can Increase Oxytocin Levels During Bed Rest after Open-Heart Surgery: A Randomized Control Trial." *Journal of Clinical Nursing* 18 (2009): 2153–3161.

Norris, P. and R. Inglehart. *Sacred and Secular: Religion and Politics Worldwide*. Cambridge, UK: Cambridge University Press, 2004.

Patel, A., J. Iversen, M. Bregman, and I. Schulz. "Experimental Evidence for Synchronization to a Musical Beat in a Nonhuman Animal." *Current Biology* 19.10 (2009): 827–830.

Pew Research Center. " Pew Forum on Religion and Public Life: Pentecostal Resource Page." October 5, 2006. Accessed February 22, 2011. <http://pewforum.org/Christian/Evangelical-Protestant-Churches/Pentecostal-Resource-Page.aspx.>.

Pierrehumbert, B., R. Torrisi, D. Laufer, O. Halfon, F. Ansermet, and M. B. Popovic. "Oxytocin Response to an Experimental Psychosocial Challenge in Adults Exposed to Traumatic Experiences during Childhood or Adolescence." *Neuroscience* 166 (2010): 168–177.

Pinto, N.R.S. and R. G. Baruzzi. "Male Pubertal Seclusion and Risk of Death in Indians from Alto Xingu, Central Brazil." *Human Biology* 63.6 (1991): 821–834.

Power, Camille. "Beauty Magic: The Origins of Art." *The Evolution of Culture*. Eds. R. Dunbar, C. Knight, and C. Power, 92–112. New Brunswick, NJ: Rutgers University Press, 1999.

Purzycki, B. G. and K. Gibson. "Religion and Violence: An Anthropological Study on Religious Belief and Violent Behavior." *Skeptic* 16.2 (2011): 24–29.

Ran, M. S. "Suicide in Micronesia: A Systematic Review." *Primary Psychiatry* 14.11 (2007): 80–87.

Rappaport, Roy A. *Ritual and Religion in the Making of Humanity*. London: Cambridge University Press, 1999.

Rice-Oxley, M. "British Ex-Jihadis Form Ranks for Tolerance." *The Christian Science Monitor*, April 23, 2008. Accessed June 16, 2012. http://www.csmonitor.com/World/Europe/2008/0423/p01s09-woeu.html.

Ross, H. E. and L. J. Young. "Oxytocin and the Neural Mechanisms Regulating Social Cognition and Affiliative Behavior." *Frontiers in Neuroendocrinology* 30 (2009): 534–547.

Rowe, C. "Receiver Psychology and the Evolution of Multi-Component Signals." *Animal Behaviour* 58 (1999): 921–931.

Rubinstein, D. H. "Youth Suicide and Social Change in Micronesia." Occasional Papers No. 36, 2002. Kagoshima University Research Center for the Pacific Islands. Accessed June 16, 2012. <http://www.hawaii.edu/hivandaids/Youth%20Suicide%20and%20Social%20Change%20in%20Micronesia.pdf.>

Shohamy, D. and R. A. Adcock. "Dopamine and Adaptive Memory." *Trends in Cognitive Science* 14 (2010): 464–472.

Smith, J. W. "Ritual and the Ethology of Communicating." *The Spectrum of Ritual*. Eds E.G. d'Aquili, C. D. Laughlin, Jr., and J. McManus, 51–79. New York: Columbia University Press, 1979.

Sosis, Richard. "Why Aren't We All Hutterites?" *Human Nature* 14 (2003): 91–127.

Sosis, Richard. "Religious Behaviors, Badges, and Bans: Signaling Theory and the Evolution of Religion." In *Where God and Science Meet: How Brain and Evolutionary Studies Alter Our Understanding of Religion, Volume 1: Evolution, Genes, and the Religious Brain*. Ed. Patrick McNamara, 61–86. Westport, CT: Praeger Publishers, 2006.

Sosis, Richard and Candace S. Alcorta. "Signaling, Solidarity, and the Sacred: The Evolution of Religious Behavior." *Evolutionary Anthropology* 12 (2003): 264–274.

Sosis, Richard and Bradley Ruffle. "Religious Ritual and Cooperation: Testing for a Relationship on Israeli Religious and Secular Kibbutzim." *Current Anthropology* 44 (2003): 713–722.

Sosis, Richard and Eric Bressler. "Cooperation and Commune Longevity: A Test of the Costly Signaling Theory of Religion." *Cross-Cultural Research* 37 (2003): 211–239.

Sosis, Richard, Howard Kress, and James Boster. "Scars for War: Evaluating Alternative Signaling Explanations for Cross-Cultural Variance in Ritual Costs." *Evolution and Human Behavior* 28 (2007): 234–247.

Sosis, Richard and Candace S. Alcorta. "Militants and Martyrs: Evolutionary Perspectives on Religion and Terrorism." *Natural Security: A Darwinian Approach to a Dangerous World*. Eds. R. D. Sagarin and T. Taylor, 105–124. Los Angeles: University of California Press, 2008.

Spear, Linda P. "The Adolescent Brain and Age-Related Behavioral Manifestations." *Neuroscience and Biobehavioral Reviews* 24.4 (2000): 417–463.

Thayer, B. A. "Causes of and Solutions to Islamic Fundamentalist Terrorism." *Natural Security: A Darwinian Approach to a Dangerous World.* Eds. R. D. Sagarin and T. Taylor, 125–140. Los Angeles: University of California Press, 2008.

Turnbull, Colin M. *The Forest People.* New York: Simon and Schuster, 1962.

Turner, Victor. *The Forest of Symbols.* New York: Cornell University Press, 1967.

Turner, Victor. *The Ritual Process.* New York: Aldine de Gruyter, 1969.

Tuzin, D. "Ritual Violence among the Ilahita Arapesh." *Rituals of Manhood: Male Initiation in Papua New Guinea.* Ed. G. H. Herdt, 321–356. Berkeley: University of California Press, 1982.

Vaish, A., T. Grossmann, and A. Woodward. "Not All Emotions Are Created Equal: The Negativity Bias in Social-Emotional Development." *Psychological Bulletin* 134 (2008): 383–403.

van Gennep, A. 1909. *The Rites of Passage.* Chicago: University of Chicago Press, 1960.

Wendrich, R. and R. Staudinger. "Controlled Induction of Negative and Positive Emotions by Means of Group Singing." *Music and Medicine* 2 (2010): 144–149.

West-Eberhard, M. J. *Developmental Plasticity and Evolution.* New York: Oxford University Press, 2003.

Whitehouse, Harvey. *Modes of Religiosity: A Cognitive Theory of Religious Transmission.* Walnut Creek, CA: AltaMira Press, 2004.

Whiting, J.W.M., R. Kluckholn, and A. Anthony. "The Function of Male Initiation Ceremonies at Puberty." In *Readings in Social Psychology.* Eds. T. M. Newcomb and E. L. Hartley, 359–370. New York: Henry Holt, 1958.

Wilson, David Sloan. *Darwin's Cathedral.* Chicago: University of Chicago Press, 2002.

Wingfield, J. C., J. D. Jacobs, K. Soma, D. L. Maney, K. Hunt, D. Wisti-Peterson, S. Meddle, M. Ramenofsky and K. Sullivan. "Testosterone, Aggression, and Communication: Ecological Bases of Endocrine Phenomena." *The Design of Animal Communication.* Eds. M. D. Hauser and M. Konishi, 255–284. Cambridge, MA: MIT Press, 1999.

World Health Organization. "Burden of Mental and Behavioural Disorders." *World Health Organization Report, 2001.* World Health Organization, New York. Accessed February 22, 2011. http://who.int/whr/2001/en/.

Wrangham, R. and D. Peterson. *Demonic Males.* Boston: Houghton Mifflin, 1996.

Yousafzai, S. and R. Moreau. "Inside Al Qaeda." *Newsweek* 156 (2010): 30–37.

Zuckerman, P. "Atheism: Contemporary Rates and Patterns." *The Cambridge Companion to Atheism.* Ed. M. Martin, 47–68. Cambridge, UK: Cambridge Univ. Press, 2006.

CHAPTER 39

DIVERGENT MODES OF RELIGIOSITY AND ARMED STRUGGLE

HARVEY WHITEHOUSE AND BRIAN MCQUINN

Some of the greatest atrocities in human history have been caused by groups defending or advancing their resourcing interests and sacred values. In order to comprehend and address the wanton violence of war, terrorism, and genocide, it is necessary to understand the forces that bind and drive human groups. This chapter explores one of the most powerful mechanisms by which groups may be formed, inspired, and coordinated: ritual.

Ritual may be defined as normative behavior with an irretrievably opaque causal structure (see Legare and Whitehouse, under review; Whitehouse 2011). Much human behavior is directed to the accomplishment of physical end-goals, even if the mechanics of the process are not always obvious. For instance, if a computer technician tells us to perform a series of actions to restore a piece of faulty software, we do so in the belief that somebody (the technician or the author of the software) could specify the causal contributions of each step even if this is opaque to us as we blindly follow instructions. With ritual actions, it is different. The causal structure of a ritual is irretrievably opaque in the sense that it would be odd, foolish, or even subversive to seek or expect a causal rationale for the content and sequencing of the procedures. Instead we justify the actions with reference to custom, reciprocity, duty, myth, and symbolism.

It has long been recognized that rituals create and renew bonds among those who undertake them together. The theory of divergent modes of religiosity (hereafter, DMR theory) proposes that ritual traditions tend to cluster around two sociopolitical "attractor positions": the one large scale and hierarchical (doctrinal) and the other highly cohesive but localized or regionally fragmented (imagistic). The applicability of the theory to religious traditions has been demonstrated by means of extensive cross-cultural comparison and ethnographic case studies, longitudinal analysis of archaeological and historical materials, and psychological experiments. Here we consider the applicability of this theory to the formation and spread of rebel groups in civil conflicts. Although the sample of case studies considered here is small, it is sufficient to demonstrate a powerful new set of tools for explaining the emergence and spread of armed groups in wartorn regions of the world.

DMR Theory

Social scientists have long observed that rituals play a role in building social cohesion and collective identity (Robertson Smith 1889; Durkheim 1912; Frazer 1922). Recent convergences and developments in cognitive science and evolutionary theory point to new directions for interdisciplinary research on this topic. One such approach, DMR theory, has sought to explain contrasting patterns of ritual and social morphology in religious traditions (Whitehouse 1995, 2000, 2004). The theory distinguishes a doctrinal mode characterized by routinized ritual, diffuse cohesion, hierarchical structure, and rapid dissemination to large populations from an imagistic mode characterized by rare and traumatic ritual ordeals and intense cohesion within small cults. DMR theory sets out to explain why certain religions spread rapidly and widely, in many cases crystallizing into longstanding traditions encompassing vast numbers of people, while others remain confined to much smaller populations even though they, too, can endure for very long periods.

Viewed within a broader evolutionary framework, the two modes may be understood as adaptations to distinct resource extraction problems (cf. Beardsley and McQuinn 2009). The imagistic mode prevails where groups depend for their survival on exceptionally high levels of cohesion (i.e., where incentives to defect are especially strong), for instance, where the extraction or protection of group resources entails grave risk and temptations to defect. The doctrinal mode prevails where group survival depends on more modest forms of cooperation (e.g., payment of tax or tribute) across much larger populations, requiring forms of cohesion that are more widely spread if less intensely felt.

Although DMR theory has mainly been used to explain the formation and spread of religious traditions, in this chapter we apply the theory to armed groups engaged in civil conflicts, some of which explicitly incorporate religious traditions while others vehemently repudiate supernatural beliefs of any kind.[1] We contrast two distinct modes in which armed groups create and maintain cohesion. The imagistic mode uses rarely performed and intensely dysphoric group rituals to create a culture of coercion that binds small groups. In contrast, the doctrinal mode produces larger rebel communities and a tendency to codify political and ideological commitments as doctrines transmitted through routinized rituals. Rebel groups, like religious traditions, may draw on the cohesion effects of both modes, but preliminary research suggests that rebels, whether or not they are religious, typically utilize either doctrinal or imagistic dynamics rather than exploiting both modes at the same time (see table 39.1).

DMR theory begins with the observation that rituals tend to be either routine occurrences, woven into the fabric of everyday life, or somewhat distinctive, perhaps unique, occasions, associated with major events in the histories of individuals and groups (Whitehouse 2004). In early formulations (Whitehouse 1995, 2000), DMR theory proposed that most rituals are either high in frequency and low in emotional arousal or low in frequency and high in emotional arousal. Systematic cross-cultural comparison has produced a somewhat more nuanced picture however. In a recent survey of 645 rituals from more than seventy language groups, the predicted inverse correlation between ritual frequency and aggregated emotional arousal has been confirmed as has the clustering of rituals around high-frequency/low-arousal and low-frequency/high-arousal ends of the continuum, but it has also been shown that these patterns are strongest for dysphoric (e.g., painful or frightening) rituals (Atkinson and Whitehouse 2010). Part of the explanation would seem to lie in the effects of dysphoric arousal on memory.

Low-frequency rituals involving physical and psychological trauma are recalled as distinct episodes in participants' lives. People remember who else underwent the ordeals and experience intense bonds with the group of fellow sufferers. The

Table 39.1 DMR Theory Summarized

Feature	Doctrinal mode predictions	Imagistic mode predictions
1. Ritual frequency and arousal	Daily collective rituals (including doctrinal repetition)	Rarely performed dysphoric ritual ordeals (with little or no doctrinal transmission)
2. Codification	Standardized body of ideology/dogma	No standardized ideology/dogma
3. Exegesis	Transmission of exegesis to all members	Meaning of rituals inferred independently
4. Scale	Large "imagined communities"	Small, face-to-face communities
5. Spread	Fast, efficient, homogenous	Slow or fragmentary
6. Structure	Highly elaborated hierarchy with designated ranking of offices	Authority exercised personally rather than institutionalized
7. Cohesion	Diffuse based on categorical ties	Intense, based on relational ties

Note: See also Whitehouse 1995; 2004.

causally opaque character of the ritual ordeals prompts long-term reflection and diverse interpretation among participants (Richert, Whitehouse, and Stewart 2005). The resulting impression of shared experience and interpretation is thought to reinforce ingroup cohesion. This "imagistic mode of religiosity" (Whitehouse 1995, 2000, 2004) creates relatively small and exclusive groups.

By contrast, high-frequency rituals (routinization) facilitate the storage of elaborate and conceptually complex religious teachings in semantic memory and thus the transmission of doctrinal orthodoxies and standardized interpretations of ritual meaning. The doctrinal mode of religiosity appeals to oratory and sacred text, capable of being transmitted widely with great efficiency by small numbers of proselytizing leaders (gurus, prophets, messiahs, missionaries, etc.). Religious communities formed in this way are able to share identity markers (such as beliefs and practices) without requiring direct interpersonal contact between all members of the tradition. The demands of policing the orthodoxy, together with the emphasis on oratorical skill and doctrinal mastery, favor the emergence of professionalized priesthoods and centralized systems of regulation. Thus the doctrinal mode produces large anonymous communities of followers and multiple levels of jurisdictional hierarchy.

Although the term *modes of religiosity* suggests that the target domain of the preceding hypotheses must be religion rather than any other type of cultural system, DMR theory is more accurately understood as a theory of modes of ritual group formation. Most ritual traditions, ancient and modern, postulate beliefs in one or more gods and largely for this reason are typically described as religions. Nevertheless the religion label is slippery and is also used to refer to cultural traditions that entail beliefs in ancestors (the spirits of dead people), creator beings (not necessarily gods in the senses most commonly used), or various kinds of magic (whether or not requiring the intervention of supernatural agents). While there is nothing wrong with referring to ritual traditions that espouse such beliefs as religions, we cannot assume that the category "religion" has underlying coherence and may simply comprise a loose assortment of ideas (e.g., about gods, ghosts, creation, magic, etc.) that have quite distinct and unrelated causes (Boyer 2001, Whitehouse 2004). We argue below that DMR theory can be extended to explain recurrent features of ritual traditions that lack many or all beliefs typically labeled religious.

LOW-FREQUENCY, HIGH-AROUSAL RITUALS
AND THE IMAGISTIC MODE

It has long been appreciated that rare, traumatic rituals promote intense social cohesion but efforts to tease apart the psychological mechanisms involved only really took off in the 1950s, much of the work inspired by Festinger's theory of "cognitive dissonance" (Festinger et al. 1956). Rituals incur costs (e.g., time, labor, and psychological endurance) often with the promise of only poorly defined or indeterminate rewards and, in some cases, for no explicit purpose at all. In the case of initiation rituals, for instance, the costs are typically extreme, involving physical or psychological tortures. In a now classic application of Festinger's theory, Aronson and Mills (1959) demonstrated that the more severe the requirement for entry into an artificially created group, the greater the participants' liking for other group members. Their explanation for this was that our feelings toward the groups we join will never be wholly positive, and the experience of disliking aspects of the group will be dissonant with the experience of having paid a price to join; this dissonance could be resolved by downplaying the costs of entry but the greater the severity of initiations into the group the less sustainable that strategy will become. Under these circumstances, dissonance reduction will focus instead on generating more positive evaluations of the group (see also Aronson and Mills 1997; Baron 2000; Berkowitz 1989).

Traumatic ritual ordeals increase cohesion and tolerance within groups, but they also seem to intensify feelings of hostility and intolerance towards outgroups. Recent studies using psychological experiments, economic games, and cross-cultural surveys suggest that within-group liking and outgroup hostility are directly correlated (Cohen, Montoya, and Insko 2006). As one games theorist neatly put it: "When Joshua killed twelve thousand heathen in a day and gave thanks to the Lord afterwards by carving the Ten Commandments in stone, including the phrase 'Thou shalt not kill,' he was not being hypocritical" (Ridley 1996: 192). Cognitive dissonance does not appear to be the whole explanation for the observed correlations. Two other factors also have crucial consequences for ingroup cohesion and outgroup hostility.

The first is memory: One-off traumatic experiences, especially ones that are surprising and consequential for participants, are remembered over longer time periods (and with greater vividness and accuracy) than less arousing events. Such memories have a canonical structure, sometimes referred to as flashbulb memory (Conway 1995), specifying not only details of the event itself but what happened afterward and who else was present. One hypothesis is that the procedures of traumatic rituals are "seared" into the memories of participants thereby contributing to the persistence of ritual traditions over many generations, even in the absence of written records or other external mnemonic supports (Whitehouse 2000; for critical discussions see Barth 2002, Houseman 2002). Another postulated consequence of low-frequency dysphoric rituals is that they produce exclusive ritual communities. There is little scope for adding to or subtracting from ritual groups whose membership derives from uniquely encoded, one-off experiences: People are either remembered as co-participants or they are not (Whitehouse 1992, 2004).

A second and related factor appears to be interpretive creativity. Since the procedures entailed in rituals are a matter of stipulation and are not transparently related to overall goals (if those goals are articulated at all), the meanings of the acts present something of a puzzle for participants. In the case of traumatic ritual experiences that are recalled for many months and years after the actual event, questions of symbolism and purpose are typically a major focus of attention

(Whitehouse 2000; see also Paez et al. 2005, 2007, 2009). In a series of experiments using artificial rituals and varying levels of arousal, it has been shown that, after a time delay, the volume and specificity of spontaneous reflection on the meanings of rituals are significantly greater in high-arousal conditions than in controls (Richert, Whitehouse, and Stewart 2005). Similar effects have been observed in field studies, by systematically comparing the interpretive richness of people's accounts of rituals involving variable levels of arousal (Whitehouse 1995, Xygalatas 2007). Since low-frequency dysphoric rituals are typically also shrouded in secrecy and taboo, participants have little opportunity to compare the contents of their personal ruminations and so form the impression that their rich interpretations are shared by others undergoing the same experience, increasing the sense of camaraderie. Activities involving high risk and temptation to defect (e.g., raiding, headhunting, bride capture, sectarian violence, and gangland disputes) would seem to be correlated with the presence of low-frequency rituals involving severe physical and psychological tortures (Cohen et al. 2006; Sosis 2007).

Traumatic and painful rituals, or "rites of terror" (Whitehouse 1996), produce intense cohesion in small groups, one of the hallmark features of the "imagistic mode of religiosity." More than simply a mode of religious expression, however, imagistic practices are best understood as a mode of group formation. Rites of terror bind together the warring tribes of many traditional societies studied by social anthropologists, for instance, in West Africa (Hojberg 2004), native America (Verswijver 1992), and Melanesia (Barth 1987). But this method of building groups also features prominently in the traditions of military cells in modern armies and terrorist organizations as well as emerging spontaneously in civil conflicts such as the 1994 atrocities in Rwanda (Whitehouse 2004: chapter 6).

HIGH-FREQUENCY, LOW-AROUSAL RITUAL AND THE DOCTRINAL MODE

High-frequency ritual (or routinization) is a hallmark of world religions and their offshoots but is also characteristic of a great many regional religions and ideological movements. Routinized rituals play a major role in the formation of large-scale identities, enabling strangers to recognize one another as members of a common in-group, facilitating trust and cooperation on a scale that would otherwise be impossible. This syndrome, the so-called doctrinal mode of religiosity, heralds not only the first large-scale societies but also the first complex political systems in which roles and offices are understood to be detachable from the persons who occupy them. As in the case of imagistic dynamics, the strengths and limitations of human memory play an important role in the formation of the doctrinal mode.

When people participate in the same rituals on a daily or weekly basis, it is impossible for them to recall the details of every occasion. Instead they represent the rituals and their meanings as types of behavior—a holy Communion or a call to prayer, for instance. Psychologists describe these representations as procedural scripts and semantic schemas (Baddeley 1997). Scripts and schemas specify what typically happens in a given ritual and what is generally thought to be its significance. In a group whose identity markers are composed mainly of scripts and schemas, what it means to be a member of the tradition is generalized beyond people of our acquaintance, applying to everyone who performs similar acts and holds similar beliefs. This route to the construction of communal identity, based on routinization, is a necessary condition for the emergence of "imagined communities" (Anderson 1983)—large populations sharing a common tradition and capable of behaving as a coalition in interactions with nonmembers, despite the fact that no individual in the community could possibly know all the others or even hope to meet all of them in the course of a lifetime.

Routinization has other important effects as well. For instance, it allows complex networks of doctrines and narratives to be learned and stored in collective memory, making it relatively easy to spot unauthorized innovations. Moreover, routinization artificially suppresses creativity, in effect producing more slavish conformism to group norms. Part of the reason seems to be that, having achieved procedural fluency, one no longer needs to reflect on how to perform the ritual, and this in turn makes one less likely to reflect on why one should perform it. Thus routinization would seem to aid the transmission of doctrinal orthodoxies: traditions of belief and practice that are relatively immune to innovation and in which unintended deviation from the norm is readily detectable.

Routinized rituals provide a foundation for the establishment of large-scale communities capable of encompassing indefinitely many individuals singing from the same hymn sheet (both literally and metaphorically). Expanding the size of the ingroup in this way has implications for the scale on which people can engage in cooperative behavior, facilitating cooperation among strangers simply because they carry the insignia that display shared beliefs and practices. At the same time, however, the cohesion engendered through common membership of the tradition is less intensely felt than that accomplished in small groups undergoing rare and painful rituals together. As cohesion is expanded to encompass greater populations, it is also in an important sense spread more thinly.

Some routinized traditions, however, manage to get the best of both worlds: A mainstream tradition constructed around regular worship under the surveillance of an ecclesiastical hierarchy may tolerate much more colorful local practices involving rare, dysphoric rituals (such as self-flagellation at Easter parades in the Philippines or walking on red-hot coals among the Anastenaria of northern Greece). While these localized practices undoubtedly produce highly solidarity groups distinct from the mainstream tradition, the resulting cohesion can be projected onto the larger community, rejuvenating commitment to its unremitting regime of repetitive rituals (Whitehouse 1995). Other patterns are also possible however. One grand theorist of Muslim society, Ernest Gellner, showed that rural tribes bound together by high-arousal rituals formed the most formidable little military units in Islam, capable of periodically toppling urban elites, whose more routinized rituals and doctrinal beliefs failed to generate the kind of cohesion needed to mount an effective defence (Gellner 1969). Other major patterns include periodic splintering and reformation (Pyssiainen 2004).

DMR Theory and the Evolution
of Religions

Although much research inspired by DMR theory has been concerned with understanding the effects of psychological affordances, biases, and constraints, efforts are now being made to model the ultimate causes of patterns of religious group formation over time (Whitehouse, Kahn, Hochberg, and Bryson, In Press). What factors favor the appearance and persistence of routinized rituals and the large-scale communities they engender? Some recent efforts to answer this question have focused on the first appearance of routinized collective rituals in the Neolithic Middle East (Mithen 2004).

A watershed in the evolution of modes of religiosity seems to have occurred around 8,000 years ago at Catalhoyuk, in what is now central Anatolia in Turkey (Whitehouse and Hodder 2010). In the early layers of Catalhoyuk, the imagistic mode prevailed, evidenced by animal bones left over from hunting and feasting activities, pictorial representations of major rituals, and human remains manipulated in elaborate mortuary practices. These emotionally intense rituals would have produced highly cohesive groups necessary for coordinated hunting of large, dangerous animals. But as hunting gradually gave way to farming, the need for such groups disappeared, and instead more day-to-day forms of cooperation across the settlement were required to sustain novel forms of specialized labor, reciprocity, pooling, and storage. Sustainable exploitation of the commons now required the dissolution of small-group boundaries and intergroup rivalry in favor of larger-scale forms of collective identity, trust, and cooperation extending to tens of thousands of individuals at the enlarged settlement.

This change in the scale of political association was facilitated by the appearance of the first ever regular collective rituals, focused around daily production and consumption, and the spread of identity markers across the entire settlement, for instance, in the form of stamp seals used for body decoration and more standardized pottery designs. The appearance and spread of routinized rituals seems to have been linked to the need for greater trust and cooperation when interacting with relative strangers. Consider the difficulties of persuading people you scarcely know that they should make long-term investments in your services based on a promise or should pay taxes or tribute in return for protection or sustenance in times of need. In the absence of more detailed information about trustworthiness of prospective trading partners or remote governors to fulfil their part of any bargain, shared insignia proclaiming commitment to common beliefs and practices becomes a persuasive form of evidence. In such conditions, groups with routinized rituals capable of uniting large populations will tend to outcompete those who lack shared identity markers of this kind.

APPLYING DMR THEORY TO REBEL GROUPS

Until now, applications of DMR theory have been most extensively explored by scholars of religion. But McQuinn, who has many years of experience working in countries torn apart by civil war, realized that the theory has potential relevance for understanding competition and evolution among warring groups, even those that eschew religious teachings of all kinds.

In this section, we apply DMR theory to five rebel groups: FARC-EP (Fuerzas Armadas Revolucionarias de Colombia—Ejército del Pueblo), AUC (Autodefensas Unidas de Colombia), Hezbollah (Lebanon), CPN-Maoist (Community Party of Nepal—Maoist), and RUF (Revolutionary United Front—Sierra Leone). In selecting these five case studies, effort was made to ensure a variety of regions were represented globally. We include only armed groups that have operated for at least ten years so as to ensure sufficient data from secondary sources for the purposes of our analysis. Moreover we consider only rebel groups engaged in conflicts that at one point reached the intensity of "civil wars," defined as within-state conflicts producing more than 1,000 battle-related deaths in one year.

Evidence for the applicability of DMR theory to our dataset is summarized in table 39.2. The predictions in the table are grouped by mode (doctrinal and imagistic respectively). The strength of evidence supporting or contradicting each major prediction of DMR theory is distinguished based on the legend below. It has five values: strong evidence for, weak evidence for, strong evidence against, weak evidence against, and no evidence. These evaluations are based on the number of corroborating sources for each prediction and the quality of each observation. Unlike many religions, rebel groups in our sample tended to exhibit the predictions of only one mode although this may be an effect of small sample size.

In the subsections that follow, we consider each of the two modes of group formation (imagistic and doctrinal) in turn, examining detailed evidence that the five rebel groups in our sample cluster around one or other of these respective modes, but not both.

Table 39.2 Preliminary Evidence of Modes Predictions

		Doctrinal Mode				
Feature	Predictions	CPN-Maoists	FARC-EP	Hez-bollah	AUC	RUF
1. **Ritual frequency and arousal**	Low arousal/high frequency	✓	✓	✓	✗	✗
2. **Codification**	Elaborated ideology	✓	✓	✓	✗	✗
3. **Exegesis**	Transmission to all members	☑	☑	N/E	N/E	N/E
4. **Scale**	Imagined community	✓	✓	✓	✗	☒
5. **Spread**	Fast, efficient transmission	✓	✓	✓	✗	✗
6. **Structure**	Highly elaborated hierarchy	✓	✓	✓	✗	☒
7. **Cohesion**	Diffuse	N/E	N/E	N/E	N/E	N/E
Imagistic Mode						
1. **Ritual frequency and arousal**	High arousal/low frequency	✗	✗	N/E	✓	✓
2. **Codification**	Absent or stagnant	✗	✗	✗	✓	✓
3. **Exegesis**	Not transmitted	✗	✗	N/E	N/E	N/E
4. **Scale**	Autonomous	✗	✗	✗	✓	☑
5. **Spread**	Group oriented/ inefficient	✗	✗	✗	☒	☒
6. **Structure**	Less elaborated hierarchy	✗	✗	✗	✓	✓
7. **Cohesion**	Intense	N/E	N/E	N/E	N/E	N/E

Legend

✓—Strong evidence for prediction

☑—Weak evidence for prediction

✗—Strong evidence against prediction

☒—Weak evidence against prediction

N/E—No evidence

Rebel Groups Operating
in the Imagistic Mode

Rebel groups utilize low-frequency, dysphoric rituals in a variety of ways but perhaps most commonly as part of the process of induction into the group. Initiatory ordeals are typically extremely painful or terrifying, including coerced acts of dismemberment, torture, or the murder of captives (Human Rights Watch 2003). Human rights observers have documented the systematic use of such practices in the Autodefensas Unidas de Colombia (AUC), concluding that "execution [was] being [used as] a significant part of the paramilitary training process" (ibid). According to one exmember of the AUC, "They give you a gun and you have to kill the best friend you have. They do it to see if they can trust you. If you don't kill him, your friend will be ordered to kill you" (ibid, 65). The inclusion of ingroup members as targets of violence ratchets up the socially forbidden nature of the experience and creates a "culture of terror" (Maclure 2006). Other documented practices in the AUC include assigning new recruits a human body part to be carried with them until it has rotted away (Botero 2002).

The Revolutionary United Front (RUF) in Sierra Leone similarly incorporated infrequent but highly dysphoric rituals. RUF inductees were usually coercively recruited (Zack-Williams 2001). The process began by inductees witnessing or being forced to participate in the murder of family or community members (Bangura 2010; Human Rights Watch 1999; Maclure 2006). Reports and interviews with excombatants[2] suggest that these ritualized murders were later augmented by periodic acts of group violence such as public executions (A. Kamara 2010a; Maclure 2006). The systematic drugging of recruits with stimulants also served to heighten the emotional and physical experience (ibid), while lowering inhibitions and intensifying cognitive dissonance effects (C. Kamara 2010b; Prestholdt 2009; Richards 1994).

As is characteristic of groups operating in the imagistic mode neither the AUC nor the RUF exhibited an elaborated body of doctrines or written texts. At its inception, the RUF published a political manifesto titled, *The Basic Document of the Revolutionary United Front of Sierra Leone (RUF/SL): The Second Liberation of Africa* (RUF-SL 1995). Yet on close analysis, the document was plagiarized from another revolutionary group in Sierra Leone with which the RUF leaders had previous affiliations (Abdullah and Muana 1998). As Abdullah and Muana describe, "Parts of it were butchered to appear as Foday Sankoh's words. But the document had nothing to do with Sankoh or the RUF; it predated the formation of the RUF, and was appropriated by the RUF-to-be before they entered Kailahun [Sierra Leone] in 1991" (Abdullah and Muana 1998: 217). Importantly, no further ideological writings were produced after the publication of this document. A number of commentators have highlighted the lack of ideologues in the RUF and AUC (Abdullah 2004; Clapham 1998; Utas 2008). Rather than providing a standardized

ideology, groups operating in the imagistic mode foster more idiosyncratic reflection on the significance of traumatic ritual ordeals. Testimonials from former AUC
members who underwent systematic homicidal initiations reveal wide variation in
participants' explanations of the purpose and meaning of the rituals they underwent (Human Rights Watch 2003: 64; 66; Bangura 2010; C. Kamara 2010b).

The small-scale and fragmented structure of RUF and AUC groups are also
typical of the imagistic mode. The AUC was created as an umbrella organization
for paramilitaries in December 1994 during a national summit of "like-minded
groups" that was organized by the AUC's future leader Carlos Castaño Gil (Sanín
2008: 14; HRW 2003: 55–58). Before its demobilization, the AUC was constituted
by as many as thirty-seven different suborganizations, each with its own history
and interests (AECID 2005). The AUC's leader described the relationship of these
subunits thus: "Each front is autonomous and responsible for its region in terms
of funds and should take responsibility for or reject responsibility for actions
that are attributed to them" (HRW 2003: 55–56). The autonomous nature of the
organizations subunits possesses challenges for the stability of the organization.
Sanin (2008: 17) observed of the AUC: "[P]aramilitarism was a social success, in
the sense that it propagated to all the country, was able to create dense and long
social networks, and consolidate regional political support. But it was an organizational no-go, as it failed to establish a minimal internal cohesion to maintain
stable regional structures, let alone build a national anti-subversive project" (Sanin
2008: 17). Although systematic evidence on the nature of the RUF's level of integration is sparser, interviews with former combatants suggests that the subelements of
the organization existed as autonomous entities with little or no sense of common
identity (Bangura 2010; A. Kamara 2010a; C. Kamara 2010b).

Preliminary evidence suggests that neither the AUC nor RUF possessed
sophisticated hierarchies (Abdullah 2004; HRW 2010). It is clear from commentators that the RUF did not have any of the committee structures prevalent in more
doctrinal rebel groups and was headed by a loose coalition of three leaders: Sankoh,
Mansaray, and Kanu (Abdullah 1998: 221). Reports suggest that the RUF's hierarchy
was made up of only three levels—senior leaders, regional commanders, and con-
scripts/captives—with little differentiation within echelons (Abdullah 1998: 232).
Anecdotal evidence from journalists and interviews with excombatants suggest
that a sophisticated military ranking structure did not exist in the RUF and moni-
kers such as Commander Blood or Colonel Kolon were simply noms de guerre and
were not an indication of military rank (Kleveman 2001). This was commented
on by one Sierra Leone specialist, "A common feature in these wars was the military hierarchical terms used by the rebels or revolutionaries. These terms made
absolutely no sense. One could meet a 14-year-old 'commander' or a 'company' of
10 year olds, an 18-year-old 'general,' a 28-year-old 'high commander'" (Golden
2005). Investigative reports of the AUC reflect this same lack of organizational
formality. Each of the suborganizations that collectively made up the AUC had
distinct identities and operating structures (Sanin 2008: 15–16).

Rebel Groups Operating in the Doctrinal Mode

Initial evidence from the CPN-Maoists, Hezbollah, and FARC-EP case studies strongly suggests that each organization relies heavily on the doctrinal mode of ritualized group cohesion. In all three groups, doctrine is typically adapted from a variety of political and religious teachings including communism, Leninism, and Maoism. The appropriation of national symbols, traditional songs, and popular narratives serves as evocative vehicles for the transmission process. In these groups, collective ritual is centred on daily political and ideology training (Brittain 2010; Dudley 2004; Hanson 2009; Harik 2004; Harper 2002; Herrera and Porch 2008; Human Rights Watch 2003, 2010; International Crisis Group 2007, 2009; Jaber 1997; Kunz and Sjöberg 2009; Norton 2007; Offstien 2003; Ortiz 2002; Penhaul 2000; Petras 2000; Ranstorp 1994; Saab 2009; Saad-Ghorayeb 2002; Sanín 2008). This includes not only transmission of ideological teachings but also group norms. Collective ritual is led by a recognized local commander or ideologue and involves elaborate and repetitive sermonizing to gatherings of combatants, usually composed of numerous subunits (Botero 2002; Eck 2004; International Crisis Group 2005; Onesto 2005).

In FARC-EP, a highly regimented daily schedule must be observed by all combatants. For example, ideological training is scheduled after the first set of morning drills and between 3 pm and 4 pm (HRW 2003). These patterns of ideological training are highly standardized and enduring, having been a consistent feature of the organization since its inception forty-five years ago (Brittain 2010). FARC combatants are also required to undertake individualized study following a curriculum that includes the writings of Che Guevara, Jacobo Arena, and Vladimir Lenin (HRW 2003: 63). The studying is done individually or in pairs (Botero 2002: 1). For the Maoists (Nepal), political training is also an integral component of the indoctrination process and combatants' daily schedule (Onesto 2005; Ogura 2008). In interviews with journalists, Maoist leaders emphasize their belief that regular ideological training facilitates cohesion and minimizes the risks of faction formation (Eck 2004: 25). Maoist combatants, like their FARC counterparts, observe a highly regimented schedule with both daily political training in groups and designated times for individual and small group study (Onesto 2005: 205; Zharkevich 2009: 30). Hezbollah represents a particularly interesting example of religious and revolutionary ideologies intermingling (Ranstorp 1994; ICG 2002: 4; Moaddel 1992: 354). Routinized schedules are also evident in Hezbollah with daily prayer and regular mosque attendance serving as central tenets of the organizational culture. The political aspects of Hezbollah's ideology are integrated into daily religious practice to such an extent that they are hard to disentangle (Palme Harik 2004:16; Schleifer 2006: 10). Regular participation in communal ideological transmission is thought to express and consolidate the strict control Hezbollah leaders maintain over the organization (Jackson et al. 2005: 53). In the initial stages of Hezbollah's formation, the emphasis on the regular repetition of ideological-religious rituals was especially pronounced, focusing on the recruitment and indoctrination of the radical Shi'ites in Biq'a area (Ranstorp 1997: 34–35).

As in many religions dominated by the doctrinal mode, Maoists in Nepal go to considerable lengths to integrate transmission of communist ideology into everyday life. The organization has prolific writers and theorists, producing thousands of publications. The organization explicitly describes Dr. Bhattrai as its chief ideologue, overseeing and developing the ideological foundation of the movement. The Prachanda path (named after the Maoist leader Prachanda) contextualized this ideology calling for ongoing urban insurrection and continued encirclement of the towns (International Crisis Group 2005). FARC-EP and Hezbollah also promulgate elaborate ideologies documented and broadcast through print, the Internet, radio, and in the case of Hezbollah, its own television network. Hezbollah's body of doctrine is unique in that it explicitly draws on Iran's notion of the *velayat-e faqih*, rule of the Islamic jurist (International Crisis Group 2002). Hezbollah ideology is grounded in the Khomeini school of thought, "a mixture of Islamic and revolutionary secular motifs, taken from the arsenal of Shi'a fundamentalism, on the one hand, and the annals of twentieth-century national liberation movements, on the other" (Schleifer 2006). In all three rebel groups considered here, stable reproduction of the orthodoxy carries a high premium, and infractions and unauthorized innovations are sanctioned.

Rebel groups operating in the doctrinal mode, much like global religions and their offshoots, tend to be hierarchical and centralized. FARC-EP exhibits an elaborated structure; its own documentation describes a ranking structure that includes seventeen levels of military rank (FARC-EP 1999). This level of sophistication is equivalent to many national military ranking structures. Various researchers with direct access to FARC-EP document the functioning of this system across the organization (Brittain 2010: 27; Sanin 2008: 8). Testimony collected from former FARC-EP combatants led Human Rights Watch to conclude "that the FARC-EP is a highly vertical, organized, and disciplined military force" (HRW 2003: 77). Other commentators have described FARC-EP as possessing a highly integrated and disciplined chain of command (Herrera and Porch 2008). Sanin's analysis mirrors this conclusion: "Internally, the FARC-EP is characterized by verticalism. There is a clear line of command and any act of insubordination can be punished with death" (2008: 13).

The CPN-Maoists structure is made up of "the standing, committee, politburo, central committee, divisional commands, regional bureaus, sub-regional bureaus, district, area and cell committees" (ICG 2005). Prachanda, the CPN-Maoist leader, sustained high levels of direct command over divisions despite growing numbers of combatants near the end of the war (Ogura 2008; ICG 2005). Just prior to the beginning of the peace process in Nepal, the International Crisis Group (ICG 2005) determined that "[t]he writ of Prachanda still runs throughout the Maoist movement, and central-level decisions are fed down to the regional, district and village levels. There have been no major disruptions to this chain of command, so to extent the movement remains united and disciplined. The reason is a well organised national command structure firmly in the grip of the central leadership" (ICG 2005: 13). As an example, in June 2002 during the central committee plenary, the organization was reorganized into three divisions with the explicit purpose to ensure discipline and control of the central committee (ICG 2005: 9). Other examples of centralized control can be seen in anecdotal reports of interventions to correct incidents of corruption. One such report concerned local commanders who tried to make money out of the medicinal *yarcha gumba* trade but were strongly reprimanded when central leadership learned of the practice and required the unit "to return the trade to its traditional private dealers, and confiscated and remitted the ill-gotten gains to the Maoist central treasury" (ICG 2005: 13).

Hezbollah also exhibits a similarly well-organized hierarchy with complex committee structures and specialized departments. A recent evaluation by Jackson (2005: 43) concludes, "H[e]zbollah is not composed of loose radical Islamic groupings but has developed a highly sophisticated hierarchical organisational structure, where decisions are taken from the top command leadership." Yet military pressure from Israeli forces has meant there is a clear separation between units to prevent infiltration and limit the effects of intelligence leaks (Cody and Moore 2006). The ability of the organization to deploy new military techniques and share intelligence among firewalled fighting units is further evidence of a highly integrated communications network (Schleifer 2006).

The modes theory predicts that routinized movements will be capable of rapid expansion through the broadcasting of ideology to new recruits by word of mouth and especially one-to-many broadcasting by proselytizing leaders. Maoists in Nepal developed sophisticated outreach strategies, propagating their ideology and training political cadres before beginning violent opposition to the government. Eck summarizes the process thus: "In 1995, the Maoists began a year-long campaign to build support amongst the peasantry in the western districts of Rolpa, Rukum, and Jajarkot. This campaign involved a number of measures, such as sending political-cultural teams into villages, organizing peasants to challenge local authorities, and mobilizing villagers for infrastructure improvement such as building roads and bridges" (2004: 13). Operas and cultural performances combined local songs and cultural symbols with Maoist ideology, narrating Maoist military victories and highlighting police brutality (Stirr 2010). Journalists and other media representatives were often invited to attend. Small teams would go door to door proselytizing Maoist values and spreading stories about the struggle (Onesto 2005).

Likewise, the rapid spread of Hezbollah in Biq'a, Beirut, and southern Lebanon is often attributed to the movement's ability to reach and mobilize the destitute Shiite community. This included working through existing networks of radical Shiite organizations and religious institutions (ICG 2002: 4). Yet it was the involvement of two imams, sheikhs Abbas Al-Musawi and Subhi al-Tufayli, that proved decisive in Hezbollah's expansion. Through their sermons and writings, each attracted large numbers of Shia followers in the Bir al-'Abed quarters of southern Beirut (Ransport 1994: 305). Over time, Hezbollah's broadcasting capacity expanded to include newspapers (*al-Ahd*), radio (*Voice of the Oppressed*), and television stations (Al-Manar). This allowed the movement's leaders to propagate its ideological message and shape public opinion (Ransport 1998: 110).

FARC-EP developed a similarly sophisticated broadcasting capacity over forty-six years of operation in Colombia. It possesses six mobile radio transmitters and can reach an estimated 45 percent of the country at any given time (Penhaul 2000). Like the Maoists, FARC-EP has also appropriated national songs and narratives as a platform for FARC-EP ideology. FARC-EP has also developed radio and television soap operas that are very popular and widely broadcast (Penhaul 2000: 5). Like doctrinal religious traditions, the spread of the organization is determined by the acceptance of the values and narratives it espouses. The more broadly these are shared in a community the more readily the group's support base can be extended.

Combining Proximate and Ultimate Explanations for Rebel Group Formation

Explaining why some rebel groups (e.g., Maoists, FARC-EP, and Hezbollah) tend to be dominated by the doctrinal mode while others (e.g., AUC, RUF) tend to be dominated by the imagistic mode can be partly explained in terms of cultural group selection (Sober and Wilson 2011). Religious organizations are adaptations to particular ecological problems. In particular, imagistic dynamics enjoy a selective advantage when access to resources essential for group survival depends on unusually high levels of social cohesion in the face of strong incentives to defect. Doctrinal dynamics, by contrast, enjoy a selective advantage where group success requires the accumulation of centralized resources from a larger and more diffusely united population. Might the same be said of rebel groups?

CPN-Maoists are a highly ideological organization spread across an inaccessible country. The group's primary source of revenue is derived from donations and "taxes" extracted from local communities and businesses in one of the poorest countries in the world (Pande 2004). This resource ecology combined with Nepal's rugged terrain make coordination and revenue collection difficult. The Maoists are a highly ideological and disciplined force not simply because its leaders are so inclined but because a doctrinal mode of operation has proved to be highly adaptive to the group's resourcing needs. In contrast, the resourcing strategies of the RUF required little investment in the hearts and minds of a large population. The ease of surface mining for diamonds combined with the geographic concentration of the mines produced high payoffs without the need for a large labor force. Under such circumstances, a highly militarized organization exhibiting limited hierarchy and intense cohesion, and hence an imagistic mode of group formation, is highly adaptive.

A new model, the Predation Profile Matrix, informs these conclusions (Beardsley and McQuinn 2009). This model distinguishes community-based and resource-based extraction strategies associated with distinct group morphology with divergent implications for levels of militarization, command structure, and relations with local communities. The two extraction strategies are cross-cut by the stated territorial goals of groups (distinguishing those seeking a separate homeland from those vying for national control). The result is a matrix that creates four categories of groups: war entrepreneurs, mercenary armies, community champions, and revolutionaries. Preliminary research suggests that when armed groups are plotted onto the matrix, they exhibit remarkably similar characteristics within quadrants and starkly contrasting characteristics between quadrants.

Conclusion

DMR theory has been used to explain a number of longstanding puzzles in the study of religion. For instance, historians and biologists have used this theory to explain why routinized religions sometimes break up into splinter groups or sects and why reformations occur (Gragg 2004; Hinde 2005; Pyysiainen 2004). Archaeologists have used the theory to account for the great transition from small-scale Neolithic societies to the vast and complex civilizations of the Near East, Mediterranean, and North Africa (Mithen 2004; Johnson 2004; Whitehouse and Hodder 2010). The modes theory has now been tested against more than a hundred case studies based on ethnography (e.g., collected essays in Whitehouse and Laidlaw 2004, 2007), history and archaeology (e.g., collected essays in Whitehouse and Martin 2004, Martin and Whitehouse 2005, Pachis and Martin 2009), and the cognitive sciences (e.g., collected essays in Whitehouse and McCauley 2005, McCauley and Whitehouse 2005). Some of the evidence needed to test the modes theory were not available from established scholarship, and so a number of new field research projects have been undertaken, targeting data collection toward areas where evidential needs of the theory were especially great (Barrett 2005, Xygalatas 2007). To obviate potential problems of researcher and selection bias, additional strategies have been adopted, including experimental research (e.g., Richert, Whitehouse, and Stewart 2005), and the construction of large-scale comparative datasets coding selected features of ethnographic descriptions of hundreds of rituals (e.g., Atkinson and Whitehouse 2010).

As research guided by DMR theory has progressed, its applicability beyond the domain of religion has become increasingly clear, and a host of new research questions have emerged. There remains much to discover about how people learn the rituals of their communities and how rituals promote social cohesion within the group and distrust of groups with different ritual traditions. Longitudinal databases are urgently needed to explore the evolution of ritual, resource extraction patterns, and record group structure and scale over significant time periods. This approach features prominently in a new program of research, funded by a large grant from the United Kingdom's Economic and Social Research Council, running from 2011 until 2016. This new project involves more systematic and in-depth research on rebel groups in North Africa and Colombia as well as controlled psychological experiments in wartorn regions of the Middle East, to explore the effects of ritual participation on ingroup cohesion and outgroup hostility.

In this chapter we have argued that the contrasting patterns of social and political organization of groups specified by DMR theory, the one small-scale and intensely cohesive and the other large-scale and diffusely cohesive, may be widely manifested in armed groups publicly committed to waging civil wars. We believe DMR theory holds significant potential for explaining broad patterns in intergroup violence and the dynamics of contemporary civil wars. Expanding the reach of the theory may change the way cognitive, social, and evolutionary scientists understand the role of ritual in coalitional behavior and decision making in explaining contemporary civil war and contribute to a richer understanding of the relationship between religion, ritual, and violence.

ACKNOWLEDGMENTS

This work was supported by an ESRC Large Grant (REF RES-060–25–0085) titled "Ritual, Community, and Conflict" (Whitehouse) and a grant from the Berghoff Foundation (Whitehouse and McQuinn). Some material in this chapter was first published by Whitehouse in *Grounding the Social Sciences in the Cognitive Sciences*, edited by Ron Sun and published by MIT Press (2012).

NOTES

1. Civil wars are internal conflicts characterized by a nonstate armed group violently challenging state authority where more than 1,000 battle deaths occur annually. The definition of civil war and civil conflict are based on the published reports of Uppsala Conflict Data Program and International Peace Research Institute, Oslo (UCDP/ PRIO).
2. All interviewees referenced in this paper are assigned pseudonyms to protect their privacy

BIBLIOGRAPHY

Abdullah, Ibrahim. "Bush path to destruction: the origin and character of the Revolutionary United Front/Sierra Leone." *The Journal of Modern African Studies* 36.2 (1998): 203–235.

Abdullah, Ibrahim and Muana, Patrick. "The Revolutionary United Front of Sierra Leone." In *African Guerrillas*. Ed. Chistopher Clapham, 172–193. Oxford, UK: James Currey.

Abdullah, Ibrahim, ed. *Between Democracy and Terror: The Sierra Leone Civil War.* Dakar: Council for the Development of Social Science Research in Africa, 2004.

AECID, Spanish Development Cooperation Office. "Plan de Actuación Especial 2006–2008 Cooperación Española: COLOMBIA." Government of Spain, 2005.

Anderson, John R. *The Architecture of Cognition.* Cambridge, MA: Harvard University Press, 1983.

Aronson, E. and J. Mills, "The Effect of Severity of Initiation on Liking for a Group." *The Journal of Abnormal and Social Psychology,* 59.2 (1959): 177.

Aronson, E. and J. Mills. "Back to the Future: Retrospective Review of Leon Festinger's A Theory of Cognitive Dissonance." *The American Journal of Psychology* 110.1 (1997): 127.

Atkinson, Quentin D. and Harvey Whitehouse "The Cultural Morphospace of Ritual Form: Examining Modes of Religiosity Cross-Culturally." *Evolution and Human Behaviour* 32.1 (2010): 50–62.

Baddeley, Alan *Human Memory: Theory and Practice.* Rev. ed. Hove, UK: Psychology Press, 1997.

Bangura, B. (2010), Personal Interview. Freetown, Sierra Leone.

Baron, R. S. "Arousal, Capacity, and Intense Indoctrination." *Personality and Social Psychology Review* 4.3 (2000): 238.

Barrett, Justin. "In the Empirical Mode: Evidence Needed for the Modes of Religiosity Theory." In *Mind and Religion: Psychological and Cognitive Foundations of Religiosity.* Eds. Harvey Whitehouse and Robert N. McCauley, 109–126. Walnut Creek, CA: AltaMira Press, 2005.

Barth, Fredrik. *Cosmologies in the Making: A Generative Approach to Cultural Variation in Inner New Guinea.* Cambridge, UK: Cambridge University Press, 1987.

Barth, Fredrik. "Review of *Arguments and Icons*." *Journal of Ritual Studies,* 16 (2002): 14–17.

Beardsley, Kyle and McQuinn, Brian. "Rebel Groups as Predatory Organizations: The Political Effects of the 2004 Tsunami in Indonesia and Sri Lanka" *Journal of Conflict Resolution* 53.4 (2009): 624–645.

Berkowitz, L. "Research Traditions, Analysis, and Synthesis in Social Psychological Theories: The Case of Dissonance Theory." *Personality & Social Psychology Bulletin* 15.4 (1989): 493.

Botero, Jorge Enrique. "Las Farc ante el nuevo gobierno: Entrevista a Alfonso Cano." *El Tiempo.* <http://www.stormpages.com/marting/lasfarc.htm≥, 2002. Accessed July 5, 2010.

Boyer, Pascal. *Religion Explained: The Evolutionary Origins of Religious Thought.* New York: Basic Books, 2001.

Brittain, James J. *Revolutionary Social Change in Colombia: The Origin and Direction of the FARC-EP.* London: Pluto Press 2010.

Abdullah, Ibrahim and Patrick Muana. "The Revolutionary United Front of Sierra Leone: A Revolt of the Lumpenproletariat." In, *African Guerrillas.* Ed. Christopher Clapham, 172–193. Oxford, UK: James Currey, 1998.

Cody, Edward and Moore, Molly. "The Best Guerrilla Force in the World: Analysts Attribute Hezbollah's Resilience to Zeal, Secrecy and Iranian Funding." *Washington Post,* August 14, 2006.

Cohen, T., Montoya, R., and Insko, C. "Group Morality and Intergroup Relations: Crosscultural and Experimental Evidence. *Personality and Social Psychology Bulletin* 32 (2006): 1559–1572.

Conway, M. A. *Flashbulb Memories.* Hillsdale, NJ: Lawrence Erlbaum Associates, 1995.

Dudley, Steven. *Walking Ghosts: Murder and Guerrila Politics in Colombia.* New York: Routledge, 2004.

Durkheim, E. *The Elementary Forms of Religious Life,* New York: Free Press, 1912.

Eck, Kristine. "Recruiting Rebels: Indoctrination and Political Education in Nepal." 2nd Annual Himalayan Policy Research Conference, Madison, WI, 2004.

FARC-EP *Beligerancia.*1999. Available online at www.abpnoticias.com/boletin_temporal/contenido/libros/Beligerancia__FARC-EP.pdf.

Festinger, Leon, Henry W. Riecken, and Stanley Schachter. *When Prophecy Fails.* New York: Harper and Row, 1956.

Frazer, Sir James George. *The Golden Bow.* New York: Macmillan Co., 1922.

Gellner, Ernest "A Pendulum Swing Theory of Islam." In *Sociology of Religion: Selected Readings.* Ed. R. Robertson, 127–138. Harmondsworth, UK: Penguin Education, 1969.

Golden, Rebecca, "Sobels, Ogas, and Green Beans." In *Representations of Violence: Art about the Sierra Leone Civil War.,* Eds. Patrick K. Muana and Chris Corcoran. Madison, WI: 21st Century African Youth Movement, 2005.

Gragg, Douglas L. "Old and New in Roman Religions: A Cognitive Account." In *Theorizing Religions Past: Historical and Archaeological Perspectives.* Eds. Harvey Whitehouse and Luther H. Martin, 69–86. Walnut Creek, CA: AltaMira Press, 2004.

Hanson, Stephanie. "Backgrounder: FARC, ELN: Colombia's Left-Wing Guerrillas." *Council on Foreign Relations,* August 19, 2009. http://www.cfr.org/colombia/farc-eln-colombias-left-wing-guerrillas/p9272.

Harik, Judith Palmer. *Hezbollah: The Changing Face of Terrorism.* London: I. B.Tauris Publishers, 2004.

Harper, Liz. "Colombia's Civil War: Revolutionary Armed Forces of Colombia (FARC)." *Online NewsHour,* 2002. http://www.pbs.org/newshour/bb/latin_america/colombia/players_farc.html. Accessed June 21, 2012.

Herrera, Natalia and Douglas Porch,. "Like Going to a Fiesta: The Role of Female Fighters in Colombia's FARC-EP." *Small Wars & Insurgencies* 19.4 (2008): 609–634.

Hinde, Robert. "Modes Theory: Some Theoretical Considerations." In *Mind and Religion: Psychological and Cognitive Foundations of Religiosity,* Ed. edited by Harvey Whitehouse and Robert N. McCauley, 31–56. Walnut Creek, CA: AltaMira Press, 2005.

Hojberg, Christian. "Universalistic Orientations of an Imagistic Mode of Religiosity: The Case of the West African Poro Cult." In *Ritual and Memory: Toward a Comparative Anthropology of Religion.* Ed Harvey Whitehouse and James Laidlaw. Walnut Creek, CA: AltaMira Press, 2004.

Houseman, Michael "Review of *Arguments and Icons.*" *Journal of Ritual Studies* 16 (2002) 18–22.

Human Rights Watch. "Getting Away With Murder, Mutilation, Rape: New Testimony from Sierra Leone." Vol. 11 (1999), no. 3(A). New York: Human Rights Watch.

Human Rights Watch. "You'll Learn Not to Cry: Child Combatants in Colombia." New York: Human Rights Watch, 2003.

Human Rights Watch. "Paramilitaries' Heirs: The New Face of Violence in Colombia." New York: Human Rights Watch, 2010.

International Crisis Group. "Colombia's Elusive Quest for Peace." *Latin America Report* 1, Bogotá/Brussels, 2002.

International Crisis Group. "Nepal's Maoists: Their Aims, Structure and Strategy." Asia Report No. 104, Kathmandu/Brussels, 2005.

International Crisis Group. "Hizbollah and the Lebanese Crisis." *ICG Middle East Report* 69. Amman/Brussels: International Crisis Group, 2007.

International Crisis Group., "Ending Colombia's FARC Conflict: Dealing the Right Card." *Latin America Report* 30, Bogotá/Brussels, 2009.

Jaber, Hala. *Hezbollah: Born with a Vengeance.* London: Fourth Estate, 1997.

Jackson, Brian A., et al. *Aptitude for Destruction*, Vol. 2. Organizational Learning in Terrorist Groups and Its Implications for Combating Terrorism (Santa Monica, CA: Rand Corporation 2005.

Johnson, Karen. "Primary Emergence of the Doctrinal Mode of Religiosity in Prehistoric Southwestern Iran." In *Theorizing Religions Past: Historical and Archaeological Perspective.* Ed.ited by H. Whitehouse and L. H. Martin, 45–66. Walnut Creek, CA: AltaMira Press., 2004.

Kamara, A. Personal Interview. Freetown, Sierra Leone, 2010(a).

Kamara, C. Personal Interview. Freetown, Sierra Leone, 2010b.

Kleveman, Lutz. "The Young Bloods Who Block Road to Peace." 2001. *Telegraph.* http://www.telegraph.co.uk/news/worldnews/1328990/The-young-bloods-who-block-road-to-peace.html, 2001. Accessed June 21, 2012.

Kunz, Rahel and Sjöberg, Ann-Kristin. "Empowered or Oppressed? Female Combatants in the Colombian Guerrilla: The Case of the Revolutionary Armed Forces of Colombia—FARC." Paper prepared for the Annual Convention of the International Studies Association. New York, 2009.

Legare, C., and Whitehouse, H. (under review). "Imitative Foundations of Cultural Learning." *Cognitio.*

Maclure, R. "'I Didn't Want to Die so I Joined Them': Structuration and the Process of Becoming Boy Soldiers in Sierra Leone." *Terrorism and Political Violence,* 18:1 (2006): 119.

Martin, L. H. and Whitehouse, H., eds. "History, Memory, and Cognition." *Historical Reflections/ Reflexions Historiques* 31.2 (2005).

McCauley, R. N. and Whitehouse, H., eds). *The Psychological and Cognitive Foundations of Religiosity*, special issue of *Journal of Cognition and Culture,* 5: 1–2. (2005).

Mithen, S. "From Ohalo to Çatalhöyük: The Development of Religiosity during the Early Prehistory of Western Asia, 20,000–7000 BC." In *Theorizing Religions Past: Historical and Archaeological Perspectives.* Eds. H. Whitehouse and L. H. Martin. Walnut Creek, CA: AltaMira Press.2004.

Moaddel, Mansoor (1992), 'Ideology as Episodic Discourse: The Case of the Iranian Revolution', *American Sociological Review* 57.3 (1992): 353–379.

Norton, Augustus Richard. *Hezbollah: A Short History.* Princeton, NJ: Princeton University Press, 2007.

Offstien, Norman., "An Historical Review and Analysis of Colombian Guerrilla Movements: FARC, ELN, and EPL." *Desarrollo Y Sociedad,* 52. (2003): 99–142

Ogura, Kiyoko. "Seeking State Power: The Communist Party of Nepal (Maoist)." Berlin: Berghof Research Center for Constructive Conflict Management, 2008.

Onesto, Li., *Dispatches from the People's War in Nepal.* London: Pluto Press, 2005.

Ortiz, Roman D., "Insurgent Strategies in the Post-Cold War: The Case of the Revolutionary Armed Forces of Colombia." *Studies in Conflict & Terrorism*, 25:2 (2002): 127–143.

Pachis, P. and Martin, L. H. (eds.) *Imagistic Traditions in the Graeco-Roman World*, Thessaloniki, Greece: Vanias, 2009.

Paez, Dario, Bernard Rime, and N. Basabe "A Socio-Cultural Model of Rituals: Effects of Collective Traumas and Psychosocial Process of Coping Concerning March 11 Demonstrations." *Revista de Psicologia Social*, 17 (2005): 369–375.

Paez, Dario, Bellilli Gulielmo, and Bernard Rime. "Flashbulb Memories, Culture, and Collective Memories: Psychosocial Processes Related to Rituals, Emotions, and Memories." In *Flashbulb Memories: New Issues and New Perspectives*. Eds. Olivier Luminet and Antonietta Curci, 227–246. Hove, UK: Psychology Press. 2009.

Paez, Dario, N. Basabe, S. Ubillos, and J. L. Gonzalez. "Participation in Demonstrations, Emotional Climate and Coping with Collective Violence in March Eleven Madrid Bombings." *Journal for Social Issues* 63 (2009): 323–327.

Pande, Sriram Raj. "Nepal National Human Development Report: Empowerment and Poverty Reduction." New York: United Nations Development Programme, 2004.

Penhaul, Karl. "Colombia's Rebels Hit the Airwaves." *Newsday,* December 24, 2000.

Petras, J. "The FARC Faces the Empire." *Latin American Perspectives*, 27.5(2000): 134.

Prestholdt, Jeremy. "The Afterlives of 2Pac: Imagery and Alienation in Sierra Leone and Beyond." *Journal of African Cultural Studies*, 21.2 (2009): 197–218.

Pyysiainen, Ilkka.), Corrupt Doctrine and Doctrinal Revival: On the Nature and Limits of the Modes Theory. In *Theorizing Religions Past: Historical and Archaeological Perspectives on Modes of Religiosity*. Ed. H. Whitehouse and L. H. Martin, 173–194. Walnut Creek, CA: AltaMira Press, 2004.

Ranstorp, M. "Hizbollah's Command Leadership: Its Structure, Decision-Making and Relationship with Iranian Clergy and Institution." *Terrorism and Political Violence*, 6.3 (1994): 303–339.

Ranstorp, Magnus. "The Strategy and Tactics of Hizballah's Current 'Lebanonization Process'." *Mediterranean Politics* 3.1 (1998): 103–134.

Richards, Paul . "Videos and Violence on the Periphery: Rambo and War in the Forests of the Sierra Leone-Liberia Border." *IDS Bulletin* 25:2 (1994): 88–93.

Richert, R. A., Whitehouse, H., and Stewart, E. E. A. "Memory and Analogical Thinking in High-Arousal Rituals." In *Mind and Religion: Psychological and Cognitive Foundations of Religiosity*. Ed. H. Whitehouse and R. N. McCauley, 127–145. Walnut Creek, CA: AltaMira Press, 2005.

Ridley, Matt. *The Origins of Virtue*. New York: Viking Press, 1996.

Robertson Smith, W. Religion of the Semites. Fundamental Institutions. First Series. London: Adam & Charles Black, 1889.

RUF-SL. "Footpaths to Democracy: Toward a New Sierra Leone." In RUF/SL (ed.), 1995.

Saab, B. Y. "Criminality and Armed Groups: A Comparative Study of FARC and Paramilitary Groups in Colombia." *Studies in Conflict and Terrorism* 32.6 (2009): 455.

Saad-Ghorayeb, Amal. *Hizbu'llah: Politics and Religion*. London: Pluto Press, 2002.

Sanín, Francisco Gutiérrez. "Telling the Difference: Guerrillas and Paramilitaries in the Colombian War." *Politics & Society*, 36:1 (2008): 3.

Schleifer, Ron. "Psychological Operations: A New Variation on an Age Old Art: Hezbollah versus Israel." *Studies in Conflict & Terrorism*, 29:1 (2006):1–19.

Sober, E. and Wilson, D. S. "Adaptation and Natural Selection Revisited." *Journal of Evolutionary Biology* 24 (2011): 462–468.

Sosis et al. "Scars of War." *Evolution and Human Behaviour* 28 (2007): 234–247.

Stirr, Anna. "Mainstream Maoism: Nationalist Music, Maoist Language, and the "New Nepal." *New Researchers' Perspectives on the Nepalese People's War* (unpublished paper, Berder, France, 2010).

Utas, M., "The West Side Boys: Military Navigation in the Sierra Leone Civil War." *Journal of Modern African Studies* 46.3 (2008): 487.

Verswijver, G. *The Club-Fighters of the Amazon: Warfare among the Kaiapo Indians of Central Brazil*. Ghent, Belgium: Rijksuniversiteit te Gent, 1992.

Whitehouse, Harvey. "Memorable Religions: Transmission, Codification, andChange in Divergent Melanesian Contexts." *Man*, n.s., 27 (1992): 777–797.

Whitehouse, Harvey. *Inside the Cult: Religious Innovation and Transmission in Papua New Guinea*. Oxford, UK: Oxford University Press, 1995.

Whitehouse, Harvey. Rites of Terror: Emotion, Metaphor, and Memory in Melanesian Initiation Cults." *Journal of the Royal Anthropological Institute* 4 (1996): 703–715.

Whitehouse, Harvey. *Arguments and Icons: Divergent Modes of Religiosity*. Oxford, UK: Oxford University Press, 2000.

Whitehouse, Harvey. *Modes of Religiosity: A Cognitive Theory of Religious Transmission*. Walnut Creek, CA: AltaMira Press, 2004.

Whitehouse, Harvey and J. Laidlaw, eds. *Ritual and Memory: Toward a Comparative Anthropology of Religion*. Walnut Creek; CA: AltaMira Press, 2004.

Whitehouse, Harvey and L. Martin, eds. *Theorizing Religions Past: Archaeology, History, and Cognition*. Walnut Creek, CA: AltaMira Press, 2004.

Whitehouse, Harvey and Robert N. McCauley, eds., *Mind and Religion: Psychological and Cognitive Foundations of Religiosity*. Walnut Creek, CA: AltaMira Press, 2005.

Whitehouse, Harvey and J. Laidlaw, eds., *Religion, Anthropology and Cognitive Science*. Durham, NC: Carolina Academic Press, 2007.

Whitehouse, Harvey and I. Hodder. "Modes of Religiosity at Çatalhöyük." In *Religion in the Emergence of Civilization: Çatalhöyük as a Case Study*. Ed. I. Hodder. Cambridge, UK: Cambridge University Press, 2010.

Whitehouse, Harvey. "The Coexistence Problem in Psychology, Anthropology, and Evolutionary Theory." *Human Development*, 54 (2011):191–199.

H. Whitehouse, K. Kahn, M. E. Hochberg, and J. J. Bryson (in press). "The Role for Simulations in Theory Construction for the Social Sciences: Case Studies Concerning Divergent Modes of Religiosity." *Religion, Brain and Behavior*.

Xygalatas, D. *Firewalking in Northern Greece: A Cognitive Approach to High-Arousal Rituals*. PhD dissertation, Queen's University, Belfast, UK, 2007.

Zack-Williams, A. B. "Child Soldiers in the Civil War in Sierra Leone." *Review of African Political Economy* 28.87 (2001): 73.

Zharkevich, Ina V. 'Becoming a Maoist in a Time of Insurgency: Youth in Nepal's 'People's War." MPhil thesis, Department of Development Studies, Oxford, 2009.

CHAPTER 40

....

A SOCIOTHEOLOGICAL
APPROACH TO
UNDERSTANDING
RELIGIOUS VIOLENCE

....

MARK JUERGENSMEYER AND
MONA KANWAL SHEIKH

THE hideous acts of terrorism committed in the name of religion at the turn of the 21st century throughout the world challenge our attempts to make sense of them as social phenomena. Do we focus on socioeconomic causes, on psychological motivation, on political strategy, or on organizational behavior? And what does religion have to do with all of this?

The religious factor is perhaps the most perplexing part of the puzzle. It is tempting to deny that such terrorists as al Qaeda's Osama bin Laden, Israel's Yigal Amir, or Norway's Anders Breivik were religious, because they clearly had political reasons for defending what they thought were attacks on their cultural communities. Yet they used the language of religion and religious history to defend their actions, and religious organizations have been their inspiration and support. Interviews with activists involved in militant acts of terrorism show that they often understand their acts in religious terms and as part of struggles for peace, justice, and a better sociopolitical order (e.g., Mahmood 1996; Juergensmeyer 2003; 2008; Jerryson 2011, Sheikh 2011). Thus, there is sufficient evidence to show that one of the factors involved in acts of contemporary violence is an effort to fulfill a religious vision.

It is easy enough to understand why violence is utilized by bad people, but what if it is invoked by otherwise good people: those whose announced intentions are pious and aimed toward advancing peace? This is the problem that confronts scholars and the general public in trying to make sense of much of the rash of violence associated with religion that came to the fore around the world in the decades at the turn of the twenty-first century. The suicide bombings of Hamas, the attack on the Hebron mosque by Baruch Goldstein, and Timothy McVeigh's bombing of the Alfred P. Murrah Federal Building in Oklahoma City may appear to have been plots undertaken by a few lone wolves, but each came from a culture in which the justifications for violence were colored by their religious understanding of social reality. Theirs were not simply strategic acts chosen by astute political tacticians in trying to achieve clearly defined goals, nor were they devious acts by a deranged few. Rather they were acts of violence that were sewn into the fabric of the religious worldviews of those who perpetrated them and endorsed by broad communities of support that shared their same religious points of view. Clearly religious thinking was a dimension of their social reality.

Understanding these perspectives has been a challenge for social analysis. Rational choice theory is baffled by choices that do not seem to be rational in worldly calculations but have a far more distant time horizon and a more imaginative sense of rewards than most materialist calculations support. Strategic analyses flounder when the strategies do not seem to yield immediate benefits. Organizational theories falter when the communities of support are diffuse, unstructured, and lack a palpable chain of command.

Many of these movements are not just organizational networks that can be understood through economic parameters of rational choice and goal-oriented behavior but also communities bonded by shared mythic and doctrinal narratives. Structural-functional approaches (such as those advanced by Neil Smelser, Ralph Turner, and Louis Killiam) and social movement theorists (including those of Charles Tilly and Donatella Della Porta) are useful in that they provide an understanding of the organization and ideology of social movements and their relation to dominant social structures and state power. But they are less helpful in understanding how the social reality looks through the eyes of religious activists. To take religious vocabulary, beliefs, and concepts seriously has long been a challenge for the social sciences. Many scholars have recognized that there is a need to approach the social phenomena of religion in new ways––not only with questions theologians normally pose but with added sociological or political queries. Yet the standard analyses are often limited.

What these and other analytic approaches often overlook is the importance of the religious worldview. Though we are aware that *religion* is increasingly a contested analytic term, because it is linked with a habit of bifurcated thinking about the secular-religious worlds that dates back to the European Enlightenment, we acknowledge that religious language and traditions provide ways of thinking about social and metaphysical reality that are distinctive. It is this that is often lacking in social analysis, an acknowledgement of the importance of religious worldviews and the way that they interact with the societies of those who adopt and oppose them. There is a clear need for an analysis of religious thinking to come into the picture in the study of social movements and contemporary currents in which religion plays a significant role.

Fortunately in recent years, social analysis has gained an increased awareness of the importance of religious ways of thinking. What has been called the "cultural turn" in the social sciences is one example of a renewed appreciation for the way that ideas and values shape social realities (Friedland and Mohr 2004). When applied specifically to the analysis of religious thinking in understanding social movements and social behavior, this trend might be characterized as a sociotheological turn. It takes seriously the logic of theology—the religious reasoning of the actors—as well as their social setting, and tries to relate the two. This chapter first defines this trend and how it has developed. Then it turns to the main area of sociotheological study, the analysis of epistemic worldviews. In the closing section, this chapter provides practical guidelines for conducting sociotheological studies. The guidelines are both normative about conducting what might be called "good sociotheology," but at the same time they are meant to be operational tools for students interested in studying the religion-violence nexus from sociotheological perspectives.

Defining Sociotheology

Militant movements such as the Taliban, messianic Zionists, and Christian abortion clinic bombers draw on specific religious myths, doctrines, and ideas. Activists in the movements often present themselves as servants of God implementing a divine command. In India, Hindus and Sikhs have justified violence in defense of their religious faiths, and even Buddhism—a tradition for which nonviolence is its hallmark—has been fused with violence in political movements in Sri Lanka, Thailand, Myanmar, and Tibet and in the activities of a new religious movement in Japan, the Aum Shinrikyo. Though often the motives of these movements can be described in non-religious terms—defending social identity, securing justice, and obtaining political order—they are simultaneously phrased in pious language and often their goals are characterized as religious. Frequently the personal spiritual mission of salvation is fused with a communal longing for a redemptive social order. Thus these phenomena need to be analyzed from both theological and social perspectives.

The interdisciplinary trend that we are here labeling *sociotheology* has emerged out of the recognition that politics has a religious side, and religion can be inherently a part of public life. It is an insight that was a part of the thinking of some of the founding figures in the field of social studies—including Emile Durkheim, Max Weber, and Karl Marx. Durkheim attempted to immerse himself in the thinking of tribal societies to understand the socioreligious significance of totemic symbols (1912). Weber adopted a posture of *verstehen* in his social analysis that was sensitive to cultural values; and he integrated both theological ideas and social theory in his studies of the religions of India and China and in developing his understanding of the Protestant ethic (1905, 1915, 1916). Karl Marx took seriously the relationship of ideological frameworks of thought to social structure, especially in his analysis of the role of religion in the German peasant's revolt (Marx and Engels 1939). Most of the sociological work on religion in the first half of the twentieth century, however, tended to be reductionist and unappreciative of the distinctiveness of religious ideas.

The trend began to turn in the second half of the twentieth century. In the beginning of the 1970s the term "socio-theology" was applied by a sociologist, Roland Robertson, in an article discussing the renewed interest in the social aspects of religion by sociologists and sociologically inclined theologians after an era dominated by the secularization thesis (Robertson 1971: 309). The term was later adopted in different contexts, denoting the tendency to take seriously religious world views in social analysis, but it did not imply any coherent methodological or theoretical guidelines. Today, however, the contours of a particular approach that we can label "sociotheological" are much more clear. We characterize this approach as an emerging "sociotheological turn" within the social sciences.

This "sociotheological turn" implies a correspondence between the social studies and religious thinking that has come as an alternative to more positivist approaches to analyzing social phenomena related to religion. Typically social scientists have felt most comfortable by keeping theology at an arm's length, and the sociotheological turn has provided exceptions. Within sociology, both Robert Bellah and Peter Berger have been hospitable to theological points of view (Bellah 2011, 1970; Berger 1967), with social thinkers such as Pierre Bourdieu and Antony Giddens accepting, albeit more reluctantly, the viewpoints from within religious traditions (Bourdieu 1980, Giddens 1991). In the field of political philosophy, Charles Taylor has been consistently congenial to religious perspectives, while John Rawls and Jurgen Habermas came around to seeing the value of taking seriously religious elements of social thought relatively late in their academic careers (Rawls 1997, Habermas 2002). Anthropologists by disciplinary habit have been more disposed to take other people's perspectives seriously, and thus have accommodated more easily religious points of view. This has been true of such anthropologists as Clifford Geertz, Louis Dumont, Mary Douglas, Stanley Tambiah, Talal Asad, and Gananath Obeyesekere. Within the fields of religious studies and the history of religion, religious perspectives are part of the objects of their studies, and some of the scholars who study religion have also been mindful of the social implications of religious ideas. These socially minded scholars of religion have included many comparativists, including, notably, Ninian Smart and Wilfred Cantwell Smith. And though theology is sometimes a closed system of thought, the political significance of religious thinking has been a theme of scholars from a variety of theological traditions, including such Protestant Christians as Reinhold Niebuhr and George Lindbeck, the Roman Catholic theologian Hans Küng, the Jewish philosopher Martin Buber, the Jewish-Christian writer Simone Weil, the Muslim legal expert Abdullahi An-Naim, the Hindu thinker Rabindranath Tagore, and the Buddhist social activist Sulak Sivaraksa. In some instances, the trend has been a steady though often minority perspective within the disciplines. At times, the scholarly attention has increased due to particular political events. For example, the Iranian revolution in 1978, the Sikh and Afghan Muslim rebellions in the 1980s, and the rise of a global *jihadi* movement that culminated in the spectacular aerial assaults on the World Trade Center and Pentagon in 2001, brought along an increased academic as well as public attention on understanding the religious motives for political acts.

In recent years, the issue of examining religion and politics together has returned, in part because of the public prominence of movements that blend religious and political activism. Religious politics has also been regarded as interesting because it appears to challenge secularism as an ideology, and this leads to an examination of the post-Enlightenment notion that religion is something private and separate from the public secular realm. This issue has been explored by Talal Asad, for instance, in his discussion of the genealogical origins of the separate spheres of religion and politics (Asad 1993; 2003), Charles Taylor's examination of the post-Enlightenment emergence of "A Secular Age" (2007), Jose Casanova's discussion of the revival of public religions in the modern world (1994), and the revival of Carl Schmitt's idea of political theology (Schmitt 1922, Meier 2006). Schmitt uses the idea of political theology in two senses, both the explicit use of religious concepts to buttress political positions, and also to imply that all concepts of modern political thought are in reality theological concepts, even if they are presented as being secular. Either way, the concept has become increasingly relevant at the end of the twentieth century and the rise of the twenty-first, decades marked by clashes between religious and seemingly secular political positions. Recent works on the idea of secularism within the field of political science and international relations theory also reflect this trend (for instance, Hurd 2007, Calhoun et al. 2011; Sheikh and Wæver 2012). At the same time, there is a growing literature on the political and social dimensions of religion within the field of theology—sometimes accounted for as social theology (see, for instance, Davis 1994)—that looks at the public relevance of religious acts, institutions, and ideas. Though isolated from other departments of the academy for decades, faculty from departments of theology are involved increasingly in incipient projects of cooperation with colleagues in the social sciences in Europe and the United States (Sheikh and Wæver 2012).

For the social sciences, this sociotheological turn means incorporating into social analysis the insider-oriented attempt to understand the reality of a particular worldview. As a result, the social sciences have recovered an appreciation for a field long banished from the halls of secular academe: theology. The insider perspective on a religious worldview is, after all, what the field of theology has classically been about, long before the advent of the modern academic disciplines: attempts to structure the social, ethical, political, and spiritual aspects of a culture's ideas and meanings into a coherent whole. It studies what Michel Foucault once designated as an episteme: the structure of knowledge that is the basis of an understanding of how reality works (Foucault 1966). These structures of knowledge have traditionally been understood in language about ultimate reality that is today regarded as religious; thus theology was—as the name implies—the study of the logic of God. By extension, it is the study of the essential moral and spiritual connections in all aspects of life.

The power of theology as an academic discipline in the early modern period was its comprehensiveness. It attempted to survey the whole range of human activity and belief and to ground it in first principles. For this reason, theology was once regarded as the queen of the sciences. Such diverse thinkers in European history as Adam Smith, widely regarded as the father of modern capitalist economic theory, and Charles Darwin, one of the fathers of evolutionary biology, began their intellectual careers studying theology. The same is true of many of the most influential scientists from the Islamic culture such as Ibn Sina (commonly known by his latinized name Avicenna), who is regarded as a father of modern medicine and creator of the concept of momentum in physics; Ibn Hayyan, known as the father of molecular chemistry; or Al-Khawarizmi and Al-Kindi, who invented algebra. A common element in their scientific approach was that they all studied, went into dialogue with, or drew on inspiration from the field of theology.

During the latter part of the modern era, theology fell into disrespect among social sciences due to the secularization narrative that represented faith as the opposite to science, and theology became isolated as a field. This was also due to three limitations in the way that theology was traditionally practiced: It was usually conducted with only one religious tradition as its frame of reference, it asserted normative truth claims about its analyses, and its analysts often ignored the social context in which the ideas they study emerge and have their life. In the present, global era, however, the theological aspect of sociotheology does not need to be bound by these limitations.

The scholars who study contemporary worldviews from the approach that we are calling sociotheology are different from traditional theologians in that they apply their analytic style to any tradition or worldview. They bracket truth claims asserted by either the subjects in the study or by the analysts studying the subjects' points of view, and they take seriously the social location in which a view of the world emerges and the social consequences of a particular way of thinking about reality. The point is to try to understand the reasoning behind the truth claims, not to verify them. In a similar vein, a sociotheological approach also avoids making judgements about why an act was undertaken—what the cause of an incident may have been. Obviously the analyst wants to gather as much information about possible motivations as possible, without accepting at face value either the activists' or their critics' judgements about why they were undertaken. For example, when Jewish activists claim that they are carrying out their acts of violence under rabbinic authority, the scholars who are analyzing this case from a sociotheological approach will try to make sense of their religious justifications—even though they might not accept the idea that the religious motives were the sole ones. They also take into calculation any information that might point to the activists' political and strategic motivations for their actions.

At the same time, although the sociotheological approach acknowledges that many motives are mixed and a mélange of political, social, and economic factors may be at play, it allows for the idea that believers can hold distinctly religious reasons for doing things. It is open to the possibility that some activists may be involved in actions and support ideas based on the perceived notion that there is a relation between individuals and the transcendent, that they hope for spiritual transformation in this life and the next, and that they long for salvation and spiritual fulfillment. Thus the possibility of multiple rationalities and perceptions to inform the individual activist's choices and worldview does not dismiss the idea that there may be something sui generis to be understood about religion and the motivating power of religious belief.

At the same time that sociotheology takes religious thinking seriously, it also takes the social context seriously. Those scholars who have been working in the intellectual style that we call sociotheology realize that much of the phenomena that modern people since the time of the European Enlightenment have called religion is related to other aspects of society, from economic and political factors to matters of social identity. For this reason, sociotheological analysis seldom is limited to a study of religion in the narrow sense, as if there were a separate cluster of actions and ideas relating to a notion of transcendence and of spiritual transformation that was unaffected by other aspects of public and private life. Sociotheology, thus, represents a third way—a path between reductionism (denying that religion can have any "real" importance) and isolationism (delinking religion from its social milieu). Instead, this trend incarnates the analytic approach that Robert Segal calls interactionism—a two-way frame of references through which religion can account for social phenomena and social factors can account for religion (Segal 2005). Though in our modern way of thinking about religion, it is granted partial autonomy from the "secular" world, it is not given immunity from the society or culture in which it is a part.

The sociotheological trend has been pushed forward by epistemological revolutions across disciplinary borders. One example is the Strong Program associated with the Edinburgh School of the sociology of science, which holds that all human knowledge and ideas, including religious ones, contain some social components in its formation process. Another relevant methodological revolution has come from within discursive psychology (Edwards and Potter 1992; Harré and Gillett 1994) and social psychology (Gee 1992) that dissolved the concepts of a mind-body dichotomy. This also challenged the subjective-objective distinction characterizing the positivist ideals of social science based on the image of the individual who has an isolated inner side that cannot be verified by positivist test methods. The dynamic view on the mind-body relationship is part of what has been called the "second cognitive revolution" (Harré and Gillett 1994) that challenged the idea that mental and psychological entities exist in a self-contained way. Instead it brought forward the idea of "socio-mental practice" (Gee 1992: 1) and positioned these seemingly psychological entities out in "the social world of action and interaction" (Gee 1992: xvii). Thus according to this standpoint, beliefs or emotions cannot be isolated or identified out of the context in which they are expressed, and as argued by Harré and Gillett, the mind (e.g., beliefs, emotions, attitudes, intentions) only comes into existence "in the performance of actions" (1994: 22).

The same sort of methodological bridge building between inside and outside perspectives has taken place within the field of theology. Here one of the pioneers was George Lindbeck, who developed a "cultural-linguistic" concept of religious doctrines by bridging anthropology and a Wittgensteinian philosophy of language that probed the relationship between language and culture, on one hand, and experience and belief, on the other. Lindbeck argued for developing a position different from both traditional cognitive-propositionalism, for which religious doctrines function as truth claims objectively pointing to realities, and modern experiential-expressivism, which holds doctrines to be expressions of inner feelings, motivations, and experiences of the divine, thereby approaching truth as something prelinguistic. Instead, he put forward a cultural-linguistic approach, arguing that language shapes experience more than the other way around (Lindbeck 1984: 37). Thus according to Lindbeck, the inner side ought not to be seen in isolation, and belief and doctrines do not reflect precognitive, prelinguistic experiences. Together, the approximation—through language—of the field of psychology and theology (the mind and belief) and sociology (the context) as two poles in the same discursive dynamics thus contributed to eroding a stonewall dichotomy between theology and the social sciences.

EPISTEMIC WORLDVIEW ANALYSIS

What is being examined in the sociotheological approach is a way of looking at the world—and, in particular, a way of looking at social reality—through religious eyes. This means that the object of analysis is not persons, things, beliefs, or actions but epistemic worldviews: the ways that participants in a particular religious perspective view the world. When activists who have supported violent actions are interviewed from a sociotheological perspective, therefore, the question is not why they did it but how they viewed the world in such a way that would allow these actions to be carried out.

The idea of an epistemic worldview is a marriage between Foucault's concept of episteme (1966)—a paradigm of linguistic discourse based on a common set of understandings about the basis of knowledge—and Pierre Bourdieu's notion of *habitus*, the social location of shared understandings about the world and how it should work (1980). An epistemic worldview is a framework for thinking about reality and acting appropriately within a perceived understanding of the world.

The idea of an epistemic worldview has much in common with the notion of religion (and other ways of thinking about the world, such as science and poetry) as being an awareness of an alternative view of reality. In a recent book, the sociologist Robert Bellah speaks about religion as one of the "other realities," like poetry and science, that "break the dreadful fatalities of this world of appearances" (Bellah 2011: 9). To understand a perception of reality—an epistemic worldview—of either conventional material reality or an alternative reality perceived through religious eyes requires the sociotheological tasks of recovering the internal logic of this perception of reality and placing it within its social milieu.

These two aspects of the sociotheological approach—internal epistemic worldview analysis and the analysis of its social location—inform each other. Take, for instance, the study of a strident Christian religious movement that ascribes to a doctrinal position that attributes subhuman characteristics to people of racial backgrounds different from the white caucasian members of the movement. This position can be understood by studying the beliefs of the movement that imagine divine blessings granted from on high to some racial groups and not to others; but an understanding of it can also be informed from social and political studies of the changing racial makeup of the surrounding society and its power implications. Other correlations between insider perception and outsider data might be less readily apparent than this example and lead the analyst into surprising new areas of inquiry that might not have been possible with information gleaned only from internal ideas or the external social data about the movement.

Sociotheology, thus, has two dimensions; the study of a group's internal epistemic worldview and the external analysis of the social world in which the group is embedded. It grounds an understanding of a particular epistemic worldview in its specific social location and seeks to understand the relation of those people who share a certain worldview to the social and power structures of the world around them. The task is similar to the hermeneutical approach to the interpretation of texts—an approach that has been employed in cultural sociology as well—in attempting to understand the range of ways that statements and social events have been perceived from various perspectives. Understanding this juxtaposition of worldviews, and locating the social and political forces behind them, provide dual levels of analysis that illumine the motivations of groups and the policy choices of sociopolitical leaders.

The attempts to discern worldviews and their internal discourses involve subjective judgments, but they are not arbitrary. Those who take a sociotheological approach to analysis do not adopt a single methodology, because the methods of understanding a worldview and locating it within a social context are many and multifaceted. The results of these methodological efforts may well be significant insights rather than conclusive data or perhaps a combination of the two. However, because an epistemic worldview is multifaceted and must be understood holistically, the studies of it focus on connections and leading principles. This approach is relevant to the study of any kind of epistemic worldview, not only frames of references that are typically thought of as being religious. One could imagine a sociotheological examination of secular humanism, nationalism, Marxism, and any other epistemic worldview that can be studied holistically.

Sociotheological analysis can be the basis of both comparative and global studies, showing how epistemic worldviews differ, how they appear to be similar, or how common experiences underlie epistemic worldviews across the globe. To facilitate the development toward a more nuanced understanding of the dynamics between epistemic worldviews and their social location, there is a need to develop a more systematic research program for the archeological reconstruction of epistemic worldviews in their social milieus. This task is enhanced when scholars from the humanities and social sciences continue a fruitful dialogue transgressing old disciplinary moats. Those who study religious literature, philosophy, and theology have much to offer those social scientists from fields such as sociology, anthropology, and political science; and they have much to learn from them as well.

Guidelines for Sociotheological Studies

Demarcating an Epistemic Worldview

One of the first challenges of sociotheological analysis is to identify a particular epistemic worldview that members of a group hold in common. While the borders of a worldview may be diffuse and overlapping with other perceptions of social reality, it is usually not so diffuse as to be unrecognizable. Like language families and linguistic communities, epistemic worldviews are identified by common features and organizing principles.

For instance, the outlook of militant Christians associated with the Christian Identity movement in the United States constitutes a fairly coherent worldview. Members of Christian Identity are united in a view of the world and of sacred history that privileges white people and identifies the continuing heritage of the Old Testament covenant between God and the chosen people to be invested not in the Jewish community—which they regard as an illegitimate usurper of the biblical Israeli tradition—but in the society of white people of European origins. They also understand redemption to be manifest in a redeemed sociopolitical order, and for this reason are deeply suspicious of secular politics.

Elements of this worldview are shared by other groups. The Aryan Brotherhood also believes in the God-given privilege of white European racial groups and the identification of Jews and blacks as second-class citizens. Yet the particular description of this prejudice—that whites are not just socially but also spiritually superior and the inheritors of the biblical Israeli tradition—is distinctive to the epistemic worldview of Christian Identity. For this reason, Christian Identity can be said to be an appropriate object of epistemic worldview analysis. The analysis of this worldview helps to understand the sociotheological background of activists who have been influenced by it, including the Atlanta Olympic Park bomber, Eric Robert Rudolph, and Timothy McVeigh. In the case of Rudolph, who claimed to be Catholic, Christian Identity teachings were imparted to him by his mother. In the case of McVeigh, he ascribed to Christian Identity–related ideas through the cosmotheism of William Pierce, who under the pseudonym Andrew MacDonald wrote the novel *The Turner Diaries*, which McVeigh regarded as his bible and which he sold at gun shows prior to his attack on the Oklahoma City federal building. Though Pierce disavowed any connection between his cosmotheism and Christian Identity teachings, the parallels are striking, and the interaction of Pierce and McVeigh with Christian Identity members is a matter of record (Juergensmeyer 2003: 31). Of course, one could begin one's study of the motives of the Oklahoma City bombing by simply focusing on the worldview of Timothy McVeigh, rather than coming at his ideas from the perspective of Christian Identity. But at some point in this analysis, one would need to relate McVeigh's thinking to those groups that influenced him in order to understand the broader context of the Christian Right in the United States to which his thinking was related. Relating his thinking to the broader context would not only show the influences on his ideas but dispel the common myth that McVeigh was a lone wolf whose actions had no connection to other currents of political and religious activism in America.

Bracketing Assumptions about the Truth of a Worldview

As analysts prepare to enter into an understanding of a particular worldview, it is important that they attempt to abandon any preconceived notions about either the truth or falsity of their subject's views of the world or, for that matter, of their own. This does not mean that the analysts have to morally approve of the destructive things their subjects' violent actions may have done or to gullibly accept their skewed visions of the world. Rather it is to accept the profound insight that all views of the world are in some ways skewed and that the business of the social analyst adopting a sociotheological approach is to understand the perceptions of others. One can judge them later; the first task is to understand how they view the world.

In some cases, a resistance to taking an empathetic stance toward the subjects' theologically informed worldview can have disastrous consequences. In the case of the Federal Bureau of Investigation (FBI) standoff at Waco, Texas, in 1993 with members of the Branch Davidian sect led by David Koresh, the FBI agents were criticized for having precipitated the fiery ending of the encounter (and the deaths of members of the movement) by not understanding the internal logic of the theological perception of history that was held by Koresh and that led him to take his tragically decisive actions. To the agents, the rationales given by Koresh in their extensive telephone conversations with him during the standoff were just so much theological jibberish. Later analyses of the conversations revealed that Koresh had a biblically sophisticated view of the eschatological end of history and a vaunted role of his own movement in the end time conflagration that helped to explain his responses to the FBI's actions.

As difficult as it may be for analysts to bracket the truth claims about the subjects' views of the world, it is often even more difficult for them to bracket the claims of their own. Most people, scholars included, are scarcely aware of their own assumptions about how the social order is constructed, especially when it comes to the role of religion within it. Since the time of the Enlightenment, it has become a dominant view in western Europe and in the United States that religion is something separate from public life, that its ideas and its practices ought to be contained within ideologies and organizations that are the domain of private life or self-contained communities.

For this reason, it can often be a challenge for the scholar embedded in the Enlightenment discourse to deal with worldviews in which religion—the ideas and practices of spiritual traditions—are seamlessly a part of the moral structure of public life. For years, Western scholars would either ignore the importance of the religiously defined roles of caste in India's social life, or they would chastise it. It took a sociologist from India, M. N. Srinivas, to recognize the importance of caste in India's modern social mobility and to analyze it from a morally neutral perspective. A French anthropologist, Louis Dumont, startled the Western academic world by building on Srinivas' insights with an analysis of a religiously rooted caste-based society as a fundamentally different kind of social organization—*homo hierarchicus*—that could be compared on an equal par with the individualistic secular social organization of the modern West, which he dubbed *homo equalis.* Neither was better than the other, they were simply different. To adopt this approach is an essential feature of epistemic worldview analysis.

Empathetic Immersion

If analysts reserve judgment on the truth claims of both their subjects and themselves, they are then able to enter into an understanding of a subject's worldview through a kind of empathetic immersion with the culture of which they are a part. This means attempting to put oneself in their positions. Empathy requires that the analyst behaves with cultural sensitivity and displays pragmatic competence; that is, he or she attempts to understand the subject's intended meaning. Being different from sympathy, empathy requires not only tolerance but the ability to understand the interviewees' frame of reference.

In a situation of cultural difference and especially in the context of social conflict, it may be difficult to take the conceptual leap to identify with the other side's point of view. But doing so may open up a vista of understanding. In an interview with Robert McNamara, the former US Secretary of Defense during the United States' Vietnam War, that was included in the documentary film *The Fog of War,* McNamara gave this piece of advice to policymakers who found themselves in a situation similar to his: "empathize with the enemy." Doing so, he implied, would have changed Americans' attitude toward the North Vietnamese and helped them understand that the Vietnamese were engaged in what they perceived to be a nationalist struggle against foreigners rather than a communist crusade. An empathetic immersion in this setting would have not only provided cultural understanding and scholarly analysis but a change in political policy.

During the Khalistani struggle in north India during the 1980s, the Sikh activists were often portrayed in the press as heartless gangs of thugs. When one of the authors of this chapter met with a group of activists who were brought to a side room in a Sikh Gurdwara (a temple) in New Delhi, their faces were initially covered with scarves and one could imagine them to be the vicious thugs that they were made out to be. But when they revealed their faces and began talking, they seemed to be ordinary young men from villages who had become swept up in a great political movement that challenged them to demonstrate their manhood and their allegiance to their faith. They did not seem to be evil people at heart but decent youth caught up in a spirit of tragic crusade. Entering into their world was, for the analyst, heartbreaking, for it was apparent that they had come to believe that their community's cultural existence was at stake and their suicidal acts of violence—which appeared to those outside the movement as horrible acts of terrorism—were interpreted by them as the brave actions of soldiers in a cosmic war (Juergensmeyer 2003: 90). Thus, talking to "the terrorists" brings analysts intellectually and emphatically closer to the topic they are studying and gives them a better sense of the situation and the issues at stake as perceived by the activists. At the same time, it reduces the risk of misunderstandings that often exist in a remote sender-receiver relation, where at times only the official manifestos or statements of the movements under scrutiny are read.

Undertaking an empathetic immersion and entering into these views of the world can be challenging for the outsider. Ordinary methods of research, such as social surveys relying on prepared questions, are often of little use, because the kinds of questions that are relevant to ask may be understood only in the process of the subject-analysis interaction. This is why interviews and prolonged cultural immersion are often the best pathways to understanding the epistemic worldviews. The most productive interviews are open-ended (rather than following a rigid questionnaire) and take a conversational shape in order to follow the logic of the subjects' arguments. Such interviews also make the subjects feel that they are not facing an adversarial interrogator but a researcher honestly interested in knowing their point of view. Yet much preparation is required to make sure that the interviewer has a sense of what to expect and can raise questions that illumine the basic values and position of the subject while keeping open the possibility that the answers will require a whole new consideration of the subject.

Thus these are not just ordinary conversations but informative conversations. They are engagements in what might be called "relational knowledge"—knowledge that is acquired not through inductive or deductive reasoning but through an interaction of ideas and worldviews with someone whose perspective on the world is quite different than one's one. It is this knowledge that is possible only though an engagement of worldviews that comes about through informative conversations.

Such conversations are not random. The point is to enter into an interaction with a clear sense of the kind of information that the analyst wants to acquire—a sense of what is important to the subject's worldview, how history and religious themes are intertwined with their perception of social reality, and how the socio-political world is infused with historical and theological meaning. But the structure of the conversation is left sufficiently flexible to let the topics shift as new areas are discovered and to allow the analyst to probe more deeply into areas that are not easily understood. As a result, analysts not only acquire new information but new understandings about their subject's perspective and their own.

Identifying Narrative Structures

One of the values of a flexible interview format is that it allows the subjects to tell stories—not necessarily made-up stories, but narrative accounts of their lives and the important events within them. These accounts are seldom narrowly bio-graphical. Rather, they can illuminate what is important to the individual about the things that have shaped his or her life. In an interview with one of the activists who planned the 1993 bombing of the World Trade Center, one of the authors of this chapter found that the pivotal moments of the interviewee's life, according to him, were moments when he felt personally rescued by Islam. He told a common Middle Eastern story about an orphaned lion cub that is raised by a family of sheep; the little lion does not know his true species until one day he goes to the watering hole and sees his reflection and knows that he is a lion, not a sheep. This, he explained, was what Islam meant to him, it showed him that he was a lion not a sheep (Juergensmeyer 2003: 67). The implication of this story was not only that his faith gave the subject a sense of social identity, it distinguished him from the alien culture of the United States in which he had lived as a foreigner. By extension, he implied, Islam is what made all Arab persons different from Americans and what distinguished the Middle East from the West in world history. His story indicated a need for true Muslims to extricate themselves from the figurative herds of sheep in which they have been trapped through the ideological, economic, and political hegemony that he thought was characteristic of Western relations with the Middle East.

Of course, it is quite possible that the subject never had such dramatic encounters with his Islamic faith and he made the whole thing up to impress the interviewer. In a sense, however, that makes no difference—even if it is his imagined history (and all histories are to some degree imagined), what he imagined and what he thought would be impressive to the interviewer tell us much about how a subject perceives what is important in his experiences in the world and what he would like to convey to others about them.

Narrative structures can illuminate a particular religious mode of justification behind violent acts, an aspect of a worldview that is of particular interest to political scientists. Often there are parallel storylines—one pointing at the worldly requirement to act, another pointing at the religious rationale—though at some point they might be fused. Analyzing the narrative structure reveals the role that religion takes in relation to justifying violence. For instance, in the case of the Pakistani Taliban, one of the authors of this chapter has found that their communication and recruitment material exhibits a wide use of religious imagery and myths that adds a transcendental layer to the explanation of jihad against US forces in Afghanistan and Pakistani security forces. An example is their restaging of important symbolic battles that have gone into Islamic mythic history as battles with special spiritual significance due to what is seen as God's intervention in them. These include the battles of Badr and Karbala and the encounter between Moses and Pharaoh. By restaging the Battle of Badr in which few followers of the Prophet Muhammad miraculously won over a large army of disbelievers and by making an analogy to their own war, the Taliban powerfully argue that God is on their side even when they may appear to be overwhelmed. In the same manner, they explain hardship and sacrifices (e.g., through the use of suicide operations) as necessary for change and order by restaging the Battle of Karbala, where the Prophet's grandson died and was sacrificed for the subsequent revolutions to take place. In their attempt to convince their fellow Muslims that they are fighting for justice and the sovereignty of God, the image of Moses's encounter with the pharaoh of his time is also referenced (Sheikh 2011). Understanding the significance of these sorts of religious myths and imagery can thus explain the mobilization capabilities of religiopolitical movements such as the Taliban as well as illuminating their view of the world as embroiled in sacred war.

From the viewpoint of the individual, telling stories allows interview subjects to place their own life stories within the larger accounts—some of them historical, some relating to their communities, and some to sacred history. In the case of David Koresh, his actions—and the responses of his FBI protagonists—were seen through the lens of an apocalyptic interpretation of biblical scripture. Koresh saw himself and his band as the chosen few standing up against the forces of evil in an end time scenario that was bound to come to a catastrophic culmination.

Many of the sacred stories in the background of contemporary instances of religious-related violence include images of war, cosmic war. A cosmic war is an imagined engagement between existential antinomies—the forces of order and disorder, truth and falsehood, good and evil—that are played out on a metaphysical level. The cosmic war has been portrayed in images in religious history and told in the narrations of sacred scriptures, including the Bible, the Qur'an, and the Hindu epics, the Mahabharata and the Ramayana. For most religious people in traditions for which these images of cosmic war are important aspects of their legendary past, the images serve as reminders of the great moral and spiritual struggles within every person's life. At times, however, conflicts in contemporary social life can appear so dramatic, intense, and consequential as to have ultimate meaning.

It is in these situations that the cosmic wars appear real. Traditional images are often grafted onto these present-day realities, and ordinary struggles are lifted onto the high proscenium of religious drama. At a striking moment during the Islamic revolution in Iran in 1978 and 1979, US president Jimmy Carter was characterized as Yazid, the Satanic figure of early Shiite history. In that moment, a contemporary political foe—the American president—was imagined to be reprising an evil role from religious history. As a consequence, he could be dealt with as early Shiites would have wanted to treat Yazid, with extreme contempt, and if possible, with a more direct and violent response. Christian activists in the United States have imagined President Barack Obama in a similar way, and plots against his life have been uncovered, plots that were justified by this image of sacred warfare and the president as a Satanic foe.

Violence in such circumstances is not so much a strategic act but a symbolic one, a performance of violence enacting a dramatic moment in a scenario of cosmic war. This means that the rational calculation, the idea that the perpetrators of violence are trying to achieve a tangible goal, is not an adequate explanation. Often when acts of terrorism are performed without any acknowledgement about what group or individuals perpetrated it, the public is puzzled. It seems reasonable to think that their goals cannot be achieved unless it is clear who did the act, why, and what measures could be done to keep such things from happening again. But what if this was not the purpose of their actions—what if they simply enacted a scene from their view of the world—a world of warfare? Enacting such a scene, like creating an arresting bit of street theater, often draws those who witness it into the view of the world of those who created it. Thus such performative acts of terrorism can be so compelling that anyone who witnesses them would be drawn into the picture and be so stunned and disturbed that they would begin to see the world as the perpetrators do, as a world at war.

This explanation seems to fit many of the more dramatic acts of religious-related terrorism that occurred in the decades around the turn of the twenty-first century, including the 2011 Oslo bombing and mass killings by Anders Breivik, whose manifesto, "2083," revealed that he thought he was enacting a scene from European history in 1683 when the Muslim invaders were stopped at the gates of Vienna. Though his action seized the public's attention, the response was not as he would have wanted, since the Norwegian public rejected his view of religious struggle and reaffirmed their policy of multicultural acceptance of Muslims and other faiths in their country. The dramatic performance of violence in the September 11, 2001, attack on New York City's World Trade Center and the Pentagon in Arlington, Virginia, had an effect that was likely more consistent with the perpetrators' staging of the conflict. The dramatic images of warfare on 9/11 did indeed draw the American public and its leaders into a mindset of cosmic war, thinking that their War on Terror in response was a part of a great moral struggle between right and wrong, freedom and slavery, civilization and chaos. The jihadi narrative of cosmic warfare was affirmed in the militant responses undertaken by the US administration under the presidency of George W. Bush.

In analyzing an epistemic worldview, such narrative constructions are instructive. Even those that do not portray an image of cosmic war often illustrate major themes and issues that will provide the analyst with points of clarity about what makes the worldview cohere. Every epistemic worldview is grounded in basic principles, guiding images and ideas that give it integrity, the basis for an integrated view of the whole. In the Islamic revolution in Iran, for example, the Shia tradition of divinely inspired leadership provides a background for understanding the powerful political role of the clergy, and its reverence for the martyrs of the tradition gives insight into the persistence of its positions, including warfare, such as the remarkably bloody border war with Iraq.

In other cases, concepts that are repeatedly used within a religious culture might reveal a central part of a group's outlook on the world. In an instructive moment during an interview with the political leader of Hamas conducted by one of this chapter's authors, Abdul Aziz Rantisi was asked what non-Palestinians understood least about the Hamas movement. Rantisi thought for a moment and then replied that Americans and other non-Palestinians misunderstood the motivation for their movement's activities. It was not about property, he said, but about pride. But instead of the English word *pride,* he used the Arabic term *izzat,* which means not only "pride" but also "dignity" and "respect," all of the traits that are opposite to a feeling of humiliation. What this indicated was that attempts to control Hamas by humiliating them were counterproductive and simply encouraged the efforts to restore a sense of pride for the Palestinian people. The marginalization of the movement and the treatment of Palestinians as citizens of an occupied territory simply fueled their anger and strengthened their cause.

Understanding these central themes—which might be in the form of images, sacred narratives, or leading concepts—is vital in understanding how a worldview coheres. It also helps to reconcile anomalies. For many it would be axiomatic, for instance, that Buddhism is a tradition of nonviolence. And yet movements in Buddhist traditions have been involved in warfare, killing, and terrorist acts. Other Buddhists are quick to condemn them—just as Muslims have distanced themselves from the terrorism of 9/11 and Christians seldom acknowledge that Timothy McVeigh had religious reasons for bombing the federal building in Oklahoma City. Yet within the worldview of the communities that have supported these activists and their plots, their religious justifications have been vital.

In the case of Aum Shinrikyo, the Japanese Buddhist movement involved in releasing poisonous nerve gas in the Tokyo subway system, their worldview was animated by an image of cosmic war, a colossal struggle that they expected to take place at the coming of the new millennium in the year 2000, which would rival the nuclear destruction of World War II in its intensity. The release of the nerve gas was intended to give an example and warning of the war to come. Yet people were killed in that event. How could this be justified under Buddhist teachings? The master of the movement, Shoko Asahara, drew from a variety of Buddhist and Hindu spiritual traditions for his pronouncements, and he found Tibetan Buddhist texts that he interpreted as saying that in a world of suffering—such as the present age in which we live—to die for a good cause was a noble thing since the merit that their souls will receive for this act would accede any merit they could possibly have accrued if they continued to live in a world of suffering, and thus they would be better off in the life to come. For this reason, those who kill for a righteous cause would presumably also be absolved of the demerit that would ordinarily be accorded to anyone involved in such an extreme form of violence. It is the overwhelming notion of cosmic war and the image of a world in suffering, however, that creates the overarching logic and the necessity of finding scriptures that will resolve what would otherwise be an anomaly in a Buddhist worldview.

Some of the same thinking was involved in the justification for the killing of Israeli prime minister Yitzhak Rabin by a student of Jewish texts, Yighal Amir. Though Rabin's widow said that neither he nor she ever expected that his life would be in danger from the hands of a Jew, Amir had received rabbinic approval for his plot to kill the prime minister under an obscure rabbinic ruling that allowed a criminal, even a Jew, to be pursued and stopped if a crime against Jews was in the process of being committed. This is how the circle of messianic Zionists of which Amir was a part interpreted Rabin's action of entering into a peace pact with the Palestinian Liberation Organization's leader, Yassir Arafat. When interviewed, other leaders in this movement revealed the central theme of their understanding of social reality: not only that Israel was under threat politically by Arab forces but also that the presence of Arabs in what they regarded as biblical Israel—the land on the West Bank that remains as Palestinian refugee territory—is sacred land that needs to be reunited with Israel under Jewish authority in order to prepare the groundwork for the coming of the Messiah (Juergensmeyer 2003:58). For this reason any impediment—including a peace-loving Israeli prime minister—had to be stopped, and the messianic Zionists found religious authority for approving it. An understanding of the dominant theme of the messianic Zionist worldview, however, was essential in making sense of what otherwise might seem to be an anomalous situation of an Israeli Jew assassinating a Jewish Israeli prime minister.

Locating Social Contexts

Though epistemic worldviews are conceptual entities, they are also tied to social realities. Others share these worldviews in a pattern of association that is usually contiguous with other social boundaries, such as a particular ethnic or religious community. Let us return to the case of the militant Christian Identity worldview in the United States. It has a social location. It is found in a particular part of the country—the mountainous areas of Idaho and Montana, part of Arizona and Oklahoma, and other pockets of the American South—and it is predominantly Protestant. But not all Protestant Christians who live in these areas share this worldview, nor do all members of Christian Identity churches buy into the more extreme interpretations of their traditions. Hence there are concentric circles of social realities that coalesce with particular epistemic worldviews: right-wing

Christian Protestants in the American rural West and South, in which some share an even more intense religiously informed worldview of the extremist Christian Identity variety. Though the inner levels of these concentric circles are not always socially distinct, often there are social markers—the movement is dominated by economically distressed, heterosexual, white men, for example, a social category in which one would find few blacks, Asians, or Hispanics, virtually no women in leadership roles, and no openly gay men or women. In the case of the extreme Christian identity militia movement, they provided their own social configurations by creating compounds such as Elohim City in Oklahoma, which Timothy McVeigh visited shortly before his attack on the Oklahoma City federal building in 1995, and the Ruby Ridge compound in northern Idaho, the scene of Christian Identity activist Randy Weaver's standoff with the FBI in 1992.

Members of a compound are rather easy to identify. But the social boundaries of followers of a movement—those who sympathetically agree with the central tenets and narrative story that dominate a particular epistemic worldview—may be more difficult to demarcate. The supporters of the global jihadi movement at the turn of the twenty-first century provide a case in point. If one thinks of the al Qaeda organization as the people who worked directly under the leadership of Osama bin Laden before his death in 2011 or who pledged loyalty to them, the numbers were likely to be only in the hundreds. But if one includes all those who were influenced by, and to some extent sympathetic with, the general jihadi perspective that identified the United States as an opponent of Islam and insisted on militant resistance on the part of concerned Muslims, the number was much greater, in the thousands and perhaps even in the millions.

The news media and many political leaders were fond of accusing the al Qaeda organization of orchestrating the rash of terrorist acts that were conducted in these decades—including those in such diverse locations as Bali, Madrid, London, Mumbai, and New York City. Yet the situation was more complicated, because each of these actions was conducted by groups that had their own identity and leadership and were only marginally connected—if at all—to Osama bin Laden and his compound. In the case of the group involved in attacking the World Trade Center and Pentagon on 9/11, for instance, it is still not clear how much bin Laden knew about the plot and how intimately he was involved in it. The 9/11 Commission Report, which summarizes the official investigation of the US government, states unequivocally that Khalid Sheikh Mohammad was the central conspirator, an accusation to which he has admitted. He has also stated, however, that he had not pledged loyalty to Osama bin Laden and did not consider himself a member of al Qaeda. In this situation, therefore, the concentric circle approach to epistemic worldviews applies, with a broad population of followers, often engaged through the Internet and other forms of electronic social media and various clusterings of activists, related at times in organizational ways, at times in a more fractured or fluid pattern of social relationships.

When locating the social context, it is also important to be aware of the significance of contested power relationships. In the Sikh separatist movement in the Indian state of Punjab, the young men from the dominant Jat caste who led the movement felt that their rightful leadership role within the Punjab was being undercut by the increasing economic success of urban Hindus from a different caste, the Khatris. It is no surprise, then, that the religious history and images that are evoked in the worldview of the members of the Sikh separatist movement are ones that extol the traditional leadership role of Jats.

In Afghanistan, the initial success of the Taliban worldview can be understood when taking into consideration the power play between different tribal and ethnic groups. Much of Afghanistan's civil war after the defeat of the Red Army was determined by the fact that Kabul fell not to the Pashto parties, but to the united Tajik forces and to the Uzbek forces. As the Pakistani journalist Ahmed Rashid has explained, this was a devastating psychological blow because for the first time in three hundred years, the Pashto groups had lost control of the capital (Rashid 2000: 21). The initial success of the original group of Taliban seizing power in Afghanistan can be explained against this background and this worldview—the Taliban were not just a political party but represented a new Pashto force, one that promised law, peace, and order. Thus an understanding of the social power relationships portrayed within a worldview can both strengthen explanations of why a given movement has success and illuminate a social aspect of its epistemic worldview.

Another important aspect of the social context is an understanding of how lines of authority are maintained, conceptually and politically. The case of bin Laden—a civil engineer who never received any religious training—shows how traditional concepts of authority are slippery since he promulgated fatwas, ordinarily the province of the clergy—and thereby expanded the notion of who is regarded as authoritative to issue jurisprudential rulings. The function previously limited to the *fuqaha* (the religious jurists) was taken out of the hands of the religiously learned elite, which gave credence to a popularist, revolutionary view of political Islam.

In order to trace the forms of authority that underpin the epistemic worldview, another relevant question to ask is what constitutes the bases of authority in the epistemic worldviews. The rationality that can be traced in the narratives of religious militants is often based on a particular rational logic. For religious militants, references to religious myths or spiritual dreams, holy scriptures or exegesis, or jurisprudential literature based on the interpretations of revelations or the will of God or gods have the same status empirical evidence would have in a scientific discourse: They are used as the basis of authoritative truth claims that can provide legitimacy to acts of violence. This perspective is important because it acknowledges that there can be a rational logic behind religious acts of violence instead of their being seen as mere irrational acts using secular criteria for what counts as evidence.

The fluidity of the social relationships related to epistemic worldviews should not be underestimated, for the epistemic worldviews are themselves fluid entities. They drift in and out and change, appearing and disappearing like clouds. Even those worldviews that seem so demanding, so ultimately important as to require the giving of one's own life, can dissipate like summer storms. An example of this was found by one of the authors of this chapter in interviewing villagers in an area of the Indian state of Punjab that had once been a center of antigovernment Sikh rebels in the 1980s. When villagers were interviewed in the early 1990s, just a few years after the movement had withered away, bombarded by police antiterrorist raids and decayed from within by the erosion of credible leadership, the villagers were philosophic about the movement and its demise. Many of the best and brightest young men in the village had given their lives to the cause, just as young men in other societies had volunteered for service in times of war, knowing that many would not return. So these young men were honored for their bravery, for their willingness to die for their faith and their community. But what about the cause for which they died? The villagers were uncomfortable with the topic. They said that what had happened earlier was then, and today was a different time (Juergensmeyer 2003: 96). Clearly their thinking about the world and their shared vision of social reality had moved on, evolved into a different perspective.

Conclusion

Epistemic worldviews can be elusive. They are shared perceptions of reality forged out of the experiences of a particular time and place and informed by the resources of images and ideas provided by religious and other cultural expressions of ultimate longing. They can shift over time, change, and disappear. But for the moments that they captivate the imaginations of those who share their understanding of social reality, they are powerful visions of the world that is and that might be, and they have generated some of the more formidable events of contemporary political life. For this reason, they must be taken seriously and analyzed with the full range of social scientific and theological comprehension that is available. This is why the sociotheological approach to studying such phenomena has gained such contemporary currency.

In a violent world, entering into the epistemic worldviews of another is crucial both to explain and prevent the escalation of violence. Often spirals of violence emerge from responses to simplified images of "the enemy" countered by actions also based on stereotypes. The lack of empathetic immersion into the ideas and images that condition the actions of each side is what the British historian Herbert Butterfield has called the "tragic element" of modern international conflict: Each side fails to see the full range of motivations driving their counterpart (Butterfield 1950). The sociotheological turn in the study of religious violence is therefore significant not only for intellectual understanding but also for policy implications.

Sociotheology represents an attempt to transcend the walls between facts and perceptions, between scientific reasoning and empathetic understanding.

The resurgence of religion in world politics and the increasing importance of transnational religious movements have presented an analytic challenge that sociotheology has risen to meet. We have found that this approach to understanding the differences among the varying epistemic worldviews of contemporary society provides analysts with the ability to bridge gaps, not only intellectually but perhaps also in the social and political conflicts of the contemporary world.

Bibliography

An Naim, Abdullahi. *Islam and the Secular State*. Cambridge, MA: Harvard University Press, 2009.

Asad, Talal. *Genealogies of Religion: Discipline and Reasons of Power in Christianity and Islam*. Baltimore, MD: Johns Hopkins University Press, 1993.

Asad, Talal. *Formations of the Secular: Christianity, Islam, and Modernity*. Palo Alto, CA: Stanford University Press, 2003.

Bellah, Robert. *Beyond Belief: Essays on Religion in a Post-Traditionalist World*. New York: Harper and Row, 1970.

Bellah, Robert. *Religion in Human Evolution: From the Paleolithic to the Axial Age*. Cambridge, MA: Harvard University Press, 2011.

Berger, Peter. *The Sacred Canopy: Elements of a Sociological Theory of Religion*. Garden City, NY: Doubleday, 1967.

Bourdieu, Pierre. 1980. *The Logic of Practice*. Trans. R. Nice. Palo Alto, CA: Stanford University Press, 1990.

Buber, Martin. 1923. *I and Thou*. Trans. Ronald Gregor Smith. New York: Charles Scribner's Sons, 1958.

Butterfield, Herbert. "The Tragic Element in Modern International Conflict." *The Review of Politics* 12.2 (1950): 147–164.

Calhoun, Craig, Mark Juergensmeyer, and Jonathan VanAntwerpen. *Rethinking Secularism*. Oxford, UK: Oxford University Press, 2011.

Casanova, Jose. *Public Religions in the Modern World*. Chicago: University of Chicago Press, 1994.

Davis, Charles. *Religion and the Making of Society: Essays in Social Theology*. Cambridge, UK: Cambridge University Press, 1994.

Della Porta, Donatella. *Social Movements, Political Violence, and the State A Comparative Analysis of Italy and Germany*. Cambridge, UK: Cambridge University Press, 1995.

Douglas, Mary. "The Effects of Modernization on Religious Change." *Daedalus* 111.1 (Winter 1982): 1–19.

Dumont, Louis. *Homo Hierarchicus: The Caste System and Its Implications*. Chicago: University of Chicago Press, 1981.

Durkheim, Emile. 1912. *The Elementary Forms of Religious Life*. Trans. Joseph Ward Swain. New York: The Free Press, 1915.

Edwards, Derek and Jonathan Potter. *Discursive Psychology*. London: Sage, 1992.

Foucault, Michel. 1966. *The Order of Things: An Archeology of Human Science*. New York: Random House, 1994.

Foucault, Michel. 1969. *The Archaeology of Knowledge*. Translated by A. Sheridan Smith. New York: Harper and Row, 1972.

Friedland, Roger and John Mohr, eds. *Matters of Culture: Cultural Sociology in Practice*. Cambridge, UK: Cambridge University Press, 2004.

Gee, James P. *The Social Mind*. New York: Bergin and Garvey, 1992.

Geertz, Clifford. "Religion as a Cultural System." Reprinted in *Reader in Comparative Religion: An Anthropological Approach*. 3d ed. Eds. William A. Lessa and Evon Z. Vogt, 168–182. New York: Harper & Row, 1972.

Giddens, Antony. *Modernity and Self-Identity: Self and Society in the Late Modern Age*. Palo Alto, CA: Stanford University Press, 1991.

Habermas, Jürgen. *Rationality and Religion: Essays on Reason, God, and Modernity*. Cambridge, MA: MIT Press, 2002.

Harré, Horace R. and Grant Gillett. *The Discursive Mind*. London: Sage, 1994.

Hurd, Elizabeth. *The Politics of Secularism in International Relations*. Princeton, NJ: Princeton University Press, 2007.

Jerryson, Michael. *Buddhist Fury: Religion and Violence in Southern Thailand*. New York: Oxford University Press, 2011.

Juergensmeyer, Mark. *Terror in the Mind of God: The Global Rise of Religious Violence*. Rev. ed. Berkeley: University of California Press, 2003.

Juergensmeyer, Mark. *Global Rebellion: Religious Challenges to the Secular State: From Christian Militias to Al Qaeda*. Berkeley: University of California Press, 2008.

Küng, Hans. *A Global Ethic for Global Politics and Economics*. New York: Oxford University Press, 1998.

Lindbeck, George A. *The Nature of Doctrine: Religion and Theology in a Postliberal Age*. Louisville, KY: Westminster John Knox Press, 1984.

Mahmood, Cynthia K. *Fighting for Faith and Nation: Dialogues with Sikh Militants*. Philadelphia: University of Pennsylvania Press, 1996.

Marx, Karl and Friedrich Engels. *The German Ideology*. Ed. R. Pascal. New York: International Publishers, 1939.

Meier, Heinrich. *What Is Political Theology?* Munich: Carl Friedrich von Siemens Stiftung, 2006.

Niebuhr, Reinhold. *Moral Man and Immoral Society*. New York: Scribners, 1932.

Obeyesekere, Gananath. *Imagining Karma: Ethical Transformation in Amerindian, Buddhist, and Greek Rebirth*. Berkeley: University of California Press, 2002.

Ralph, H. and Killian, Lewis M. *Collective Behavior*. 3rd ed. Englewood Cliffs, NJ: Prentice, 1987.

Rashid, Ahmed. *Taliban: Militant Islam, Oil and Fundamentalism in Central Asia*. New Haven, CT: Yale University Press, 2000.

Rawls, John. "The Idea of Public Reason Revisited." In the *University of Chicago Law Review* 64.3 (Summer 1997): 765–807.

Robertson, Roland. "Sociologists and Secularization." Sociology 3 (1971): 297–312.

Schmitt, Carl. 1922. *Political Theology; Four Chapters on the Concept of Sovereignty*. Translated by George Schwab. Chicago: University of Chicago Press, 2005.

Segal, Robert A. "Theories of Religion." In *The Routledge Companion to the Study of Religion*. Ed. John R. Hinnells, 49–60. London: Routledge, 2005.

Sheikh, Mona K. *Guardians of God—Understanding the Religious Violence of Pakistan's Taliban*. PhD dissertation, University of Copenhagen, Department of Political Science, 2011.

Sheikh, Mona K. and Ole Wæver. "Western Secularisms: Variation in a Doctrine and its Practice." In *Thinking International Relations Differently*. Eds. Arlene B. Tickner and David L. Blaney, 275–298. London: Routledge, 2012.

Sivaraksa, Sulak. *A Socially Engaged Buddhism*. Bangkok: Sathirakoses-Nagapradipa Foundation, 1999.

Smart, Ninian. "Religion, Myth, and Nationalism." In *Religion and Politics in the Modern World*. Eds. Peter H. Merkl and Ninian Smart, 20–32. New York: New York University Press, 1983.

Smelser, Neil. *Theory of Collective Behavior*. New York: Free Press, Glencoe, 1963.

Smith, Wilfred Cantwell. *The Meaning and End of Religion*. New York: Macmillan, 1962.

Srinivas, M. N. *Caste in Modern India and Other Essays*. New York: Asia Publishing House, 1962.

Tagore, Rabindranath. *The Religion of Man*. London: Macmillan, 1931.

Tambiah, Stanley. *World Conqueror and World Renouncer: A Study of Buddhism and Polity in Thailand against a Historical Background*. Cambridge, UK: Cambridge University Press, 1976.

Taylor, Charles. *A Secular Age*. Cambridge, MA: Belknap Press, 2007.

Tilly, Charles. *Social Movements, 1768–2004*. Boulder, CO: Paradigm Publishers, 2004.

Weber, Max 1905. *The Protestant Ethic and The Spirit of Capitalism*. Trans. Peter Baehr and Gordon C. Wells. New York: The Free Press, 2002.

Weber, Max. 1915. *The Religion of China: Confucianism and Taoism*. New York: The Free Press, 1951.

Weber, Max 1916. *The Religion of India: The Sociology of Hinduism and Buddhism*. New York: The Free Press, 1958.

Weil, Simone. *Oppression and Liberty*. London: Routledge & Kegan Paul, 1958.

Index

CPSIA information can be obtained
at www.ICGtesting.com
Printed in the USA
BVHW060946111221
623602BV00002B/7

9 780190 270094